Forever Mine

Kyra Jones

PublishAmerica
Baltimore

First printing

ISBN: 1-60563-911-7
PUBLISHED BY PUBLISHAMERICA, LLLP
www.publishamerica.com
Baltimore

Printed in the United States of America

DEDICATION

I would like to dedicate this book to my love, the hero in my life, my husband Michael, because without him in my life I would not be the person I am today. I owe him everything.

Secondly, to my mother, the most loving caring woman I have ever met in my life. She, too, taught me how to be strong and how to love.

To my sister Amber, for whom I have always had the utmost respect. I loved her dearly. She was my protector and much more than just a sister. She was a loving friend as well. Her passing left a great gap in my life, one that could never be filled.

To my loving sister, April, also one of my protectors. She, too, showed me many things in life, how to cook, how to keep a nice home, and how to love. She was also one of my best friends as well as my sister and always gave so very much of herself. She sometimes gave until she had nothing left. Her life is to be commended. She took such great care of the handicapped women that were left in her charge; always putting their feelings first and always making sure they had everything they needed even when she wasn't on duty. She was a loving, caring sister, and a fantastic loving, caring aunt. She will live in our hearts and our memories forever.

Then Robert Clay, a sweet, loving and caring friend who always worked so hard to put a smile on his children's faces as well as everyone else's around him. He was a caring, loving soul that this earth will surely miss such as I do.

Also all our neighbors that were lost and all our friends that Michael and I always had so much fun with, playing pool, dancing, and partying with. These are fond, fond memories, memories that will always bring a smile to my face. I miss them all so much, and I miss all the good times that we had together.

I consider myself really blessed to have known so many great people in my life. There have been so many heroes, but my main hero will always remain my husband. The other half of my heart, the other half of my soul will always be with him until we can be together again some day. He holds that part of me.

Now all I have are my memories of all the love and the laughs my family had, and these memories will get me through the bad times.

Most of all I would like to dedicate this book to God, because without His love and His guidance, I would have never gotten through the horrifying heartbreaking times when He stood by me. He repaired my fractured heart and my fractured soul as only He could, and I pledge my heart to Him. I will try my hardest to do good every day because of the love He showed me. I know this is what He wants me to do. I will honor Him and those loved ones I've lost for the rest of my life every day. I will try my best to make them proud of me.

There is one other thing I just want to say. Anybody can do what I do, to feel the spirits of your loved ones that have passed. All you have to do is stop telling yourself you can't. Just try praying and ask God to help you do this. Then open your mind up and keep it open and watch for the signs. There will be signs and feelings, but you have to be open to them. Believe me; I am no one special. If I can do this, so can you. It just takes time. This book truly has been a labor of love and love never dies.

ACKNOWLEDGMENT

This is for my two sons, who are also my best friends and my confidants, and I theirs. They were so much help to me while I was writing this book. I truly believe I couldn't have done it without their support. They, like I, truly believed this book needed to be written, and they supported me the whole time I was writing it. They, themselves, made many sacrifices, because while I was writing this book I wasn't able to be with them and do things with them. However, they always understood and allowed me the time to do what I had to do. They put up with me on the bad days, the days I would have to relive in my mind the most heartbreaking times in my life. They never wavered in their support and their love for me. For this I will always be forever grateful.

My two sons and I now share an incredible bond, a bond of both love and pain as well. Unfortunately, we will never forget this pain and heartache, but the three of us have emerged out of this pain ever stronger. It is very true what they say, "What does not kill you will make you stronger." We are living examples of this, but we have found a way to put the pain away and remember only the love, the laughs, and the good times. These memories are what carry us through the bad times. When we speak about their father, their grandparents and their aunts who have now gone, we speak of them as though they are still here with us, because in our hearts they still are. That love will forever live on. We also know that they are not far away from us, and they will always be a part of us. The three of us choose to remember only the love, the laughter, and the happy times, not that very moment before they passed. That terrible memory we have tried to erase from our memories. I do know for a fact that this is how they would want to be remembered, not by the final last moment of their lives.

My sons have become strong and honorable young men I will always be proud of, and they will always have all my love and respect. There is one example, one conversation that Teddy and I had not too long ago. It took place in the kitchen while I was making dinner. I was putting his plate in front of him, and he looked up at me and he said, "You know, Mom, you know how you're always calling me a man's man?"

I said, "Yeah."

He said, "That may be true, but you're forgetting one thing. I may be a man's man, but I'm always going to be a momma's boy." This statement warmed my heart and brought a tear to my eye. That my sons loved me that much, and we are that close, is incredible. There is nothing I wouldn't do for them and nothing they wouldn't do for me.

I had to raise my children under the most heartbreaking circumstances. I always did the best job that I could, but as a parent you always wonder if it is enough. With a statement like Teddy made, it shows me that maybe, yes, I did do enough to protect them, and they are going to be fine. They are both very compassionate, loving young men that I am so proud to call my sons, and I know Michael would be as well. I am proud to say they are both their father's sons. They always have all my love and respect.

Teddy's plan for the future is to own and run a restaurant. Martin I am not sure of yet, but I am pretty convinced he is going to do something with art. He is extremely talented in this area. I am going to support them and help them 100% of the way.

I would also like to thank Mrs. Sonja White. She is the wonderful transcriber I was lucky enough to find. She has been transcribing books for over 20 years now, and she worked very, very hard on this one for me. She had to listen to many hours of tapes, and she did such wonderful work. As you know, it is not the easiest book to get through, emotionally speaking. I look forward to many more years of friendship and working closely with her on future books.

Last but certainly not least, I thank Izzy, my best friend and the woman that I consider my sister for planting the seed in my mind about writing this book many years ago. Later on when I remembered her comment, and I began writing this book. I found it was the very thing that saved me.

I am so grateful to have these four people in my life, and I thank them all so very much.

I would also like to thank PublishAmerica, LLLP, for believing in me and publishing my work.

CHAPTER ONE

I wrote this book for many reasons, one of which is that I hope my story, my words, will help other people. Most important, I seek to find justice for my beloved. I speak from my heart. This is really Michael's story. I dedicated my life, and now I dedicate this book to him. My life has become a test of love and faith—about losing your faith and then having it come back to you tenfold.

My life began in a small New England town on March 23, 1962. I was the youngest of three daughters. There was a great age difference between my sisters and me. My sister April was eleven years older than I was, and my sister Amber was sixteen years older than I was. I guess you can say I was quite the surprise package for everyone.

My mother, June, was forty-two, and my father, Frank, was forty-three years old when I arrived. Even though I was a surprise, I can say I never felt unwanted or unloved. We were very poor, but we always had a lot of love. My mother saw to that. She was a very strong woman—strong in heart, soul, and spirit. I do not think I would be the person, the woman, and the mother I am today without her as my role model.

My father, on the other hand, was just the opposite. He was not someone to model your life after. He had a lot of problems, to say the least. I guess looking back at it, he had his reasons. His own childhood was horrible. At the age of six he lost his own father to murder. His father, after a long time in the Navy, retired with a high rank. I guess even back then the military pension was not enough to support a wife and six children on, so he found employment with a detective agency. One night in 1924 he was guarding a warehouse in Brooklyn, New York, when men broke in. My grandfather was horribly mutilated and murdered in the break in. They never caught these men, and no one was ever brought to justice for his murder. When the police found my grandfather, his nose and ears were cut from his head. I can only imagine the horror my family went through. I guess in this time in history they would bring the body back to the house. The family would take care of it and have the wake in the house, because that's what they did. The police brought my grandfather's mutilated body back to the house and laid him out on the couch in the living room in full view of his children. My poor father—he was only six years old at the time. For him to have seen that must have been a heartbreaking thing. I truly believe in my heart that this is what set the tone for the rest of my father's life.

On that day my father not only lost his father but something very important in himself that he was not able to regain. My father's older brother, who was sixteen years old, and whom my father loved dearly, had a total mental breakdown over this. He had to be put in a mental institution where he stayed for the rest of his life. So you see, my father not only lost his father, but he also lost his older brother to whom he was very close. As I said, I think this set the tone for the rest of my father's life and also the lives of his wife and children.

After his father's murder my father became a very angry young man. He would skip school and get into fights. I guess it got to the point where my grandmother could no longer handle him. She was forced to put him in a boys' home for troubled youths. I think this must have broken her heart. Now not only her husband, but also now two of her sons were lost to her.

My father had a very hard time in this boys' home. He was beaten and abused. Looking back at it now, this must have really added to the anger he already felt. By the time he was old enough to leave the home and start a life of his own he was a very screwed-up and angry man. He needed a lot of help and never got it. He started hanging around a local gym where his talent for fighting was cultivated. He became very good: too good. He went on to win the Golden Gloves of Brooklyn. He was to hold that title for three years until the Boxing Commission took it away from him. My father's anger-control problem was so bad that when he was told to stop during a fight and go back to his corner of the ring, he could not. This happened time and time again, and this left them no choice. After this he started drinking and gambling.

At this time he was around twenty-one years old. He went from job to job, never really finding himself. Then World War II broke out, and he did what every red-blooded American man did. He signed up for the Army. I am really not sure to this day how he found himself in this small New England town. Maybe he was visiting a friend he made in the Army. All I know is that he found himself in a little diner in our little town were a lot of military men ate, and on that day my mother happened to be having dinner there with friends. She told me many times how she met my father and how handsome he was in his uniform—his blond hair his blue eyes and his beautiful smile. I guess he was able to sweep any girl of her feet, and boy, did he! They started dating right away and fell deeply in love with each other. They were married within months of their first meeting. They wanted to get married before he was shipped out.

My poor mother had no idea what she was getting herself into. She had spent all of her life in this small town. She really did not know what the world was about or what it could do to you. She had two sisters and one brother. Her mother was so loving and caring. She was a great mother and wife. She was a very talented seamstress, and she could make anything she wanted. She made her own wedding gown, and it was beautiful.

Her father was the same way. He was a great father and husband. He worked very hard every day in the stove factory where he made cast-iron, potbelly stoves. My mother was very intelligent and beautiful. She was very slim and petite. She only stood about five feet one inch tall, with long black wavy hair and large brown eyes. My mother was also a very talented artist. She could draw very beautiful portraits of people and landscapes. Just about anything she drew was beautiful. When she was in high school she entered a drawing contest and won the first prize. The prize was a full scholarship to an art school in New York City, but my grandfather would not hear of it. He was a loving father, and I am sure all he was trying to do was protect his daughter at the time. What he did, though, was crush her dreams and spirit and leave her with very little to look forward to in life besides becoming a wife and mother, because that is what proper women were expected to do back then. It makes me feel so sad inside to think of what could have been, what kind of great and exciting life she could have had, and all the things she could have seen and done.

Instead, after high school she went to work in one of our local silver factories. My mother worked there for two or three years before she met my father. Shortly after they met they were married. He was shipped out to Europe where he spent a little over a year in combat. When he came home he was worse than ever. His bad side, the side my mother had not yet seen, had just gotten worse. A year after his return home my mother gave birth to her first daughter, Amber. My father moved them back to New York. This was the beginning of many years of moving back and forth. We would spend a couple of years in New England and a couple of years in New York. We would never stay in one place too long.

Shortly after my sister Amber's birth, the cycle of abuse began toward my mother and my sisters. My father's drinking and gambling destroyed our family. It went on for close to thirty years until my sister Amber became an adult and was able to save enough money to get my mother a legal separation from my father. I was ten when this happened. My father suffered from posttraumatic stress syndrome. In World War II they called it being shell-shocked. He could have and should have gotten help for this, but he simply chose not to. Instead he just destroyed and then lost his family.

He tried to keep in touch with us, though he never returned back to my mother's home after the separation. At this time it was now just my mother and I. My sisters were married and lived on their own. He would go and stay a week or two with one of them, which made for a really tense time in their home. Thank God this only occurred once or twice a year. They simply could not have stood any more of him than that.

I guess the earliest years I can recall from my childhood were when I was three or four years old. These memories were of my sister April taking me to the Bronx Zoo. She and I just about lived there. She would bring me there almost every day in order to get me out of the house and away from our father. We lived right around the corner from the Zoo, which was very convenient for us. As I said, we would move back and forth from New England to New York every couple of years.

I remember the move back to New England when I was about six years old. My family rented an apartment on a really nice street with really nice houses. I made friends with two little girls across the street. Their names were Sue and Ashley. I can remember how nice their whole family was to me, their father especially. He was what a dad should be. He took me under his wing and treated me like one of his own daughters. I would sleep over, I would eat dinner, and I would spend most of my day over their house.

There was one day in particular I will never forget. Sue, Ashley, and I were playing the board game Candy Land on their living room floor when all of a sudden I heard this voice I did not know. I looked up to see this very handsome soldier in uniform. All I can think of was he looked like a movie star. He was just so handsome. Believe me, I do know just how very odd this all sounds, but when our eyes met I just got such a strange feeling. Chills went up my spine, and I had no idea why. After he left I asked Sue who he was, and she told me that he was their cousin who was about to leave for Vietnam. Being six years old I really did not understand much about the war only what my father told me about the one he was in. This chance encounter is one I will never forget.

About six months after that we were on the move again, but at least this time we stayed in the same town. My family only moved to another apartment. I lost touch with Sue and Ashley. I missed their family very much. They were the first normal family I had known. We moved into a third-floor apartment. It was a very big house. There had to have been at least six other families living there. Most of the families were nice, but there was one family that lived in the apartment in the back. In this family there were four boys, and they were horrible. They used me as their own personal punching bag. Every time they saw me, one of them would find a reason to hit me.

I remember particularly one winter at this park right down the street from where we lived. On one cold winter's morning I took a shortcut across the big frozen pond that was located in the center of the park. There were many children skating and enjoying the winter's day. I was half way across the pond heading toward our neighborhood milk store to buy my mother some milk, when all of a sudden I felt someone hit me from behind. They knocked my legs right out from underneath me. This was the last thing I remembered. The next thing I knew I was waking up on my mother's couch, not knowing how I got there. My mother said I just came in the house and said nothing. I just went to the couch and lay down and went to sleep.

When I awoke I told her what had happened to me on the ice. She was beside herself. She went down to the park to find out what exactly had happened to me, and when she found out that it was one of the boys that lived in the back apartment that did it. For her this was the straw that broke the camel's back. My mother then went to see the boys' mother and told her all about what her sons had just done. She also informed the boys' mother about everything they had been doing to me since the day we moved in. My mother then went on to tell her she was to handle her sons and punish them accordingly, or my mother was going to call the police this time. After this day, let's just say I never had any more trouble.

My mother had enough on her plate. As it was she worked very hard and long hours as a C.N.A. at our local hospital. My sister April worked very hard as well in a local plastic factory. My father was no longer living with us. It was only the three of us at this point. My sister April was about to leave soon to be married. I was about eight years old when she got married. My other sister Amber had already left to get married a couple of years earlier, so now it was just my mother and I. It was nice and quiet. I was busy going to school, and my mother was very busy working. She loved her job very much and everyone at the hospital where she worked loved her too.

After school I would often go to visit my grandmother at the nursing home. After the death of my grandfather, she sold their family home and moved into the nursing home. It was beautiful, converted from an old hotel. It had red plush carpeting everywhere and a beautiful old staircase. At the entrance there was a big beautiful lobby. To one side of the lobby was a large sitting room. There were also four large, old-fashioned sitting chairs. Beautiful mahogany wood trim ran through the entire lobby and staircase leading up to my grandmother's private room. Her room was on the second floor, which faced the street. Across the street was an A&P grocery store. I would sit on her turn-of-the-century Singer sewing machine she had received as a wedding gift so many years before. She made all of her children's clothes on the machine. My grandmother was a very talented seamstress.

I would visit with her on an average of three days a week. I looked forward to our visits very much. I would sit on the sewing machine and eat penny candy she bought for me, and I would also look down onto the passing traffic below. We would watch the people come and go out of the A&P as we sat there and talked. We would talk about a lot of things from when my mother was a child, to World War II, to what was going on now in the world. She would always ask about my father. Now I know why she would. It was to make sure he was no longer around. He was not her favorite person in the world. My grandmother was not the type of person to hate anyone, but I think she hated my father.

We would also talk a lot about God and the Catholic religion. God and the church were very important to her. In her words, "If you have faith, Kyra, you can get through anything. God will help you. He will always be there for you, and always remember, you are his child."

I would study my prayer book with her and attend my religious education classes. My grandmother helped me to prepare for my First Communion. On the day I received my First Communion, my grandmother was very happy and proud of me. I could tell this was something that was very important to her. I made her happy. I felt good about myself on that day.

We continued our visits, and over the weeks and months we spoke more and more about God. I think she knew she was not going to be here for much longer. She was 76 and not in very good health, but of course she did not speak about this to me. We instead spoke of only cheerful things—of God and Heaven and how some day we would all be together again in Heaven back home with God.

Now looking back on these talks, I can see how she was trying to prepare me for her death. When this day came I remember my mother telling me that I could not go for my regular visit with my grandmother because she had fallen ill. I remember getting so mad and giving her such a hard time about this and yelling at her, telling her I was going to go anyway. It was then that she told me how sick my grandmother was, far too sick to visit with me. "When she begins to feel better, we can resume our visits," my mother told me. But that day never came. I never saw my grandmother again. She died the very next day. I would later find out she had suffered a stroke. She was gone in a day. I never got to say goodbye or see her one last time. I was not even allowed to go to her funeral. I guess back then they thought they were protecting me, when in fact all they did was make me even angrier and make my hurt even deeper.

This was to be the first time my heart would be broken. The loss of my sweet grandmother left a hole deep down inside of me. I was trying very hard to deal with the loss the best way I knew. How I tried to remember her words, her strong belief of God and Heaven. These words gave me much comfort until one night I overheard my sister April and my mother talking in the kitchen. They did not know I was listening. I overheard them talking about the day about a year before when my grandmother had gone to church. She went up the stairs of the church and arrived at the front door. Just then she remembered she had no money. She felt ashamed to go in with no money. She felt as though if she had no money to put into the collection basket she had no right to sit in church. My grandmother did not feel welcome in God's house, my mother said. My grandmother just turned around and walked back down the church's stairs without even going in.

I cannot even begin to tell you how empty and cold this made me feel inside that my sweet grandmother was made to feel so ashamed of herself at the one place she had loved most in the world, church. I not only lost my grandmother, which was hard enough, but on this night I lost my faith, my faith in God, my faith in the church, and my faith in everything that I thought to be true. I was only nine years old, and I felt so empty and sad. I lost my faith when I needed it the most. I pushed it away. I pushed God away. This is how I stayed for the next twenty-six years of my life. What a mistake that was.

It was a few months after my grandmother passed away that my mother started getting sick. She began experiencing a lot of pain in her back and legs. She would go to work many days in pain. She did this day after day for months until she could not go any more. She became unable to work, which broke her heart because she really loved her job. We ended up on welfare and having to move yet once again. We moved into a very large project in town. I was just turning ten. I did not like it at first, but when I got to know some of the other children and their families, I began to feel right at home. There was a group of us kids with whom I became close friends. We would play baseball and football in the backfields, and we would walk back and fourth to school together. Often we walked along the railroad tracks. This was our shortcut. We would also stop at this little corner milk store for snacks on our way to school.

As I said, it was a very large project. It had eighteen units, and in each unit there were six apartments attached together, side by side. You got to know the people very well in each unit. In the apartment right next to us there lived an elderly couple, Mary and her husband Jim. Their son was missing in action in Vietnam. They had their daughter-in-law and her two sons living with them as well. In the next apartment over lived another elderly couple, Tony and his wife Sara. Tony was much older than his wife, yet he was the one who took care of her.

It should not have been this way. She was only a diabetic, and there was nothing else physically wrong with her, yet she claimed not to be able to walk or do anything for herself. She would just lie there day after day and have her husband wait on her hand and foot, until one day while Tony was at the grocery store their daughter popped in for a visit and found her mother walking down the stairs carrying a small television. Well, I guess the cat was out of the bag. She could no longer do her "Poor little me" act. After all, Tony, by this time, was over seventy years old and getting very tired and becoming ill himself. His wife wore him out and damn near killed him. Come to find out, she was severely mentally ill, to say the least.

Jean was the name of the daughter that discovered her mother coming down the stairs that day. She had four young children of her own. She was not really able to keep as close an eye on her parents as she would have liked. The day when she walked in on her mother coming down the stairs by herself when supposedly she was not able to even walk, she became very angry. She realized right then and there just how badly her mother had taken advantage of her father. After she saw this she was bound and determined to get her father out of that house and as far away from her mother as she could get him.

Jean spoke to her father's doctors and told them what she had seen and asked them for help to get her father out of there. They worked together and found him a really nice nursing home where he would be taken care of for a change. He did not want to go at first, but when Jean told him what she had seen her mother doing that day, he quickly had a change of heart. That poor man was awfully hurt because he had been lied to for so many years by the woman he loved. To him this was unforgivable.

He and his daughter both packed up his belongings, and she had him moved in a matter of two days into the nursing home where he lived very happily until the time of his death in 1978. The doctors arranged for Sara to have a home health care aid. This aid came to her house every day for two hours a day. This attention was not enough for her, and she became increasingly more and more depressed. She eventually ended up committing suicide by slitting her own throat a year after her husband moved out.

In the next apartment over from theirs lived a very nice young couple named Cathy and Joe. They had one daughter named Mary. They had moved into their apartment a few weeks after my mother and I had moved into ours. Their daughter was about six months old. I became very close to them and their baby. They would often take me with them whenever they went any place special. I remember they would go mostly every weekend to Lincoln Park. I think they were hooked on the live country music bands that performed there. I would always have fun, and they were always nice to me. I also babysat for them from time to time. My mother allowed me to do this because she was only two doors away from where we lived. One day I overheard my mother and Cathy talking, and Cathy told my mother that I was the only young girl in the whole neighborhood that she and her husband trusted to take care of Mary. They knew I would never let anything happen to her. It made me feel really good to hear that I was trusted that much.

This was also around the same time my love for Roller Derby was cultivated. Every Wednesday night I would go over to Cathy and Joe's to watch it with them. My mother was not a big Roller Derby fan, to say the least. She hated it, and I think she became a little worried about my fascination with it. I do believe she envisioned me trying to do this for a living, and I'm sure it sent chills down her spine. Well, of course I did not, and my love for Roller Derby died out, although it took a couple of years to do so.

In the next apartment down, which was the last apartment in our unit, there lived a family consisting of two boys and one girl. They were all much older than me, so I really did not get to know them very well because of this. I quickly made friends with the other children in the project that lived in several different units. One of my friends was named T.J. She came from a rather large family that consisted of three brothers and one sister. In one of the other units lived another friend named Lisa. Her family was also very large. She had four older brothers. Only one of her brothers joined our little group of friends. His name was Tim. In the last unit lived my other dear friend Angel, who also came from another large family. She had three brothers and one sister. So this was my little group of friends: Lisa, T.J., Angel, Tim, and me. The five of us would walk to school, hang out together listening to music, talk, and just enjoy each others' company. On rare occasions when we would have a dollar or two to spend, we would walk downtown and hang out at the Woolworth's soda fountain where we could enjoy an ice-cold Coke on a hot summer's day.

None of our families had very much money. In fact we were quite poor, so when we were able to do this little thing, it was a real treat. Even though I was poor, I would not have traded my life for anything. I grew up being able to get to know all different kinds of people. My childhood, my life, has made me the caring and tolerant person I am inside today and has given me the ability to be able to place myself in another person's shoes and also the ability to feel another person's pain. I thank God for this. Sure, my friends and I went without a lot of things, but it gave us an appreciation for what was really important in life and that is people—friendships, caring, and tolerance.

Do not get me wrong. There were a couple of things I would have changed if I could have, mayonnaise sandwiches for dinner being one of them, better-looking furniture being another, but most of all those damn mayonnaise sandwiches really sucked. Our food stamps would always run out about a week before we were to get more. We would only get them once a month, and they really gave you only enough to go three weeks. Welfare back then and today does not give you enough money to even live, period. If you were at all able to work, this would be a much better life. Most of my friends' families were in the same boat. Even though their mothers were working, they could not make enough money to support their household, so they were getting assistance to try to make ends meet.

This was not an easy way to grow up. My poor mother, who had always worked, found herself not able to any longer because of her health. My mother often went without so I would not. There was very little money for anything, even clothes. I do not know how she did it, but she always made sure I had nice clothes for school, and I always looked good. She was a great mother. She taught me what was really important, love, and never to let anybody bring you down or to make you feel bad about yourself. She taught me to always stand my ground and to stand up for my friends and for people that cannot defend themselves. She taught me to protect the weaker among us and to always hold my head up high. She would tell me it does not matter what you have. You could have very little in your home, old cheap furniture. Just as long as whatever you have is clean and neat, you can always be proud. I can remember the maintenance man coming into our apartment. They would always comment on how nice and clean it was.

My mother was one of the strongest people I have ever known. Her spirit and her love for her children were strong. She was always very much a lady at all times. She did not smoke or drink, and I always looked up to her. She was not only my mother, but she was my best friend. I can only hope to be half the woman she was. She was my hero. I always felt safe and protected as a child with her as my mother. She gave me many things, things money could not buy besides her strength. I also inherited her artistic ability. We would sit and draw together for hours. She taught me about lines, shadows, and depth. She showed me how a little line and a slight shadow could make a big difference in a drawing. She also taught me how to sew and embroider. One winter she and I designed and made by hand a winter coat for me. It was a lot of work, but it looked great, and I was so proud to wear the coat that she and I created together on the first day of winter. We also enjoyed watching T.V. together. Our favorite shows were *All in the Family*, (we watched the first episode together) and also the first episode of *M.A.S.H.* and *Little House on the Prairie*. My mother and I spent a lot of time with each other just talking. This time was so nice.

Meanwhile my sisters Amber and April were very busy with their husbands and their lives, but they always found time to stop in for a cup of coffee and a visit at least once a week. My sister Amber worked very hard and put in a lot of overtime in her job. She had just gotten out of a very bad marriage and had just begun dating a very nice man. His name was Steven. At this time my sister April had been married for about three years and was also putting in a lot of hours working overtime at her job. She and her husband Christopher seemed to be very happy in their marriage. They had just purchased their first home. It was small and what you would call a fixer-upper, and when I say, "fixer-upper," I mean it. This house did not even have a toilet or plumbing in it. Her husband and his three brothers were very handy with tools and could build just about anything, and believe you me, they really had their work cut out for them with this house.

It took almost a year to complete the work, but when they were done it was beautiful. They made the upstairs into a separate apartment for my sister Amber, while April and her husband Christopher lived on the first floor. It was very nice. They all got along very well. It was as though my sister April and Amber were more than simply sisters—they were best friends. They went everywhere and did everything together. My mother and I would spend every Christmas and most holidays at my sister April's house. She would always have her house beautifully decorated, especially for Christmas, with a huge, beautifully decorated tree. She would bake delicious pastries, cookies, and fruit breads all from scratch. Her dinners were incredible as well.

This time of year was such a happy time for my mother and me to spend the holidays with my sister April and her husband, and my sister Amber and her new husband, Steven, without my father ruining the holidays with his drinking. For a change we found our selves able to simply enjoy each others' company and share the love that a family should be sharing at this time of year. My mother had always tried hard to make our Christmases happy ones, but no matter how hard she had tried, it was impossible with my father there. My father would always find a way to ruin all of the happy times. I have spoken to many people who were very bitter about not having a father in their lives, people that come from single-parent homes. They tell me they always felt as though they were missing something in their lives, and I guess sometimes that feeling is correct. It has been my experience that sometimes it is worse if they stay.

There are people in this world that should just never become parents. My father was one of them. So when our home became a single-parent household, when my father was finally gone, and it became just my mother and me, we had a true appreciation for the peace and quiet of everyday living. I was able to get to know my mother as a person and not just as a mother. I not only loved her, but I liked her as well.

I remember my eleventh birthday when we had been living in the project for about a year now. Our neighbors Cathy and Joe had given me the sweetest, most beautiful, pure white angora kitten with big blue eyes for my eleventh birthday. I named her Cuddles, and she would sleep with me every night at the foot of my bed. This was so nice of Cathy and Joe. You know, people are under the impression that people that live in projects are low class, but in fact, it is just a matter of low income. Most of these people have not had the advantages and the privileges in life that other people have. This is what puts them in the projects to begin with and keeps them there. A lot of people think people who live in projects are there because they want to be there, and that simply is not true. They think people that live in projects are lazy or stupid or simply just do not care. Most people do not really know what it is like living in a project as families and what it is like to struggle every day to try to keep your family together. I will tell you right now, projects have received a very bad rap. Eight out of ten families are good. It is the other two that give projects a bad name and make it hard on the rest of us to simply raise our children with safety and with love.

The seventies were the turning point in our small New England town, as it was for most of America. Drugs were invading our town and our communities. Of course the projects felt it the worse because the drugs and the racial tensions were becoming worse by the day. Our project that had been such a close-knit community was slipping away. It was very confusing for me and hard because most of my friends were black and Puerto Rican. I quickly found myself having to choose between my white friends or my black and Puerto Rican friends, and I did not know why. All of a sudden I had to choose, and it did not make any sense at all. We were all the same people as we were before, but now if I were seen playing or talking with one of my black friends, my white friends would shun me at school. At one time I was actually called a "nigger lover" by one of these white so-called friends. On that day I came home crying.

I spoke to my mother about what was going on, and she explained to me that it was not the children that were to blame for this; it was their parents. It was what they were being taught at home. All I know was it was very stupid. I remember one night I was watching TV with my mother when they showed the clip of Martin Luther King's famous "I Have a Dream" speech. When Dr. King Spoke about judging people not by the color of their skin, but by the content of their character, I was, as many people where, very moved by his words of love and compassion for our fellow men. He was a great man, and his death left an unfillable hole in the heart of the human race. Listening to his speech I thought, *How funny this is. His words have already been taught to me all of my life by my mother.*

My choices suddenly became very easy and very clear to me. I came to the conclusion that my white friends were not friends at all—no one that I had anything in common with outside of our skins. Looking back at this now, I can clearly see that their parents had brainwashed them into thinking just as they did. How sad! So my true friends remained my friends, and all the others just drifted away out of my life. My friends and I continued to be close at home and at school as we continued to walk together as usual to and from school.

There was one fateful day when we were coming home from school. It was 1974, just before summer vacation was about to begin. A group of three boys always walked behind our group. They were a year or two older than us and a bit more mischievous. I guess you can say they were just being typical 13-year-old boys. The railroad tracks that ran just behind the project were one of our regular shortcuts. Although our parents had warned us all of the danger, we, of course, did not listen.

On one of these days the three boys that always lagged behind decided they were going to try to jump onto one of the trains as it was going by. They thought this would be a lot of fun. The rest of us thought they were nuts. We could all think of better ways to have fun, but then again all people has their own idea of what fun is. My friends and I continued home. We were just entering the project when we could hear the train's whistle blowing. I approached my front door. Just then I could hear the train's wheels trying desperately to stop. The screeching of the wheels was almost deafening. I thought to myself at that moment, *Man, those boys are going to be in a lot of trouble.* My first thought was they put something on the tracks so that the train would have to stop. I quickly realized that this was not the case at all. Just then I could see one of the boys run into one of the other boys' house. I stood there and watched as the mother came running out of the house with the other boy, and they both ran quickly down the street to where the railroad tracks were.

What I heard next I would never forget—this poor woman's screams. I had never in my life heard anyone scream this loud. Her screams of anguish tore through the heart of our community. At that moment we all felt her pain, and it was horrible. I cannot even imagine what she saw or what she felt coming upon her son's mutilated body just lying by the railroad tracks. What a horrifying sight that must have been!

We would later find out that the boy was trying to jump the train and his legs got sucked under the wheels. He lost both of his legs and almost his life on this day. He was never the same person after this, and neither was his mother. Even though he went through an enormous amount of physical therapy, mentally he was never the same. He and his mother became somewhat reclusive. They seemed to cut themselves out of the community forever, and within a year's time they had moved. I never ran into them or heard anything about them after this.

I am sad to say they were not the last ones to move out of our community. Things were really heating up in our project. The drugs were flowing freely through our community, and most of the teenagers had begun experimenting with them. Many of them became hooked, and it breaks my heart to say that my closest friends were among them. When they started breaking into apartments in the projects to support their drug habit, one by one all of the decent families began moving out. All of the families that I had talked about in our unit in a year's time had moved out. A lot of them had been broken into and no longer felt safe living there.

My mother and I were the last ones in our unit to move after we got broken into. My mother still could not afford to move out of the project, so she did the next best thing and that was to move us into the last unit of apartments in the project, the unit closest to the main street. We felt a little safer, but things there just went from bad to worse. One of my friend's older brothers started taking drugs, and because he really did not know how strong they were, he overdosed one day.

It happened right in front of me while I was over there playing with her. He fell to the floor and just started convulsing. His eyes rolled back in his head. All you could see was white. Foam started coming out of his mouth, and then all of a sudden everything just stopped. He had stopped breathing. He died right there in front of me. I was in shock. I had never seen anything like this before in my life. This was the first time I saw death. Just then the paramedics came in and started CPR on him. They were able to bring him back. They rushed him to the hospital, and he survived, but I will never forget that day and that sight.

On this day I swore to myself I would never take or have anything to do with drugs or people who did them. This scared me so much to see what drugs can do to your body and how quickly they can kill you. Even though this got around the project, it did not discourage any of my other friends from trying them. More and more of my friends were starting to experiment with them, and I was spending less and less time with them because of this. One by one I watched them slowly slip away. There was nothing I could do about it. The more I tried to talk them out of doing drugs, the more they began to avoid me. They just did not want to hear about it. We drifted apart forever.

This was one of the saddest times of my life so far. I started staying in my house and in my room more and more. I had no reason to go out. I could no longer stand what I was seeing my friends turning into. Thank God my mother enrolled me in a summer work program called CETA. It was for teenagers 13 and older from low-income families. It at least gave me a reason to leave the house and kept me away from the drug scene. It was a great program. It allowed kids to have their own money and be able to afford to buy their own school clothes and have a little spending money for themselves. When you have nothing, this opportunity was a really great thing.

I loved my first job. I had just turned 13, and my job was to do filing work at our local welfare office. I really loved it. The welfare office had air conditioning. I remember I did not mind it a bit, spending my long, hot summer days there, and I was getting paid for it to boot. I would walk to work every day and most days I would get a ride home from one of the social workers. One day toward the end of the summer, I think, when I had about one or two more weeks left to work before school started up again, one of the social workers dropped me off about a block away from the project. I remember walking down the street toward the project and hearing people yelling and screaming, along with police sirens. I was not sure where all these noises were coming from. The closer I got to the project the louder the noise got. I started to run down the street toward the project. I turned the corner and ran right smack dab into a line of police dressed in full riot gear.

I could not believe what I was seeing. It was like peering into Hell. There was a police car tipped over onto the roof and set on fire. There were other smaller fires all around, and my friends and other teenagers along with adults were running all around with the police at their heels. I saw one of my friends fall to the ground, and then try to get back up when a policeman jumped on her and hit her so hard in the head with his nightstick it looked as though her skull had been cracked like an egg shell. After seeing this I totally lost it. I tried to break through the police line only to be pushed back, and I fall to the ground by one of the policeman. He, at this time, yelled at me saying, "No one is getting in here, and no one is getting out!"

What concerned me most at this moment was my mother. You see, almost all of this was taking place right in front of our apartment. My mother was all alone in there. I had to somehow get in. I had to know if she was hurt or if they had gotten into our apartment and were just holding her there. I was so scared for her at this point that I really did not care about what could happen to me. I looked for an opening in the police line and found a place they were not guarding at the back of the project. Right next to the project was a factory with a big chain-link fence. I went down far enough so the police could not see me jump it. I made my way over the fence and ran as fast as I could to our back door. I began banging on the door yelling, "Mom, it's me, Kyra. Open the door. Let me in."

I do not know if my mother could not hear me over all the noise, but she did not open the door right away. I am sure it was just a matter of a minute or two that I was standing out there, but it felt like forever. I was really scared. Just then as she was opening the door for me, one of my friends came running around the corner of the building in cuffs, and quickly on his tail was a very angry cop with a very large nightstick. My mother quickly pulled me into the apartment and out of harm's way. Just as she closed the door the cop caught up with my friend and began beating him. I watched this out my back window. I would later find out that my friend ended up with a broken arm, broken nose, and shattered cheekbone. I guess he was lucky to still be alive.

It took hours for things to begin to calm down. They must have arrested half of the people that lived in our project. I later found out how all of that began. It started when the police came to arrest one of the neighborhood teenagers for breaking and entering. He was one of the teenagers that had been breaking into the apartments. I guess the boy decided he was not going to go peacefully, and the police began to get rough with him, slamming his body into the police car. I guess it was his mother that saw this and came running out and tried to protect her son. She began attacking the cop, and things just started exploding from there. Before they knew it they had a full riot on their hands. This small-town police force did not know what hit it. It was around midnight when things finally came to an end.

Going to sleep that night for me was very hard. The images of what I had just seen kept replaying themselves in my mind. The terror that I experienced that day reached into my own bed and made sleeping impossible. It was around four in the morning when I finally just got up and gave up trying to find any peace for this night. I sat at the edge of my bed, heartbroken.

Over the next year and a half, things went from bad to worse, to really bad. It got to the point where I never went out of the house except to go to school and food shop. My mother knew we could not really stay there much longer. She could see how very sad and lonely I had become. I was slowly slipping into a very bad depression. When I was 15 we finally moved. We moved into a nice four-room apartment downtown in one of our city's oldest buildings. It was over a clothing store. It felt funny at first to live right downtown, but the change was just what I needed to lift me out of the depression that had taken hold of me.

The winter of 1977 was pretty much like every winter in New England, cold with about six to ten inches of snow by Christmas. It was always very pretty. As usual my mother and I spent the Christmas holiday with my sisters, April and Amber, and their husbands. As usual, we all enjoyed ourselves very much. April was always the perfect hostess. Everything was always so lovely. She worked very hard to make it this way.

The following February of 1978 at my sister Amber's birthday party, we decided to spend the night. We had no idea of what was just about to hit the East Coast. Our one-night sleep over turned into a week. It was incredible and slightly scary. The blizzard of 1978 was upon us. Our whole town had come to a screeching halt; in fact, all of Massachusetts had come to a screeching halt. They simply could not clear the streets fast enough. The street department simply could not keep up with all that snowfall all at once. Our streets were impassable for close to a week. No one went anywhere. We had snowdrifts that reached up to people's second-floor windows. We were buried in snow. The storm system that produced all of this was very strong. It developed a pattern that would dump a massive amount of snow on us. Just when the forecasters thought it was blowing out to sea it did, but then it would return time and time again to dump even more snow. We were so completely buried in snow it took a week of digging out to make the roads just barely passable. It was very scary to see. It was certainly something I will never forget.

Winter turned into spring and spring into summer, and the Blizzard of 1978 became a distant memory. I had just turned 16. I was a high school student looking for a summer job. I submitted my application at a jewelry factory the next town over. My sister Amber was working in another factory close by. I thought it would be fun for us to ride into work together, and it was. I was hired for the summer, or it was just supposed to be for the summer, anyway. Summer was coming to an end, and I was supposed to be heading back to school, but just before my final day, the personnel manager called me down to his office to speak to me. He told me he was very impressed with my work ethic and honesty, and he said he really did not want to lose me. He offered me a permanent full-time position with the company, which also included a dollar more an hour raise. I found it impossible at the time to turn it down. I was just a sixteen-year-old kid that had nothing. I was finally given an opportunity to be able to afford to buy the things I wanted in life. I just could not pass this up. After all, my sisters were all factory workers themselves, and they did not finish high school. They seemed to be perfectly happy. They were able to own their own homes. They went on vacations and owned their own cars. Back then if you were willing to work hard, you were able to obtain these things and have a comfortable life, not like today.

So I made the fateful decision to quit school. It was easily the biggest mistake of my life, and one I would live to always regret. When I made this decision I was also thinking about my mother. For the first time in my life I would be able to help her a little. After all the sacrifices she had made for me and never once complained, she deserved so much more than this life had given her. My mother was a true believer in the idea of, you give to your children, and you take care of your children. Your children are not supposed to take care of you. She did not like to bother anyone for anything, not even her children. She was a very strong and very independent woman. The day I came home and told her I was quitting school she became very upset and tried her best to talk me out of doing this, but I think she knew all of her talking was a waste of time. All I can remember today is her yelling at me and telling me how stubborn I was, but she realized once I had set my mind to doing something, nothing, not even her yelling at me, would make me change it. Her last statement about this was, "I guess I cannot fault your stubbornness too greatly because I know you get it from me!"

CHAPTER TWO

After much yelling and much discussion, the following week I began my first real job. It felt great being able to help my mother and to buy the things we needed and wanted. My first week at work went very well, and my sister Amber, with whom I was riding to work, asked if would like to stop on the way home from work and get a beer. I was only sixteen and a half. At the time the drinking age was 18, but I looked like I was 20. I was never carded, and I unfortunately I never had a problem getting alcohol. Alcohol was an accepted thing in my family between my sisters and me. My mother, on the other hand, absolutely hated the idea of her daughters drinking. My sisters as well as I had inherited from our father his four worst personality traits. These were alcoholism, gambling, a very strong willingness to fight at the drop of a hat, and a very bad temper. Most people have their own personal demons that they must fight. These are my demons, and I have had to fight them all of my life right up to today.

Amber and I would stop for a couple of beers once or twice a week on our way home from work. I very much enjoyed this time of the day. We would just sit and talk over a couple of beers. Also, at this time I had begun going out with a few people from work on the weekends. This was the seventies, and disco was just reaching its heights. I discovered I loved to dance, and it was one of the few things I was really good at. Unfortunately, along with the disco scene came drinking and drugs. The drugs I had no problem staying way from. As I said before, they scared the hell out of me. But the drinking, on the other hand, I embraced even though I hated my father for his drinking and how he let it destroy our family. I found I took to it like a duck takes to water. To this day I do not understand how you can hate something so strongly and at the same time desire it just as strongly. The human mind is so complex.

I began more and more to find myself not being satisfied now with just going out on the weekends and getting drunk, nor was I satisfied with just one or two beers with my sister after work. I would continue drinking at night in my bedroom, and I began sneaking in shots of whiskey. I don't know how, but so far I was successful in hiding this from my mother. This continued on for months. I would get drunk every night alone in my room. The alcoholism that had run rampant through my family had finally taken hold of me. The urge and the craving was so powerful, it just snuck up on me before I knew it.

At the age of sixteen and a half I was now a full-fledged alcoholic. I became very good at hiding it, and actually so good I was even able to hide it from myself. I guess I could not accept the fact I had become the very thing I hated most, an alcoholic. I was so deeply into denial I could not see what was right in front of me. Denial is a powerful emotion. I found it to be at least as powerful as alcoholism.

On November 4, 1978, I was getting ready to go out to my favorite disco. I put on my favorite outfit, which was a cocoa-brown, nylon wraparound skirt, a matching body-suit top, with my bronze-colored stiletto-heel sandals. One of my girlfriends from work was supposed to go to the club with me, but at the last minute something came up, and she had to cancel. Well, I was all dressed up, so I decided to just go by myself. After all, I knew most everybody at the club and felt comfortable enough going by myself. On my way there I remember thinking to myself, *I have a lot in my life that I am grateful for— good friends, a good job, and my family.* I was happy for the most part, but I always felt there was something missing in my life. I always felt incomplete and did not know why. Perhaps it was something from my childhood or maybe something else.

I arrived at the club around eight. Two of my friends were already on the dance floor. I took a seat at the end of the bar, and that is when I saw him. He was sitting about five seats away. I took one look at him, and he took one look at me, and at that very moment when our eyes met, it was just like fireworks going off. I don't mean just these little firework displays that they set off for the Fourth of July, but a whole damn factory's worth. I lost myself in his beautiful hazel eyes. They reached down into my very soul.

I never before this night believed in love at first sight, but that is exactly what this was, love at first sight for both of us. It was so strange. We just sat there staring at each other for the longest time. He finally worked up enough courage to come and talk to me. He started walking toward me, and all I could think of was that there was something strangely familiar about him, though I cannot

28

imagine from where. As he came closer to me he began to smile. It was the sweetest thing I have ever seen. He had a full beard and mustache and shoulder-length, wavy, dark honey-blond hair, and of course those beautiful hazel eyes. He was built like a lumberjack. He was wearing jeans and cowboy boots and a baby-blue silk shirt that showed every muscle he had. He was incredibly looking and very sweet and soft-spoken. He walked up to me and introduced himself to me as Michael. Then he reached over and gently took my hand and asked me what my name was. I told him my name was Kyra. He then asked me if I cared to dance, and of course I said yes. That very moment was our beginning. I felt as though I had just truly started to live. We danced the night away. Time went by so fast. Before we knew it, it was 2 a.m. The club was closing, but we just could not say goodbye. We ended up in an all-night coffee shop, where we talked until the sun came up.

From that moment on we were inseparable. Every day after that we were together. I felt as though I had found the other half of my heart. For the very first time in my life I felt whole and complete. I could not bear to think of my life now without Michael in it. Every day after work he would come over to pick me up, and we would sometimes just go for a long drive and talk. Other times we would go on long walks sometimes through the woods his mother owned. His mother owned a house with about 15 acres of land in the back. As far as the eye could see there were pine trees and wild blueberry patches.

Michael and I would spend hours just walking and talking. He told me all about his childhood living there. He had horses, goats, and donkeys. He had become so good at horseback riding he was able to ride bareback, which is a very hard thing to do. Michael also loved and was very good at fishing and hunting. He had spent countless summer days at the pond down the street from his house fishing. When he became a little older, around 12 or 13, he began hunting. His father had bought him his own shotgun. He particularly liked hunting rabbit. I thought to myself, *Oh, my God, I have fallen in love with a cowboy.* And I also thought how very different our childhoods were, as different as night and day.

I remember the first time we made love like it was yesterday. It was a couple of days before Thanksgiving, and it was unusually warm. Michael packed a picnic lunch, and we went for a long walk in the woods. Michael spread out the blanket in the middle of a clearing next to a pine grove. We sat down and then lay down. We held each other close looking up at the sky. I remember the crystal clear blue sky and a few puffy clouds dancing by. The air was so crisp and clear. Michael reached over to kiss me, and there we made love for the first time. Under the beautiful blue sky our love was born and that was also the first time Michael and I proclaimed our love for each other.

This is a day that I will keep alive in my heart and in my mind forever. From that day on Michael always made me feel safe and protected. He told me he would always be there for me, and he was. Michael was a good and loving man that always stood by his word. He always considered himself a man of honesty and honor. These two traits were always important to him.

One day after work he picked me up at my mother's house as usual, and we went out for a drive and to eat. We ended up at the lake to watch the sun set. I loved watching the sunset with Michael at the lake. Everything was so quiet and peaceful. The sunsets were so beautiful with magnificent colors of brilliant reds, oranges and violets. I look at a sunset as though the sky is God's canvas with beautiful brilliant strokes only he could paint.

Michael and I had been dating for about a month when he felt safe enough in our relationship to start confiding in me. He told me he had been in Vietnam and that he had been drafted into the army at 19 years old. Just like most of the men drafted at 1967 when he was, they weren't even men yet, they were still just boys that were forced to grow up really fast or die. He started opening up and telling me all about his experiences there, the horrors he witnessed, the images and the feelings. These images had embedded themselves forever in his mind. No matter how hard he tried he just could not get them out of his head. Michael described it like a bad horror movie playing over and over again in his head. When he slept, when he was awake, it was just always there. Drinking was the only thing that provided him the ability not to feel this. While he was drunk, he was numb. That was the only time he truly felt at peace even though this peace only lasted a short period of time like so many other Vietnam vets that were not provided the proper help that they all so desperately needed after Vietnam. Just like so many other men, Michael crawled into the bottle.

To start off with, it was bad. His platoon was stationed in Fort Carson, Colorado. He was a member of the armored cavalry. His platoon trained twice as long as a normal platoon would have because it was picked to go and avenge the platoon that had gone before them and had been wiped out. I guess the Army was trying to make some sort of a super troop out of these guys.

After six months Michael's basic training was complete, and then he and his platoon were off to Vietnam. Michael then told me about his first impression of Vietnam. He felt as if he had just been dropped into the middle of a John Wayne movie. It just seemed so surreal. The helicopter that he was riding in would not even land. They had to jump out of it. When there was a lot of firing going on they called this a hot LZ (landing zone). Michael felt as though he had landed right in the middle of Hell. There was gun fire going on all around him, and the first thing Michael's platoon leader said to him was, "Don't shoot until you get shot at, because it is very hard to tell who the enemy is and who is on our side."

Michael thought at that very moment, *You have got to be fucking kidding me.* Michael learned very quickly about how to survive. At the age of 19 he had become an infantry soldier and an expert marksman, and he was also one of the men who were assigned to run the mortars. He hated the mortars. They were very hard to run and very loud. He was not there very long when the Tet Offensive hit. Tet is a huge holiday in Vietnam. It is like our Thanksgiving, Christmas, and New Year's all rolled up into one. The Vietnamese government asked for a cease-fire for this holiday, and being the honorable people we are, our government agreed to this. Well, they took full advantage of our honor and hit us with everything they had. You could say we got caught with our pants down!

Michael was back at base camp along with most of his platoon. Michael was relaxing in his bunk, taking a well-earned rest from all the madness that was going on. He could escape this at least for a few days. Just then all Hell broke loose. When the first bomb hit it threw him right out of his bunk and across the barracks. It was total chaos. All of the men just started running around, scrambling to find their weapons. As they were being hit with bomb after bomb, Michael ran out of the barracks. Just then another bomb hit, and he was thrown to the ground. While he was lying there, a live grenade landed no more two feet away from him. He thought to himself, *Dear God, this is it. I'm dead.* Then a miracle happened. It did not go off. It was a dud, but within those few short seconds of waiting to get blown up, Michael said his life flashed before him. His first thoughts were of his mother and father and how devastating his death would be to them. After a few seconds passed he realized the grenade was a dud, and he felt as though at that moment anyway, he had cheated death. He got up, shaking, and joined the other soldiers in getting the mortars and all of the other weapons up and running so they would be able to start fighting back.

They did just that. This battle lasted for days. That first night during the battle a few of the Vietnamese infiltrated the camp. They were quickly shot down. At this point Michael was lying on his stomach shooting as the enemy ran in front of him. He had one in the cross hairs of his rifle and had his finger on the trigger ready to shoot. The figure was about one hundred feet away when another bomb went off. Just then Michael saw blonde hair. That was the only thing that saved that soldier's life that night. Michael knew there were no Vietnamese blondes! It turned out the man was a medic, and he was bravely running across the battlefield to pull our wounded soldiers to safety. Michael could not believe what he had almost done. When he realized he had almost shot one of his own men, he felt so sick. Later, after everything was over, he told the medic what had happened and if he did not have blonde hair, he would have been dead. Michael told me after that fateful night it seemed to him like the battles and the war itself hit a fever pitch. The men had to fight all the time. They had very few days of rest. Michael was so tired he actually fell asleep while standing up leaning against a tree.

Through all of this there would be one battle that would affect and change his life forever. This was the day when his platoon and another platoon a little further away were both engaged in battle against the enemy. The other platoon found itself surrounded by the enemy. The men were being picked off one by one, and they could not escape. They all faced certain death if they did not act quickly. Their platoon leader radioed over to Michael's platoon leader for mortar rounds to be dropped in their area in the hope of eliminating some of the enemies. The coordinates of the mortar rounds were given by the other platoon's commander, and Michael, along with five other men who were running the five other mortars, was given these coordinates by his commander. The condition of the ground he was in was muddy and soft, so every time Michael and the other men shot off a mortar round, the mortar would sink further and further into the ground. They had to reset the coordinates after every round so the mortar shells would land on their targets like they supposed to.

At this time the other platoon was beginning to become totally overrun by the enemy, and they started calling the mortar rounds in faster and faster. Michael's commander was just shouting at them, "Fire! Fire! Fire!" Michael and the other men were not given the proper time to reset the coordinates. They were all just ordered to keep firing. The result of this was horrific. Most of the other platoon was being killed and maimed by our own men. They call it "friendly fire." I really hate that term, and so did Michael. Michael, along with his platoon rushed to their aid and killed any of the remaining enemy that were still alive. The few men from that platoon that were still alive were very badly blown apart.

As they were bringing them out on stretches and putting them into the helicopters, they passed by Michael and the other men that were on the mortars. One soldier who had his arm and half of his face blown away started screaming at Michael and the other men. "Why, why did you do this to us? You killed us all!" Those were the exact words this poor man used. This cut so deeply into Michael's heart and soul he had to try and find out which one of the mortar rounds landed where all of these men were killed.

After this horrifying incident with the friendly fire, Michael would never again return to the mortars; he would simply be an Infantry soldier. There was a small investigation as to exactly what went wrong that day, but there were no conclusions made. It was just simply a horrifying accident, but this horrifying accident would live with Michael for the rest of his life. This was something that would haunt his dreams and haunt him. The guilt that he would carry now would sometimes be completely overwhelming.

While he and the other men remained in Vietnam they had to somehow deal with this and put it away so that they could live and fight, at least for the time being, anyway. Michael and his platoon had already survived the worst fighting of the war, and that was the Tet Offensive, and now for this to happen. It was just too much, too much pain for one man's heart and mind to take. But Michael would survive this and the rest of the war to come back home from Vietnam with no physical scars but many, many mental scars. He would punish himself for the rest of his life over what happened there, even though he was just following orders just like all the other men were. It wasn't fair.

Michael suffered from what you would call "survivors' guilt." Why did the soldier standing next to him get killed and not him? Why was he lucky enough to make it back home and not one of his friends? He could never understand this. You know, when you are wounded in battle and you have your scars, your wounds eventually heal. I think it's much, much harder to heal a brain, to heal a mind and to forgive yourself. I don't think Michael ever truly did this.

I was very grateful that Michael loved me enough to open up and tell me all of these horrible things that happened to him. He told me throughout his life that I was the only person that he felt comfortable enough to tell all of this to. I can't even begin to tell you how good this made my heart feel. We were the closest that two people could ever be. We shared our deepest, darkest secrets. I would tell him about my childhood and about my father, something that I had never told anyone before. We trusted only each other with these secrets.

I realized Michael had me to talk to, but there were so many Vietnam vets that had nobody to reveal all their secrets to, things that they were ashamed of for no reason. A lot of these men, too many of these men, just suffered in silence. Before Michael met me he did find a source of relief, and that was the alcohol. He called it a shot of Novocain to the heart. With every drink that he took he would forget a little more, and that was his mental relief. He didn't feel anything, and he didn't think when he was drunk. He just was.

Throughout this first year together, Michael would tell me many, many things. He also told me about how he felt toward his fellow soldiers. They were not just fellow soldiers, but they were brothers, brothers in arms. So I guess when you lose one of your brothers, someone that you consider a brother, the cut is very deep and the pain never goes away.

Many, many nights throughout this coming year Michael and I would sit by the lake talking, and he would also tell me about the climate in Vietnam and other little things, including the bugs and the heat. He also mentioned this defoliant that our government sprayed on the brush. The brush was so thick and so high that our enemies would hide behind it and ambush them, so they had to find some way to get rid of it, and Agent Orange was used. This chemical defoliant worked quickly and effectively.

Unfortunately it wouldn't be until much later that we would find out the side effects of it, and these side effects were horrific. Men were coming back from war having children that were horribly deformed due to this chemical. I suppose these were the men that had it directly sprayed on them. Michael said he saw them. They would go over in little planes like dust croppers and just spray it. Michael, fortunately, did not have it sprayed directly on him, but he and his platoon would come through later on, kicking up this dust through the dead brush. He thought to himself, *How strange this is and how weird it was to see all this dead brush.* He, just like all the other men, had no idea at the time exactly what they were kicking up, what kind of horrible poison they were ingesting.

I guess what really upsets me to this day is that our government had other choices to make. They could have gone with other chemical agents, (ironically) Agent Red, White and Blue, but these were not as effective. Our government didn't give any thoughts to what this chemical could do to a human body in the long run. They just wanted it done quickly. They wanted the foliage dead, and they just didn't care that the men that they were spraying it on were going to be dead, too. Many of these men later on would die of horrible cancers caused directly by Agent Orange.

About a month after the friendly fire incident, Michael through our conversations told me about when he again found himself in the middle of yet another battle. All of a sudden a helicopter landed nearby. The sergeant got out of the helicopter and went over to his commanding officer asking him where Michael J. Jones III was, and his commanding officer pointed to Michael.

The sergeant then went over to Michael and asked him, "Are you Michael J. Jones III?"

Michael said, "Yes, I am."

He said, "You need to come with me immediately."

Michael had no idea what in the hell was going on. He followed the sergeant back into the helicopter, and they took off. During the journey the sergeant told Michael that he was needed at home immediately because his father was very ill. This was a total shock to Michael, because throughout all the letters that his mother had sent him she had never mentioned his father being ill. Michael had also done something else while he was over there. He sent most of his pay back home to his mother and father to help pay the bills. He had no idea at the time that he was doing this that all they were living on was the little bit of money that he sent home every month. Michael would only keep enough money to buy cigarettes and a beer when he was on leave. He had no idea how much they needed that money because she never let him know. She was afraid that thinking of his father would preoccupy his mind, and he could possibly be killed, so she kept the bad news from him. This all came to him in a crushing blow. After everything else that he had just experienced, now finding his father close to death was just more than he could handle.

They got Michael on a flight back home. He landed in Boston still dressed in his fatigues. Remember, he was literally picked up off the battlefield. He had about $35 in his wallet, and he had no way to get home. Boston is about a 45-

minute drive from Morton. He wasn't thinking correctly. His brains were scrambled. He should have called a family member to come and pick him up, but he wasn't even thinking that way. He wasn't thinking at all. He got into a taxi and told the cab driver where he had just come from, what was going on at home and that he needed to get home as soon as possible. He told the cab driver that he had just been picked off the battlefield.

The cab driver turned around and said to him, "So what?"

Mind you, a lot of the Vietnam vets did not get a very good reception at their homecoming. A lot of them were spit on and called "baby killers," so I guess for the cab driver to just simply say, "So what?" was not such an unusual thing at the time, but this floored Michael. He just shook his head, and he said to the cab driver, "Take me as far as $35 will bring me."

The cab driver turned around and just started driving. He ended up dropping Michael off on the side of the highway, leaving Michael to hitchhike the rest of the way home.

In the late '60s, standing on the highway dressed in battle fatigues, Michael began hitchhiking. Thank God a van of, I guess you would call them hippies, picked him up and gave him a ride back to Morton.

He immediately went to the hospital without stopping at home to wash or change. He went to the ICU Ward where his father lay dying. Michael told me what he looked like when he walked into the room. He said it was incredible and devastating. My father looked like a human balloon. His father was dying of severe cirrhosis of the liver. Michael went over to him and touched his hand, and his father opened his eyes and he began to cry.

He said, "Michael, is that really you?"

His father thought he was hallucinating. He said, "Yes, Dad, it's me. I'm here."

His father asked again because he simply couldn't believe it. He said, "You haven't even changed."

Michael said, "No. I just got here as soon as I could." Michael didn't want to leave his father's side, but he realized he had to get washed up, so he took a cab home after spending a couple of hours with his dad.

The first thing he said to his mother was, "Why didn't you tell me that Dad was so sick?"

That's when she began to explain that she didn't want him distracted because she was afraid he would be killed. That's also when he found out how important that money was that he was sending home every month, and he thought to himself, *Thank God I did that,* because he really didn't know. Michael then quickly got washed up and changed his clothes and headed back to the hospital, where he remained for the next three days.

It was on July 3 that his father passed away. This devastated Michael, but he thought to himself, *Thank God I was at least able to be there at that very last moment of my father's life.* Michael composed himself as much as he could and went with his mother to make the funeral arrangements.

On the day of his father's funeral at the grave side, Linda Davis, a congresswoman from Massachusetts, attended the funeral. You see, Michael's father was a World War II vet and also a member of the Local Four, a huge construction union. Perhaps that's why she was there. I really don't know, but Michael told me he remembers it like it happened yesterday. She turned to Michael as he stood there in his full dress uniform and asked him if he would like to stay home or return back to Vietnam. He looked at her and couldn't believe she was actually asking him this.

He told me he looked at her as though she had three heads and said, "Yes, I would rather stay home. I don't want to go back to Vietnam."

So she helped get him a compassionate reassignment where he was able to stay in the United States and serve out the rest of his time in the military. Thank God for this, because it was only a couple of months after this happened *that Michael got word that most of his platoon had been wiped out, and he couldn't help but think, My God, if my father hadn't died, I probably would have.*

This was yet another devastating blow to Michael because he remembered all the men in his platoon, and he wondered how many of them made it back. During all of this he was trying to take care of his mother and his two little brothers. He had two younger brothers, John and Joe. His mother suffered from severe rheumatoid arthritis, which just about crippled her, so Michael had his hands full. He tried to do his best, but he had been so scarred from Vietnam. There was only so much he could handle, and it became just too overwhelming. He crawled into a bottle, and that is where he remained for the next ten years. Becoming numb and self-medicating himself was the only way for him to avoid a complete mental breakdown at this point.

Throughout all of these stories that he would tell me, my heart would break for him. I knew I couldn't stop his pain. I could only sit there and listen to it, and this hurt me deeply because I loved him so much. I began to think that perhaps with his talking about it and letting all the painful emotions out, somehow it would begin to heal him. This is what I hoped for, to somehow help him heal his heart. I knew I could never erase these memories, but I was hoping to somehow replace these bad memories with good memories, memories that Michael and I would make together. Maybe the good memories could override the bad somehow. I knew I had a long road ahead of me, and this became my heart's work. All I knew at this point right now I was in it for the long haul because my heart left me no choice. He was my first love, and I had a feeling deep down that he was going to be my last, my only love forever.

It was now also around this time, I would say about a month and a half to two months after we had started dating, Michael told me something else that he was keeping a secret. He had a son, Michael Jr.

I asked him, "Why did you keep this a secret for so long?"

He just told me he was afraid I would think badly of him because he wasn't able to stay with his son's mother because they just didn't get along.

I told him, "Don't be ridiculous. Things happen, and I understand."

Then he told me he wanted me to meet Michael Jr., and he thought we would hit it off. Michael then told me that he was going to arrange to pick up Michael Jr. that weekend. I was so excited. I couldn't wait to meet this little guy.

That day came, and I remember it like it was yesterday seeing Michael Jr. for the first time. He was so cute with his curly blond hair. He was three years old, and he was absolutely adorable and so sweet. I leaned down and gave Michael Jr. a big hug. I introduced myself, and he just smiled so sweetly at me. Michael and I took him for a ride to get an ice cream, and then the three of us just sat in the car talking. Michael seemed to really like me. Thank goodness our first meeting was a success.

On the same day after Michael and I dropped Michael Jr. off at home, we went for a ride. We just happened to pass Webster Street, the street that I mentioned earlier where my mother, my sister April, and I lived. This was our final move back home from New York. This was the apartment where I had met Sue, Ashley, and their family. This was the family that lived right across the street from us, the family that I had spent so much time with and of whom I had so many fond memories.

Michael told me then, "Oh, that's where my Uncle Charlie lived."

I then asked him, "Did your Uncle Charlie have two little girls, Sue and Ashley?"

Michael turned to me and said, "Yes, they're my cousins."

I said to myself, "Oh, my God, is this a small world or what?" I then asked Michael, "Do you remember going over to your Uncle Charlie's house just before you were ready to ship out to Vietnam?"

Michael replied, "Yes."

I then asked him, "Do you remember seeing your two cousins and another little girl sitting on the living room floor playing a board game, and looking at the little girl?"

He thought for a moment, and he said, "My God, yes."

I then told him, "Michael, I was that little girl."

We were both completely blown away, and for me to realize at that moment I actually saw him before all of this happened to him. I got to see the real Michael before he was scarred for life. Then it came to me that night we first met in the disco, when I looked into his eyes. He looked so familiar but I just couldn't place him until this moment. I have to tell you this blew both our minds.

It was this first summer together that we decided to get our own place and move in together. We thought it would be really nice to be able to have Michael stay over on the weekends. It was just a small, one-bedroom place, but it met our needs and we were very happy there. So just as we planned we had Michael Jr. sleeping over on the weekends, one or two weekends a month, and he would sleep between us. We were a nice little family, and it felt so right. I remember Michael Jr.'s favorites were a plain, cheese pizza and vanilla ice cream, so we would always try to have plenty of that on hand. His favorite show to watch was *The Dukes of Hazard.*

At this point in our relationship Michael and I had been together for about eight months. On one of the weekends that we weren't taking Michael Jr., Michael asked me if I would like to go down the Cape and spend the night at a hotel. I said, "Yeah, that sounds like fun. Sort of a mini-vacation."

You know, if a woman is lucky she gets at least one perfect weekend, one perfect moment that will live in her memory forever. It is one of those moments that during the hard times and your painful times you can look back on and gain comfort from. Well, this weekend was to be mine, my one perfect weekend. My one perfect memory, a memory that will remain in my heart and my mind until I draw my last breath. That weekend Michael and I began packing up our car, and then we headed down the Cape to Onset Beach. This would be a place that we would revisit many times in our lives.

Once we arrived at Onset we checked into a hotel called the Oakcrest. It was a cute little Bed and Breakfast right across the street from Onset Harbor and Beach. It was about three o'clock in the afternoon. After we got settled in our room we changed into our bathing suits and walked across the street to sit on the beach. We sat there, me sipping my piña coladas, and Michael drinking his Jack Daniels. We went for a long swim and just enjoyed the cool water on a hot, hot summer's day.

Before we knew it the day was coming to an end, and the sun was beginning to set. Michael and I sat there on the beach with only a few people left. Michael was holding me in his arms as we sat there watching the beautiful sunset over the horizon. The brilliant oranges and reds were magnificent. While the sun was setting, the last few people on the beach were beginning to pack up. Soon we had the beach to ourselves.

We were sitting there now in the dark, under the midnight blue sky a quiet peaceful cool breeze blowing across our faces. Michael began kissing and caressing my neck. We both fell backwards onto our warm blanket.

He then began caressing my stomach working slowly to my breasts, and I told him, "Michael, we are on the beach. There are people around."

He said, "There is no one here but us."

I looked, and I realized he was right. We were alone, and we began making love under the midnight blue sky. I felt as though I was in a dream, a dream I never wanted to wake up from. I could feel him inside of me, and it felt so right and so good as I lay under him trembling with both our passions exploding. He held me in his arms, and I felt so safe. Afterwards we just lay there in each other's arms, neither one of us wanting to let the other go.

He then turned to me and said, "Kyra, let's go get something to eat and maybe do a little bit of dancing. How does that sound?"

I looked at him, and I smiled and said, "That sounds terrific, my love."

We started back to the hotel room, and after we got all washed up and dressed we headed down the street where there was this really cute seafood restaurant. It had a juke box in the back if you wanted to dance, so of course we did. The first thing Michael and I did was to hit the jukebox. Michael played a song for me, "Only You," and took my hand and led me onto the small dance floor where we held each other tight. Michael sang along with the song softly in my ear.

That was that one perfect night, that one perfect dance, that one perfect song, and that one perfect man. This memory alone sustains me to this day. I could feel our hearts beating together during this dance, and it made me feel so strong. Our love was strong, and this is something you could definitely feel. I felt with Michael beside me there was nothing I wouldn't be able to accomplish. Just as he would always have me to lean on, I knew I would always have him to lean on as well.

It was so strange. He made me feel strong, but at the same time, every time he held me in his arms, I would turn to Jell-O. His very touch would send shivers down my spine. We danced after this to a few more songs. By this time we were working up quite an appetite, and Michael ordered two seafood platters. Oh, my God, they were just overflowing!

I looked at him, and I said, "I hope you have a really good appetite, because I really don't think I can finish all of this."

I was correct. I was only able to eat about half of it. Michael did make a pretty good dent in his. Both of us at this point were exhausted, and now we were completely stuffed. It was a fantastic day!

After we finished our dinner we headed back to our cozy little hotel room where we got undressed and just lay there in each other's arms for the longest time. It wouldn't be long before the passion would overtake us again. We made love all night long, and just as the light was breaking through the blinds, we fell asleep, holding each other close.

Like I said, I wished everyone could have one perfect moment. We should all be allowed that one perfect moment that we could freeze and go back to when we need to, when things are so hard we can barely handle them. But only being human, all we have are our memories, and those will have to be enough and this is mine.

That next afternoon we returned back to the beach to spend the rest of the day before heading back home. That afternoon, when we arrived back home and were unpacking the car, I thought to myself, *I don't think anything will ever compare to the weekend that we just had.*

There would be many, many more weekends that Michael and I would return back to Onset Beach, mostly with Michael Jr., to fish or just to have fun, but nothing would compare with this. The rest of that summer flew by. Before we knew it, it was our one-year anniversary, November 4, 1979.

Michael and I enjoyed living together very much and being able to hold each other every night, but somehow our drinking was getting worse, both mine and Michael's. I don't exactly know why. I guess it's just that slippery slopes and the nature of the beast, an alcoholic only gets worse, not better while drinking. We found ourselves instead of going once or twice a week to our favorite bar to play pool with our friends and have drinks; we were going practically every night now. It was strange. It seemed like the happier Michael was, the more he drank. I think it went back to that guilt, that survivor's guilt. I don't think he truly believed he had a right to be happy. The happier he was, the more he wanted to numb himself.

Michael always had a hot temper. His nickname was "Wild Man." That was his father's and his grandfather's nickname as well, so it sort of ran in the family. The more he drank the more his temper would come out and the more fights he would get into. It seemed like practically now every time we went out and tried to enjoy ourselves, he would end up getting into a fight with one of the guys, sometimes one of his friends at the bar. But right or wrong I always had his back, and he knew it, and I always knew he had mine. A lot of the time I would intervene, especially when it was one of his friends he was about to punch in the face for no good reason, and I mean intervene. I would actually stand in front of the man that he was ready to throw a punch at.

Michael told me one time, "I wish you would stop doing that. Out of reflex, I'm going to hit you, and I don't want to do that."

I told him, "No, you won't. I know you won't," and you know, he never did.

I knew Michael had reached a new low in his life when the bartender took me aside one day and said to me, "You know, Kyra, I really hate like hell to see Michael coming without you because you are about the only one that can control him."

Even though he was arguing and fighting a lot at the bar, our relationship somehow remained ever strong. I can count on one hand how many arguments we had, and they were usually about something stupid, but even through all the fights and the drinking, we did enjoy going to our favorite bar. We enjoyed playing pool with our friends, two friends in particular, Alex and his wife, Corey. Most of the other guys had known Michael for years, so I was accepted into their little circle, and I always felt welcome and respected. For the most part we all had a lot of fun together.

It was just before Christmas that I would receive a crushing blow. One night

Michael and I decided to go to Alex and Corey's apartment to pay them a visit. Michael and I walked in the door, and we went into the kitchen and sat down at the kitchen table. On the table was this newspaper, The Gazette. On the front page was a face staring up at me, a very familiar face. It was one of my old childhood friends, Angel. The headline read, "Girl found murdered in her own bed." My blood ran cold. I couldn't even talk.

I said to Michael, "I can't stay here. I have to go."

He looked at me and said, "Why?"

I said, "This was one of my best friends," and I pointed to *The Gazette*.

As we were walking out the door Alex said, "I'm sorry, Kyra."

I was choking back the tears, I just said, "Goodbye."

Once we got into the car, I broke down and cried my heart out. I felt so sick inside. The more I read, the sicker I became. Here was this young innocent girl who was found suffocated in her own bed. Just like my grandfather's murder, they would never find out who did it. Michael held me in his arms as I sat there in our car, crying uncontrollably. All these memories of my childhood just came rushing back to me all at once, memories of Angel and me along with our other friends walking to school together, walking back home from school, playing baseball in the backfield, and just having fun. For her to end up this way was inconceivable.

Michael and I went back home that night, and I just went to bed and cried myself to sleep thinking of her last moments on earth and how horrifying they must have been to her. It made me sick.

As the days passed by I couldn't get the thought of Angel out of my mind. I guess it was a week later Michael had to stay with his mother because she was sick with the flu. This left me home alone. All of these memories of my childhood were just too overwhelming. I began drinking, this time scotch. I drank, and I drank, and I drank until I couldn't remember anymore. I went into a blackout, and the last thing I remember was sitting at the kitchen table. I remember nothing after that. I woke up on my living room floor. I never told Michael about this. I never before drank that much to cause me to go into a blackout, and it scared the hell out of me.

It was now maybe a month after this happened that something else strange began happening in our relationship. Michael was starting to experience night terrors and flash backs. I'll never forget the first time Michael had a night terror. He was screaming at me in Vietnamese, and he punched me in the face.

Thank God it wasn't hard enough to leave a bruise. It was just hard enough to hurt like hell. Once the night terrors started, they happened more and more frequently. First it was maybe once every two weeks, and then it was once a week, and then it was two or three times a week. One night I woke up to find him crouching down beside the bed on his side hiding behind the bed, speaking again in Vietnamese and looking up over the bed in terror. The look that was in his eyes I will never forget.

I quickly put the light on to see this, and I kept yelling to him, "Michael, Michael, it's me, Kyra."

He snapped out of it and just sat there crying not knowing what in the hell had just happened to him. Again that look in his eyes when he was going through this was like he was seeing me but not seeing me. He was there but some place else at the same time. It was truly terrifying and heartbreaking to watch, and then before I knew it, it stopped as quickly as it started. He would fall back to sleep again. Sometimes he would remember, and sometimes not.

I remember one night in particular, by far the worst flashback he had ever had. He had picked me up from work, and we went to the bar. We shot a little pool, and we had a couple of drinks. Actually he wasn't even drunk that night. We went home, and I cooked supper. It was a nice steak dinner, and after eating he relaxed on the couch. I was doing the dishes in the kitchen when all of a sudden I heard a crash. I came running out of the kitchen to see Michael standing there in the middle of the living room, screaming and yelling at me again in Vietnamese, and I said, "Oh, no!" because from the look he had on his face he looked like he wanted to kill me. I knew what he was seeing. He wasn't seeing me. He was seeing the enemy, and I didn't know what to do. It was a small apartment, and outrunning him was not an option. He then began to rip things off the walls and throw all of our glass things around, our decorations, breaking them on tables and smashing our stereo.

He totaled the whole apartment, and then he came at me. I was trying desperately to avoid him by going around things. But he finally grabbed me, and when he did, I thought to myself, *This is it!* He grabbed me, and he threw me so hard against the wall I slid down it. I could not feel my legs, I hit my back so hard. As I lay there with him four or five feet away from me yelling and screaming in Vietnamese still, I knew what was going to be coming because he had showed me hand-to-hand combat before. He was going to come and smash my head. I knew I had to somehow get up. I had to move or die.

Just then I began getting the feeling back in my legs, thank God, and I crawled away from him and got up and ran into our bedroom, barricading the door. From the phone in our room I called my sister Amber. I didn't know who else to call. I didn't want to call the police because I knew Michael wasn't Michael, and I didn't want him to be arrested. Amber said that she would be right over. I explained to her what was going on, and she told me to stay in the room.

In the meantime things started to quiet down in the living room, so I thought I could get out the door. I knew I would have to go through the living room to do so, but I did, and I did reach the door. I got out, and I stood on the porch. I could see Michael through the window sitting there on the couch with his hands over his face.

Then all of a sudden he spoke in his own voice, and the words that he uttered just ripped right through me and broke my heart. He said, "Kyra, Kyra, where am I?"

He had no idea of what he had just done or even where he was. As he sat there in the middle of all this rubble that used to be our beautiful little apartment, he began crying hysterically. I didn't know whether I should go back in or just remain out on the porch and wait for my sister Amber to come. I didn't know what would be the right thing to do, but as I always did I followed my heart, and my heart told me that my Michael, the real Michael, would never hurt me. So I took a deep breath, and I walked back in. I went over to the couch, and I put my arms around Michael, and I held him as he was crying and shaking. He was totally traumatized, even more than I was.

As we sat there looking around at the mess, he looked at me and said, "I did this?"

I said to him, "Michael, yes, you did."

Then he asked me, "Did I hurt you?"

"No," because you see Michael didn't hurt me, something else did, something that he had no control over. My Michael would never hurt me.

Yet one more thing that I kept from him because I didn't think he needed to know. I told him, "No. I just grabbed the phone and ran out to the porch, and I called Amber when you started." That's all he needed to know.

It was a few minutes after this that my sister Amber arrived. She had stopped for a 6-pack of beer. She said it sounded like we could use a few drinks.

I just looked at her and laughed. I said, "Yeah, maybe," and she began looking around.

She said, "Oh, my God. It looks like a bomb went off here."

I said, "Yeah," and I took her aside and said, "Michael doesn't know anything. Just forget it." She and I just started cleaning up and salvaging what was left.

All Michael kept saying was, "I'm sorry, Kyra, I'm sorry."

I told him, "You don't have anything to be sorry about, Michael."

So Amber stayed for about 3 or 4 hours, and we got things straightened out.

That night when Michael and I went to bed I prayed that this was going to be it for that night anyway. We held each other so close that night. I was so afraid for him. I had no idea how much worse this may become, and I worried for his sanity. Thank God, though, this was a one-time occurrence. This never happened again, although the night terrors did. They continued to increase now to three and four times a week.

Looking back on all of this now I think I realize what was going on. It seemed like the more I got Michael to open up about what happened to him in Vietnam, the more the memories came flooding back to him. This was how he was dealing with it. This is when the night terrors began, after months of talking and opening up. It was as though I was his counselor at that time, but I was no counselor. I didn't know what I was doing, and I truly believe I was opening up a floodgate. Now the more he talked about it the worse his night terrors became, and I didn't know how to stop it. There were no magic words. I could only love him and support him, but this would not be enough to stop the terror that grew inside of him. The fighting at the bar just went from bad to worse. Practically every night now he was getting into a scuffle over one thing or another. If someone just looked at him the wrong way that would be enough.

It was around this time that Michael and I decided to go out for a night of dancing, which we hadn't done in a while we went to the Pickle Barrel, a local country and western type bar. We were drinking and we were actually having fun. We were dancing, and we stayed there until closing. For the first time in awhile we had fun. We decided to grab something to eat at the local fast-food restaurant before returning back home. While placing our order at the drive-through, Michael put the car in park, got out, and went to the car in front of us to the person that was placing his order. He opened up his car door and pulled him out, threw him over the hood of our car and began punching him in the face.

He got two punches in before I grabbed his arm, and I screamed, "Michael, what in the fucking hell are you doing? Why are you beating this man up?"

He said, "Oh, this guy broke into my friend's house."

I said, "What?" The guy was just lying there with his face bleeding, looking totally bewildered because he had done no such thing.

Then Michael got a really good look at the guy, and he said, "Oh, I'm sorry," and let the guy up like this was just going to be fine.

The guy just got back in his car, and he said, "I don't know what in the hell's the matter with you, man, but you're nuts," and he drove off.

Michael and I sat there, and I just shook my head and said, "Michael, this has to stop before somebody gets very badly hurt. This has to stop!"

At this point in our relationship Michael and I were having no fun at all. There was no fun to be had. It was drinking and violence, the two things I should have tried to avoid in my life but was weirdly drawn to. Now every time when we would go out, something would happen. He would have a fight with one person or another. It always ended up this way, and I told Michael at this time that something had to give. All this fighting was beginning to take its toll on me, on us. Now night after night Michael and I both found ourselves in a drunken haze, not really enjoying life or our relationship anymore, just sort of stumbling through it all. I knew I didn't want it to be like this. We had too much love between us to just merely exist.

The winter of 1979 had turned into the summer of 1980 when I got a letter from my Aunt Cathy in New York, one of my father's sisters, informing me that he had died of spinal cancer. I knew he had cancer for about year because I had seen him at my sister April's house. That was the last time that I saw him, and he informed me he had cancer. I had shown no emotion just as he always liked it. I leaned over, kissed him on his cheek, and I said I was sorry. Then I walked out the door.

So his death really did not come as a surprise to me. I truly, truly wish I could say I was heartbroken over it, but I cannot. The truth is, I had no feelings toward him at all, not hate, not love, nothing. So his death to me was no more important than a stranger's would be. I think that's what hurt me the most. A daughter should not feel that way, but I was made to by him. He died in a veterans hospital in New York all by himself. I suppose it's just what he deserved.

A funny thing happened—well I think it was a funny thing anyway. The first time that Michael met my father was about two to three months before my father found out he had cancer, so he was healthy. I introduced Michael to my father. They extended their hands and shook, and then Michael punched my father right in his face. My father then landed on the couch, looking up at Michael. Michael leaned over him and said, "That is for June and the girls," and then Michael turned and walked out the door.

So that was my father's introduction to the true hero in my life. He deserved that punch so much, and I was so glad he was put in his place by my hero Michael. It was funny, because after that Michael thought my sisters and I would be angry with him.

We just sat there and laughed our asses off and said, "Good, he deserved it."

So when I read the letter to Michael about the news of my father's death he said to me, "Kyra, I'm sorry."

I said, "I'm not," and he just shook his head and walked off.

The night that I received that letter I did get a little more intoxicated than I usually did. I don't know why. Perhaps I was thinking of what could have been or what should have been. A father and daughter's relationship is supposed to be something special and instead it was just pain, from emotional to physical. That was the legacy my father left behind. So should I cry over him now? Should I drink a toast to him? I don't know. All I know is I wished things could have been different, but you can't change the past. All you can do is look toward the future and try very hard not to make the same mistakes that you've seen your parents make.

This news on the other hand did hit Amber and April rather hard. Amber's drinking had become just as bad as Michael's and mine. She was getting to the point where all she was doing was working and getting drunk to the point of blackouts. One morning shortly after my father's death she told she woke up, looked in the mirror, and had a hallucination. She saw nothing but a skull with eyes, and this totally, completely freaked her out. She knew right then and there that the drinking had to stop. She had gone over the deep end. When she actually looked in the mirror and saw nothing but a skull looking back, she knew there was something terribly wrong. Her drinking was out of control now. Her marriage was falling apart. She and her husband were arguing all the time.

My family and marriage just do not mix. It seems like someone just flips a switch as soon as you say, "I do." All of a sudden Amber wasn't allowed to go out to the bars with her husband anymore because she was a wife. So she sat at home and drank. He continued to go out and have fun with his friends.

Their relationship had totally dissolved.

After Amber suffered this hallucination she knew that was it, enough was enough. She had to do something. She was miserable in her life and she was miserable in her marriage. She started going to AA Meetings, and it was there that she learned about detox and that was a place you could go for a week just to be by yourself and to get the help that you need to stop drinking. She knew she had to stop drinking at this point. She was afraid of losing her sanity.

Amber came to our house one night and told me all of this, all of what had been happening to her and what horrible sights she had seen. She told me that she had made arrangements to go to a detox and that she was leaving her husband. I thought to myself, *What a brave woman she is for taking such a huge step in getting her life together.* I knew this was not going to be easy for her, and I let her know that she had my full support and how proud I was of her.

Unfortunately this kind of affected my life in a negative way, but it didn't matter. How it affected me was that I was getting a ride back and forth to work with Amber every day. We only had one car, so this left me without any way to get back and forth to work. Michael brought me in before he went to work himself and would pick me up. However, it was like three or four towns over from where he worked, so it was very, very difficult. I tried desperately to get a ride from someone that I worked with, but this didn't work out. I thought to myself, *Well, if it's only a week that Amber is going to be away in the detox, maybe I could get just a couple of days off from work.* Then she called me and let me know that she was going to a sort of a halfway house, and this program would last for thirty days.

Michael and I were both very impressed with Amber's actions and very proud of her. After the thirty-day program was completed she was offered a stay at another house, and this house was a little bit more structured for everyday living. She was allowed to go to work and to have her own money in this particular house. So Amber remained in this house for the following six months.

CHAPTER THREE

Amber liked it very much, she told me. It provided the structure that her life most desperately needed at this moment and something she had not learned before. Hopefully when she leaves this house, she can take with her these coping tools that will help her stay sober for the rest of her life.

Meanwhile, Michael and I were still going through our own difficult times. We were going on our second year together and things were not looking too good for us. One day Michael had decided to go to welding school on a government grant, and I was forced to quit my job because of no transportation. You see, Amber and I always rode in together, and with her not working and living away, I had no way to get to the next town. Michael needed our car to get back and forth to school which was about an hour's drive away. I tried desperately to find another ride with someone that I was working with, but I was not successful, and I ended up having to quit my job. I hated that because that was one of the best jobs I have ever had—one of the best paying ones—it was for NASA making plastic parts for space shuttles. So the pay, you know, was really good. With Michael having very little income and me none at all at the moment, we were forced to give up our apartment. I ended up for the time being moving back with my mother, and he moving back with his. We both hated this, but we had no choice at the time.

I thank God that quickly I found a job near my home, one that I had never tried before, waitressing. I found it a very fast paced but very exciting and very fun. It was an all-night restaurant and it never closed. I started on the third shift. As I was doing this, Michael was doing really well at school. However, our drinking at this point had not changed. One night in the late winter of 1980, Michael and I went out partying with his younger brother, John, and one other of my friends, Joe. All four of us ended up at Alex and Corey's house where we proceeded to get very drunk. We were all drinking heavily, but things appeared to be fine among all of us. That is why what came next came as a huge surprise. As we were leaving Alex and Corey's, John turned to Joe and punched him right in the nose for no apparent reason. Joe began bleeding, and Michael jumped on John and just kept screaming at John.

What the hell are you doing? Why are you doing this?

John offered no explanation. He just told Michael, "Fuck you."

Michael replied to him, "Fuck you, John; just get in the car and shut the hell up, now."

The four of us got into the car with John sitting directly behind Michael. Michael had begun driving us all home when John leaned up and tapped me on the shoulder. I turned around to look at him and our eyes met, and he said to me, calmly and clearly, "Kyra, I'm going to kill you."

I was shocked at his statement and replied, "What did you just say?" and he calmly repeated himself.

Michael, hearing this statement, looked in the rear view mirror at John, and he said, "Are you serious?"

John just replied, "Yes, I am," and then John proceeded to repeat it again for the third time to Michael, "I am going to kill Kyra."

Michael then flipped. I mean, he totally lost it on John. He then began screaming at John, "You sick son of a bitch. Don't you realize that no woman has ever stayed by me the way Kyra has, taking care of me in the kind, loving way she has? Don't you realize that I love Kyra, and you dare to speak to her like this?" Michael then called him a mother fucker and told him he was completely nuts.

Michael then continued driving, keeping his eyes on John the whole time in the rear view mirror. We drove past John's house. As soon as we did this, John knew something was up. As we proceeded to drive, it was only half way down the street to the Morton State Hospital. As we drove through the gate of the State Hospital, John really started flipping out in the back seat. Realizing what he had said and then what his brother was about to do to him. Morton State Hospital is a very well known Hospital and has been there for over 100 years. The grounds of the hospital are huge. On the property it has around 10 very large buildings. Once through the gates we proceeded to the admittance building.

Once arriving at the building, Michael and I both got out of the car. It was a small car—a 1975 Nova, 2-door, powder blue—and it was so pretty. But it was also quite small. So John was pretty much pinned in the back seat along with Joe. Joe got out and grabbed one arm. Michael grabbed the other arm and literally dragged John kicking and screaming into the Admittance Building. Michael was strong enough to hold onto one of John's arms, but Joe was rather tall and thin and didn't have much muscle. John was beginning to slip away from Joe's grip, so I went to assist.

While the three of us entered the Administration Building holding onto John for dear life as he thrashed around screaming and yelling and spitting. Seeing this, one of the nurses ran to get a wheel chair for restraints. The nurse proceeded to strap his arms and his legs to the chair. I will never forget this moment. I remember looking at his face and in his eyes. He looked like a man possessed. It sent shivers up my spine—just screaming and spitting and thrashing his whole body back and forth. He wouldn't stop. It was horrible to watch. Michael then began telling the nurse why we had brought him there because of what he had said to me because he had threatened to kill me, and he took this threat very seriously. And then what else Michael had proceeded to tell the nurse, I did not find out until this very moment. I had no clue. He proceeded to tell her that John had tried to kill him three years earlier. That is why Michael took this threat so seriously. Michael began telling the nurse about this day—that John had tried to kill him.

It was a beautiful summer's day. They had picked up some beer and decided to spend the day fishing, and Michael at the time had this big black van. Michael had parked the van alongside Lake Sabbatia, his favorite fishing hole. After a few hours had passed and they were both feeling the effects of the beer and the heat of the sun, Michael was sitting there in his van with the side door open baiting a hook, when all of a sudden totally out of the blue, John came up from behind him and put him in a chock hold almost blacking him out. Thank God a fellow fisherman had seen what was going on and came to Michael's aid, because at this point he was seeing stars. If he had not helped Michael, Michael probably would have died. Michael, of course, never trusted John again after this incident.

Right after this happened while Michael was trying to recover, he was packing up his things, and he told John, "Just go. Just walk home. I don't want to see you."

It was 2 or 3 days after this happened that Michael went to John's apartment, and he asked him why, why would he do this to him? He thought he loved him.

John's only response was, "I'm sorry, Michael. I'm sorry. I don't even remember doing it." You see, John was quite a Jekyll and Hyde character. John sober was one of the sweetest, most kind men you would ever want to meet. He would literally give you shirt of his back. But John drunk, that very same sweet, loving person would turn into something you would not even want to stand next to. He would turn into a complete animal. As a matter of fact Michael's nickname for John when he was drunk was "Mad Dog," and that was exactly what he became when he was drunk.

But now, not only with his drinking, he began taking drugs which would make his behavior even more bizarre and unpredictable. Michael also told the nurse this as well. Michael also went on to tell the nurse that John had been in and out of trouble for most of his life, and in and out of jail starting at the age of 14. John started off by stealing cars, setting fires and just always getting in and out of trouble. Michael really felt that John needed desperately some kind of intervention or something really horrible was going to happen to him or someone else. However, after all of this information that Michael had just given the nurse in hopes to get him some help, and even though I and many people thought that a mental hospital would be the best place to find John the proper help, I could not believe my ears the response that we received from this nurse after everything that Michael had just gotten through telling her.

Her response was, "It appears to me John is just drunk, not crazy." She said she was very sorry but because of his being intoxicated there was no way she could admit him for help. She then told us the only thing she could do at this point was to call the police. They would arrest him and put him into protective custody for the remainder of the night.

We could not believe that that was all that they were going to offer him, a night in jail. The nurse called the police, and while we were waiting for them to arrive, John continued his thrashing and spitting and swearing at everyone. The look on the officer's face when he entered the lobby and saw John sitting there behaving as he was, and by the look on the officer's face, I could read his mind. He must have been saying to himself, "Oh, God, no." It took three officers to restrain John in order to put the handcuffs on him to place him in the back of the cruiser. They then placed John in the back of the cruiser and came back into the building to get more information from Michael and me. Michael reported to the police that his brother needed psychiatric help and not to be arrested. Trying to get this through to the police officers and the nurse was impossible and very frustrating. All they could see was a drunken maniac that needed to sit his ass in the can for 24 hours to sober up, and then everything would be just fine. They just did not get it.

While we were in the lobby talking with the police officers, John was in the back seat of the cruiser, flipping out. He started kicking and kicking the back window until he kicked the whole window out. We exited the lobby just in time to witness John kicking the last part of the back windshield, out of the cruiser. Even after this happened, they still would not admit him into Morton State. All they simply did was call for another cruiser to take John into jail.

But oh no, he was not crazy. Well, I ask, "What kind of sane person does these actions and what kind of sane person tries to kill the brother he's supposed to love so very much?" There was no other explanation outside of a man needing psychological help. We tried to get him this help and were just turned away.

Michael felt terrible about what had just happened. He truly wanted to get his brother some help, not locked up. Michael and I dropped Joe off at his house and then proceeded to the police station. Before going to the police station we picked up a sandwich and hot coffee to bring to John. Morton has a very small police station, and upon arriving at the police station, Michael went in, and he could hear his brother in the back screaming and yelling. In all this time, he had not calmed down at all.

One of the police officers that Michael had known for years told Michael, "Don't worry. John will just burn himself out, and end up going to sleep. He'll be fine come morning."

The officer would not allow Michael to see him, but he told Michael not to worry. That as soon as John started calming down, he would make sure that he would get the sandwich and the coffee that he brought to him. Michael knew he could trust this officer to do this for him. As much as Michael hated leaving John there like that, he knew there was nothing more that he could do for his brother. Michael would return to the police station in the morning to accompany his brother to court, and after John saw the judge in the morning, he was free to go.

Michael had talked to John about what had happened and his actions that last evening, and again John replied he simply did not remember much of what took place. Michael then pleaded with John to please get some help. John then just agreed to think about it. In America even though it is a loving brother trying to get you help, you cannot force someone to get help if they don't desire to. All you can do is try your hardest to talk them into it, and Michael did, to no avail, unfortunately, although John did seem to calm down a little bit after that night. There were no more explosions or violence, although we did not spend a lot of time with John after this incident. The little time that we did spend with him, he did seem to be becoming a calmer person.

Michael continued going to welding school, and I continued waitressing. We would see Michael Jr. only about two days a month now because our drinking was really reaching its peak and becoming totally out of hand. It was one drunken hazy night after another. That spring Michael received his welding certificate. He really tried hard in class, and it must have been very hard for him with a hangover every day, but he never gave up. I was very proud of him for graduating in his class.

Michael received his certificate and began right away applying for welding jobs. I remember one day when we took a drive to Quonset Point Shipyard where they make ships for the military. Michael filled out this huge application that took well over an hour, and they said they would give him a call later. But I think Michael really knew that he didn't stand a chance in Hell of getting this job. Well, one week past, then another. Michael finally called them, and they told him that they were very sorry that they had all the men that they needed at this time, and they were looking for men that had had a little more experience.

Michael then thought perhaps he stood a better chance of getting a job in one of the smaller shipyards. There he could gain the experience that he needed that they were looking for at Quonset Point. So this became his goal. He would look through the newspaper on a daily basis and apply to all different welding positions in our area. Month after month he would fill out application after application. He tried so hard, but each and every job interview that he went on, it seemed like there was a younger, more experienced man there before him. After all, if you have a 25-year-old healthy man sitting in front of you with 5 years' welding experience, and then a 32-year-old man who had just received his welding certificate, who are you going to pick?

This is what happened to Michael, time and time again, and he became discouraged. He began to realize that he could not continue doing this. He realized he needed some sort of steady employment. He began putting in applications for employment to all the factories in our area. It broke my heart to see him do this because I realized how hard he had worked for his welding certificate, and I felt he was going backwards instead of forward. But I guess it was just not meant to be.

It was a couple of weeks after he had started going regularly to factories to apply for jobs. At this point in history Mount St. Helen erupted. It would be a couple of more weeks before he would hear of a factory in the next town over that was beginning to manufacture face masks for the workers around the Mount. St. Helen area. It was the 3-M Company, and it paid pretty well. Michael put in his application there and got hired there right away. He began working there, but the pace was very fast and very stressful. It was a very hard job, but he did it. They worked 10-12-hour shifts, 6 days a week, but for Michael this was especially bad because he was not able to drink. At the end of the 12-hour shift, he would be shaking and extremely irritable until he was able to get his first drink.

This went on for months. He was not in very good shape mentally, and I was really beginning to worry. We would talk about his day and the stress, and I always tried to make him feel better. I don't know if I succeeded or not, but I tried. I do know it's always better to get the aggravation of the day off your chest, and being able to always talk to one another about anything, is one of the reasons we have such a strong, good, loving, close relationship. This is what kept us going through the good times and the bad. We always knew we had each other.

It was about a month after Michael had started this job when our car was stolen and found burned. I remember feeling very sad and angry over this. This was the car that he had when we first met, and it held special memories for me. It was a pretty car. It was a baby blue, 2-door Nova. I just loved that car. But I guess things have to change whether for the good or the bad. Things are always in a constant state of change. If you are very lucky, it is for the better, not the worst. But no matter what, life does not stand still for anyone.

Michael and I began looking for a replacement car. We looked at a few other Novas, but we ultimately decided to buy a van instead. We thought a van would be a lot more fun. We could use it to go camping down at Sabbatia Lake during the summer. The van was 3 years old. The color was black, and it was just perfect for what we had in mind. The price was right and we even had a little money left over from the insurance payment from the Nova to buy some camping equipment for the summer. At first I found it rather strange going from a little blue Nova to a huge black van. Driving it and parking it was quite difficult at first for me, but I became accustomed to it, and I am proud to say, I did not have one mishap while learning to drive such a different-sized car. So by the time summer rolled around, we were really looking forward to having some fun.

The first warm weekend of the summer, we packed up the van and headed down the Cape to Onset. Our friends, Corey and Alex, owned a cottage down there. Michael and I had planned to spend a day at the beach and then go back to Corey and Alex's and camp out there at night. We arrived at Onset at about 2 o'clock in the afternoon, and we spent the day drinking and swimming and just relaxing and enjoying the beach under a beautiful, crystal clear sky. The sun was so great and so warm, but there always seemed to be a nice cool breeze blowing. I loved the smell of the salt air.

It was around 8 o'clock at night when Michael and I started packing our things up and headed out to get some dinner. We went to the Beach Side Restaurant to get some fried clams and French fries and watch the sunset. As we were leaving the restaurant we saw a very small cruise ship docked at Onset Harbor. The cruise ship was offering a moonlit cruise down the Cape Cod Canal. Michael saw this and thought it would be a really romantic ending to a beautiful day we had just spent together. I probably would have felt this too, but for one thing, my fear of drowning. I really did not like boats because of this, and I also did not like large bridges that ran over water because of this. To this day I really could never figure our why I had such a fear, a dread. So for me to go out in the middle of the night in the middle of the Cape Cod Canal (and when I say dark, I mean pitch black, there was no moon out that night)— so it was pitch black looking out at the water.

Michael knew of my fear, but I don't think he really realized how bad it was. Michael assured me that it was going to be fine. This boat was very safe and it went up and down the Cape Cod Canal all the time, and there was really nothing at all for me to be afraid.

He told me, "I would never let anything happen to you. Please, just trust me." He assured me we would have a lot of fun and this was going to be really romantic.

I was afraid, but I also trusted him. So what else was I going to say. I agreed. So, Michael and I boarded the boat. (I think it was around 9:30) There were about 25 other people aboard. You had your choice to stay on top deck or go below where they had a lounge where they served cocktails. Michael and I chose to stay up top for most of the cruise. The boat left dock as we stood there on the deck. We watched as the beach that we had just spent a beautiful day on slowly disappeared out of sight.

Michael could see the apprehension in my eyes and feel my sweaty palms. Michael held me in his arms and told me, "Kyra, for Christ's sake will you please just try and relax and enjoy yourself?"

I thought, *Yeah, easier said than done.* I hate fear. I absolutely hate feeling afraid of anything or anyone, so when I was hit with an irrational fear of drowning and of bridges, I would become very angry at myself. All of my life I have needed to be in control of my emotions, and when you fear, you are not in control. I felt so uncomfortable standing there on the deck with a pitch-black ocean surrounding. I felt as though I had been swallowed up. I was no longer in control of my surroundings, and I didn't like it one bit. I tried, I really tried, to keep myself calm and not let Michael see the fear that lay inside of me.

After awhile I asked Michael if we could go down below to get a drink. I thought if we went down below I could for a while forget we were even on a boat. And this did seem to work for a little while. I felt my anxiety level dropping, and I felt a little more relaxed. But after an hour Michael wanted to go back up on deck to get some more fresh air. The cocktails were beginning to catch up to both of us, so I thought perhaps this would be a good idea. Standing on the deck Michael held me in his arms. We stood there looking out into the black ocean, and onto the distant shore we could see the lights in the houses. While looking out at all of this I began to appreciate the beauty and the majesty of the ocean. It was quite breathtaking.

The cruise was almost coming to an end now, and we were heading back to the dock on Onset Beach. The boat was halfway back to the shore when everything all of a sudden went black, the motor went silent, and the only lights that you could see were coming from the houses on the distant shore. We were floating dead in the water, and the current was very strong and was just pushing the boat side to side. It was just so dark. The sky was black and so was the water. You could barely see the hand in front of your face. The captain of the boat went around telling everyone to get below for their own safety. The boat had begun tossing around like a little toy in a child's bathtub, so all of the passengers went below, and after about 15-20 minutes they were able to get a few of the lights back on.

When I looked at Michael's face, I was not comforted by what I saw. He was beginning to worry as well. Michael had spent many of his summers down the Cape and was quite familiar with the Cape Cod Canal and just how deadly it could be if you didn't know what you were doing. He knew the current and the undertow could be very vicious there. He knew this was nothing you could swim in and survive. I could tell by his face he was becoming more and more concerned as time went on.

By this time they had been working on the motor for over an hour with no success. Meanwhile, my anxiety was building to fever pitch. I began breaking out in a cold sweat. I could hear my heart in my ears, and I was just gripping the edge of my seat, my nails imbedding into it. It was getting so bad I felt like I was going to pass out. I had never felt this type of anxiety before in my whole life, and all I could think was, *You stupid bitch. You put yourself here, and now you are going to die here.* This is all that I could think as I sat there, imbedding my nails into the side of my chair. I made myself a promise right there and then, if I were to live through this night that I would never, ever again set foot on another boat. I just kept saying to myself over and over again, "Please God, help me."

Just then one of the crewmen got the motor running again. After well over an hour and a half floating dead in the water I had had just about enough. Thank God the motor's starting. We then made it back to the dock, and as I was getting off the boat and putting my feet on the ground, I was never happier in my life to feel this. It took every ounce of self-control for me not to drop to my knees and kiss it. The captain apologized to all of us about this horrible mishap and offered each and every one of us a free cruise for the next night. I guess the captain could tell as I was walking away laughing that I was not going to be amongst the ones returning for the next night.

Michael and I proceeded to the nearest bar and had ourselves a few more drinks. I had at least four or five piña coladas, and Michael had as many boiler makers. Within an hour and a half we were both very drunk. We decided we were going to get something to eat and ended up in a little pizza parlor right around the corner. The pizza parlor was half full and had about 15 or 22 people. Michael and I went up to the counter and placed our order and then took our seat. We sat there for about 20 minutes and in those 20 minutes we would see people coming in and out picking up their orders which consisted of mainly sandwiches which were a lot quicker to make than a pizza. But Michael, being drunk, did not see it this way. He saw everyone being served before us, and he was becoming very agitated.

I told him to stop being ridiculous, that this wasn't the case at all, and then I went up to the counter, and I asked the man how long our pizza would be. The man replied, "Only a few more minutes, ma'am."

I returned then back to our table and told Michael what the man had just said, and Michael for some reason or another (probably because he did have a lot to drink) was not happy with this. He began yelling at the top of his lungs, "What in the fuck do I have to do to get some service in this rat hole?"

I was so embarrassed I felt like dying, like crawling underneath the table, and as I mentioned earlier in my book, it just seemed like every fun night out, every time we would be having a great time, it would always end up in a disaster. This night would be no different. Michael always ended up by getting into a fight with one person or another. One big difference between this night and all the others was I did not just have my ass stuck on a boat floating dead on the Cape Cod Canal and having the shit scared out of me, going through a horrible anxiety attack and fearing for my very life. So all and all with everything that I had already been through that night, I had no patience left. I had no sense of humor left.

This was not the night for Michael to be pulling this shit, and I certainly was in no mood for a brawl in a pizza parlor. Michael then started with his bullshit, and I gave it right back to him. This was to be without a doubt the worst argument that we had ever had or ever will have again in our relationship. You see, deep down inside I was already angry at him, but I did realize it wasn't his doing. However, I was still angry that he had talked me into one of the most terrifying nights of my life, taking "the moonlit cruise from hell," as I would always refer to it after this night. But now this. *Oh, no, not tonight.* I suppose after this night in the terror that I had just gone through, I was actually looking to kick someone's ass myself, and it was going to be Michael's.

After Michael yelling out what he did in the restaurant, I stood up, knocking the edge of the table toward him, knocking the sodas into his lap, I began screaming at him, "I have had it. Every time we go out and have fun it always ends up in a disaster, and if you want to be a fucking asshole tonight, be one by yourself!" I told him I was finished with him—we were done. I said, "You bring me on a cruise from hell and now this. I'm done."

I left him sitting by himself in the middle of the pizza parlor with two sodas in his lap with his mouth hanging open and looking very shocked at me. I then walked back to our van parked on the side street and sat on the curb waiting. For what, I don't know. I had no idea of what Michael's reaction was going to be to all of this, but I really didn't care. I had never spoken to him so cruelly before, but this night I was at my breaking point.

I sat there for about 20 minutes, and then I could see Michael coming out of the pizza parlor and walking toward me down the street, carrying the pizza and laughing at me which only pissed me off even more because it was as though he did not take anything that I said to him in the restaurant seriously. All of tonight just seemed to be one big joke to him. Before he even reached the van I was becoming madder and madder at him.

As Michael approached me sitting on the sidewalk, he laughed again and he said to me, "You're not going anywhere, and you're not going to leave me."

I said to him, "Oh, really?"

He said, "Yes." He did stop laughing and asked me to please just get into the van.

I did get into the van with him, but the only reason I did was because at this point I had no other way to get back home. I would have been stranded there in Onset if I had not. Once in the van the argument continued. He then told me he had no idea how he could have ever fallen in love with a woman that was a spineless jellyfish and that I had no guts and never stood up for myself.

He had no idea of whom he was saying this to and what I had been through already in my life, and the fuel he was adding to the fire with every taunt and every insult that he threw at me. I could feel the anger boiling inside of me with every insult and every taunt until all at once it just boiled over and it boiled over all onto him all at once. He did not even see it coming. I then saw in between the seats of the van a half full bottle of vodka. I reached down to grab it, and while holding the bottle in my hand, I looked at Michael's head and just wanted to smash it in. If I had let loose with all the anger my whole life gave to me at that moment onto Michael's head, I surely would have killed him. But within that split second of time I turned instead to smash the windshield with the bottle, and thank God I did.

Thank God my heart ruled over my anger, and all the anger that I had held deep down inside my whole life, I had exploded onto that windshield. It flowed out of me like a volcano erupting and a bomb going off all at once. Thankfully it was all directed to that windshield. I smashed that bottle through the windshield time and time and time again until three-quarters of it was missing.

It happened so quickly Michael didn't realize what was going on. The force of my anger spewed out of me. It took Michael a few seconds to realize exactly what was going on, and as soon as he did, he grabbed me and grabbed my arm to try to get the bottle away. We wrestled for a few seconds, and he was finally able to get the bottle back. Michael was stunned. Everything happened so quickly.

When he was able to get the bottle out of my hand, I just looked at him and said, "Fuck you," and got out of the van.

He sat there in shock as I walked down the street. Michael was very particular about his cars. He always kept them very clean and in good running condition, so for someone to just go smashing through his windshield like that was unthinkable. No one before has ever done anything like this to one of his vehicles.

While I was walking down the street the only thing I could think to do was go back to the bar that Michael and I had been to earlier that night. It was one of the few things that were still open, but even they were getting ready to close. I went in and told the bar tender what had happened. He had been very nice to Michael and me, and he had a great personality. He was a nice guy, and I explained to him that I had left my pocketbook in the van, and I had no change and needed to call someone from home, one of my sisters, to come and get me. He then told me I don't want you going back to that van. I will give you some of my change from the tip jar. He then handed me it and told me to take whatever I needed out of it.

I was stranded there, and I just expected Michael to take off. I went over to the pay phone with the bar tenders tip jar and began dialing my sister April's phone number, but just then I saw Michael come walking through the doors of the bar. I thought to myself, *Well this is it; now it's going to get physical.* I prepared the best way I could to fight. The bar tender watched as Michael slowly walked toward me. He was getting ready to leap, but Michael very much surprised me. He just came calmly walking up to me and gave me a hug. I could not believe this. He just put his arms around me and said he was sorry. Everything got just completely out of hand and it was really stupid. He said this whole night had been a disaster from the cruise to this moment.

While walking back to the van Michael had his arm around me and he said to me, "You know, you are going to fix this yourself."

I said, "Yeah, I know. I'll be more than glad to pay for the damages."

He said, "Oh, no. I don't want you to pay for the damages. You are going to go and buy a windshield, and you're going to put it in with your own two hands." He said, "Don't worry; I'll help you, and I'll show you how to do it. We'll do it together because it was both our fault."

We cleaned up the glass from the dashboard and seats and headed over to Alex's cottage. By this time it was around 2 o'clock in the morning. It was very late, and Alex and Corey were already asleep.

We then set up our tent in the back yard, and Michael said to me, "Let's just try to get some sleep. We will talk about it in the morning. Right now both of us have had way too much to drink." As we lay in the tent Michael put his arm around me, and he said, "Don't worry. Everything is gonna be okay."

But I knew it was not going to be. As soon as he said that, something went off inside of me. I began to think of what I had just done to the most important person to me in the world, to the man that I loved. I almost killed him tonight, the man that I loved more than life itself. You see, at this moment Michael did not realize that I was going to hit him upside his head with the bottle instead of the windshield, but at the very last second turning my anger onto the windshield, thank God, instead of his head. He had no idea, but I knew. All the anger that I felt rushing through my body at that moment was almost inconceivable. The only thing that stopped me from hitting Michael instead of the windshield was my deep, deep love for him. Thank God it seemed to have overridden all of the anger and furry that was rushing through me. It scared me so much to think of how close I came.

The longer I lay there beside Michael, the more I thought and the sicker I became. My mind became consumed with my father and all of his drunken rages beating my mother after he had lost all his money on any given day at the track. I saw too much of my father in myself tonight. I had become the person that I hated most in the world, my father. There was no way I could allow this to happen to me. I simply could not allow myself to become this person. I knew deep down inside I was stronger than that, and now came the time I had to start fighting my addiction. I had no choice.

Thinking of all of this I began to cry. I felt so sick inside. I would rather die than become my father and to begin to hurt the people that you are supposed to love and protect. I simply would rather be dead than to do this. I knew I had a fight ahead, but I knew deep down inside I knew it was a fight I could win. I had to win.

Michael heard me crying and woke up. He tried to comfort me the best way he could, but I was beyond any comforting. I refused to discuss what I was feeling at that moment with him. I just felt so ashamed of myself. I just told him I was feeling sick because I had drunk too much. I could not tell him what was going through my mind and what I was feeling at that moment. And while lying there I also began to remember it was just one year earlier, almost to the day, that we had our perfect romantic weekend together, the one that I would remember for always. While remembering this, my heart truly began to break. I just cried myself to sleep feeling nothing but despair.

We awoke a few hours later. The sun was out. We could hear Alex and Corey's voices in the yard. We could hear them over by our van discussing what happened to the windshield.

Michael and I then came out of the tent and Alex turned to Michael and asked, "What the hell happened to your windshield?"

And he just simply said to Alex, "Ask Kyra." I remember Alex just saying while he was looking at me, "No way in hell did Kyra do all this."

I then explained to Alex what had led up to it. Alex just shook his head and said to Michael, "Well, I'd think twice before pissing her off again," which made me feel even worse.

Alex and Corey had made a good breakfast, but our appetites weren't the greatest. We were still hung over, so we ate very little. We packed up the tent and our camping gear and left. On the way back home we stopped at the liquor store to get a bottle of vodka. I wasn't too sick myself. It seemed like I never really got a severe hangover. No matter how much I drank, I never really got sick.

While going into the liquor store Michael asked me if I wanted anything to drink, and I said just a Pepsi. He asked me if I was kidding, and I said "No." I still had not told him about last night and what I was feeling and how I had decided last night was enough. It was going to be my last time. You see, no matter how hard it was going to be for me and how much pain I had to go through, I was not going to drink anymore. I loved Michael with all my heart and soul. There was nothing I would not do for him, including protecting him from me, or the me I was becoming when I drank. So that meant never letting that "me" ever come out again, and the only way to do this to be assured that would never happen again was to not drink, period. One day at a time, they say. Well, this day was my first, the first day of the rest of my life and hopefully a long and loving life with the man I loved most. I knew that my love for Michael would be all the strength I would need to do what I had to do.

After Michael took a swig of vodka, we headed back toward Morton to a garage where we knew they had windshields for sale. We looked through windshield after windshield after windshield. We finally found the one that would fit the van. I paid for it and then we went to the hardware store to get the glue and caulking we would need. We decided to go down to the lake to work on it. It was a very hot day, and we thought down by the lake we would get a little bit of breeze anyway. The job took a little over four hours to complete, but we did it together just like Michael said we would. After the work was done it was beginning to get late, and I told Michael I just wanted to go home.

The next few days following this, I would spend alone. The first week was the hardest for me. My head and my body just ached. The emotions were off the chart—high, low, crying one minute, laughing the next. I felt like I was losing my mind, and every time I tried to go to sleep I would wake up soaking wet. This was really bad for the first three days, and then the chills started. After this, I just slept. I slept a lot. I would only wake up to go to the bathroom. The only communication I had with Michael through this time were two phone calls, and in those two phone calls our conversation consisted of me telling him I could no longer drink. I had to stop for both our sakes. Well, I guess the words, "I don't want to drink any longer," are not the correct words. I will always want to drink. The correct words would be, "I can no longer drink."

After this week passed I asked Michael to come and pick me up so we could talk. I was beginning to feel much better, and I really needed to get out and get some air. Michael picked me up and we went down to the lake, our favorite spot. We parked there and talked for hours. I told him everything. I told him how I was feeling that night when I broke his windshield and how I was desperately afraid of becoming my father. We also began to discuss the fighting that would occur. Every time we had a good evening together, he would always end up in a fight with someone over absolutely nothing and how this would ruin our good evening. Michael did agree with me on this. He realized it was a problem and he had to stop. He promised he would really try hard to keep his drinking under control, and for a while he did. But as Michael and I would later find out, his alcoholism was just the underlying problem of the main one. The alcoholism was just masking his real pain, but for now all we could do was deal with the alcoholism only.

This summer was turning out to be a very hot one. It was the end of June. We picked up Michael Jr. It was on a Saturday afternoon. It was so hot that day we thought it would be nice to bring him swimming down the lake, and we knew all our friends would be there along with their children. So I packed up a nice lunch and we headed to the lake.

As we drove up the winding pine-tree lined dirt road toward the lake, when I turned to Michael Jr. and said, "I can't wait to dive right in that nice cool lake; can you?"

I will never forget what he said next. I will always remember this one. He looked at both his father and me and said, "No, no, Daddy, too cold, too deep!"

Michael and I just looked at each other and started laughing. Michael Jr.'s statement was so cute and he was so cute and very, very smart. I had fallen in love with both of them.

We parked in the spot next to our friends. Now you have to keep in mind this was only my second week of sobriety, so being around people who were drinking of course made me want to drink. I felt slightly uncomfortable, but I fought the urge. When I was offered a drink at first, I told my friends I wasn't feeling very well. I think I was coming down with the flu or something. But a few hours into the day I confided to Corey and let her know that I had stopped drinking. I was surprised, I don't know why I was surprised, but I was. They were very, very supportive. But even with them being supportive I still felt rather uncomfortable and slightly out of place. Trying hard as they may, I still did. But you know, I actually don't know who felt more uncomfortable, me or them. After all when people are partying, drinking and having a good time, a lot of time they make a fool of themselves, and the last thing they want is a sober person sitting across from them watching all of this. They would much rather have you joining in with them. Having one sober person at your party kind of sucks all the fun out of it. But I know they were my true friends, and they respected my decision for stopping.

While Michael and our friends partied on, Michael Jr. and I spent a lot of the day in the lake in the nice cool water. We had a lot of fun together, but the day was coming to an end. It was just after sunset and everyone started packing up their belongings. All the children were pretty wiped out from all the sun and the water, including Michael Jr. Michael and I then dropped Michael Jr. off at home and headed off home ourselves.

It would not be for a couple of more weeks that Michael and I would return back to the lake. It was July 13, and yet another hot, hot day. So considering the weather we decided that we would spend a couple of days camping out where we could get some cool breezes. At the lake they also had camping spots that you can rent by the day. Michael and I shared a campfire with another couple that was camping right next to us.

That night was so much fun. We roasted some hot dogs and marshmallows and listened to some music. Michael did as he promised and kept his drinking under control. He only had a couple of drinks that day, and we stayed up until early, early in the morning listening to the radio with the other couple and talking. I guess it had to be around 2 and 3 in the morning when we all turned in for the night.

Michael and I woke up around 9 o'clock and went down to the local coffee shop for some coffee and breakfast. We returned back to our camp site about an hour later with coffee for our new friends. Michael and I decided to take our beach chairs down by the water's edge and listen to the radio. As we sat there sipping our morning coffee, we just sat back in our chairs and let the cool breeze blow on us. It was so peaceful and so quiet.

Then the morning news came on the radio station. It was breaking news. They announced that overnight there had been an armed robbery and a car chase that expanded to three other towns all the way up to the city of Boston. It had all come to an end in the next town over from us, Raynham, where they were finally able to stop the car at the roadblock and apprehend the occupants of the vehicle, none of which were the owner. So that left the police to wonder where exactly was the owner or who was the owner. Then the news reporter went on to say that the three men that they had removed from the car were covered in blood, but yet had no wounds to themselves. So this led the police to wonder if perhaps the owner of the car had met with some foul play. Then they went on to report the names of the three men. The first were two brothers, Ron Herman, 19. The second was an older brother, Paul Herman, 21, and the third man was John Jones, 30.

Michael and I then sat up quickly in our seats, and I looked over to Michael. His face went white and all he could say was, "Oh, God, no," and he repeated this over and over again. As Michael sat there holding his head in his hands, I jumped out of my seat to go and hold him.

As I held him in my arms, I just told him, "We don't know the whole story yet. Please, let's not jump to conclusions."

I remember this day as though it happened yesterday. I then told him, "Michael, let's just go to the police station and find out for ourselves what's going on." But Michael knew it wasn't going to be good. When Michael lifted his head up to look at me, it was as white as a sheet and the look of pain and horror that was in his eyes. My heart broke for him. I never saw that look of horror on his face before, and I never wanted to see it again.

We proceeded to pack up as quickly as we could our campsite. We got to the state police station in Middleborough. It was just before noon, and it was so unbearably hot that day. I think it reached over 100 degrees. I can remember my head feeling like it was spinning. Between the unbearable heat and the horror that was unfolding in front of us, Michael went in to speak to one of the police officers, an officer Michael had known for years.

The officer told Michael, "This is bad." This officer also knew John and said to Michael, "This is much worse than anything John has ever done in the past." Then the officer went on to tell Michael that they had just recovered a body from the Oakcrest Dam and that two boys this morning found this body while they were fishing. The body was yet to be identified because it was so badly beaten. Most of the man's face was gone.

This left identifying him very difficult, but they believed it to be the body of Mr. Robert Smith, the man who owned the car that John and the other men were found in. Poor Michael—he just stood there numb and in shock. He then told the cop that he had tried to get John some help, and he had tried to stop something like this from happening, but no one would listen to him. The police officer allowed only Michael into the room where he could speak with his brother. This was very upsetting to me because I did not want Michael to have to face John by himself. I was very concerned with Michael's mental frame of mind at this point. I had never seen Michael so devastated before.

While I was waiting out in the waiting room, Ron and Paul's mother and father came in. They looked as devastated and as sick as we felt. Our eyes met as they passed me to go into a private room to speak with their sons, and I will never forget the pain that I saw in that poor mother's eyes at that moment. About half an hour passed when Michael came out of the room where he was speaking to John. Michael's eyes were red and swollen, and I could tell that he had been crying.

He walked up to me and said, "Kyra, let's get the hell out of here. I'm done."

We got back into the van and started home, Michael not saying a word. For the first ten or fifteen minutes there was just a sickening silence. Michael just looked like he was in shock. Then all of a sudden he pulled off to the side of the road. He then jumped out of the van and started running into the woods. He then dropped to his knees and began crying and vomiting. Of course, as he jumped out of the van so did I, running after him. I was so scared for him at that moment I had no idea of what he was going to do. I knelt on the ground beside him and put my hand on his back, rubbing it until he was finished vomiting. I then held him in my arms close. I think we may have sat there like that for over an hour, and in all this time there was not one word spoken. After all, what were we to say at this point?

After this time passed, Michael pulled himself together and we both got back into our van and began driving back home. On the way we stopped at Dairy Queen and got a couple of sodas. Sitting outside at the picnic bench Michael began telling me about his conversation with John. Michael at this point had no desire to have anything stronger than a Pepsi. He was just feeling so sick, both physically and emotionally. Michael began telling me what John had said to him which was not very much. Michael told me to start off with before they brought John into the room where they were to speak. One of the state troopers told Michael everything that John and the other two men were being charged with and what they had done to Mr. Smith, and he went on to tell Michael what the body had looked like when they pulled it out of the river. It was horrible what they did to that poor man. They literally punched, kicked and clawed him to death. The trooper told Michael the man had looked like he had been attacked by a pack of wild animals which I guess, in fact, he had. And all of this was laid on Michael's shoulders two minutes before John came walking into the room. Just as the trooper was finished, John came walking into the room and sat down at the table across from Michael.

Michael then told me he looked into John's eyes and asked him, "John, what have you done?" and asked him if what they were accusing him of was true. "Did you do this horrible thing?"

Michael said all John did was look down at the table and shook his head, and he said, "Michael, I can't remember a thing."

Michael then thought, *This is insane. How do you murder a man and not remember anything, and then after murdering a man, going on a crime spree in that man's car, holding up a gas station at gunpoint. How do you not remember such things?* But that was the only response that he would get from John. He simply did not remember any of it. Michael at this point simply wasn't buying it. Even in his worst blackouts, he would remember little bits and pieces of what took place during a black out. Never had Michael experienced a complete and total blackout of an entire night like that, like the one John was saying he experienced.

John also went on to tell Michael that besides drinking a lot of booze that night, the three men also started taking a lot of drugs. John claimed that is why he experienced such a complete and total blackout. No matter how many questions Michael asked him, John would not budge from his story that he did not remember. Michael told me he was just so sickened and disgusted with his brother's actions at this point and his lack of caring, remorse. or remembering, that he had nothing more to say to him. Michael just got up and walked out of the room. To the best of my knowledge this was the last time that Michael saw his brother face to face.

In the following weeks John and the other two men would be indicted for murder. It would take the Commonwealth of Massachusetts 10 months to get the trial underway, and in these 10 months John would try to escape, stabbing and injuring the guard in the process. Thank God the guard's wounds were not fatal or John would have had another soul on his hands. This of course was just added to the other charges that John was already facing.

The trial began in late spring and ended almost to the day of the first anniversary of the murder. John's sentence was life. He was found guilty on all counts, and this would become yet one more nightmare, one more burden that Michael had on his shoulders. You see, besides all the nightmares that were now coming to the surface from Vietnam, he now had to live with the knowledge of what his own brother had done. To this day only a few people know how hard Michael tried to get his brother some help before something like this happened. It was as though Michael could actually see this coming and he tried so hard to stop it and was just turned away and not taken seriously.

One of the sad parts about this story is that I realize how much Michael loved John and also how much John loved Michael. But I guess no matter how much you love someone, sometimes you can't save them from themselves. Michael loved John because he knew the real John, the sober John, the John that would give you the shirt off of his back. But the drugs and alcohol poisoned John. They were toxic to his brain. They turned him from a good man into a murdering animal, a Mr. Hyde, you might say. But he could just not manage to stay away from them, and he could never get the help that he desperately needed. Time and time again John fell through the cracks of our system, and poor Mr. Smith was the one to pay for this. Of course, no one can be completely sure of what role John played in the murder of Mr. Smith, and what exactly John's actions were that night and exactly who did what—and I suppose it doesn't really matter. The outcome will remain the same.

I do believe John when he said he didn't know and he doesn't remember anything that happened that night. I also believe there is only one person outside of God himself who truly knows the role John played that horrible night, and that is Mr. Smith. I also believe that some day the score will be settled between John and Mr. Smith. I believe no one goes before God without judgment. The ill deeds that you do here on this earth you will be forced to face the consequences of when you pass away and your soul returns back home. But these are just my beliefs.

My heart broke for Michael. He took this so unbelievably hard. His drinking became much, much worse. It was to the point where he started drinking in the morning, and it did not stop until he'd passed out in bed at night. He was almost constantly drunk, and I really don't know how he did this, but he made it to work every day.

I was still waitressing and Michael was still working at the 3-M plant, but the bars that Michael and I had always gone to for fun, to listen to music and to shoot some pool were all of a sudden becoming very uncomfortable for Michael to go into. He began to feel like our friends and other people there were somehow blaming him for John's actions. Michael always thought they were thinking that he could have done more to stop John. But these were just things going through Michael's head because of the guilt that he was feeling. None of them were real. Our friends didn't feel this way at all. I tried to tell Michael this, but he just did not want believe it. I tried to explain to him, John was an adult, and the only way he could have stopped John was by literally tying him up and sticking him in the house for however long it took for John to get the drugs and the alcohol out of his system so he wouldn't want to do this anymore. But even then when he left the house he would still be on his own. There was literally nothing Michael could have done to stop this, but you could not tell Michael this at that time. I remember telling Michael this was something he was just going to have to accept and somehow try to live with.

Michael's drinking was spiraling out of control, but it was weird. It seemed like the more he drank, the less I wanted to. I felt as though I had to stay sober and in control of the situation. I was beginning to feel like I had to start protecting Michael from Michael. We had stopped going to the bars and cut off all contact with our friends. Michael would pick me up from work every night, and we had somehow gotten into a cycle of going and sitting down the lake and him getting drunk, or should I say drunker.

It went on like this for months, and we were both living at his mother's house at this time. Michael also worried about his mother. You see, this is a very small town and everyone knows everyone else, and Michael was afraid that she would be attacked or something would happen to the house because of John's actions. That they would take vengeance out on the family. But of course this too was only in Michael's head. No one was seeking vengeance. No one had ever planned a retaliation against John's mother or the family. As far as I was aware, the people in our Town felt sorry for Michael's mother as well as for Mrs. Smith, Mr. Smith's mother, who at the time of his death was 84 years old and who had shared a home with her son, Robert. I cannot even imagine the pain that that poor woman had to endure.

For that following year Michael's mother would receive phone calls in the middle of the night. There were never any words spoken. It was just a sobbing woman at the other end. She would remain on the line for only a minute or so and then hang it up. We all assumed in the family that this had to have been Mrs. Smith perhaps wanting to speak, but not able to get the words out, although I could pretty much guess what she wanted to say, and that would be why. Every day Michael felt worse and worse. Between the demons he was already dealing with from Vietnam and now this. It was all becoming just too much for one man to handle.

Our second anniversary was quickly approaching, but given the past year's event, I certainly was not in any mood for any kind of celebration, and I was pretty sure that Michael wasn't either. But Michael surprised me as he often did in life.

On November the 4, our second anniversary, he came home and told me, "Kyra, get dressed. We're going to go out for the evening."

I couldn't believe that he remembered after everything that had just gone on this past year, but he did. He actually remembered our anniversary, and he said to me, "How could I ever forget that night that we met? That was the luckiest night of my life." And I told him I felt the same way.

Michael and I got all dressed up and went to this little romantic restaurant called Ann's Place. It had a lake front view, and we both ordered the prime rib. This was the one thing Ann's Place was famous for. It was a perfect dinner and a perfect night. After our dinner we went out dancing, and this is something we have not done in months. It was as though a breath of fresh air had been blown back into our relationship. Michael managed to keep his drinking under control for this night anyway.

I remember it was a couple of nights after this. Michael received a phone call from Michael Jr.'s mother, Bertha. She was frantic. I guess she was having problems of her own with alcohol, among other things. On that day Child Services came into her home, removed Michael Jr. from it and placed him in foster care. Michael got the name and the address of the people who were now taking care of his son from Bertha. We went over there the next day to see what was going on. We were not sure exactly what to expect.

We found the woman was very nice and extremely understanding of the circumstances. Her name was Lisa and she had been a foster parent for many years, so she really knew what she was doing. She really knew how the system worked and what was going on, and she was able to explain it all to Michael and me. She was very loving and caring and only had the best interest of Michael Jr. at heart. Michael and I explained to her about our situation and the problems we were going through at this point in our lives and how we knew we were not going to be able to take care of a child. Michael knew in his heart he was barely able to take care of himself at this moment in his life. The situation Michael and I were in was not one that you would want to bring an innocent child into. I simply didn't think it was right to have Michael Jr. watch his father get drunk night after night. I grew up in that type of household, and I would not wish this on any child.

After meeting with Lisa, Michael and I decided without a doubt this would be the best place for Michael Jr. to live for now until we were able to get our acts together. We knew she could provide stability and he would be safe there, and we would still be able to see him on a regular basis and take him out for the day. But even though we knew all of this, it still hurt. We so wanted Michael Jr. with us.

So with yet one more blow it seemed like, Michael was being pushed to the edge. Things just got worse and worse with his drinking. I could see him getting worse every day. I really did not know how much more he could take before he completely snapped. I prayed that nothing more would happen, nothing more would be thrown our way for him to handle for fear I would lose Michael forever to depression and alcoholism, the two things that had begun to consume his life. I was beginning to feel so helpless myself. I felt so inept, so powerless. I felt there was nothing I could do to help him. The only thing I could do was what I did and that was listen to him talk for hours and hours about his feelings, about the sadness and the anger he was feeling every day, and how his heart broke over what was going on with his own son. He was consumed by all of his memories and all of these thoughts every day. The more he remembered and the more he thought, the more he would want to drink. He only hoped that some day, somehow Michael Jr. would be able to forgive him for letting him down so badly.

And as the weeks passed by, Michael and I would see Michael Jr. less and less. With Michael's drinking getting worse, it was harder to make plans we would be able to stick to. I would never know from one day to the next just how much Michael would drink and how drunk he would become. On one of his lesser-drunk days we had gone to pick Michael Jr. up. Lisa had taken me aside and told me something that broke my heart. She told me that Michael had called her a couple of weeks earlier, something I did not know about at the time, and asked if he could pick up Michael Jr. that coming weekend. Of course she said that would be fine, but this would be the second weekend now in a row that he would have called to make plans to pick Michael Jr. up and not show up as he did the time before. Each time Michael called, Lisa would hand Michael Jr. the phone and Michael would tell Michael Jr. he would be picking him up on a certain day, and Michael never showed up to do this.

Lisa said to me, "Kyra, I know how much you love Michael Jr. This is why I am telling you this. You see, I love Michael Jr., too, and it breaks my heart when he is sitting out there on the curb waiting and looking for his father to show up. As time passes by he realizes his father isn't coming. I just can't stand to watch this over and over again. I don't want it to ever happen again."

I told her, "Neither do I," and I went on to tell her, "Lisa, I had no idea that Michael was making these phone calls and setting these plans up."

She said, "I realize that you didn't."

I told her I would discuss this with Michael after we dropped Michael Jr. back off at home today. That afternoon we did take Michael Jr. out to the playground, and we spent most of the afternoon having fun and throwing the ball around.

Michael would drink, but he would keep his drinking under control for his son's sake while he was with us, and I knew his being pretty much sober by the end of the day would be the perfect opportunity I would need to discuss with him about what Lisa had told me. After we dropped Michael Jr. back off at home, Michael and I want to the lake to talk. I told him everything that Lisa had told me. I asked him just what in the Hell did he think he was doing making plans with Michael Jr. and then not showing up to pick him up? I asked him why he did this. Why was he calling Michael Jr. and getting his hopes up and leaving him sitting on the sidewalk for hours waiting and looking for him? I expressed to him how cruel I thought this was. I said, "Didn't you even think to make a phone call to him and let him know that you weren't gonna come?" I asked him, "How could you do this to your own son. Are you fucking crazy?"

Michael's only reply to this was, "Yes, I think I am," he said when he was making these phone calls he was very drunk, and because he was so drunk, he forgot about the plans and he even forgot to let me know about the plans.

I told Michael, "This cannot go on. You cannot keep doing this to your son."

I don't know if I was right or wrong in this next statement to Michael, but I told him, "It would be better if your son never saw you again than for you to keep calling and setting up times to pick him up and leaving him sitting out on the sidewalk brokenhearted like that." Then I made him promise me that he would never do this again. Michael agreed, and he felt horrible about what he had done.

Michael and I both knew that the alcoholism was beginning to take him over completely. It was tightening its grip on him. It was clear that Michael was no longer in control. The alcoholism was. It was slowly taking him over and ripping his life apart, but he did not know how to stop this or if he was even strong enough to win the fight against it.

It was a few days after this conversation when Michael and I found ourselves over our friend Alex's house. Michael and Alex were both drinking heavily that night, and Alex started in on Michael about what was going on with his son, and particularly his son being in foster care. Alex asked Michael why Michael Jr. was there.

Now you have to remember the dynamics of their relationship—how they first met. In the fifth grade they were both forced to walk home after missing their bus because they had to stay for detention, a detention that they earned because of their fighting in the classroom. Well, this just seemed to be the theme of their lifelong friendship. They loved each other like brothers, but they also fought like brothers as well—the sibling rivalry. It was a rather strange relationship. I could never figure it out, and after a while I stopped trying to, but it seemed to work for both of them. But at this time in Michael's life he really didn't need it nor did he really want to hear it. He told Alex to please shut up, and to my surprise Alex did what Michael asked for the first time that I knew. Alex dropped it, but it was far from being the last time he would bring it up that night.

The four or us decided to go out and get something to eat. The closest place to Alex's house was a little burger joint called The Jack in the Box. We went through the drive through, and then we decided to eat there. We just parked our cars in the parking lot, and we all got out to sit at the picnic table.

Sure enough after we were through eating, Alex started in on Michael again making cruel and stupid statements like, "Well, it's too bad Michael Jr. couldn't be here to join us right now."

Michael screamed at him, "Alex, will you just shut the hell up?"

He reminded Alex that he didn't need the shit right now, but instead of shutting up, Alex just went on and on. When Michael could stand it no longer, he lunged at Alex, punching him square between the eyes, almost breaking his nose. Alex being much larger than Michael was able to grab him and put him in a neck hold. Michael then broke out of the hold, and they both ended up on the ground. It was just like they were back in that fifth-grade class fighting and duking it out. It was ridiculous at their age that they would act like this.

Alex ended up on top of Michael, punching him in the face, and as I said before, Alex was no lightweight. At this point in his life he was like 350 pounds and very strong. I started trying to pull them both apart. Trying to pull 350 pounds off of the man that you love was no easy feat, but it is amazing what you can do when you have to when your adrenaline gets pumping, and your anger takes over. At this point I just wanted to slap the hell out of both of them for acting like such juvenile delinquents. I then exploded. Michael was on the ground. Alex was on top of Michael. I got on top of Alex. I hooked my arms underneath his as he was trying to throw the next punch to Michael's face. I put my knee in the small of his back, and I pulled with all my weight and all my force with my knee imbedded into his back, pulling up. I knew that he had a bad back, and this would cause him a lot of pain, perhaps enough to let Michael go. This was all I wanted him to do.

I knew I had two things going for me at this point. You see, Alex, along with all of Michael's other friends, really liked me a lot, and I liked all of them as well. I always tried to fit in, to be just one of the boys, and they also knew that I never took any shit and they respected me for this. They knew I never put on any airs, and I always was just me. What you saw is what you got. I never held back any punches with any of Michael's friends. I always spoke my mind. That was the first thing. The second thing was, I was very strong for a woman. I always had physical jobs where I had to do a lot of heavy lifting, so that always kept me in really good shape.

I always believed a woman should be strong both mentally and physically and should always be able to stand on her own.

So I sat there on top of Alex in the hold that I had him in, screaming, "Are you going to stop? Are you gonna stop? All I want you to do is stop hitting Michael."

He finally after a few moments agreed and said, "Yes, I'll stop. Get off me."

Alex and I then rolled to one side, getting off of Michael. Alex sitting there began to laugh. He said, "I'm amazed that you were able to get me in a hold like that."

Michael got up off the ground with his nose bloodied and his eyes bruised. We sat there for a few moments while he composed himself. He called Alex a fucking asshole and told me to get in the car, and we both took off, leaving Alex and Corey sitting there.

After the fight Alex and Michael did not speak for a few days. Michael was very angry with him, but as usual it only lasted a few days and then they were back talking and laughing again like nothing had ever happened, just as usual.

A few weeks would pass. It was now the middle of January and it was proven to be a typical New England winter. It was particularly cold, the coldest I could ever remember it being. It was so cold that it froze the entire Sabbatia Lake, the lake that Michael and I always went to just to talk every night. It had frozen so solid it was able to support the weight of at least 50 cars and vans along with snowmobiles. Everybody had so much fun that winter on the ice. Michael and I drove our van out into the middle of the lake. Michael began doing doughnuts all around. It was a blast.

It must have been around the second or the third day, people started setting up games to play on the ice with their snowmobiles, little races they would have.

And the cars began their own racing games. We would go from one side of the lake to the other. I'll never forget all the fun that Michael and I had for those few days before the Police had to come down and break it all up. It was probably for the best anyway. God only knows how much longer the ice would have held out.

This was the first time in quite a while that I had seen Michael smile and laugh. We both needed this—just to kick back and have some fun for a change. One night after Michael and I got off of work, we started driving back home to his mother's house as usual. We were about halfway there when Michael looked at me and said, let's go shoot some pool and have a little bit of fun. This was kind of a breakthrough for Michael because up to this point he really didn't want to go back into the bars. He was still thinking that people were holding him responsible for John's actions. So now with him wanting to go back, I could clearly see he was no longer feeling this way.

We walked into the bar and a friend of ours came over to greet us. He asked where we had been.

Michael just replied, "Oh, I've been really busy at work." Then Michael could clearly see for himself that no one held any animosity toward him, but Michael still was not feeling very comfortable there.

Michael and I went up to the bar, and Michael ordered a beer, and I ordered a coke. Halfway through the beer Michael turned to me and said, "Why don't we get out of here now? Why don't we go and visit Alex and Corey for a while?"

Alex and Corey lived only around the corner from the bar, so we just left our car there and walked. After visiting Alex and Corey for an hour or so, I was beginning to feel sick to my stomach, and I felt like my temperature was rising. I was not feeling well at all. I felt like all I wanted to do was go home and go to bed, but Michael would not hear of it. The longer I sat at Alex's the sicker became.

I told Michael again, "I really need to go home now."

Then we began to argue, and I told Michael if we did not leave right now, I was going home to my mother's house to spend the night. You see, my mother also lived right down the street from Alex, so it would have been very easy for me to walk there. But he kept refusing to bring me home and all I wanted to do was lie down.

I was in no mood to put up with this bullshit, and Michael yelled at me and said, "Go ahead. Do whatever you want. I'll see you tomorrow."

So I got up and I said, "The hell with you," and then I walked to my mother's house.

When I arrived at my mother's door she was very surprised to see me there so late at night. I told her Michael was in a party mood tonight, and I was too sick to remain with him.

She then told me, "Yeah, you look like hell. Come on in, and I'll make up a bed for you."

I spent the night there, and the next morning when I woke up I felt like hell. I could barely stand up and my body ached from head to toe.

When my mother came in to check on me I was burning up. I had a 103° temperature, and she told me, "Kyra, you have the flu. You're not going anywhere." My mother was such a loving and caring woman. She told me, "You just lie there, and I'll take care of you. Don't worry about anything." Then she said, "You know, Kyra, no matter how old you get, you'll always be my baby."

I called Michael before he left for work that morning and let him know I had the flu, and I was going to be spending the next few days at my mother's house. He told me he would come over after work that night to see if there was anything I needed. I told him, "I love you," but I did not want him to come up because I was afraid he would catch the flu from me. I told him to just stay away for a few days until it passed, and it took about a week before I started feeling normal again. Within this time Michael would call me every single night to check on me.

At the end of the week, he came to see me. It was so nice to see him again after being apart for a whole week. You see, since the day we met, we have been together every single day, and because we were so close and we had spent every day together for over two years now, I could see something was wrong in his eyes. I don't know how I knew. I just knew. He had cheated on me. We were too close for him to have hidden such a thing from me.

I looked in his eyes, and I asked him, "Do you have something to tell me?"
He said, "What?"

I said, "I think you know what." Then I just blurted it out. "You cheated on me, didn't you, you bastard."

Michael then replied, "Who told you?"

I said, "No one. No one had to. I just knew by the look in your eyes. I could just tell." Then I asked, "How could you do this to me? How could you break my heart like this?"

Then he began to tell me the whole story. He said it happened that night I left him at Alex's house. He said he got very drunk. He then went on to tell me that he and Alex ended up at Dunkin' Donuts around midnight to get something to eat and some coffee to help sober him up. Michael said this woman was just sitting there at the end of the lunch counter.

He kept saying over and over again, "I was so drunk I didn't know what I was doing." I then I asked him what Alex did if anything to try to stop him. Michael told me he did remember Alex telling him to knock it off and trying to get him out of there, but he remembers little after that. He remembers arguing with Alex, and Alex calling him an asshole and taking off and leaving him there with this woman.

Michael says he doesn't know how he got to the woman's apartment, but he did and they had sex. Michael went on to tell me it was around 5 o'clock in the morning when he woke up, and he had no idea of where he was. He told me he was in a blackout that he didn't know if I believed him or not, and at the time I did not. He also said when he did wake up he called my name because he had no idea where he was, and he expected me to be in the next room. He told me how sorry he was and that it would never happen again.

I just sat there crying my eyes out and my heart shattering into a million little pieces. He just kept telling me how much he loved me and how sorry he was. I had never felt so completely empty as I did at this moment.

As I was drying my eyes, I stood up, and I looked at him and told him, "You have just hurt me deeper than anyone has ever hurt me in my whole life. I have put up with a lot in this relationship, but there is one thing I will not put up with, and that's a cheating, low-life, son of a bitch. Now get up and get the fuck out of my house."

As he kept saying how sorry he was and for me to reconsider what I was about to do, I said to him, "I hope you can at least remember where this woman lives, because I no longer want you. Go back to her. You are hers now, and not mine. Now the only thing I want from you is for you to go away."

It was the next night that I would take a cab to his mother's house to pick up my car and my belongings. I entered into his house and explained to his mother what had happened, and I told her "I am sorry but Michael and I are finished." It was just then that Michael came driving into the driveway, and I told his mother, "I'm just going upstairs to get my belongings, and I'm going to leave."

When Michael came into the house, he heard me upstairs in our room. He immediately went up there and began trying to talk me out of this. He followed me all the way around the room as I packed my clothes in a suitcase.

I just kept repeating to him as I said earlier. "She's your girl, not me. You need to go back and be with her," and that I wanted nothing more to do with him.

We began having a tug of war with my suitcase. Michael refusing to let me leave, but I won.

As I was walking down the stairs he began screaming at me. "It's not over."

As I went out the door I said, "Yes, Michael, it is." I then went to my car and placed my suitcase in it and drove off.

On the drive back to my mother's house, I began crying. I never knew my heart could actually break so badly. I had never before felt such pain and betrayal in my life, and I feared that pain would never stop, and again, how could he betray me so badly after all we had shared. Everything he told me about his life, all the painful parts, and all the horrific parts in Vietnam. Every night we would sit and talk. How can someone share their heart and their soul and their love and their deepest, deepest emotions like that and then turn around and stab you in the heart. And then I began thinking about our most perfect evening down in Onset where we danced and we loved so perfectly and deeply and how we would never again have this. I would never again feel this way toward him. And now how Michael and Michael Jr. were both out of my life now forever and it made me feel physically ill.

After this, Michael would continue to call my mother's house every couple of days and plead to her to please have me speak to him, but I refused time and time again. There was nothing neither Michael nor my mother could do to make me speak to him.

After one of his phone calls to my mother, she turned to me and said, "Kyra, you know, people can do really stupid things when they're drunk."

I told her, "Mom, I know that, but there are certain things maybe you just can't get past or forgive, and this I think for me may be one of them." I told her, "I really don't think I could every forgive Michael for this. The betrayal just cut so deep into my soul."

It was now going onto three weeks since Michael and I had broken up when one morning as I was getting off of my night shift, leaving the restaurant, and heading toward my car in the parking lot, I saw the big black van parked right next to it. I walked up to him sitting in the van. As I was approaching I could see he had been crying. His eyes were all swollen and his voice was shaky. But my anger ran so deep still; all I wanted to do was punch him in the mouth. In a shaky voice he asked me to please get into the van so that we could talk.

I said, "If that is what it is going to take for you to leave me the fuck alone, then yeah, we'll talk a little bit more. I don't know what more you have to say to me. Nothing is going to change."

He said, "I don't care. I just need to talk with you. I need to be with you for a few minutes."

When he said that I became even angrier. I don't know why, but I ended up by calling him a fucking asshole and told him he was going to be sorry that he was still tormenting me.

He then again said, "Please, I just need to talk with you."

But when I got into the van he just repeated what he had said earlier about how sorry he was and about how much he loved me and missed me. He told me if he could take back that night, he would in a heartbeat. But he couldn't turn back the hands of time. He told me how very badly he wanted to start making it right again between the two of us. He went on to tell me how badly he needed me, and he never wanted to be with anyone else and he would never be again for as long as we were together. I just told him how angry I still was at him, and I asked him how could I ever trust him again or how I could ever believe him again. He had broken that trust and he had broken my heart. I didn't know how or where we were going from here.

Then he asked me if I still loved him. I sat there for a few moments in silence thinking about this question and wondering to myself, if I could be this angry and so hurt still to this moment, my heart must still love him.

I then answered him, "Yes, I do love you."

He said that was all he needed to know. From here on out, he said, he would spend every day trying to win me back, to win back the trust that he had utterly destroyed and the respect and the close, close bond that we once shared."

And he did, but it took well over a year for me to begin trusting him again, and for my pain to diminish. I also realized the pain that I was feeling paled in comparison to his pain. His nightmares that he suffered through every night from his brother back to Vietnam. But still, I was not the one that caused his pain. He was the one that caused mine, though. We had been lovers, best friends and each ones confidant, and in time we would get this back again. We were such a part of each other, such a part of each other's hearts, it actually hurt not to be with him. It was as though we were always meant to be together and as though we had always been together. It was very nice and strange to feel so completely a part of another person like the way we felt toward each other. These feelings at times were so overwhelming it scared me. But my heart left me little choice but to be with him.

Make no mistake, I entered back into this relationship with much caution, but I always knew in my heart, this was the right thing to do. This was the right choice. The only choice my heart would allow me to live with, and as I said, I moved back into this relationship slowly.

Michael wanted me to move back to his mother's house with him right away, but I could not. I told him it would happen when I am ready, and that is not right now. I told him it would probably be a couple of months before I was ready to jump head first back into this serious relationship and thus live together again. Even though we were not living together, we would see each other every single day.

This was all happening in the early spring of 1981. By late spring, early summer, John's trial had begun. Michael and I avoided the courthouse and pretty much all of downtown. Our little common which was in the center of Town where the courthouse was, had become a complete media circus. All the television stations, newspapers, from all around basically set up camp there, right there on the courthouse lawn for the duration of the trial. It was probably the most notorious murder trial since the trial of Lizzy Borden one hundred years earlier, but although her trial did not take place in our courthouse, she was a guest in our lovely jail cells for the duration of her trial which took place in Fall River only one town over. I believe probably not since then did our little Town receive such publicity.

Michael and I both stayed away from the courthouse but followed the trial closely in the newspaper and on television. Unlike last year when the murder was first committed, Michael and I had avoided all the newspapers and television. Michael probably would have been better off doing the same thing this time as well, because of course, during the trial all of the details about the murder case came to light. Things that we did not know and had no wish to know.

One particular detail about this case was that Mr. Smith was not even supposed to have been in Morton on this fateful day. I really don't know what you would want to call it, destiny, fate or just some really horrible timing. It came out in the trial that Mr. Smith had been in Boston that day undergoing stress tests, and he was supposed to have spent the night there, but instead he decided to come home. Soon after that he would be dead. How these four men's paths crossed at just a precise moment to me is incredible. Out of these four men, one would end up dead and the other three would end up behind bars.

As Michael sat there reading this newspaper article to me, all he kept saying was, "Oh, my God," as the details unfolded of how these four men came to be. Michael said all the man did wrong was come back to Morton and give these three assholes a ride on a hot night so they would not have to walk. The more Michael read, the more he drank, and the drunker he got the more upset he became. I tried to persuade him just to put the paper down and stop reading it for now and come upstairs to bed with me, but he insisted on staying up so he could also catch the late news on the television. I asked Michael why he was he doing this to himself, and he told me he couldn't continue to stick his head in the sand. He had to know the truth; he had to know exactly what his brother did and the role that he played in this poor man's death. So I went over to the couch and sat beside him as the news came on.

They began telling about just how the murder happened. It seems like one of the men knocked Mr. Smith unconscious while he was pulled over the side of the rode. They pulled him in the back seat and then one drove the car to the Oakcrest Dam where they pulled him out and began beating him and clawing at his face like a pack of wild dogs. They kicked and they punched until he was no longer breathing. They beat him to death, and then they tossed his body into the Oakcrest Dam. Then they used the man's car for a crime spree where they held up a gas station and just went through one roadblock after the other, until they were finally stopped.

The only thing during this trial that was never established was why. What made them do such horrible things? It did, however, come out that it had been a very hot, long summer's day, and they had started drinking very early in the morning and using drugs, so by evening they were quite out of their minds. All through the trial John insisted he had no memory of any of it.

Then I would hear this tidbit of information. I don't know if it is fact or not, but this is what I heard. Dr. Troy who was my doctor and many peoples' doctor for years in this town, was quite old, but he doubled as the coroner. From what I heard and understood, the other doctors in our hospital would not allow Dr. Troy because of his age to perform this autopsy on Mr. Smith because the body was in such horrific condition. They were afraid Dr. Troy would have a heart attack. They were afraid he was simply too old to be able to witness such a horrifying sight. I heard this from another doctor.

You know, I think a lot of things in our lives come down to simple choices, whether to stay or whether to go, whether to be with a certain person or not, and sometimes these choices we make every day can be life altering or live ending. Hopefully most of us will make the right choice.

After the news ended, Michael and I just sat there in silence. We didn't really know what to say. As Michael took one more drink, I told him we really needed to go to bed. This had just been too much. He agreed, and we both went upstairs and quickly fell asleep in each other's arms. About four hours passed, and I was abruptly awakened by Michael jumping out of bed. I thought, *Oh no, he is having one of his flashbacks,* but it was not that. He could not breathe. I saw him holding onto the wall and gasping for breath. I quickly jumped out of bed, ran over to him and started rubbing his back, telling him to calm down and try to relax. I yelled to him over and over again to relax and try to concentrate on his breathing. He was hyperventilating. He was getting too much air in. I just stood there rubbing his back, and Michael finally started breathing normally again. I told him, I thought he was having an anxiety attack. I got him to finally sit down on the edge of the bed as I continued to rub his back, but he was afraid to lie down because he was afraid it would start up again. So we both sat there for what must have been over an hour. I gave him a back rub and he fell back to sleep. As I lay there watching him sleep, the thought came to my head, *I don't know how much more his heart and his mind can take before something snaps.*

As the trial went on and the weeks passed, Michael's drinking along with the hot summer was coming to a boiling point. At this point it could not get any worse. Michael now was drunk almost constantly. He was barely holding onto his job and he began taking days off because of this. Finally the trial was coming to a close, and the jury as I said earlier, came in with a verdict of guilty on all counts. John received life in prison, and I thought, or should I say was hoping with this behind us, Michael would be able to get some kind of hold on his drinking again. But that would not happen. Michael was slowly killing himself, and I did not know what to do to stop him. I felt a little part of me dying right along side of him. I felt so utterly powerless and useless.

Now not even while visiting his son was he able to stay sober. It was a week or so after the trial ended when we went and picked up Michael Jr. for the day. We had not seen him for a couple of months now. With everything going on and his father being in the mental frame of mind that he was in, I thought it best not to even bring Michael Jr. into this insanity. But too much time was passing by, and we had to keep in touch with Michael Jr., so Michael and I picked him up on this day.

Michael was not quite drunk yet so I suggested that we all go fishing and then maybe out for some ice cream. I thought being with Michael Jr. in the sunshine and the fresh air would lift Michael's spirits for today at least anyway. It did turn out to be a good day. Michael Jr. spent most of the day running back and forth on the shoreline and wading in the water. I could tell that being with Michael Jr. was taking Michael's mind off of all of the horrible things that had happened. I could see the happiness on Michael's face as he watched his son play in the sunshine. He loved Michael Jr. much, and this I believe was truly the only bright spot in Michael's life right now. But even through these happy moments, Michael still was drinking. He sat there and sipped on a bottle of vodka and was pretty much drunk by the end of the day. As the day was ending, I suggested that we stop for Michael Jr.'s favorite cheese pizza and then go get some vanilla ice cream.

It was becoming late, and after we did this we started back to Lisa's house where Michael Jr. lived. I turned to Michael and I said to him, "Why are we doing this? Why are we dropping him off here? Why don't we just keep driving? You are his father, and you have just as much right to him as anyone, even more than anyone."

I don't know what I was thinking at the time. I was just so upset about everything that was going on in our lives. Everything else seemed so wrong, except this. Michael, Michael Jr. and me being together; that seemed right. It was the only right thing in my whole life right now. I thought perhaps if we could just get away and escape from everything that was around us. Have a change of scenery and go to a place where the three of us could just live our lives together and get away from all this insanity. I thought Michael Jr. and I would be very happy, and Michael would come to his senses and stop with all the drinking. A fresh start, I guess you would say. I told Michael, "For real, what are we truly leaving behind here. Two crappy jobs, our mothers are certainly capable of taking care of themselves. We need to concentrate on our little family. We need a fresh start."

Michael looked at me and he asked me, "Are you crazy, Kyra? How can you even consider doing such a thing?"

I said, "How could you not consider this?"

He said, "Do you want me to be in jail right beside John for kidnapping, because that is what I would be charged with, and we would be found."

I thought about it for a moment, and even though I did not want to agree with Michael, I had to. Michael continued driving to Lisa's house, and even though we hated the thought of having to drop him off and leaving him there, we did know in our hearts that she was a good woman and she loved Michael Jr. as well. This is the only thing that made it bearable. As Michael and I drove up the driveway to drop Michael Jr. off, I opened the door to the van to get out. Michael Jr. did not want to go. He did not want to get out of the van. As young as he was, I guess he understood what I was saying.

As Michael Jr. sat there refusing to get out of the van, Michael told me to get out and close the door so he could speak with his son in private. To this day I have no idea what Michael said to Michael Jr., and I never asked Michael. I figured it was a private conversation between a father and a son. After the talk they both of them got out of the van and Michael Jr. ran over to me and gave me a kiss on the cheek and the biggest and strongest hug I have ever received in my life. My heart breaks to say this but I had no idea at the time that this would be our farewell hug.

After this day, Michael's drinking did become worse. Just as I thought it couldn't get any worse, it did. He spiraled completely out of control. He began seeing things like little white bugs crawling on his arms at night while sitting in his chair watching television. While this was happening to him, he kept control of himself. He did not mention what was going on to me at the time that it was happening. I often wondered why he kept looking at his arms so strangely. I said nothing to him because I probably just didn't really want to know. You see he knew enough about the DT's to not totally freak out. He knew that he was seeing things and it was not real. It was only in his mind. So because of his knowledge, he was able to keep a little control over himself until it passed.

From here on out, every day would be a struggle for Michael. He would start off by heaving his guts out. He then would shower and shave and drop me off at work on the way to his job. Then on his first break of the day, around 10 o'clock in the morning, he would head to the liquor store where he would buy his first pint of vodka for the day. Out in the parking lot he would proceed to take a couple of good swigs from the bottle. He preferred vodka because it left little smell of alcohol on his breath. Then he would proceed back to work where no one would be any of the wiser. At lunch time he would go out to the van, eat a little of the lunch that I had prepared for him and finish off the bottle of vodka. He would of course return back from lunch drunk but not so drunk that it was noticeable to the boss. He avoided the boss until it was time to punch out for the day. Then he would head back to the same liquor store where he started off that morning's break to get yet another pint of vodka.

Thank God it was a short trip back to Morton, just one town over. He started on that bottle in the parking lot and continued to drink it all the while he was driving to pick me up from work. By the time he reached my job he had consumed three-quarters of the bottle. He sat out in my parking lot waiting for me to come out from work, finishing off the second pint of vodka. On most days he would get out of the van and say, "You are driving, Kyra." He was already drunk, and it was only 5 o'clock in the afternoon. As a matter of fact he was too drunk to walk, let alone drive. He drove from one town to the next in that condition every day. After waitressing all day and putting up with the general public, I was in no mood to put up with this bullshit.

There were days that I was just so frustrated with him. I would yell and scream, "You stupid asshole. You can't even stand up, and you are driving a van like this. You are going to kill yourself, or you are going to kill somebody else. When are you ever going to stop? And just how would you be able to live with yourself if this happened? Picture yourself wiping out an entire family. You think you are dealing with a lot now; try dealing with that."

Even this did not deter him. I told him, "You had better start thinking straight and using your fucking head," all the while realizing I knew it wasn't as simple as just not drinking. I knew all the while why he started drinking, and I knew why he was continuing to drink, but I remained powerless to help him. I saw myself becoming an enabler. This is something I thought I would never be, and I knew until I found him the professional help that he needed, this was not going to stop, and I saw no good end to it for either one of us. Michael had too many emotional problems to deal with on his own, and I was not a professional. I was only the woman that loved him, that listened to him but I guess as far as giving

88

him any constructive help, I simply couldn't do it. I didn't know how.

Meanwhile though all of this, my sister Amber was still in the half-way house working very hard to overcome her alcoholism and getting the counseling she desperately needed to overcome my father's abuse and my father's alcoholism and the emotional pain that was inflicted on her by him. My sister Amber was left feeling so much hatred and resentment toward my father because of his actions that her emotional scars ran deep. She was just as screwed up as Michael but for very different reasons. Like Michael, she too numbed herself so she wouldn't have to feel these emotions. This was her escape. But unlike Michael, it caught up to her a little bit earlier. Her mind, her body could no longer take all of this abuse. She broke before Michael did.

With the knowledge that Amber was providing me about these houses and these programs, I spoke with Michael about perhaps going into one of them and reminded him how well my sister Amber was doing. However, each time I would speak to him about this, all he would say to me was, "I don't want to leave you alone."

My response to this was, "If you were to kill yourself or kill someone else and go to jail for the rest of your life, would you not be leaving me alone then?" I told him this was what I was afraid it was going to come to. I reminded him that there were no easy answers and this was not going to be painless. I told him I realized it was going to be hard, and it was going to be painful, but this is the only way we are going to ever have a happy and long life together. If he continued on the road that he was going down now, it would end one way or it would end another, but it would end.

I asked him, "Don't you realize, can't you see as we sit here today together we have no future?" I told him, "Michael, apart we are very strong people, and together there is nothing that we cannot do. Michael, in my heart and soul I truly believe there is nothing in our lives that we are not going to be able to overcome together, nothing. You remember this always, Michael. We can beat this, and we can win if we stick together."

Michael thought for a moment really hard about what I had just said and asked me, "You really would be willing to go through all this hell with me?"

I said, "Of course. I love you."

CHAPTER FOUR

After this conversation Michael began to seriously think about getting some help for the first time in his life, but his addiction remained very strong and continued to take hold of him until he finally broke. The day that I had dreaded had come. He reached his boiling point and snapped. This happened on one crisp fall day. It was on a Friday, and we both had just gotten paid. It seemed like just the same old shit. He was again drunk when he picked me up. We stopped to cash our paychecks, and he headed right for the liquor store where Michael proceeded to get his third pint of vodka for the day. He went into the liquor store and came out. I was driving of course. He opened up the bottle of vodka taking one huge swig from it, when all of a sudden he began crying. He threw the bottle and the remainder of the vodka out the window of the van. As I sat there in amazement with my mouth hanging open, not yet pulling out of our parking spot at the liquor store, I remember seeing a lot of people coming in and out of the liquor store that day. They looked over at the van while Michael sat ranting and raving and crying like some kind of a madman. He began rocking back and forth uncontrollably and just started screaming, "I can't do this anymore. I can't do this anymore!" over and over again.

I was very scared for him. I had never seen him like this before. I had never witnessed him being this distraught. He looked as though he was losing his mind. What would happen next would be truly terrifying. Michael leaped out of the van and just started running into the oncoming traffic trying desperately to get hit by a car or a truck. Honestly to this day I have no idea why he was not hit. The speed limit on that street is 40 mph, and the traffic was very heavy with people just getting out of work. Thank God the traffic somehow was able to avoid Michael which really pissed him off at this point. As the cars slowed down around him, he began kicking the sides and trying to break the windshield. I had no idea what was running through the minds of these poor drivers at the time. They all had such a look of horror on their face.

Michael had finally snapped and was having a complete and total nervous breakdown right in front of me and right in the middle of the street. Everything all at once finally caught up with him. The nightmares from Vietnam, the thing that had just happened with John and now his son. All of his pain could no longer be held at bay by alcohol. It just came flooding out. Clearly there was not enough alcohol in the world to kill his pain any longer.

Once I realized what was going on, I began chasing him down the street in the traffic. Thank God he finally got onto the sidewalk, but he only began running faster. I could no longer catch up with him, so I decided the next best thing was to run as fast as I could back to the van. With the van I thought I could catch up with him and get him back in before the police would hear about this incident. I was fearful of him being arrested or worse, taken to the very place that we wanted to take John, Morton State for observation, even though maybe at this point he needed a little rest. Maybe he needed to be there. I just didn't want him to go there. I knew he wasn't crazy, he was just handling too much.

I reached the van and jumped in heading back to where I last saw him, but he was no longer there. I drove up and down the street but I could not find him anywhere. I continued driving all around looking for him. It was as though he had just disappeared. I was driving so erratically because I was in such a frantic state, I almost got into a head on collision myself. I then parked the van and began looking into some wooded areas around where I thought he might head, but still no sign of him anywhere. I drove around for hours after that looking and hoping and praying that I would find him. I then began going to all of our friends' houses, hoping maybe he would have ended up there, but still nothing. I was beside myself with worry, and by this time all of our friends were out looking for him as well. And then I thought maybe he would go to my mother's house, so I stopped there and let her know what was going on and if he were to show up to please keep him there, that I would be back later to get him. On my way out of the door the phone rang. I prayed that this was Michael on the phone and it was. Thank God.

I said to Michael. "What the hell did you think you were doing?" and I told him all of his friends were out looking for him, and we were all out of our minds with worry. I also told him that if we were not able to find him tonight, the next step would have been going to the police.

Michael then went on to remind me of our conversation about him getting help. He said, "Kyra, that is where I am right now, getting help."

He then told me that he was at the Brockton Detox. He went on to explain how he walked from where I had last seen him downtown to the Drop-In Center and spoke with one of the counselors there explaining to them what he had just done and asking them for help. They quickly accommodated him and gave him a ride to the Brockton Detox. I had never been so relieved in my life to hear this, but at the same time feeling so furious as to what his friends and I had just gone through.

He kept calling me his Baby Doll. This was his nickname for me, and he always called me this when he knew he was in some deep shit, and I remember telling him, "Don't you dare call me that right now. I am so angry with you. You scared me to death with the stunt that you just pulled." I went on to tell him, "I almost got into a head-on accident while I was frantically driving around looking for you because I was afraid you were going to kill yourself. You don't have the right to call me Baby Doll, not now, not right now."

Michael then began telling me how sorry he was. He said Kyra, "I just snapped. You saw it coming, and I knew it was coming; I could feel it. I lost all control. My heart could no longer take any more pain, and the alcohol was no longer numbing it sufficiently. I just could not stand one more day of feeling like this."

He again said how sorry he was, and I told him I understood. I could see it coming. I told him I knew he was at his breaking point, and he then said, "You know what I mean then."

I said, "Yes, I do, Teddy Bear." You see, "Teddy Bear" was my nickname for Michael. But unlike him I only called him that out of love, not when I had done something wrong. Right at this moment, I wanted to show him how much I loved him and how much I was supporting him and his decision, and we both realized at this moment how much we owed my sister Amber for breaking ground and letting us know that help is out there if you want it. Thank God in Michael's fragile mental condition, he remembered this.

While speaking with the counselors at the Drop-In Center in our town, Michael realized maybe this would work. The counselors there were so kind and understanding because they had been through the same thing. They too also realized it was only a matter of time before Michael killed himself or someone else, because Michael also told them how he was driving and how much he had to drink every day while he was driving.

So the counselors began work on how to get Michael to the Brockton Detox and to make sure there was a bed available. Once at the detox the counselors spoke with Michael. They explained to him everything he was going to feel and what he was going to go through. This was going to be very, very hard but it was well worth it and not to give up.

They also explained to him that he could not go from drinking over a quart of vodka a day to nothing without having his body go through certain changes, but they said they would be there for him and not to worry.

Michael was especially scared that first night, but with all the counselors and the medication that they provide there, he got through that first night with little incident.

The next day as the counselors were talking with him, Michael kept repeating that he was doing this for me, as well as for himself.

The counselors told him, "Michael, you can't be doing this for anyone else but yourself. That is the only way it is going to work. Kyra can be a help, she can be a part of the recovery, but she cannot be the reason that you are in recovery. You truly need to understand that you cannot do this for anyone else but you. You cannot control other people—only you."

I would stay at my mother's house for the next week while Michael was at detox. I just could not stand sleeping in our bed without him beside me.

The next day when Michael called me to talk, he told me about this conversation that he had with the counselor and how he was supposed to do this for himself. I told him I agreed wholeheartedly.

I said, "The only one you need to be doing this for, the only one you need to be concentrating on right now is yourself."

I reminded him of how much I loved him, and I would stand by him through anything. I told him our love is true, and he need not worry about this or ever doubt it for one minute.

At the end of our conversation, I told him I would see him tomorrow. I would be up right after work, but Michael then told me no visitors were allowed for the first three days. You see this was only a five-day program, and usually the first three days people were too sick to be having visitors anyway.

This was the one part that I hated the most, not being able to be with Michael, to hold Michael in my arms as he went through this pain. I had no choice but to agree. How my heart ached for him. I just so wanted to be in his arms at this very moment, but they had their rules so I would have to wait until the fourth day to see him again.

After this phone conversation with Michael, I called his mother to let her know what was happening. She too was very happy to hear that Michael was finally getting the help that he so desperately needed, although in this conversation with my mother-in-law, I did leave out the fact that her son had run into traffic and had what I considered a complete mental breakdown. I figured she just didn't really need to hear all the details.

After the three days were up, I was finally able to see Michael. I went straight to the Brockton Detox from work. I picked up a few packs of cigarettes for him because I knew by now he must be out and the last thing he needed was to be withdrawn from the cigarettes as well as the alcohol. I found the detox with little problem. I walked into the building and into the visitor's lounge, a little room they have off to the side which was very nice. I remember it having large windows where a lot of light and sun could shine through.

I don't know quite what I was expecting to see there, perhaps *One Flew Over the Cuckoo's Nest* type of deal, but I was pleasantly surprised. It was nothing like that at all. It was very cheerful, and the staff and counselors were very, very nice. They worked very hard to keep people's spirits up while they were going through this most difficult time. The counselors there worked with people through the most painful process of trying to get their lives back.

As I stood there looking out the window waiting for Michael, I thought, *Could this truly be the beginning of our lives together? Our lives filled with joy and love and happiness and most importantly sobriety? Maybe now we can actually hope for a normal life.*

Just as I was thinking that, I turned around and Michael was standing behind me. We wrapped our arms around each other and just stood there holding each other for the longest time. I remember him looking so pale and so drained. He looked like hell, but it didn't stop him from looking into my eyes and smiling from ear to ear. We then kissed, and he told me how very much he missed me, and I told him how much I missed him. We then both sat down in the chairs, and we began talking. We talked for hours just as we always had, but this conversation would be drastically different. He would be sober.

He told me about the first three days and how hellish they had been for him. He told me about the crawling sensation he had all over his body and how he just wanted to explode, wanting to break out of his own skin. Between the cold sweats, the chills and the nightmares, he felt as though he was losing his mind at this point but he knew he had to keep going. He couldn't stop. He couldn't stop now. Although they did provide medication for him, it wasn't strong enough to stop all of the withdrawal symptoms, but without this medication I cannot even imagine how sick he would have been.

Michael shared his room with one other man, and as sick as Michael was feeling, he still felt luckier than this man. Michael went on to tell me about his first night there. How this man woke up yelling and screaming. He just kept screaming over and over again, "Would you shut up? Can't you see you are keeping me awake?" Michael then sat up and put his light on and saw that there was no one else in the room.

He said to the guy, "Who are you talking to?"

He said, "All these people. Can't you see them? They just won't shut up. I can't get any sleep."

When Michael told the man that there was no one else in the room but him the man became irate and began screaming louder and louder, "Shut up; shut up!"

By now one of the staff was hearing this and came in. They calmed the man down and took him to a more private room where they could more closely monitor him. The man would stay in this private room for the next two nights, while Michael lay there sweating and then freezing to death. He tried as hard as he could to get some sleep.

On the third night they brought the man back to the room to share with Michael. He was doing much better and his hallucinations had just about stopped. Michael said he just lay there thinking, *I just want all of this to be over with.*

The next day he began talking to one of the counselors about what he was going to do after he left. The counselor then asked Michael if he was interested in going into one of the halfway houses that they had in the area for a little while. Michael replied, "No. I realize the only thing wrong in my life is me."

You see, when you are an alcoholic and you start reaching out for help, whether it be through counseling or half-way house, or a detox such as Michael just did, you and the counselors have to work very hard together to try and figure out exactly why you want to be drunk. Why do you want to drink and why do you want to numb yourself? Is it family issues, is it job issues? Or are you in a relationship where your partner is drinking or doing drugs. What is the cause?

This sometimes takes a long time to find out and to figure out. So naturally they look at the person closest to the alcoholic. In this case it would be me. When the counselor began trying to get our relationship, the dynamics of our relationship, out of Michael, Michael did tell them that I used to drink. Alcoholism ran in my family, but I had not drunk in over a year. In fact I was trying to get him to stop drinking. I was standing by him and supporting him through all of this, and then he told me he went on to tell the counselor that I was the last thing in his life that was making him want to drink. Michael told him it was his scars from the past, long before he met me that were making him want to drink, to stay numb, so he wouldn't have to relive it. So he wouldn't have to think about it.

Then Michael began telling them about all the nightmares from Vietnam. Ones that he just could not get out of his head. Ones that played over and over like a bad movie in his mind. All the things that he did and all the horrors that he saw in Vietnam, he just had to escape from them. Michael then told them he called it taking a shot of Novocain to the heart every time he got drunk. That is the only thing, the only way he could escape it.

He then went on to tell the counselor that the day after his father's funeral, when he had just gotten back from Vietnam, was the day he crawled into the bottle, and there he had been ever since. Michael told him, "This is the only way I can deal with my life. The only reason that I am sitting here right now trying to get help and trying to get cleaned up is because I love Kyra, and she loves me. We hope to just have a normal life together."

He told them he realized that if he didn't take this step to help himself, there was a good possibility that he would lose me forever, and he couldn't let that happen.

The counselor then went on to remind Michael that he couldn't do this for me. He had to do it for himself. That is the only way it would work.

By now Michael was getting a little sick of hearing this statement. He asked, "For me to stop killing myself and stop drinking and not lose Kyra, isn't that doing it for me? Isn't that making my life better? I am sitting in front of you because I love Kyra, but when all is said and done, isn't having a long happy, normal life for me? What I am supposed to be trying to achieve here? If it is to be with Kyra, the woman that I love, what is so wrong with that?"

You know I give counselors and psychiatrists, people that work with alcoholics and drug abusers a lot of credit for they are really understanding. I know we can be among the most difficult to work with. Alcoholics can be so hardheaded and stubborn.

You know, it wouldn't be until years later when I became much older that I would realize what that statement really meant. You had to do it for yourself. You could not reclaim your life in someone else's name, and you could not go through all this pain for another. It must be for you, because one thing that stays constant in everyone's life is looking at yourself in the mirror every morning when you get up. You must face who is looking back at you whether you accept this person or like this person or not. You see, other people leave you, other people will divorce you, they will walk out and they will turn their back on you. Ultimately in the end you, yourself, is all you will have. If you are doing this for another person, and if that person were to leave you, where would you be? Back at square one again.

You can't change for someone else, because there is no guarantee that someone else will always be in your life, but you will always be in your life. You will always look at yourself in the mirror every morning, and you are the one you must do this for.

Furthermore, if you are taking drugs or drinking to numb yourself, you must find out why. Why do you feel as though you have to go through life numb? If you cannot figure this out for yourself, then please get a counselor to help you. This is what they do, and whatever the problems are that are making you want to go through life numb, you must address. You must face them and figure out how to work through them whether they were your fault or not.

Sometimes things just are not within our control, but whatever the situation is, it can be worked through. There are people who will help you deal with it and work through it and hopefully you will get past it, so that you can continue on with your life, with a normal life—a life without drugs and a life without alcohol. You cannot control other people's actions, things that other people may have done in the past to you, but you can control your future. You are the only one that can.

This was my first lesson. I learned I could not control other people. I could only control my own actions, and I was only responsible for myself. I was the only one that could choose whether I was going to be sober or drunk. I don't know. Perhaps it was from my childhood and not being in control and not being able to stop the things that I saw my father doing. That I felt as though I always had to be in control. And of course, I was anything but when I was drinking.

This was one of my driving forces that helped me stay sober.

These are one of the few things that Michael and I did not quite get at first. The counselor asked Michael if I was receiving any counseling for myself. Michael told him "No. All of this is fairly new to us. You see, Kyra's sister Amber is the one who first opened our eyes to this help."

He then went on to explain how Amber was in a halfway house for alcoholics and was in a recovery process of her own. Michael's counselor then strongly recommended that I attend regular counseling sessions with him considering I had a family history of alcoholism myself.

He told Michael, "If you are going to get through this together, you are both going to be needing counseling, and you are both going to have to be strong for each other for this to work." He also told Michael that he had a very long and difficult road ahead of him, and it was not going to be easy. But then again, nothing worthwhile is. Michael then told me that the counselor wanted to meet with me the next day before Michael left the program. That would have been his fifth day there. I told Michael to tell the counselor I would be happy to.

By this time it was getting rather late, and Michael had an AA meeting to attend. Every night a representative from the local AA would go to the detox to speak to the patients there. He would bring information about the areas that the patients came from, the local AA meetings, and the counseling groups that were available to them in their town.

I then gave Michael a big kiss and a hug goodbye and reminded him of how proud I was that he was doing so well. He just said, "Baby Doll, I love you so much, but we have a long road ahead of us. You know that, right?"

I said, "Yeah, I know," and I told him I loved him again.

Before leaving he asked me if I would please bring some candy bars tomorrow night when I came for our visit. I reminded him that he was coming home with me, but he said, "That is okay; bring them anyway. The guys here really have a sweet tooth, and I wanted to leave them with a little something."

I was rather surprised to hear about this new sweet tooth Michael had developed. You see Michael had never been big on sweets. He just told me that he had a craving for chocolate. I guess it was because he wasn't getting all the sugar in his body anymore from the alcohol. Alcohol is loaded with sugar, and the body still craves that sugar long after you have stopped drinking.

So before returning the next day, I stopped and picked up a large box of individually wrapped candy bars—Babe Ruth, Hershey bars, all different kinds. When I showed up at the door of the detox, I was surprised to discover how many friends I had made rather quickly. When I opened the box of candy in the visitor's lounge, all of the other guys gathered around and Michael told them, help yourselves. I stood back and watched. It reminded me of children opening their stockings on Christmas morning. They then ripped through that box of chocolates like a swarm of locust, and as I was sitting there Michael's counselor came out and asked to speak to me now.

He started our session off by asking me about my drinking and how I was handling it. I told him I had my good days and my bad ones. I said, "I am not going to lie to you. There are days where I do feel like drinking, but I continue to fight the urge, and I have every intention to keep on fighting."

I then went on to tell him, "Strange as this may sound, it was actually Michael's drinking and meltdown I could see coming that kept me sober." I told him that I felt as though I had to be sober to protect Michael from himself, because I never knew what he was going to do next and one of us had to be in control.

Then he asked me something that really surprised me. He said, "Well, if Michael were to stop drinking now, what incentive would that be for you to continue to stay sober? Surely you wouldn't have to feel as though you needed to protect him any longer."

I looked at him as though he had two heads. I said, "That answer is simple. My incentive is to have a long and happy and normal life with the man that I love. That is all the incentive I need." I also told him, "I will be there by his side at every AA meeting and every counseling session that he will have, and I will be getting help for myself as well to stay sober."

The counselor was very happy to hear this. He then began setting up counseling sessions for Michael and me in our town. He also gave me a list of all the AA meetings in our area. He then called Michael into the office and said his goodbyes and wished us the best of luck. He said that if we needed any help any time in the future, to please call him.

Michael and I began our counseling sessions at the Community Counseling Center. At first we were seeing our counselors three days a week. Every night after work it seemed like we were either seeing our counselors or going to AA meetings. As a matter of fact, we were so busy we hardly had time to even think about drinking. I guess that was the idea. Michael at this time was becoming quite the connoisseur of chocolate and in the process had gained a few pounds, but he looked really good. Michael always looked nice; he dressed well and took care of his appearance. However, in the few weeks prior to him sobering up, he had started to let himself go. His hair and his beard were beginning to look all straggly and that was just not Michael. So to see him now looking so handsome was really a good sign. Our relationship was a bit strange at first. It was like we were getting to know each other all over again, but it was exciting.

Michael's nerves were a bit raw at first from the withdrawals. I tried to keep him out of stressful situations as best I could, but I could not be with him 24 hours a day and especially while he was at work. He was under tremendous stress at work. The air masks that he was making and the coating process had to be precise or it was no good, and it was very, very difficult to get this perfect every time because the machine kept messing up. He stuck with it however, and most importantly he stayed sober. Every day sober, every day that passed was a victory for us.

The first thing that AA teaches you is just that to take it one day at a time. That is what both of us were doing. They say this because if you actually sat there and said to yourself, "I can never have another drink again for as long as I live," that is precisely what you will want to do, so therefore you take it one day at a time. This saying, along with another popular one among alcoholics is, "One drink is too much," and "Ninety-nine is not enough." This is something that every alcoholic knows all too well.

Now about a month and a half have passed, and Michael and I had been attending our meetings and our counseling sessions on a regular basis. We were doing very well until one night Michael picked me up from work. As I was walking out to the van, I could tell something was terribly wrong with Michael. He was sort of slumped over the steering wheel. I went to the van. I thought he was sick. I opened the door. He then stepped out of the van and fell flat onto his face. It was surreal. I couldn't believe my eyes. He was without a doubt the drunkest I had ever seen him, and he actually drove all the way to Morton in this condition. To make matters worse, it was snowing out, and the roads were very slippery. It was the first snowfall of the winter season. The sight of him lying there made me sick to my stomach; I almost threw up. I helped him up off of the ground and got him back into the van.

I drove us both home, and ironically we had a counseling session to go to that very night. I went alone of course and told the counselor what had just happened, and how I could not believe Michael could do this to me and most importantly to himself, especially after the hellish week he had just spent at detox and the month and a half that followed with all our counseling and AA meetings. It was like all of this was for nothing.

She then told me to please try and calm myself down, and then she went on to tell me that this happens a lot more than not. "He just had a slip up, Kyra. You see, people that have been drinking for as many years as Michael have found it almost impossible to stop their first time out."

She told me that my situation was much different than Michael's. For one, I hadn't had the years of drinking, the years of addition and craving that he had, and also our reasons for drinking were vastly different. I drank because this is something that was just accepted in my family. All my sisters did it. My father did it. My mother was the only one who didn't. For Michael his reason was to numb the past, to try and forget the past and drown it out and that is much more difficult to recover from.

She said, "The most important thing now is that Michael try again as quickly as he can." She asked me to please get him in here tomorrow to see her. She also went on to tell me that sometimes it can take years and many, many tries before an alcoholic can actually stop for any extended amount of time. This I have to be honest with you, left me rather discouraged, but my love for Michael remained stronger than ever. I knew that was the one thing that would get us through this hell. She also reminded me that alcoholism is a disease, a disease for which there is no cure.

An alcoholic must constantly be aware of this fact, and even as time passes and the desire becomes less, you always do have the urge to let your guard down and sometimes want to forget that you have this disease and have a social drink with your friends. But a social drink to an alcoholic can be disastrous. You always have that desire to feel normal, to want to fit in. You will have to live the rest of your life with your guard up, always knowing that the next drink could possibly be your last. The last one that will push you back into the alcoholism, back into the vicious cycle. So it is a disease that you have to stay ever vigilant and aware of in your own self, in your own mind, in your own body and you have to stay in control and avoid situations you know are going to make you fall back.

I will always be an alcoholic. This I have come to terms with, and this I will live with the rest of my life. I have this choice, and I choose sobriety. I choose to feel things, and I choose to live. I choose to love, and I choose to laugh and with God's help, I will stay strong. I do know that there are many, many alcoholics in this world that lead normal lives, and have happy lives, and I hope Michael and I will be among them.

Michael and I would soon learn that there are certain rules that every alcoholic must follow in their lives to stay sober. One of these rules is knowing your limits. You cannot do everything and you cannot control everything. When you discover this, you can stop beating yourself up for it. This adds to the guilt and the grief and makes the drinking and escaping more desirable. Once you learn these rules and try your hardest to live by them, things are a little more acceptable, and maybe even some day you will be able to help other people, fellow alcoholics, learn the rules and help them lead a normal life as well.

As the counselor sat across from me explaining these very important rules, ones that I would eventually learn to live by, I couldn't help but think to myself, *If I can barely understand and accept what she is saying, how on earth is Michael ever going to be able to?* This led me worrying even more, but she told me the sooner you learn these rules and start living by them, the better chance you will have to stay sober and the better chance that you will have to help Michael stay sober.

As I sat there struggling to understand exactly what she meant, I felt less and less hopeful that I would ever be able to help Michael. I would continue the counseling meeting with her three times a week, but along with Michael I had stopped the AA meetings. Although I tried my hardest to get Michael to return to counseling, he refused and his drinking continued. I thought, *Perhaps if he sees me going the three times a week to see our counselor and how it is helping me, it will give him incentive to return,* but the alcoholism just took him back over again.

His drinking would continue for the following three weeks. This time though worse than ever. He would experience blackouts on a regular basis now and be violently ill every single morning until one day he showed up out of the blue at his counselor's office after not seeing her for a month. Thankfully she was not in the middle of a meeting with one of her clients, so Michael was able to speak with her immediately. He sat down and began telling her he had not gone to work that day. Instead he had gone directly to a bar and proceeded to get drunk. While he was there, I was at work.

I received a phone call from her letting me know that Michael was in her office drunk, and he wanted to go back to the Brockton Detox. She then asked me if I would be willing to bring him there. I said that yes, of course I would.

She called over to the detox to make sure they had a room for him. I walked into her office, and I saw Michael sitting there, slumped over in his chair. I began apologizing to her for Michael's actions, and she told me Michael owns his own actions. I have nothing to apologize to her for.

She then confided in me by telling me, "Kyra, I did worse things when I was drunk," which really shocked me because I had no idea that she was an alcoholic.

She then told me that she had had a problem with alcoholism for most of her life, and she is an alcoholic. She just hasn't had a drink in 10 years. She went on to tell me that most alcohol counselors are alcoholics themselves. That is how they can identify so well with their clients.

She said, "I know the pain that you and Michael are going through, because I went through it myself. That is why I told you about the rules, the rules that I also had to follow in order to stay sober." She also told me that she attends AA meetings on a regular basis and continues to see a counselor herself. She also said that she had just received her 10-year chip from her AA group.

I suddenly felt no longer embarrassed about what Michael was doing. With her standing in front of me, a person that seemingly had her whole life together and was doing very well for herself, I saw hope. Something that I desperately needed to see, a light at the end of the tunnel for Michael and me. I then thought, *If she can do this, possibly Michael and I can as well.* She provided the strength that I needed at that moment, in time to help Michael and to carry on.

The three of us spoke for about a half an hour. Michael had some coffee and began sobering up a little. You see, the detox will not take you if you arrive at their door drunk. By the time Michael and I reached the detox, he at least passed for sober.

The counselor that Michael had had the first time he went was not surprised at all to see us back. He said to me, "Kyra, don't worry. Very rarely do people make it on the first time." These people that work with alcoholics are truly amazing people. They do truly care and are very driven in their cause. They know themselves, because they were there themselves that it can be a very long road to recovery, but they only wish to help. They only wish to have you back on the road to recovery. Whatever way they can help you achieve this, they do. It is a true calling for them to help their fellow alcoholics in their time of need. They are truly special people, each and every one of them.

So Michael that night was welcomed back with open arms and now had to begin detoxing all over again. Although this time it was not nearly as hard as the last time. The cold sweats were at a minimum and his nerves were not as raw. Just as before, I was able to see him on the third day. I remembered the chocolates and instead of bringing one box, this time I brought two. I brought one box just for Michael and the other box he could share with his friends. As I stood in the visiting room, waiting for him to come in, I again was looking out the window, but this time with a little bit more knowledge than I had the last. Again as I turned, I saw Michael standing there. I gave him a big hug and a kiss and reminded him again of how much I loved him. We sat down and to my surprise he didn't look nearly as drained or worn-out as he did the last time.

We found ourselves sitting in the very same room that we had just been in a month earlier with so much hope and expectations that we were going to start this wonderful brand-new life together. Then came the cold slap in the face of reality, and the reality is people do relapse. People do fall off the wagon, but the important thing is to get help immediately. Michael and I both realized that to get back on the right path again there are no quick fixes. Nobody is going to come and wave a magic wand and make it all better. This will be a lifelong battle that we will fight together.

We spent most of this time discussing what exactly drove him back to drinking. Was it the job? Was it me? What exactly was his breaking point? What exactly made him stop and get that bottle of vodka? We had to try and figure out why he relapsed.

He quickly told me, "Kyra, it wasn't you. The stress from my job and just the old demons that are coming back into my head about Vietnam when I am sober, that is all I can think about. No matter how hard I try to push them away, to push it out of my head, it just keeps replaying itself, and I don't know how or if I ever will be able to push them out of my head."

He then went on to tell me that every day since that friendly fire incident happened, "I see that man's face, that man, that other soldier that they carried out on the stretcher, and I can hear his voice asking me, 'Why? Why were they trying to kill them?'" The poor man's bloody face. The face that was half blown away, and Michael didn't know and would never know for sure if it was his mortar that did this horrible thing to this man and killed so many in the other platoon.

All of these images would forever be seared into Michael's brain even after all this time. Michael tried so very hard to stop thinking about it and to try and put it out of his mind so that he could remain sober. So he could have a life. But he had not yet found a way to do this. Until he did, he feared he never would be able to stop drinking.

He then went on to tell me how sorry he was that we were back here again. I then told him what our counselor had told me about it taking sometimes many, many times before people can successfully stop drinking. I told him it took many years for you to get here, many years of drinking, and he was not going to be able to stop overnight. I realized this, and now it came time for him to realize this as well. I reminded him of how much I loved him and that I would always stand by him, and I told him not to beat himself up over this relapse.

As we were talking our counselor at the detox came in and asked to speak to both of us. He had a few questions he was wondering about.

He asked us one. "Are you still associating with the same people that you were associating with when you were drinking?"

Michael and I both said, "Yes, we are, but not as much." We explained to the counselor that we simply really didn't have the time to hang around with our friends anymore. Between the working, the AA meetings and the counseling sessions, most of our free time was taken up.

Then the counselor looked at me and asked me if I was staying away from alcohol, if I was drinking or had I gone back to drinking, or drinking in front of Michael, and I said, "Of course not."

Then the counselor turned to Michael and asked him, "Well, then, what exactly do you think led to this relapse?"

Michael simply said, "My job. It is driving me crazy. It is very stressful. Then one night, I don't know why I did it or how I even found myself parked in the liquor store parking lot, but I was there. Before I knew it I went in and got a bottle of vodka and proceeded to drink it."

He also went on to tell the counselor that on that day, he had had an argument with one of the men that he was working with on the machine. "So between the stress from the job and the argument on that day, as I was driving home and driving past the liquor store, I just stopped. I didn't want to, but I did. I knew it was wrong. I sat out there, and I consumed almost the whole pint of vodka. While driving home, halfway from Middleboro to Morton, I must have gone into a blackout, because I don't remember arriving at Kyra's work to pick her up. But what I do remember is feeling instantaneous relief, relief from all the stress. As soon as I took my first drink, I could feel the stress just melt away from me and a sense of euphoria overtake me. As I said, I don't remember entering the parking lot where Kyra worked. I didn't snap out of it. I didn't start remembering until about 2-3 hours later when the alcohol began wearing off.

"The next day Kyra told me just how horrible I was. How I got out of the van and fell flat on my face, and the look that she had on her face when she was describing all of this, the hurt and the disappointment in her voice overwhelmed me. I had started again, and the cravings started again. From that day on, I went back to drinking, even though I could see what it was doing to Kyra. I just couldn't stop myself. The alcohol once again took me over. The craving for alcohol overpowered my love for Kyra, and then the next day at work, it started all over again, just as it was before. At break time I would go out and get a pint of vodka and take a few swigs and then return back to work.

"Although this time around, it didn't seem to take as much alcohol to get me drunk as it did before. It seemed as though my system was a little bit more sensitive to it, and it just seemed like my craving for alcohol, my craving to be drunk, overrode everything else that I was feeling. Everything else that I knew was right and everything that I had learned in AA and the counseling sessions that I was going to just didn't seem to help at this point. I know it was wrong, but my body just craved that escape, that euphoria. There was nothing else in this world that could make me feel like that but alcohol."

The counselor strongly suggested to Michael he seek other employment, perhaps less stressful at this moment in his life. He would be much better off doing this. But Michael then reminded him of the job situation in our area and just how bleak it was, and he told the counselor how long it took for him to find this job. He explained to the counselor how he had been on job interview after job interview and got nowhere. Because of Mount St. Helen's erupting, this factory opened up a new branch and that is why they needed to hire people. He explained to him how this kind of just fell into his lap, and he said it was a really good paying job. He could just not stand the thought of leaving it right now and having nothing again. He said what would be worse would be his staying with a job that was driving him crazy, or being total broke and unemployed. Michael told the counselor, "So you see, I really don't feel as though I have a choice but to stay here for now anyway."

Michael also said all of this might be a moot point, because of all the time he was taking off to try and get help here. The counselor told Michael, "Don't worry about it. They can't fire you. Alcoholism is a disease, and it is covered by your medical insurance." So he told Michael not to worry about that. The counselor told Michael, "The only thing you have to worry about with this job is staying sober on it and not letting the stress get to you. That is what you need to be worrying about now."

The counselor went on to ask Michael if he had kept up with his counseling sessions at home, and Michael said, "No, I haven't."

She said that was a shame because she might have been able to help him through the stressful job and to avoid this relapse. She may have been able to teach him how to handle the stress instead of crawling back into the bottle. "So you see, Michael, instead of turning to the alcohol for help, you should have turned to the one person who could have helped you, your counselor."

Michael said he didn't think of it that way, and he told her she was right. He said, "Perhaps if I had done that I wouldn't have relapsed." Michael then agreed to start seeing his counselor again on a regular basis which still was three times a week.

After his detox time was up, which was the fifth day, Michael did keep his word and he resumed seeing the counselor again, and we would also resume the AA meetings. But sadly to say, despite all of this, Michael only stayed sober for a week and a half before his next relapse. He once again picked me up from work, and he was almost as drunk as he was the first time he relapsed. It was so heartbreaking to see him this way. I drove us home, and all the while I was fighting back my tears. It was coming to the point where I didn't know what to expect anymore, if I would come out of work and see him sober or falling down drunk. I just remember feeling scared and empty inside. I just felt like a raw nerve. I just tried desperately to remember everything that the counselor had told me prior to this, but at the time it didn't make it hurt any less. As I looked over at Michael sitting there drunk, I found little comfort in her words.

Michael would once again stop his counseling sessions, but I did not. I would continue seeing my counselor twice a week. I believe at this point, this was the only thing that was keeping me from losing my mind. I at least had someone to talk to, someone that understood what I was going through.

Also, along with Michael's relapse and going back to drinking, came his night terrors. He was experiencing them more and more frequently, and they were becoming more and more violent. On the average, they were happening about 2-3 times per week and when he was experiencing these night terrors, it was so strange, it was as though he was there, but not there. He spoke in Vietnamese, yelling and screaming at me and it was almost getting to the point where I was actually afraid to fall asleep, never knowing when I was going to be woken up by Michael yelling and trying to punch me in the face or grabbing me by the throat and trying to choke me.

All I could do when these things happened was try to slide myself out from underneath him, onto the floor and put the lights on. It seemed like once I put the lights on and began yelling his name, he would stop, and I could clearly see he was disoriented, not knowing really where he was at that moment. It was as though he was awakening out of a horrible nightmare, and you must realize that after every attack, this would bring back horrifying nightmares of my own childhood and seeing my father hurt my mother in the way that he did.

These were my own private nightmares and my own private hell that I had to deal with, which made dealing with these episodes even more difficult for me. I called them night terrors. I don't know if that is the correct term for it or just mini flashbacks he was experiencing. Whatever they were, it terrified both of us, and after each one he would hold me and cry, telling me how very sorry he was that he scared me or hurt me. I could tell this was truly something he never wanted to do, and it seemed like every time that he had stopped drinking for any period of time, and then he would have a relapse, these night terrors just became worse and much more intense. It was as though he was uncovering the pain, continuously picking the scab off and not being able to heal it. It was clear he was not receiving the proper help, the help that he needed.

It was about two weeks after he started drinking again when he picked me up from work, and I could tell he was pretty sober. He had only had a couple of drinks. I guess he was trying to take it easy this day, or maybe he was hoping that he could start back on sobriety again, just doing it himself this time; I don't know. It was the dead of winter, and in New England in the dead of winter there is not much to do, so we just headed on home, and on the way we passed our favorite hangout place. Michael turned to me and asked me if I wanted to go in and shoot a couple of rounds of pool. It now had been months since we had been out, and I figured, *Sure, what the hell? He was drinking anyway and I was really in no rush to get home.* I had been so stressed out and unhappy myself lately, I figured maybe we would have a little bit of fun. Michael and

I went in and sat at the bar. He got a beer, and I got a coke, and we could see that there were some guys playing pool at that time so we just sat there talking, waiting for them to finish up their game.

So as Michael and I were sitting at the bar, waiting for the table, this man came in and sat down beside Michael. He ordered a drink and glanced over at Michael and me. He had olive skin, and he stood about 5 feet 11 inches, with a slim build and jet-black wavy hair, big brown eyes, a mustache, and the most perfect, beautiful, white smile I had ever seen. His smile lit up the room and would knock any girl off of her seat. Just then Michael got up to go to the men's room, and that is when our eyes met. He looked deep into my soul and warmed my heart. We just sat there across from each other staring into each other's eyes, and I had not felt this way since the first time Michael and I met. Just then Michael was returning back from the men's room, and although I did not know this man, Michael seemed to and our other friends as well. Michael told me oh this is Christopher, and he introduced us, and Christopher took my hand and our eyes met once again. I knew that I loved Michael, and I knew that these feelings that I was having toward Christopher were wrong, and I fought them, ignoring what I had just felt when I looked into his eyes.

Christopher was a very nice guy. He was quiet. He played pool with the guys and he didn't like to fight. He seemed to get along with everyone. There was sort of a standing joke in the bar with all the guys about Christopher, because he was a little bit darker skinned, and he was Portuguese. He spoke with a little bit of an accent. All the guys would call him a Puerto Rican and tell him go back to Puerto Rico where you came. Christopher would laugh at them and tell them, "Sure. If you wouldn't mind buying me a plane ticket, I would love to visit." This joke was just all done in fun.

After my and Christopher's first encounter, when our eyes first met and it was obvious that the sparks were flying, I did my best to avoid him for the rest of that night. After this, I went over near the pool table and sat down and started to talk with our friend Corey. I just knew I had to get some distance between Christopher and me. But while Michael and Christopher sat there at the bar talking, Christopher turned his seat completely around and sat there staring at me, and just then the pool table became available, and Michael suggested that we play doubles. It would be me and Michael against Alex and Christopher. I could not believe my ears because as I said I was trying to keep some distance between Christopher and me, and I had no idea of how Michael was not picking up on this.

So the four of us spent the rest of the night playing pool together and throughout the night, I would learn that Christopher was not only very, very sexy but he was sweet as well. Something I did not want to learn. And his smile was only suppressed by his personality. I found myself being drawn in by him, by laughing at his jokes and enjoying myself with him. Just feeling genuinely happy, something I had not felt in a very, very long time, but I knew what I was getting myself into here, and this would be very dangerous. For Michael after all was very jealous, and he could be very dangerous, so I knew I was walking a thin line. And after this night came to an end, I promised myself that I would not put Christopher or me in this situation again. I would just try to simply avoid the bar and in doing so, avoid Christopher.

But the next night when Michael picked me up from work, he wanted to go back to the bar and play some more pool with Alex and Christopher. I made up the excuse that I was not feeling well and this would not be such a good idea. I came up with every reason that I could think of for us not to go back, but it didn't work, Michael insisted. I had no choice. Once we arrived at the bar, I told Michael that because I was not feeling well I thought I would sit out the night of pool and just sit at the bar and watch. I then went over to Corey and asked her if she would take my place as Michael's partner at pool. So she agreed to, and I stayed at the bar trying to keep as much distance between Christopher and me as I possibly could.

This worked for a while, but it seemed like every time it was Michael's turn up to shoot, Christopher would come over and talk with me at the bar. Even though I was trying to put up that wall between us, he somehow was able to break it down, and he got me laughing and kidding around with him, just as we did the night before. There was an undeniable and heated attraction between us, and we knew it. I also knew after tonight there was no way I was going to be able to go back to that bar with him there. I knew I would never be able to be this close to him again without something happening between us, and I could never allow this to happen. I was in love with Michael and until this point in time, this moment, I had never thought about being unfaithful to him. But Michael and I had been going through such hard times emotionally, it seemed like we never laughed, and we never had fun anymore, and I just missed that so much. And I knew deep down inside what I was feeling for Christopher just was not right.

Of course, the next night when Michael picked me up from work, he suggested the same that we go back to the bar and play some more pool, seeing that we had such a good time the night before. I told him absolutely not, and I am putting my foot down. I said, "I really, really feel sick tonight, and I feel like I am coming down with the flu." But I knew I couldn't use this excuse forever. Thank God it did work for this night, and we went straight home.

A few days would pass and Michael was hitting the bottle really strong. There was only one good thing about this, at least he stopped suggesting that we go to this bar. This continued for a few more weeks until one night after work Michael asked me if I could call the Brockton Detox and see if they could take him again. Of course I wholeheartedly agreed to this. I made the phone call, and the counselor there told me, "Yes, bring him in," and once again Michael was welcomed with opened arms even though this was now the third time.

On the fourth day I showed up with of course, two boxes of chocolate bars. I went into the visitor's room where Michael was sitting waiting for me, but one big difference between this time and all the others was Michael was sitting with all his clothes on waiting for me. You see before, they kept them in their pajamas. You were not allowed your clothes back until you were ready to leave. Well, evidentially Michael was ready to leave.

I walked over to him, and he looked up at me and smiled and said, "I am ready to go."

I looked back at him, and I said, "Like hell you are. You are not going anywhere. You need help. If you leave now, what is going to happen? I will tell you what is going to happen. You are going to go right back to drinking."

Then he said, "I probably will anyway, whether I spend the full five days here or not."

I then asked him, "Why did you ask me to bring you here to begin with?"

His reply was, "At that moment I wanted to stop drinking."

I said, "So you have changed your mind, and now you don't want to stop drinking. You don't want help."

He said, "I want help, but I just need to get out of here right now. I just want to go home, and yes, I need to get a drink. And this, for now, is all I want."

I told him to wait right there and don't move from his seat. I quickly went to see if the counselor was available for us to speak with, but that day he left early. So instead I spoke to a couple of the staff people. They came into the visitor's lounge with me and tried to talk Michael into staying, but nothing that they said made any difference. He was bound and determined to leave that night. One of the staff persons just looked at me. They said they were very sorry, but there was no way that they could make him stay there against his will. He could only be there if he wanted to be; if he wanted help. He explained it wouldn't do him any good right now anyway because he doesn't want the help, and they told Michael, "You know you are always welcome here. If you ever change your mind, please come back, and we will try to help you. Perhaps in a couple of weeks you will want to try again." They reminded Michael to never give up.

I looked at Michael and said to him, "Come on, let's go home."

While this was going on I felt like there was a pressure inside of my head just building up and building up until I was ready to pop. I felt a wave of so many emotions at once; anger, frustration, fear, but most of all sadness. For at this point in my life, I just felt like crying. I felt like my heart was breaking all the time. I had to fight these emotions on a daily basis now. I loved Michael so much and all I wanted to do was spend the rest of my life with him, grow old with him and die in each other's arms. But I realized if he was not going to be able to stop all this madness, to stop drinking, we would not be able to have anything, and I would never truly be able to have him. I feared that the alcohol would always be his first and only love, a love that was slowly killing him. I feared his body breaking down, he becoming ill from it, and if it didn't kill him physically, then perhaps on some snowy night while he was driving home in a blackout, he would crash into a tree and kill himself that way. But either way, the alcohol would have him and the thought of this broke my heart. I knew we had to fight, but I couldn't fight this alone, and I couldn't fight this for him. He was the only one that could do it for himself. I could only love him and stand beside him.

At this point I saw no happy ending for us, and I sank deeper and deeper into despair with every passing day. I had to think very hard about what my next move was going to be. Was I going to stay with the man that I loved and watch him kill himself slowly little by little and with himself a part of me as well, or was I going to have to make the toughest, most heartbreaking decision of my life, and that would be to leave him. But how could I turn around and just walk out the door and leave my only love, my first love.

As Michael and I were leaving the detox, Michael insisted on driving, and I knew why. He knew I wouldn't stop at the liquor store, so he wanted to be in control of the car. I knew at this point all he had on his mind was to get his next drink. So he did just what I expected him to do and that was stop at the liquor store and go in for his pint of vodka. He came out and proceeded to chug it down, and by the time we arrived back home, he had a pretty good glow on but he was not drunk. So I thought this would be a good time for us to talk about what had just happened before he got any drunker. We sat on our bed, side by side, and I told Michael everything that I was feeling. I told him I really just needed a break. I needed some time alone to think. In short I needed a vacation from all of this madness that had consumed our lives. I told him how unhappy I had been and that most of the time I just felt like crying, and I told him I didn't know how much longer I could live this way. "I just need a rest," I said.

He asked me to please not go and my reply to him was, "I asked you to please not leave detox, to please stay for the help that you needed, and you refused to listen to me. Now I am refusing to listen to you. I need to get away. I need time out, and I really feel as though I need to leave here now."

He replied, "Well, go right ahead," he said. "That will really help me not drink by you walking out on me."

I turned around and told him, "Michael, obviously you are going to drink, whether I am here or not. The only question that remains is whether I wish to sit here and watch you drink night after night and slowly kill yourself, and right now I do not." I began to yell at him. I told him as far as his recovery process seemed to be going, I had been putting more work into it than he had, and he could see how well this has worked out for him. I told him, "It seems to me you are right back at square one."

As he sat there on the edge of our bed, holding the bottle of vodka, I looked at him, and I never felt so utterly useless in my whole life. I just could not seem to get through to him and perhaps the shock of me walking out would snap him back into reality. I did not know.

I got my suitcase out of the closet and began packing up a few of my things. I told him I was going to go back to my mothers for a while, and as I was packing my things, I began to cry. Michael got up from the bed and tried to comfort me. He put his arms around me and started to kiss me. I pushed him away. The way that I was feeling, it just hurt too much for him to even touch me, and all I kept thinking was, *How could such a loving and beautiful beginning turn into such a heartache?* I was beginning to feel like our relationship had become toxic to me, and all the hugs and kisses and *I love yous* in the world could not stop my heartache. I think he began to realize that this could really be the end for us because he began crying too, and asked me again to please stay. He promised me that he would try again to stop drinking. That he would get help tomorrow, but sadly these words I had heard time and time again.

What I did remember is what the counselor told me from the beginning and that was Michael would have to do it for Michael and not for me, and he was yet to realize this. At this time I also reminded Michael of this, and I asked him, "All this time have you been doing it for me, and perhaps this is why it wasn't working."

He looked at me with tears in his eyes and he said, "No, Kyra, I have been doing it for us." He went on to tell me that the program and learning to live his life without alcohol was just so hard. That is why he kept having the relapses. He said he just could not stop thinking about alcohol and the euphoric feeling he received from it. And he told me that the euphoric feeling that he got every time he drank was very hard to live without, but then he said to me that the love that we shared would now be ten times harder for him to live without than that euphoric feeling that he has when he drinks.

"So the only conclusion you can come to," he said, "is that the alcohol is the one that has to go because I don't want to live without you," and he could clearly see he couldn't have both. I truly believe he meant this when he was saying it, but after so many years of drinking and his body being used to the alcohol, it was physically painful for him not to do this, not to drink. So besides the emotional reasons why he was drinking, he now had the physical. When you enter into one of these detox programs, or the 30-day programs, you have to learn how to live all over again. You have to learn how to act in relationships, how to interact with coworkers, how to socialize, how to become a responsible adult. This whole process is very painful. It is very painful to grow up and have to live in the real world, day by day. There is no escape from reality.

I told Michael, "Until you are ready to accept this and to take this fight on, we are just going to keep bouncing in and out of detox, and this is precisely what I need the break from, the madness. Don't you see how you push me out of your world? Every time you make that decision to crawl back into the bottle, can't you see the pain that you are causing me, or don't you even give a good fuck?"

Michael said, "Of course I do. I can see the pain in your eyes, and even that is not enough to push me into sobriety. The alcohol seems to override everything and everybody that I love. I just don't know if I will just be able to completely stop, Kyra."

I then said to him, "Well, it seems to me that you also have a lot of thinking to do as well as I do. You have to decide what you want to do with the rest of your life, whether we are going to be together or not. It is completely up to you now."

I told him this as I was walking out the door. I went out to my car and put my suitcase in my trunk, and he was standing behind me. I gave him a big hug and a kiss, and I told him I would call him in a couple of days to see how he was doing.

I cried all the while I was driving to my mother's house, and when I arrived there she opened the door to see me holding my suitcase in my hand, and she asked me, "Oh, God, what happened now?"

Over a cup of coffee I told her all about it and she agreed perhaps maybe a little time apart was exactly what Michael needed. As I lay there in bed that night, I tossed and turned. I may have only gotten an hour or two of sleep. I lay there thinking about the last week and what I had just said to Michael kept running over and over in my mind. I didn't want to hurt him, but I had to shake him up. I had to make him realize that he had to start working on his problems. I couldn't do it for him.

I called him the next morning on the phone to see how he was doing. All he kept saying to me was, "Please come back," and I told him I would in a few days. I just reminded him of our conversation that we had the night before of how I needed this time alone to think, and after this we would talk every night on the phone, but we would not see each other. Every night on the phone he was sober. He told me he went directly from work, right straight home. He was trying to detox himself.

I guess it must have been about four days after this that I received a phone call from Alex, and when I heard his voice on the other end of the line, I panicked. I thought to myself, *Michael really did it this time, he must have wrapped himself around a tree*, because Alex never called me before. Alex heard that I was back home with my mother and asked me if everything was okay between Michael and me, and I said to him, "Yes, it is." I made up an excuse that my mother was sick and that I needed to take care of her.

I asked Alex why was he calling me, and he kind of scared me because he never did call me before, and I assumed that something had happened to

Michael. He then told me Michael was fine. He then went on to tell me that Michael had stopped over his house the day before, and he was pretty wasted. I guess Alex caught me in a lie because Michael told him everything that had been going on between us. He said, "You know, Kyra, Michael is my best friend. He is like a brother to me, but I do realize how hard he can be to be around sometimes, especially when he is drunk. When he told me that you said that you needed a break, I told him that I agreed with you, that maybe this would be a good thing for now."

He went on to tell me that he was just calling me to invite me to a party that was being held downstairs from where he lived by a new neighbor. The party was 7 o'clock the next evening. He thought I could use a little bit of fun at this time in my life. So Corey suggested that he call to invite me. At this point I would have to agree with him. I did need a little bit of fun in my life. I told him sure I would be there, it sounds like fun. I told him I would bring my deviled eggs which is what I had become known for at all the parties that Michael and I went to. Alex said that would be great.

Then I thought quickly, and I asked him, "Did you invite Michael as well?"

He said, "No, Kyra, I wouldn't do that. I know right now you are taking a break from each other."

I said, "Thank you Alex. I will see you tomorrow at seven." And then I hung up the phone.

After I hung up the phone I realized what Alex had said about Michael being up there the night before, really drunk. This would explain why he had not called me. Well, I could see detoxing himself was no more successful than him going to the detox itself. The next day I began making my deviled eggs, and as I was working on them, I thought to myself how weird this all felt. This was the first party that I was going to be going to without Michael, and by now Michael and I had been together for over three years.

It was now late January of 1982, and I also realized that we had not moved any further ahead in our relationship since the time we had started dating. We had not accomplished much together. We were right in the same place as we were at the start, and this thought, itself, was very discouraging. We had put all this energy over the past year into Michael's sobriety and neglected our relationship. We could not set any goals because we simply didn't know from one day to the next what was going to happen, and if Michael continued to drink and continued to carry on the way that he was, I knew that we would never get anything accomplished. And I just said, *To hell with it all for tonight.* I wasn't going to be thinking about anything; about Michael, about the drinking, about myself, about anything. I just wanted to give my brain a night off and leave all my worries at home.

I began getting ready for the party. I got all dressed up, just like I did when I used to go out dancing at the discos with my friends. I decided to leave my car at home because I was expecting to have a few drinks myself tonight, and seeing that I only lived right down the street from Alex's, it was kind of ridiculous for me to drive there. I arrived at the party and Alex introduced me to the couple that was hosting it, the new neighbors Cheryl and John. They wanted to throw this party to get to know everyone in the neighborhood. They seemed like a really nice couple. They seemed like a very normal couple. I wasn't sure quite how they were going to fit into our little group, but they were a lot of fun and they seemed to have very little trouble getting along with everyone.

I sat down by Corey on the couch, and as we sat there talking I happened to glance over by the door, and I could not believe my eyes, but who came walking in? Christopher.

I turned to Alex and asked him if he had invited Christopher, and he said, "Yes, why? Is he here already?"

I replied, "Yes, he just walked through the door."

I don't know if this is what really happened or not, but I was beginning to feel like I had been set up, although I don't know how Alex could have known how Christopher and I felt about each other. I am sure Christopher didn't say anything. Before I knew it Alex yelled to Christopher to come here and sit beside him. Christopher then signaled to Alex that he was going to get himself a drink before he came over. All I could think to myself was, *Oh, shit, I am in trouble.* I said to myself, *I should probably just get up and walk out the door right now,* but I did not. I knew I should have, but the feelings that I was feeling for Christopher were so strong that I should not have trusted myself to be in the same room as him because at this moment I was feeling too vulnerable.

And when I saw Christopher, I must have had a very strange look on my face, because Alex leaned over and asked me if I was feeling okay. I just told him, no I wasn't feeling very well at all right now. Of course I could not tell him what I was feeling and the thoughts that were running through my mind. Half of me just wanted to get the hell out of there before Christopher had a chance to even come over, and the other half of me wanted to fall into his arms. And I knew once he came over and began talking to me, I would be in trouble.

In the meantime, Alex just said to me, "Oh, Kyra, you are going to be fine. You are probably just feeling a little nervous because this is the first party that you have been to without Michael beside you." He reassured me and told me not to worry and that we were all just friends here. Boy, if he only knew what I was thinking at that moment. He also reminded me that all of Michael's friends are now my friends, and they will always have my back. So he wanted me to just sit back and relax and enjoy myself for the night.

Alex then said, "Why don't you just have one drink, and maybe it will relax your nerves." He then got up and got Corey and me a drink, and along with our drinks, he also brought Christopher back to sit with us. I couldn't believe it. Then Christopher sat beside me and asked me how I had been. He remarked that it had been a long time since he saw me. I told him I was doing fine but all the while thinking I really should get out of here. You see, I never had any intentions on cheating on Michael, but Christopher was bringing out something in me. Feelings that I had not felt for a while with Michael because of everything we had been going through, and I liked that feeling even though I knew it was wrong to have toward Christopher. I knew right then I should have left, but I didn't want to.

The four of us sat there joking and talking for hours, and the more beer I drank, the more I became relaxed about the whole situation. I had a lot of fun and a lot of laughs that night. Something I had not had in a very long time. It was around midnight and everyone was beginning to leave.

At one o'clock only the three couples remained, Christopher and me, Alex and Corey, and our hostesses. It was around this time that Alex suggested that we start up a game of strip poker. And for one I didn't gamble, and I wasn't supposed to be drinking, so I was anything but happy with his suggestion. Things looked like they were taking a turn toward the really weird, so shortly after that I was out of there. I proceeded to get up and put on my coat. I went over to the hostesses and thanked them for a really fun night. Alex wanted to give me a ride home.

It was just then that Christopher stood up and said, "Alex, you don't have to bother yourself with going out right now. You're having a good time. I'll be more than glad to give Kyra a ride home. I'm leaving anyway."

Alex then looked at me and asked if this was all right.

I said, "Look, I don't even need a ride home." Once again I reminded them both, "I just live down the street, and for God's sake, just leave me alone. I'll get home fine, and then I just turned and started out the door.

Christopher came running behind me and pulled me by my arm to his car. He said, "Kyra, just get in and stop being so stubborn."

I was so afraid of what was going to happen if I did. We had an undeniable attraction to each other. It was like moths to a flame, and you know what happens when a moth gets too close to the flame. They get burned! However, even knowing this and knowing better, I got into his car anyway, and sure enough, Christopher leaned over to me and cupped my face in his hands. He looked into my eyes, and his stare penetrated my soul. His sultry brown eyes melted all my inhibitions, and for now anyway, I could forget all about my worries. Our lips touched, and I tingled from head to toe. We were both completely consumed with the passion that we felt toward one another. My whole body just went weak, and as he pulled his lips away from mine, he began staring into my eyes once again.

As he brushed his hand across my cheek, he said to me, "You knew this was going to happen, didn't you?"

"Yes, I did. That is why I tried to keep my distance, and that is why I avoided you at the bar and didn't want to play pool. I could tell by the look in your eyes you were feeling the same way toward me as I was toward you. That feeling was there even before we were introduced that night."

He said, "I know. When I looked over at you at the bar and our eyes met then, I knew I wanted to be with you. I had to be with you."

Just then Christopher leaned over to kiss me again, and with each kiss it was more passionate and intense than the kiss before. While we were embracing each other, he asked me to please come home with him and be his.

I could not help myself. I could not resist the feeling that we had toward one another. I said, "Yes."

All the while driving to his house he held my hand, caressing it. As soon as we walked through his door and closed it, the passion exploded. All the feelings that we had been denying and trying to keep a lid on erupted all at once. He began kissing the back of my ear and slowly working down to my neck, and then softly caressing my breasts. We began undressing each other as we worked our way toward his bedroom. He gently laid me on his bed, and as I slowly removed my last article of clothing, he then leaned over me and began caressing my neck again, and my breasts, slowly working his way down my stomach. He caressed every part of my body and my soul. He then slowly worked his way back up until our lips met once again. I tingled from head to toe as I felt him slowly penetrate me. I became short of breath and trembled all over. The deeper he penetrated me the more euphoric I felt.

As we lay there with our bodies intertwined, it seemed to take very little time before he was able to bring me to climax. All the passion and the heat we felt toward one another erupted in one huge explosion. As I lay there trembling during climax, his hands were shaking as well as he brushed back my hair from my face. As we lay there staring into each other's eyes, I begged him to stay inside of me. I so desperately didn't want this moment to ever end, and I could tell, neither did he.

We held each other tight our bodies entwined and our lips locked in the heat of passion, and he slowly began caressing my neck once again, and then my breasts. I could feel him growing larger inside of me. He penetrated me so deeply with every thrust. Our bodies fit together as though they were made for each other. All the while he pushed deeper inside of me. He caressed my neck and my lips. The passion was so overwhelming I felt like I was on fire. He then pinned my wrists above my head and began penetrating me harder and harder, over and over again, until I was in a fit of frenzy.

As I lay there climaxing, I felt as though my head was going to explode, and as I lay there shaking, he would not stop. It was as though the passion had overtaken him completely, and I had no choice but to submit to him. As he would climax for the third time now inside of me, he had exhausted himself and was just lying there wrapped around me. I had never felt so completely satisfied in my whole life. That night we fell asleep in each other's arms. I felt so safe and secure with him.

The next morning when the first rays of light came through the window, he leaned over and kissed me telling me how happy I had made him and how happy and complete he felt at this moment. He then began talking about what we were going to do tonight. He wanted to take me out for dinner and a movie.

At that moment I didn't know quite what to do or what to say to him. I had not planned to leave Michael, nor was I going to, but I didn't want to hurt Christopher. I found myself completely torn. He told me he wanted to start seeing me, but I was not free to see him, and I told him dinner and the movies probably would not be such a good idea right now. He asked me why, and I began explaining to him about what Michael and I were going through, the rough times that we had had. But even though we were going through our rough times, I still loved Michael.

Christopher was not very happy to hear this. I told Christopher that Michael and I were working through this, and I could not leave him right now. Then Christopher reminded me that I could not just forget what happened last night and what we felt toward each other. I told him I realized this, but my relationship with Michael was very complicated, and I really didn't know what I want to do right now. I told him I needed time to think.

I could tell by the look in Christopher's eyes he was very disappointed and very upset. He made us both breakfast. We sat there eating in silence. After we ate, we began getting ready to leave. He would drop me off at my home.

Christopher said, "I don't care what kind of complications you and Michael are having right now. I just want to be with you. I don't care about anything else," and I reminded him I just had to think.

He asked me for my phone number, and then asked if he could call me that night, and I said, "Yes."

When we arrived at my mother's house, he gave me a passionate kiss goodbye and said, "I will call you tonight."

Just as he promised, he did. We talked a lot about what had happened the night before, and how good we both felt about it. I told him I did feel good in one way about it and bad in another because the last thing I wanted to do was hurt Michael, but now I have found I don't want to hurt you either. I asked him to please not call for a couple of days so I could have a chance to think about everything that has just happened and try desperately to figure it all out.

In the meantime I had been talking to Michael on the phone every night. He was trying his best not to drink, although he was failing. I could tell he was drunk. He just wanted me to come back to him. I just kept telling him that I needed more times.

It was now a couple of days after Christopher and I had been together when he called me again and asked me to come out and have a cup of coffee with him so that we could talk. I agreed. He picked me up at my mother's house, and we went to Dunkin' Donuts and sat out in the parking lot drinking our coffees and talking. I tried desperately to explain my relationship with Michael, everything that we had been through together, and everything that he had been through in Vietnam and that he was desperately trying to stop drinking. In other words I wanted Christopher to know this would not be an easy decision for me to make choosing between him and Michael.

After I got through telling Christopher about the past three years Michael and I had spent together, he did not seem to change his mind one bit about me. All he did was lean over and kiss me and told me he wanted me to be his. I knew right there and then this was not going to be easy. I had gotten myself into the middle of something, and I didn't know how to get out of it. Then he went on to tell me that he wasn't afraid of Michael, and I told him he should be.

I knew if we were going to start seeing each other, it would have to be very discreet, and we would not be able to be seen in public in our own town together. I was not the type of woman who could go sneaking around like this. This wasn't me. I was always up front and forward with Michael and honest. I was just so confused. I never thought in a million years I would find myself in the middle of a situation like this where my heart didn't know which way to turn.

Christopher began caressing my neck again, and our lips met in a passionate embrace, and he said, "Come home with me again, please."

The passion was so overwhelming I agreed, and so I found myself right back where I was two nights earlier, back in bed with Christopher with a passion like a title wave engulfing us both. It was so all consuming it just took us both over. It was so intense it scared me. I knew I was in real trouble now. It seems my heart had taken some kind of twisted detour, and if I would ever find the right path again, or did I even know what the right path was at this point in my life. Was I supposed to be here with Christopher in a passionate embrace or with Michael? I had more questions about my heart, myself, and my actions than I had answers for.

Each time I was with Christopher it just made it harder and harder for me to choose. You see with Christopher it just wasn't the passion or the sex, it was how he was as a person. He was kind and giving. He always treated me tenderly and he made me laugh. But there was something he was not and that was Michael, because Michael was the only man that ever had my heart hook, line and sinker. Even with all these positive things about Christopher, they simply were not enough to override the feelings I had toward Michael and the all-consuming love I felt toward him.

It was that following night that Michael called me and wanted to see me.

He said, "The only communication that we've had over the past week and a half has been over the phone, and I really need to see you so that we can talk."

I agreed because I wanted to see Michael. I wanted to be with him again.

After this conversation on the phone, Christopher called and he wanted to see me as well. I told him I was meeting with Michael, and he and I were going to try to work through our problems. Christopher just hung up on me. He then quickly called me back and told me that after I was done talking with Michael, if I wanted to call him, he would be at the bar playing pool. I then told him that I probably would not be calling him tonight because Michael and I did have a lot to talk about, and I probably wouldn't get home until very late. Then Christopher did just as he did before—he hung up on me.

I was almost afraid to face Michael. I was afraid that he would be able to see in my eyes what I had done. I had no sooner gotten off the phone with Christopher than Michael pulled up outside of my house. He beeped the horn, and I came down the stairs walking toward the van. I got such a sick feeling in my stomach. Would he know? Would he be able to tell? Could he see in my eyes I had been with another man? All these thoughts came rushing through me before I hit the door of the van.

As soon as I got into the van, I leaned over and gave Michael a kiss and a big hug. I could tell by his kiss he suspected nothing. After all, why would he? I had never deceived him before, and believe me I was feeling no pleasure about doing it now. It felt horrible, and also with his kiss, I could tell Michael had been drinking, but he was far from being drunk.

We went down the lake and parked in our spot. We began discussing our feelings and where this relationship was going. He went on to tell me how he wanted me back in his life and that he loved me and missed me terribly. I told him how much I loved him and missed him as well. Then I went on to say I didn't miss the craziness that had consumed our relationship and our lives. I told him I couldn't go back to that nor was I ready to go back to him yet and start dealing with this all over again. I could no longer stand by and watch him slowly kill himself anymore.

"I just cannot do this," I said. "I cannot live this way. You have no idea what that does to me. I can actually see a little piece of myself every night when you get drunk die right alongside of you, and I just can't stand that feeling anymore. I really mean it when I say I love you. You are the only man that I've ever had in my heart."

For these reasons we decided to stay separated for a few more weeks, and Michael was going to try to stop drinking on his own.

He told me, "I will go to work every day and then go straight home. I will try to do it this way. I'll call you every night so we can talk." I agreed to this.

The days went by and Michael called me every night as he promised, and to my surprise, he was sober. I am ashamed to say, though, every night after Michael's phone call, I would see Christopher. I knew this was wrong, but I just needed some happiness back in my life, and Christopher right now was making me very happy. I just longed to feel that love, that passion, that togetherness that Michael and I once shared. When I was in Christopher's arms, I felt alive again, but this came with a hefty price. For you see along with the love, the tenderness and the sharing came guilt, this guilt was eating me up inside. I couldn't have it both ways. I couldn't have both of these men. I knew this right from the beginning, but I chose to start it anyway. I knew it was only a matter of time before my guilt would get the better of me, and this day was coming soon.

It was now a couple of weeks since Michael and I had decided to just communicate over the phone. When he called me and wanted to see me, I quickly thought, *Oh, God, he has heard something,* but he had not. He still had no idea that I was dating Christopher or anyone else. Michael and I then decided to start seeing each other every night just as we always had. We had been back together for a week when he started drinking again. Things were going right back to the way they were before we separated. So at this point, I was juggling Christopher and Michael. It was totally crazy.

I quickly found myself never being happy now because whenever I was with Christopher, all I could think about was Michael, and when I was with Michael, all I could think about was Christopher. I felt as though I was being torn in half and the guilt of my actions was eating me up inside.

It went on like this for over a month until one night Christopher exploded at me. He began yelling at me and telling me he didn't want me seeing anyone else, meaning Michael, and I told him I could not do that. I told him I was not ready to make that kind of decision yet and that he was just going to have to give me some more time. I guess some more time to Christopher meant two days because it was exactly two days after I said that he suggested we move in together. I told him I couldn't even think about doing something like that and that I was sorry.

Christopher again was very upset with me and told me he was only going to put up with this for so long, and I told him maybe perhaps we should take a break. This being a Tuesday, I told him I wanted the time off to think, and to get back in touch with me on Friday. In this time that he had to himself, he had planned a romantic weekend for the two of us at a nearby hotel. He had gone earlier that day to set up some wine and candles.

That night was so romantic, just the two of us surrounded by the warm glow of all the candlelight. While Christopher opened the wine, I went into the bathroom to put on my new red negligee. By the time I came out of the bathroom, Christopher had all the candles lit and was sitting in a chair sipping on a glass of wine. He looked up at me, and his mouth hung open. He took me by the hand and told me how beautiful I was and how badly he wanted me. He stood up and pulled me toward him, and we both fell onto the bed.

He began caressing my neck, and my whole body went weak. The explosive passion that we felt toward one another was undeniable. He then began softly caressing my breasts all over, and consumed in passion, he started tearing at my new negligee and quickly ripped it off of me, and after slowly worked his way down from my breasts to my stomach, gently kissing every inch of me. He worked his way to my inner thighs, and as I lay there tingling from head to toe, he aggressively worked his way toward my clitoris, first caressing it with his lips and then circling it with his tongue.

He knew exactly what he was doing to me. Then I felt his fingers penetrate me. I could hear my heart beating faster and faster as I was hitting a passionate frenzy, and the deeper he penetrated me with his fingers, the closer I was coming to climax, but he did not want to bring me to climax this way. He began slowing down, removing his fingers and going back to caressing my inner thighs, slowly working his way back up my stomach and my breasts where he circled my nipples with his tongue, slowly running his tongue over every inch of my breasts. He then began caressing my neck, and as he was doing this, he was penetrating me deeper and harder and harder, over and over again.

The passion was all consuming. I felt as though my heart was going to burst in my chest, and inside I must have become so tight because I was on the verge of climaxing. The tighter I became, the harder and deeper Christopher penetrated me. As I wrapped myself around him, my nails imbedded into his back, that wave of euphoric relief washed over me as I lay there climaxing and shaking under him. Christopher quickly followed, but before he did he was whispering in my ear, "God, I don't want this to end, my love."

Afterwards we just lay there in each other's arms holding each other tight, and as we lie there he looked down at me and with his hands he pushed my chin up so that we were looking into each other's eyes. That was when he told me how much he loved me. He said, "There's no denying it any longer. I love you, Kyra."

Until that moment I never thought having someone say, "I love you," could feel so bad. I then sat up in bed, and I looked him straight in the eye and told him, "Please, don't love me. I don't want to hurt you." But all the while what I really wanted to say was that I love you too, Christopher, for that is truly how my heart felt. But I couldn't let him know that. I had made such a mess of everything.

He told me, "Don't worry about hurting him. He's a big boy. He can handle it."

But I knew I couldn't, and so the following few minutes we just sat there in silence. I didn't know what else to say. My heart was breaking so badly. Here I was with a man that I loved so much and couldn't tell him how I felt, and I truly had no choice but to hide these feelings from him. I feared if he found out that I loved him as much as he loved me, then he would fight Michael for me I didn't want him to do this. I was so afraid of one of them being hurt or worse. I knew Christopher didn't have a violent streak in him, but Michael did, and I really didn't know what Michael was capable of doing if Christopher were to confront him about all of this.

Then I just made it worse. I told Christopher I didn't love him. I didn't feel the same way toward him as he felt toward me, and I was sorry. I couldn't help it. I had to lie to Christopher. I thought this would be the safest thing and the only thing that I could do right now. Never, ever could I have ever imagined being able to love two men at the same time so deeply as I loved Michael and Christopher.

How on earth could I be feeling so much love toward both of them yet be in so much pain all at the same time. I literally felt like I was being split right down the middle with half of me so deeply in love with Michael and the other half so deeply in love with Christopher. Nothing in my life was making any sense anymore, and I also realized now that I had to break it off with Christopher. Things had gone too far, and when I realized this, I could feel a little piece of my heart breaking. That piece of my heart that only Christopher will ever have for he will ever stay in my heart until the day I die. You see, Christopher was my beautiful oasis in the vast desert that had become my life.

It also saddens me to think, and I really don't want to believe this, that perhaps Christopher was no more than a delightful distraction from my reality, my reality being my life with Michael. When it came down to choosing between Michael and Christopher, there really was no choice. My choice was Michael. It was always Michael. We had a bond between us that no words could adequately describe, and it took a shocking statement like Christopher telling me, actually using the words "I love you," to snap me back into reality. The reality was I could only be with one man. I could only love one man. I could only have a life with one man. I could only grow old with one man, and that one man was Michael. It was always Michael.

When Christopher and I left the hotel in the morning, as he dropped me off at my mother's, I told him that I wanted two days by myself. I had a lot of thinking to do. He wasn't happy with this, but he agreed to it. I then made a phone call to Michael and told him the same, that I didn't want to have any contact with anyone for the next two days. I needed some time by myself, but I already knew what my choice was going to be. For better or for worse, I knew where my heart truly lay. No matter what Michael and I were going through at the time, he always had my heart and my soul. We were just meant to be together. I could see this clearly now.

After these couple of days passed by, I called Michael, and I told him I wanted to see him. To please pick me up, and we had a lot to talk about. He came over my mother's house and picked me up, and we went down to our spot on the lake. Thank God he was pretty sober, because I was about to tell him something I knew would send him into a rage.

I then began telling Michael everything. I told him the truth. I had to because I could not live with this between us. If we were going to go on with this relationship, I had to be honest with him about everything. I began telling him what happened and why it happened. I also told him if we are to be together, things are going to have to change. He is going to have to stop drinking, and then I reminded him of how much I loved him, and I wanted to spend the rest of my life with him. How between the two of them he is the one that I wanted to be with. He is the one that I love most.

As I spoke to Michael, he just sat there staring out onto the lake. I could tell he was in shock. He began gripping the steering wheel tightly in his hands. He continued to just sit there not speaking a word. We both sat there in complete silence as we watched the sun set over the lake. The silence was becoming nerve wracking to me. I sat there not knowing what to expect next. I knew I was wrong, and I was prepared to take whatever he had to throw at me.

After the longest time he finally spoke the first word, and that word was, "Who?" Who was this other man, he wanted to know.

I said to him, "Wouldn't the better question be 'Why?' Why is it that I needed to find comfort in another man's arms? Can you only imagine how sad and how empty I was feeling to do this thing, and you are the one that made me feel this way. You, in fact, pushed me into another man's arms with all the madness of your drinking, the night terrors and the worries that have consumed our relationship. I couldn't stand any more, and yet you still have not completely stopped drinking, and all you can ask me is 'who?' when you should be concerning yourself with 'why?'"

Michael said, "I do understand why you did this. You know, in a weird way I don't blame you. I realize how shitty things have been between the two of us, and most of that was my fault, and I know my drinking is slowly killing our relationship. However, it seems the hardest thing in the world for me to do right now is to stop drinking. No matter how much I fight it, the urge is very powerful and overwhelming, and even though I saw it coming between us, I could not stop. All I know is that I love you, Kyra, and I don't want to lose you, so I will keep trying to stop no matter how long it takes. No matter how many visits to the detox I have to do, I will stop."

We then hugged each other, and I told him again how much I loved him. He then asked me again who was this man, and again I told him, "'Who' is not important, and no, I will never give you his name."

He then asked me, did he know him.

Of course I lied and said, "No." I could never allow Michael to find out that it was Christopher in fear of what he would do. I couldn't live with myself or the guilt if Michael were to hurt him. This became my deepest, darkest secret that I must always keep, and until writing this book, I have.

All the fears that I had of Michael hurting Christopher were all confirmed with Michael's next statement. He told me, "If I ever found out who this man was, I would put him in the hospital for a very long time. You know that don't you, Kyra?"

I told him I suspected as much. I also went on to tell him I don't know why he would do this. After all it was not this man's fault, it was mine. It was my choice and my decision to be with him. He then told me he had to be alone to think, so he dropped me off at home.

While he was leaning over to give me a kiss goodbye, he began to cry. I tried to talk to him some more, but he told me, "Please, Kyra, just go into the house. I'll see you tomorrow."

Again I reminded him of how much I loved him.

He said, "I love you too, Baby Doll."

I stood there on the sidewalk as he drove away. I began to cry. I never felt so horrible in my life as I did at this very moment. I felt as though someone had driven a knife right straight through my heart.

As soon as I got into the house, you talk about perfect timing, my mother told me that Christopher had just called and he was down at the bar. He wanted me to call him as soon as I got in. I then just dropped my body onto the couch and began to cry. She looked at me and told me how wrong I was. What I was doing was wrong. I shouldn't be doing this to Michael and it wasn't fair.

I told her, "Ma, I know."

She told me I had to make up my mind quickly, whether I was going to be with Michael or with Christopher, but choose one.

I looked up at her, and I told her, "I already have chosen. I choose Michael, and now I must talk to Christopher and tell him that we are over."

She then asked me if Michael knew whom I had been seeing.

I told her, "No. This is the secret I must keep for the rest of my life."

She said, "Good luck with that. Keeping such a secret in such a small town is nearly impossible. Everybody knows everybody else's business, and you will not be able to keep the secret forever. Somehow, someday it will come out, and you've got to be ready for that."

I told her, "I'll cross that bridge when I come to it. For right now, I have to settle things with Christopher."

After I got through crying I regained my composure and made the phone call to Christopher, who was down at the bar playing pool. He said he wanted to see me tonight, and I said that was a very good idea because we had a lot to talk about. He picked me up and we drove to a little bar on the outskirts of town. We went in and sat at the table and began to talk. I told him I had just seen Michael, and I told Michael everything, that I had been seeing someone else. Then I told Christopher that I had planned to go back with Michael, and I could no longer see him anymore. Whatever we had between us had to end.

Christopher's reply was, "No. It's not going to. I'm not giving you up that easily." He said he didn't care about Michael and that he wasn't planning to let me go.

I told him he had no choice. I had made my decision and that I could not go on dating him and Michael. Then I assured him that Michael would never find out who he was. Christopher just looked at me and said he didn't care if Michael found out his name or not.

I said, "You should, because he may just kill you if he does." I told him I couldn't live with myself if he did. I just didn't want anything to happen to him, and I said, "We just have to end this here and now."

He refused to accept this. He just wouldn't let it go. He just kept saying, "You're not breaking up with me."

I told him, "Christopher, this is what I want."

Christopher was becoming more and more enraged about the whole situation, and I didn't want to turn this into a huge thing. So I told him, "Let's just go home and sleep on it, and if you want to talk more tomorrow, we will. Just know this; it is over between us."

And he just said, "Kyra, we definitely have a lot more to talk about. This is not over yet, and as far as I'm concerned, we have not broken up, and I have no intention of breaking up with you. So you just deal with that, Kyra."

On the long drive back home we argued back and forth about this. He was constantly reminding me about how deep his feelings were toward me, and of course, I still said nothing about the feelings, the true feelings I had toward him. I denied it to him, and I denied it to myself. I felt as though by keeping my love from Christopher, letting him know how I really felt, had to become as deep a secret to keep as his identity to Michael. After all, Christopher was behaving this way not knowing how I felt about him, and how deep my love ran for him. Can you only imagine how he would have acted if he had known the truth?

When we arrived at my house, Christopher used his automatic door locks to lock my door, and as I tried to get out of the car, he leaned over toward me and took my face in his hand and our lips came together in a passionate embrace.

As he began kissing my neck, I pushed him away. I told him, "Please, Christopher, just unlock my door." I just wanted to go. I had to put the distance between us, because really all I wanted to do was submit to the passion that ran so deeply between us. I knew I could no longer do this. I had made my choice, and I had to stand by it.

As I pushed him away, he did finally unlock the door. He told me as I was getting out, "I want to see you tomorrow. Be here and be ready by 8 o'clock."

It hurt me so badly to be so deeply in love with someone and have to push them away, and to push them out of your life forever. How does a person do this? I was finding it nearly impossible to do, and I thought once I had made my choice and my decision, everything would just fall into place. Everything else would be so clear-cut, but I was finding that it was not. It was anything but.

Things just became increasingly more complicated as time went on. For the next night when I was supposed to meet with Christopher, Michael showed up at my work at the end of my shift with a huge bouquet of flowers. He gave me the most passionate kiss he had ever given me before, right there in the middle of the restaurant, and asked me if we could please just start over.

I said, "Yes, I would love to!"

We then went out to dinner and talked, and all through our dinner he only had a couple of beers. We began talking about our future together, and he told me he was going back into counseling and would begin attending AA Meetings on a regular basis.

I quickly agreed to attend every meeting with him. I reminded him, "We are in this together, and as long as you keep trying, I will be here."

In my mind I knew this thing with Christopher was not going to be easy. I had made a real mess of things. It was around 6:30, and I knew that Christopher was going to be at my house to pick me up at 8, so I had to come up with an excuse for me to go home. I told Michael that I had started work earlier than I usually did, and I was just dead on my feet. I really wanted to go home and sleep. He asked me to go home with him. He said our bed felt big and empty without me there lying beside him, and then he asked me to please move back in with him. I told him I wanted to, but I thought we needed to take things slowly. I wanted to just see him on a daily basis and take it from there.

I said, "Perhaps in a couple of weeks, we could go back to living together. We will just have to see how things work out." I told him I didn't want us making the same mistakes that we had made in the past by rushing back to each other because it always seemed to end up with him drinking. "If we take it slowly maybe this time we'll make it, and then we'll never have to separate again."

I told him how much I loved him but that we needed to take it slow.

He agreed, but he said, "I want a decision within a couple of weeks. I want you sleeping beside me every night just as it should be."

I agreed to this and said, "Just give me two more weeks." I figured within those two weeks I could certainly get things straightened out with Christopher.

It was now 7:30, and I knew Christopher would be here at 8 o'clock on the dot. I gave Michael a kiss goodbye and told him again how much I loved him. I then headed upstairs and got ready for my date with Christopher. Sure enough, Christopher pulled up his car 8 o'clock on the dot in front of my mother's house and beeped the horn.

As soon as I got into Christopher's car I began to cry. I told him, "I can't do this anymore. I cannot be with Michael one hour and with you the next. It has to be over between us. Can't you see how it's tearing me apart? Won't you please let me go, Christopher?"

Christopher's reply was, "You are free to go any time you want, but just remember this, Michael will never make you as happy as I know I could in or out of bed. You and I have a very special connection, Kyra, and you cannot deny this no matter how hard you may try. If this is what you really want, I will not stand in your way, and I will not try to stop you." With his hand he turned my face toward him, and with tears streaming down my cheeks, we kissed goodbye for the last time.

With this kiss my heart broke inside of me. I felt so empty inside. I just wanted to scream out, "I love you, Christopher," but I knew I could not, I must not. I just kissed him goodbye, and without another word I got out of the car. I went upstairs to my room and cried myself to sleep. All I know is that I never, ever wanted to feel this way again, and it was now over between Christopher and me. I would not allow myself to think of him any longer. I had to begin to work very hard at blocking him out of both my heart and my mind.

A week or so passed by, and Michael and I were working very hard on rebuilding our relationship together. We were really getting along great. We were back in each other's arms and hearts just as we were before. We were falling back in love with each other all over again, and it felt so good and right. Michael's drinking remained under control even though he had not completely stopped yet. We were going to AA meetings regularly and counseling sessions together.

It was one afternoon on a Saturday, there was virtually nothing to do, he suggested that we stop in and play a game of pool just for fun.

I told him, "I'd really rather not, Michael."

He said, "O, come on; it's been ages since we've been in here. We can at least stop in and talk to some of our friends."

I smiled at him and was thinking to myself, *Oh, this is not going to be fun at all.* I prayed that Christopher would not be there.

As Michael and I drove up to the bar, I looked around to see if Christopher's car was there, and it was not. I thought maybe everything was going to be fine, and I could relax, so Michael and I went into the bar. Alex and some of our other friends were there playing pool. We went over to the pool table and asked if we could join in. They remarked how long it had been since they had seen us and asked how we were doing. Michael wrapped his arms around my waist and pulled me close for a kiss, he said, "Oh, we're doing just fine now."

Alex then suggested that we play doubles, Michael and me against Alex and Charlie. Just then as I was making my shot, I heard Alex yell out, "Hi, Christopher. Come here and join us in the game."

Well, needless to say I completely missed my shot and almost fell face forward into the pool table. Christopher then came over to the pool table and asked how everyone was. Then he came directly up to me staring me in the eyes asking how have I been, and remarking that it had been a couple of months since he saw Michael and me there. He asked me what I had been up to.

I realize now that he was interested in playing a little cat and mouse game with me, and I was not appreciating it at all, nor did I find it funny. My reply to Christopher was, "I've just been keeping myself busy at work," and then I just turned and walked away. I went up to the bar and told the bar tender to give me the strongest drink he had available, which was a Cherry Bomb that I proceeded to down as fast as I could. Then I quickly asked for another.

He said, "Kyra, are you sure? You haven't been drinking in awhile and this is gonna hit you like a bag of bricks."

I said, "I've never been surer of anything in my life." He was right. It did hit me like a bag of bricks, and the smell of it, the strong, strong cinnamon was overwhelming. For months after that I wouldn't be able to smell cinnamon spice without wanting to vomit, but it did the trick. It numbed me. At that moment I needed it, and I just wanted to be anywhere but here.

This day had become a nightmare come true, and I just wanted to wake up from it. I consumed two of the Cherry Bombs at the bar and brought the third one back to the pool table where all our friends were. I sat down on one of the stools by the pool table. Michael pulled the other stool over to sit beside me, and it really shouldn't have been any surprise to me when Christopher then pulled the third stool over and sat on the other side of me. I found myself sitting there, me in the middle, Michael on one side, and Christopher on the other—a fucking fool sandwich. I felt like a piece of raw meet just sitting there in the middle.

As the knot in my stomach grew larger by the minute, I just sat there waiting for Christopher to say something stupid. The longer we sat there, the bigger the knot became in my stomach. I was working on my fourth Cherry Bomb now when all of a sudden I could feel my stomach coming up in my throat. I just about made it to the ladies' room. I had never been so violently ill in my whole life.

After I got through vomiting, the room started spinning in circles. I just sat there with a cold cloth on my forehead wishing today would just end. Then I began getting the severe pain in my chest. I was afraid I was having a heart attach. Just then Michael came in and asked me if I was all right and why I was taking so long. I said I was fine. I told him I guess the Cherry Bombs just caught up to me.

He laughed at me and said, "I've never known you to be such a light weight." Then he began telling me about a few of our friends including Alex and Corey that were going out later on that night to a country and western bar and we were invited to go along with them, and I told them that we would meet them there.

I thought to myself, *God, please just take me now,* and as I sat there with a wet paper towel on my forehead, I just looked up at Michael, and I said, "Sure, why not? It sounds like fun."

He said, "Yeah, I think so, too," and then he turned around and walked out.

Meanwhile I'm thinking, *I'd rather have brain surgery.* When I came out of the ladies' room, I told Alex, Corey, and Michael I had to go home and change first, and maybe we could meet them there in about an hour or so.

They all said, "Fine."

I was almost out the door, almost through with this horrible evening and away from Christopher, when Michael then turned as we were leaving and yelled to Christopher, "We're going to the country and western club. Why don't you meet us there in about an hour?"

I felt like I was going to drop to my knees and just die right there. I honestly don't know who I wanted to slap more, Michael, or Christopher for accepting his offer, but I guess Christopher just wanted to have a little bit more fun with me or perhaps torture me a little longer.

I stopped by my mother's house to pick up a change of clothes for the night, and then we proceeded to Michael's mother's house where we both got dressed up. Michael looked really good. He had a baby blue silk shirt on with his jeans and boots. Blue was always his color. I had my silky low cut black dress on with my black Stiletto heels. I pulled myself together as much as I could, still recovering from all those Cherry Bombs.

Michael said, "Are you ready to go, Kyra?"

I said, "Yep."

He gave me a big kiss and hug and remarked on how beautiful I looked that night. We arrived at the nightclub around 9 o'clock. All of our friends were there—Alex, Corey, Cheryl and her boyfriend, Charlie, and of course Christopher. They were all sitting at a big table waiting for us. Michael and I sat at the far end of the table away from Christopher. I chose the seats, and as Michael and I sat down and ordered our first drink, Christopher decided he was going to change his seat. He now sat directly across from me.

As the country and western band played on, Michael asked me if I would like to dance, and I said, "Yes, I would." We danced to a few songs, and considering the circumstances, I was having a really good time. It had been a long time, too long, since Michael and I had slow danced together. It felt so good and so right. I loved being in his arms and the way he held me as he danced. After about four dances Michael and I were pretty tired, so we returned back to our seats.

It was a little more than twenty minutes when the band began playing, "Love, Lift Us Up Where We Belong." Christopher came over to my seat, put his hand out, and asked me to please have this dance with him.

I looked at Michael, praying he could tell Christopher to get lost, "My lady isn't going to dance with you," but he did not. He said, "Sure, Kyra, go ahead."

I could not believe Christopher was doing this. I mean, after all, how much more uncomfortable could he possibly make me feel? He knew this wasn't right, and as we entered onto the dance floor, I tried to keep my distance and dance with our bodies apart formally, but he pulled me close to him and wrapped his arms around my waist.

I asked him just what in the hell he thought he was doing, and he said he was dancing with the woman that he loved, with his woman. I told him he was crazy and that I wasn't his woman any more.

He said, "Yeah, sure." Then he began looking deeply into my eyes, just as he did in the past, the looks that melted me, and he knew it. He then whispered in my ear, "You know, when we're ninety years old in a rocking chair in a home, I want you to look back on what we had together and smile." He then asked me to make him a promise.

I said, "That all depends on what."

He wanted me to promise that I would go to his funeral if he were to go before me. He said, "I just want to know that you are going to be there on my last day on earth," and he told me, "I promise to go to yours if you go before me."

I thought this was a strange thing to be talking about, rather macabre and very depressing. I then asked him, "Do you know something I don't? Are you sick?"

He said, "No. I just want you to promise that you are going to be there."

I agreed to this. I promised him. Fortunately thus far I have not had to keep this promise.

Then Christopher began pulling me closer, too close, and I told him, "Christopher, you have to stop this."

Before I could get out another word, there Michael was standing beside Christopher and me as he was holding me that close, too close. Michael looked at Christopher, and he said, "I'm cutting in now." Christopher had no choice but to let me go. As he walked back to his seat, Michael took me by the waist, and we danced to the next song that they played. Michael asked me what the hell was going on. I told him,

"Nothing, Christopher was just drunk," and Michael hesitantly accepted this answer.

Michael and I returned back to our seats after this dance. Once we were sitting down, Michael put his arm around me and pulled my fact toward him and gave me the biggest, longest kiss he had given me in a very, very long time. When Michael was through, we both sat back, and I looked across the table at Christopher. He sat back in his seat and he had a look of pain and disbelief on his face, one I never wished to put there. He didn't need to see that, or I don't know, maybe he did. Maybe he needed a slap in the face of reality in order to let me go. All I know is I couldn't stand any more. I never ever wanted to hurt Christopher, but I was.

I turned to Michael and told him I wanted to leave that I was getting very tired and it had been a long night. They were going to be calling "Last Call" in a few minutes anyway, so we might as well just leave now. Michael and I proceeded to say goodnight to all of our friends, and as we headed out the door I turned to look at the table and our friends sitting there, and I saw Christopher. He looked at me, and then all he did was look down at the table.

Michael and I then headed home to his mother's house, and although I hadn't moved back in completely, I was spending most of my nights with him. We arrived home and it was very late. We were both tired and both of us had a little bit too much to drink. We went straight to bed and fell asleep in each other's arms.

As soon as the first ray of sunshine came beaming through our window blinds, we awakened still in each other's arms. He ran his hand down my cheeks and pulled my face close to him. Our lips came together in a long passionate embrace, and his kiss made me tingle from head to toe just as it always did. That old feeling was still and always there, that tingling, that passion, that romance that we felt so strongly toward each other. It had been rekindled and came rushing back more powerful than before, and we made passionate love that morning.

I knew right then and there I had made the right choice. Here is where my heart truly lay, and as I felt our tongues entwine and then his lips gently kissing my ear and then my neck, working slowly down to my breasts, running his tongue over every inch of them, circling my nipple with it. As he slowly ran his tongue from my breast down to my stomach, I was growing increasingly moisture and wetter inside, and began throbbing with anticipation. As Michael gently began caressing my inner thighs, he slowly worked his way to my vagina, where he penetrated it with his tongue. My God, I had never felt anything like that before in my life. I was slowly reaching a state of sexual frenzy.

I looked down at him, and said, "My God, what are you doing to me?" I then grabbed the headboard of our bed as he continued to penetrate me with his tongue wiggling it ever faster inside of me. He told me let him know before I was ready to climax.

The feeling was so intense and so completely overwhelming, it wasn't long before I was ready to climax. As I lay there clutching onto our headboard with my body tightening, and on the verge of climaxing, I told Michael to stop. I was ready. Then he began slowly working his way back up, running his tongue over my entire body. He then began kissing my neck, and I could feel him penetrate me so deeply I felt like I was on fire inside, so hot and so wet, I felt like I was going crazy. He began pushing harder and harder inside of me growing ever larger inside of me until both of us just exploded from all the passion. He held me down as I lay there shaking and climaxing, and then I could feel him explode inside of me.

After this we were so exhausted and sweaty, we just lay there in each other's arms, him still inside of me. Neither one of us wanted this to end. It felt so good and so right. With my inner muscles I pulled him deeper inside of me, releasing and then tightening again. I did this over and over until I could feel he was coming to a full erection all over again. He once again began penetrating me harder and harder. He had never penetrated me this deeply ever before. I felt as though we truly had become one.

We lay there with our bodies entwined, him softly kissing my neck and my ears, and then our lips firmly pressing against each other's in a heated embrace, and our tongues twisting together. The passion was overwhelming us, and we both began to climax at the same time, as we lay there shaking in each other's arms, he softly whispered to me, "Kyra, I love you." After we made love we lay there together wrapped in each other's arms for the longest time. Neither one of us wanting to let the other one go. We spent much of the Sunday afternoon like this. We never did get up. We lay in bed talking about the future, and he asked me to please move back in permanently now. I agreed to this. I told him I would move the rest of my things back in on that Tuesday.

On that Sunday night Michael brought me back to my mother's house because I had all of my uniforms there, and I had to go to work that Monday morning. I told Michael that after work on Monday I would finish packing up all the rest of my things, and he could pick me up after work on Tuesday. We could go back to my mother's house and bring them back to his.

So that Monday after work when I came home, I began packing up all my things. I was pretty tired, and I had an awful lot of packing to do. I guess it was around 9:30 that evening when I received a phone call and it was Christopher. He was calling me from the bar, and he told me that Michael was there. I was unaware that Michael was going to the bar because I hadn't seen him after work. I told him that he was just to pick me up on Tuesday, so he pretty much had the whole Monday after work to himself, but I didn't think he would be going to the bar so I was rather surprised to hear this.

Christopher remarked how surprised he was to see Michael without me there, and then he thought to himself, *Well, if Michael's here, then Kyra must be at her mother's house.* He thought this would be a good opportunity for him to talk to me alone for the last time. He went on to ask me if he could please pick me up tonight. He just needed to see me and talk with me about something very important to him. I then told him that the next day, that Tuesday, I was going to be moving all of my belongings back to Michael's mother's house for good, and I also reminded him that we were through. He assured me that he had nothing funny in mind, but he just simply wanted to talk to me as a friend. He needed to talk to me. He said that after everything that we had shared together, I owed him at least this much, so I agreed so long as we stayed in a public place and just talked.

A half hour went by, and I was wondering where the hell he was. It was getting very late, and I was very, very tired at this point. Just then I saw him drive up. He beeped the horn, and I came out. I got into the car, and I looked at his face. He had a look of horror on it. We then drove to Dunkin' Donuts. We sat in the parking lot in the car talking. I asked him what in the hell happened to him and what was wrong. He had such a strange look on his face. Why?

Christopher went on then to tell me that Michael had cornered him in the men's room at the bar. Christopher said, "I guess Michael heard something through the grapevine about you and me. While Michael had me cornered in the men's room, he asked me flat out, 'Are you the man that Kyra has been cheating on me with?'"

Christopher told me he just said, "'No,' and I told him I didn't know what he was talking about. I don't know if Michael believed me or not, but he let me go." Christopher then said that he went out to the bar and finished his beer and waited a few minutes before coming and picking me up, wondering all the while if Michael was going to follow him.

I told Christopher I was afraid of something like this happening. "You could have been very badly hurt, and it would have been ultimately all my fault."

Christopher said, "It wouldn't have been all your fault, Kyra. I wanted this as badly as you did. You didn't force me into anything, and I didn't force you into it. We both wanted this." Then he looked at me deep into my eyes and told me he still didn't want to lose me. He said, "Please, Kyra, just stay with me and we can work this whole mess out somehow."

I told him, "No, we can't. This is impossible, and we can't continue this without one of us getting very badly hurt."

He said, "I'm hurt already."

I reminded him that he wasn't hurt as badly as he could be. "This has to end here and now. Can't you see that I love Michael, and Michael is the one that I need to be with and that I want to be with? "I don't have any feelings for you, Christopher, and you need to let it go and let me go."

I loved Christopher, and I had to lie to him for his own good, for his own safety. I thought if I hurt him a little bit now it would save him an awful lot of pain in the future. I know this was cruel and harsh but I couldn't think of any other way to make him let me go. My heart broke having to say these things to him. His love had opened a window into my soul and let in the fresh beautiful air that my heart had so desperately needed at that moment. But I knew that my life was with Michael although Christopher had become a part of my heart and will forever stay with me. This man that sat before me, this man that I had all these feelings for but couldn't show them to him, I had to deny my love. I must now have to leave him forever without ever letting him know just how I truly felt and what he meant to me.

It was quickly approaching midnight, and I told Christopher that I was extremely tired and that I really needed to go home now. "I think we have said everything that we needed to say to one another."

Christopher just turned around facing out looking through the windshield. He lowered his head and shook it, and said, "I can't believe this is happening. This is it; it's really over, isn't it?"

I said, "Yes, it is."

He then started the car and drove me home. Once we arrived at my mother's house, he leaned over in the car and took my face in his hands and began kissing me just as he did the first time we were together. He asked me to please reconsider my decision.

I then pulled away from him and told him, "Please stop, Christopher. Please just let it go." I again said it was over, and it was the way it had to be.

As I was getting out of the car he grabbed me by my arm, starting to pull me back in. I said to him, "What are you going to do, follow me up the stairs like some kind of little puppy dog?"

He said, "I gladly would if I thought it would make a difference." He then released my arm, and I got out of the car.

At that very moment I felt terrible and my heart was broken as I thought to myself, *This is the last time I will ever kiss him,* but I also knew in my heart that I had made the right choice, and I had to be strong and stand by this. I told him, "Goodbye Christopher," and I turned and walked up the stairs to my home. Once upstairs I looked out the window and his car was there. He hadn't driven off yet. For a few minutes he just sat there, and as I continued to watch I then saw his car slowly pull away for the last time and drive out of my life forever. It was truly over now, and it was now time for me to begin a new life with Michael and to make a fresh start of it all.

This was exactly what we did. Michael and I rekindled our lives and rekindled our romance to begin this bright new life together. We both returned to counseling and attended regular AA meetings together. As usual it helped for a while.

During my counseling sessions my counselor asked me if I had been drinking, and I told her, "Every now and again I do."

She asked, "Do you get drunk?"

I said, "Yes."

I didn't tell her about Christopher and me. I don't know why. I just kept this to myself. Perhaps it was something that I wasn't particularly proud of. I told her that when Michael and I did go out to the bar and play pool, I would have a few drinks, but a few drinks don't seem to be enough for me. I do usually drink until I get drunk. I said that it was only maybe once a week or once every two weeks.

She told me I was playing with fire. I asked her what she meant by that, and she said, "Kyra, what you're doing is called 'binge drinking,' where you don't drink for a couple of weeks and then you get really drunk. On one of these binges you may never come back; you may never be able to stop again." She told me I was an alcoholic, and of course I agreed. She said, "Even binge drinking for an alcoholic can be disastrous."

You see I was under the delusion that just so long as I wasn't drinking every single night or getting drunk every night, that I had my alcoholism under control. But an alcoholic will never have the alcoholism under control. The alcohol will always control them, and I will forever have to be on guard and live my life by the certain rules that I have to set up in order not to be put in a situation where I feel weakened, where I want to drink. But I did not know quite how to do this yet. I was young, and I wanted to have some fun, and to me having fun was being with my friends, and all of our friends drank. I now had to learn how to have fun and be with my friends without drinking, and I didn't know if I could do this or not. What my counselor told me about never being able to return back to sobriety after a binge quite frankly scared the hell out of me.

After this one particular counseling session, I came out extremely depressed and realized I should never, ever drink again but wondered if I was going to be strong enough to do this. I realized I was basically born an alcoholic, and I would die an alcoholic. It would be my choice whether I let it destroy my life or not. This is a disease I can fight. I can go through my life intoxicated and not knowing what I am doing, lose my self respect and ultimately my friends, or I can fight, fight to stay sober, chose to live life and not just stumble through. I chose that night. I chose life, and I promised myself with every ounce of strength that I had left in me that I would try and stay sober.

It was also around this time that the restaurant that I had been working in and liked so much was going out of business, so I had to start looking for other employment. I was very lucky and found another job almost immediately working in a bookbinding factory. It was very hard work with a lot of heavy lifting, but I didn't mind it. After all, I was used to being on my feet, moving around and lifting heavy trays of dishes. I thought myself very lucky to have found another job so quickly.

CHAPTER FIVE

Considering how many people were unemployed in our town, Michael and I both worked very hard every day, and we spent our nights together either counseling or at AA meetings. We had been sober now for weeks and were becoming closer and closer. With the absence of alcohol clouding our brains, our relationship flourished. We were best friends and lovers. We knew each other's most intimate, deepest darkest secrets. Our love life had become incredible. We had become as close as two people could possibly be. We were avoiding all of our friends that continued to drink and just concentrated on each other. We felt that the only way we were going to be able to stay sober was to avoid the people that remained drinking. I compare this to a severe diabetic having a bunch of bakers for friends. If you do not see it, it's easier to avoid and to be tempted, for that temptation will always be there.

Michael and I decided it was time that we got our own place again, so we began looking at apartments, but Michael had another slip before we were able to find one. This time he would remain sober for two months before this last slip up. Michael spent a week back on the bottle before he asked me to please take him to the Brockton detox once more. This was now the fourth time back in the detox in a little more than a year. At least this time he stayed the whole five days, but this time around would be slightly different. This time the counselor would strongly suggest to Michael, seeing this was his fourth attempt and in the past did not work, why would he think it would work now. He suggested this new place that had just opened up, this new facility called Seacrest. It was in Newport, Rhode Island. Michael had health insurance from where he worked and the health insurance had to cover this. It was a very, very expensive program that lasted for thirty days. The facility sounded great. The only bad part about it was it was about a two and a half hour drive from where we lived. I was only allowed to see Michael on the weekends which were when visitors were allowed in to visit the clients. Michael did not care for this at all, so he began giving the counselor a little bit of a hard time about the whole thing.

I looked at Michael, and I told him, "Teddy Bear, we have the rest of our lives together. If this place is going to help you, please go. We need this, and it is such a small amount of time—only four weeks. We can certainly get through four weeks. If we are ever to move on with our lives together and succeed the way we want to and have a home and children, this is the only way we are going to be able to do this, and the only way for you to stop. If a place like this can help you stop, then you must go."

Michael finally agreed and our counselor set up all the preparations and filled out all the necessary paperwork for Michael to get a room. This was now the fifth day, the last day Michael was able to stay at the detox, so the counselor wanted to get him a room immediately at Seacrest. He was lucky enough to get Michael in the very next day, and they even set up the transportation for him. Thank God because I don't think I would have been able to find my way alone down there. I had never driven out of state before.

After Michael signed all the necessary paperwork and everything was all set up, I then returned home that night and packed up a few changes of clothing and toiletries for Michael. I brought them immediately back to the detox so that Michael could take them with him in the morning. As I returned to the detox the next morning, I gave Michael a huge hug and a kiss. I reminded him how much I loved him and that he was doing this for us, and I would be up the next weekend to see him. I asked him if he would call me when he got there to let me know that he was all right.

The next morning he did just that. As soon as he arrived at Newport he called me, and I told him that I would be there to see him the following weekend with a lot more clothing, enough to last the month. Through our conversation that morning I felt like crying. I missed him so much already because now it was over a week since we had really been together. Since he went back to the detox I had only been able to see him twice, and I was used to being with him every single day. I held off my tears until I hung up the phone, and then I cried. My heart longed for his arms to be around me. You see, whenever Michael and I were apart I always felt this way, and when we were apart I always felt like half a person, like half of me was missing, like half of my heart was missing, and this was a terrible feeling. Why were we having to go through so much pain and so much turmoil in our lives when we clearly loved each other so much, just to have to fight for a normal life? What had we done to deserve this?

Michael called me again the next night and told me about his first day there and how everything was going really well and the grounds were so beautiful. It was a brand new facility and he was one of the first clients there. Michael continued to call me every single night and tell me about his progress there and what they had discussed in therapy and in all the group meetings that they had. I in turn would tell him about how my day went which was basically the same thing day after day.

Finally the weekend, thank God, was quickly approaching, and I would be able to hold my Teddy Bear in my arms again, but there was one problem. As I stated earlier, I had never driven out of state before, and I had no idea of how to get down there. I realized I needed a little help. I thought about it for a while, and then it came to me. Alex was like a brother to Michael, so maybe he would help me out here. I gave Alex a call and explained everything to him and asked him for his help. He agreed to give me a ride, and on Saturday morning he was a man of his word. He showed up with Corey, and they both helped me load up the car with Michael's clothes. It was a bright, crisp, sunny October morning, and we got a very early start because Alex was not exactly sure of how to get their either and he wanted to have plenty of time in case we got lost, and we did. We got lost two or three times taking wrong turns, but we eventually found our way there.

The entrance was beautiful. We drove through large cast iron gates. I could see what Michael meant when he said the grounds were beautiful. Although the facility itself, the main building, was only two stories high, the building was very long and formed into a crescent shape with a beautiful flower-filled courtyard with a pond in the center of it. The grounds themselves were quite large with massive amounts of trees, and they had just started turning all the beautiful colors that you could only find in New England—the vibrant reds, the brilliant yellows, and the bright oranges. These gorgeous colors were everywhere that I looked, from the tallest trees to the beautiful flowers growing in the courtyard. Off in the distance I could see two large brick towers that you could still go into and walk all the way up to the top. They must have been there for well over 100 years. I don't know what this land held on it before they built this facility, but it must have been a beautiful estate. By the looks of the grounds and the two towers I could almost imagine a castle being there in place of this facility. These two towers sat on the outskirts of a small forest, a forest where the clients from the facility could go and take long walks just for a little bit of peace or to meditate. It was a beautiful, restful place to spend some time. The entire landscape was simply breathtaking, and I was so happy that Michael was in such a beautiful place. He certainly deserved it after everything he had been through in his life, and I thought, *Maybe, just maybe, he will finally find the help that he so desperately needs here.*

Upon entering the building I found myself in a small lobby. The interior of this building looked like some kind of posh hotel. As I entered the lobby there was a receptionist sitting at her desk. I went up to her and told her my name and who I was there to see. She then escorted me to the visiting room where I waited for Michael. Just then I saw Michael coming walking through the lobby through the door to the visiting room. He was accompanied by his counselor. It was so good to see him again. He walked up to me and we gave each other a huge hug and a kiss. The counselor then began explaining to me that they like to keep the first visit the patient has with his family brief. She said we liked to keep it at about a half an hour or so. Then she explained to me that starting the following weekend, the regular visiting hours would start, and I would be able to spend the whole day there walking and talking and visiting with Michael. However, for today we had to keep it brief which I absolutely hated. I could see Michael wasn't too happy about this himself. After all, we were used to being together all the time, and now all of a sudden we had to put limits on our time together. This quite frankly sucked, but it was for a good purpose.

I told Michael that Alex and Corey were outside in the car waiting for me, and that I had brought all his clothes with me. Michael and I then went outside and Alex and Corey got out of the car. They went over to Michael and gave him a big hug. The four of us brought all of Michael's clothes into the lobby, but that was as far as we could go. They didn't allow anyone else in the bedrooms outside of the patients, so Michael had to carry all his things up to his room by himself. I told Alex and Corey we were only able to visit for about half an hour today because this was the first visit. They then turned to Michael and gave him another hug and said that they would wait outside in the car so that Michael and I could have some privacy.

Michael and I had only about a few minutes left to talk. We went back into the visiting lounge and sat on the couch together. Michael put his arm around me. We cuddled together and talked a little. The little time that we had left passed so quickly, and before we knew it, our time was up. Michael's counselor came out to the visiting lounge to get Michael. It was time for his next session. We both stood up and kissed and hugged each goodbye and yet once again I found myself choking back my tears. I could not allow him to see how much this separation was hurting me. He needed to concentrate on but one thing and that was getting sober and staying sober and healing himself in both his mind and his soul. I knew that it would take all he had to do this, and I didn't want him to be distracted or worried about me. After one more kiss, I quickly returned to the car where Alex and Corey were waiting for me, and I got in.

We headed back home with me still fighting back my tears. Alex tried to distract me. He started telling me stories about when he and Michael were children together. This saddened me even more, and I could no longer hold back my tears. I began thinking if only we could turn back the hands of time to before Michael went to Vietnam, when he was still that child playing with Alex in the school yard, before Vietnam, before John, before all the wasted years he spent drinking. If only Michael could go back to the age of 12 and start all over again, how marvelous this would be. I don't know if it was my tears or the trip down memory lane Alex was sharing with me, but before I knew it he was pulling into a liquor store parking lot. He asked me if I would like anything.

I told him, "Sure, just a Pepsi though."

He quickly returned back to the car with my Pepsi, a pint of vodka, and some o.j. for Corey and himself. As with most alcoholics, the more he drank the more stupid he became and the more stupid he talked.

After a few drinks he started questioning me about why I was even staying with Michael and made the statement, "You could do a lot better." I was disheartened to hear Alex speaking about Michael like this, and I could also see clearly now that Michael and I were alone in this fight. We would not get a lot of help from our friends, and you know, this was just fine by me. If this is the way it had to be, then this is the way it had to be.

Alex went on to ask me, "Do you really think Michael is going to stop drinking? Kyra, how many times now has he tried to stop? What does this make—four, or five or ten?"

He was quite insulting and belligerent at this point, and I felt like smacking him across the head. Then he went on to say, "Kyra, can't you see that Michael likes his life like this? He likes to drink, and he likes to get drunk. There is nothing you are going to be able to say or do that's going to make him change. Can't you see you're wasting your time? You bring him to these places time and time again, and you stand by him time and time again to get where? Nowhere. As soon as he gets out he goes back to drinking again, and how many times exactly are you going to put yourselves through all of this before you wake up and realize it's a losing battle with Michael?"

I could feel my blood pressure rising and going through the roof with every nasty remark that Alex came out with, and I swore to myself once I got out of this car, I would never talk to Alex again.

Then I guess he just ran out of things to say, because all of a sudden he just shut up finally, but now it was my turn to talk. I really, really let him have it. I asked him how could he possibly talk about his best friend like this, a best friend that he has had since childhood, and then I asked him, how could he ever turn his back on his best friend and then try to get me to do the same?

Then I told him, "Alex, I thought you cared about Michael, but I guess I was really wrong. You are no friend of his, nor of mine. One more thing, to answer your other questions about how many times is Michael going to go back to detox, and how many times am I going to stand by him? The answer to that questions is, 'For as many times as it takes' because my heart lay with Michael, and quite frankly I don't care if it takes 50 more fucking times, I will remain by his side always, unlike you. Furthermore, Alex, while we're on the subject, it wouldn't kill you to check out one of these detox centers, because it seems to me you do an awful lot of drinking yourself. One more thing. Michael will eventually stop drinking, and we will have a long, happy normal life together, and obviously it will be just Michael and me without our drunken friends. Can you say the same for you and Corey?"

Looking back on this conversation I think Alex was slightly jealous of Michael because for the first time in Michael's life, he actually had a woman who wanted to stand by him no matter what. After I was finished we said no more to each other. The rest of the ride home was in silence.

Upon arriving back home, Alex turned to me and asked if I would like to go to the bar with he and Corey to shoot a couple of rounds of pool. I looked at him in amazement. After everything that we had just said to each other, he expected me to just go and have some fun. I don't think so.

I said, "No thanks, Alex. I've had about enough for one day."

As he dropped me off at home, I got out of the car and thanked him and Corey for their help. The following weekend I would take the bus down to Newport, and I did this for the remainder of the weekends when I went to visit.

I couldn't believe that I'd almost forgotten that it was going to be Michael's birthday on that following weekend. I had never forgotten Michael's birthday ever. Ever since we had been together I had always given him a birthday present and a cake. If I had shown up that following weekend empty handed, I knew he would have been heartbroken, but considering everything that had been going on, I could see it slipping my mind. So Friday after work I ran around getting his birthday cake and his present.

That next morning, Saturday, I drove to the bus station. From there I took a bus down to Newport. From that bus station I took a cab to Seacrest. Once I arrived at Seacrest I went into the main lobby and told the receptionist that I was there to see Michael and gave her my name. I went into visiting lounge and waited there for him. When he saw me, he had a smile from ear to ear. I was sitting there with his birthday cake in one hand and the present in another.

He said, "I thought you had forgotten."

I said, "Never." We gave each other a huge hug and a kiss, and he said to me with everything that had been going on, it wouldn't have surprised him if I had forgotten, and he certainly would have understood. I told him I confessed I almost did forget, and we both laughed.

As I handed him his cake, I said, "Happy Birthday, my Teddy Bear," and I kissed him again and told him how much I missed him and how very much I loved him. The two of us then went into the cafeteria, and I removed the cake from the box.

His roommate walked by at that moment and patted Michael on the shoulder and said, "You're a lucky guy," and wished him a happy birthday. Michael introduced us and he said, "I'll just leave you two alone to enjoy your time together."

I then turned to Michael and asked him why he didn't invite his roommate to sit down with us and have a piece of cake. Michael just smiled at me and he said, "I don't want to share you or my cake with anybody. We haven't even had a chance to be alone in two weeks, and I want to enjoy every minute with you alone together." Also, I guess you could say Michael really didn't like this guy very much because he went on to tell me what a real bummer he was. He said he hit rock bottom. He was a lawyer with a family and a successful practice before the alcohol consumed his life and took him over. He lost everything. First went his practice, and then his wife left him and took their two teenage sons and even their family dog, which the man affectionately referred to as his "little pooch." Michael then laughed and said he sounded more broken hearted about losing his little pooch than he did losing his whole family or his practice. Michael went on to tell me that he was yet to receive any visitors. Michael also said that most of the men here were like his roommate, they were all professionals—there were lawyers, doctors, business people—very, very successful people that lost everything.

Michael told me he felt like he was out of his element. He said it was very hard for him to even know how to begin to relate to most of these men. This came out most of all in the group meetings where everyone had a chance to talk about what happened in their lives and to share with the other men. In group meetings they insisted on your sharing.

Michael told me about when all the other men started talking about their college years and the reunions that would come years later. Also, because of their drinking, what asses they would make of themselves at those reunions. He told me how his roommate's wife had threatened him at one of these reunions to leave him because of his excessive drinking and promised him if he ever acted that way again in public that she would. He did and then she did. That is how he found himself at Seacrest.

Michael told me he felt very little sympathy for any of these men. While at all of these meetings all Michael could think to himself was, *Yeah, you stupid bastard. Big deal. You made an ass out of yourself at your college reunion. Whoop de do! Sure, while you were in college getting a career started and goals that you could reach and making a future for yourselves along with the millions of dollars you had earned, I was in frickin' Southeast Asia getting my ass shot at on a daily basis. What is your fucking problem.*

It was overwhelming clear to Michael at this point that he and these other men had absolutely nothing in common.

He felt as though he wasn't really receiving much help there, but he agreed to stick it out and keep trying. Michael desperately tried to find something in common with any one of these men. There is one thing that they all had in common and that was alcoholism and the drive, that overwhelming compulsion, to drink—a deep, deep craving. This is what they all had in common.

You know sometimes when an alcoholic is sobering up, they can tend to act very childish, closer in age to a 14 or 15 years old instead of 35 years old. When they want things, they want them right now, and their patience is very short.

I know why, because that craving is just eating at them and they can't do anything about it except try their hardest to ignore it and to keep their minds occupied with other things. I was seeing this in Michael's behavior. He was short-tempered and very moody.

He went on to tell me about yet another meeting he attended where his roommate now was speaking. He went on to tell everybody about himself and how he had lost his practice and his family left him.

Michael said, said, "I swear to God, the man really did not start crying until he started talking about losing his little pooch."

Michael then told me he began laughing at the man and simply lost all control of himself. It was what you would call, nervous laughter or a laughing jag, and the harder Michael tried to stop laughing the more he laughed. Michael said he finally had to excuse himself and walked out of the meeting.

He went out into the hall and his counselor followed and asked Michael if he was going to be okay. She told Michael not to be embarrassed about what just happened. She said it does happen a lot. It's called nervous laughter, but Michael confessed to me it wasn't just a laughing jag. The things that this man was coming out with were so outrageous and ridiculous, it was funny, and whenever he had started crying about losing his pooch and was more broken hearted over losing the pooch than he was over losing his family, I just lost it. It was so ridiculous.

Michael and I continued to talk about more of these sessions as we sat there having a delightful lunch. After lunch he opened his present. I got him a beautiful brown leather jacket. He loved it so much. I said yes, perhaps he could use it today as we go for a long walk. As I was cutting into the cake, I could see Michael's roommate sitting over in the corner by himself looking out the window. I suggested to Michael that he bring him over a piece of cake. Whether he liked this man or not, the sight of him sitting there all alone broke my heart.

Michael said to me, "No, I won't."

I said, "What do you mean, you won't?"

Remember what I said earlier about the alcoholics acting a little bit childish, well this was Michael's proud moment. He simply refused to bring the poor man a piece of cake, and we argued back and forth, Michael telling me, "No, I won't, and you can't make me."

I couldn't believe what was coming out of his mouth and how utterly ridiculous he sounded. Then I told him, "All right. I'm not going to argue with you about this, but would you please just for me bring the poor man a piece of cake?" I told him how ridiculous and juvenile this argument was quickly becoming.

Then Michael said no again and he said, "I just don't want to share my cake."

Then I told him, "You are really being ridiculous. If you don't bring the poor man over a piece of cake, then I will."

He hung his head down and shook it and said, "Okay, I will, I'll bring him a fucking piece of birthday cake if it will shut you up."

I said, "Good and thank you very much."

As I sat there watching Michael walking across the cafeteria toward his roommate with this piece of cake in his hands, a horrible thought popped in my head. Given the fact that we had had the most juvenile argument we had ever had in our relationship, I don't know if he was in quite the frame of mind to be doing things he really did not want to do. I don't know if perhaps I had pushed where I shouldn't have. In my mind's eye I could see Michael walking up to this poor man and smashing it into his face, the cake, the plate, everything. At this point I wasn't sure what Michael was capable of doing. Thankfully Michael did nothing but place the cake in front of the man. The man then thanked him, and I breathed a sigh of relief as Michael headed back toward our table.

He said, "Well, are you happy now, Kyra?"

I said, "Yes. You did a good thing."

After Michael and I had some of the cake for desert, Michael wanted to bring the rest of it back to his room. I sat there in the cafeteria waiting for him to return. We had planned to go for a very long walk around the grounds. It was such a beautiful fall day, a perfect day. The air was crisp but not too cold, and the warmth of the sun's rays felt so good on your face. We first went into the courtyard behind the building where I saw the most beautiful fall flowers I had ever seen before. The colors were incredible. There had to have been every color under the sun. The beautiful mums, daffodils and sunflowers all mixed together. We sat there for a few moments just taking in the scenery, and then we began to venture off into the small forest where people often went for walks. We covered the entire ground. It took us almost three hours to do so. I'm telling you, the place was huge.

Michael and I ended our walk with the exploration of the two towers. We entered into one of them and it looked like something out of an old pirate movie, old English dungeon, the bricks you could tell were very, very old. We followed the staircase all the way up to the top where there were five window openings. Michael and I walked over to one of the windows, and from there you could see the entire grounds and even beyond to the outer street. The view was breathtaking. As we both stood there holding each other, Michael cupped my face with his hand and gave me a long, passionate kiss. He pulled back away and stared deeply into my eyes, and then leaned back in where our lips pressed ever so hard together. I wanted him so badly.

I started kissing Michael's neck, working my way up to his ear lobes. I gently caressed him as I pulled him closer. I then began unbuttoning his shirt, all the while kissing his neck softly. When I had his shirt totally unbuttoned, I began running my tongue over his chest. Just then he took my face with his hands and pulled it close to his. Our lips once again met in a heated embrace and our tongues twisting in each other. He began unbuttoning my blouse and his lips quickly found their way to my nipples. He caressed my breast as he unzipped my pants, and as we fell to the floor in a heat of passion, he then began to unzip his pants revealing a full erection. As I could feel him slowly penetrate me, it grew larger and larger. He penetrated me so deep and so hard, and it felt so incredible.

It had been so long, too long, since I was able to feel Michael inside of me like this. It was over two weeks now since we had been together, and I was cherishing every moment of this. The larger he grew inside of me, the tighter I became until I was on the verge of climaxing. I then gripped on to the brand new leather jacket that I had just bought him almost ripping it in half. As the passion was erupting inside of me, I just held onto Michael shaking, and as that wave of relief came over me, Michael then in a fit of furry penetrated me harder and harder until he erupted deep inside of me.

After this as we lay there in each other's arms, Michael still inside of me. He said, "I wish we could stay like this forever, Kyra."

I said, "Yes, so do I, Honey," but the reality was, we could not.

We kissed for a while, and then Michael said, "We really have to get dressed."

We then sat there in each other's arms, hating the thought of having to leave the ivory tower that had just become our refuge from the world and all of its worries. We both took one last look out of that window, admiring once again the beautiful view, while standing there with our arms wrapped tightly around each other. I told him how I missed this, how I missed holding him in my arms so tight, and how our big bed at home is so lonely and empty without him beside me. We quickly reminded each other that it was only going to be a couple of more weeks now, and we could certainly do that. Then we would be able to hold each other every night from here on out for the rest of our lives.

I hoped and I prayed that this would be the last time that we would be separated like this. These thoughts I kept to myself, though. So as we stood there holding each other tightly, the sun was beginning to set, and oh how magnificent this was. It looked like an orange ball of fire hanging in the sky, slowly dipping down over the horizon, and all the oranges and greens and yellows that were on all the tree tops just below this orange ball. This sight was just magnificent.

I thought, *My God, I'm not going to be able to touch him until next weekend.* I stared into his beautiful hazel eyes, and how my heart broke, for this week was going to feel like an eternity.

He said to me, "Baby Doll, we really need to get back. The sun is setting, and it's going to get dark quickly."

So we both walked down this tower and headed toward the main building. I cherished every moment that we had just spent together, and I know he did too, but our day was coming to an end. I know I only had a week of loneliness ahead of me. I was in no hurry to get back.

Upon arriving at the main building, Michael and I both went into the cafeteria and got our dinner. We sat there and ate, but I didn't have much of an appetite. I choked down every spoonful. I just so did not want to leave him there. I hated that empty feeling in the pit of my stomach when I wasn't with Michael, and I knew once we were finished with our meal I was going to have to once again say goodbye.

I was finding this increasingly harder to do because whenever I was forced to say goodbye to Michael, I always felt as though I was leaving a part of myself behind, or perhaps just a part of my heart.

After we finished dinner I called a cab to take me to the bus station. As Michael and I sat there in the visiting room waiting for the cab to arrive, we held each other close. I could tell he did not want to let go of me anymore than I wanted to let go of him, but we had to. As I saw the cab driving up, I gave him one last kiss goodbye, and I told him how very, very much I loved him and how proud I was of him. He told me how much he loved me and he reminded me that we would have a life together. He was going to see to this.

I said, "I know, I can feel it, Michael." With one last kiss outside of the taxi, he then opened the door. I got in and he closed it. As the cab drove off, I waved to him goodbye. After a long bus ride home, it must have been about 9 o'clock when I arrived at my house, I called Michael's mother to let her know just how he was doing and the progress he was making. She was very happy to hear that and very happy to hear from me.

That following evening Michael called me. We would talk every night on the phone an average of an hour. He would tell me about his therapy sessions, and I would tell him about my day. We always ended our conversation with, "I love you."

It was this week that I received some information concerning my sister Amber and her recovery process. Amber called me on the phone and we must have talked for well over two hours. She was telling me everything about where she was living, her roommate and how very well she was doing in her recovery program. She wanted to come for a visit to get together with April, my mother, and me, a little family reunion you might say. During this visit, Amber let us know that she was ready to leave the halfway house and to get her own apartment. She decided to stay in Boston, and she had just started a new job that was paying very well. She was a very experienced circuit-board solderer. She had worked for many years at TI. She looked really good. It was the healthiest I had ever seen her, but most importantly she was happy. She sounded happy and she looked happy for the first time in her life, and I was so happy for her.

Her second marriage now had officially ended. She had received the divorce papers just a few days earlier. She told me she was happy about this and that the marriage had probably ended the first day she went into the detox. Her husband never stood by her, and he being an alcoholic himself, certainly wasn't for her detoxing and stopping drinking. She told me once she entered the detox, he never called, he never visited. He did nothing. It was like I stopped existing, she said. He forgot all about me. She went on to tell me that he could never see that there was a problem, and he never intended to stop drinking because of this. He never thought he had a problem. She told me what triggered her desire to go to this detox. She said that life just caught up to her. All the years of drinking just caught up to her. She was working seven days trying to make all the payments on all the bills that she had. In every spare moment, she drank, so her life was coming down to working and drinking and little else. Certainly no room left for having fun or feeling happy about anything.

I said to her, "Well, you are much better off without him in your life."

She said, "Yeah, Kyra, I know."

It was also around this time that my other sister April was also contemplating a divorce, and as a matter of fact, she had begun looking for her own apartment. She was ready to leave her husband, and as a matter of fact, I would say it was around two to three weeks after this little reunion we had, that April moved into the apartment right next to my mother's. Just like Amber, she was so much happier.

I tell you, there are a lot of bad things in this world, and being stuck in a bad marriage has to rank right up there with them all. All the while I was growing up I saw nothing but heartache come from marriages, first my mother's of course, and then my sister Amber's first marriage, now her second, and now April's. It seemed as though in my family, as soon as the women said, "I do," everything just fell to shit. It really wasn't so much us as the men. The men were the ones that changed. It seemed like as soon as that ring went on the finger, we became a piece of property instead of a partner, and with our personalities in our family, this simply did not work.

So I would go through life very leery of marriage when most little girls dream of the day they'll walk down that long church aisle with their beautiful flowing white gown on up to the man they love and give their wedding vows to one another. I would cringe at the thought. As much as I loved Michael, and as much as he held my heart, I could not override this feeling. I was utterly terrified of getting married. I just looked at it as the beginning of the end. I didn't want to lose Michael. I could not deny the facts, and the facts were there was never a successful marriage in my entire family.

April was married for thirteen years before she got her divorce. I guess the unlucky thirteen strikes again. Over the thirteen years her marriage had just fallen apart, and it simply became too painful for her to stay. There was not just one particular reason, there were many reasons, and perhaps they had just grown apart.

Then our conversation turned to Michael and me. They asked me about Michael and how he was doing, and I told them. He has his slip ups, but he always goes back and he tries even harder the next time. As a matter of fact that is what he is doing right now, and I went on to explain to them about this new facility in Newport and how beautiful it was. I told them how very proud I was of him.

The four of us just sat at the kitchen table laughing and talking all night. Before we knew it, the sun was coming up, but I guess this was a really good thing because we had a lot of catching up to do. It had been such a long time since we had all been together like that, and I so missed my sisters in my life. I really needed this reconnecting, and it made me feel not so much alone because really I had no one else to talk to about Michael and I and the recovery processes we were going through.

This week passed by really quickly, thank God. Before I knew it, it was Friday, and I would be able to see Michael the following day and hold him in my arms once again. That Saturday morning I arrived at Seacrest around 11 o'clock, and we went into the cafeteria and had lunch. Then Michael and I went out into the courtyard where we sat and talked for a couple of hours. We spoke mainly about the progress that he was making and a little bit about my work although there wasn't much to say about it. Again he made the remark about him not really feeling like he was fitting in, and he told me it just seemed like his problems were just so very different than everyone else's here. He went on to tell me he didn't even feel his own counselor truly understood him. He said she was simply not used to talking to and counseling a veteran. Her other patients were all businessmen with college degrees such as herself, and he just felt as though she wasn't understanding anything that he was telling her. He told me when I tried to explain to her about all the horrors I witnessed in Vietnam and what I went through, she just sat there in silence not sure of what to say to me.

"I can tell she is simply not getting it," he said, "And there was no way she could possibly comprehend what I was telling her." Michael then went on to tell me he felt more frustrated after a counseling session than he did before, and she was providing no help at all. He then went on to describe his counseling sessions to me comparing it to trying to explain a sunset to a blind man, a blind man who had never seen colors before. How do you explain such things, and how on earth could they ever comprehend them? Even though he was feeling this way, he still wanted to stay and wanted to keep trying. He assured me he would never give up.

This now was going into his third week. He would only have one more week left. Then he made this statement to me. This would be the first time he would say this to me, and he would repeat it many, many more times throughout our life together.

He told me, "Kyra, it's okay to sit back and take a break when things get too hard, but after you've regained your strength, after you've taken your rest, come out fighting and never, ever give up."

The first time he made this statement to me I was very impressed, and I thought to myself, *I would really like to live my life by this rule.* This is just one of many lessons Michael had taught me in life, and perhaps this was the most important one and that was how to be strong. Although I always thought of myself as a strong woman, I didn't know what strength was until I met Michael. He was a true survivor and a true hero in every sense of the word. What he went through in Vietnam, all the horrors and the suffering he had to endure, and still he left there, he left Vietnam with his sanity in tact. That's a strong person, and that's my hero. I felt as though if I could only have half of his strength, there would be nothing that I would not be able to accomplish in this world. I also realized at this moment if he was this strong a person, I knew for a fact someday he would beat the alcohol. He would regain control over it. If he truly wanted to, he would, and I could clearly see he did.

The following year I would learn yet another valuable lesson from Michael. I would learn from him to never let your pain show. Try your hardest to keep control over your emotions at all times. Although I had already learned this earlier in my life as a little child with my father, I learned quickly never to show any kind of emotion in front of him. If I felt like crying I would run into the bathroom, because he looked upon this as a weakness. To show any kind of emotion in front of my father was equal to waving a red flag in front of a bull or having an open cut and going swimming in shark-infested waters. As soon as he saw that first tear streaming down your face, he knew he had the power over you to hurt you, and that was something that I never wanted to show him. I never wanted him to see that he had any sort of power over me, because he did not. I didn't hate him, I didn't love him, I felt nothing, and because of these actions, he didn't know quite what to think of me.

My sister April later on in life would tell me this. It is true, he didn't know what to think of me. Because I showed him nothing, I think in some sort of twisted sick way I became his favorite, not only because I was the baby of the family, but I think he saw a strength in me that perhaps he didn't see in my sisters. While they would always cry in front of him and express their emotions, their sorrow for being hurt by him, they also did anything and everything to gain his approval, something I could have cared less about.

So you see, this strength was developed really early simply because I looked upon the strength of being able to hide my emotions, a matter of survival in my own home. But over the years, I kind of let my guard down. I opened up my heart and soul to Michael, and I showed him every emotion I had. Showing Michael this was fine, but I needed to remember that the rest of the world didn't need to see this. This was something that I had forgotten, so I had to learn again how to put up that shield, that shield that no one but Michael would be able to penetrate. Once you learn how to put up that shield you are in control. You are in control of letting other people only see what you want them to see and not your true heart, the heart that can be broken. With this shield up it is very hard for co-workers, family members or friends to hurt you. If you try to remain in control of your emotions and your surroundings, you're less likely to go back to drinking.

After our lengthy conversation in the courtyard, Michael and I then went for a long walk and eventually ended up back at the tower where we had made love the weekend before. Then, once again we walked up that long twisting staircase to the very top where we once again found ourselves in each other arms, where our lips met in a long passionate kiss. I tingled from head to toe. Then he began caressing my neck softly with his lips. Before we knew it we were overtaken by the passion that we felt, and we began making love. How I longed to feel him inside of me again. We truly became one, and with our lips locked and a passionate embrace I never wanted this moment to end. I was completely and totally consumed by our love. Each and every time Michael and I made love I felt as though he touched me straight down to my soul. Afterwards we lay there. We were holding each other. Neither one of us wanted to let go. I believe it was at this moment that both of us realized there could never be any one else for either one of us.

I always had a sense of destiny with Michael, like this was where I was supposed to be. Our souls were supposed to go through life together on this earth. There was nothing else that felt so right in my life than our love for each other. You see, I was a damaged soul and so was he, for very different reasons, though. Together we made each other strong. You see, when I was feeling down he always had a way of bringing me back up, and when he was feeling down I did the same. We somehow drew strength from one another, and our love carried us through the rest. Throughout our lives together, I never, ever feared Michael. I never felt as though he would every hurt me, and he never did. No matter how drunk he became or how severe the flash backs or the night terrors were, even then I felt safe with him.

Maybe at these points in our lives I should have feared him because he didn't know what he was doing at that moment, but I couldn't. I just didn't because I knew underneath all of it his love for me was stronger than anything that was happening to him at that moment. Just like that horrible, horrible night, that life-altering moment, that fight that we had in the van where I knocked out the windshield with that bottle instead of hitting him in the head with it and possibly killing him or injuring him for life. My love is what stopped me. My love is what made me turn the bottle from his head to the windshield at that split second, and his love for me was what prevented him from hurting me when he was in either a blackout or a flashback. Sometimes love is so strong it can overpower every other emotion.

As we lay there in each other's arms we told each other how much we loved one another. We remained lying there for a few more moments, and then Michael told me, "It's time to get back, Kyra. Baby Doll, I don't want to let go of you, but I have to."

We got ourselves together and headed back toward the main building. We had a delightful dinner together in the cafeteria and once more I choked down almost every bite. It made me feel so heartsick to know that I was going to have to be leaving him in only a short time. The only thing that was making this even bearable was the knowledge that Michael would be returning back home with me the following weekend. This would be the last time that we would have to say good-bye. It was now time for me to leave him once more. We called the cab and he opened the door to the cab and gave me a kiss good bye. I got in, and as he stood there on the sidewalk, I waved as the cab drove off.

A few days had passed by now and it was Thursday. I realized that we would need a ride because Michael had all of his clothes there. We couldn't possibly take the bus. So against my better judgment I called Alex. He was the only one I could think of that would be able to help me on such short notice. Please believe me when I say, I really hated to do this, but I did. I gave him a call. I explained the situation and that we had all of Michael's clothes to bring home along with Michael, that his 30 days would be up on Saturday. If he and Corey could help me out once more, I would really appreciate it. He agreed to help me once more not mentioning the conversation we had had two weeks prior, one that I would never, ever tell Michael about because I knew it would hurt him too much. So for the rest of my life, I kept that to myself. During the conversation with Alex he told me, "Kyra, Corey and I will always be there for you and Michael."

I really could never figure this man out. How Michael and he could fight and insult each other, and then the next day act as though nothing was wrong, nothing every happened. I could never figure it out, and this was the way Alex was acting with me. It was as though that conversation never even took place. Alex was rather glad to hear from me because he was wondering what was going on, so he agreed to pick me up about 9 o'clock that Saturday morning.

After this rather strange conversation that I had with Alex, I called Michael to let him know about the arrangement that I had made with Alex and Corey and that we would be there around 11:30-12:00 to pick him up.

Through this conversation with Michael, he told me he had begun taking this medication called Antibuse at the beginning of the week. It was something his counselor strongly suggested he start taking. So I was really hoping between all the counseling he had been receiving (even though he didn't feel too in touch with his counselor or that she was getting it), it was working and relieving a lot of problems that he had.

So between that and this new medication, Antibuse, I thought he had a really good chance of success this time and so did he. This medication, Antibuse, was discovered in of all places a tire factory. You see, the workers would go out and have a beer with their lunch and then return, and when they returned they would become violently ill. They figured it out. It was a new chemical that they were adding to the new tires, and this new chemical had an adverse reaction to alcohol that would make people feel violently ill, and actually the worst-case scenario, could possibly kill you if you were to drink while taking it. They did have an antidote for this, but you would have to get to the hospital in time. For a few people, they didn't make it.

So Michael and I realized this was nothing to mess with. If he was going to be taking this medication, he absolutely and positively had to stay away from alcohol or risk dying. A person that would start this medication had to be completely dedicated to stopping drinking.

Michael told me, "Baby Doll, this time I am completely, totally dedicated to this. I love you so much; I know this time it's going to work."

I had never been prouder of him than I was at that very moment. I realized how painful all of this was for him and how hard he had worked to get where he was at this moment. I told him, "Teddy Bear, I love you so very much, and my respect for you right now is beyond words."

That Saturday Alex picked me up at 9 o'clock as he promised and we arrived at Seacrest about 11:30. This time Alex and Corey went in with me, and Michael greeted us. He was waiting in the lobby. His counselor came out and asked me if she could speak with me privately for a few moments, and I agreed, of course. We went back to her office where she began explaining to me all about this new medication Michael was on and just how strong it was and how serious it was if he were to drink while taking it. She then went on to explain to me what all the side effects were and what would happen to Michael if he were to drink. She said not even a drop of alcohol can be ingested into his system. That means no mouthwash with alcohol in it, no after-shave, and no cough syrup. There was a whole sheet of items that he was not able to take or ingest any longer while he was on this medication. She said, "In short, anything that contains alcohol could possibly kill him."

I went over the sheet of paper with her, and I looked down at the bottom was vanilla extract, rum extract, lemon extract, any of the extracts that you would use in cooking. She said, "In case you don't know this, and many people don't, read the back of it. It has a very high content of alcohol."

I was amazed to hear this. I really hadn't realized this before, and I thought to myself, *I hate the thought of Michael having to put something this vile into his system in order for him to stay sober.* I asked her then, "How long do you think he'll have to take this?"

She said, "As long as necessary. Until he gets a hold on his sobriety. This is what they call a strong deterrent on the days that he's feeling weak. On the days that he would go to that liquor store in a moment of weakness. Just knowing the consequences would stop him, and sometimes that's all it takes is that split second of having to think about it. Once the craving passes, once whatever annoyed you during that day that drove you to want to drink will pass. This helps them get past this moment in their lives so that they can stay on the road to recovery. It may be a year, maybe two years before he is fully confident that he can handle the pressures without turning to the alcohol, and then he would be able to go off of the Antibuse. Until then this is the little extra that I think he desperately needs right now."

When she put it that way, I had no choice but to agree.

Then she asked me, "Do you realize how much Michael loves you? There was hardly a session when he didn't bring up your name and tell me how much he loved you and how badly he wanted a life with you. With the Antibuse and your help and your love he has a good chance of making it, Kyra."

I told her we had been together now for four years, and I loved him more than life itself, and I reassured her I would be there for him every step of the way. In fact I felt exactly the same way toward Michael as he felt toward me. We had a very strong relationship, and she told me she found that the stronger the relationship, the better the chances were for success, so she was very happy to hear me speak like this.

She then went on to tell me that she had set up appointments for Michael to meet with the counselors that he was seeing before. He had expressed to her that he was very happy with his counselor at home. Then I told her that I was seeing the same counselor as well and that she had helped us very much in the past.

She then led me back down to the lobby where Michael, Alex and Corey were waiting for me. Michael had all his clothes packed and was ready to go. She told Michael pretty much everything that she and I had discussed, and she wished us both the best of luck. As she shook our hands, we both said goodbye to her and then the four of us began loading up the car with all of Michael's clothes. This did not take us very long, and we were quickly on our way.

Alex and Corey were both impressed on how well Michael looked and how happy he seemed to appear to be, but all I could think was I finally had my Teddy Bear back in my arms for good now, not just for a day but for always. Alex suggested that we stop for fried clams. Newport was famous for their delicious seafood. Michael and I both jumped at the idea. We had not had fried clams in a very long time and we loved them. Alex soon found this little out-of-the way restaurant. He pulled into the parking and the four of us went in and order four huge plates of fried clams. When the waitress brought the plates to us, they were overflowing. Then she asked us for our drink order, and it just didn't hit me until that very moment. Oh, God, Alex and his alcohol, his beer, but he very much surprised me. Thank God he ordered a coke. I guess he remembered where Michael had just come from.

Believe me when I say this was a very large bullet that I felt as though I just dodged. I don't know what Michael's reaction would have been if Alex had ordered that beer. Maybe he wouldn't have said anything at all or maybe it would have driven him crazy. I don't know. I was just very grateful that Alex was showing Michael a little respect and a little courtesy and actually using his brain. I realized also that after this bullet was dodged, if Michael and I were to be successful at staying sober, we were going to have to avoid situations such as this in the future and also avoid all of our friends who drank. Unfortunately, you can't separate the people from the alcohol. We realized the kind of relationships we had with all of our friends that we always had a lot of fun with came as a packaged deal. If you couldn't take the alcohol, you couldn't be around them because they were not going to give alcohol up.

So Michael and I had no other choice but to give them up at least for the first few years anyway until we both had a strong handle on our sobriety. Neither one of us was exactly sure how long this was going to take. We only knew that we had to avoid situations. We had to avoid at all cost making ourselves vulnerable to another relapse. Alcoholics always walk a very thin line between sobriety and drinking. You must be aware of your situation at all times.

The four of us finished our dinner of these delicious fried clams and had a great time laughing and talking with no alcohol at all. I wish they could have seen and realized that we were having such a good time with no alcohol and that this can be done. However, Alex and Corey were alcoholics, and I knew deep down in my heart that they wouldn't be able to do this ever again with us. They were alcoholics that were in denial. They never did realize that they had a problem. Even after what they saw Michael and I were going through, they still didn't realize that our problem was also theirs. You know something I found out about denial? It's a nice place to visit, but you can't live there. You can't spend your life there.

After this delightful day, Alex drove us home back to Michael's mother's house where Michael and I chose to remain and not get our own apartment right away so that we wouldn't add more pressure onto Michael. We decided and agreed to wait at least two months, possibly longer, before we were to get our own place. Michael really felt as though he needed these months to get a little more sobriety under his belt so that he wouldn't fall back.

It must have been around 7 o'clock that evening when we finally arrived back home. After Michael and I unloaded all his clothes from the car, Michael gave Alex and Corey a big hug and thanked them very much for all their help and told them how much he appreciated it. I, of course, thanked them as well for being good friends. After Michael and I got through unpacking it was rather late when we finally got to bed.

That night we made the deepest most intense love that we had ever made before, because you see when alcohol and drugs are taken out of the picture, out of the relationship, you are then truly awake and alive and can feel absolutely every touch, every caress and every heartbeat. Your senses suddenly become so sharp and so intense by not being numbed by anything. You are alive again, and every single emotion you can truly feel right down to your inner soul. Your senses are awakened once again. After this intense love making we fell asleep in each other's arms and we spent most of the following day in bed, holding each other and talking.

In the following weeks we both resumed counseling and were doing very, very well. We were avoiding all temptations with alcohol, and we also resumed parking at our spot down at the lake every night after work. That's where we would go to talk, our favorite spot. This spot that I call "our spot" overlooked the entire lake, and we would sit there night after night watching the most beautiful sunsets. I swear to God it was the most peaceful place in the whole world. It was just so calming and quiet, a place where Michael and I went to just get away from it all and it felt like we were the only two people on earth.

The longer Michael stayed sober, the more he talked to me about Vietnam. He opened up a little bit more and more each day. This had become a daily topic that I very much encouraged, and I told him, "Please tell me about it." I really, really wanted to know everything about his time in Vietnam, and how I wanted to know every little detail because I wanted so desperately to feel everything he felt. I realized this was the only way I would be able to help him by actually putting myself right in his shoes and in his head. I thought if we could face all of these nightmares, these ghosts together, both of us would find a way to finally be able to put them to rest. He had already told me before about Vietnam, but I wanted more detail. I wanted it detailed because what he was telling me before was just skimming over the surface. I needed to get deep down inside. I knew the only way that we would be able to get on with our lives and to have a life together was for him to let go of the past and to release all of his pain and guilt that he felt.

So I guess you could say I tried turning into Michael's own private counselor. Even though he was seeing his counselor on a regular basis, I knew he couldn't open up to her the way he could to me. We knew everything about each other, but I needed to go deeper.

So day after day we would go to our spot at the lake, and he would tell me story after story, each one more terrifying than the last. I am sorry to say I was only too successful in entering into his mind and into his nightmares. I found myself being able to feel all of his pain and all of his anxiety. Each and every nightmare he had I was visualizing as he was talking to me. I had grown up listening to all my father's war stories from World War II. They all paled in comparison to what Michael was telling me now. Many times after Michael would get through telling me one of his stories, we would just sit there and cry together.

After weeks and months of this, I truly believe we had become as close as two people could ever become, and it left us both emotionally drained. Besides the stories of the mortar incident, the friendly fire incident, where most of the other men in the platoon were killed and the ones that did survive were horribly maimed, he told me other stories.

One story in particular was about this Vietnamese soldier that his platoon had come upon lying on the ground. He was dying. The medic leaned over him and tried to give him some aid. The medic had a cigarette hanging from his mouth. The Vietnamese soldier took it and began smoking, and Michael said you could see the smoke coming out from behind him as he lay there. They turned him over to see a gaping hole in his back. The medic said, "Don't worry; I'll give you a shot," Michael thinking all the while the medic was going to pull a syringe out of his backpack to give him something like morphine to ease the man's pain. Instead he pulled a gun out of the holster and shot the man in the head.

That was just one of many, many horrifying stories, things Michael had to witness and endure at the age of 19, because you see Michael didn't see a Vietnamese soldier lying there. He just saw a human being lying there, one that was put out of his misery as you would a mad dog. Michael was in shock after he witnessed the medic shoot this man.

Then another story was about these Vietnamese children that would come to the gate of their base camps with these bottles of juice and sometimes beer, and all the men were warned that they could be poisonous. I guess a couple of them drank it and became violently ill. So they couldn't even trust a 7-year-old whom our men were trying to defend over there and help get the people's lives in order.

Our men never knew who the enemy was. They were all Vietnamese. You never knew whether it was just a farmer protecting his crops and his family or it was a farmer with heavy military capability that would wipe out half a platoon. They never knew.

Then yet another story of how they would go in after they set off the mortars into villages known to be harboring the Vietcong. That's why they would fire upon them and clear them out, and they would go in and have to collect body parts in order to get an accurate body count. Michael told how he would have to go digging through the rubble to find one leg, then two, then one arm and another. Michael told me the first time he had to do this with his platoon he went and picked up a leg and the veins and the arteries were hanging from it. He said he threw up, but he had no choice. He had to continue.

He felt as though he was stuck in the middle of Hell. Between the heat and all the pain and suffering that went on around him on a daily basis it did something to his very core, to his very soul. He left the real Michael, the innocent Michael, the Michael who grew up on a farm that rode the horses when he was a little boy. He went out hunting for fun. This innocence would forever be lost to be replaced by heartache and nightmares that he would have to endure for the rest of his life.

Then he went on to tell me about yet another strike where they had to send in mortars and bomb yet another village where they suspected the Vietcong were hiding and being protected by these families. Michael told me how he came upon a collapsed hut, and after removing all the debris in that hut, he found an entire family with the father on top of his wife and their two children trying his hardest to protect them, but he could not. He perished right along with them.

An entire family killed, and Michael wasn't even sure for what. When he began removing the father from the top, then he would find the wife and a little boy and a little girl underneath the wife. Each and every one of them had a look of horror on their face. These faces Michael would never erase from his memory.

Through all these nightmares there was one that stuck out in Michael's memory more so than any of the others and that was the day that his platoon was right in the middle of the jungle. From nowhere this little girl appeared. She couldn't have been any more than five or six years old. An angel-faced little girl with long, shiny black hair, and he told me that he would remember this most of all because of the look in her eyes. She had a dead stare. It was as though there was nothing at all behind it, and he looked right into these eyes, these dead eyes.

When the commander saw this girl, somehow he knew probably from past experience that this was not good, and he ordered the men to run and duck for cover. Michael said it was only a matter of seconds between the time he and the other men had found a safe place to hide behind when it happened. The little girl exploded right in front of him. She was a human bomb. The top part of her blew one way, and the bottom part of her the other, and then Michael and the other soldiers found themselves completely surrounded by the Vietcong. They were receiving fire from every spot, every direction, and they got to their guns and began returning fire. They were able, thankfully, to wipe out most of the Vietcong soldiers who were trying to kill them. But that little girl's eyes Michael would never forget. They were void of any human emotion, of any light, of anything. Michael and his platoon survived yet another battle.

Then there were the traps that the Vietcong would set up for our men. The pits that they would dig and insert these long spears into, and each of these spears was covered with feces. Then they would disguise the hole to look like ground, so when our men dropped into them. A lot of times they would go feet first and a massive infection, of course, would immediately set in. If they were not able to get these men help immediately, a lot of times they would get blood poisoning and die. The Vietcong were very inventive. They had been doing this for many, many years and many generations, so they had it down pat. They knew exactly how to hurt and how to wipe out the enemy that crossed their path. The way that they fought the war was quite disgusting. For any country to use their own children as weapons in my book is about the lowest and the most evil that you can be.

However, I also want to make it very clear that not all of the Vietnamese people were this way. There were many, many soldiers that joined our side to help make their country better, to bring the country together. Along with the bad, there were also many good men that died, many good Vietnamese men, soldiers that died right alongside our own. I don't believe they truly got the credit that they deserved, just as in the way America never gave the Vietnam soldier the respect and honor that they deserved, and I don't think they ever will. That is why I believe the time has come for books like this to be written. Every story that I tell about Vietnam comes from Michael's own words, the soldier that had to endure his time there.

Where the time was not right for Michael to write a book to let everyone know just how badly the war affects not only the men, but the people that loved them and their lives, this is now left to me. I bear the burden of telling all these horrible stories to let everyone know, to let all Americans know just how horrible war is and how our men and women, now that the women are on the front lines just as much as the men are, never come back the same. They lose a part of themselves, a part they will never get back. There is no forgetting what you see. War will change them forever. They will never come back the way they left.

I believe wholeheartedly that they deserve so much more than what America repays them. They are not shown nearly as much respect and as much honor as they should be. They completely alter their lives for our society, for our America and for our freedoms. I believe special honors should be bestowed upon them.

After so many weeks and months passed by hearing all these stories, each more horrific than the last, something strange began happening to me. I know I asked Michael to put me in his shoes, but I didn't think psychologically I actually would be able to do this, but it seemed as though I was. I noticed myself becoming anxious at work, anxiety ridden for no reason at all, angry for no reason at all, and becoming extremely startled by loud noises. Then it happened, the first time my foreman walked up behind me as I was busy working and tapped me on the shoulder. I almost took a swing at him. He startled me so badly. I felt like I was absorbing all of Michael's fears and anxieties, and instead of me being able to help him through these nightmares, I was going deeper and further into them myself. Instead of me pulling him out, I was being pulled in. To this day, even with all my counseling, I never could figure out exactly how this happened. However, I did realize that it was happening, so I became aware of my actions and tried to keep a hold of myself at all times.

After months of us talking now and Michael telling me in great detail everything, it was my turn to speak. I began trying to emotionally counteract all of these horror stories. I would tell Michael, "I understand about all of your nightmares now, and I also realize that you will never be able to completely forget about them, and you will never forget all the fallen soldiers that did not make it home, all of the men that died over there. You can never forget, and maybe you should never forget, but there is one important thing you need to start thinking about. It is how you can honor them all by living your life; your living a normal happy life would be honoring their memory, by living each day from here on out the right way, sober, making a life for yourself. Don't you think that they would want you to do this, and if the situation were reversed, wouldn't you want them to go on with their lives and have happy lives and not be sitting here every day slowly killing themselves, wasting the life that they have been given, the chance to have a happy life that was so horrifyingly taken from them? Don't you think they would want you to do this, not waste the gift that has been given to you? You survived. You are a survivor, and you always will be."

I believe that was one of Michael's main problems. It was called survivor's guilt. Why was it he and not I? Do I have a right to even be living? Of course he did, and of course that man would want him to. That other soldier that lost his life there would not want Michael to just waste his life here. He survived, he got out alive, something that that soldier that died wanted more than anything. Here Michael was just wasting it.

I told Michael, "How do you think that man would feel? How do you think any of them would feel to see you sitting here wasting what was so grandly given to you? It wasn't your time. You weren't meant to die there. You were meant to come back and live. I know that's what I want us to do, have a long happy life together. We have to find some way to put these nightmares behind us in order to do this, and I believe we've taken the first step, and that's talking and dragging all the ghosts out of the closet, dealing with them, and then putting them in their proper place, in the past where they belong."

I went on to tell Michael, "I will go even one step further here, say, I think that you actually owe it to these men who never made it home to live, to truly live, to taste life and to cherish every moment of it. In fact believe that you owe it to each and every one of them to do this."

Just as before it seemed like the more we talked about it, the worst his night terrors were and the more flash backs he was having. It was almost like poking a stick into a beehive and rattling it around, but I didn't know how else to help him. I did know for a fact that talking about problems was the only way to solve them. I couldn't help him without talking about it and talking about it somehow in many ways made it worse. I suppose looking back at it now, I really should have seen this coming.

Michael began drinking again. It seems as though he had secretly stopped taking the medication, Antibuse, that the doctor at Seacrest had prescribed for him, but this last time was the longest he had stayed sober and it was two and a half months before he slipped. Through all our talks and all the things that he shared with me, the nightmares that he relived with me time and time again, I realize now it was just opening painful wounds time and time again. The pain of all these wounds was becoming just too much for Michael to bear again, so he crawled back into the bottle, where he felt safe and numb. Once again, in his words, he was "receiving that shot of Novocain to my heart so I can't feel the pain." However, this time, unlike the last, he continued to see the counselor on a weekly basis. I, on the other hand, was staying sober and had no desire to return back to drinking.

Although Michael's drinking was not as bad as it was before, he was still drinking, but it was just to ease his nerves. He never drank enough to be falling down drunk again like before. I suppose because Michael was drinking, he all of a sudden became obsessed with finding out who I had been with before, the man that I had had an affair with. He was desperately trying to find out his name even though it had been months since this happened, months since I had broken up with Christopher. It was as though Michael slid back in time right after this happened.

He started questioning me almost on a nightly basis asking me where this man and I went and what we did and how we were able to keep everything such a secret from him. He wanted me to go into detail, and every night he would become more aggressive about his questioning.

I asked him, "Michael, why are you bringing all of this back up again? Do you think I am seeing him?"

Michael's reply was, "No, I don't. I just want to know who he was. I want to know his name. I realize how close we have become, as close as two people could possibly be, and I love you very much. I know this, but I just want to know his name."

I again asked Michael why was it so important for him to find out his name, and Michael said, "So I can take care of him and move past this."

I then told Michael, "You are going to have to find another way to get past this, because I will never tell you his name." Then I went on to ask Michael if he would like to be sharing a jail cell with his brother John, because if he went out and did something stupid and really injured this man or killed him, where did he think he'd be then? The past four years would be for nothing. I then begged Michael to please just stop, stop the questioning and forget about it.

Right now in my life between Michael and my job I was becoming increasingly aggravated. Every day at my job at the book-packing factory I had to lift huge numbers of books that were very heavy, and I was beginning to have a lot of trouble with my back. I was in pain a lot of the time. These boxes that I had to lift every single day weighed between 50 and 75 pounds, and I would lift on the average of 50 to 75 of them. After almost three months of this job, it had begun to take a toll on me.

Then one day one of the women that I was working with told me about a nightclub that was doing some hiring for a cocktail waitress, and she had heard that I had waitressed in the past.

She said, "Kyra, why don't you go and put in an application? The job is a lot easier than here."

As soon as I heard about this I jumped at the opportunity. The next day I went and applied at Jim's Place, a nightclub. It was owned by, two very, very nice people. Their names were Jim and Tina Gold. They had owned that nightclub for around 20 years. Although I had never waitressed in a nightclub before (I had previously served only food), it looked a lot easier and a lot simpler of course. I so desperately needed a break from the factory work I had been doing. Jim and Tina were an older couple and they were very respectable. They didn't put up with a lot of bullshit from the customers, so I knew as a waitress I would have a little sense of security there, a little sense of protection. Most of the clienteles were respectable couples and older couples that would just go there to listen to the live band and have a few cocktails. It wasn't what you would call a rowdy crowd. It was a classy little out-of-the-way place, and I quickly found I could make more working Thursday, Friday, and Saturday at this waitress job than I did working five to six days a week busting my back at the factory job.

After I talked to Jim and Tina and filled out my application, they told me, "Well, Kyra, you got the job," and I was only too grateful to accept.

Now all that was left was for me to tell Michael, and I realized he wasn't going to be happy about this change of careers I decided to make. I explained how absolutely miserable I was at the factory, and he could see that I was in pain every night. When I had waitressed in the past, I really liked it. I enjoyed meeting people and talking to my regulars. I really missed this in my life. I believe the only reason Michael allowed me to work there was that he did know how respectable this nightclub was and he knew Jim Gold. He knew his reputation, and he didn't put up with a lot of bullshit. The clientele was very nice and very respectable and Michael knew that I wasn't getting in over my head. Even though I was working around alcohol all the time, you could not drink while you were working. I think that's a common misconception. They think if you work in a bar then you're drinking, when in fact if you drink, you would get fired on the spot. They had a live band there every night. I always enjoyed music and dancing.

This was a little uplift in my life at this moment, something that I desperately needed. I was ever so grateful that Jim and Tina hired me. There were three rules to this job that I must follow in order to stay employed there. One was as I said before about not drinking on the job. If someone were to buy you a drink or wanted to buy you a drink, you would have to drink this after your shift ended. The second rule was no boyfriends or husbands allowed in while you were working. This made for difficult situations. If someone were to flirt with you and you had a jealous boyfriend, a big fight could happen so the owners set this up as a rule to avoid a lot of confrontations. Third was never, ever dip into the till. If you were caught taking one penny that didn't belong to you, that was automatic dismissal. Of course I never did on any job. In fact, I never stole anything from anyone at anytime. Believe me, I heard many stories about other waitresses. If you're known to do this, you will not get hired anyplace.

I soon grew to love this job. It was like a little family there. There was only one other waitress besides me, and her name was Sue. There was only one bartender, David. He was about 25 years old. He was very handsome and very intelligent. He was a nice, sweet guy. He had just graduated from college with a degree in accounting, but yet he was standing behind a bar handing out drinks most of the week. It really didn't make a lot of sense to me. I did know one thing. If I had a college degree in anything I certainly wouldn't have been standing in the middle of a nightclub serving drinks!

It was after a couple of weeks of working there. David and I started talking and getting to know each other a little bit better. We became friends, and he began telling me a little bit about his life. This is when I found out that he had just graduated from college. I just stood there looking at him as if he had two heads, and then I asked him, "Are you crazy? What in the hell are you doing here serving drinks, or for that matter even staying in this small town? My God, you should be in Boston applying to firms and getting your career started. Why are you here?"

He simply replied, "Kyra, I'm just not ready yet, and I really don't know if I ever will be. I can't imagine a huge Boston law firm hiring me, and I would always fear that I couldn't do the job."

He didn't think very highly of himself, and he had obvious self-esteem issues.

The longer we worked together, the closer we became, and the closer we became the more I tried lifting his self-confidence. I told him how good looking he was and how smart he was, and if he really put his mind to it, he could do anything he wanted. I mean, after all, he did graduate from college. He was able to do that, so why didn't he think he was able to start his career? He just needed to take that next step.

I then began trying to convince him, and I would try to brainwash him. The three nights that we worked together I would ask him every single night, did you call that firm yet. There were a couple of firms in Boston that he was interested in, and I would continuously be on his back about it.

I told him, "What do you have to lose? What do you think they're going to do? Pull out a gun and shoot you? You have absolutely nothing to lose. You're working as a bartender. You could be making ten times the amount at the end of the week as you're making now and for something that you are trained to do. You have nothing to lose. Go for it. All they can say to you is 'no,' and quite frankly, who cares? It would be their loss."

I told him, "Start small. Start at the smaller firms and work your way up to the larger ones. This way your first interview, who cares if you get the job or not? You gain experience, interview experience. You only grow better and better by each interview. By the time you hit the really big one, the one that you really want, you will have a better chance of getting it, but you must start trying because years can slip away before you even know it. Do not become too comfortable in your bartender's position because you are not meant to be here. That's obvious to me and to everyone who walks through that door."

Quite often after work Sue, David, and I would go to a little after-hours club where all of the waitresses and bartenders gathered after their shifts were over. They stayed open all night long. When we didn't go there, we would often go to the other nightclubs that would be closed but we would gather there with the bartenders and waitresses from all the other nightclubs and just stay until 3, 4, 5 o'clock in the morning with the owners partying. There were about five major nightclubs in our town, and we would go to a different one every night. Thursday, Friday, and Saturday, the after-hours club partying would begin. The three of us would head out after work and just have a blast, just some good clean fun along with about thirty other waitresses and bartenders in the area.

Of course, Michael was not happy with me coming home at 5 and 6 in the morning from my job that ended at 1:30. But I told him what I was doing and whom I was with and that it was all just innocent fun. He knew in his heart that I wasn't doing anything wrong. I had no interest in dating anyone else or sleeping with anyone else, I only wanted him. Still he told me this was becoming a habit, one that had to stop. We argued a little bit about it. Then I agreed, but I told him I wanted to be able to go out at least once a month with my friends after work. I would cut it down from three days a week to once a month, and he agreed to this reluctantly.

Michael and I had continued to see our counselors, and I told her all about my new job and the nights I was spending out on the town with my new friends. She of course was not happy to hear about this. She reminded me again about the binge drinking and how very dangerous this was for me, and how I was playing with fire. Although I had always listened to her about other things, I just couldn't take this binge drinking seriously. I thought if I was only drinking one or two nights a week that this was acceptable, and it seemed to have been working for me. So I wasn't as terrified about this as I think she wanted me to be.

I do, however, understand now that an alcoholic is an alcoholic whether it is two days a week or seven days a week. Alcohol is poison to an alcoholic, and as with any alcoholic you can trick yourself into believing and thinking that certain things are acceptable. The desire is always there. That craving will always remain. It's up to you whether you act on this or not. She was so afraid, she was so scared that I was going to fall and fall hard, and I did realize I was standing on shaky ground.

I went home that night, and I told Michael everything that I had discussed with our counselor, and I told him, "I guess she's right. I have to make a final choice here, and my choice is you and sobriety. I love you, Michael."

He smiled and leaned over to give me a big hug and a kiss. From that moment on I stayed sober. I continued to waitress, but I did not drink anymore, and the partying every night stopped. After this day I only went out once more with my friends after work, but I still am proud to say I did not drink. It was very hard but I resisted the temptation to drink even though everyone around me was. I stayed strong, and I stayed sober, and I realized I could not keep putting myself into these situations, not if I was going to stay sober.

My luck being what it was, it just so happened that that last night I was out with my friends, guess who showed up with one of his friends a bartender from another club: the one person that I truly didn't want to see, and that was Christopher. I had not seen him since we had broken up, but there he was sitting there as Sue, David, and I walked into the club. The three of us went in and sat at the bar, David sitting beside me. Christopher was looking over, and I think he assumed simply because David and I were together that we were now dating and nothing could be further from the truth. When I glanced over to look at Christopher, I saw a look in his eyes that I had never seen before and that was anger and furry. Christopher just sat there staring at David and me. The longer he sat there staring at us like that, the more alarmed I was becoming. I had never seen Christopher's violent side before, and I wasn't looking forward to seeing it now. Then Christopher made his move. He got up from his bar stool and slowly walked over to join David and me. He walked past David and sat on the other side of me.

As he sat down, he said in a loud voice, "Hi, Kyra, how have you been? How have you and Michael been doing?"

I replied, "Michael and I are doing just fine," and then I introduced David to Christopher. In my introduction I told Christopher that this is the bartender that I work with, and we are just very good friends. Christopher seemed to have a slight look of relief on his face, but I could tell he was still suspicious. It was only too clear to me at this point that Christopher had not completely gotten over our breakup.

Christopher began striking up a conversation with me about the old days, all our old friends, Alex and Corey, and how nobody had seen Michael and me for quite a while now. Christopher went on talking about all the fun that we used to have together, all the drinking and music I used to play on the jukebox, and how the bar just wasn't the same without me there. While David was listening to our conversation, he began entering himself into it. Christopher did not like this one bit, and every question that David would ask Christopher, he would ignore. When David started talking, Christopher would talk over him not letting him get a word in edgewise. I could see David becoming increasingly aggravated by this. He felt as though Christopher was trying to make a fool out of him. I told Christopher to stop acting so ignorant, that David was a friend of mine and to please let him into this conversation.

While all of this was going on people were partying and having a good time in the background. As I sat there with my Pepsi, David on one side and Christopher on the other, they getting increasingly drunker as the night went on and more confrontational. All I wanted to do was get the Hell out of there. What Christopher did next gave me the perfect excuse to leave. Christopher stood up and poured his beer right down the middle of my cleavage.

David stood up, his eyes bugged, and I quickly laughed it off, saying, "I guess Christopher had a little bit too much to drink tonight."

I then just began cleaning the front of my blouse with a few napkins. I told David to sit down. Everything was fine, and I took this opportunity to quickly make my exit. I was finished. I was finished with Christopher. I was finished with partying after hours. I was finished with the whole foolish mess. This would be the last time that I would ever see Christopher. I don't know if he moved out of town or not, because we had stopped running in the same circle. This would also be the last night that I would ever go partying with my friends.

I then stood up and told Sue, David and Christopher that I was going to go home. I was very tired, and I had had enough for one night and said goodbye to all of them. I went out to the parking lot and got in my car.

By now it was about 3 o'clock in the morning. I had gotten off work at 1:30. I went straight home, and Michael asked me as I was getting into bed how my night was and if I had had anything to drink. I told him, "No," although I'm sure he could tell that I hadn't. I informed him that this would be the last night that I would be doing this, and he was very happy to hear this.

Although Michael was still drinking I was able to stay sober. We had stopped altogether going out to the bars, playing pool with our friends or going out clubbing. When Michael did drink, it was now at home and it was not very much, much less than he ever had before, but still I worried about him and how long could he keep this up.

It seemed as though he had now turned into a maintenance drinker, just drinking enough to keep the edge off and still being able to hold down his job. But still my counselor's words rang through my mind constantly. If we went on binges like I did, or did maintenance drinking like he did, we might someday reach a point where we would not be able to every stop again. We were alcoholics, and that meant not drinking at all and finding a way to live your life without alcohol. Michael had not quite found this yet.

A few weeks would pass by and for the most part they were uneventful until one Tuesday night after work Michael came home, and I could tell he had been drinking a little more than he had been. He asked me if I would like to go out to dinner that evening and maybe see a movie, and because I could see he was a little bit drunker than usual, I did hesitate for a moment, but then I agreed. I thought it would be good for us to both get out. We went out to eat at this little restaurant called The Gondola, and then went to the drive-in to see *Cobra,* the new Sylvester Stallone movie.

Before going to the drive in Michael had made a stop at the liquor store for a pint of vodka, and I said to myself, "Oh, no, not again." As soon as we arrived at the drive in he downed about half of the pint, and as the movie began, Michael was very quiet through the whole movie which was very uncharacteristic of him. I could tell something was bothering him. I just couldn't quite put my finger on it, and as we sat there watching the movie he continued to drink, finishing the pint of vodka. I told him that I wanted to drive home and that he had had too much to drink, but he would not let me drive.

We were about halfway home when out of the blue and all of sudden he began questioning me again about the man that I had had the affair with. I could not believe this. He just would not let it go, and as the time passed by he simply could not forget, even though by now a year had passed by.

I told him, "Michael, just let it go. I am not going to tell you the man's name."

Then he began screaming and yelling at me at the top of his lungs, over and over again. He just kept yelling, "Tell me his name! Tell me his name!"

Over and over again I refused. It was then that he began driving faster and faster. He began really losing it and going crazy, banging on the steering wheel, yelling at me, as he started to call me all kinds of names like "bitch" and "whore." As soon as he began insulting me something inside of me just snapped. I went numb and everything seemed to be moving in slow motion all of a sudden, and until this day I have never quite figured out what that was all about.

It only lasted for a minute or so, and then I snapped back. I then began yelling back at Michael. I asked him if he really thought he was going to intimidate me into telling him this man's name by driving like a maniac. I told him, "You really should know me better than that by now," and then I screamed at him, "What's the matter, asshole? You can't drive any faster?"

Looking back at this statement now, I really should have known better than to say something like that because right after this statement Michael began to floor it. We hit a sharp corner of the road going at least 85 mph in a top-heavy van, and how or why we didn't simply just roll over and keep rolling is anyone's guess. But I guess luck was on our side this night. Instead we just went into a terrible spin and remained in the middle of the road spinning, completely missing huge oak trees that would have surely done us in. As we were spinning in the van through centrifugal force, I was sucked right out of my seat and right out of my shoes, and I was thrown right into the back of the van like a little rag doll.

Michael began fighting with the steering wheel trying to regain control of the van. He held on for dear life, he told me for as long as he could until the centrifugal force then sucked him out of his seat. He then landed in the back of the van right on top of me with full force. I felt as though the hand of God just came down and held onto this van, it suddenly stopped right in the middle of the street.

I remember to this day, Michael looking at me, asking me if I was okay, and then asking me if we were dead.

My reply to him was, "I really don't know."

He then pulled himself off of me. I had sharp pains in my chest and my rib cage because of the force of Michael landing on me. It hurt like hell, and we both just sat there in the back of the van for a few moments trying to regain our senses. He then asked me again if I was all right, and I told him, yeah, I was just a little sore. I asked him if he was okay, and he told me yes. Neither one of us could believe that we both walked away from something like this without one little scratch. I guess it's true what they say, "God protects children, fools, and drunks," because Michael and I were both acting like all three of these this night.

After we regained our composure we then got out of the van. Standing there in the middle of the street by our van we could clearly see the line of trees on both sides of the street, these huge trees that, if the van had hit them, would probably have put us both through the windshield and would have badly injured us if not killed us. We stood there with our mouths hanging open in amazement looking at the circles in the middle of the street that led up to the van. It was as though something was keeping us on that one direct path because Michael certainly at that point had no control over it, and believe me, we both realized how lucky we were to still be alive.

We stood there regaining our composure and taking deep breaths. We then got into the van and on the fourth try Michael was able to start it up. This was only down the street from Michael's mother's house so we were able to drive there. When we got out of the van at home we looked at it to inspect the damage. There was not one scratch, and again we just stood there looking at each other in amazement. Both of us then went into the house and washed up. We then went upstairs and went straight to bed without saying another word.

The next morning when we awakened we both sat up on the edge of our bed our bodies feeling as though we had been hit by a Mack truck. We were both so sore at this point we could barely walk. As I sat there on my side of the bed, I looked at Michael standing now at the foot of our bed. I looked him dead square in the eye and asked him, "Were you trying to kill us both last night?" and I asked him just what in the hell was he thinking.

He then sat down beside me and put his head in his hands and said, "I don't know what I was thinking about. I guess I wasn't thinking at all."

I then went on to tell him just how horrible my body was feeling at this moment. I told him I felt as though someone had hit me in the chest with a sledgehammer. My chest, my rib cage and my back were in such severe pain, and I said, "All you have to say about last night is you weren't thinking. No, I guess you weren't."

I did not say another word after that. I then got up and began getting dressed. I got my suitcase out of the closet and started packing up my things. Michael said, "Please, don't go. Don't leave me again."

I then turned to him and said, "When my chest stops hurting, and my back feels normal again, I will then think about coming back to you. Until then you know where you can find me."

You know the weird part about it was I wasn't even angry with him at this point. I was just numb, and I once again showed up at my mother's door suitcase in hand.

Now by this time April had taken the apartment right next door to my mother's. It was really nice. I had both my mother and my sister to talk to, although I said nothing to either one of them about what had just happened the night before. I told my mother I just needed a few days' break from Michael. Starting this day I could feel myself becoming increasingly more depressed. My relationship with Michael seemed to always be taking one step forward and four steps back, and this was really wearing on my heart, my nerves and my mind, and I was depressed.

It was about 9 o'clock that evening that first night back at my mother's. I was going to take a nice hot bath, and just as I was running my bath water Michael called. I caught my mother just before she answered the phone. I asked her if it was Michael, could she please tell him I had already gone to sleep and that I would call him back in the morning. I ran my bath water as hot as I could stand it. I needed the heat for my sore body. I was in such pain physically and mentally. I just felt as though my whole world was collapsing around me, and I wanted out. Before I got into my bath, I took a razor blade from the medicine cabinet. I then got into my bath. As I sat there holding the razor blade to my wrist, I felt so totally disconnected from everyone and every thing in this world.

As I sat there trying my hardest to make that first cut, the strangest thing happened to me. I started thinking about my grandmother. I started remembering all the things she had taught me and her unwavering and undying love for God, a God she believed so strongly in, one that she tried so hard to teach me about. Then I would just keep coming back to what I had overhead my sister April and my mother talking about after she died. I realized I too believed in God. I never stopped believing in God. I just lived my whole life very, very angry with him, but because I never stopped believing in God, with God there is also a heaven. I then began to worry about just where my soul would end up if I were to commit suicide, and every Catholic knows suicide is the one thing that is unforgivable in God's eyes. Even after all these years I could not forget my grandmother's words, her teachings, even though I hadn't prayed since she died. I guess I just had nothing to say to God, and I figured he had forgotten all about me.

I began thinking about my life and all the horrible things that have happened to me and all the people around me, my friends, the one in particular my dearest friend who died such a horrible tragic death before she even had a chance to live, Angel. Then I started thinking about Mr. Smith and his coming back home early that day from Boston only to end up being murdered, and then just so many other horrible things that Michael told me about when he was in Vietnam.

I just had an overwhelming feeling that God somehow was asleep at the wheel. How could he let all this pain happen?

Then just as I was thinking this I put down the razor blade and began to cry. As I lay there in excruciating pain in my hot tub, I wondered to myself what was going to happen in my life next, and I realized suicide was not the answer. I could not possibly go through with this. I also thought to myself, *When you decide to stand beside someone that you love more than life itself, and I mean stand beside them through everything, the night terrors, the flashbacks, the alcohol rages, and all the other self-destructible behavior, when exactly is it enough? Where do you draw that line, and at what cost do you stay?* Looking at myself sitting in this tub with the razor blade, the cost perhaps is much too high. It now is coming down to the cost of my sanity.

Have I come to such a point in my life I could no longer see the light at the end of the tunnel? I could see no help. Everything in my life had just become so painful, too painful to bear any longer. I felt as though I could no longer live with Michael, and at the same time I realized I didn't want to live without him. Living without him would be unbearable. I could not bear the thought of never touching him again, seeing him, or making love to him again. I had already tried living without Michael in my life only one time and that was when I was with Christopher. So you see, I realized I could not bear life without Michael no matter how hard I tried. Neither one of us could stand to be without each other. So what choice did I have? I felt so alone and so stuck, and I just kept thinking this is not what love is supposed to feel like, or is it? I didn't even know anymore. I got myself out of the tub, and I went straight to bed, trying not to think about all the pain my heart was in right now.

I no sooner went to sleep when I started having the most horrific nightmare of my life. It started out with me lying there in a casket in a funeral parlor. I could hear and see everything, but I could not move, and as I lay there I could see the lid of my casket. It was a dark, dark blue, with beautiful stars, like in a night sky. This dream seemed very real, and I was terrified. I couldn't get anyone to notice that I wasn't dead, but I couldn't move either. My mother was there and my two sisters. They were there standing at the head of my casket looking right at me and crying. Then Michael came up and gave me a kiss on the cheek, and then he began to cry. They were all standing there crying. I could see them, I just could not speak or move. As hard as I tried, I just could not. Somebody then closed the cover on my casket, and all of a sudden I could move but the casket lid was locked and no one heard me crying out for help. I could feel myself being carried out and sliding into the back of the hearse, and even though now I was pounding at the lid, no one responded. I then felt the motion of being taken out of the hearse and lowered into my grave. I then began clawing at the silk lining, and then all of a sudden I awakened, thank God, out of this horrifying nightmare to find the sheet over my face. I began screaming hysterically. My God I never had a dream that felt so real in my life, and I hoped I never would again. I then sat up in bed and my mother and sisters both heard my screams. They came running into my room asking me what was wrong. I told them it was nothing. I was just having a bad dream.

By this time the sun had begun to rise, and I could not possibly get back to sleep now. I just got up and made myself some coffee. Sitting at the kitchen table I tried my hardest to just forget this horrible nightmare that I had just woken up from. After I regained what was left of my sanity at this point, it was a couple of hours afterwards that I called Michael. He asked me if he could pick me up after he got out of work that night, and I agreed.

That night as I saw the van driving up I thought to myself, *Is he going to be sober or is he going to be drunk?* I was very relieved to see he was sober. We picked up a couple of coffees at Dunkin' Donuts and drove to our spot by the lake. He asked me how I was feeling and if my pain had passed. I said that all depended on what pain he meant, my emotional pain or my physical because neither one of them had subsided. I assured him I would be fine in a couple of days, and he was very relieved to hear this.

I then asked him how he was feeling, if his pain was still as great as it was the day before. He said he wasn't really in that much pain. "After all, I was the one that landed on you, remember?"

I said to him, "Your emotional pain should be much greater than your physical pain right now. Don't you remember? You are the one that tried to kill us both, and that is totally fucked up."

He then said, "I was not trying to kill us."

I said, "Well, what would you call it? Because in my eyes this is exactly what it looked like and it felt like."

He told me, "I just start getting a little crazy when I think about you with that other man. I just can't help it."

I then asked him, "If I were to tell you his name and you went out and beat the shit out him and put him in the hospital, what possible difference would this make in our relationship outside of us not being able to be together because you'll be in jail? What is this going to change? Is this going to make our relationship better? You do not need to know this man's name, and I will never tell you this man's name because I know what you would do, and this bullshit has to stop. It has to end, Michael, right here and right now, today. I never want you to ever bring this up again or to ask me for his name. This has to end Michael or I am afraid we will."

Michael then told me, "I just don't want to lose you again, Kyra. I just can't stand the thought of this happening to us."

I assured him this would not ever happen again. "I don't want to be with another man." I only wanted to be with him but we had to find some way to move on from this if we were to have a future together. We could not keep rehashing the past and keeping that hurt alive. We have to find some way to forget because this is the only way we are going to be able to move on and have a life.

Until this point I hadn't planned on telling Michael what I was contemplating doing last night in my bath, but I thought perhaps he needed to hear it. He needed to truly appreciate the pain that I was also going through. I also told him about the horrible nightmare I had, following this.

Michael said, "Although what you have just told me sickens me, it does not surprise me." Michael then went on to tell me about the sick feeling he was getting in the pit of his stomach last night. He said he was getting the feeling like someone close to him had just died, and at the time he had no idea why he was feeling this way. He said, "That is why I called you. I wanted to talk to you because of this feeling."

Ironically this was just before I got into the tub with the razor. This I found very bizarre for Michael to be telling me. He was many things, but a liar wasn't one of them, and I knew if he told me he was feeling this, he truly was. I realized our connection was that deep and he was picking up on my emotions.

Just as I was able to feel his pain, he was now beginning to feel mine. Then he went on to tell me he assumed everything was fine because my mother had told him that I had gone to sleep. He told me, "The next time, I'm going to trust that feeling in the pit of my stomach, and I will come to you, Kyra, when you need me."

I then went on to tell Michael about how I was feeling and how the stories from Vietnam were affecting me by my anxiety level, my sharp temper, my distrust of other people, and how I am now able to become startled very easily. It's like your emotions have rubbed off onto me. I said, "We love each other so much we're actually feeling each other's pain." Along with this love has come much pain.

I asked him, "Michael, is this really what love is supposed to be like? Is one person supposed to cause the other person so much pain they actually contemplate suicide, something so unforgivable in God's eyes? How can we keep hurting each other like this? It has to stop."

Michael then took me in his arms, and we both began to cry. He said, "I know, it has to stop, and it's going to right now. I truly realize how lucky I am. I have a good woman who loves me very, very much, love that I perhaps don't even deserve. Kyra, I am going to get it together."

However, for the following few weeks I did remain at my mother's house and he remained at his. In the next couple of weeks Michael quit his job, the one that was causing him so much aggravation and stress. He thought this would really help his sobriety, and in this time he stayed in the house. He only left to see me and to go to the counseling sessions. He fought so hard against the urges, the demons that kept trying to make him drink. Michael, in fact, had put himself into a self-imposed exile in order to avoid all temptations.

In one of his visits to our counselor he told her that he had quit his job and things were really bad financially. She suggested he go to see the VA counselor down at City Hall. Perhaps he was eligible for some benefits to help him through this tough time until he was able to get back to work. However, there was only one thing wrong with her suggestion, and that was Michael. Up until now wanted absolutely nothing to do with our government, and with good reason. He looked upon the VA as being a part of the government, so needless to say he was very hesitant about going down there and talking to anyone. So many of our Vietnam vets felt exactly the same way. They simply just wanted to forget.

So it took a lot of talking, a lot of persuading on our counselor's part to try to convince Michael to go see a veteran's representative. Even after Michael was convinced that this was probably his only option right about now, it still took him two more weeks to get down to the office. One day Michael just decided, *Fuck it, I'll go. I know they're not going to do anything for me, but I'll go anyway.*

I went along with him for moral support, and he told the VA representative what he was going through, how he was drinking and desperately trying not to, the programs, the detoxes, everything else that he'd been through, including the counseling, the AA, and how horrible his life was going. He told him also how the tremendous stress from his last job seemed to repeatedly throw him back into the bottle.

Michael said, "From here on out, I am at a loss. I don't know what else to do to stop. I've stuck myself in my mother's home. I try to avoid all stressful situations. I have essentially taken myself out of life. I don't know how much more I can stand or what else I can do to stay sober."

Then the veteran's rep went on to tell Michael, "I'm not the least bit surprised that none of these programs worked for you."

Michael asked him what he meant by that and he said, "You see, my friend, alcohol is not your problem. That's why those programs didn't work for you." He then went on to explain to Michael about what a lot of the Vietnam vets were going through, people similar to him, men who were suffering just like he was, and each and every one of them crawled into a bottle of alcohol or a bottle of pills. It doesn't matter really which, but they crawled into it to escape, to escape the memories, to escape their pain.

"You all fought over there for your lives and to help the Vietnamese people, but what most of you did not realize is the real fight was yet to come when you came back home, the fight for you sanity again, to regain the normal life again. It was almost an impossible dream. Although many men did achieve this, many more did not, many men like you, Michael.

"It takes years for them to realize that they can't hide from themselves. They can't hide from the nightmares no matter how much they drink. When you wake up, they're always there, and this, my friend, is what you need help with, not the alcoholism. What's making you want to drink? It's not your job, not family; it's the horrors that you had to witness in Vietnam, the ones that you have to remember on a daily basis. This is what's keeping you in a bottle and preventing you from truly living.

"You need help from the people that can truly understand you, that can truly identify with you because they've been there, and they know exactly where you are coming from. Just as it takes a recovered alcoholic-turned-counselor to help fellow alcoholics, it takes a fellow veteran who has gotten his life together and who has crawled back out of that bottle. It takes a man like this to be able to help a man like you for that man has truly been in your shoes. These men and only these men can you truly respect and listen to and follow. They are the only ones that will be able to help you now."

Then the VA rep went on to ask Michael, "I see here that you were at the Brockton Detox. You know what a shame that was. You were so close but yet so far. The Brockton VA is only down the street from here, the place where you belonged. As a matter of fact, I'm going to call over there and see if they have a room for you. You can enter into the detox, which is 5 days. Then they have a program which is 30 days, where you will get intense counseling for your specific needs, from people that really know what they're doing and who they're dealing with. This is a place that is tailored specifically for a veteran."

He then got up and walked over to Michael and put his hand on Michael's shoulder and he told him, "I can see you want to get your life going. You need to get your life started after, how many years now, 12? 13? It's time you started living, Michael, and this place will help you start. I promise you that."

Believe me, the irony was not lost on Michael. The very entity that screwed up his life to begin with, the government, was now the only one that would be able to help him regain his life. The veteran's rep made the necessary arrangements and that very night I brought Michael to the Brockton VA. As Michael and I got to the front desk of the Brockton VA, we signed him into the detox.

Michael said to the counselor then, "I don't know why I need to be detoxed. I haven't had a drink in over two weeks."

The counselor said, "It's a rule. Everyone going into our 30-day program has to go through the five days of detox first." I guess the counselor thought Michael was giving him a hard time because he then asked Michael, "Do you really want this?"

Michael said, "Of course I want this. I need this desperately, and I want desperately to get my life back on track. I will do whatever I have to do to achieve this."

As soon as Michael was all signed in and set up, we once again had to say goodbye. We gave each other a long hug and a kiss.

It seemed that was happening all too frequently all through our lives now. It never became any easier, but this one unlike all the other programs that Michael had been in I thought this program was going to truly be able to help him. I thought perhaps seeing that the military is the very thing that screwed him up so badly to start with, now I thought perhaps another branch of the government, the VA—the veterans, would be the only one that could help him. I felt as though he truly was in the right place this time.

My feelings were correct. This was the place he needed to be. They were the only ones that did help him, that were able to help him, because you see, this is the first time he was truly able to completely open up and tell his counselors everything that happened to him in Vietnam. Prior to this he never felt comfortable telling other counselors all of these horror stories because he was afraid of what they would think of him. He was finally able to open up to a person who could truly help him. So he told them everything, all about the night terrors, the flashbacks, and everything else he was experiencing. Michael told me he felt as though a weight had been lifted off of his shoulders.

I then asked him, "Didn't you get anything out of Seacrest the 30 days that you were there? All the group meetings that you had? What did you talk about if you didn't talk about Vietnam?"

He said, "I didn't talk about a lot." He reminded me that all of these other men were doctors, lawyers, and businessmen. "If I had gone into details, great details about Vietnam, half of them probably would have thrown up, and my counselor there really didn't have a clue as to what I was going through." He felt if the men after hearing his story didn't throw up, what they would do is pass judgment on him, so he simply did not feel free to talk. In this case at the VA all of the other men he was with had all gone through similar situations, and they knew exactly how he felt. He told me that he felt very much at home there, and he felt like these other men were his brothers.

My heart felt so good hearing him talk like this. I could see a change was happening already. He was happier than I had ever seen him, even though it was difficult to discuss it. I could actually see that first week that the weight had been lifted off his shoulders, and I could see he was final starting to heal all the wounds that he carried for so many years. He was slowly becoming a new person both in mind and in spirit. I watched his eyes, over time, slowly regain a light of love, a love for life, and that light slowly uplifted both of us. That was our light at the end of this deep, dark tunnel, the tunnel that we were trapped in for so long.

All of this was not easy for Michael. He had to overcome a lot, not only his alcohol addiction but he had to force himself to speak for the first time openly about everything he experienced and all the horrors that he witnessed in

Vietnam. This was not an easy thing for him to do, but he pushed himself and he eventually overcame the fear of judgment because he knew the other men understood exactly how he felt.

Michael went on to tell me about his private sessions with the psychiatrist. He said, "As much as I tried not to, my anger would overcome me when I started discussing certain things that happened to me in Vietnam, the friendly fire incident for one. I became increasingly angry about talking about this to him. Then I went on to tell him about the nightmares and the flashbacks that I was experiencing from this, and how this haunted me on a daily basis, and how he could never seem to get these faces out of his mind. All the faces of all the other soldiers that died there just kept replaying in my mind like a horrifying movie over and over again. The only way I could make them stop was to get drunk."

After many sessions with the psychiatrist and all of the information that Michael shared with him, he was finally diagnosed. Michael's diagnosis was he suffered from severe post-traumatic stress syndrome and depression with overwhelming feelings of guilt and remorse. All of this led to the night terrors and the flashbacks and the anxiety attacks he suffered from.

At the beginning of Michael's recovery at the VA, Michael was like a big ball of raw nerves, and each day that I would visit him, I was never quite sure what to expect. I guess it would all depend on how his psychiatry sessions would go that day and whether he was talking about something particularly bad or something a little bit lighter. I could tell by his mood how that session had gone. Each day it was pretty much a crapshoot. If he were having a bad day I would try my best to lift his spirits and talk about anything but what had gone on in the session.

At the beginning I always felt like I had to have a guarded conversation with him, always leery of saying the wrong thing and setting him off or making him feel worse than he already did. So I always had to choose my words carefully and tried very hard not to bring the outside world in with the complications and troubles the outside world held. Then other days he would be so up and so happy, and I would be thrilled to see him this way. He would be almost euphoric, and as I said, I never knew what to expect. Michael would meet with his psychiatrist on a daily basis while he was there.

After a couple of weeks, the psychiatrist started Michael on some medications. They started him on anti-depressants, anti-anxiety medications, which at first made Michael a little spacey, but I figured better spacey than angry, or worse, getting drunk. Michael was learning a lot in his sessions with the psychiatrist. He was learning how to open up even more, and he began confiding in me even more than he did before. He told me something that he had always been hesitant about telling me before, and that was ever since that friendly fire incident in Vietnam he was always afraid to be responsible, responsible for any other human being. The thought of him holding someone else's life in his hands absolutely, completely terrified him. He told me how that one incident completely changed his life.

After Michael told me all of this, I began to think to myself of that van incident where we could have been killed and then asking him if he was trying to kill me, and then my thoughts of suicide that I was really open with him about. I think it really shocked him, shocked him back into reality, and the reality is you do have to care about other people. You just can't go through life as an island, alone, and the things you do will affect other people whether you want them to or not. I felt like taking my own life because of him, and he almost took mine in that van that night. He realized no matter how hard he might try to avoid being responsible for someone else, there is no way he could. No man is an island and no matter how much you don't want to touch other people's lives, you do.

I truly believe these two incidents really pushed him back into reality, and that is reality. There is no avoiding this, especially if you choose to love a person and accept love from that person, whether you like it or not the reality is you do hold a certain amount of responsibility for your actions and for your treatment toward that other person. I believe these two wake-up calls were just what Michael needed to finally take life seriously again and stop muddling through it in a bottle. I think he realized he could not and did not want to face another tragedy again like losing me to suicide or us dying in a van. Unlike in Vietnam, here he did have control over this part of his life. So, yes, I do believe this was Michael's wake-up call.

Through this period of time I had quite a few chances to speak with Michael's psychiatrist. He met with me as well. He first asked me about my life, and then he would ask me about my life with Michael.

The first question out of his mouth to me after he got a little bit of my past history was, "Are you done with drinking? Are you still drinking?"

I told him, "No, I'm finished, and I'm finished this time for good."

He was very relieved to hear this, and I told him also, "The man that I love is here fighting for his sanity. He's fighting for sobriety, and he's fighting for us. He's fighting for our future together and our life together."

I asked him, "Do you really seriously think I could go out and get drunk after I visit with Michael?"

After I got to know the psychiatrist a little bit better, I began opening up and sharing my thoughts with him about war, particularly Vietnam, and my total lack of understanding war at all. I told him, "Doctor, when you have children, you raise them, you teach them and you protect them, and most importantly you love them. You also teach them how to protect themselves as well as other people. You teach them how to treat other people with kindness, caring and love, and how to be responsible and respect every life, and to always fight for the weaker among us. In short, a parent does his best to turn this little human being into a loving, caring, and responsible adult that may some day make this world a better place for everyone to live in. If you are religious you take them to church," and I explained to him how my grandmother took me. I also told him that Michael was a confirmed Catholic, so he had a religious upbringing as well. Michael and his family would attend church on a regular basis, and what is the first thing a Catholic learns?"

He looked at me kind of with a blank look on his face, and then he said, "Thou shall not kill?"

I said, "Precisely. We teach our children all these very important things, these rules that we expect them to follow, and through their lives we are basically brainwashing them, but that's okay, because it's a good brainwashing. Then all of a sudden one day when they are 18, 19, they are snatched away from us like gypsies stealing a baby in the night and told, 'You must forget everything you were taught now. None of it is important.' They pick these young men up, they teach them how to kill, and then they drop them in the middle of the jungle. Our government just expects all of them to simply forget their life's teachings. Instead of 'Thou shall not kill,' it's 'Kill or be killed.' No more caring, no more love, no more respect for human life."

I then asked the doctor if Michael told him about the first day that he was dropped in the middle of battle and how surreal it all felt to him. How he could not wrap his brain around what was going on, and how he felt he was just being dropped into the middle of some kind of crazy John Wayne movie. All the death, all the killing that Michael had to witness on both sides. His own men that he had to witness being blown apart right in front of him, and then of course our enemies the Vietcong, and the delightful job Michael had collecting body parts for an accurate body count. These are visions that he will never be able to erase from his memories.

Then I asked the doctor, "How in the hell does our government really think our men can now just come back home the same as they were when they left, and resume their lives as if nothing ever happened? We cannot witness such things and simply forget about them. That is exactly what our government expects our soldiers to do, "Suck it up and go on." They were expected to come home and resume their lives where they left off, which is impossible to do because they are simply not the same men as they were when they left. They have changed and changed forever. How on earth does our government expect all these men to slip back into society after seeing what they've seen?"

I reminded him of what Michael told me that there was also another factor that came into play here that made Vietnam very different from World War II and the Korean War and that was the mobility factor. Instead of it taking soldiers three or four days to reach a battle, it would take only a matter of hours if not less. Our men went from battle to battle with very little rest in between, very little time to collect their thoughts and to hold on to what sanity remained. Their brains simply were not given enough time to adequately take in what just had happened to them before they found themselves facing yet more horror, the biggest horror being watching their fellow soldiers die right in front of them and wondering if they were going to be next. A lot of them tried very hard not to think this way, but they could not deny what was unfolding right in front of them and wonder this. Then after all of this, after all the horror, all the shock, they come home to our own people spitting on them and calling them "baby killers" or simply being told "Big deal," like the cab driver's remark to Michael after he had just gotten through telling him where he had just come from.

I do not know how the government expected any of these men to just come back and lead normal lives after all of this with no help, no kind of support system offered to them. The government offered little if any help at all integrating our Vietnam soldiers back into society. All of these men were pretty much left on their own in America to deal with the horror and all the nightmares. It just felt like America tried very hard to forget all about them along with the Vietnam War altogether. But our government was forgetting one very important thing. You see, all of these Vietnam vets were fighters and they did just that. They fought and they fought hard just to get the respect they deserved, but not only for respect but for the honor that they deserved.

Because I was a woman very deeply in love with one of these men, a proud honorable vet, all of this knowledge about our government simply infuriated me. Because of my love for him, I could feel all of his pain, despair, and hopelessness when I lay beside him in bed every night and had to endure the night horrors and the flashbacks right alongside him. Right along with of all of these memories came a huge distrust of our government, and for as long as I live I will never forget Michael's night terrors, the painful screams that would awake me. Try hard as I may, I could not protect him from this. I could not push them away. I could not stop him from hurting. You cannot fight against memories with a gun or a knife. Only words and love can help. I promised Michael as long as he was trying to help himself and trying to stop drinking, I would stand beside him no matter what. I knew with both Michael and me working together we could achieve some sort of normalcy, some sort of normal life and stop this insanity and perhaps have a chance of having a long and happy life with the man that I love.

At this point I had no idea what the future held in store for us. I only knew this. We were both looking at the fight of our lives, for our lives. We had no idea if we were going to win. The only thing that I was sure of at this point in my life is that I loved Michael with every fiber of my being. Even though Michael and I, at this point, had already been together for four years, with him being sober for not long now, I felt as though we were just starting to get to know each other. I felt as though we were starting a new relationship, a new life together. I felt as though we were coming out of the darkness and into the light. For the first time in four years I could truly see the light at the end of the tunnel, and this light was beautiful, the light of hope that shined clearly through the darkness of despair.

Although it was so hard for Michael and so painful to face all of his memories, he was making so much progress in his therapy sessions. I was so proud of him. The psychiatrist went on to tell me with the right balance of medication and therapy he felt Michael would have a good chance for success and a good chance of leading a halfway normal life. They had to work on the right combination of medications, and this sometimes was very difficult to find. It seemed as though they were switching his medications almost on a weekly basis, and with the changing of medications came mood swings, sometimes more depression, and sometimes euphoria. It seemed like it was a crapshoot.

You never really knew what pill was going to do what to him. Then it happened, they found the right combination for Michael and he seemed like a different person. He seemed to have control of himself and of his emotions, and he seemed genuinely happy. This is what we were looking for.

They only came upon this right combination it seemed like at the end of the 30 days. Now Michael was ready to come home, but he was also to meet with his psychiatrist back there three days a week. So Michael's schedule was to continue taking all the medications that the psychiatrist had prescribed and seeing him three days a week, but now would come the real test, and that was living in the real world again and facing all of life's aggravations. Was he going to be able to remain sober through all of this or not? In the meantime I quit my cocktail waitress job. I began thinking about it, and the more I thought about serving people alcohol, the less appropriate I thought it was for this time in my life, when I was so desperately trying to push alcohol out of it. I knew how happy my decision would make Michael.

Thankfully I found another job rather quickly in the next town over. It was a machine operator's job. I was working putting stickpins together, and it was a sit-down job, so I wasn't totally exhausted at the end of the day. The pay wasn't great but it suited my purposes for this moment even though it had to have been the most boring job I had ever had in my life. I was bored to tears every day.

After a few days out of the VA Michael began applying for factory work. He must have put an application in every factory around our town. There were few jobs for women and even fewer for men. The many factories that had sustained our town had moved either to another state or another country, and Michael was becoming increasingly more desperate to find employment.

A month and a half passed by, and still no job. Then one day while Michael was fishing he was talking to another man who told him about a farm that was hiring.

Michael said, "Farm? I've never worked on a farm."

The man said, "You don't have to have a lot of experience. It's taking care of the chickens." There was a large chicken farm in the next town over that was looking for help.

Michael thought about it for a while, and he said, "Well, this will probably be a good idea. It's low stress." Having a low-stress job was very, very important to Michael right now, because along with the stress came the desire to drink to stop the stress. So Michael thought for now anyway, this would be a good job for him. He went and applied and spoke to the gentleman that owned the chicken farm, and they hired him immediately. Michael would be in charge of the feeding machine. There were thousands of chickens, and then the collection of eggs at the end of each day. The farm itself housed thousands of chickens but Michael would be in charge of only 600 of them. The pay was not that great to start off with, but Michael thought, *It's an honest living, and the stress level is minimal.*

Being able to make an honest living to Michael was everything because Michael was a man of honor and being honorable was very important to him. He always thought, *To live life without honor a man might as well be dead.* Michael, in fact, was one of the most truthful people I had ever met in my life. He told me early on in our relationship how much he hated liars. Another thing we had in common.

Michael was a good man, a man of integrity. He had more integrity than anyone else I had met in my life, and as far as what Michael felt about being truthful, his philosophy on this was, "If you don't want to know the truth, then don't ask," because he would always speak it.

This ironically was also my father's position on the subject. He also hated liars, and as screwed as he was, I can honestly say he never lied to me. He would tell me, "Kyra, never trust a liar," and my father also used to say, "I would rather lie down beside a murderer or a thief. At least you know what they are going to do. A liar you never know, and a liar is never to be trusted." Through my own experiences in life, I had found this to be true. The first time I would catch a friend in a lie, I would feel betrayed like that bond of trust had been broken. Maybe this is why Michael and I had always been so painfully honest with one another, telling things that we knew the other one didn't want to hear, but it was the truth. We could live with the truth. We couldn't live with lies, and you could never build a loving relationship on them. When I found Michael, I found the two most important traits any human being could have and that is honesty and honor. These perhaps were the two personality traits that I first fell in love with, the reason I fell in love with him. Our love now was beginning to grow stronger with every passing day.

We had both remained sober now for six months, and it felt rather strange to me because even though we had now been together for nearly five years, I felt as though I was meeting him for the first time. We were getting to know each other all over again, this time without the fog of alcohol, and I was so happy. Our relationship was blossoming like a beautiful flower, a flower that would only grow stronger with each passing day. At this point in our relationship it seemed I would learn something new about Michael every day.

It was during this time that I not only loved Michael, but I really liked him, too. I cherished every moment that we spent together. He was truly my soul mate and my best friend, and I felt there was nothing that I could not tell him. We were reaching a point in our relationship where I would know what he was going to do even before he did it. I even knew sometimes what he was going to say before he said it. It is very difficult to put it into words. How can you even begin to describe being that close to another person and feeling so completely a part of someone else? This feeling that we were feeling was just so good and so right. It made us feel like together there was nothing we could not do in this world. We knew as long as we stayed sober, the sky was the limit.

We did everything together—camping, swimming, and fishing. We would go on long walks in the woods until we would come upon a clearing where we would sit and talk for hours. We would even work on the van together. At one point I remember visiting with my mother and my sister April and explaining the fine art of how to gap a spark plug. I believe I was the only woman in the family that could actually give my own car a tune up. I don't believe April or Amber even knew what a spark plug, but Michael not only taught me about cars and how to give a really good tune up, but he taught me so much more. He taught me about life and about love.

Michael and I worked so well together, side by side. He was like an extension of me, and together as long as we stayed sober, there was nothing in this world that we would not be able to accomplish. As long as we stayed sober, we were a team, a team to be reckoned with. You see, we were also both fighters and neither one of us was willing to give up on the other.

A year now has passed, a year of sobriety for both Michael and me, a year of rediscovering each other and our love flourishing. In this year Michael's love for guns was reborn. You see he had always had a gun before the service. When he was a young boy he used to go hunting for pheasant in the back woods, and even though he lost the desire to kill anything, target shooting he thought would be a lot of fun for us to get into. A hobby that he had always loved as a child, he wished to introduce to me and share this with me just as he shared everything else in his life with me.

I will never forget the first time Michael and I went out target shooting. Michael had just bought a new shotgun, and we went to the sand pits to try it out. Michael began setting up eight cans on a wooden fence. He then proceeded to load the shotgun, and then much to my surprise he handed it to me. Then he came up from behind me and held my arms as I held the gun, and he showed me how to pull the trigger and how tight to hold onto it so that the kick from the gun would not send me flying onto my butt. Of course, the first shot I missed completely and the second shot, I didn't do much better. However, with much amazement on my part, on the third shot I hit the target dead on. With Michael standing behind me, helping me hold the gun, we went right down the line and hit can after can. It was a lot of fun.

Next was his turn, and of course, his being as experienced as he was, he hit the first can straight out and then right down the line. I stood there watching him, watching his aim and how he handled the gun, and for a moment it brought me back to one of his nightmares. I could picture him standing in the middle of the jungle catching a Viet Cong in one of the cross hairs, and at that very moment, I could actually visualize all of this.

A strange look must have come over my face as I was standing there thinking this, because he asked me, "Kyra, what's the matter?"

I just replied, "Nothing." I knew for the first time out shooting again, things like that must have crossed his mind as well, but neither one of us said anything. I desperately tried to block these thoughts from my mind so that Michael and I could just enjoy the day. It was now my turn again to shoot, and while holding the gun I realized just what a powerful weapon this was, a weapon that can take someone's life in a heartbeat. I became surprisingly good at this, surprisingly fast. This time on my own shooting I knocked out six cans out of eight, as Michael stood there with his mouth hanging open in amazement.

He asked me, "Are you sure you never fired a gun before?"

I said, "I'm sure." I don't know. Maybe this was one good thing that I inherited from my father. The only good thing I ever did. He was a sharp shooter when he was in the military in World War II, so maybe I just had a natural eye for it. I don't know.

Then it was Michael's turn again and as he stood there holding the gun ready to take his shot, he looked at me and smiled and he said, "Kyra, there is something I need to say, and I know it's going to sound really strange, but I need to say it anyway because it's what I feel. I feel like you are more than just my love. Sometimes I feel like you're my little sister. We are so close, and I have never shared my emotions and my heart with anyone else the way I share them with you. Only siblings share what we have shared, our deepest darkest secrets, secrets that we would be too ashamed or too afraid to tell anyone else."

He looked at me and smiled again, and he said, "I told you it was going to sound strange. It is just something I felt as though I had to tell you. I just feel so close to you, a feeling that goes beyond love. It's something else altogether, and I have never felt this before. This feeling that I have toward you is a little strange, but it's very good."

I smiled back at Michael, and I told him, "I know exactly what you mean. Sometimes I feel that you're like a big brother to me, and I have never been closer to another human being in my life than I am to you, my love."

As time passed by these feelings would grow even stronger. Neither one of us wanted these feelings to ever end, and if they did I think we would surely have died.

Michael had been working on the chicken farm for over a year when he decided it was time to move on. The more sobriety he had under his belt the stronger he felt. He put in an application at Smithville College for grounds crew and was hired immediately. It was physically tiring work, but again the most important thing was that it was low stress. His body would be sore every night, but I would always be there with a back rub for him. I would rub his back until he drifted off to sleep. I would always love this close time together. It seemed like through all of my loving back rubs every night, his therapy sessions twice a week, the medication that he was on, and my love for him, they were all a combination that would help keep his nightmares, his night terrors, and his flashbacks at bay. Everything was working well in combination. He seemed to really be making it this time. He was staying sober now with no problem (both of us were), and I thought to myself, this last time away from me, the last time he was at the 30-day program at the VA would be the last time that we would be separated. Thank God, Michael had one more important thing on his side and that was his own character. Michael was a very strong person and he never gave up. He was in every sense of the word a fighter. The road to sobriety for him was rocky and very hard, but he finally did it.

It was 1983 when Michael took his last drink of alcohol. Exactly fourteen years had passed by since he took his first step off of the plane that brought him home from Vietnam. Fourteen years of his life wasted and fourteen years he will never regain. Now the rest was up to us. The rest of our lives we have ahead of us, and we could not make any more mistakes. We could not waste one more day.

The year now was 1985 and we had been together for seven years. With everything we had in common and all our hobbies and everything we loved doing together, we never ran out of ideas on how to have fun and enjoy every moment. Our love and passion for one another just grew stronger by the day. It was so perfect, and some days I could hardly believe that we knew such happiness. Sometimes it didn't even seem real but more like a dream, a dream that I would never want to wake up from. It seemed like while all our other friends, the couples that we knew and had partied with for so many years were all breaking up and getting divorced, Michael and I just grew closer and closer.

It was now early 1985 and Michael decided to sell the van. He explained to me why. He said, "We are starting a new life now, and I wanted a brand-new car to go along with it." Michael then told me, "That old van just holds so many bad memories, I really won't miss it one bit."

Michael and I then began looking at new cars but they were a little pricey and out of our price range, so we had to settle for a secondhand one. That was okay because it was still new to us. Michael just hated the thought of buying a new car right off the lot anyway. He told me the damn thing depreciates drastically as soon as you hit the pavement. He said, "Right now it would be a ridiculous investment for us." I had to agree. We were trying to get money together to get an apartment and to start our new life together, so the money we had needed to be spent elsewhere rather than on a car. Michael found a really nice low-mileage, tan, Cutlass Supreme. It ran like a dream and Michael and I were both happy with it. Michael knew how to pick out a good used car. He knew what to look for because he always did his own work on all his cars. All of his cars ran beautifully. This knowledge he passed down to me. He taught me how to maintain my own car.

Just as in every other aspect in our life, we were a team. We stood side by side through life, through the good and the bad. It seemed like at this time in our lives, luck was really shining on us. I also made a job change to a factory that was right in our city. This job paid twice as much as the one I had left. It was a glass factory called The Glassworks where I would be on the assembly line mainly packing dinner plate settings and other glass products as well.

Unfortunately for me along with this job came again a lot of heavy lifting. These boxes of dishes weighed a ton, but I knew to take it slow, and be very careful for my back. The money that I would be making from this job, and that Michael made from his combined was a really good income. So Michael and I decided to start looking for our own apartment again.

We quickly discovered though along with the shortage of jobs in our area, there was also a shortage of really good decent apartments so it would take us awhile to find one that we really liked. This took us over two months, but we finally found one, one that both of us liked. It was a complex called Garden Place, and in the complex there was a total of five buildings. Each building housed twenty-four apartments, and our new apartment was on the bottom floor toward the front of the building. It was a beautiful two-bedroom apartment with wall-to-wall carpet, air-conditioned, dishwasher and laundry room facilities right down the hallway. Michael and I were thrilled to have found this. It also had a security system where you would have to buzz someone in the main entrance. Along with all of these attractive features, this apartment had way out in the back behind all the buildings a beautiful, huge, built-in swimming pool for all the residents. Michael and I both knew as soon as we saw the pool that we certainly would be making good use of this during the long hot summers.

Okay, now that we found our beautiful apartment, we had to furnish it. So the next step was going furniture shopping. Both of us were hit with sticker shock. My God, the price of brand-new furniture was through the roof. It was almost as ridiculous as that new car, but we sucked it up and went for it. After all you can't live without furniture.

As Michael and I stood there in the middle of the furniture store looking at all the new styles and trying to decide what we were going to get, Michael told me he wanted us to have a nice home and he wanted us to start our new lives together with something nice. We picked out a really nice three-piece living room set, a maple dinette set for the kitchen, and Michael really is the one who picked out the bedroom set on his own. He said, "This is so beautiful. I want to give this to you, Kyra." It was a maple canon-ball bed with matching dressers. The large long dresser would be mine. It had a beautiful mirror on the back with shelves on both sides of the mirror. His dresser was tall with many drawers. All pieces had the beautiful carvings and shiny finishes. It was simply beautiful. In this bed I knew we were going to spend many, many happy years.

Two weeks later we were all moved in. Everything was so beautiful—the apartment, the new furniture—everything. It was all fresh and new, just like mine and Michael's life together. This was our new beginning, and as I sit here today as I close my eyes and try really hard, I can remember even the smell of the fresh paint on the walls and the way the new furniture smelled so clean and so good. This was the happiest I had ever been in my life.

Our first night in our brand-new apartment was incredible, and I wanted something very special for our first night's dinner in our brand-new apartment. I set up a candle-lit dinner. We had sea scallops, baked potato, and a green salad. This dinner was one of Michael's favorites. After this romantic dinner Michael and I went and sat on our brand-new couch to watch some TV. As we sat there he held me in his arms. Watching TV with Michael holding me on the couch would not be the end of our very special evening, our first evening in our new apartment. I had a few more surprises up my sleeve for Michael, but while still in Michael's arms on the couch, he leaned over to me and looked deeply and lovingly into my eyes. Our lips came together in a passionate kiss. His lips moved from my lips to my neck, and as he began caressing my breasts I suggested to him that we move this into our bedroom.

Once we were both in our bedroom, I told Michael to wait here. I had another surprise for him. Ten minutes later I would emerge out of the bathroom wearing nothing but gumdrops. I then went to our bedroom and struck a pose. Michael sat there on the edge of our bed with his mouth hanging open. I then slowly walked over to him, his eyes growing wider with each step I took. I stood in front of him holding his face in my hand. He smiled from ear to ear at me, and then our lips met in a long passionate kiss. I then began kissing his neck and nibbling on his ear.

He threw me onto the bed, and I told him, "Be careful; you just knocked off a couple of gumdrops."

He looked me in the eyes, and he said, "You know, you really are my Baby Doll, and I love you so much."

I told him, "I love you, too, babe."

He began kissing my neck slowly working his way down covering every inch of me with a kiss. Then he began licking off each and every one of the gumdrops, one by one. I think it must have been around the seventh or eighth gumdrop that he had eaten when he looked up at me and said, "Baby Doll, you are just so beautiful and so sexy, and you know how much I love you, but please the next time could you find another candy that doesn't take so long to eat? Perhaps M&Ms!"

At this point we both began to laugh, but even through the laughter the passion between us was not lost. The intensity of the love and the passion that we felt for one another each time and every time we made love only grew more intense over the years and more powerful. There just are no words for me to adequately describe the true intensity of all of these emotions when you are sober. How very different love feels. How very different life feels when you are sober, because only when you are sober are you truly able to feel every kiss, every touch, and every emotion so much more deeply than you ever could when you were drinking. The feeling is simply amazing and quite overwhelming at times.

This would turn out to be a night that neither Michael nor I would ever forget. After he finished with all the gumdrops we made passionate love. Our first night in our new apartment was so memorable. Everything just went absolutely perfect.

As the days and weeks and moths passed by, we were so happy. Michael continued with his medication and meeting with his psychiatrist twice a week, and most of the time I would accompany him. More often than not I would speak with the psychiatrist myself. His questions would always be mainly the same: How is Michael doing, and how were we doing in our relationship and in our new apartment? I would tell him the truth; things were great.

At one of these sessions the psychiatrist asked me if Michael and I socialized very much. I explained to him, "No, we don't, because most of our friends are still drinking. The dearest friends that we have we no longer feel comfortable around, and none of them seem to want to stop drinking. They all seem to be happy living the way they are, so who are Michael and I to come in and criticize what seems to be working for them? That kind of leaves us out of the loop and with very little social life. Michael and I enjoy just being together," and as I told him we had a lot of hobbies and we were always keeping busy. Of course, both of us were working full-time jobs as well, so actually it left very little time for socializing anyway.

The psychiatrist's reply was, "Well, so long as both of you are happy with this, that's all that really matters."

It was now quickly approaching the 4th of July, and the psychiatrist asked Michael and me if we had any plans or any celebrations to go to. We told him,

"Yes, as a matter of fact we were planning to head over to the high school and watch the fireworks that they had there every year."

The doctor said, "That's good. It sounds like fun."

A couple of days later 4th of July was here. Michael and I headed over to the Festival and both of us had a lot of fun. We ate hot dogs and hamburgers and listened to some music. The only bad thing about that day was that it was extremely hot, but I guess that's to be expected for the 4th of July.

It was becoming dusk now and Michael and I went over to the fried dough stand and got us some, and then over to the lemonade stand and got ourselves some frozen lemonade. We then began scoping out a good place to sit to watch the fireworks. We found a perfect spot in between two trees. It provided the shade that we needed to cool off a little bit as the sun was still there, the heat was still there, and it seemed to be taking forever for the sun to d sappear over the horizon. The sunset that night was so beautiful. It looked like a big fireball disappearing slowly into the horizon. With the sun disappearing, the sky slowly turned from light blue to black with just a few twinkling stars in the sky, until finally it was dark enough for them to start the firework display.

Michael and I sat there with our arms around each other lear ing back and resting. I remember the first firework. It was beautiful. It was a flower burst of colors, red and oranges and yellows, but I quickly became distracted when I could feel Michael's body jolting and this was something he never did before. We had seen fireworks before, but then it dawned on me he was drinking at all of those times, so this would be the first time that we would see the fireworks together sober. I was surprised, although maybe I shouldn't have been, with his reaction, how he was startled and upset by the sound. Then I realized the sounds sound very much like mortar rounds. I think he was as surprised as I was to have this reaction.

After the first jolt, the first fireworks, he said nothing to me, and I said nothing to him. When the second firework exploded in the sky, he shook yet again. I could feel the tremor of his body, and still he said nothing to me, but I could see the agony he was experiencing sitting there. With every tremor my heart broke for him. I knew I had to get him out of there but I also knew he wouldn't leave because he would not want to spoil my good time. I didn't care, I wasn't having a good time if he was sitting there being traumatized, so I quickly began thinking of an excuse I could use to get out of there. I decided I had to lie to him even though I didn't want to, and I hated to.

I turned to him, and I told him, "Michael, I have to go home right now or I'm going to be sick right here. I guess it's the combination of the heat and the hot dogs, hamburgers and fried dough. I don't know, but if I don't get out of here now I'm going to throw up." He quickly agreed, and we left for home.

Because I wasn't really sick, later on that night I began trying to make love to him, and he looked at me and he said, "That was a quick recovery."

I remember just smiling at him and saying, "Yeah, I know. I guess I just needed to get out of the heat."

After we made love that night I just lay there in his arms. After a few moments we began to talk. I said to him, "It is really odd how fireworks sound just like mortar rounds, don't they."

He looked at me and he said, "How the hell did you know that?"

"I said, "Well, it doesn't take a genius to figure it out, and I've seen enough movies in my life to know."

He looked at me and he said, "You knew then how I was feeling."

Then I told him, "Michael, I felt your body tremble with each and every firework's explosion. How could I not know how you felt?"

He said, "I didn't realize that you were picking up on my emotions at that time."

I said, "Of course I was. Michael, you and I are so close I can feel your pain. I know when you're hurting, because I then hurt too, and thank God I can." Then I asked him, "Why in the hell did you not say anything to me? Why did you just sit there putting yourself through this without saying a word to me, and it was just as I suspected?"

He told me, "I didn't want to ruin your evening." He said, "We don't really get out much, and I wanted you to have fun today."

I told him, "How could I possibly have fun when you are sitting beside me being traumatized like that? The next time anything like that happens, please let me know, if I don't pick up on it. I don't care if you think you're spoiling my fun. You're more important."

He promised me that night that he would never try to hide anything like that from me again. He promised me that if he were ever in pain like that again, he would let me know. I then realized trying hard as we did, we would never just be a normal couple. We would always need to be vigilant and be careful when we made plans to go anywhere or to do anything. I would never want to put Michael in that particular situation again where he was being traumatized. So that meant having to think before we acted upon any kind of invitation or made future plans for entertainment. Having a father who was in the military, I had learned early in life about just how delicate a vet's nerves can be and how easily they can be startled. Now with Michael, I tried very hard to avoid making sudden loud noises and never, ever sneak up behind him. In other words I tried my hardest to keep a quiet, peaceful household because I realized then pretty much everything would go smoothly.

On the other hand there is one thing Michael and I would love to do, and it was anything but peaceful, and that was play jokes on one another. We loved pulling pranks so much so it was starting to become a sick little pastime for us, but it was always in good fun.

Looking back now on one of the pranks Michael played on me, and this one had to be the worst he ever did. It was one day just before the fall in 1985. I had taken the day off of work and planned to spend my day by the pool because I realized this was probably the last day I would be able to do this before winter came. So I just wanted this one day, one day to do nothing, and one day just for me, for myself.

That morning Michael and I woke up, and I told him my plan.

He replied, "I don't get a day off; why should you?"

I then suggested that he call in sick and take a day off and lie beside me by the pool. He said, "No, I don't think so." I reminded him that he hadn't taken any days off since he started, but it didn't make any difference. He went to work anyway.

In a couple of hours after Michael left for work I headed out to the pool. I did feel a little bit guilty. After all, Michael was working hard, and I was just out there hardly working, or should I say working on my tan. I stayed out at the pool until about 2 o'clock, swimming and sunbathing. I was beginning to get a little burned and knew I had to start supper anyway, so I headed back toward our apartment.

I no sooner walked through the door when the phone rang. It was Michael at the other end, and he asked me a rather strange question, "Where have you been all day?"

I told him, "You knew where I was. I was over by the pool."

He said, "Oh, yes, I forgot." He then went on to tell me he wasn't thinking too clearly because of all the medication the hospital had just given him for the pain.

I yelled out, "The pain! What pain?"

He then told me he had an accident at work and had been at the hospital most of the day trying to reach me on the phone.

I then yelled, "You're in the hospital?"

He said, "Yes." Then he went on to tell me he wouldn't have bothered calling the house repeatedly if he had remembered that I was going to be sitting out by the pool all day.

I then tried to get out of him what had happened. He then told me he had an accident with the riding lawnmower, and he had lost two of his fingers. It happened shortly after he began work that morning.

I instantly felt my stomach coming up in my throat, and my heart sank into my knees. I began crying. I felt so horrible. Here I was sitting by the pool all day while the man I loved was sitting in the hospital being operated on.

When I began crying Michael realized he had gone too far with this joke. As I stood there holding the phone, sobbing, he yelled at me, "Kyra, it's just a joke, I'm joking. It's not real. Baby Doll, I'm just kidding," he kept repeating over and over again.

I screamed into the phone, "What!" and then I proceeded to call him a son of a bitch and told him he almost gave me a heart attack. At this point I was still crying, but now it was for a different reason. Not because I felt bad, but because I was furious and quite frankly wanted to kill him. I then began screaming at him over the phone, "You just wait until you get home. You are going to be slapped like you have never been slapped before in your life!"

Michael just kept repeating, "Baby Doll, I'm sorry, I'm sorry!"

I said, "Not yet you're not, but you are about to be." I was so mad at him this day.

I could count on one hand how many arguments Michael and I had, but this was most definitely one of them, and it was one of the worst. Michael and I hardly ever got mad at each other. All there was between us was love, so when we felt anger toward one another, it was so odd and it felt so wrong and weird. As I stated, I could count on one hand how many arguments we had, and this was by far without a doubt the worst practical joke he had played on me or would ever play on me again.

This night Michael was very late getting home. He did not dare come home until he knew for sure I had had enough time to cool down which was only just before bedtime. I think he spent the rest of the afternoon hiding over his mother's house because I was in bed by the time he came home, or should I say sneaking back into our apartment. I could hear him from our bedroom opening up the front door very quietly using his key, and then I heard him tiptoeing into the bathroom before coming to bed. I could hear him standing beside our bed in the dark quietly getting undressed and then slipping his sneaky little body between the sheets just like a little weasel.

I lay there facing the wall waiting until he became very relaxed and then I spoke which surprised the hell out of him because he thought I had been sleeping. After he realized I was awake and before I could say another word, he moved close to me which was probably a stupid move on his part. He leaned over and tried to give me a hug. I pushed him back and said, "Are you out of your fucking mind?" and I yelled at him, "Don't even touch me right now. I am so furious at you." I told him, "You know what this means."

He said, "What?"

"Payback, my love, and payback is a bitch, and now it is my turn to play a joke on your ass, but first I have to think long and hard. You won't see it coming, and you will have no idea what it is going to be, but I guarantee one thing, my Teddy Bear, it's going to be a doozie. Watch out," and then I said, "Good night. I love you."

He said one last time, "I'm sorry, Baby Doll, and I love you, too."

The next morning I thought to myself, *What can I do to top this last practical joke he played on me, this horrifying practical joke he played on me? What can I possibly do to top it?* Just as I sat there thinking of all the horrible things I could do to him, all of a sudden dawned on me. I smiled and said to myself, *I don't have to do anything. His torture will be anticipation. I'll let him walk around for the next two weeks wondering, 'Is today going to be the day when she is going to get me back, and what will she do?'* That was better than anything I could think up.

This proved to be so true. For the following two weeks I watched him every day slowly open that cabinet door waiting for something to jump out at him, checking his side of the bed every night for tacks, right down to smelling his shampoo each and every time before he used it to make sure I didn't replace it with Nair (hair remover). Every time I caught him doing one of these things, I just turned around and chuckled to myself, although I have to say I was tempted in one situation to add a little bit of shaved Ex-Lax to the hot fudge sundae that I made him one night, but I resisted the urge. I was just having too much fun watching him every day flinch and twist at certain things, but I knew two weeks was long enough. It was time for it to end.

That night I sat him down, and I explained to him everything about what I was doing and that I realized I didn't have to do anything at all. He in fact was torturing himself for two weeks. I was just standing by and enjoying it. I could tell he was torn between relief and anger himself, anger over being so easily sucked in to believing something horrible was going to happen at any moment. It was this day that we swore to one another that we would play no more practical jokes. Enough was enough, and that last one was way over the edge. He admitted that, and he again apologized.

Later on that evening we were sitting on the couch watching television, Michael had his arm around me and we were very relaxed and very happy again. Michael then sat up to blow his nose. He pulled his handkerchief out of his back pocket where he would always keep one, and I saw that little piece dangling from his handkerchief, a little corner. I don't know, the devil made me do it is all I can say, all I could think of, but for some reason I couldn't resist. I pulled the handkerchief from his hands. He then blew his nose into his hands, and as he sat there with mucous dripping from his fingers, he looked over at me and he said, "I thought we had called a truce."

I told him, "I know; I know. I don't know what made me do it."

Michael then leaned over to me and tried to wipe his hands off on my shirt. I quickly jumped up from the couch. Michael then began chasing me all around the apartment with his mucous-covered fingers. Thank God I was able to make it to the bathroom in time to lock the door where I remained for the next half hour.

I came out of the bathroom waving a white towel, signifying the white flag of truce and that I gave up. We both stood there in the hallway laughing hysterically at one another, and I am happy to say, things after that returned back to normal in our happy little home.

The date now was October the 5th, just two weeks before Michael's birthday, and it began like every other day. Michael and I both got up in the morning and went off to work. When I arrived at work they told me today that we would be packing crystal dinner bells to be shipped out for the quickly approaching holidays. I would say it was maybe three or four hours into my shift and the day so far had been going fine when all of a sudden I picked up one of the bells to put into the package and it exploded like a little bomb in the middle of my hand. I saw it and I heard it. I received a huge gash right in the middle of my palm.

It seemed as though the dinner bell was blown too thin and simply the heat of my hand just made it pop as I picked it up. I dropped on my workbench the remaining glass that was in my hand, and I looked down to see blood gushing out of my palm. I couldn't believe this was happening to me. I didn't squeeze the dinner bell, I simply held it in the palm of my hand, nestling it, as I would pack it into its box. I applied no pressure to it so I couldn't imagine how it could just pop like that. It wasn't until later I would found out it was defective which is why it happened. The blood was just pumping out of this huge gash. Before I knew it I was standing in a puddle of my own blood. The foreman came running over and rushed me into the ladies' room where he began applying pressure to try to stop the bleeding, but it did not stop. All he could do was wrap it up the best he could and get me to the hospital.

Although it only took a little over five minutes to get to the hospital, I was feeling faint. I had lost that much blood. Once in the Emergency Room they saw me right away. They began soaking my hand to make sure all the glass crystal particles were out of it. The doctor then came in and sutured my hand. It took almost twenty stitches to completely close the cut, and believe me when I say, it hurt like hell. Up to this point I had never had stitches in my life, and I really wished to hell I wasn't getting them now.

The nurse then came in to bandage the rest up, and she told me because of the medication for the pain that they had to give me, I could not drive home. I told her I had planned to take a cab from the hospital back to work and get my car and go home, but she said, "No, you can't do that."

She then asked me, "Don't you have anyone that you can call to come and pick you up?"

I said, "Yes, my boyfriend."

I then told her he wasn't home yet, but I knew he'd be arriving there within an hour or so. Then I began thinking to myself, *How can I possibly call Michael and actually get him to believe my story knowing what happened the last time a prank was played, the prank he played on me?* I thought for sure he would just think I was trying to pull something back on him even though we had come to a truce, but I knew I had to try anyway. Realizing what Michael's reaction was going to be, I then decided to use the phone nearby one of the doctors so that they could confirm my story.

I waited until the time I knew Michael would be arriving home, and I called. As I was explaining to him everything that happened to me, I just kept hearing his practical joke ringing over in my ears, and I realized he thought I was so full of shit. He allowed me to finish my tale of woe, my storytelling before he commented.

I told him, "Michael, just come and pick me up at the hospital."

Before I could say another word he started laughing hysterically and said, "Baby Doll, haven't we been here and done this before?" He then told me, "Please, just get your ass home and stop playing around." Then he hung up the phone on me.

I couldn't frickin' believe it. I'm standing there with my hand throbbing listening to him laughing at me, and then he hangs up on me. I could have killed him. I just stood there with a blank look on my face holding a dead phone. I turned and looked at one of the doctors, and I asked him if he could please redial the phone for me and tell my boyfriend where I was and that he really must come and pick me up. The doctor looked at me as if I had two heads. He probably couldn't believe my boyfriend didn't believe me, and I really didn't know him well enough to get into details about our relationship and the pranks, so many pranks that we had pulled on one another in the past. He dialed the phone for me and Michael answered. I told Michael, I will put the doctor on the line and he will tell you the truth and please believe him. Michael thinking all along of course that I'm still pulling this prank on him didn't expect to hear a doctor's voice at the other end. He was completely shocked and horrified when he did. The doctor explained to him that he had to pick me up from the hospital because I wasn't allowed to drive.

Boy, did I have a cold slap in the face of reality this day. I saw what could happen when people play jokes and pranks on one another. When you really want someone to hear you, to believe you, they won't. That's the dangerous part of pulling pranks, and this only stood to reinforce our commitment to one another that we would not play anymore pranks or jokes on one another. After the doctor finished speaking to Michael, he then handed me the phone and Michael apologized to me up and down. He felt absolutely horrible for not believing me.

I told him, "How could you? This would have been almost a perfect setup. It was almost exactly what you told me, short of losing two fingers. I don't blame you, Michael, I expected it."

Michael then immediately drove to the hospital to pick me up. When he came into the Emergency Room and he saw me sitting there waiting for him, he came up to me and gave me a huge hug and told me how much he loved me and he was so sorry.

Then he thought to himself he said, "These doctors must all think I'm crazy."

Michael then helped me out to the car and we drove home.

CHAPTER SIX

That night it was impossible to sleep. The pain was so bad. My hand was throbbing all night like a huge toothache. I felt as though someone had smashed me right in the palm with a sledgehammer. It was so stiff and sore. I would not be able to return back to work for two weeks until I had the stitches removed, and believe me when I say these were the longest two weeks of my life. I was going stir crazy just sitting around the apartment, and even though I was in pain, I couldn't just stand sitting there all day. I had to do something. I tried cleaning the best I could with one hand, and I had to go slow, so this took up a good portion of my day. I just couldn't wait for those two weeks to pass by so I could get back to my normal life again. I realized Michael's birthday was right around the corner, only a couple of days away now. I wanted to do something special for him. Lord knows, I had the time.

I remembered Michael pointing out this pocket watch he saw in a jewelry store and how he would really like to have it. Although he always wore a wristwatch, he really wanted to switch to this pocket watch, so I thought this would make the perfect birthday gift. The next day I went to the jewelry store where we saw it, and I purchased it. On the cover of the pocket watch I had his initials engraved and on the inside cover I had my feelings for him engraved which were "*All my love until the end of time, your Baby Doll,*" and this was truly how I felt. It was a beautiful gold, shiny, almost antique-looking watch. It was beautiful. I had the jeweler wrap it in beautiful gold wrapping with a big gold bow on the top.

Two days after this was his birthday, and while he was at work I worked all day on the perfect dinner for him. In between I ran out and got his birthday cake, chocolate, his favorite. I picked up twenty balloons and decorated the whole apartment with them and streamers. When he got home from work that day on his birthday, he was so surprised. As I could hear his key turning in the door, I greeted him as soon as he opened it with a huge hug and the longest, most passionate kiss. I said to him, "Happy Birthday, Teddy Bear." He told me how great the apartment looked and that he was amazed I did all of this with one hand. He later told me he was really surprised because of the condition my hand was in.

"I thought you were in too much pain to be doing all this work," he said.

I told him, "Honey, I would never forget your birthday no matter what else was going on in our lives. This is your special day and my lucky day, because this is the day you came into the world. This was at least something positive, something that took my mind off of the pain in my hand."

He was so thrilled with his birthday dinner, which consisted of a two-inch-thick New York sirloin steak, baked potato, corn on the cob, and a huge green salad. It was a romantic candle-lit dinner. Then of course we had the birthday cake for desert.

This whole night was turning out to be absolutely perfect, and I so loved making Michael happy. After dinner we went into the living room and cuddled up on the couch together, and that is where I handed him his birthday gift. He proceeded to open it up, and his eyes lit right up. He was so surprised.

He told me, "Kyra, I didn't even realize that you were paying attention when I pointed this out in the jewelry store that day."

I told him, "I pay attention to everything you say, even though it may seem like sometimes I don't. I thought you knew that."

He said, "Well, I do now." Michael then proceeded to take the watch out of the box. He saw the engraving, his initials on the front, and he said how beautiful that was.

"You haven't seen anything yet," I said. "Open it up."

When he read the engraving, he almost cried.

I told him, "Honey, that's how I truly feel. That's my heart speaking. You do have my love until the end of time."

He then held my face in his hands and our lips came together in a passionate kiss. He then began caressing my neck, moving down to my breasts, and removing my shirt. We made love right there on the couch.

That night like many other nights, we didn't even make it into the bedroom. We would often find ourselves just so overcome with the passion that we felt toward one another, it would simply overtake. Whenever Michael and I would make love, I would never feel so alive as I did at that very moment, but yet so close to death as well. I could feel my heart beating faster and faster. The feeling was so intense I felt like my heart was just going to burst inside of my chest. At that moment I would gladly die right there in his arms. I could not even imagine a better way to leave this earth. With Michael I had found my other half, and my other half of my heart which he held in his hands. I have found that one love, that one love that makes you whole. If you were lucky enough in life to actually find another person that completes you so perfectly, you would never want to continue with your life without him. If you were to lose this in your life now after knowing this feeling, your heart might just as well stop beating.

After his birthday we would have yet another celebration. November the 4th would be our seventh anniversary, and this would only be two weeks away. I remember thinking how amazing this was, seven years together, and our love and our passion had not diminished one single bit. It had only grown stronger. We found that we were as attracted to one another today as we were the first day that we laid eyes on each other. When our eyes first met and that passion was lit, we never grew tired of one another, looking at each other, and each time we made love, it was just more passionate than the last and much more intense.

Our close relationship made us stronger in both love and in life. We were always lifting each other up spiritually and mentally. We truly were a team in every sense of the word. When one would grow tired, the other one would pick up the slack. I never thought in my life that I would be lucky enough to find someone like Michael, someone I knew I could count on through anything with no questions asked. Up until the time that I met Michael, my life had not been very lucky or very happy. There are some days I really can't believe that this was all true that this was all real and that Michael was mine. That he was mine, and I was his, all of me. Mind, body, and soul he owned them all.

In between his birthday and our anniversary, just before I had the stitches removed from my hand, I was trying to do the housework. I was a little aggravated because of course I only had one hand. This is where the team comes in that I speak of. What chores I couldn't get done because of my limitations, Michael did even though he was working a full time job. We went through the apartment cleaning it from top to bottom together. I didn't ask him. He just got up and started helping me.

Thank God the day finally came when I had the appointment with the doctor to remove my stitches. As I sat there in his examining room, he unraveled my bandages from my hand, and he noticed the skin had grown over the stitches, which was something he found very unusual. As I stated I had never had stitches before, so I didn't know what was normal and what wasn't. All I knew was this was going to hurt like hell because he actually then had to start digging through the skin that had grown over the stitches to reach the stitches to cut them. My hand began bleeding all over again. This moment was not a fun time for me to say the least. He did this with no Novocain, nothing. I sat there holding on with my right hand to the edge of the examining table squeezing it and grinding my teeth together as he cut through the layer of skin.

As the doctor was removing the last stitch from my hand, I looked at it and it looked like raw meat. It looked horrible. It was bloody and throbbing. Thank God I had an extremely high threshold for pain or I probably would have passed out at this point. When the doctor was finished he rebandaged my hand and asked me what type of job I did. I told him I was a packer in a glass factory, and I really needed to return back to work.

Then he told me, "Well, Kyra, you're not going to be able to return again for another week, or at least until your hand heals." He then wrote me a prescription for a mild painkiller that helped a little, but nothing could stop the pain.

When I returned home Michael asked me how it went at the doctor's, and as I was telling him what went on he was becoming more and more furious.

He said, "I can't believe that the doctor just cut into the palm of your hand like that without injecting it with Novocain first or giving you some sort of a pain killer."

"Well, he did," I said.

Michael then said, "The next time you have to go to see this doctor, I will be with you."

I looked at Michael and laughed, and I said, "You really don't think there's going to be a next time, do you?"

It was the following week when I began experiencing more pain instead of less in my hand, and the pain now was working its way up to my elbow. I found when I tried to grab or hold onto anything, no matter how light or how small, this shooting pain would go from the palm of my hand right to my elbow. It didn't affect my entire hand; it was just the last three fingers of it. The pain remained from my last three fingers to my elbow, and the pain in my elbow grew ever stronger. The only thing I can compare it to is when you hit your elbow and you hit your funny bone by accident. You know that nauseating pain that you feel from this? Well, this is pretty much how it always was. It never subsided.

I didn't know what to do because at the end of this week, the beginning of the following week I should say, I was supposed to return back to work. I didn't know how I was going to be able to do my job with the pain. I did return back to my job that Monday, and I tried, I tried my hardest. I thought perhaps maybe it was stiff because I hadn't used it that much. I didn't know what was going on, so I told them I was ready to return back. I guess it was about an hour into my shift when the pain became very excruciating. It seemed like no matter how hard I tried not to pick up anything the wrong way, there just seemed to be no way I could do it without writhing in pain. I lasted for two hours, and believe me, these had to have been the longest two hours and the most painful two hours of my life. I went to the foreman and explained to him how I was feeling and how much pain I was in. He told me he felt horrible for me. He felt very bad about the pain, and he hated to lose me. He complimented me.

The foreman told me, "Kyra, you were one of the hardest workers I've ever had here." He then told me to just go home and give the doctor a call. He assured me he would handle all the necessary paper work there.

I walked out of the factory. I went out into the parking lot and sat in my car and just began to cry. I realized the mistakes I had made in my life, especially the lack of education that left me with only the option of being a factory worker. Now I was a factory worker with only one good arm and a whole lot of pain. Then I thought of that old joke, the joke about the one-armed paper hanger, and how good is he?

I had no idea what I was going to do next. I felt as though I had just lost my livelihood. I was scared, and I was very, very angry. I then went home, and I called the doctor. I proceeded to tell him about all the pain I was in, and he saw me the following day.

I went into his office, and he examined my palm, which seemed to be healing normally, but he said, "Given the amount of pain you are in, Kyra, I would suggest exploratory surgery would benefit you right now. Perhaps there was glass that was left in that is now causing the problem."

So I agreed against my better judgment. I was never quite thrilled with this doctor considering the way he removed simple sutures from my hand. I didn't think he was that good, but since I had already been seeing him, I felt more comfortable with him than I would a new doctor, a stranger. It was a couple of days after this visit that he booked the operation. In the operating room they gave me what they call an IV Block where it numbed my whole arm all the way down to my fingertips. He then began operating on my palm, removing all of the scar tissue. He told me everything looked good, everything was clean, and he didn't detect any glass left behind. He finished cleaning out the area and then he stitched me up.

After a day or two passed I felt no different. The pain remained right up to my elbow. Then I began thinking well perhaps once it's all healed again the pain will subside. So I tried very hard not to become discouraged, but even after it healed and he was removing the second set of sutures and having to dig through my palm just as he did the first time, there was absolutely no difference. If anything, the pain was more severe. Through x-rays and physical therapy the pain remained. I felt like I was losing my mind. There seemed to be no logical explanation as to what was going on with my arm. The doctor at this point was looking at me like I was nuts.

I realized I had to see another doctor. By this time Michael's mother had heard what I was going through. She suggested a doctor she had been seeing, and ironically he was in the same building as the quack that I was seeing. He was very good, and he had the state of the art testing equipment. He tested me with different things including very high-tech thermography. The normal x-rays didn't pick up anything, but the thermography did. This would probably be equal to what an MRI machine could pick up today in the human body. Thank God he was able to find out why I was in so much pain. It was only a matter of a couple of days after his examination and the testing that he got the results.

On our next appointment the week that followed he told me what I had. He said, "It's a very rare disease that happens usually after a surgery. It is caused by a severe cut or severe trauma to a certain area, usually in the extremities—the arms, the legs," he said, however, that he had also seen it in the back. "This is called Reflux Sympathetic Dystrophy, RSD for short."

I remember sitting there on the examining table looking at him, and I asked him, "What in the hell is that? I had never heard of such a thing."

He said, "You haven't heard of it before because it is that rare. Only a few people have it."

I said, "Well, I guess I was lucky enough, huh?"

The doctor said, "You are lucky in one aspect, because it seems to have stopped at your elbow instead of going all the way up to your arm."

Then he went on to tell me that there is no cure for this. "Physical therapy does help to ease the pain a little bit, but this is basically something you are going to have to live with for the rest of your life."

I can't even begin to tell you how devastating this news was to me. I counted on having two good arms to be able to make a living. Now what in hell was I going to do because also along with the pain, my concentration level had dropped because of having to deal with the pain? So, going back to school at this point really was not an option to me. I had to first learn how to live with pain, chronic pain, and the anger that was erupting inside of me because all of a sudden I wasn't strong. All of a sudden I couldn't do anything I wanted to. I now had limitations, physical limitations. The anger that grew in me over this realization was almost as crippling as the pain itself.

The next thing the doctor did was pull out his prescription pad. He began writing me prescriptions for painkillers, two different types.

I told him, "Forget about it. I don't want them." I then began explaining to him about my addiction, and I told him, "I'm an alcoholic, but I haven't had a drink in years now, but I will always be an alcoholic. Any prescription that you give me I will eventually end up abusing; I know this. So please do me a favor and keep your pills. I'll have to learn how to handle this my own way. I'm 23 years old, and you're telling me I have to live the rest of my life with this pain. If I start on these painkillers now at the age of 23, what in the hell am I going to be by the time I'm 50? Probably dead."

I had no choice. I had to figure it out on my own. I began taking Excedrin, and this did help ease the pain slightly. After this doctor's visit I went home, and I told Michael what the doctor had just explained to me. I also told him perhaps this physical therapy would ease some of the pain, and I was going to start on this immediately with the doctor. I could tell this news devastated Michael as well. He felt terrible. He knew how active I was and how physical I was and now I had limitations placed on me. I didn't know, and I don't think he knew how I was going to handle this, but I knew together our love would keep me strong and it did.

As Michael sat there stunned at this news of this rare disease and how unlucky I was that I got it, he spoke and he told me, "Kyra, you've overcome a lot in your life, and we will overcome this. We are survivors, and this is just yet another curve ball that has been thrown our way."

From that moment on I was determined not to let this one moment destroy the rest of my life, a life that Michael and I have worked so very hard to gain.

Along with the physical therapy that I would begin would be the Excedrin that I took to control a small portion of the pain. The other part had to be up to me. I sat there one day on my couch while Michael was at work and as the pain was throbbing in my arm, I began trying to focus on a picture, an object, anything that could take my mind off of the pain. I could control my own pain if I tried hard enough. I knew I could, and I eventually became an expert at this. Whenever the pain would start becoming almost unbearable, I started focusing. I started thinking about anything else but that, completely totally taking my mind off of it. Each and every time it worked like a charm.

It worked better than any medication I could have ever taken. But I should say this didn't happen overnight. The first time I tried, I felt a slight relief but it only lasted for a few moments. It only lasted while I stayed focused, and at this point I was inexperienced. I didn't know what I was doing, so I needed an object to focus on instead of simply being able to escape in my mind and push the pain away through that by thinking of other things, distracting my own brain from the pain.

With experience I eventually got to the point where I didn't need an object to concentrate on any longer. I could do it with my mind. When the pain became severe, I would think of shopping. I would think of laundry. I would think of what I was going to paint the apartment. I would think of absolutely anything but the pain. Thank God this worked. From here on out I would always have to be careful not to forget and reach out to grab something, because once I did this the pain would be absolutely excruciating, and it would send a shock wave right up to my shoulder. The pain is similar to being hit in the funny bone with a hammer. Though I was experiencing this pain, I tried my best to keep it from Michael. I didn't want him to know. I didn't want to share this with him. I didn't want him to hurt or feel bad for me. I knew sharing my pain with Michael would only hurt him. In the past I could not protect him from his own pain, from his own nightmare, but I could protect him from this. This is one thing that we need not share.

I was now finding sleeping almost impossible. This is one time of the day that your mind can't be in control and it seemed like as soon as I got to sleep, as soon as I lay on my arm or I bent it the wrong way, I would wake up in pain. Many nights I would just go into the shower and sit there and cry as Michael lay sleeping. I fought the anger and depression on a daily basis, and actually

I had fought depression my entire life. Thank God I somehow was able to pull myself out of it each and every time. I would fight the urge to just lay in bed and think of the sad thoughts that kept popping into my mind. I pushed myself out of bed when I was younger, and I will do it now. I fought my depression. I would not allow it to consume me, and just as when I was younger, now it was even more important for me to fight, to fight against the anger, and to fight against the depression. I had to beat it, and I had to win because I just had too much at stake now. I had my whole life with Michael to lose, and there was no way in hell I was going to allow this to happen.

So I dragged myself out of bed every morning half awake, not being able to sleep very much, and fought every day. I took the Excedrin for the pain. I went to physical therapy twice a week, and I practiced the mind control that would help me block the pain. I did all of these things for months, not to mention the physical therapy sessions themselves being excruciating. I was clenching my teeth through one of these sessions so hard one of my teeth broke off. It actually cracked, but I continued in hopes that it would help somewhat.

After these sessions I would meet with the doctor until during one of our visits I told him how many Excedrin I was taking a day. I was up to twelve a day. He wasn't too thrilled with this. He explained to me how this would eventually destroy my liver.

Then I asked him, "The pills that you would be giving me would do about the same, right?"

He said, "Not necessarily."

"Well, if they didn't destroy my liver they would turn me into a legal junkie. What's worse? What kind of time frame are we talking about here, doctor? How long would I have before the Excedrin would start affecting my liver?"

He couldn't tell me how many years exactly. "Everyone is different. Some people take medication, and their system does better than others. It could be five years or it could be 10, 20, or 30. It all depends on your system."

I then asked him, "You mean it could take years for this to even begin affecting me?"

He said, "Yes."

That's when I told him, "Well, I think I'll just stay on the path that I'm on. The Excedrin seems to be keeping my pain bearable."

I explained to him about the mind control that I had begun trying to focus on other things and taking my mind off the pain. That too seemed to work very well for me. So this is how we left it. I was going to continue doing what I was doing along with my physical therapy. I reminded him again of my age. I told him at least I would have these years ahead of me, years of sobriety and being able to live life without being in a fog from drugs. I told him I would switch later on in my life and choose the pain medication if the pain became too unbearable for me to handle, but for right now, I was happy this way.

So the next few months I slowly began to feel a little bit back to my old self, my old personality, my happy personality. This took a lot of work. I had to deal with anger and depression, but I tried to keep them in their proper place and began enjoying the small things in life again. As far as my anger went, it was simply because I felt like I was given such a raw deal. Michael and I had just started our life together as a normal couple without the fog or alcoholism haunting us, and for the first time thoroughly being able to enjoy each other. Then this happens, something that would cause me pain now for the rest of my life and severely limit my ability to do the things that I wanted to do in life. Yes, I was angry and for a very good reason. However, like all of my other pain I had to learn how to put it in its proper place in my life so that I could live. Eventually through a lot of hard work, I did this.

Michael through all of this was fantastic. He stood by my side through thick and thin. He was so incredibly supportive and incredibly loving, and as I mentioned earlier, my confidant. I could tell him anything, and this is how we made it through this most difficult time by being open and honest with one another and being able to talk about my anger and how incompetent I felt at that moment and how I hated that feeling. But we were always a team, the team that no one or anything could ever destroy. We always seemed to know what was in each other's head and hearts.

The year now was 1986, and it was just before my 24th birthday when Michael came to me one evening after we finished supper. He sat beside me on the couch, held my hand and asked me to marry him. As soon as he asked me this question, I must have had a very shocked look on my face, because as I said earlier this is something that I never, ever planned to do. Then again, I never ever planned to love someone as much as I loved Michael, so my answer was very hard for me to come out with.

I just looked at him, and as much as my heart wanted to say, yes, so desperately wanted to say, yes, my head said, no, which was the worst decision of my life and a decision I would live to always regret. I was just so afraid of marriage. There had never been a successful marriage in my entire family, ever. In my family there just never seemed to be any happily ever after. The only side of marriage I had ever seen was pain and tears, and I was just afraid of screwing everything up with Michael, everything we had worked so hard to achieve, a good relationship, and a loving relationship. I was afraid of losing all of it. I was so sure in my heart that if we were to get married it would all end. Sooner or later it would all end in just as miserable a way as it ended for my sisters and my mother. I didn't want this to happen to Michael and me.

After I told Michael "No," I told him I didn't think this would be a good idea.

I told him the reason why, and he said to me, "Just because this happened with your sisters and your mother that doesn't mean it is going to happen to us."

"Can you guarantee this?" I said.

He looked at me and said "There are no guarantees in life. You know that."

I told him, "Yes, I do. That's why for now I think we should stay the way we are, in love and happy. We don't need a piece of paper to keep us together." You know, they say hindsight is 20/20. I would have given anything now to go back and say, yes, and have a beautiful church wedding, but you can't change the past, and you can't turn back the hands of time.

Michael was upset, but he tried to understand how I felt. I mean, after all, it was because I wanted to stay with him that I didn't want to get married, not because I didn't love him, and he knew this.

He got up from the couch and nodded his head and looked down and gave me a big kiss on the cheek, and he told me, "I understand, Baby Doll. We'll talk about this maybe in a few more months, because maybe after a few more months of living together, your ideas will have changed."

The following week on my birthday, I figured he had recovered from my answer because he got me this beautiful low-cut white negligee with a matching robe with pearl buttons and lace trim. The cake that he got me for that birthday was so adorable. It was a white cake with white frosting and little pink roses around the edge with a sweet little ballerina in the middle. When I first saw it I laughed, but I thought it was really sweet, and I asked him, "How come the ballerina?"

He said, "That's because you love dancing so much and also you are my little princess, my little Baby Doll." He gave me a big kiss and a hug and said, "Happy Birthday, Baby Doll."

The spring quickly turned to summer and between my physical therapy sessions and doctor's visits and Michael's working and his psychiatry sessions at the VA twice a week, we always still found time to live and love. We just so enjoyed spending quiet nights at home together, sitting on the couch after dinner in each other's arms watching TV. Other days on the weekends mostly we would go fishing and we would go target shooting. I could no longer hold the rifle because of my arm, but I would go with him anyway and we would talk and laugh and just enjoy being with one another. Other times during the week after supper sometimes we would take a ride down to the lake and sit in our favorite spot to watch the sunset and just talk. It didn't really seem to matter what we were doing as long as we were doing it together. Then there were a few really hot nights during the summer when Michael and I would just go for a drive down the Cape. Our favorite spot down there was Onset Beach because of all the memories, both good and bad, they were ours.

During the day when the sun was at its brightest, Michael was not able to go to the beach because of all the different medications he was one. Most of the medications have the warning to avoid the sun, so we had to pick our time wisely. It was always about an hour or two before sunset we would arrive at Onset Beach about 5:30-6 o'clock to sit there and watch the beautiful colors, the brilliant oranges and red and the fireball that the sun became sinking into the horizon. It was so beautiful. We would sit there on the beach in each other's arms and just take in the beauty. These were our relaxing moments, ones that we very much enjoyed spending together. Before going to the beach to watch the sunset, we would indulge ourselves with some fried clams and French fries from a nearby stand. On very hot nights we would go for a dip in Onset Bay to cool off. These loving nights will forever live in my memories.

It seemed like before we knew it the summer of 1986 had come to an end. It was now October again and Michael's birthday once more was right around the corner. I had the usual romantic dinner and the cake with a few decorations of balloons and streamers in his favorite color of blue around the apartment just for him. But unlike the other birthdays, this time he seemed a little depressed, a little off, not quite himself, and I asked him what was wrong.

He looked at me and kind of smiled, he said, "Oh, Kyra, it's really nothing. I guess it's just because I'm turning 38, and I'm starting to feel a little bit old, I guess. Also there's a fear that lingers in the back of my mind that as I get older, you are going to be beautiful still, and when I'm sitting here an old man, I'm afraid you are going to leave me for someone younger."

I guess because of our age difference, 13 years between us, this fear did always linger in the back of Michael's mind, but of course this fear was unfounded. I loved him so much I didn't want to ever think of myself with anyone else, and I told him that much.

After he made this statement for the first time, I sat down in my chair, and I laughed. My reply was, "You don't realize, my darling, my Teddy Bear, you are stuck with me for life now. I love you so much. I can't believe you are even thinking like this, and I hate to bring up such a sore subject right now, but I feel I must."

I reminded him about the time that he and I were separated, and I was with another man. I told him, "When I was with him all I could think about was being with you, and every time I pictured your face all I could remember was how desperately in love I was with you."

I went on to tell Michael, "I fell in love with you at first sight. I loved you almost from the first time we laid eyes on each other, and the passion and the trust has just become so strong between us, and it grows stronger as the years pass. I can't even begin to imagine my life without you by my side. You truly have made my life worth living, and these words come straight from my heart, Michael. This is truly how I feel. My heart and my soul are in this relationship for the long haul. You have me, Michael, heart and soul for always."

We then held on tight to one another and after a long embrace, we retired to the living room where we sat on the couch holding each other close.

Michael then all of a sudden turned and looked at me and said, "Kyra, I want to have a baby with you, and we should really think about doing this now. I'm 38 years old, and I want to be able to enjoy a family before I get much older."

He kind of threw me, because this was one subject that never seemed to have come up before. It was just something that we never spoke about, but I knew someday it would come up, and I guess today was the day. I knew some day I did want to have a baby of my own, and I wanted it to be a part of Michael as well as me. However, it always seemed in my head to be somewhere off into the future that we would be talking about this, not here or today. You see the two of us had tried and fought so long and so hard to find this little piece of sanity that we were now finally enjoying a normal life together.

Through all the crazy years that had passed, we were finally here, a normal couple, but through all the time and all the work through all the years that had passed by, Michael Jr. had become lost to us. It took so long for Michael to finally find himself, to find his sanity, and in the meantime something very precious slipped away. It was another part of himself, and that was his son. This is something Michael did not want to have happen, but it did. Later on both Michael and I would find out the tragedy of Michael Jr.'s life, and how he had spent years being passed from foster home to foster home. All the years that Michael fought to regain his sanity and to recover from his alcoholism, this is what was going on in his son's life. The fact of the matter is Michael was simply incapable of taking care of himself, let alone a child at that point in time in his life. To make matters worse, he had no legal right to his son. It was a huge mess, a mess that broke our hearts.

It was a month or so before Michael had asked me about having a baby when he was talking with Michael Jr.'s mother's brother. The information he gained from him is what made Michael decide on our having a baby. He knew Michael Jr. now was lost to him forever. The man who would have been Michael's brother-in-law told him that Michael Jr. had been placed in a very loving home in the next town over with an older couple who did this for a living. They took in children and raised them, and they were very, very loving to all of the children they took care of. Also he told him that there was a rumor going around that this couple wanted to adopt Michael Jr. for their own.

Michael just sat there, and he told me, "I screwed up this kid's life enough. He loves these people, and they obviously love him if they want to adopt him. What right do I have to stand in his way, his way of happiness, his way of being happy? I have no right to stop him, and I will not. What do you expect me to do, Kyra, just burst back into this child's life and blow his little world apart, a little world that took him a lifetime to create? He doesn't probably even remember me. I won't do that to him. I can't do that to him. I owe him more than that. I'm going to leave them alone and let them be a family. I think that's the only thing I can do right, and that's the right thing to do.

"I have always loved my son, Kyra, and now I have to love him enough to let him go, to let him be happy and to live a normal life with a normal family that he loves and that loves him. I now have to put his best interests before my own. This is not what I wanted to happen with my child, but nevertheless, this is the way things are, and I must accept them. Perhaps when Michael Jr. is older I will have an opportunity to explain just what went on and how very sorry I was and how I never stopped loving him. For now, however, I will not cause him any further heartache than I already have."

As Michael sat there telling me all of this, I just sat there numb and in disbelief. I always thought that someday I would be raising Michael Jr. as my own son. I had hoped. I now realized that Michael was 10 years old. It had taken just so long for his father and me to get our acts together and his father to get the help that he truly needed.

Michael still wasn't completely recovered. He was seeing the psychiatrist twice a week and would remain doing this for quite awhile. He still had a lot of recovery left ahead of him, and for me to be faced with the realization that Michael Jr. would never be in our lives again, and there would be a part of the man that I loved more than life itself out there. I would never be able to see him again. I truly hated the thought of this, but I had to put all of my emotions aside. What Michael was telling me did make sense. Heartbreaking as it was, it was the most logical thing for us to do. I also resented the fact that he was to be adopted and raised now by another woman. I wanted to be that woman, and I wanted to be his mother.

All I knew at this moment was that I had an awful lot to take in and to sort out. First of all Michael was asking me to have a baby and then telling me everything that he had just found out about his first son. I had a lot of thinking to do, and I told Michael this.

I said to him, "I need a week or so to think before we decide to bring a child into this world. Both of us need to be very sure that we are making the right decision before I become pregnant."

Digesting everything that Michael had just told me, I wasn't all that sure at that moment that this would be the right choice for us. I worried that he wasn't quite ready. I realized that he had many more years of therapy in front of him. Would this help him if we now had a baby of our own? Would this give him encouragement? Was he ready for this massive responsibility? To be honest with you, I wasn't sure even if I was ready. The only thing that I was completely sure of was that we loved each other with all our hearts, and this love we could give to our child. But is love enough?

I began to think, and I began to worry that the stress of having a newborn baby would send Michael back to the bottle. Stress was always a huge trigger point with him, but he seemed so sure that this was truly what he wanted more than anything right now, and that was for us to create a life together. I also realized a child would be the ultimate testimony to our life. I could only imagine just how wonderful it would feel to be carrying around a part of Michael inside of me, and watching it grow over nine months, and knowing all the while that the love that we shared with one another is what created this wonderful little human being. What more could my heart ask for?

Michael by now was going on his fourth year of sobriety and intense counseling, and I knew he never had any intention of picking up another bottle again in his life. I thought having a child would be the next natural step for us to take. So after four years of sobriety and eight years of being together practically every single day, I thought a child could only bring us closer. He was ready for this next step, and I decided so was I.

It was a week or so after Michael's birthday, after we had first discussed having a baby, when I told him, "Yes, I would love to have a baby with you."

It was in the morning over a cup of coffee when I told him exactly how I felt and how much a baby would be the next natural step in our relationship. He just smiled from ear to ear and completely agreed with me. It was this morning that I stopped taking my birth control pills. We began trying that very night to conceive.

It took us two months for me to get pregnant. Finally in January of 1987 we achieved our goal. The funny part about this was it would not be until March 23, on my birthday, that we found out we were expecting. You see, I continued having my period from January to March. Although I did have the morning sickness, I didn't realize that's what it was because I had never been pregnant before. I thought it was just a bad stomach virus or something that I had eaten. Looking back on it now, why would this last two months?

As I said, it wasn't until my birthday. My mother gave me a Mr. Coffee machine. Michael and I had never bought one before because quite frankly we just weren't big coffee drinkers, and I usually had a little glass of Pepsi or orange in the morning instead of coffee. So I was rather surprised when she gave this to me as my birthday present.

She said, "Oh, just try it. The percolator coffee is much better than instant. Maybe you and Michael would like it better."

So that morning after my birthday, I cleaned the coffee pot following the directions to a T (I cleaned it not only once but twice just to be on the safe side), and then I ran the first pot of coffee. As soon as the smell hit my nose, I almost threw up on the kitchen floor. I went to the bathroom just making it in time and vomited my brains out.

Michael asked me, "What the hell's the matter with you?"

"I don't know," I said. "I think there's something wrong with the coffee machine because it just doesn't smell right."

He said, "It smells fine to me," and he poured us both a cup.

On my second sip I found myself back into the bathroom vomiting yet again. I swore up and down to him there was something wrong with the coffee machine. He said, "Kyra, I feel fine. It's not the coffee machine. It's you."

I said, "Well, I've never had that reaction before to coffee."

He responded, "Well, I don't know."

Later after Michael left for work I called my mother and told her what had happened. I asked her if she had saved the receipt for the coffee machine so I could return it because I think there was something wrong with it.

She then asked me if I got sick before I even took a sip of it, just smelling it? I said, "Yes."

She said, "Kyra, I think you're pregnant.

Now mind you, I had told no one about our trying to have a baby. I didn't want to jinx it. I wanted this to stay just between Michael and me until I found out for sure that I was pregnant and then I would pass the good news along to all my family members.

I then asked her, "How did you know we were trying to get pregnant?"

"I didn't," she said. "I didn't." She then went on to tell me that through every pregnancy that she had with my sisters and me, this is the one thing that hit her the worst, smells. Even just the slight smell of coffee would start her vomiting.

I told her, "I had no idea. You never told me that before."

"Well, I never really had a reason to." Then she told me I should pick up one of the pregnancy tests, and I did. I went out later that day to the drugstore to get one. Later on that night I tested it, and it was positive. Michael and I were pregnant.

I did not let on to Michael about anything that was going on, including the conversation that I had with my mother earlier that day. I wanted this to be a total surprise. I remember coming out of the bathroom as he sat there on the couch, relaxed, watching television, and handing him the pregnancy test stick, and him looking at it. He threw it up in the air after he looked at it. He jumped up and gave me a huge hug.

He said, "Oh, my God, Kyra, we did it!"

I said, "Yes, we did."

He was absolutely glowing. He smiled from ear to ear, and as we held each other so tight I told him how very much I loved him, and he told me how very much he loved me. This was easily one of the happiest moments of our lives together.

Then Michael began kissing my neck, working down to my breasts, and I told him, "Your job's over now."

He said, "Yeah, I know; now we can just have fun." It was on this night we made passionate love. So now we were truly connected in every way two human beings could possibly be, our hearts our bodies and our minds, and now a beautiful baby growing inside of me. From this day on both of us knew that we would forever be as one.

It was the next morning that I would call my obstetrician to make an appointment to see him. I told him about my pregnancy test coming back positive and asked if he would see me right away. He did so that I could start on my vitamins and checkups.

After the conversation with the doctor I called my mother and let her know. She told me, "Kyra, I already knew."

I said, "How could you be so sure, Mom?"

She said that's because this is how it happened with her. She said, "One morning I was sitting there having coffee with your two sisters when they were younger, and the next morning at that same kitchen table, the same cup of coffee, I became violently ill. That's how it always was. That's how I could tell I was pregnant, and obviously I handed this talent down to you, or should I say, curse."

I realized how hard this must have been on my poor mother. She lived on coffee. As I was growing up she easily drank ten to twelve cups a day, so for her all of a sudden not to be able to do this, must have been utter torture.

My mother was excited about this great news. She was finally going to be a grandmother for the first time. This gave her something to look forward to and a lot of happiness she knew was going to come her way in the future with her new grandchild. She told me how thrilled she was for Michael and me, and she realized, she said, how much we loved each other. So I guess this was just a natural step.

Then she went on to tell me, "I know you and Michael are going to make great parents. You have so much love. It's only natural to be sharing that with a part of each of you, which will be your child.

It was that following Monday that I saw my obstetrician and he gave me a test in his office and an exam, and he told me, "Kyra, you aren't just pregnant, you are about three months' along."

I asked him, "How could that be? I was getting my period on a regular basis?"

He said, "Well, some women do. That's nothing to be alarmed about."

He said, "It should stop."

Actually that month I didn't get my period. I started on my prenatal vitamins and exercises. He also asked me about childbirth classes. I explained to him my worries about drugs being given to me while I was delivering and that I didn't want them. I wanted natural childbirth, so the Lamaze classes seemed to be perfect for Michael and me. I thought I was already practicing pain control with my mind, and this is a large part of the Lamaze class is focusing on certain objects and taking your mind off of the labor pains. So I was already one step ahead in that aspect. I thought Lamaze would be perfect for Michael and me.

The doctor told me that I was about three months' pregnant, so counting back we figured it was around New Year's Eve that Michael and I conceived. I also told the doctor the concerns that I had about my vomiting, and about the morning sickness. The morning sickness wasn't only happening during the morning but in the afternoon and evening as well. I said I was eating and keeping the majority of it down, but that nauseous feeling just wasn't going away.

He said, "Well, maybe through this pregnancy it won't. It's just something you are going to have to deal with." He told me to try saltines and ginger ale, and they helped a little bit, but nothing completely stopped it.

The doctor gave me the due date of September 2, give or take a day. After the exam the doctor left me alone in the room. As I was getting dressed I looked into the mirror, and my face had never looked like this before. It had a glow to it, a glow of love, and I thought to myself at that moment, *This is the look of a woman in love and a woman that is about to share the most precious gift of all with the man she loves and that is their child.* I was simply beaming with joy.

After my doctor's visit I remember stopping at the grocery store to pick up Michael's favorite dinner. I wanted to make this meal special because it was a special night. I picked up some large sea scallops, fresh potatoes and green salad fixings and his favorite desert, chocolate cake. By the time Michael arrived home after work, I had dinner fully prepared. As we sat there eating I explained to him what the doctor told me about the due date.

I told him, "I think we must have conceived on New Year's Eve. While the rest of the world was having their celebration, we were having ours, but ours was much more spectacular."

He laughed. "Well, you can say that again."

After supper we sat on the couch together pouring through all the pamphlets the doctor had just given me about what to do during the pregnancy, the importance of rest and a good diet. Michael and I figured it was just all a matter of common sense. Of course you're supposed to take care of yourself. There were a few pamphlets in there just for him. To explain to him the emotional roller coaster some women do go on during pregnancy, and their backaches, and the having to get up throughout the night to go pee, what I like to call "The Warning Pamphlet" for all expectant fathers.

It was on my next visit to the doctor when he handed me a bunch of pamphlets on the Lamaze class that were held at the medical building next to Oakland Hospital. As Michael and I sat there reading all of this literature, Michael turned to me and he said, "Are you sure that you want to do it this way?" He said, "It sounds awfully painful."

I said, "I know, but I think it would be better for the baby where both of us are alcoholics. I just simply want to make sure we give our child a fresh, clean start not to be born with drugs in his system already. I quite frankly can't stand the thought of that happening. So for me to go through a little bit of pain is well worth it."

There would only be one problem here and that was I was sure that Michael was not going to be able to go through this with me. I knew if I were to take the Lamaze classes I would have to take them alone. As much as Michael loved me, I knew he wouldn't be able to stand there for hours listening to me scream and yell in writhing pain. Because he suffered from post-traumatic stress, I feared these things would trigger an episode of flashbacks or the nightmares again. So I told him I realized that he didn't like the sight of blood for one. It would make him light in the head, and everything that was going to be happening to me. I preferred he not be in the labor room or the delivery room. I think knowing all this was the reason that he wasn't too thrilled to begin with that I was choosing the Lamaze method of childbirth instead of just having a quick delivery or keeping me drugged so I wouldn't be screaming. He knew what he was in store for, and he did agree. He was glad that I understood.

He told me he had spoken to his psychiatrist about this, and even the psychiatrist didn't believe that that would be a good place for him to be, beside me, listening to me scream for hours on end. This would not be a good thing for Michael to go through mentally at this point in his recovery, especially when we had so much riding on this, riding on him staying sober. After all, he would now have a family to support. He could not afford to be thrown in a rubber room. So during my next visit to the doctor I would explain this to him and everything that Michael and I had gone through and how we struggled for our sanity and our sobriety. I told him, "If I go through this Lamaze class, I will be going through it alone which was just fine by me."

After I explained everything to the doctor, he did agree that this perhaps would not be a good thing for Michael to do, but he told me it would be much better for me if I had a coach. He asked me if there was anyone in my family who would be willing to do this with me. I explained to him, "I have two sisters and a mother, but my mother is getting on in years and my two sisters never had a child, so all of this would be quite shocking to them. So, no, I think I would rather just do this alone."

The doctor told me, "Well, Kyra, that's up to you."

It was very early in the morning after this doctor's visit, and Michael would not be home until much later, so I thought I would pay my mother a little visit and get her caught up on everything that was going on. I explained to her during my visit that I would be doing Lamaze because this is the way I wanted to have my child free of drugs, and she agreed. She thought that would be a very good thing as well. Then I went on to tell her I would be doing this alone, that I didn't think Michael would be able to take all the yelling, the screaming, the blood, and everything else that goes along with child labor.

She also agreed, but she said, "You can't do this alone."

I said, "Well, I can physically. There's no law that states you have to have a coach in the delivery room. It helps, but you really don't need one."

She was rather upset about this and said, "Perhaps I can go in."

"Ma, please, I think you've been through enough in your life. You don't need to see what I am about to go through."

We continued with our conversation. We started talking about baby furniture and clothes, and getting the nursery together, and how much fun we would have doing this together, as Mother and daughter. And we did. We had a blast shopping for all the pretty little baby things.

Later on that evening after supper I received a call from my sister April telling me that she had spoken to our mother about the Lamaze classes and how I had planned to go through this alone, and she offered to do this with me. It would not be until at least two years later that I would hear the truth from April, which was that our mother had browbeaten her so badly into offering to do this with me, she had no other choice.

She said, "Oh, my God, I had no idea of how I was going to do this, but Mom insisted that I at least try and go through the classes with you."

So during our conversation that evening when she offered to do this with me, I said to her, "Do you have any idea of what you are getting yourself into?"

She said, "Not really, but I guess neither do you."

"No, I don't." So we both agreed. I thanked her very much.

It was a couple of days after this that I signed us both up for the Lamaze class with my sister April as my coach. As I was telling Michael about the conversation with April and her offering to be my coach, I could see the look of relief come over his face.

Then he told me, "If April did not offer, I knew I could not let you go through this alone; I would have to do this. I am very much relieved to know that your sister will be beside you."

He then again said to me, "Kyra, no matter how much I love you and how much I know it would be the right thing for me to do is to be there for you and our baby, you realize I wouldn't be much help for either one of you if I was passed out on the delivery room floor. This is exactly what I am trying to avoid, and this is exactly what I fear will happen, but because I love you so much I would have tried. No matter what the outcome would have been. I would have had to be there for you. I would not let you go through this alone."

After he got through speaking, I leaned over, gave him a big hug and a kiss, and I told him how much I loved him and how much I appreciated his being willing to put himself in that position. I also told him, "You don't have to prove anything to me. You have proven your love to me time and time again."

I could tell by the look on his face he did feel as though he was letting me down. After all, we had always been a team and we had always shared everything. This just seemed to be so unnatural that we were not sharing this most important time in our relationship. However, both of us realized why and both of us realized that this was the best decision for us to make is having April as my coach.

The remaining five months of my pregnancy, thank God, was pretty much uneventful but extremely uncomfortable. All in all it was a pretty normal pregnancy. I remember our first ultrasound test. It blew Michael and me both away to actually see our sweet baby's face for the first time. The feelings were almost indescribable. It was a miracle, and this was taken in my seventh month of pregnancy. Although we could see the sweet angel face, we couldn't quite make out the rest of the body. We couldn't tell whether it was a boy or a girl just looking at it, and we didn't want to know. We wanted to be surprised.

In the seventh month a lot of other things started happening. The baby was shifting and moving around constantly. He never seemed to sleep, and therefore I never slept. One day I guess he shifted on my sciatic nerve in my back, because the pressure became so great that the pain in my back went all the way down from my hip to my foot. I couldn't sit down, I couldn't lie down, and it hurt to stand up. There wasn't a comfortable position I could get into, and this lasted for over two weeks. Just before the end of this two weeks while in the middle of washing my kitchen floor, I went completely dead from the waist down. Thank God we lived in a one-floor apartment. I literally crawled to my bed and threw myself into it. Thank God Michael was coming home shortly. After about an hour of lying there, the feeling started to return back to my legs, and the pain in my hip had stopped. I guess the baby had shifted into a more comfortable position for itself, thank God, and had taken the pressure off that nerve.

In my eighth month I couldn't seem to quench my thirst no matter how much water I drank. I would literally stand there in front of the refrigerator with a gallon of water, drink three-quarters of it down, and two minutes afterwards still feel thirsty. Then of course I would spend the remainder of the day running in and out of the bathroom either vomiting or peeing.

Then one morning in the middle of the eighth month, Michael had just left for work, and I sat down in my chair, which was a feat in itself. The only things harder than my sitting down in the chair was getting out of the chair, but I was so tired I just sat back, and I relaxed. I watched my stomach roll up and down. I felt like I was watching an alien movie! I could actually see my baby's head rolling up and down my stomach. The baby must have been doing somersaults. I followed the bulge from the middle of my rib cage all the way down to the right side of my bladder and then come back up again. Without a doubt this was the freakiest thing I had ever seen in my life, and I didn't know babies did this. I heard they were active, but this was ridiculous.

When Michael got home that evening, I told him. I tried my best to explain to him exactly what I had experienced right after he left for work. He told me, "The baby does that all the time while you are sleeping. I lay there watching and feeling it as it moves around, and through my amazement you sleep right through it, Kyra." He told me that was his favorite time of the night when the baby was the most active and he could actually see it. He told me some nights he even talked to it, and when the baby heard his voice, he quieted down, so he tried not to talk too much because he wanted to see the baby move. I know as long as the baby is moving, it's happy and it's healthy.

I asked Michael when exactly was he going to let me in on this little secret? He said, "I thought you knew. I thought this happened outside of the bedroom, outside of when you were sleeping."

I said, "No, not quite that bad, not quite that active. This really blew my mind to sit there and watch all this."

"I know; it blew mine the first time I saw it, too."

It was also along this time that we were almost finished setting up the nursery. Michael, my mother and I had gone shopping, and we got these beautiful wall hangings with a plush teddy bear. It was almost like a stuffed animal but not quite, holding balloons, big silk balloons, four of them. The nursery was going to be Bambi along with teddy bears because we weren't quite sure of the sex of the baby yet, and we didn't want to know.

Michael and I had taken a trip a couple of towns over about an hour's drive to this baby furniture store where we bought a beautiful bassinet. It took us about an hour to pick out everything we needed. When we got it home, and were assembling the furniture and the crib, we took the bassinet out of the box, and we discovered that the skirt for the bassinet, the beautiful lace skirt that they had on display, did not come with the bassinet. It had to be purchased separately. I was so disappointed.

Michael saw the disappointment on my face. I guess he just couldn't stand to see me that way, so he said, "I'll be right back. I have to go do something."

He went all the way back to the furniture store and bought me that beautiful lace skirt. When he brought it home I was amazed. He just handed it to me and gave me a kiss on the cheek and told me, "I love you Baby Doll."

Now we were all set and ready for the baby to come. We had everything that we needed. I remember going into the nursery before the baby was born and just sitting there in the rocking chair looking around at how everything was so beautiful and so nice, just like the new life we were going to bring into the world. I felt so happy about it. It felt so right.

It was a couple of days after our visit to the furniture store when I was putting all of the little baby things away, the clothing we had bought, when all of a sudden I was struck with such a horrible feeling, a feeling of complete despair. I had no idea where this was coming from. I was feeling fine physically and everything was going very well. I had no clue as to why I was getting this feeling, but it came over me like a tidal wave. I knew something horrible was going to happen. Then I began to cry, and it was becoming uncontrollable. I did remember the doctor telling me that sometimes pregnant women have ups and down with their feelings and sometimes the downs can be very hard, so I wrote it off to that, to a lady just being pregnant. But I felt it was just more than just the passing blues. I knew what depression felt like, and this was not it. This was something else altogether, and I knew it. Then a flash came into my head, *Oh, God, did something happen to Michael?* This kind of sick feeling you only get when your heart is being broken, and I knew, I just knew something had happened to Michael. I could feel this now inside.

It was a couple of hours after this that Michael called me. He was in the hospital and he wanted me to come right away. He told me just go to admittance. They would have his room number. I couldn't believe what I was hearing, and the way that I had felt. I actually picked up on his pain. When I walked into his hospital room, I saw him just lying there. He wasn't in any pain because they had just given him some pain medication.

Then he began to try and explain to me what happened. He said he and another co-worker were moving this very heavy file cabinet when the co-worker that was in front of him at the top who was pulling it up let go of it, and it all came crashing down onto Michael. Michael strained his back trying to stop it. Michael explained to me that it really was nobody's fault. The man had just lost his grip because it was so heavy.

Remembering the feelings that I had earlier that day, I asked Michael, "When exactly did this happen? What time of the day was this?"

Whenever he told me it was right after lunch, it floored me because that was exactly the time I was experiencing that horrible feeling of dread. I then told him about this feeling that I had and how it was driving me crazy because I didn't know where it was coming from or why I was even having it. I guess this explained it.

Then I told him, "My love, I don't know if you are going to believe me or not, but I could actually feel your pain at that moment when you hurt yourself. I felt so horrible inside."

Michael just nodded his head and said, "Of course I believe you. I know when you're hurt; I can feel it. I feel upset for no reason sometimes, and then later on I'll find out that you've either hurt yourself or you're having a bad day with your pregnancy. I can definitely feel your pain too."

Thankfully this was no big thing. It only turned out to be a slightly pulled muscle in his back. Michael was able to return to work in a few days, but he had to stay on light duty for a couple of weeks. He had now been back at work for a week. It was a couple of weeks before I was due to deliver our baby when I received another call from the hospital, telling me to come down. I couldn't believe it, and I had been feeling weird that day but not as bad as when he hurt his back.

This time Michael had been taken to a hospital by ambulance with severe chest pains. He thought he was having a heart attack. They did an EKG on him and a stress test, and everything came back negative. It seemed as though he was just having a horrible anxiety attack. He was so worried about the baby and me and about what was going to happen in a couple of weeks. It seemed as though the closer my due date came, the more nervous he became. I guess it's not only the woman that's carrying the baby, but the father too that goes through his own anxieties and his own worries and also some physical changes. Michael began to have morning sickness right along with me, and he had also gained about fifteen pounds.

He began telling me exactly how this occurred at work. He told me he was riding on the lawnmower when he began thinking about the baby and me. Then he began thinking about everything that could go wrong in the delivery. The more he thought, the more his chest hurt. I assured him that I was feeling fine and the baby obviously was very, very active and very healthy. I told him he had to stop doing this. He couldn't think and worry about us to the point where he was putting himself in the hospital with chest pains. He had to get a grip.

He just said to me, "I'll be glad when all of this is over, and the baby's here and healthy, and I'm holding it in my arms."

"Me as well." I then told him how tired I was of having to get up so many nights twenty to thirty times a night it seemed like. I was going every 15 to 20 minutes to the bathroom to pee, and half of the time I fell asleep in the bathroom. I said if this doesn't stop soon I'll be so exhausted by the time the baby comes. I won't be able to take care of it. I was so huge I felt like a balloon in the Thanksgiving Day parade. I felt like I was ready to pop. My life had become a vicious circle of drinking water and going to the bathroom, and it seemed like that last week that's all I did.

In this last week of my pregnancy when I sat on the couch, I needed assistance to get back up. All day long when Michael was at work, and I was there alone, I had to make sure I sat in the right chairs, so that I would be able to get back up by myself. It was only the couch that I had trouble with at this point. Michael literally had to take my arm and pull me forward in order for me to be able to get off the couch. This is how huge I had become, but I would not have traded one second of it for all the money in the world. This is our beautiful baby that I was carrying. This was our testimony of love to one another. All through the pregnancy I would talk to it. I would listen to soft music with it, and I would rock in the rocking chair loving it. I was in love with this baby before it was even born, before I even showed. I made a promise to the baby before it was born that it would know only a loving, caring, always supportive environment and nothing bad would ever touch it. This was a promise I intended to keep until my dying day.

It was only but a few days away from my delivery date when Michael brought home a piece of mail that was delivered to his mother's house. This letter would break my heart and Michael's as well. It was a letter stating that Michael Jr. was going to be adopted and they wanted Michael's signature on the papers so that the adoption would go through smoothly. Michael and I just sat there, stunned, on the couch, looking at each other as he read the papers.

He asked me, "Should I just sign it and let them finalize this adoption?" The two of us began crying.

I told him, "This isn't right."

He said, "I know."

Then I said, "I feel like we have made some kind of fucked up tradeoff here. We've just traded one baby for another."

Michael as heartbroken and tearful as he was looked at me and said, "That's really not the case, Kyra. We haven't traded one for the other. Michael

Jr. has grown up with these people now. He's twelve years old, and he loves them, and they obviously love him or they wouldn't be wanting to adopt him."

As much as this made sense in by brain, my heart felt differently. My heart still felt we were trading one for the other. Michael said he could not bring himself to destroy what Michael Jr. had with this family by fighting this.

He said, "I've never done anything for that boy. I can at least let him have a life with a happy family if nothing else."

I then begged Michael not to sign the papers. "Rip them up and throw them in the trash," I told him. I don't care if it takes longer to finalize this adoption. At least later on in years when Michael Jr. looks at these adoption papers, he won't see your signature on them indicating that you just freely gave him away like a piece of furniture. If you don't want to fight it then don't, but don't make it easy either."

Thank God I was able to convince Michael of this. He told me, "You are right, Kyra. When he looks back at these papers, these adoption papers, he won't see my signature on any of them. He won't think that this was my idea, and I didn't care and just wanted him to go away, because it is not what I wanted at all."

Michael and I always had hopes of raising Michael Jr. right along with this baby that I was carrying. We were going to try to get it together after this baby was born and have Michael Jr. come and stay with us as a family, live as a family, but this was not to be. In the process of us getting ourselves together and getting a stable life together, we had lost him forever. This broke our hearts.

The following two days after Michael received this letter, he went to bed and he stayed there. He was so depressed and so heartbroken he couldn't think of anything else to do. He didn't talk to me. He didn't eat. He didn't do anything but sleep. The depression had completely taken him over.

On the third day he finally emerged from our bedroom. He sat at the kitchen table and had coffee and toast, and he looked at me and he said, "Kyra, I will never make the same mistake again as I made with Michael. I will never, ever do this. I will never let one of my children go again like that."

I told him, "Michael, I know that, and I know how much you loved Michael Jr. I also know how much you love this baby that's growing inside of me. As far as Michael Jr. went, there were a lot of things that were not in your control. Until you were able to get the help that you so desperately needed at that point, you weren't able to be a father. Now you are, and I have full confidence you are going to be a great one. I love you so much, and I know our baby will as well."

I assured him then that he did the right thing by ripping up these papers and throwing them in the garbage where they belonged. I told him when Michael Jr. looks at the paperwork later on in life when he is an adult, he'll know. Hopefully he'll know how you felt toward him by not signing him off.

There was yet just one more thing for Michael to bear. It was now September 2, and I went into labor. Finally it was all going to be over with, and we were going to be holding our beautiful newborn baby in our arms. I was hoping that it would take the sting out of Michael losing his son, although I knew one child could never replace another child in your heart. I was just hoping and praying that it would lift his spirits just a little bit.

So on September 2, 7 p.m., I went into labor. I began first getting mild stabbing pains in my stomach and then the pressure all around. I called the doctor and let him know the feelings I was getting, and he told me to get to the hospital because my labor had started. At this point they were only coming about 10 minutes apart so I didn't feel as though I was in any rush. Michael and I then calmly and cooly began getting ourselves prepared. I had the bag already packed. I had it packed for weeks waiting for this date with my nightgowns and a few other personal articles and the wrap that I was going to bring the baby home in. I had gotten undressed already for the evening, so I had to get dressed again, and while I was doing this Michael called April and Amber to let them both know that it was time. April said that she would meet us at the hospital.

I had never had a baby before, so I was not quite sure what to expect. I could only go by what Lamaze classes taught me. One thing I realized through life is you can take all the classes and you can read all the books, but there is nothing like experiencing things first hand. The books just don't cover it, and I was soon to learn this. As prepared as I thought I was, I had fooled myself into believing. Nothing quite prepares you for motherhood. Absolutely nothing can adequately describe the feeling that you feel when you hold your baby for the first time in your arms, a baby that you've taken care of inside of you and talked to for 9 months and have loved more than life itself. I was soon going to find this out as well. The pain that the human body has to endure before this miracle can take place is beyond description. I never knew such pain before in my life, and I never knew the human body could endure such pain without passing.

As Michael and I arrived at the hospital, the pain was still coming 10 minutes apart, so Michael and I calmly went into the emergency room and explained what was going on. They quickly brought me up to the delivery room. April would soon follow. Michael waited out in the waiting room while April and I were in the labor room. They strapped a fetal monitor to my stomach so they could keep track of the baby's heartbeat and make sure he was fine. After about an hour, it was about 8:00, 8:30, the pains started coming closer and closer together. In the dilation process you go from 1-10, 10 being the delivery process. I reached 5 within that hour.

The doctor said, "That's good. We're going to have a quick delivery, it seems like. You're halfway there, girl." That's what he kept telling me, "You're halfway there."

As I lay there in excruciating pain, April rubbed my back and was trying to talk to me. I was trying my focus exercises and also my mind-control exercises that I had practiced on my hand and arm pain. Nothing, though, seemed to be overriding this pain that I was feeling. I couldn't stay focused no matter how hard I tried on something other than the pain. The pain just completely took me over.

I remember being so thirsty. Remember, I had been consuming at least two gallons of water a day, and this nurse was coming in with a little tiny cup of ice chips.

I said, "Are you kidding me?"

She said, "No, that's all you can have."

I said, "Oh, my God," as I consumed the ice chips like a person that hadn't seen water in a week.

My sister April was raiding the refrigerator that the nurses had in their lobby trying to find me a Popsicle or something to quench my thirst. April had never experienced childbirth before. She didn't have any children. Neither did Amber, so they had nothing to go on either. All of this was as new to them as it was to me. As Amber and Michael sat out in the waiting room, April would give them hourly reports on me and my progress.

Before we knew it, it was 12 o'clock, and I was still only dilated to 5. I didn't seem to be progressing quickly in that area, but on the other hand the pain had become even more severe. I felt as though I had a Hoover Deluxe Hose put into me and turned on full blast. The pressure was so incredible and so painful, and it was coming like two minutes apart at that point. I felt as though my organs were being sucked out of me, and the pain was becoming so intense through every contraction. Every time it would begin, I would pass out from the pain and awaken as soon as the pain stopped. I was passing out and coming to. This lasted for hours: seven, to be exact.

It was around 3 or 4 in the morning. April just couldn't stand it anymore, and she went out and told Michael, "You're going to have to take over. I'm exhausted." She told Michael, "I can't stand there and watch my baby sister experience such pain and not be able to do anything to help her. I simply can't stand to watch this any longer."

Michael then realized he had to do what he had been desperately trying and hoping to avoid. He had to go in there with me. He had to face his fears and he had to face me. He honestly didn't know if he was going to be able to do this without passing out.

He took a deep breath and he walked in. He said, "I wasn't going to let you go through this by yourself."

While I was coming in and out of consciousness, one time I looked up and saw Michael standing there, and he told me, "I'm gonna be the coach now," and he began rubbing my back. Just then I had another contraction, and I passed out again.

It would be like this for the following seven hours. I would come in and out of consciousness only to see Michael standing there crying, leaning over me and patting my forehead with a cold compress. It was around 9:30 that morning, exactly fourteen and a half hours later when I would begin to dilate further. During these fourteen and a half hours I was stuck at 5. It quickly went to 7, 8, and then it reached 10. That was when I was able to deliver our baby.

They rolled me into the delivery room and Dr. Wilson said, "You're ready, finally, huh?"

"I was ready fourteen and a half hours ago," I told him.

As the doctor was telling me to push, he had to cut me a little bit so that the baby could come out.

As Michael stood there holding my hand, and I was squeezing his, he asked me, "Kyra, will you marry me?"

I couldn't believe it. I just could not believe it. I'm lying here screaming my brains out, delivering our child, and he asks me to marry him again.

I screamed at him, "Shut the fuck up!"

The doctor looked up at both of us, and he said, "Can't you argue about this later? We're kind of busy right now aren't we?"

After that the doctor told me to push. I pushed twice, and our baby was delivered. As they were cleaning him up, the doctor said to Michael and me, "You have a beautiful healthy baby boy."

The doctor then laid the baby in my arms, and Michael kissed his forehead. The doctor said to Michael, "What are you just standing there for? Get to work," and he handed Michael the scissors wanting him to cut the umbilical cord.

Michael looked at me with a look of such horror that I had never seen before. He said, "You want me to do what?"

The doctor said, "You heard me. Get to work."

Michael took a deep breath, and he said, "Kyra, if I pass out, don't be shocked."

I said, "Oh, just do it," and he put the scissors to the umbilical cord and cut right through without passing out, without fainting, without even throwing up. I was so proud of him.

On September 3, 1987, at 9:45 our son Teddy Jones was born. He weighed 8 pounds and he was 19 ½ inches long. He was the most beautiful precious baby I had ever seen in my life. As I lay there in the delivery room holding our beautiful baby, Michael leaned over and kissed me and told me how very much he was in love with me. Then he kissed our baby again, and he told me how much he loved him. After this they rolled me into the recovery room where Michael stood there holding our son, Teddy.

As April walked into the recovery room with Amber, Teddy actually lifted his head to turn to her voice because it was a familiar voice he had heard so often. I didn't know babies could actually do that, but he did. As I lay there they gave me the telephone, and I called my mother to let her know everything was fine and that we had had a beautiful baby boy. She was so happy she cried. She told me she was coming that afternoon to see us.

It wasn't until a couple of days later that Michael began talking about what was going on in his head while I was lying there in pain, why he kept crying. He told me he was so terrified that he was going to lose us both, that we were both going to die on him. He said he had never seen a woman in labor before, and he didn't know exactly what to expect. He didn't know if this was normal or what was going on. All he knew was that he was terrified of losing us both. That's why he was crying.

I remember the first day, the first time they brought Teddy in for me to feed. They placed him in my arms and the feeling was indescribable joy, a feeling of so much hope. I had a brand-new life in my hands, and I was going to do everything right. I would work my hardest to keep all the evils away from him, the drugs, the alcohol, the gambling, and the violence, everything that I was forced to grow up with. I was determined all of these things were going to be absent from his life. Here was a new soul in this world, one that I could mold and shape into a good human being, a responsible honorable man, a loving man.

That was my goal in life now, for when I held my baby in my arms, I held hope, hope for the future, hope for breaking this vicious cycle in my family, this vicious cycle of abuse. I was determined to do this. Michael and I had already got the ball rolling on it, and there was no way after looking at this precious child that we were ever going back to the way things were. We were on the right path, and Teddy was our guiding light, the light that would keep us on the right path always. For him we would now be strong.

I find it so funny that Michael and I had always been a team, and we had always done everything together. We supported one another through everything, and him not being there, April being my coach and Michael not being the part of the team, during the most important time in both our lives, just didn't seem natural. So, when it ended up with Michael having to do what he had to, it was almost like fate intervening. He was supposed to be there. He was supposed to be by my side. He was my other half, and he was the other half of the team. He needed to go through what he went through just as I did.

The first time Michael held Teddy in his arms he glowed. Michael actually glowed. I had never seen that look of utter complete content and happiness on his face. In the nine years that we had been together, I had never seen him with a look like that before. It was so funny, when Michael would come to visit me and the baby in the hospital, I would be holding him, and Teddy would always be sleeping. He slept all the time, and Michael would try to wake him up by tickling the bottom of his feet, and this would do it.

He would wake up, but I told him, "The baby needs to sleep."

He said, "I don't care. I only have a few hours here to visit, and I want to be able to visit with my son."

Teddy was so adorable. He didn't have very much hair, just a little bit of peach fuzz on top. He had the roundest face, fat little cheeks and a cute little nose. He resembled slightly a Cabbage Patch Doll. He had the sweetest smile and the fattest little legs. He was simply adorable. The first time Michael and I both laid eyes on him, trust me, it was love at first sight. Here was a living, breathing testimony of Michael's and my love for each other that we held in our arms. At times it just felt so surreal like I was living some kind of a beautiful dream, a dream that I didn't want to wake up from ever. For the first time in my life everything was perfect. I had a man that I loved more than anything in the world, and now a beautiful baby. I couldn't have asked for more.

Now it was time for Teddy and me to go home. After four days the doctor released us. Michael arrived at the hospital very early that morning, and we prepared to go home. We got all the formula together, the doctor's orders, we packed up the car, and we put our precious little package in his car seat for the first time. We drove home. When I opened the door I was floored. The place was decorated in a party atmosphere with balloons and streamers, and a big beautiful cake awaited us. My mother and sisters got this together. There were so many pictures taken of Teddy with everyone. It was such a happy day, one that I will never, ever forget.

My mother took a picture of Michael and me both holding the baby, and she looked at the picture after it came out turned to me and said, "Kyra, I don't know if you realize this or not, but Michael actually looks like he is glowing, and I have never seen this look before on his face."

I told her, "Ma, I know it. I saw the same thing."

She said, "He truly looks like a man in love, in love with both you and his new baby. That twinkle that is in his eyes in this picture is indescribable."

That night after the party was over and there was just Michael and I and our new baby, I sat there watching Michael give him his first bottle at home. I felt like crying. I never felt so happy in my life and so fulfilled, knowing that this baby was a part of Michael and me and our love. I felt so good inside being able to give Michael something so precious. I felt so good being able to make him so happy. Our life and our love was truly now complete.

I also realized at that moment how strong a man Michael truly was to be having to deal with everything from his past, from Vietnam, from the alcoholism, and now losing his first-born son to adoption, and yet still being able to hold it all together for his baby and me. How strong this man was emotionally not to let life destroy him. He picked himself up always, dusted himself off and kept on going.

As he always told me, "It's okay to take a break, Kyra, if things get too hard and too overwhelming at times. It's all right to just sit back and take a break. But remember this as well, Kyra, take your break and then come back strong, and come back fighting, and never, ever give up."

Those words I tried so hard to live by, and to this day I still do. These words have gotten me through a lot in my life. This is how Michael survived his life, all the horrors that happened to him and all the painful memories. He dealt with them finally, and he was able to move on with his life and find happiness with me and now with our new family. He is a hero in every sense of the word, and these are the thoughts that ran through my mind as I sat there watching him feed our beautiful baby boy, Teddy, knowing he would be teaching him the same things that he taught me—how to be strong.

CHAPTER SEVEN

I also thought at this moment, who was I to be so blessed in this life, as Michael sat there, holding and feeding Teddy so gently and so lovingly. I made a promise to myself that I would never, ever take their love for granted, my beautiful baby boy and the man that I loved more than life itself. I would hold their love in my heart and protect it always.

Michael was a great father from the word, go. He was always so gentle and so loving with Teddy, and our little family got into a beautiful routine where every night after we bathed Teddy we would place him between us in our bed to give him his nightly bottle and just stare in amazement at this beautiful human being that we had both created a living, breathing testimony of our love.

Unfortunately it wasn't always this easy, you see when I first brought Teddy home from the hospital he was colicky, and for the first three months of his life he didn't sleep very much. He took twenty-minute naps here and twenty minute naps there. Every time I would feed him he would end up vomiting. It became a succession of feeding and changing his bed after he threw up. The doctor tried everything. It seemed every other week we changed his formula because the doctor thought perhaps this was making him sick.

It wouldn't be until years later that I would finally figure out what exactly had gone wrong. I think Teddy had acid reflux. It did run in the family. Michael had it very badly, and I think this is what was going on with Teddy. It was just that the doctor did not diagnose it. So for the first three months, as I said, there was a procession of keeping his little baby tub out by the sink and giving his nightly bath, his nightly bottle, and laying him down in his bassinet, only to hear him vomiting all over. Then I would have to change the bassinet, and I would have to bathe him again. Then, of course, he would be hungry again, because he just got through vomiting up all his food, so I would have to feed him again. This went on night after night after night after night for three months. At the end of the three months I was almost psychotic, with very little sleep, and of course Michael wasn't able to help me very much because he had to work. He had to get his sleep to be able to do this. So I would take Teddy out in the living room. We would go through this every night.

Thank God for my mother. She would come over almost on a daily basis to help me out with Teddy. She would take care of him while I was able to do some cleaning, the laundry and a little bit of cooking. She would become Teddy's second mother. They had become so close.

It was only after these three months that Michael and I were able to truly thoroughly enjoy having our new baby. Before that it was very stressful, but we made it through. I can still remember the first day that Teddy slept completely through the night. I had put him in his crib in our room about 9 o'clock that night knowing that it was ridiculous for me to do this because he would just end up by throwing up, and the same thing would be happening over and over again, but I tried it anyway. It wasn't until 9 o'clock the following morning, twelve hours later, that I woke up.

As I was waking up, I looked at the clock, and I said, "Oh, my God." All I could think of was my child was dead because he had never slept like that before. Mind you it was twenty-minute naps here and twenty minute naps there. Now all of a sudden it was twelve hours. I jumped out of my bed in complete horror. With my heart in my throat, I ran over to the crib expecting to find a dead baby, and much to my relief I picked him up crying. I was crying, not the baby, and held him in my arms. He just looked up at me and smiled. This was the end of the colic phase, and believe me when I say, I would never want to repeat this, ever again. It was after this that Michael and I were able to really enjoy him after his baths with his bottle lying there between us.

While I was going through all of this with Teddy's colic, Michael's mother told me that Michael was the same way when he was born. It was over three months before Michael actually had a good night's sleep. Again I don't believe it was colic. I believe it was that acid reflux, because Michael had that all his life, and now, so does Teddy. Even after the colic stopped my mother continued to come over almost on a daily basis, actually about four days a week. She was a fantastic grandmother and she loved her grandson so much. As with any good grandmother, she spoiled him rotten. In her book, whatever Teddy wanted, Teddy got, which from time to time made it rather difficult for Michael and me, but that was okay. It was a good trade off. He was happy, my mother was happy, I was happy and Michael was happy. That's all that mattered.

Most mornings in good weather, I would put Teddy in his carriage, and my mother and I would take him for a long walk up and down the street. As he grew older and was able to walk on his own, she would take him all around the complex showing him off to the neighbors. He truly was her heart, and they so enjoyed spending time together. I remember we had a little table with matching chairs in Teddy's room for snack time, and every lunchtime she would take him in there with peanut butter and crackers and chocolate milk. She would tell him, "It's time for our little picnic lunch," and they would both sit there together looking out the window snacking on their goodies. She would spend hours every day with him either playing games of watching Sesame Street. This was his favorite show of all.

I remember one day in particular. Teddy must have been about two. When I was walking by his room I overheard their conversation. She was telling him about God and his son, Jesus, and how heaven was. Up to this point I hadn't really thought about how I was going to raise him as far as religious went. I still felt the way that I felt about the Catholic Church, and I was still angry with God. So I was not all that sure about his religious teachings yet. I stood there and listened to their conversation and how nice she made it all sound, and it brought me back to my grandmother teaching me. I didn't know whether I liked this or not, and I didn't know if it was right or wrong. I wasn't sure if I should say anything to her about how I have been feeling all my life because she really didn't know and I decided not to. I decided he could learn worse things I suppose, and he needed some sort of a grasp of who our Creator was. Mind you, I never stopped believing God was there; I just didn't like him. I didn't like the decisions that he made, and I felt a lot of times he was simply just asleep at the wheel. However, I kept my anger in check toward God, and I let my mother continue her teachings. I never said anything to her, and I certainly never said anything to Teddy. I could see in Teddy's eyes that he had the same love for his grandmother that I did for mine, and this made me feel good inside. So I thought to myself, *How could this possibly be wrong?*

Now as I sit here today I am very grateful to my mother for teaching him his first lesson about God because at that time I simply was not able to. My mother was easily the strongest, most talented, and the most intelligent woman I have ever met or ever will meet in my life. She had always taught me to be strong, and now she is going to teach my son the same. I felt truly blest to have a mother like her, and I also realized I could never hold a candle to her as far as being a mother and a woman goes, and I would never try to fill her shoes. If I were only half as good a mother and a woman as she was I would consider myself truly blessed. My mother and I had always been more than just mother and daughter. We were best friends as well, for I knew there was nothing I could not tell her, and I knew she would never stand in judgment of me. We did not always see eye to eye on everything. There were a few decisions that I made in my life that she did not agree with, but I always knew in my heart and soul she would stand behind me no matter what, and she always did.

I will cherish all of these days that my mother spent with Teddy and me forever. These were special times for both my son and me, memories that will live in our hearts and our minds forever. Many a night at the dinner table I would look across and see Michael, my mother and Teddy in his little highchair, and I would thank God for them all. I realized how truly blessed I was to have such a loving, caring wonderful family.

Little did I know Michael was thrilled with this as well but wanted to add on to our little family. It was around Teddy's second birthday when Michael approached me on the subject of having another child. You see, neither one of us wanted Teddy to be alone in life. We always wanted him to have someone else to turn to after we were long gone, a brother or a sister, someone else in this world that he could truly count on to be there. Although I wanted another baby with all my heart, and I felt this way toward giving Teddy a sibling, I feared that the stress would just be too much for Michael. I was worried about this. So far he was handling everything fantastically. He was such a good father and a great husband, but again with another child more stress would be added, more stress to the budget, needing more money. I had to think about it, and I told him he should as well. Through all of this he was still continuing to see his psychiatrist and was on medication.

You see posttraumatic stress and the trauma that he suffered isn't anything that they have a cure for. It can only be treated through a regiment of medications and talking with a psychiatrist. He was doing so well with this regimen I was afraid to rock the boat. You see, with any veteran that suffers through these mental illnesses, you don't know. They are always walking a fine line. You are truly living on a tightrope, and one push one way or the other could send them tumbling. This was something I was trying desperately to avoid by doing my best to make a nice home, a nice quiet home. I did my best to do everything perfectly—to have meals on the table at a certain hour, to have the house always clean and to have Teddy well taken care of. I felt as though if I did this, this was one less stress on Michael. So when he did get home even though he may have had a bad day, he would always come home to a place where he was happy to be and could spend time with his child and his loving wife, a sort of refuge from the world. I worked hard every day trying to achieve this for him. So after Michael approached me with the suggestion of having another child, we both gave ourselves a week to seriously consider the move before we would make it. Both of us went over the pros and the cons. Ultimately, we did decide we wanted to have another child.

I began trying to get pregnant again. It was in February of 1990 when we conceived our second child—on Valentine's Day to be precise. We both thought to ourselves, *How appropriate. On this day of love we created something so wonderful.* I was to find out the same way I did the first time with Teddy that I was pregnant. The day after Valentine's Day I would wake up, and I ran to the bathroom vomiting. I then went into the kitchen and tried my hardest to make a pot of coffee and became violently ill at just the smell of it. I knew then, and I told Michael, "We did it, Honey. I'm pregnant." The rest of that month I spent throwing up, and I was not being able to stand the smell of coffee let alone the taste of it. I told Michael we would have to wait to be sure.

It was at the end of that month when I got a home pregnancy kit, and I took the test. Sure enough, it was positive. After I took the test in the bathroom, I came out holding the stick, and as Teddy and Michael sat there on the couch watching television, I walked up to Teddy, and I kneeled down beside him and gave him a great big hug, and I told him, "Guess what, Honey? You're going to be a big brother."

Michael then jumped off the couch and gave me a huge hug. He said, "I don't know why I'm surprised after this last month of seeing you vomiting and your aversion to coffee, but it's nice to get confirmation," and we hugged each other and kissed. Then we both hugged Teddy.

Although Michael's reaction was what I expected, Teddy's was not. Teddy jumped off the couch and ran into his bedroom crying. Mind you he was only two and a half at the time and had no clue what to expect. He had no idea what exactly was going to happen to him, and of course at this age, children believe the world revolves completely around them. He was wondering how this little brother or sister was going to fit into, and of course he didn't want anything to change in his life so he was less than happy to hear this news.

Michael and I then both went into his room to talk with him. Firsts of all we wanted to know why he had as bad a reaction as he did. Then we tried to figure out what exactly he was thinking about. I asked Teddy why he was crying.

He shouted at both his father and me, "Now that you're gonna have a brand-new baby you won't want me anymore!"

Michael and I both looked at each other and laughed at first, but as soon as we realized Teddy was serious, this was no laughing matter. We had to convince him that our love for him and his place in his home would never change.

As much as we tried talking to Teddy, all he kept yelling out was, "You won't want me anymore; you'll just want the baby," and he really truly believed this. Then he said, "After the baby is born you won't even want me to live here with you, will you? Where am I supposed to live if I can't live here with you? Where am I supposed to go?"

I then sat on his bed beside him, and I held him in my arms, and Michael sat on the other side. The two of us both tried our best to explain to Teddy that his worries were completely unfounded. He would always be our baby, and he would always live with us. I tried to explain to that him this baby was not a replacement for him but an addition to our family, a loving addition. I said, "Our family now is going to consist of Mommy, Daddy, Teddy, and a new brother or a sister."

I also told Teddy that he would have a responsibility as well with the baby. Being a newborn baby and his little brother or little sister, he would have to teach him things. It was his turn to be the teacher now and to protect him always. Then Teddy looked up at me with tears in his eyes, and quickly replied, "I only want a new baby if it's a little sister. That's all I want."

I looked down at him and smiled, and I told him, "No one but God knows what this baby is going to be; there is no way I can possibly guarantee that you are going to have a little sister." I told him, "You're going to have to take what God gives us and love it."

Knowing that my mother had already taught him these lessons and spoken to him about God I thought it would be a helpful tool now for me to use because he understood God created us. I just kept reminding Teddy, "This baby is going to rely on you to protect him from the world, from bad things like Mommy and

Daddy protect you. You have a very, very important job, which is now to be a big brother. No matter whether it's a boy or it's a girl, we will love it, just as we love you, Teddy."

I also told him, "Whatever it is, it will always look up to you as his big brother, and look toward you for guidance. You're going to be like Superman in this baby's eyes, a hero." I knew Teddy would be able to identify with that because he did enjoy watching all the Superman movies. "Wouldn't you like to be like Superman if you had a chance?"

He said, "Yes, I would."

"Well, here's your chance. You can now always be this baby's protector, this baby's super hero."

Teddy looked up at his father and me and smiled at us. He said, "This is cool, Mom."

Michael and I then both hugged him, and reminded him of how much we loved him. I held his little face in my hand, and I told him, "You will always be a part of me, a part of my heart. No matter how old you get, you will always be my baby," and I told him, "Don't you ever forget that."

This talk that we had with Teddy did seem to squash some of his fears. I didn't know if he was still completely happy with the idea of being invaded by another baby. Only time would tell. I knew we would have to have a few more conversations during my pregnancy for him to truly accept this, but for now we seemed to have gotten things smoothed over.

It was March now of 1990 and there was a late winter's snowstorm. It was so beautiful out that night, with its cool, crisp air. All the stars had come out and we felt on this special night that they glowed in the night sky just for us. By about 9 o'clock the snow had stopped falling and it was eerily quiet out. You see Michael and I had always loved going for drives at night after a big snowfall. Just after the plows cleared the streets everything was so beautiful, so white and so clean looking. We loved how the new fallen snow glistened in the moonlight. It looked as though there were millions of tiny little diamonds sprinkled all over, and the trees were beautiful with the snow clinging to every little branch. To me it was just simply magical looking. It was as though God had sprinkled our little corner of the world with pure beauty. The air itself just smelled so clean and so crisp.

Through these drives that Michael and I would take, we would often stop at Dunkin' Donuts for a delicious hot chocolate, and then we would continue our drive just admiring the beauty of it all. We would often spend two, three, sometimes four hours at night driving around after a fresh snowfall. These were one of our simple pleasures of life, things that we enjoyed doing together. These drives lived in my memory for always, every one of these nights with the quietness, the tranquility and the beauty. Each and every one of these special nights as we drove by tree after tree glistening with snow in the tranquility of our surroundings I will hold in my heart forever. The tranquility of it all would make Michael and me feel as if we were the only two people on the face of the earth. Michael would always make me feel so safe and so secure. I always felt so protected with him beside me.

So on this very special night Michael and I thought, *Why not do this? Why not go for a nice long drive? Why not end the evening doing something that we both loved to do so much?* We both then turned to Teddy and asked him if he would like to go for a ride in the snow. He jumped for joy, he said "Yea, Mommy, yea!"

So I bundled him all up, Michael and I put our coats on, and we headed out to the car. I put Teddy in his car seat in the back. Michael and I got into the car and we started our little adventure. I remember Teddy looking up at the full moon and pointing to it and asking, "What is that, Mommy?" I then explained to him what it was. I didn't realize that he had not seen a full moon before, but perhaps he did but was too young to realize just what it was.

So with the full moon and the twinkling stars we had a most magical trip. Well, I should say at least Michael and I did. Halfway down the street I looked into the back seat, and Teddy was fast asleep. I guess 9 o'clock was just a little too late for him, and I just sat there looking at Michael driving and Teddy in the back seat. I thought to myself, *The two men that I love most in this world, the two men my heart beats for, my whole world was sitting right beside me.* How totally and completely fulfilled and happy I felt at that very moment. Michael and I had created a beautiful family together, and there would only be more love to come with the birth of our second child due in the fall.

As Michael and I drove down the street taking in all the majesty, the beauty of the fresh fallen snow, we drove to Dunkin' Donuts to get our traditional hot chocolates. As we sat there in the parking lot of Dunkin' Donuts watching the plows go by, Michael turned to me and asked me yet again to marry him. But now I thought to myself, *I had even more at stake to lose.* Now we were going to have a second child, and all my old fears came rushing back to me. I was just so petrified of losing everything, of losing Michael if we were to be married and it didn't work out, I would be left to raise my two children by myself. I couldn't risk it. I just could not. Everything was too perfect, and I was afraid of throwing a wrench into the works. I was so terrified of taking the next step and that would be marriage.

So I quickly reminded him of why I didn't want to get married to begin with. I told him, "You know, I really don't believe in curses, Michael, but I swear my family has one on it. There just has not been a successful marriage in my family." I told him, "I truly feel and believe in my heart that if we were to get married it would destroy everything that we've worked so hard to build. How can I possibly get married feeling this way? I'm just not willing to take that chance, not yet, not now."

Michael told me I understood, but I don't think he really did. I only hoped he never felt as though I didn't love him enough. If anything, I loved him too much to destroy what we had built and to take that chance. This is a fear that I would never be able to get past.

It was now about 11:30, it was getting late and our hot chocolate had turned cold. We decided to head back on home. Michael carried Teddy into the house where he remained in a deep sleep. After every one of these long winter night drives, Michael and I could hardly wait to get back home and crawl under our nice warm comfortable covers to hold each other. This is just what we did. After we tucked Teddy in for the night we crawled underneath our covers and we held each other close, our lips meeting and our bodies entwining warming every inch of ourselves that had been touched by the winter's night air.

Although Michael and I had been together now for eleven years, the fire and the passion had never diminished, and the bond and love that we felt toward one another grew ever stronger year by year. Each and every time we would make love it just seemed to be more passionate than the time before. This night in particular would stand out in my memory forever, because Michael and I were so thrilled about finding out we were going to have another child. I can remember every little thing about this evening, and after we made deep passionate love, we lay there in each other's arms and spoke about the wonderful future our family was to have and wondered if the next child was going to be a boy or a girl. But I honestly have to say neither one of us cared what it was as long as it was healthy and happy. We lay there for the rest of the night talking until we saw the sun coming up. We fell asleep in each other's arms.

The next few weeks to come would prove to be quite a transitional period for my family. With the settlement for my hand coming through, Michael came to me and asked me what I thought about his going to Tractor Trailer School to get his CDL license. I have to say, I had never seem him quite so excited about any other career choice he had made in the past as he was about this. He explained to me with a CDL license he would be able to make enough income to put us in the life style that he wanted to. We would be able to get our own home and be able to start putting money away for the children's education. He would finally be able to support us the way he wanted to, and he hoped someday it would lead to him owning his own business that perhaps he could hand down to Teddy and this next baby that would be coming.

I could see he had definite plans for our future, and he explained to me that although the college job was secure, it was not enough money to do the things that he wanted to do for his family. He knew he would never make the income that we truly needed if he were to stay there, and I told him, "Michael, I see how happy you are about wanting to do this, but you really have to think long and hard now before you just throw a job away, because you do have people relying on you for this income." I reminded him how hard it was to get what he had. He told me he realized all of that, but he knew he could do better now. He was feeling a lot better, and the medication and the psychiatry were really working. He was feeling normal for the first time in his life, and he knew he could do this.

Again, I reminded him of the few jobs that were in our area, and he had a decent paying one so he needed to really, really be sure before he turned his back on it. I told him they would probably never hire him back. He told me, "Kyra, sometimes you just have to take chances in life. You have to take that leap of faith in order to do better, in order to be able to provide better for your family and give them the lifestyle that you want. Sometimes you have to take chances, and this is going to be mine." Then he looked at me and he said, "Baby Doll, I really need to do this. I need to do this for myself, and I need to do this for us. I need to move on. I need to better myself as a man."

I then told him, "Michael, I don't need a big fancy house; I don't need big fancy cars or to go on vacation. All I need is you. All I want is you, so if you're doing this just for me, don't."

"I'm doing it for you but for myself as well. Please try to understand, Kyra. This is something I just need to do. I need to try this."

I hesitantly gave my blessings. "Michael, if you really want to do this then go ahead, just so long as you realize what you are leaving behind, and that is a secure, decent-paying job."

He said, "I know, and I know I can do this."

I told him, "I'm behind you all the way, Michael. As long as it makes you happy, I'm all for it."

Then Michael quickly reminded me that he was just following in his father and grandfather's footsteps, and he told me perhaps our son would do the same. "After all," he said, "my father and grandfather made good incomes. They were able to provide nice homes for their families," he said, "I just want to have the opportunity to do the same."

Then he quickly reminded me about when he had come back from Vietnam he was in the construction union, and he had been a heavy equipment operator, so he really did like that type of work. He said, "The only reason I screwed up on that was because of the drinking and the problems that I had that I didn't even know I had. I was just straight out of Vietnam. That's why I couldn't make that work at that time, but I can now, Kyra. I promise you I can."

He told me, "You realize that without a college education I would never be able to make the kind of money I know I can make driving a truck."

So we came to the agreement that, yes, he was going to give the college two weeks' notice, and as soon as my settlement came through, which was only a matter of days, that I would receive the check. He would enroll then in Tractor Trailer School.

Now at this time I was in my fourth month of pregnancy and Michael was going to school full time. I was staying at home taking care of Teddy, and everything seemed to be going smoothly. With the settlement I was able to pay off all of our bills—the furniture loans, the car loans, and I was even able to afford to by myself a Camaro. In the back of my mind I was always worried whether Michael was going to be successful at this. I could see Michael was working so hard and doing well in school.

As my pregnancy progressed I found it was very different from the first one. The baby was so calm. I was not used to this at all considering Teddy spent 90% of his time doing somersaults in me. I began to worry, and I spoke to the doctor about this, and he said, "If it would ease your mind we could do an ultrasound." I quickly agreed to this. So we did the ultrasound. Michael and I, along with Teddy went to the appointment, and he saw his little baby brother or sister for the first time.

We got a picture, and the doctor told me the baby was absolutely perfect. He told me, "There's nothing to worry about, Kyra. He's just a little bit calmer than Teddy was."

Again, Michael and I did not want to know the sex of the baby. We wanted to be surprised. I thought immediately to myself, *Well, maybe it is going to be a girl because it is so calm and so different from the first pregnancy when I had a boy.*

Also something else pleasant happened to me. The morning sickness on the fourth month finally stopped. I was able to rest and enjoy my pregnancy without always worrying about having to be around a bathroom. So my pregnancy was going well, and Michael was studying his brains out (this was a habit he had to get back into because it had been many years since he had studied). In between the studying and the school, he also was worried about the baby and me. Just as he did during the first pregnancy, he worried about us both being okay. Michael had a tremendous amount of pressure on his shoulders at this time, but he was handling it very well.

Michael quickly found one other way to relieve some of the stress besides speaking to his psychiatrist about it. He remained going there twice a week. He started taking Teddy fishing. After school he would come home and pick up Teddy and the two of them would go down to the lake to our special spot and throw in their lines. They would spend hours every day just doing this. This made me feel so happy inside to see father and son bonding so closely together. The first day out Teddy caught two big-mouthed bass. Michael was so proud of him. When he got home with the fish we took pictures, lots of pictures. As Teddy stood there in the living room with the fish dripping onto the rug, he proudly held up his first catch, but his father was even prouder.

Even this was not enough to relieve all of Michael's stress: the stress of school, the stress of worrying about me and the baby, worrying about Teddy, and making sure he was spending enough time with him. Michael was now finding himself staying awake half the night worrying about the baby and me and the other half of the time worrying about how he was doing in school and trying to study.

It was now the first time in years that he had an episode, an episode of night terrors. It was one of these nights that in his sleep he kneed me in the stomach and punched me in the mouth while screaming in Vietnamese just as he did in the past. I just lay there stunned. I couldn't believe this was happening, not after all this time, but I guess this is what happens when too much stress is put on a person with post-traumatic stress. Thank God neither the baby nor I was injured. Michael snapped out of it quickly when I jumped out of the bed and switched on the lights. The two of us were quite alarmed at this apparent regression in his behavior.

The next day Michael met with his psychiatrist and explained to him everything that had taken place that night before. His psychiatrist explained to Michael how people with the problems that he had had with post-traumatic stress handled things differently, much more differently than other people. They find it very difficult to handle every day stress and pressure. They fool themselves into thinking that since they are handling it during the day, and it may appear they are, at night it will come out. The stress will take over, and this is when we see a regression in the therapy. Quite often the psychiatrist sees the night terrors returning. In most of the cases it is only for a short time that they will return. As soon as the stress is relieved, the night terrors will stop again.

He then told Michael, "Whether you realize it or not, you are under tremendous stress. You have a new baby on the way, you have a baby to take care of, and you have a career that you are trying desperately to start. You see, you have stressed yourself right out. No wonder you're having nightmares. You must learn how to deal with all this stress while you are awake, or it will come out at night."

This was something that Michael never quite learned how to do, so the doctor ultimately ended up by changing a couple of his medications. These medications did not agree with Michael at all. They left him very, very tired, and he found it nearly impossible to stay focused at school. Surprisingly enough tractor-trailer school was very difficult. People think that it is just as simple as getting behind the wheel and driving, but you have to remember that it is an eighteen-wheeler. It's enormous. Unless you know what you are doing, you are driving a killing machine. As a matter of fact, this course was so difficult that a few men dropped out of it because they could no longer take the pressure. Michael did not let this influence him at all. He stayed and pushed through it. He was never one to give up on anything, whether it is in his personal life or at work. He was a very, very strong-willed man who had a lot of integrity, a trait I prayed he would hand down to his children.

Meanwhile, at home now, the days for me were passing rather quickly. After breakfast my mother usually came over to visit. She did not visit as often as she did a few months earlier. Her age was beginning to catch up with her. After all she was close to 70 now and living the life that she had led and all the crosses she had bared, she had a right to be tired. She was also a diabetic and this disease was slowly stealing her eyesight. It seemed like every year her eyesight diminished a little more.

Teddy, my mother, and I had a routine of watching *Sesame Street* together. By this time I was beginning to teach Teddy his colors, his numbers and a few letters from the alphabet. Every day Teddy and I would work on something different together. On most days Teddy and I would go for long walks and each day there would be a new color I would have him point out. I would call it the "Color of the Day" and the "Number of the Day." Every day I would play this game with him. I would have him count the trees as we walked by. I would have him tell me the colors of the leaves or the pretty flowers that we passed, and he would always try to find a little bit more than he had the day before.

At night after supper and his bath, we would sit there in the rocking chair together and read nursery rhymes and Dr. Seuss. He so enjoyed me reading to him. My nickname for him was Honey Bunny. I couldn't help it. He just looked like one with his cherub like cheeks and his twinkly eyes. He was just so sweet and very, very smart. Teaching him was a breeze. It seemed like all you needed to do was show him something once or twice, and he would just get it. He amazed me at times at just how fast a learner he really was.

One night after supper, Michael and I, along with Teddy, were all snuggled up on the couch watching TV when on the show that we were watching appeared a very intoxicated man. Teddy looked up at me with his sweet little face and asked me, "Mommy, what is that man doing? What's wrong with him?"

I looked down at Teddy, and I said to him, "That man is drunk," and that is when it hit me. It suddenly occurred to me Teddy had never been exposed to anyone who had been drinking, because when Michael and I had stopped drinking in 1983, we stopped associating with all of our friends that remained drinking. We never even thought of having alcohol or drugs in our home. This was simply not accepted by either Michael or me or allowed in our home, especially around our children, so Teddy had never been exposed to any of this at all.

I looked over at Michael, and I said to him, "I guess this is just as good a time as any to start our campaign of no drugs and no alcohol in our home. Let's start our teaching."

Michael looked at me and said, "Yes, I guess so." We knew by teaching our children about the downfall of drugs and alcohol this was the only way that we were going to be successful in breaking the cycle of alcoholism in our family. It had to start here. It had to start now when they are at the most influential age. So you see just as I taught Teddy about colors and about numbers, I now had to teach him about the downfalls, the dark side of life, the dark side that his father and I crawled out of. So Teddy was taught from the time he was two and a half years old how bad alcohol and drugs were and how people did stupid things while on them. Mommy and Daddy didn't do this, and we didn't expect him to do this. This would never be accepted in our home. I associated alcohol and drugs with poison, and I told him I don't expect you to drink or to take drugs any more than I would expect you to drink poison because in our minds it is the same thing.

Every opportunity after this that I had to educate Teddy about this I took. I was determined to break the cycle in our family. I was determined that our children were going to be the first generation in both Michael's and my family to not have alcohol take over their lives and ultimately destroy them. I wouldn't let this happen, not to my children. I realized I would have to make this my life's mission to ensure that this did not happen to them, and I would.

Throughout out all of this I did also realize one other thing. Children learn by example. If they went their entire lives seeing their father and me never taking a drink, I prayed that they would never have the desire to. They would always see their father and me dealing with our problems, dealing with life and enjoying and loving each other with the absence of alcohol. Children after all want to do what their parents are doing, and if they never see their parents doing certain things, why on earth would they even think about doing it? This is what I hoped would happen. This in essence was my game plan.

Also, more often than not, what you are, your children are going to become. So, if you are sitting there drinking and getting drunk every night, why on earth would it be so surprising to you if your children grew up doing the same exact thing. They mimic what they see. More often than not, your child will become you. So before you pick up another shot of whiskey or whatever you do to numb yourself, please, for your child's sake, take a good, long look at his or her face and ask yourself, "Is this the legacy I want to hand down to them, a legacy filled with heartbreak and loneliness and sorrow?"

You see, this is what I saw whenever I looked at my father. I saw him choosing the alcohol over me, over my mother, over my sisters, and over life, and the cruelty that would follow after he became intoxicated. The only thing that saved me was having a clean and sober mother, a strong woman who deeply loved her daughters. She was the one and only thing that saved me.

So before you take that next shot of Whiskey, think about what I am saying. Put it down and go and get help, if not for yourself, for your children. They deserve, just as every child deserves, to live a normal happy life with normal parents, parents that are not in a daze and parents that can truly love them. Ultimately all a child needs to survive is love, and when you are numb, your heart is numb and you cannot give that to your child. As much as you think you are or want to, it's not happening.

I grew up in such a bizarre home. On one hand I had my father, abusive, alcoholic and gambler who was self-serving, self-centered, and who cared basically for no one but his own self. He was an evil bastard. Believe me when I say that I fought my whole life never to become him, to never let that evil in, to never let it take me over as it did him. I instead tried my hardest to become like my mother. Although I know I can never hold a candle to her, I would like to think of myself as being as strong and loving a woman as she was. If I could achieve this in my life, I will find myself very fortunate, and if I am sure of only one thing in my life that is good will always win out over evil. I am a living example of this.

Every day I looked at both good and evil; my mother the good, my father the evil. As physically strong as my father may have been, my mother's will, her inner strength and heart, always beat the shit out of him. Because I recognized my father as being what he was and that was in my heart I truly believe evil. I gave nothing of myself. I showed him nothing. I showed him no fear. I showed him no hate, no anger, and certainly no love. I gave him nothing, and I am sure he hated me for this. He thrived on people hating him. He thrived on feeling people's fears. He thrived on things that would sicken a normal father. So now you understand when I say, the last thing I wanted to do was to be like my father. As far as I'm concerned, the day he died is the day the evil died and left my life forever. This is why I wanted to raise our children in a clean loving atmosphere. All of the evil that my father spewed out over the years, over my lifetime, was going to end here and now. It was not going to be passed on to another generation, another generation of addiction. I was breaking the cycle.

I turned my back on the past, on that part of my family's history, and I will never look back. I will only now look ahead, look ahead to a normal life with my family, my children and the man that I love more than life itself. I will never forget what I must do. I must always be vigilant with my teachings, with my children. I turn my back on my family's addictions, but I will never be able to forget them, nor should I. I also realize that my own addition can always come creeping back up on me. I must always be careful because my family's past additions could rear their ugly heads at any time.

I promised myself I would teach my children well. I would teach them about all these things, and as they grow older, hopefully they will be able to use the knowledge that I passed on to them and to be able to fight it as well. So right along with the A, B, C's I will teach them these facts of life. Hopefully the time will never come when they are going to need this, or they are going to need my words. Hopefully, they'll be able to stay clear of alcohol and drugs, but if they fall prey to it, I hope they can remember my words, my teachings and follow in the footsteps of their father and mine. Dear God, all I want is for my children to lead normal lives, happy lives, and if I need to work my whole life keeping them away from the things I know are going to destroy them, I will do this. I will do this for them.

Recently I have heard that alcoholism and drug abuse are not only passed down from generation to generation simply because this is what you see while we are growing up, but they've also found that it's in the genes. They have found that the alcoholism can be physically passed on. I'm hoping that this isn't true, and if it is, that my children somehow do not inherit this, but I know I'm playing against the odds here.

Michael was now on the verge of graduating from tractor-trailer school, and I was so very, very proud of him. I knew just how hard he had worked for this day. We had two things to look forward to because I was also on the verge of giving birth to our second child. As a matter of fact, it was exactly two weeks after Michael graduated that this occurred. It was November 26, 1990. Michael drove me to the hospital after my water broke, and I was in labor for ten hours. This time April was not there and Michael waited out in the waiting room. This is the way I wanted it. The stress was just way too much on both of them before.

After ten hours had passed, and I was still only five centimeters dilated, just as the labor before with Teddy, I couldn't stand any more. I told the doctor to please give me a "C-section," and I also discussed having my tubes cut and tied because two children were all that Michael and I were planning to have.

As I lay there screaming in agony in labor, the doctor leaned over me with his tie tickling the end of my nose, he asked me, "Kyra, are you sure? Are you sure you want to do the C-section?"

I grabbed him by his tie, pulled him close, nose to nose to me, and said, "What do you fucking think?"

He said, "Okay, okay," and they wheeled me into the operating room.

They put me under anesthesia, and before I knew it I was out. I awoke about an hour later in the recovery room where Michael was standing. He leaned over me and gave me a big kiss, and he said, "We have another beautiful baby boy, Kyra." On this day, Martin Jones was born. Martin weighed seven and one-half pounds and was 20 inches long. He was absolutely perfect.

The first time they brought our baby in and laid him in my arms, he took my breath away. I swear he looked just like an angel. His skin was so light it glowed. His face was angelic and just soft fuzz covered his whole head. If you can stop for a moment and think of what a little baby angel would look like, this is truly what he looked like. He had the biggest, most beautiful blue eyes.

The first time that his father and I first held him, we fell so deeply in love. I remember looking into those beautiful blue eyes and saying, "You are my angel. You are my angel on earth." I looked up at Michael and said, "My God, God sent us one of his angels."

Michael chuckled at me, and then went to take Martin into his own arms. He looked down at his beautiful face. As he was staring into his big blue eyes, Michael then looked at me and said, "Kyra, I would have to agree with you; God did."

Michael and I already had the most perfect name already picked out for him. Well, actually two names. You see, if he were going to be a girl, we were going to name him after my sister, Amber, her full name, Amber Ann Marie. If it were a boy we were going for the pure Irish name of Martin, and this seemed to fit him perfectly.

So, after a very long, long week in the hospital away from my other precious baby, Teddy (although he was allowed to come in and visit a few times to see his new little baby brother) I was so looking forward to coming home again and getting into a routine now with my two beautiful baby boys. Believe me when I say, Martin Patrick Jones and Mommy were just itching to go home. I was extremely sore, and I found a C-section to be much harder on the body than a normal delivery like I had with Teddy. The pain actually was tremendous, but I have to admit well worth it.

Michael was telling me a day or so before we were due to go home, how hard it was on Teddy coming to see me with the new baby, and then their having to go home alone. So I knew as far as the psychological standpoint went, I really needed to get out of there and back home with Teddy. Michael said, "Yes, we both want Mommy back," and thankfully finally that day came. Martin and I began getting ready. I got him dressed in his swaddling clothes, and I got myself dressed. There we sat on our bed in the hospital waiting for Daddy to come and pick us up.

My first day home as before with Teddy, my sisters and my mother had a little party for us. Teddy really enjoyed himself although it was a bit strange for him having this new little person in his life. After all, there were three years' difference between them. Teddy had just turned three in September two months before Martin was born. It quickly became apparent to me that although I had two little boys, this age difference did make a huge difference in our home because both of them required my time and my attention and of course my love, but for two very different reasons. One, Teddy would want to go for walks and want to do different things with me that I physically couldn't do at the time because I was still healing. Martin of course required me to take care of him because he was a newborn baby. So there were some very different needs from equally loved babies, and it took me a little bit of time to adjust to this.

There were some days I felt as though I was being pulled in three different directions, being a wife and being a mother. Michael, thank God through all of this time, this time of adjustments for me, was marvelous. He helped out so much, and as always in our relationship we found we worked perfectly as a team to get the job done whether it was a tune up or our two children. When I was busy with Martin, Michael would take care of Teddy and his needs. When I was busy with Teddy, Michael would take care of Martin and his needs. It was like a tag team.

Michael was so funny. It seemed like he was always holding Martin on his arm. He nicknamed him "Peanut." Now, how cute was that to see this big man holding this little tiny baby all the time! I once made the remark, one that I don't think Michael appreciated, but I told him you look like some sort of big hulking pirate holding a little parrot on your shoulder. Because of the way Michael used to hold Martin, that's exactly what it looked like. Martin was such a good baby. He hardly ever complained or cried, and he slept fifteen hours out of twenty-four. I know this is going to sound terrible, but sometimes I would forget, completely forget, that he was even there. That is how quiet he was.

I remember my sisters visiting, and every time they would go to leave they would say goodbye to Teddy and of course give him a big hug and a kiss and Michael and me. As Michael would escort them to the front door, holding Martin like he was holding a little parrot, as I explained earlier, and as they were closing the door he would always yell at them, "Did you forget somebody?"

They would look at him with a bewildered look on their faces wondering why he was getting so angry with them. He would yell at them, "April, Amber, what about Martin?" and they would crack up laughing. He was just so quiet. Every time his father was holding him, he would fall asleep in his arms, so you could easily forget that he was even there. Michael would actually become insulted that they would forget his little "Peanut." He let them get away with this a few times, and on the fourth or fifth time of them visiting, he couldn't stand it anymore, and he yelled at both of them for forgetting Martin.

They apologized profusely and said it would never happen again.

He said, "Well, I hope not!"

After they left and all was calmed down again, Michael and I and our two beautiful sons retired to the living room to watch TV for the evening. Michael was sitting in his favorite overstuffed chair with of course Martin in his arms fast asleep. Teddy decided he was going to join his brother alongside his father, so Teddy climbed up onto Michael's lap and lay in the other arm.

I could not resist. This was the perfect picture. Michael yelled at me, "Don't do that. Both the kids are going to wake up."

I said, "I don't care. This is too good to pass up. This is the sweetest picture, the sweetest thing I have ever seen in my life."

Michael said, "Go ahead if you have to," and after taking the picture, Michael looked up at me and puckered his lips so that I would go over there and kiss him, and I did. He whispered to me, "Thank you Kyra."

I said, "You're welcome, for the picture?"

"No, for giving me two beautiful sons." Then he said, "I love you so much, Baby Doll."

I replied, "I love you too, Teddy Bear."

So as my Teddy Bear sat there in his big chair holding Peanut in one arm and Honey Bunny in the other, I sat there on the couch looking at the three of them feeling like my heart was going to burst from my chest. I never knew that my heart could hold so much love. I actually had to pinch myself to make sure this was for real, and I realized that some people, some very unfortunate people never get to experience for one moment all the love and complete fulfillment I now will feel for the rest of my life. This made me feel so completely blest. After an hour or so of us just relaxing and the baby's fast asleep, Michael realized it was getting late, and he had a big job interview in the morning.

This would be his first job interview since graduating Tractor Trailer School. Michael was rather nervous because it was for one of the larger trucking companies in our area, and it was a really good paying job so he had a lot riding on this interview. First I took Teddy and carried him into his bedroom and tucked him in for the night. Then I came back to get Martin and placed him in his crib and tucked him in for the night, both with sweet kisses and prayers for a safe night's sleep. Michael of course following behind me with his own big Daddy kisses, and then we proceeded to our bedroom where we crawled underneath the covers and snuggled up together, falling asleep in each other's arms.

The next morning Michael and I both got up bright and early. I made sure Michael had a good breakfast so that he could be the sharpest he could be, but even though I made all his favorites, he was only able to eat about half because he was simply too nervous. Before leaving the house, the look on his face was terrible. He looked like he wanted to throw up. Even though I tried my hardest to reassure him, telling him he had just as good a chance of anyone else to get this job, but it seemed like no matter what I said, it just didn't help much. He put his coat on and started heading out the door. I ran after him and gave him a big hug and a kiss, and I wished him luck. I told him not that he was going to need it, but good luck anyway.

I reminded him of everything that we had already been through together and how hard we had both fought to get where we are today. With me it was just a matter of remaining sober, but with him it was a lot more. He was handling it and he was overcoming it, and I told him, "You are a very strong man, Michael. This is a piece of cake compared to what we have already been through, and please keep this in mind when you are talking to the man from this company."

I also reminded him of just how hard he had worked to get to this moment, and I told him, "The only thing that would stop you is you. Now get over the nervousness, and start thinking back about what you have already accomplished. Take that self-confidence into that interview with you." I told him, "You are a winner. You already are a winner whether you get this first job or not. Nobody can take away from you what you have struggled so hard to achieve. Don't you ever forget that."

He did not say a word to me but gave me the biggest smile and the biggest kiss and turned and walked out the door.

About two hours had passed, and I was getting our sons up for their breakfast when Michael returned back home with the greatest news of all. He had gotten the job, and he was to start in a week. The week passed quickly and Michael was so looking forward to his first day's work. He knew this was the start, the opportunity he needed to finally give his family the lifestyle that he wanted. The first day of his new job finally arrived, and he was looking forward to this day with great expectations, but unfortunately once again Michael's nerves seemed to be taking him over. I suppose the first day on any new job would be slightly nerve-wracking in itself, but for a person like Michael who is suffering from post-traumatic stress, it was even more nerve wracking because, you see, the post-traumatic stress will always make nerve-wracking situations much more stressful than what a normal person would be going through. Even with the therapy and the medication that he was receiving, even with all that help, it still was a very real struggle for him every day. Michael always just pushed himself, pushed ahead and pushed through all the anxiety, the nerves and the stress.

That morning the first morning on his new job, I made a beautiful breakfast for him which again he could only eat half of, and I gave him a huge kiss at the door. I reassured him that things were going to be fine, and I reminded him of how much, how very much I loved him and his sons as well. They both loved their daddy so much, and they were so proud of him and that is all he needed to remember.

He told me how much he loved me and our two beautiful sons as well, and he said, "Honey, I'll see you after work." He took a deep breath, gave me a kiss and then he headed out the door.

I then went into the baby's room and awoke Teddy and Martin for their breakfast. The morning seemed to just fly by. Before I knew it, it was noontime, and I began to wonder how Michael was doing on his first day. I could hardly wait for him to return back home to tell me all about his day. I guess it was around 3 o'clock when I happened to be looking out the window. I saw Michael driving in, which struck me rather odd, because he wasn't supposed to be home until around 5:30-6:00. I met him at the door with a big smile on my face holding Martin in my arms. He took Martin from me and gave both of us a big kiss.

Then he went over to sit in his favorite overstuffed chair with Martin in his arm, and then Teddy jumped up into his lap. Teddy asked him, "How was your first day driving the big truck, Daddy?"

Michael just kissed Teddy and looked at me. I could tell by the look on his face and in his eyes he was searching for the words to be able to tell me everything that had just happened to him, and I knew this was not going to be good.

Michael then began to speak. He told me about the horrible thing that had just happened to him. He began by telling me he arrived there at 7 on the dot, just as he was supposed to, right along with seven other new drivers that they had hired at the same time they hired him. He told me that they were all called into the cafeteria by the personnel manager, and then they were all told the most horrible news they could get. None of them had a job. It seemed that the company had been expecting a government grant to come in. The grant was canceled, so all the new drivers that they had just hired were now going to have to be let go, Michael being among them. This was devastating news for all eight men. The company manager apologized profusely, but he didn't see any way that he could hold all eight new employees on the budget that they were given. He simply had no choice.

Michael along with these other poor men had lost their jobs before they even had a chance to begin. Each and every one of them knew what the job situation was in our area, and there were not very many of them and certainly not for well-paying companies like this one. So they realized that it would probably be a while before they were going to find employment. This was crushing news to my family. Michael then told me after this meeting, he and the other men left the building. He went and sat in his car just staring ahead. He told me, "Kyra, I just felt so numb inside. I felt as though the rug had just been pulled out from underneath me."

Michael then told me he really did not know what to do next. He said that he just felt as though he needed to escape, he needed to get away for a few hours and be by himself. He told me that he went to our place down the lake and sat there for most of the day, just sitting there staring out over the lake. That night Michael didn't even eat supper. After he kissed me and the boys goodnight, he just went straight to bed. It must have been about 6 o'clock. That was the earliest I had ever seen him go to bed. I know this was horrible for him. It was a crushing blow to his ego. It just seemed like the poor man couldn't catch a break, and my heart felt for him.

I, too, became very depressed that evening. The following day, Michael remained in bed for the entire day only to emerge out of our bedroom to use the bathroom. This just floored him so much. On this day he didn't even eat or drink anything and spoke not a word to me. I thought it best just to leave him be, give him time and give him space. I took the boys out that day to play in the playground for a few hours. I came back home just in time to give our sons their supper and their baths and to put them to bed.

I went to bed early that evening around 7, and I tapped on Michael's shoulder. He lay there with his back toward me, and I asked him if he would like me to make him a sandwich or get him a drink. He said, "No thank you. I'm not hungry," and then I asked him if he would like a back rub. He said, "Yeah, I think I could use one of them."

So I gave him a nice long back rub, and when I was done I just wrapped my arms around him and held him close to me.

He began crying and told me, "Kyra, I don't know what I'm going to do now."

I told him, "Honey, Teddy Bear, don't worry. Something will come to us; it always does." I told him we didn't have to figure all of this out tonight. "Let's just go to sleep. Tomorrow morning when we wake up we can start figuring things out."

That night I held him in my arms all night long, and I never let on to Michael that I was just as scared and just as worried as he was. I was trying to lift him out of his depression, not make it worse. I always tried my hardest to keep a smile on my face and look at the bright side of things when it came to Michael, but inside sometimes I felt very differently. I didn't want to let on. I loved him too much to make him feel even worse than he already did.

Quite frankly, saying I was very worried was putting it mildly. I was petrified, because right now here we were with two beautiful children who were counting on both of us to hold it together. Here I was, with a screwed-up arm, in pain, and I was not able to work, and now Michael was not able to find work. My money from the settlement was quickly disappearing with household costs and feeding two children. Yeah, you could say I was becoming a little petrified at this moment, as would anybody in their right mind. Though I was in bed by 7 o'clock I can honestly say I only had maybe two hours sleep that night. My brain just couldn't shut off. I realized that night I had to get Michael out of this depression that he had sunken quickly into and fast.

That morning when we woke up I remembered that my sister Amber was on vacation. I asked her if she would mind coming and watching the two boys for a few hours that day so that Michael and I could go out and do something together, either go fishing, just taking a long walk, or perhaps drive down to Onset and sit there on the beach remembering the happy days, that one perfect day that we had. I was hoping I would be able to snap Michael out of this depression. Amber agreed to come over and take care of the children.

I then went into our bedroom and woke up Michael and told him, "Come on; get dressed. Amber is coming over, and you and I are going to spend the day together alone just like we used to. We're going to have some fun today."

At first he protested and then he thought about it and he said, "Maybe that's just what we need." So both of us proceeded to get dressed, and I got the boys up and gave them their breakfast. Amber came over, and Michael and I took off.

We didn't know where we were going yet. We just drove, and I did suggest the Cape, but then he said maybe a little bit of target shooting would be fun. So we went and spent an hour or so doing that and then we drove down the Cape. We took a long walk along Onset Beach, and we did talk about that most perfect day that we had and it brought back a lot of good memories. We also chuckled about how we used to make love right on the beach we were walking on.

Michael and I spent a great day together. We had a lot of fun and quite a few laughs this day, and I tell you, this was better than any kind of medication Michael was on. This was medication for the soul and for the heart, and I could see in Michael's eyes that the depression was lifted. Thank God I got my old Michael back, my sweet loving Teddy Bear.

We finished off our day by getting some fried clams and French fries by the Onset Dock Restaurant. It was about 8 o'clock at night when we finally returned back home. Amber had quite a story to tell us once we arrived. The three of us sat at the kitchen table while the two boys were asleep in their room, and Amber asked me, "What in hell have you been telling Teddy about alcohol?"

I smiled at her, and I said, "Why?"

She said, "My God, Kyra, I opened up a beer about 1 or 2 o'clock in the afternoon to have with a sandwich, and Teddy totally flipped out. He started screaming. He started yelling at me. He told me I was going to turn into a monster if I drank that. Teddy then ran to his bedroom where his little brother was taking a nap and tried to protect him from me."

Amber said, "Don't be ridiculous. I'm not going to turn into a monster."

He said, "Yes, you are."

Amber told him she would pour the beer down the sink. This was the only way to calm him down. After she poured it down the sink, he came back to his normal self.

I proceeded to tell her, "Yes, I have been teaching him quite a bit about alcoholism already at this age because I want him to get an early start." Every opportunity I explained to her that is given to me I would take and run with it. I would explain to him the stupid and horrible things people do while they are drunk.

She told me, "You could have given me a little bit of warning, Sis," as she sat there laughing.

Michael looked at me, and he said, "I thought you were going a little bit overboard, Kyra, but I didn't want to say anything."

I told him, "Bullshit, you can't be too educated too early, and my philosophy is by the time he is old enough to be able to drink, that will be the last thing he will want to ever do. This is what I am hoping and praying for, for him and Martin."

Amber actually agreed with me. She said, "Yeah, given our family's history, this is the one sure way to break the cycle. At least you are giving it your all, Kyra, and they can't come back to you later on in life and say, 'Why didn't you warn us, Mom?'"

I told Amber, "Yes, you're right." I thanked Amber very much for being such a good sister and such a good aunt and having to put up with my children's neuroses that I was pushing onto them. I gave her a kiss and a hug, and she left.

That night when Michael and I went to bed we had the most passionate lovemaking that we had had in months since I was six month's pregnant with Martin. It was this night we found each other once again. All of the passion and the romance that we had always had came washing back and this felt so good and so right. After that day and after that night Michael and I had both escaped the depression that we had sunken into.

After our love making we lay there in each other's arms. Michael said something really funny to me. He said, "Baby Doll, I have a feeling I'm going to be chasing you around nursing home when I'm 90 years old."

I said, "You're absolutely right," and I told him, "Yeah, and guess what. I'll always let you catch me."

After this we just lay there in each other's arms and fell fast asleep.

It was a couple of days after this when Michael began going around to all the trucking companies in our area and filling out applications. He had little luck with any of these companies, so he began filling out applications in the factories. The few factories that were left in our area didn't seem to be doing a lot of hiring. It was after about a month of Michael doing this on a daily basis when he finally got a call back. It was one of the factories that he had applied at. They needed a part-time driver to deliver the merchandise. They were an extremely small company and only needed but a few drivers, so Michael took the job. He figured part-time was better than no time at all, but he told me he was running into the same problem that he had before he was sobered up and that was that there would be a twenty-year-old man sitting there applying for the same job, and of course they would choose him over Michael.

Now it was even worse because Michael was quickly approaching 42 and he had just graduated Tractor Trailer School. He had driven truck in the past for a moving company after his union job with the construction company fell through because of his drinking, so he had a little bit of experience driving tractor trailers to begin with. But no matter how much experience he had and what kind of license he had, he was still competing with men half his age and who didn't have nearly the problems that he had. This was very, very difficult for Michael to handle. He said, "Kyra, you wouldn't believe it. I would walk into one of these driving companies, and there would be sitting two or three other men, and the oldest couldn't have been more than 25. He said, "I do not stand a snowball's chance in hell of getting a job over them with less experience than they have." This would just make Michael pull his hair out.

The frustration of it all sometimes overwhelmed him, and this just got worse as Michael got older. He felt as though when he walked into the room and saw these other men sitting there filling out the same applications, he already had two strikes against him; his age and the lack of experience in driving. It just always seemed as though Michael was taking one step forward and constantly being shoved back two steps.

The city that we lived in certainly didn't help. All the jobs were few and far between, and there didn't seem to be very many good paying jobs. Our city in the past was a thriving one. We had many silver factories, good decent paying factory jobs that a man could work in, put a hard day's work into and get an honest day's pay. But no longer did these jobs exist.

At this time in our city's history I would say at least 60% of the factories that were decent factories a man could support his family working at were gone, long gone. What few moved in their place and the ones that did remain seemed to be lowering their pay as the years went by instead of gaining. I truly felt our city was becoming another death valley, and through the years, I'm sorry to say, it has not improved. It seems that they are trying to turn this into what they call a "bedroom community" where people work in Boston and surrounding towns and have their beautiful homes here. There were many beautiful homes built, but I never saw very many Morton residents being able to afford them, so I don't know who were buying them up. The developers destroyed our woodland areas, our rivers, and our lakes and gave us nothing back except heavy traffic and strangers that invaded our little city.

With the rise in population and the dwindling of jobs in our area, the high crime started to hit. In our past history, we never had such a high crime rate as we do today, and to me it is obvious why. There just simply are no decent paying jobs in our area. This city is holding less and less opportunity for our youth with every passing year. I have to say it was truly sad to watch a city that had been thriving at one time go so drastically downhill to the point it is just floating dead in the water. People who live here now are lucky to make enough money to cover the rent. Where do they get money for food, utilities, and clothing for the children? I don't know. I suppose that is where the high crime rate and the drug dealers come in. If they can't make it one way, they have to make it another which then of course destroys a community even more. It seems to me the developers and the city planners are the only ones that made out and became rich in our city.

Now after Michael got this part-time job I thought I would start looking around for some work myself, because there was no way we were going to be able to run a household on part-time pay. I figured once Michael got off his shift, I could go on to mine. Perhaps being a woman and having worked in a factory, I was more apt to get a job sooner than Michael would. However, I was also going on interviews with one strike against me and that was my bad arm. I literally only had one good arm and wasn't quite sure of what I would be able to do in a factory job any longer. I knew I couldn't do what I had done in the past because I simply didn't have the strength. The pain I had to deal with hindered this, but I had to try. I had to at least try to see if there was anything out there for me at this point. I had no choice. I figured that even if I could only work a few hours a week it would be that much more money that would be brought into the house. So as soon as Michael started working his part-time job, and as soon as he got home in the afternoon, I then took off and put my application in every factory that I could find.

After about two weeks I got a call back. The pay was only minimum wage, but again it was something. It was a full-time packing job, but during my interview they told me I would have to be able to lift at least 40 pounds. I then quickly explained to them about my hand and my arm, and I told them I did write that down on my application. I was becoming rather irritated and upset with them for even calling and offering me this after I had made it clear to them that I was limited. I guess all they were looking at was my past experience in the factory work that I did, and they thought I was the best candidate for the job.

I told him I was sorry but I was going to have to decline the job. I knew there was no way that I could do the heavy lifting that was going to be required of me. I knew the rent was coming due and there was very little money left in our bank account. I really didn't know what we were going to do. I had to face reality. With my hand being in the shape that it was in and the pain that I was constantly in there was no way I was going to be able to work in a factory again. With no formal education I was pretty much stuck.

It was the next day when I realized I had to do something drastic, something to tied us over so that we could get back on our feet again. I hated like hell to do this but I felt as though I had very little choice in the matter. I had to feed my children, and I had to keep a roof over their heads. I was forced to go down to the local Welfare Office and apply for assistance for food and our bills. Believe me when I say, I knew this would only be a temporary solution. There was no way I had planned to raise my children on Welfare, and what I got from Welfare was just enough to pay our rent and utilities, buy the baby's Pampers with not a penny to spare. This was not the life I was going to give my children, but my back was against the wall, and I was very, very desperate.

After being accepted for this aid, we found it to be the most depressing time of our lives. We both felt like such failures as human beings and most of all as parents. It was absolutely horrible. After everything that Michael and I had fought so hard to achieve, sobriety and building a life, everything that Michael was hoping to be able to accomplish with his CDL license, everything had just simply fallen apart.

Believe me when I say, our fight every day with alcoholism was true, it was a battle every day, but we won every day. Everyday we would stay sober was another day under our belt. We were winners! We fought so hard to be productive human beings and to lead normal lives, and we were. All of the fights that we fought, we won, but now we found ourselves in such a predicament that we can't even afford to feed our own children by ourselves.

I often thought, *What is all this fighting for? Is it to end up with nothing, or to end up a big fat failure, a sober failure but nevertheless a failure?* The most painful part was being a failure in our children's eyes. I couldn't stand this thought. We fought so hard every day to be just normal, only to be shoved back down time and time again. We had both become more depressed about our situation.

Michael's hours at work now had changed. They were from noon to 5 o'clock in the afternoon. No matter how many times he spoke with the foreman, he just couldn't get any more hours than that. The financial stress and the depression were starting to take its toll on our little family. Michael would come home from work, eat supper with us, and instead of watching TV or playing games with his sons as he always did, he would now just go straight to bed. Our depressing situation was now beginning to overtake us both. I felt as though I must do something now, something quickly to put a stop to this.

So I began looking at other apartments, something more in our price range, and I could find nothing. You see there was another phenomenon that was taking place in our little city. It seemed as though the wages were going down. A lot of them were simply minimum wage at this point. But on the other hand the rents magically stated doubling and tripling in some places. It made no sense what so frickin' ever, and this in itself had become extremely frustrating for me. Then I realized on our budget there would be no way that I would be able to afford any of these rents, any of these apartments that we had looked at. We couldn't even afford where we were right now.

After a couple of months of looking at all of these other apartments, it was the last apartment that I looked at, that the landlord told me was about $300 more than what I was paying now. I went home that night and just cried myself to sleep. I had no idea what I was going to do. In the morning when I awoke I decided I had to do something that I never in my wildest nightmares imagined I would be doing and that was going to the Housing Authority and looking for an apartment from them. This was basically going back to the projects from where I came.

This devastated me more than anything else that had just happened, but again I had to think of my children. I also had to think of Michael and what this was doing to him. It was shoving him deeper and deeper into a depression, and I prayed he wasn't too far in where he wouldn't be able to recover. I had to keep a roof over their heads, and getting an affordable apartment was my only choice. This was my only choice because in the private sector there were no affordable apartments. It was coming down to the wire. The rent was owed, and I had no choice. It was either moving into a project or a shelter, and I thought, for my children's sake, a project at least would be better. Again, I prayed that this was only a temporary situation that we were in and that something would open up for us.

So I went down to the Housing Authority that morning, and I filled out an application. After my application was filed with them it took a couple of weeks, but we were eventually shown an apartment. Actually it was not that bad. In fact it was really nice. The project was a very small one, and there are only a few families that lived there. The community was quite tight knit which I loved. Every family seemed to know the other, and we always watched each other's children. I was pleasantly surprised to find all of this out and realized that maybe this wasn't such a bad place after all. Our boys would have a nice backyard to play in where we would set up a swing set.

In reality they had much more fun living here than they ever would living in the apartment that we were living in now. The apartment was mainly for couples with a swimming pool and the playground in the back, but that was all that they had for children there. There were no private yards. There were no places to set up a little wading pool for the little ones. So this place all in all did offer more for my children, and with the pleasant neighbors and neighborhood, I thought, well, maybe we're going to be okay. This location also offered another good thing for me and my children. There was an elementary school right down the street where I could walk them every day. So after seeing this apartment and hearing about the neighborhood, Michael and I decided right away to take it.

Our little family moved in on October 16, 1991. Martin was not a year old, and his first steps were taken here about 2-3 days after we moved in. I was lucky enough to capture them on film. Teddy had just turned four, and he wasted no time meeting and greeting all our new neighbors. Everyone seemed to love him. Teddy had become quite the little social butterfly. He always had the gift of gab, and he always seemed to be able to make friends so easily. He had a great personality. Michael and I spent the following two weeks getting things put in their proper places, turning this apartment into our family's home. After we were done it looked quite cozy and quite comfortable for our two babies. Michael and I were really happy with the outcome.

The first summer there we spent fixing up the yard for our two boys. Michael put up a fence, and my sisters April and Amber put their money together and got Teddy and Martin a beautiful big swing set. My mother bought a picnic table for our back yard, a picnic table where I hoped we would have many, many happy family gatherings. Michael and I bought a mid-sized swimming pool for the boys and a sandbox and a grill for our family cookouts. So with the help of my loving family, Michael and I were able to give Teddy and Martin a spectacular childhood backyard. I have to say they made good use of this yard.

Those two boys were out there from morning until late at night. They were outside kids, and they enjoyed every moment of it. I would even give them their breakfast at the picnic table. They sat there eating while I cleaned up the pool and set it up for that day's play. I loved spending the afternoon with my two babies just playing and having fun and watching them splash around in the pool.

Then at night when Michael would come home from work, we would have a cookout. I cooked out every single night. That's where I made my family's supper, and they enjoyed it so much. I would have grilled chicken, hamburgers, and hot dogs. They never grew tired of my cookouts. With the stress relieved from Michael's and my shoulders about how we were going to keep a roof over our children's head, we were finally able to enjoying ourselves again and love each other without all that stress on us. Quite simply we could just enjoy being Mommy and Daddy to two beautiful baby boys.

I can honestly say Michael and I were truly happy now, and this is something we had not felt in months. I used to do a funny thing with the boys. After they would get through eating summer I would soap them up while they stood in the pool, and then I would hose them down and they would jump all around laughing and having fun. By 7:30 they were both passed. They were totally exhausted. This happened on a daily basis. This was our routine, and I loved it. It was such a fun routine.

As our two little ones would fall asleep on the couch with their father sitting beside them, he would then carry them up to put them in bed and tuck them both in as I followed closely behind. After our little ones were tucked in for the night, Michael and I would then go down and sit on the couch and snuggle up close together.

You know I have quite often thought to myself, *No, this didn't turn out exactly the way we had planned it.* Having a little bit more money would have helped, but you know, I wouldn't have traded this moment for anything. Michael and I were both so very happy with our family and the time that we had to spend with them. We enjoyed all the fun that we had every day with them learning and experiencing new things that you can only learn through a child's eyes. I figured it was some sort of a trade off. Even though we didn't have money, we had each other. We also had a lot of love and a lot of fun. So if I had to choose between money and this, I would have chosen this. That's what truly counts. That's what truly matters. Not so much that you are just living, but it's how you are living, and what kind of happiness you have in your heart and your soul every day. I feel sorry actually for people that are constantly struggling to keep up with the Jones's, getting the next best TV or the next best car. It's all a matter of stopping and smelling the roses along the way that truly matters.

At the end of the day, how do you count happiness? Do you count it by dollars or do you count it by memories and kisses and love? Yeah, I think our little family is going to be just fine. As a matter of fact, I know we are. You can never put a price on a person's heart, and my heart beats only for Michael, Teddy and Martin, for this love that I feel in my heart toward the men in my life cannot be measured. There is no way you could put a price on it. I would not trade this feeling for all of the money in the world.

I also realized dealing with failure is a matter of giving in to your circumstances which I refused to do. I refused to let it beat me. Instead of giving in to my circumstances, I changed them, and I would work hard every day to improve them. Improving my circumstances in my heart and mind means working with my children every day, and bringing them up with a great heart, a great mind, and a great soul and making them people who can feel other people's pain, and of course that never ending teaching that I will always do with my children against alcohol and drugs. I am hoping to create two beautiful men; men with honor, integrity, self-confidence, and most importantly love in their hearts for everyone else. If I can achieve this no matter where we live, whether it is a mansion or a project, I will feel as though I have been a great success in my life.

As the days and the weeks had passed by I could see every day that did pass a little more relief on Michael's face and a little less weight on his shoulders. Our relationship was returning back to normal, that closeness, that passion and the love that we always felt toward one another was stronger than ever now. We had gotten into a very, very good routine with our little family, and all four of us were very happy.

As our children grew older, we now had to teach them along with the dangers of alcohol and drugs a whole lot more, and that was to be wary of strangers. Later on we would develop a code between us, a word that only Teddy and I would know (and of course Daddy) and a word that Martin and I and Daddy would only know. They were not to go with anyone else and certainly no one that didn't know that secret word if they were in someone else's home that they were visiting and playing, on a playground or at school. We taught them this word, and this was the word that would forever keep our children safe we hoped. While teaching them this word, this secret word that we would only keep between us I would tell them, "It's like a secret code, a special secret code that would only be shared by us." So I tried to make it as exciting as I possibly could to them. I emphasized the importance of them keeping this word just in the family.

Then the next lesson in life would be racial tolerance, or should I say just tolerance of anyone else that doesn't look exactly like you. I taught them to never ever judge anyone by their appearance, by what clothes they wear, or where they live, or what they drive. I taught them to look past all of that, to look into the person's heart because truly it's what's inside that counts, nothing else.

It's what kind of person they are and what kind of heart they have and what's in their head that counts, and to never judge anyone by their skin color.

I also explained to them, "If you do, you will be cutting out a lot of good people from your life, people who could truly be good friends to you, people that you have a lot in common with and that you could have a lot of fun with. That's why you must keep an open mind and never pass judgment on anyone simply by their appearance. You get to know them by talking to them and finding out exactly what you have in common and what you guys like to do, but most of all what they hold in their hearts. If they're good people then you certainly want them in your life, and if they are bad, then you do not. But make sure you are choosing them for the right reasons."

It was very important to me to be able to teach my children this, because this was the way I grew up. My mother taught me very well, and she taught me how to look beyond appearance. You see it doesn't matter to me at all whether a person's eyes are round, almond shaped, or his skin is yellow or black or white. What matters to me is what a person holds in their heart, what kind of person they are, and what they stand for in life.

One of my favorite speeches is the one that Martin Luther King, Jr. delivered, "I have a Dream." In that speech one particular line hit me like a bag of bricks and that was when the doctor spoke about judging people not by the color of their skin but the content of the character. These are words that I lived by and these are words that I taught my children to live by because we are all God's children. We are all created equally in God's eyes. So really, who are we to put a person down and make them feel less than human simply because of what they can afford to wear on their backs, or where they can afford to live or afford to drive? Who are we to pass such judgment upon our brothers and sisters?

And I would also tell my children about all the friends that I had growing up, how some of them were Puerto Rican, and some of them were blacks. It didn't matter to me. They were all good friends, friends who I would never forget, and friends who would always welcome me in their home and them into mine.

As I was telling my boys this, I realized something very important. Being a parent is so difficult because you have a human life in the palm of your hand, and you have to make sure that you mold that life correctly.

There are so many things I have yet to teach my children, important things that I know I must, and I have to get it all right. I also realized that parents are children's first teachers, in fact the most important ones they will ever have. They are the ones responsible for teaching them respect, respect for authority, respect for their teachers and respect for other children. This is a great deal of responsibility that is placed on each and every parent's shoulders and something I did not take lightly. But I never quite realized this until this moment when I had to begin teaching my children certain important facts in life such as these.

Among all of these other very really important lessons in life, Teddy experienced first hand the lesson about stealing. He was about three years old when this occurred. I had taken him grocery shopping at the nearby supermarket, and while unloading the groceries into the trunk of my car, I turned around and he held up a package of gum to me and asked me if I would like a piece. I said, "Thank you, but no," and then I asked him where he got it.

He said, "Oh, I just took it off of the stand."

I said, "Mommy didn't pay for that."

He said, "I know."

I asked him, "Do you know what that's called?"

"No."

"That's called stealing, and that's against the law. People get arrested for that."

Then he became quite upset because he thought the police were going to come and arrest him at that moment. I told him, "No, they're not," I said, "No one knows that you took it. No one but you and me." I saw an instant sigh of relief come over his face.

I said, "No, you're not out of the woods yet, though."

I proceeded to unload the rest of the groceries into my trunk. I closed the trunk, and I took Teddy by his hand, pushing the cart back to the grocery store. We pushed the cart in the holder, and when I told him, "We are going back into the grocery store, and you are going to tell the lady exactly what you did, that you took something without paying for it."

He started to cry. He said, "Mommy, I don't want to do that."

I said, "I know but it's something you have to do because what you did was wrong, and I never want you to do this again."

I took him up to the register where I had purchased my groceries, and I had him hand the woman at the register the package of gum that he had opened and explain to her what he had done.

Through his tears he told her, "I took this."

She said, "Did you know that was wrong?"

He said, "I do now, and I'm sorry."

I gave him the 50 cents to hand to the woman at the register, and I told him, "Do you see what that's called. That's called purchasing. What you did was called stealing, and this will never happen again, right Teddy?"

He said, "No, Mommy, I promise."

Doing this worked like a charm because he never, ever again stole anything from a store or from a person. This I have to say was one of the easiest lessons that I had to teach him.

Once we got back into the car from this last lesson that he so quickly learned, I looked at him, and I said, "Have you ever in your life seen Mommy or Daddy take anything from anybody without paying for it?"

He said, "No."

"So why on earth would you expect this to be fine with us, that this would be acceptable to us when you know we don't do this?"

He just sat there with his head down. Then I informed him that that was his ice cream money for the night. So when the ice cream man came around in his truck, he was not to expect to get anything. Upon arriving home after bringing all the groceries in, I sent Teddy to his room for the remainder for the day as his punishment.

It was around suppertime when I went up to his room, and he was there, just as I left him two hours earlier, sitting in his little chair. I kneeled down to him, and I asked him if he though long and hard about what he had done and how very wrong it was to steal, and then I asked him, "Do you think this is something you are ever going to do again?"

He said, "No, Mommy, no."

I know what I did next was wrong because it was kind of like reinforcing bad behavior, but I couldn't stand it. I leaned over, and I gave him a hug and a kiss and I told him, "That's okay. Everybody makes mistakes. As long as you learn from them." I told him, "Daddy and I have made mistakes in our lives, too, and we, too, have tried to learn from them and not repeat them." Then I took him by the hand and walked him into the kitchen. I sat him at the kitchen table and gave him his supper.

That night after supper he was looking out the window as the ice cream truck drove in. He sat there and watched all the other children get their ice cream and he didn't say a word to me. He knew. He realized, and that was all I needed to know. As a parent you really truly never know what is exactly the right thing is to do with your children. They don't come with Owner Manuals unfortunately, but I felt as though in my heart this was the right way to handle this. It seemed to have worked for Teddy.

That's basically what I did as a Mother. I followed my heart. I let them know right from wrong. I taught them everything I knew, and I hoped that they listened. One other important thing that I taught them was that Mommy and Daddy would always have their best interests at heart.

"We love you, and we are your teachers. We must teach you right from wrong, so no matter whom you meet or what kind of friends you have, you listen to us, not them. They don't love you the way we do, and they are not looking out for you the way we always will."

Michael and I work together so well, just as we always did. It was a team effort. What I couldn't teach them, Michael did, and thank God we were blessed with very, very smart children that were able to understand what we were telling them and listen to us.

As Michael and I navigated through the tricky waters of parenthood, I must say these years were the happiest years of our lives. We sat back and watched our children grow and watch them learn and develop their own personality. It was quite incredible to see how they developed their own likes and dislikes, and how we could see a part of each other in both of them. Thankfully, they were the best parts of us. As they would grow into their own personality, it was just the most incredible thing to watch.

As they grew it was becoming quite clear how incredibly different both of them were in their personalities. Teddy was the rough one. He loved to get our there and ride his bike, and go on his skateboard and his roller blades. He was so physical. Martin on the other hand was more delicate. I guess you would say more of the artist-type personality. He would love drawing. He loved collecting little pictures and doing just about anything with arts and crafts.

So as the children grew, Michael did more of the physical things with Teddy with the bikes and all the sports that he was in to. I spent a lot of time with Martin with the drawing and the crafts. Everything just seemed to balance itself out beautifully. Michael and I would both do everything we could to encourage these traits that had developed in their personalities.

Even though money was extremely tight at this time, it was quite a balancing act trying to pay bills and food and still have money left over to do things with our children. Michael and I were both determined never to let this bring us down. We were not going to allow our financial circumstances to interfere with our children. We were not going to sit there daily worrying about bills and let them depress us to the point where we wouldn't be able to have any fun with our children at all. We would not let this happen, and whenever something really bad hit that we would need money for immediately, and we would start becoming stressed out. Ironically enough it was Teddy or Martin that would snap us back into reality. We could only do so much, and we were giving it our all. Our two children were the ones we were going to be thinking of, not bills.

We were never able to afford family vacations like a lot of the people we knew or be able to afford to take our children to ball games, things that we would have loved very, very much to have been able to do with them. The money simply wasn't there. What was there was us, their Mommy and their Daddy, and we spent all of our time with them. Michael and I always tried our hardest to make the best of the situation. Instead of a summer vacation I spent every day with my children by the pool teaching them things about butterflies, about insects, playing games with them in the pool, and teaching them how to swing on their swing sets. I tried my best to make up for my shortcomings, for the lack of money that our family had.

Certainly what Michael and I lacked in money, we more than made up for in love. I have to admit if we could have only had both, it would have been perfect, but life is not like that. Life is not perfect, and this I had learned at a very early age. Always when Michael was not working, he was with our sons doing one thing or another, either taking them fishing or bike riding, or just simply working on the car. He taught them a lot about that too.

Michael's first passion as far as hobbies went was fishing, and he would take our sons at least three times a week to the lake where Michael and I always used to go. By the time Teddy was six years old Michael took him out for his first target-shooting lesson. During all the times that Michael took Teddy target shooting, he would teach him a little bit more each time. The most important thing was to always respect guns. That guns kill, and he explained to Teddy what we are doing now is just target shooting. I told him, "Daddy doesn't kill anything."

Teddy loved this. He took to it like a duck to water, and it took Teddy probably about six months before he actually started becoming good at it. Michael was so proud.

One day he came home with Teddy, and he told me, "Kyra, you wouldn't believe how many targets Teddy actually hit. I think it was like 7 out of 9."

After each time they would go out, they would come back home and go down to the basement. Michael taught Teddy how to disassemble a rifle and how to clean it properly. He reminded him that he must do this after every use. Michael went very slowly with Teddy teaching him all the important rules as far as guns were concerned.

I did have a slight concern about Teddy's age because he was only six. Michael told me that this is the age that his father started teaching him how to target shoot. Where he grew up, mainly the woods, they would hunt for pheasant and deer. But Michael, of course, by this time had lost his taste for the kill. So it was only strictly target shooting. This is the way he wanted to bring Teddy up, not to kill anything and to respect life.

Through these times they bonded very closely. Michael would drill into Teddy's head the value of human life. He told him, "You never, ever point a gun at anyone or any living creature to kill."

This time that Michael and Teddy spent together was very, very precious to both of them. In this time that they would spend together, Michael would not only have developed Teddy's mind, but his heart as well by teaching him how to have the utmost respect for all of God's creatures, big and small. Michael so loved all of these things; target shooting, bike riding, and of course, fishing. He felt privileged to be able to do all of these things with his sons.

Then he added one more to the list, and that was skating. Michael had never been very good at it, but he thought maybe with his two kids falling around him, he wouldn't look so conspicuous. I declined the offer. I said, "I'll just sit on the sidelines and watch."

So we went to the store and we bought three pairs of ice skates that winter. It was the winter of 1993. They laced them all up and hit the ice, and when I say hit the ice, I mean hit the ice! All three of them fell right on their butts. Martin lay there like a turtle on his back. I had him so bundled up he couldn't move. He actually had to get on his knees to get up. Michael had to stand him back up, and as I sat there on the bench watching the show, I thought to myself, *What a fantastic father Michael is. What a loving father he is.*

I hate like hell to have to admit this today, but way deep, deep down inside a little twinge of jealousy came over me. I wished I had a father like Michael. As I was thinking this with just a little tiny twinge of jealousy or envy, another feeling came rushing over me and that was a feeling of utter complete happiness that my children now have such a fantastic father. I knew things were going to be fine, and they had a great man to follow. I knew all through their lives Michael would teach them valuable, valuable lessons about life. I also knew as soon as they were old enough to understand about Vietnam, he would tell them all the stories that he told me, and of course that other part of our lives that we were not too proud of, the times when we were drinking. But I need them to know this as they would grow older in hopes of warning them not to follow down that path. Things that were on that path we would have to tell our children for their own sake, and I knew this, and I also knew it wasn't going to be easy.

But I didn't have to worry about this now. Our sons were still babies, six and three. It wouldn't be until much later on in life that we would have to sit them down and talk to them about our past. So for now I would just enjoy the moment, enjoy watching the three of them falling down and getting back up. I could tell they had their dad's personality because neither one of them gave up. No matter how much their feet hurt or their legs or Teddy's butt, they never gave up.

This went on for about an hour and a half when the three of them came back to the car with their teeth chattering looking for hot chocolate. I told them, "Mommy doesn't have any hot chocolate. We'll have to go to Dunkin' Donuts for that." They quickly removed their ice skates, put their boots back on, and we were off to find our hot chocolate.

It was that night during supper that Michael started complaining about how sore he felt, and Teddy quickly followed.

Then Teddy asked me, "Mommy, how come you didn't try skating?"

I said, "I know better." I told him, "When I was a little girl I tried roller-skating, and I tried ice skating, and I failed miserably at both. My feet were just meant to be on the ground. I'm simply not very coordinated, evidently."

It was at this point Teddy started calling "Chicken" and making chicken sounds at me. Michael quickly followed, as did Martin. So the three of them were sitting there at the supper table eating making chicken sounds at me simply because my back wasn't sore as were theirs, and I told them that.

I said, "Yeah, but you see, Mommy can sit down and enjoy her supper, can't she?" We all had a good laugh.

While I am discussing supper time here, I will say that this was another rule of mine and that was that every single night, no matter what, our family would sit down at the supper table together and discuss the day. I felt this was very important for children to do. So whether it is in the house at the supper table or out in our backyard at the picnic table having grilled hot dogs and hamburgers, we were to sit always together at this time of the day. An extra bonus would be if Gramma or Aunt April or Aunt Amber could join us. This would make it even more special.

I am happy to say, most of the time this was the case, and most of the time it was my Mom. They not only learned from their fantastic father, but they also learned a lot from their fantastic gramma, two things I will always forever be grateful for, and I know my children will be also.

I would like to take you back now a little bit to our first summer there. My sisters, my mother, Michael and I did all that work in the back yard to set it up for Teddy and Martin, their dream yard. I guess it was a week or so after we had finally finished all the work when I was lying in my beach chair right by the pool watching my sons splash and play around and just have a blast. I lay my head back only for a few seconds, and something caught the corner of my eye. I turned to look and over by the trees I saw this little girl. It was the strangest thing I had ever seen. She was dressed in period clothes, turn of the century. She had on a long brown dress just past her knee, with little brown shoes, an angelic face with two long blonde braids in the front. To this day I will never forget the look in her eyes, the look of utter hopelessness, of such profound sadness.

This sight was quite disturbing to see, and I was quite confused by it all because I had not seen her in the neighborhood. We didn't have that many small children. I guess she was about four, five. My hair stood on end. A chill came over me at the way she just stood there staring at me. I turned my head away and rubbed my eyes and looked back and she was gone. I then jumped up out of my beach chair and ran toward where she was standing. I looked up and down the street, and I couldn't see her anywhere. I knocked on a couple of doors in the hopes of seeing her standing there, but she was nowhere to be found. She completely disappeared.

After the third and last door that I knocked on, it hit me out of the blue. I couldn't believe I had done this, but I actually left my sons unattended in the pool. I ran as fast as I could back to my yard. Thank God they were okay. I sat in my beach chair. I must have had a completely puzzled look on my face because Teddy asked me, "Mom, what's the matter?"

I told him, "Oh, nothing, Honey," and dropped it.

This image disturbed me for the rest of the day. I couldn't get her face out of my mind. I couldn't forget the sorrow that was in her eyes and what she looked like. She was just a whisper of a little thing, and the dress that she wore was just not of this time. No one around here dressed like this. They hadn't for 100 years. After giving this much, much thought I had to come to the realization of what I saw. The only possible explanation for it was a spirit. I know this to be true now because I had never seen her before, and I never saw her afterwards. She did simply vanish. Believe me when I say I searched, and I searched hard for a logical explanation.

After Michael got home from work I proceeded to knock on the remainder of our neighbor's doors asking if they had a relative they had come to visit that fit this little girl's description. They looked at me like I had two heads. There just is no other explanation than that she was a spirit. After I got through making a fool out of myself to our new neighbors I went home, and I told Michael what I had seen, and I asked him, "Have you ever seen this little girl?"

He said, "No, Kyra." He told me, "Kyra, just let it go. Forget about it. Forget about her. You know what it was you saw." He asked me to please not talk about it any further with him, and I agreed.

Michael already knew this side of me, of course, but up until now I had chosen to leave this out of my book for this is something even my closest, dearest friends don't even know. I wasn't sure if I was going to include this or not, but I'm hoping times have changed and people are more open minded because this would be the first time that I would speak openly about how I feel. I'm not even sure quite how to explain it myself or what you would call it, but I have always been able to sense a spirit. I've never been able to see them or hear them, but I've always felt them. It seems that perhaps the angrier they are, or the more upset they are, they come through stronger. The best way for me to describe how I feel when a spirit is in my presence is if you yourself were speaking with a friend and both of you stopped talking at the same time and you closed your eyes, you can't see them, you can't hear them because they are not speaking, but you can feel them, you can feel that person's presence. That's how I feel the spirit around me.

This is something that I've also had to deal with all my life since I was ten years old. That's when it first started happening. It runs in my family. My sister April has it, my grandmother had it, my mother had it, and my great-grandmother had it. There was talk that with one of my grandmothers being from Ireland there was practice of white witchery. You would call it wicker. They were good. They never did anything evil. This is the blood that ran through me, but it just weakened over the centuries.

When I was ten years old I began feeling the presence of certain things—spirits, ghosts, whatever you want to call them. It started one night just before my tenth birthday. I had a horrible nightmare, and my dream just seemed so real. I saw a hunter in the woods but he was in a lake. He was drowning, and he couldn't get his coat off, and the water was just pulling him under. He tried to grab on to the wire fence that was close by the water's edge, but he couldn't quite reach it. I saw him die. I saw him just slip under the water.

That night I woke up in a cold sweat. I couldn't go back to sleep for the rest of the night. The next morning at the breakfast table I told my mother what had happened, and she wrote it off to just a really bad dream. I was upset for that whole day. I felt as though I had been kicked in the stomach.

When I got home that night after school, after supper my mother and I went into the living room and watched the evening news, and there he was the hunter I had seen in my dream. It happened the night that I had the dream, the night before. It was as though I was standing there watching it all unfold in front of me, watching his death unfold in front of me. For a ten-year-old this was just a little too much to absorb.

The news report went on to mention that the hunter drowned. Hypothermia had just taken him over and he wasn't able or strong enough to pull himself out. I saw it all. I couldn't believe it. I remember then turning to my mother and asking her how could this be. How could I be seeing this as it was happening because I described it to a T?

It was at this point she let me in on our little family secret. She told me she was holding off talking about this waiting for something like this to happen. She wasn't sure if this part of our family history was going to affect me, and if I was going to be sensitive or not, so she was just waiting until she had a sign and boy was this a sign! She then went on to tell me how she was always able to pick up on things before they happened and dreams or just really sick feelings like the feeling of getting kicked in the middle of the stomach but not knowing what was going to happen or were. That's the frustration. You have just enough to feel it but not enough to do anything about it.

Believe me when I say from the beginning I wanted nothing to do with this so-called gift. Some people would call it a gift. I don't. A gift is something you want not something that's forced on you through bloodlines. She then explained to me about my grandmother in Ireland and a rumor that went through our family and that was she belonged to a wicker group. Evidently they did the best they could to fine tune their gifts and put them to work for good.

As she sat there explaining all of this to me, I have to tell you, I felt sick inside. I couldn't believe the things that were coming out of her mouth and the things that she had felt all her life. Oddly enough they started at about the age of ten just as mine did. I actually have this on both sides from my father's mother and my mother's mother, both grandmothers. I am only now finding this out. This is when she told me about her mother, the Portuguese side of the family that was also sensitive. So I got it from both sides. I got it but I didn't want it.

I asked her, "Am I going to keep having horrible nightmares like this? Am I going to see people dying? This is something that I don't want."

She said, "No, not necessarily. It can come another way, the foreboding, the feeling, telling you something is going to happen."

"Oh. Will I be able to stop these things from occurring?"

"No, nine out of ten times you can't, because you never know where it's going to hit. If it's going to be directed at you or a friend or across the road, a horrible event could happen. You could feel that it's coming, but you will not be able to do anything about it."

She told me to let her know when I was getting feelings or having nightmares, and she and I would talk more about it. She also started drilling into my head about how to keep this in the family. I was never, ever to talk about this, and she told me if I did, people more than likely would think you were crazy.

This was 1972. A lot's changed since then I hope. When this started in my life after the age of ten I have told only a hand full of people what I felt and what I could pick up on. One of them of course was Michael. I told him from the get-go, when we first started dating. So you see when I told him I saw this little girl was no big surprise. But I had never, ever seen an apparition before this day. I had never seen anything. I had never heard anything. I could only sense, and every time I did sense a spirit I tried to push it away. I tried to block it out, just as I would block out the pain in my arm, I would block them out of my mind. I never wanted it to go any further.

Actually I would have been very happy if it had stopped altogether. I don't know if I was given a gift. I don't know if these spirits were reaching out for me to help them, and I just didn't know how to use this gift I was given. If that's the case, I'm really sorry. But you have to realize the life that was given to me was not very easy, and I have had a hard enough time dealing with reality and what was here in front of me, physical never mind trying to deal with something I couldn't see or hear, only feel. I never felt as though I could handle it. I had no desire to fine-tune my gift. I simply just found it too disturbing. So as my mother taught me, I kept it to myself until now.

CHAPTER EIGHT

You see just as my writing this book has freed me from all my pain, me now being able to talk openly about what I can feel, the spirits, is also a relief. I feel like a great weight has been lifted off my shoulders, and it is liberating. I no longer have to consider it a dirty family secret, but yet just another part of my life that I have had to deal with. Seeing this little girl, this apparition, was greatly disturbing to me because I thought, *Oh, my God, I've somehow gone on to another level. Now I'm actual able to see them instead of just feeling them.*

I really did not want this. Just seeing this little girl was so disturbing, so shocking to me. I never wanted to see anything like that again. That's why I ran through the neighborhood desperately searching for answers, desperately searching for her to show me she was there and that she was a real person. This wasn't something that I just saw myself. Unfortunately I found nothing, and I had to face what I saw, what she really was. That's why when Michael told me to let it go. I knew he knew how I felt and how disturbing all of this was. I remember telling him afterwards, "I hope to God I never see anything like that again."

He told me, "Kyra, I hope so too, but if you do, try to realize what it is and hold it together."

I never said another word about this little girl to Michael again, and I thought to myself, *Hold it together.* How in hell do you hold it together when you clearly see something standing before you that no one else can? It's not just anyone standing in front of you. It's an appearance, the horrifying sad look in that little girl's eyes. I found it just incredibly disturbing. I'd rather be able to just cut it out of my life, but it is a part of me.

I realized what I had to do now was try to perfect the art of being able to block it, block seeing it and block feeling it. However, I knew this was going to be easier said than done because blocking out these feelings was something I did try to do all my life. I was never quite successful at it, and they were still

293

able to get through. Now I could only pray that it hadn't gone on to another level.

That dream of the hunter dying seemed to be the catalyst. It was after that dream that I started being able to pick up on spirits. Although I am very happy to say that after that dream it would be many, many years before I would have another quite like that. I remember after this dream (I would say it was a month or so) when I first felt a spirit's presence, and I remember where I was. It was my schoolyard, and I thought my friend had come up to stand beside me near the swing set at recess time. I turned to look and there was no one there, but I could feel that there was someone there. This was my first experience. I dealt with it, and when I got home that night I told my mother about it and she said, "Yes, you just sensed a spirit. We can pick up on them, and you are now able to feel them. I feel the same thing."

It was during this conversation that she also taught gave me one very valuable lesson, and that was to never, ever under any circumstances play around with a Ouija Board. She told me that later on in life when I am at parties, if they ever bring one out, find any excuse you can to get the hell out of there. She tried to explain to me exactly what it was that we had. She said, "Picture a little pin light in the vast darkness. That's what you are, and that's why they are drawn to you. If you open yourself up with a Ouija Board, it is as though you are opening up a door and inviting anything in that could be floating by at the time. Sometimes what you invite in you will not be able to handle. Sometimes they are not very nice, and more than that, you may never be able to get rid of them. So if you play with a Ouija Board, it could be very disastrous." She really drilled this into my head.

About four more years passed by. I was 14 when I was sleeping over my sister Amber's house. My sister Amber lived just above my sister April. She and her husband had an apartment. He was away at boot camp for the National Guard. Amber and I had gone to the movies, and we came back home. Now, keep in mind that up until now I had only been sensing the spirits here and there and not very often. So once Amber and I returned back home, we stayed up watching TV for a couple of hours.

It was around 12 o'clock when we went to bed. She slept in her living room giving me her bed, which I thought was rather odd, because I certainly didn't mind sleeping on the couch. She insisted upon this, and at the time I had no idea why. I always felt a little strange in that bedroom. As a matter of fact I felt strange in the whole house. I did pick up on spirits a lot in that house, but I just wrote it off and let it go and tried to block it because after all it was my sister's house. So when she offered her bedroom to me, I thought it was rather suspicious, but I just shrugged my shoulders. I went in there and got undressed and got under the covers. She had fallen fast asleep.

I could hear her snoring in the living room, and then I drifted off to sleep only to be awakened fifteen minutes later. It was exactly 12:15—I saw the digital clock on her night stand lit up. I was so tired, but I was so abruptly awakened. I awoke to my heart beating in my ears. I felt as though I was going to have a heart attack. With me lying there in the dark facing the clock, I could feel something coming toward me from behind. I then felt a hand on my shoulder, and the hand slowly worked down to my waist and then my hip. The best way to describe it is I felt as though I was going to be attacked, to be molested I guess you could say. As I lay there I could hear my heart beating faster and faster in my ears, and I felt as though if I didn't get out of there I was going to die. My heart was just simply going to burst.

I had never, ever experienced anything like that before in my life. I was utterly, completely terrified. I knew I had to make a move before it was too late. I threw the covers back, and I jumped up on the bed and took what couldn't have been any more than 2-3 giant steps out the door. I ran into the living room that was right across the hall from this bedroom, and I screamed to Amber, "Wake up, wake up!"

She had been drinking that night, but even so, she had never been in that deep a sleep. I literally had to shake her to wake her up. It was as though she was in a coma. Then I went over to put the light on, and she said, "What's the matter? What's the matter?"

I described to her what had just happened to me. She started laughing. I couldn't believe. She just sat there and she laughed, and by this time I was so terrified I was almost in a complete frenzy. I yelled back at her, "What in the fucking hell are you laughing at? Didn't you hear what I just told you?"

She said, "I know. I felt it myself," and then she went on to tell me about our cousin and her children that she had over a few months earlier. The little boys were playing in her bedroom while she and my cousin sat at the kitchen table. The little boys came out of that room like a bullet, screaming and crying, tears coming down their cheeks, yelling, "The man's gonna get me. The bad man's gonna beat us with a belt."

Evidently there was an apparition in that room that chased those little boys around the bed with a belt in his hand trying to beat them. They were absolutely, completely terrified, and that's exactly what I sensed as I felt this unclean hand running down my arms and onto my hip. I felt the presence of a very, very large man, a very intimidating large man, a spirit that in fact enjoyed scaring the hell out of people. Perhaps it made him feel more powerful than when he was alive, or perhaps he didn't even know he was dead and this is how he acted when he was alive. But now he was stuck there after death. Who knows?

All I knew was I was never, ever going to sleep again in that room. Amber told me she herself would not get undressed in that room. She felt as though there was someone staring at her. I said, "Thanks a lot for telling me all of this now."

"Why do you think I didn't want to sleep in the room without Steven?"

That next day Amber and I went downstairs to April's and were sitting around having coffee at the kitchen table. April then started telling me her own stories of that room. She said, "It seems to be the darkest place in this whole house. There is a woman that remains downstairs actually where her bedroom is now, and she's a nice woman, a lovely woman." She could feel that, but April said there was no way that she would ever sleep in Amber's bedroom. Even if Amber were to move out she would not do this.

Then she went on to tell me about the night she and Christopher were sleeping in the bed in that room before they renovated the upstairs into a separate apartment. She was awakened just as I was with a complete sense of terror, and her heart was beating in her ears. Unlike me, she looked to see what was there. I could not bring myself to do that. Instead of looking back over the room, I just focused on the living room across the hall. I could not bring myself to see whatever was there, but she did, and it covered the door. It was a very, very large man, and she watched it go from the closet door to the entrance door of the bedroom. It took up the whole doorway, just this dark black figure. As she watched it move toward her she began clawing at her husband's back trying to wake him up because her screaming was just not doing it. She clawed and clawed and finally he woke up, and just as he was waking up the thing disappeared.

She then told Christopher everything that had just happened, and unlike Michael who seemed to try to understand what I was going through, he did not. Christopher just thought she was insane. The feelings that she had, the visions that she saw he wrote off to insanity. So she got no support or help from him in trying to deal with what was going on in that house at the time. It had gotten to the point if Amber hadn't moved in that she was going to sell the house because she no longer felt comfortable staying there alone during the day while Christopher worked.

She told me she would be downstairs at the breakfast table, and she would hear footsteps coming down the stairs and back up the stairs, down the stairs and back up. This would happen 4-5 times a day, and now we didn't know if it was us bringing this out in this house or if this was something that was always there. We never did find this out. What we did find out in the past history of that house was that there was an overseer that died in that bedroom. He was not a nice man, a nice overseer. He took care of the slaves, but he was very, very cruel to them. He was also cruel to his family that lived in that house. The best we could figure out was that he was very cruel and very cheap and treated his family with little regard. You could say he was much like my father.

April would go on to tell me the first year or so that she and Christopher lived there after they got through renovating the whole place, she began talking to her neighbors. What she found out was quite incredible in itself. It seemed as though a group of teenagers from the neighborhood broke into the house one night (this was way before April bought and renovated it so it was run down) and this was their hangout. They brought flowers and candles. There was one girl and two boys. Along with the candles and flowers they brought alcohol and some sandwiches. They brought everything up to this room, this notorious bedroom, and placed them on the floor. Three of them went downstairs to make some sandwiches. Upon returning back upstairs the three of them found the flowers placed in a perfect circle with candles lit in the middle. After finding out that neither one of them did this because they were all together, they went running screaming from that house, never to return.

April found this out from one of the parents of these children. It seems her son was about 17 at the time that this happened, and she always told them to stay away from that house and not to enter someone else's property to party. The place was just really creepy to begin with. So she got this information from the horse's mouth, one of the children's mothers.

So you can only imagine what my next question was to April and Amber. I asked them, "Why in the hell did you ever let me sleep in that room?"

She and Amber just kind of chuckled, and April said, "We just wanted to see how strong you were getting with being able to pick up on spirits, so we didn't want to give you any information in advance. We just simply wanted you to experience it yourself and see what was going to happen."

I said, "Thanks a lot. I almost had a heart attack is what happened." I told them "Don't ever pull any shit like that again on me."

I can honestly say this was really the first conversation that all three of us had concerning what you would call the gift. They began telling me about the experiences that they had in their lives. They both had a dream just like mine that started it all off. Then they really started getting into it with me, and they started describing the feelings that they had always gotten. They too could sense when a spirit was close. April could very well, but not so much Amber. I think it was maybe the alcohol that numbed her to this or maybe a lot of it she just wrote off to hallucinations. I don't know. She was not very talkative about this. She wanted to just simply forget and simply block everything out. I guess she felt like I did. We could barely handle reality, never mind something we couldn't see or hear, just feel.

As a matter of fact it was about a year after this occurred that Amber did move out with her husband. They moved right down the street to Garden Place, the very apartment complex Michael and I would share many years later. So that just left April and her husband Christopher in the house. I would come every now and again to visit and sometimes spend the night.

There was one night in particular she and Christopher had a poker night with their next-door neighbor, so April and her husband went over there. I was sitting alone in their living room downstairs watching TV. I did not want to join them for poker. That was when I heard what April told me about. For the first time I heard them, the footsteps. You could clearly hear footsteps, and they went up and they went down, up and down. At one point they came down the stairs and they stopped right before the living room where I was sitting. I was absolutely petrified once again, and I could feel the spirit and it was he, the man I felt in the bedroom.

When you feel evil spirits, bad spirits, it is bone chilling. I don't know if it's evil or not. All I know is the anger and hate that they had in life they carry in death. When you feel these spirits it gives you a sick feeling inside because it is just so wrong. It's wrong the way they lived their lives, it's wrong what they're doing now, and for some reason they can't cross over or they don't want to cross over, or maybe they don't even know that they're dead. I don't know what it is, but with the dark spirits, the feeling is just so bad. It always took me a long time to shake it off. I could always tell good spirits from bad by that feeling. All I could feel with a dark spirit was utter hopelessness and anger. Again, it's like receiving a kick to your stomach and not knowing quite how to handle it, so you try to block it, you try to listen to the television, you try to think of anything and everything else except what you're feeling at that moment. Hopefully this feeling passes quickly, and the spirit moves away from you. Thankfully the footsteps returned back upstairs, and they stayed there. Thank God.

The only thing that I have found that is actually worse than feeling a bad spirit is the feeling of foreboding, a feeling that can just overwhelm you, a feeling that you know deep down into your inner core that something horrible is going to happen, something you will not be able to do a damn thing about, not even knowing what it is, just having that horrifying feeling that you know something horrible is going to happen. Having to deal with that feeling is much worse than having to deal with a bad spirit. It could last up to three days this feeling, and then something bad would always happen. Thankfully, I don't get these feelings very often, but when I do, something horrible always follows; a tsunami, an earthquake, a plane crash. It seems like only within days of my feeling this way, something horrible happens. It has never failed, and it is oh, so very frustrating to feel this and to know something is going to happen but not knowing when or where or what, just knowing that something bad is going to happen.

April and Amber, my mother, and I have all these feelings. All four of us would know when something was going to happen. We would all experience this all at the same time. Sometimes it would be enough to drive you crazy. I would call my mother telling her I was feeling this way, and she would tell me, "Yeah, I do, too." Then I called Amber and then April, and they would all describe the same feelings I was getting, and all of us knew there was nothing we could do about it. I just prayed it passed quickly and nothing too bad would happen. We all realized we did not have the power to stop it.

I often wondered what that foreboding feeling came from. Was it the people that were going to die? Was it their souls reaching out before their death? I don't know. There are so many questions I have, and I have found little answers about the experience. I am afraid to go forward with this and try to seek the answers to all of these questions that I have had all my life. I am afraid. I don't want to take that next step. I don't want to open that next door. I am afraid if I start researching or talking too openly about it this is what will happen whether I wish it to or not. I might go on to the next level that I desperately avoided all my life. So maybe I should just stay in the dark and not look for answers. This is the only way that I can assure that door that I never wanted to open will remain closed forever.

My mother and my sisters all felt exactly the same way. My mother all the while I was growing up had a really great saying. She always used to say, "Kyra, if you don't want to know the answer to something, don't go looking for it," and I chose wisely to listen to her. After all, who in their right mind wants to be able to see dead people? I have enough problems dealing with the living. So for me to start opening doors that are best kept closed I felt would be a really stupid move. I chose to live my life by another famous phrase and that is, "Ignorance is bliss," as far as this gift went anyway.

I decided at a very early age there would be no upside to trying to fine-tune this gift that I had been given. Just stop and imagine for a moment, if I actually was able to find out what was going to happen when I would get these horrible feelings. If I were able to find out when and where, would anyone listen to me, or worse, would they think I did it if it were a bombing or something else like that? No, there was no upside that I could see to this gift. So I am secure in the knowledge that I made the right choice, really the only choice I could make, and that was to go no further.

I also took solace in the knowledge that I wasn't alone in the world feeling this way. My two sisters and my mother felt exactly the same things, and I know we would always be able to talk to one another about these feelings. This helped me in my life immensely.

It was exactly two years after that horrible thing happened to me in April's house when I was around 16, just before I met Michael, when April and Christopher sold their house. April could no longer stand living there. She explained to me how it was getting worse, and she didn't know if it was her bringing this out in the house, or if this was something that was in the house to begin with. With the kids that had broken in that night to party, with that happening to them, she figured that maybe it was just a little bit active, but then when a person with her gift moved in, it became completely awakened, we weren't quite sure again what we were dealing with. April knew she had had enough after eight years of living there and she was ready to get the hell out.

It seemed as though these footsteps had not only continued going up and down the stairs, but she actually heard them in the rooms overhead.

After Amber moved out, she and Christopher remained in the apartment downstairs, never again returning to the bedrooms or anything else upstairs. So she knew darn right well there was no one up there and she told me about hearing footsteps going across what was Amber's living room and of course that bedroom. One thing she knew she couldn't remain there much longer because it seemed as though whatever was up there was getting stronger.

She and her husband, thankfully, were able to sell it rather quickly. They moved next door to Amber and Steven at Garden Place, their apartment complex. April kept in touch with her neighbors, good friends that she had made while she lived there and from what she could gather, there was absolutely nothing going on in the house after April left. It seemed to just die out. So with her being rid of the house, my mother, Amber, April, and I just wrote this off as another weird family experience.

Even though Michael knew all of this about me, this was not a subject that I would bring up too much in our relationship, because I could see this made him uncomfortable. He believed what I was saying to be true. He had no doubt that what I was feeling was real; it just disturbed him, and he, like I, really didn't know what to make of it. So you see that afternoon when I told him about this little girl, it really came as no shock to him. He just didn't want to discuss it, and I suppose much like I, just wanted to push it away and make believe it didn't happen. It was very, very difficult for me to get this poor little girl's face out of my mind. For days afterwards I would find myself looking for her seeing if she was hanging around the house by the trees where I first saw her.

To this day I am not exactly sure what I would have done if I had seen her again, and perhaps was able to talk to her. I don't know if I would have taken that opportunity or not or would I have just closed my eyes and prayed she disappeared again. I suppose the most disturbing thing about all of this is wondering if they are trying to reach out for help. If something that happened in their lives was keeping them here or perhaps it was the way they died. Perhaps something in their death was so quick and so dramatic. Possibly they don't know that they are dead. Being a mother now the look she had in her eyes broke my heart as she just stood there watching me laughing and playing with my two little boys, and I wonder if thoughts came back to her. Perhaps her mother played and laughed with her the same way I did with my sons, and perhaps she longed for the love of her mother. Maybe that's why she appeared to me. I went around in circles for over a week thinking about this little girl, and I had to stop. The more I thought about it, the more my heart broke for her. As the weeks passed by that summer she became little more than just a memory to me although I will never forget her, and I will never forget the look on her face.

In the weeks that followed we would host many family cookouts, and I wonder if she was standing by taking it all in and hoping that someday she would be reunited with her own mother. My cookouts consisted of my mother, Michael's mother, and my two sisters. We would all congregate in the backyard. These days I will cherish for always. We would laugh and talk about the old days, and both the grandmothers had loads of fun playing with Teddy and Martin. These were mine and Michael's happiest days.

Michael and I especially after the two boys were born had now just become so incredibly close. We had become completely a part of each other, and looking at our two children they were both living and breathing parts of each of us. Even though as close as Michael and I were, I actually couldn't imagine two people being closer. Every now and again we had our arguments, arguments I could count on one hand that we had over the years. But still, we had them and they always disturbed me because I never liked hurting him.

The job situation in our area was horrible. Michael just seemed to be stuck as far as employment went, not going backwards but going no further ahead either, with still only that part-time job. Things were difficult financially for us always, but we never lost sight of what was truly important and that was our beautiful little family. We would cherish so much these moments at the cookouts we would have, and all the family gatherings, because we knew in our heart that was what was important.

Even though we didn't have money we always knew deep down in our hearts without a doubt we would always have each other. Knowing this is the one thing that got us through all these hard times. We remained that strong team always and partners in life. We knew deep down inside that this would always keep us together even after the passion would eventually begin to diminish over the long years. As passionate as we were toward one another, I couldn't see this happening too soon because by this time it was 1994 and we had been together already for 16 years. To me it just didn't seem like that long at all. Even Michael commented, "My God, I can't believe we're celebrating our 16th anniversary already. I feel like we've been together maybe, 5 years."

I said, "I feel the same way. It's incredible how time passes so fast."

All I know is he had been in every beat of my heart for the past sixteen years, and I was so looking forward to another fifty. Our love was so strong, and it just felt so right. It stood the test of time. It stood the test of poverty. It stood the test of alcoholism, and all of our struggles that we had to go through, it only drew us closer together. We were true partners in every sense of the word, and he truly was my heart. People refer to their partners in life as their "better halves." I'm not going to do that. I refer to Michael as my "other half" for half of my heart beat only for him, and I was convinced our souls were intertwined.

I don't know, some people believe in reincarnation and some don't. I happen to, and I felt like with Michael and me this was a prime example of reincarnation. I felt as though we had always been together. It was that comfortable and that close. I felt as though we had shared the same things we are sharing now before, perhaps in another life. I don't know. I would like to think this is true, but I guess this is yet one more thing I will never know for sure.

Every holiday and every birthday that would come up for our children, Michael would desperately try and get more hours at his job so that we could have a little bit more money to put toward these things. Sometimes he was able to, other times not, but we always made due with what we had. We always tried our hardest to give our children good childhood memories, ones that they would always cherish. This was really important to Michael and me.

What was equally as important to us was giving our children a sense of family and family values. So of course, with all the holidays and birthdays, both of our mothers were there and my two sisters. Not only on these special times, but all through the year I would have to insist on my two sisters coming at least twice a month on the weekend for a cookout with us. My mother was over the house practically every day, and she would more often than not enjoy nice dinners with our little family that she was very, very much a part of.

It was Michael's mother that was not quite able to make it every time there was an event going on. This I felt very bad about, but she suffered with rheumatoid arthritis and sometimes it was very painful for her. All in all, the holidays, the birthdays, the family gatherings, the cookouts, and the dinners were all memories that I hope my children will hold in their hearts forever.

These special events were particularly important to me because this is what

I never had growing up because of my father. Most of our family stayed away to avoid him. So that is why it was so important for me to give my children a true sense of family. It would fill me with such joy to look at my beautiful Christmas table with a huge turkey in the middle of it and my beautiful family surrounding it; my mom, Michael, my two children, my sisters April and Amber, and Michael's mother. This was what the holidays were all about to me, family. At these dinners looking at everyone's face with them drooling over my turkey, I felt so blessed and so overwhelmingly happy. I thank God so much for these special memories. All the laughs and all the love that my whole family shared through each and every one of these events were priceless. What our family lacked in income we more than made up for in love.

One thing I found to be very, very true was that it doesn't matter where you bring your children up. Whether you bring them up in the poorest of neighborhoods and projects or in a mansion, it is not where you bring them up, it is how you bring them up. If you are consistent in your teachings and you are caring and loving, they will grow up with a sense of security. Love, your love, will make them feel that way, and they will always feel protected with that love. There are a lot of good men throughout history that have come from poverty, and they have pulled themselves up from much, much worse circumstances than what my two sons are having to deal with, and they were tremendous people that made a good life for themselves and helped other people as well. I hope and pray that my children would follow in their footsteps and make a difference in this world for the better. Compassion, honor and to help the less fortunate among us, these were the most important values I desperately tried to instill in my children. Through the love of their family, the strength that the family would give them, I hoped they would take all of this as adults out into the world and truly, truly make it a better place.

Now mind you I bonded with my children through arts and crafts and spending time with them in the pool and teaching them the ABC's, numbers and colors. Michael had quite a different version of bonding. He liked the rough and tumble things like the target shooting that he would do with Teddy. Most recently he had purchased a BB gun that Teddy could use target shooting while he used the shotgun. It was lighter for Teddy to handle and it was easier for him to aim. Remember now, in 1994 Teddy was only 6 years old and Martin only 3, but Michael hated the idea of leaving Martin out when he and Teddy went target shooting, so he thought he could set up a little thing in the basement of our home. The basement door was just off of the kitchen, and one day about two weeks after he purchased the BB gun, when I was in the kitchen cooking their favorite dinner, homemade chicken pot pie, I heard a *ping*. Then I heard Michael scream, "Hit the floor!"

I said, "Oh, no." I quickly ran to the head of the stairs and screamed down, "What in the hell is going on?"

Michael yelled up, "Oh, nothing, Honey."

"Nothing, my ass; I just heard that ping."

I went down there and I saw the setup Michael had. He had a huge box that he had stuffed old newspapers rolled up with a target taped over the front of the box, and he was helping Martin take his first shot with the BB gun. Martin shot the BB gun, and of course, it was way off target. It hit the cement on the wall and ricocheted all around the basement. I suppose that was when Michael yelled, "Hit the floor." I quickly took my baby Martin upstairs and told Michael he was insane.

"I'm just trying to have a little fun with Martin. He said he hears about Teddy and me going target shooting all the time, and he just wanted to give it a try."

I said, "Do you know how crazy you sound right now? He's a baby. He's three years old."

Michael said, "I know, but I made a huge target. I don't know how he missed it."

I told him, "Maybe because he's only three years old!"

Needless to say this never ever happened again. The next time Martin would hold this BB gun would be outside about two summers from then, when he was six years old.

It was about five minutes after I took Martin safely in my arms back upstairs away from the two loonies down in the basement when they followed. The three of them sat in the living room saying not a word. Michael put on one of Martin's favorite shows, *Sesame Street*, and I just stood there shaking my head.

To tell you the truth, I did think it was rather funny! It was a huge lapse of judgment on Michael's part, but I suppose when the male bonding begins to take over, men are liable to do just about anything for a kick. It got to the point when the three of them got together I never knew what to expect. They always seemed to be getting into trouble, and I would hold my breath every time the three of them would go down the basement together.

After this he had a dartboard set up. Once I saw the dartboard, I said to Michael, "What are you doing?"

"Don't worry about it. I make them wear safety goggles."

Michael had truly begun looking at Teddy and Martin as his closest buddies. Everywhere Michael went, they went, and as the days and the weeks passed I could see that bond growing ever stronger, and I loved it. I loved to see the three of them together. Partners in crime—they always had such a blast. I thought to myself, *Well, after all, they can't always be coddled by their mommy. They have to become little men.* Michael was so looking forward to teaching them absolutely everything about what a good man does and how to have fun.

It just seemed like the years were passing very quickly. Teddy had just turned seven September 3, 1994, and he was in the second grade already. He was doing very well there. He really thrived at school. He was very, very smart, and he absorbed everything like a little sponge, but what I also was seeing was that Teddy had started to become quite the man's man, a real little man, a real little tough guy who loved riding and jumping his bike. The higher the jump the better he liked it. He seemed as though he loved anything outside that was physical, and he was a little bit crazy. It seemed as though he just didn't care whether he crashed his bike or landed right up. He got just as much enjoyment either way. It seemed as though he had inherited my high threshold for pain because when he did crash his bike, he very rarely complained. He simply got up and brushed himself off, made sure his bike wasn't broken, and would get right back on his bike and ride off. He would do this again and again. He would continue making the same jump until he got it right, just the way he wanted to land. It seemed as though he had a plan in his mind of just what he wanted to do, and he kept trying until he achieved this. He even talked his father into building a bigger ramp that he could jump, and Michael went along with this. I couldn't believe it, but he did.

Michael then explained to me, "Well, Kyra, he has jumped all the other ramps that I have made, and he is getting bored. It has to go up to another level now."

The first few times after Michael had built this larger ramp, Teddy crashed. While I was standing there beside Michael watching our sweet child go through all this pain but yet not be bothered by any of it, just brush himself off as he always did, and try it again, I said to Michael, "Are you crazy? Why did you build such a huge ramp?"

He explained, "Teddy has become quite a high-spirited child. He loves going on to the next level. He loves challenging himself, and he loves riding his bike, roller blading, or skate boarding. He loves the action and the thrill of it all. He is high spirited." He turned to me and said, "Kyra, please don't ever crush that spirit because that is a part of Teddy. That's what makes Teddy, Teddy." Then he said, "We should be cultivating this spirit, not try to crush it. I'll always stand by him," Michael said to me, "no matter what Teddy decides to do. I'll back him 100%."

I looked at Michael, and I told him, "I'm not trying to crush his spirit. I'm just trying to prevent him from crushing his skull."

That's when Michael told me, "Well, why do you think he's wearing a helmet?"

I just shook my head and continued watching Teddy go over the ramp and crash again and again and again. I think it was on the sixth or seventh jump where he made it, the perfect landing that he was trying to achieve, and I turned to Michael and I said, "Okay, that's good. I'm proud of him, and I'm proud of you, but I don't want to see any bigger ramp. This ramp is big enough." Michael did agree. It was quite an impressive size.

This is how very different Martin and Teddy were in their personalities and their likes and dislikes. Actually you could not have had more opposite children. At the age of seven Teddy was jumping these humongous ramps and Martin not quite four wouldn't even get onto a tricycle. I literally had to put him on his tricycle, and he sat there crying and screaming for me to take him off. I have no idea how they came out so differently, but I realize you can never push one child into being like the other. They each had their own personality, and Michael and I had to respect this. So Martin sat on the sidelines with Michael and me watching his insane brother doing these jumps time and time again. Perhaps it was seeing this that scared the hell out of Martin. Maybe he thought his father and I, too, expected him to be able to do this, and there was no way in hell he was going to do it.

So what Michael and I quickly discovered is that we had one son that was trying to follow in Eval Knievel's footsteps, and the other son was trying to follow in Picasso's footsteps, the sensitive quiet artist. Needless to say catering to both of these personalities were, at best, very difficult from time to time.

Now and again I would refer to them as the Odd Couple, right down to their bedroom. Martin's side of the room was always kept neat as a pin, and Teddy's side looked like a bomb exploded in it. I always felt rather sorry for Martin because he had to wake up every morning looking at the mess on the other side of the room. That is why I tried to get in there every day to make it as neat as I possibly could for Martin, more than Teddy, because Teddy quite frankly could have cared less if he lived in a mansion or pig sty at this point.

It was also around this time that Martin had developed a fascination for bugs. Thank God just plastic ones, not real. He must have collected seventy or eighty different kinds of insects from centipedes to ants to beetles. Any bug, you name it, he had it. Like most little boys that played with their matchbox cars, he lined all these bugs up on the edge of his bed, on his bureau, and on his toy box. I have to tell you walking into their bedroom was quite the adventure. On one side, as I mentioned, it would look like a bomb had gone off, with clothes everywhere, toys everywhere, and the other side neat as a pin except for a line of bugs all over. Talk about two quirky kids. I loved them so much, though, and I loved their personalities and what they were turning into. They were both great in their own special way.

It had always blown my mind, though, about how very, very different they were. I mean, after all they both grew up in the same household with the same parents who taught them the same things.

The year 1994 held a lot of change for us. We realized the children were no longer babies, and Michael's job situation seemed to be changing for the better. He woke up one morning and decided to give his old boss a call at the moving company where he had worked years earlier.

I asked him, "Are you physically still able to do this? It is very, very hard work"

He said, "I love driving, and as far as the work goes, there are other men there that will be able to help. I think my body is strong enough for me to be able to do this work. Regardless, I have to give it a try anyway. I really want to improve our income, and this is the only way that I can see to do this. It is the only trucking company that knows me well enough to trust me with a truck."

Of course, he did have that CDL license now that would entice the employer. Michael's psychiatrist at the VA had also just changed his medication and this made Michael feel a lot better and certainly a lot stronger, strong enough to be able to go on long hauls and to make some decent money for his family. His psychiatrist had prescribed Prozac for him.

About three weeks after he began taking it, Michael started really feeling much better, much happier, and much clearer in his thoughts. I thank God for Prozac. There was such an incredible change in Michael's personality. I actually could see that twinkle in his eye again. He was alert, he was sharp and he felt great.

He told me, "Kyra, applying for this job I have nothing to lose. If I can't do it, I can't do it. At least I can give it a shot." He also reminded me that driving would easily triple our income and with our children growing older and wanting to get into more things like bigger bikes, the money he was making before was not going to cut it. He said, "I have to at least try."

So I agreed, and I said, "Go ahead. Give it your best."

It was now October of 1994, just before Martin's fourth birthday and just before Michael would begin his new truck-driving job. The leaves were turning and everything was so beautiful outside with all their magical colors. There were orange and brilliant reds and yellows that I loved so much. This was my favorite time of the year. As I have mentioned, Martin and Teddy's personalities were very different. Michael spent time with Teddy on his jumps and working on his ramps, and he spent an equal amount of time with Martin doing things that Martin liked to do. He drew with Martin, played board games and would help him rearrange his bug collections.

Among these things, his favorite thing to do with Martin was to take long walks, especially in the fall. So that is exactly what happened. Michael and Martin both headed down to the corner variety store where Michael purchased a soda for both of them. They would often take these long walks and just talk and spend time together.

On this one particular day after purchasing the soda, Michael decided to head back home instead of going the other way for an extended walk. It was getting kind of chilly and he thought that Martin might catch cold. So they decided to come back home to get their jackets and then go down to the playground about a quarter of a mile from our house as they often did. While on their way back home, Martin pulled a packet of gum out of his pants pocket and offered his father a piece. Michael couldn't believe it. It was the same thing that happened with Teddy and me. Perhaps if we had kept our children away from gum this never would have occurred. I don't know. Maybe it was our fault, but it was that damn gum yet again.

Michael asked Martin, "Where did you get that?"

Martin told him, "I took it from the stand at the store we just came from, Daddy."

"You took it?"

"Yes."

Michael then said, "Daddy didn't pay for that," and he quickly remembered how I handled the situation with Teddy. He did exactly the same thing with Martin. He explained to Martin that was stealing, it was wrong, and it was also against the law. He walked Martin back to the store and he told Martin, "You show the man the gum that you took."

Martin placed the gum on the counter. The man looked down at Martin and said, "Do you know this was wrong? You just took it without paying for it."

Martin broke out into tears and said, "Yes, I'm sorry."

Michael then paid for the gum and showed Martin this is what you do when you go to a store. You never walk out with anything unless you have paid for it. This is money. Michael handed the man at the counter the 50 cents for the gum.

Martin took the gum and turned to Michael and said, "Thank you, Daddy." He turned back to the man and apologized once again.

They both left the store, and while walking home Michael tried his best to explain to Martin how he was never to do this again, and how he had never, ever seen Daddy or Mommy take anything from any store without paying for it." We don't do that because it is wrong." Michael told him, "I don't want you to do wrong things in this world or bad things, so please promise you'll never steal anything again," and he promised. He, too, kept his word.

When they arrived home Michael told me what had happened. I looked at Martin and said, "You realize it was wrong, and I hope you listened to Daddy."

He said, "Yes, Mommy, yes."

Teddy was sitting at the kitchen table doing his homework at the time, and he looked up at Martin, and he just laughed. He said, "That was a really scary thing you had to go back and do, right?"

I looked at Teddy, and I said, "Yea, you can speak from experience, huh?"

"I sure can. I'll never forget that," and he never did. That was burned into his memory. Teddy had a good chuckle and returned back to his homework.

I told Martin, "Now you can go and sit in your room until supper is ready and you think hard about what you just did."

The lessons with our children just went on and on. We seemed to be teaching them a new lesson every other day.

With Michael on this new medication, it was like living with a different person. I have never seen him so alive and so high-spirited in all the time we had been together. I had only seen this a few times. The first time was when he was put on his first medication. He seemed a lot happier, but it still wasn't the same as now. He was tired before. It seemed like every medication that they would switch him to, this would be the side effect, but not this one. The Prozac gave him the energy he needed, the happiness and just feeling alive again. This drug was a miracle for our family and for Michael's mental state of mind, and by far this is the best medication that he had ever been on.

As Michael started working at his new job, the money situation improved dramatically. We were finally able to take our children to different places that we had never been able to before. Michael and I both found that we could breathe just a little bit easier being able to cover all the bills we had. That Christmas was great.

Just before Christmas was Martin's birthday, November 26, right after Thanksgiving, and we were able to throw him a really great birthday party. Afterwards we took him to the Christmas parade that our little town had every year, and then the four of us went out to eat. Things seemed to be looking up for the first time in a long time financially, but there always seemed to be a flip side to my life.

When things in one area begin going very well, things in other areas of my life seem to always turn to shit. While Michael and I were enjoying a little relief with a little bit more income, my mother's health on the other hand started going downhill. Instead of her spending four or five days a week at our house, it was down to two or three and then to two and then to one. This was beginning to affect the boys because they loved their grandmother and they loved spending time with her. They had gotten use to her being there practically every day. As I mentioned, she was their second mother. She was much more than just a grandmother to them. I have to admit especially with Teddy because he was the first-born, there was a special bond between them, so I suppose it was hardest on him. It wasn't so much my mother's health that was deteriorating, but her eyesight. She felt unsure of herself in her footing. The worse her eyesight became, the more hesitant she was about leaving her apartment, and this was due to diabetes. She developed Type II Diabetes when she was about

50, and through the years it slowly began stealing her eyesight to the point where she was no longer able to take care of her own bills or cook her own meals because she couldn't see to follow recipes or the stove settings.

All of this just became very difficult, and I could clearly see that this was quickly becoming very depressing to her. I saw her mental state decline dramatically, and this worried me most of all. I told her, "Mom, don't worry about it. I can do the bills for you. There is no problem there." I took over her finances and her meals and made sure she got to all her doctors' appointments. All the while I was doing these things for her, I could tell she hated it. Remember, my mother was one of the strongest women, most intelligent and most independent women that I had ever met. For her to have to hand over all this responsibility to me had to have killed her inside. Of course, I never complained. I never looked at it as extra work for me. I looked at it as being able to repay a huge debt to her, and I was grateful that God gave me this opportunity to repay her. I owed my mother so much.

So I guess you could say, in a weird way I kind of enjoyed taking care of her for a change and making her life a little bit easier and being ever grateful to be able to do so. But still I know she didn't look at it this way. She hated not being independent, not even being able to make one of her own favorite recipes, a chicken bake with rice and breadcrumbs. Even though it was a simple thing, her eyes had gotten that bad (she must have been close to blind at this point), I knew as far as the cooking went this was a problem easily solved. I simply got her a little toaster oven, and I made her a huge marking on the side of where the temperature setting would be. I picked up aluminum trays like TV dinner trays, and I would spend one entire day cooking a week's worth of meals for her. She would take them home and put them in the freezer. I made sure that they were very nutritious with vegetables and a side dish along with the meat, either beef, hamburger or pork chops. The steak didn't fare too well. Her favorite was my homemade chicken soup. It seemed to be not only her favorite, but also Michael's, Teddy's, and Martin's as well. This would last two or three dinners because I would make a huge pot of it along with homemade biscuits. I made sure my mother's lunches and suppers were covered. All she had to do was simply take them out of the freezer and put them into the little toaster oven, setting it on the marking I had made. So that left only breakfast, and she usually only had coffee and toast for that.

Her bills I simply had transferred to my address, so every month when she received her Social Security check I would take her to cash it, and we would make out the money orders for the bills. I would take her grocery shopping, and we would plan her meals and my family's meals together. Many times I would try to persuade her to simply come to my house for dinner because the boys really enjoyed having her as well as Michael and I did.

A lot of times she did this, but I believe with her sight getting worse as the days went on, she was developing probably an anger issue. I remembered when I hurt my hand, the limitations I had to deal with and the anger I felt. Many people don't understand how anger can set in after you have had an injury. It's just simply the limitations that you now have to deal with. You can't live your life as you always did. You have to now stop and think before you go and grab something, or now in my mother's case, she couldn't even see the oven well enough to work it. So, yes, I would imagine she was having anger issues as well. Perhaps she just didn't want to show this to us. That's why she cut down the visits to two and then one day a week instead of the four and five she always did.

On the days that she didn't want to come over to the house, we always talked on the phone two or three times a day. Remember, my mother wasn't only a mother. She was my best friend, and she was the one woman, the only woman that I ever admired in this world. So believe me when I say, the privilege of being able to give back to her after all of these years that she has given so much to me, I was truly, truly grateful for. Believe me, I let her know this. I let her know how I felt toward her.

She told me, "Kyra, don't be so ridiculous; I was your mother. That was my job to teach you things, to teach you right from wrong, and to love you. I brought you into this world and that was my responsibility as a Mom to love you the best way I could." She also told me, "You know, I might not have been able to give you everything that you wanted, but I gave you everything I had. I certainly don't expect to be repaid for a job that I was supposed to do to begin with, and I don't want anything."

You know, she never did. She never asked me for anything. She was always giving, and my mother was the type of person that would literally give you the shirt of her back if you needed it more than she did. So you can only imagine what she gave to her daughters, all the love and all the caring. I have no idea how a woman so small had so much love in her heart.

This woman did not deserve the life that was handed to her, but I could see how her life strengthened her. She somehow through her life was able to turn her pain into her strength. I watched this, and I tried to learn from this. Looking back at the way I behaved as a teenager, quitting school and the drinking. How this must have disappointed her after everything that she had taught me. I knew that there were many times I broke her heart, and that is why now it was even more important to me to try and somehow make up for my past, for my teenage years. This is why I was so grateful to be given this opportunity to do so. I would try so hard in my life after my teenage years to never again let my mother down, and now she finally needed me.

Something odd occurred. It was that Christmas, Christmas Eve of 1994. After Michael and I got through wrapping the children's and the family gifts and placing them under the tree (some of course from Santa), we filled up Teddy's and Martin's Christmas stockings and placed them by the tree. We put all the lights out. It was getting pretty late; I'd say probably 2 in the morning by now. We had to make sure that the kids were fast asleep before we started our work as Mr. and Mrs. Santa. We didn't want them coming down the stairs and surprising us.

It was after all this work that Michael, and I put all the lights out, except the Christmas-tree lights. We lay there cuddling together on the couch with the soft glow of the tree lights. I remember lying there in Michael's arms feeling so safe and so secure. He leaned down and our lips met in a soft embrace, and he told me how very, very much he loved me, and I told him how very much I loved him. As we lay there just relaxing and taking in the beauty of the Christmas tree, (we loved our Christmas trees) all of a sudden completely out of the blue a wave of sadness engulfed me. I couldn't control myself. I began crying, sobbing uncontrollably. It was that feeling of foreboding, and I had no idea where it was coming from. Of course, as I mentioned earlier I would never find out what was going to happen until it did. But this was the worst one yet. This was completely devastating and crippling to me. I had never experienced one so strong before. I was completely engulfed in sorrow and pain, a tidal wave of despair. I couldn't understand it. I had never been hit so hard with these feelings before, and no matter how hard Michael tried to console me, nothing worked. Nothing could make this pain go away, and when I say it came from out of the blue and sucker punched me, I mean it.

We had had such a fantastic month. Michael and I for the first time in a long time had the money that we needed to provide a great Christmas for our kids and our family. We got some beautiful gifts that year. Everything was going perfectly, so when this hit me, it was a total shock, and it was the worst foreboding feeling yet that I had ever gotten. I must have lain there in Michael's arms crying for over an hour. I felt at the same time horrible for Michael as well because everything had been going so well. He thought he was doing everything right. Why was I all of a sudden so sad, and reminded him of these foreboding feelings that I had gotten in the past, and how bad things always followed. I told him I had never felt anything so strong before in my life—a kick in my stomach, to put it mildly. He asked me if there was anything he could do to make me feel better, and I told him, "No, there's nothing. I just pray that it will pass quickly." As I lay there crying in his arms, my heart was breaking, and I had no idea why.

A little over an hour had passed by now, and Michael told me we really should get to bed. I had stopped crying, and he reminded me that we had all the relatives coming in the morning, our two Moms and my two sisters. He said, "You better pull it together, Kyra."

I agreed. I told him, "I know." The feeling was quickly leaving me, thank God, although I began to realize all the feelings of foreboding I had had in the past had never ever been this strong before and always horrible things followed. So when I got one this tremendous, this strong, I had no idea of what was going to happen, but I knew it wasn't going to be good. Quite frankly, I didn't even want to think about it.

Michael and I went up to bed for the night. He held me in his arms until we fell asleep. Before we knew it, Teddy and Martin were jumping on our bed yelling, "Mommy and Daddy, Santa came! Santa came! Come downstairs." I sat at the edge of the bed feeling as though I had a hangover. I was still drained from the night before. Thank God for my two little angels who seemed to be able to take my mind off of everything, off of all the bad in the world.

As soon as we hit downstairs, they went underneath the Christmas tree and began pulling out their gifts unwrapping them in a fit of frenzy with wrapping paper flying all around. They were thrilled. They had gotten exactly what they wanted. Teddy was especially happy with his new game boy and his games, and Martin, his science kit. After they got through searching for their last gift underneath the tree, they then started on their Christmas stockings. They were special stockings made a few years earlier just for them. I believe Martin was one when I made his. I made it out of an old red tablecloth. The stocking actually was as big as Martin was. I used a piece of their "blankie" that they had held close and loved for years and slept with every night for the toe and the heel. On top I put a ribbon of holly, and in the middle of the stocking was their name in gold letters. Also on each of their stockings were little pendants, Christmas pendants, little teddy bears, one depicting each personality. Teddy's teddy bear had skis, and Martin's was on a rocking horse. Oh, how they loved their stockings, and I enjoyed every stitch that went into making them for my babies.

After the frenzy of them opening all their gifts and their stockings was over, they began to play with all the new toys, and I started the Christmas turkey. I always loved a big turkey. Mine had to be at least twenty-six pounds. I found the larger the better. The more leftovers and the more leftovers for me to be able to give to our Moms to take home. As our mothers arrived along with April and Amber, they of course went directly to the living room to be with Teddy and Martin and see all the new toys that Santa had just brought them, and go through their stockings. April was particularly interested in the stockings. She loved them. Remember she's the one that always made a beautiful stocking for me.

As the turkey was cooking in the oven I stood at the entrance to the kitchen looking into the living room at my whole family enjoying Teddy and Martin. I tried so hard to live in the moment, to join in with their laughter and the fun that they were having, but at this moment all of this happiness eluded me. I couldn't shake that feeling of being kicked in the stomach no matter how I tried. I was angry that it was interfering with the real world and my life now, something I had never let happen before, but it was now preventing me from thoroughly enjoying this Christmas with my children and my family. Nevertheless no matter how I was feeling, I was determined not to ruin it for everyone else. I put on a smile, and I went through the day trying my best to just enjoy it, if not for myself but for them.

It wouldn't be until later on that evening after everyone else had gone, I was cleaning up, and my mother was sitting at the kitchen table and we were talking. I told her about what happened to me last night and how terribly sick I felt all day.

She said, "I could see something was wrong. I wasn't sure what it was, but you were a little off, and you didn't seem to be as happy as you usually are."

I told her that was why, and then I turned to her and asked her if she had felt anything last night, because quite often when one of us has this foreboding feeling, all of us did.

She told me, "No. I'm fine." Then she looked at me and she said, "Kyra, you know there is so much sadness and despair in this world right now, maybe none of us has a right to be truly happy anymore, whether it be Christmas or any other day. I don't know," she said. "Perhaps that's what you are picking up on, just the world's sadness."

I just nodded my head and began drying my dishes, and I told her, "I would rather not be picking up anything. I just want to live a normal life. I don't want to have feelings like this thrown on me like a tidal wave."

"Like it or not, that's what was given to you."

"I don't like feeling as though my heart is breaking for no reason." I went on to tell her that's how intense that feeling was and that it was the strongest that I had ever felt.

It did take three or four days after that happened for me to start finally feeling normal again and truly happy. Again it was Michael and my children that finally pulled me out of the funk that I was in. We took our boys over to the hills next to our house and watched them slide with the sleds that they got for Christmas. Up and down the hill for hours until we were frozen. I then began laughing and the happiness returned back into my heart.

It was now a week after Christmas. It was New Year's Eve, and Michael and I would spend it much like we had spent all the prior ones (after we had stopped drinking) cuddled up on the couch watching the clock in Times Square bring in the New Year, just the two of us. This was our special night. I would make deviled eggs, tuna rolls and chicken wings with some potato salad. That was Michael's favorite. After putting the boys to bed we would come down and enjoy a little snack together and lie on the couch, holding each other, cuddling by the soft glow of the Christmas tree lights and watching the clock. As always, just after the stroke of midnight of the New Year, Michael and I would kiss and embrace, and there we would always make love, that feeling of passion burning ever so bright. Even after sixteen years he still had a way of making me weak in the knees. It's funny how the love and the passion just overtook us, and he still gave me goose bumps while caressing my neck. We simply would just lose all self-control. Afterwards we would remain on the couch still in each other's arms until the sun came through our window blinds.

When Michael and I awoke that morning, we found a fresh blanket of snow had fallen overnight. I remember getting up off the couch and looking out the window at it and saying to Michael, "It's as bright and as beautiful as our love." He came up behind me and gave me a huge hug and started kissing my neck again, and I told him, "I don't think you want to do that right now," as we heard Teddy and Martin's little feet pitter pattering down the stairs. So as we stood there in each other's arms, Teddy and Martin came running up toward us, Teddy grabbing Michael's leg and Martin grabbing mine. They quickly began begging their father and me to take them out sledding. They had already looked out the window and seen all the new beautiful snow, snow that they wished to plunge their little bodies into.

Teddy looked up at me and said, "Mommy, can you take us to the big hill, not this little tiny one over by our house? You know, the big one."

I knew immediately what he meant. It was a farm house about five miles away from where we lived, and a lot of the city kids would go there with their brand-new sleds after Christmas. It was a huge hill, and the kids would have such a blast on it. Of course Michael and I said, "Yes."

I made them their breakfast, which they seemed rather perturbed at because they didn't even want to eat. They were too excited and they wanted to be the first ones on the hill. But I made them eat a little bit of breakfast anyway, just oatmeal and hot chocolate, just enough to give them the energy that I knew they were going to need. They gobbled it down as fast as they could, and I proceeded to get them all bundled up in their snowsuits, their winter boots, hats, gloves and scarves. My sons were so bundled up, if they had fallen they probably would have bounced back up again. Then Michael and I got all bundled up. Everyone got into the car as Michael loaded the sleds into the trunk. We then took off.

The roads were still slippery because they had yet to be plowed. We found ourselves just down the street from the huge hill, and the closer we came to it the more Teddy could see all the other children which kind of disappointed him because you see at this age he thought everything did belong to him, including other people's land. He so wanted to be the first one on the hill, the first one to make a mark in the fresh fallen snow with his brand-new sled.

We would park our car on the side of the road just like everyone did, and as I was getting the boys out of the back seat; Michael was getting their sleds out of the trunk. We walked up to the top of the hill. The snow was up to our knees, and the boys loved it so much, that fresh, clean, crisp snow. There is nothing like it. There my two babies began their day of bumps and bruises and near misses with other sleds. I would stand there holding my breath from moment to moment and other times nearly having a heart attack watching my two sweet babies get into collision after collision with other sleds. Then of course was the treacherous trek back up the hill with everyone still wanting to go down. The ones that had already gone down were trying to work their way back up to go down yet again. Quite a few times Teddy would have his feet knocked out from underneath him by another child that was coming down the hill when Teddy was trying to drag his sled up. I kept telling Teddy when he saw a sled coming to get out of the way because they can't stop. After a few bumps and scrapes, they both got the idea. Martin seemed to have caught on quicker than Teddy as far as this went. He only got plowed down once before he learned his lesson to simply jump out of the way when he saw someone coming.

After a few tries on their own, Michael decided to start going down with them. I was always afraid of injuring my arm further, so this kind of prevented me from having as much fun with my children as I had wished. This being one of the cases, I really wasn't looking forward to having my arm run over by another child's sled, so I stayed put on top of the hill watching the three of them. They were having such a blast, and once again I thought to myself, *How lucky my two babies are to have such a father as Michael, and how much I love him.*

This morning seemed to pass by so quickly. Before we knew it we were out there for five hours. All four of us were frozen to the bone by this time, and it began snowing again. That is when Michael said, "Okay boys. We have been here long enough." I could tell they were freezing as well. Their little teeth were chattering, but do you think we could get them off the hill? Hell no. The boys continued pulling their sleds up the hill and quickly flying back down them just out of Michael's and my reach.

We kept yelling to them, "Come on, boys. It's time to go. Mommy and Daddy are cold, and we have to go home now and get warmed up."

They just yelled back at us, "No, we don't want to!"

We realized we had quite the struggle on our hands, and we even tried playing the sympathy card. I yelled down to them, "Mommy's feeling sick, and we need to go home now." I don't know if they heard me or not, but if they did hear me they chose to simply ignore my words. By this point it was quickly reaching six hours. I was beginning to lose the feeling in my lower extremities and feared that I would never feel my legs once again. Their father and I had to quickly come up with a plan. We walked away from the hill backward, where they couldn't see us, in hopes that they would panic, and they did. As soon as we were out of eyesight, they came rushing back up the hill with their sleds. That's when Michael and I grabbed them, Michael grabbing Teddy and me grabbing Martin by the waist. We carried them back to our car, kicking and screaming all the way.

On our way back toward the car with our children under our arms like a sack of potatoes kicking and screaming, I turned to Michael, and I laughed. I said, "I'm glad we did not have any more children. We would have been outnumbered."

We tried to brush Teddy and Martin off before we placed them in the car. The ton of snow that was clinging to each of their snowsuits was hard enough to brush off without having a child kicking and screaming, but we did it. Michael put Teddy into the car, and I put Martin in. We put their seat belts on while they were still kicking and screaming. "No, we don't wanna go. We don't wanna go."

I said, "We have to go, or Mommy and Daddy are going to die out here."

Michael then threw their brand-new sleds into the trunk as quickly as he could because at this point they were still trying to take off their seat belts. The four of us were now in the car, and the heat was finally defrosting my legs. I looked back at both of them yelling and screaming still and thrashing around, and I swear when I looked at Martin, my littlest angel, growled at me. I couldn't believe it. This was the first time he ever did such a thing. I swear we were not in the car but 10, 15 minutes at the most trying to get warmed up before we drove home when they actually both passed out in the back seat. Their father and I could not believe it. We turned around and they were both fast asleep. Here were two children who only 15 minutes earlier refused to come off a hill. Michael and I both just shook our heads and proceeded home.

When we got home Michael and I both woke up Martin and Teddy, our two little sleeping snowmen in the back seat of our car. They walked into the house very slowly with their eyes half open. They stood there in the kitchen, Michael removing, or should I say peeling off Teddy's drenched snowsuit, and I, Martin's. I then went upstairs and got their Dr. Denton's, their little bunny suits I used to call them, their pajamas with the feet in them, and I put them both on. They quickly passed out on the couch, one at one end and one at the other. As Michael and I sat there in our chairs looking at their sweet little faces sleeping, they looked like two little cherubs, completely and totally exhausted cherubs.

Outside the snow had begun to fall at a very steady pace. It was becoming quite deep. To Michael and my surprise it was becoming a blizzard outside, a complete whiteout as a matter of fact. It was so bad you couldn't even see the house next door. Michael said, "Thank God we left the hill when we did, because driving home in this would have been very, very hard. As Michael and I sat there watching this new falling snow, we sipped on a nice hot cup of chocolate, just relaxing and taking the day's events in and trying our hardest to defrost our frozen bodies. After I regained the feeling in my legs, I then went out to the kitchen and began making New Year's Day dinner.

It was now a little after three, and I had gotten kind of a late start on it because of what we had done earlier that day. However, I didn't really worry too much about this because we weren't going to have any of the family over for this dinner. New Year's Day dinner my mother always spent with my sisters April and Amber. Looking outside at all of the snow I was relieved at this because I didn't want anyone driving in it anyway. So I began making the potatoes and the squash, and I put the honey-glazed ham in the oven and had everything going. I knew it would take at least a couple of hours and the children more than likely would be awake by then. So as Michael sat relaxing in the living room alongside of our two little boys, I cooked New Year's Day dinner.

About an hour had passed when I heard a tap, tap, tap at the door. Given how great the snow was falling by this time I couldn't imagine who it could be. I couldn't imagine April just out of the blue showing up at my door with Mom. So as I walked toward the door I had no idea who I would be opening it for. As I opened the door, I saw this cute little guy standing there, and it was Joey one of Teddy's best friends wondering if Teddy would like to come out and play with him in the snow.

You can only imagine the thought that went through my mind. It was, *My God, kid, you have no idea of how many hours we had just spent out there*, but I knew Teddy, being the snow lover that he was, there was no way he would be able to resist this. He did hear the knock at the door, and he did wake up. He ran to the door with his little Dr. Denton's on and said to Joey, "You want to go out and play in the snow?" I could not believe what he was saying. I thought this child was frozen to the bone, but I guess after his short little nap, he had he regained all of his strength. As Joey stood in the doorway Teddy jumped up and down, begging me to let him go out and become a human snowman all over again.

I said to myself, *Oh, my God, now I have to get him all dressed up all over again.*

Thank God he had three winter suits, for the simple reason that I knew how much he loved the snow. He was constantly getting soaking wet outside, and I would constantly have to put a dry new one on him. So I made sure I had plenty of backups for both him and Martin. Martin, thank goodness, didn't hear this conversation going on. He was still passed out, dead to the world on the couch, so I took time out from my preparation of dinner and got Teddy all dressed up again.

He and Joey played in our front yard. The first thing they started doing was making snow angels, and then they moved on to bigger and better things. They tried to build their own snowman, but it seemed like the balls of snow that they were able to get from this huge snowstorm were bigger than they were. You should have seen the two of them out there trying to roll this huge ball of snow. I have no idea what it weighed, but it took both of them and all their strength to push it.

Joey was a really good kid. I loved him. His family had moved in about a year earlier and how we met was a funny story. I was walking Teddy to school as I would every morning. I would put Martin in the carriage and as we walked to school Joey just started joining us. I would go to pick Teddy up from school with Martin in the carriage. Martin was old enough to walk, but it was quite a distance for his little legs so it was easier for me to just put him in the carriage.

Anyway, Joey one day asked me if it was okay if he walked with us. I looked down at him and said, "Certainly, you're more than welcome to."

Then he introduced himself to me, and I introduced myself to him. He asked me, "Could I come over your house and play with Teddy some day?"

"Certainly, Honey." He was such a sweet kid, a well-mannered child. Joey was about a year and a half older than Teddy, but this year and a half didn't make very much difference at all. Their personalities just clicked. They had the same likes and the same dislikes, and I completely encouraged their friendship. I had met his mother and his whole family, and they were so very nice and so kind. I thought to myself, *Teddy was lucky to find a friend that was so nice so early in life, and I hoped that they would keep this friendship forever.*

I will tell you that later on in years this bond between Joey and Teddy, this friendship, would carry Teddy through some of the most difficult times in his life, times that were yet to come. I stood there looking out my kitchen watching Teddy and Joey build their huge snowman, or attempt to, anyway. Michael and I actually were no help with this because we were still too frozen to venture back out into the winter wonderland that Joey and Teddy so completely embraced.

I stood there watching them both, and Teddy reminded me so much of my mother. She used to tell me stories about when she was a child out in the snow and how much she loved it. She told me she was the first one out in a snowstorm to play and the last one to go back into her house, and this was Teddy. You give him a good snowstorm and there would be no way to keep him in the house. My mother and Teddy were both extreme snow lovers, and this was just one more of his passions, just another part of his personality, his wonderful personality.

By this time our New Year's Dinner was almost ready to be put on the table, and that left the dreaded deed of trying to get Teddy back into the house. But much to my surprise he didn't give me very much of a struggle. I guess even he had had enough of the cold for one day. So he came in the house after only two times of me having to call him.

I asked Joey if he would like to stay for dinner with us. He thanked me but said, "No. My mom's got dinner cooking, too."

Just then I heard Izzy, his mom, yell out the door for him. "Joey, it's time to eat."

I said, "OOPS, I guess you're right," so he headed off back home, and Teddy came in the house with no problems. I then peeled his snowsuit back off of him, dried him off a little bit, and put his little Dr. Denton's back on.

I tried my best to wake Martin up, and succeeded after 10-15 minutes. His eyes were still droopy. He was still exhausted from his big day on the snowy hill. He staggered to the table. He sat down, and he looked as though his face was going to fall into the plate of food that I set before him.

I told him, "Martin, wake up. You have to at least eat New Year's Day Dinner with us."

"Mommy, I'm so tired."

"I know. Just take a few bites, and then you can go upstairs if you'd like."

He said, "No, I just want to go back on the couch to sleep," and I agreed to this. So after he took a few bites of his ham and some mashed potatoes, he stumbled back to the couch where I covered him up with a nice big quilt. After he finished his supper, Teddy followed his brother back onto the couch, but he stayed awake. He and Michael sat there watching their favorite TV show, *The Cosby Show*.

After cleaning up and doing the dishes I then retired to the living room. We watched TV together for a couple of hours. It was now around 8 o'clock, 9 o'clock and the two boys were completely passed out. Michael carried Teddy upstairs, and I carried Martin. We tucked them both into their nice, warm cozy beds, and then Michael and I returned back to the living room to watch a couple more hours of television before we went to bed. We sat there laughing and talking about the day's events, and that's when I told him, "You know Martin growled at me?"

He laughed and asked me, "When did he do that?"

"Just before he passed out in the backseat of the car."

It's completely amazing to me even today how two sweet little boys, two sweet little cherubs could turn into such utter complete monsters at the drop of a hat. I thought to myself, *Well, I really don't care as long as they turn back into my cute little cherubs as long as at the end of the day I get my angel and my Honey Bunny back.*

That night after Michael and I crawled underneath our nice warm covers for the night, we talked a little bit about the year to come. We spoke about how things were looking up for us financially and how great our children were doing and what kind of great people they were growing into. Michael was really counting on gaining the experience he needed, along with his CDL license, to go to a better-paying company, perhaps long haul. Eventually we would have our dream come true, and that was to be able to buy our own home and to do things with our children that we always wanted to do. One of them was being able to go on a family vacation. Just simple things like that in life, Michael was planning on being able to give to us now that he had begun gaining experience through this furniture moving company. He knew he couldn't stay at that job for too long, perhaps another year or so of gaining experience because his body would not allow him to. It is very hard work moving furniture all day. So that was his plan, to stay there, to gain experience driving, and then go to a better company, perhaps return back to the company that he had put in his first application for that was really paying great. This was his plan.

Now it was the beginning of 1995. A whole brand-new year lay before us, a year with challenges, with growing, with experiencing many marvelous things with our two boys. This year was filled with hope for both Michael and me, and this year did hold so many changes in our family's life. Some of them were not so good. This was the year that I had begun experiencing pain in both of my hands and arms. I had dealt for ten years now with the RSD in my left hand and forearm. In that left arm, the arm that I had the RSD in, the pain was becoming increasingly worse. My right hand and forearm, an arm that I never had any problems with before, was now also beginning to cause me much pain and numbness. I had no idea what was going on. I had no idea what it was.

I began trying to handle the pain in both of my hands and forearms just as I did when I first got the RSD and that was mind control. I tried to block the pain, but this was beyond pain. It was also a sense of numbness. When I would be driving the car my hands would go dead. When I would try to do a lot of activities with my hands or lifting, my hands would go dead. I still tried blocking it the best way I could, but every day trying to do my regular household chores or simply driving became increasingly more difficult.

You see when I first started noticing this happening with my hands going dead, it would take a little bit of work before this would happen, a little bit of movement. It seemed like it was getting worse and worse. Instead of it taking 10 to 20 minutes for my hands to start going dead, it now was only up to a minute or two. It seemed like this happened as soon as I started using them.

This was driving me crazy because I had no idea what was going on with me. I hadn't injured them in any way. Not like I did when I received that very deep laceration when I was working and developed the RSD, so I had no idea. All I knew was it was terribly aggravating and terribly painful, but I found ways to handle it. As I said, I tried blocking the pain just as I was doing with the RSD and this did help along with the Excedrin. Soaking my arms in the sink in very hot water for a few minutes a day brought some relief to me, enough that I was able to continue doing the things I had to do and that was taking care of my family.

As time went on and after a few months passed, blocking out the pain was working better and better. Just as I had to practice when I first got my RSD, I would now have to practice with this new pain, but it was working. I would now find the only time I was not able to do this was when I slept, because of course your mind just shuts down and goes somewhere else. You no longer have control over it, so every time I would move the wrong way or God forbid sleep on my arm, I would wake up in agony. This would occur four or five times a night, and then it would take me a half an hour or so to get back to sleep.

This was beginning to disrupt my life dramatically. I mean, I could deal with the pain during the day, but I at least had to be able to sleep. I found I could not do this any longer. I could not get a full good night's sleep as the human body requires. Out of desperation I then began self-medicating. I was forced to take a couple of Tylenol PM before bed every night, but even this didn't work. This could not stop the pain during the night. They provided very little relief if any at all. I could clearly see this wasn't the answer to me obtaining a good night's sleep, but I just didn't know what else to do. So I took the pills, and I suffered through the nights.

This all began in early spring of 1995. Right along with my problems, Michael's mother's health had also started a sharp decline. You see, she had suffered for so many years with rheumatoid arthritis it was beginning to take its toll on her body. I believe it was in late February early March of 1995 where she took a really bad fall in her home. Thank God she was able to reach the telephone. She called Michael up very distressed of course, and Michael went over there to help her off the floor. It was after this she saw her doctor, and the family decided in her best interests she no longer could live alone. That left her with only one choice and that was a nursing home where she would be able to get the help that she desperately needed. So Michael and his brother Joe began looking at different nursing homes, and they found a beautiful one for her. There was a beautiful garden right outside of her window, and after a month or so of her just getting use to the place, she was very happy there. Michael and Joe would visit her every weekend, and quite often Michael would take Teddy and Martin along with them so that they could spend time with their grandma.

It was also around this time when Michael received a phone call out of the blue from Michael Jr.'s mother, Bertha. I answered the phone and Bertha told me that she had some big news for Michael, news that she knew he would want to hear and if I could please give the phone to him. He was in the shower at the time, and all I could think of was that something bad had happened to Michael Jr. I banged on the bathroom door, and I told Michael to please come out now. Bertha was on the phone and she had something very important to tell him, and I didn't know at all what it was. She told him that Michael Jr. who was now twenty years old had joined the Marines, and he was doing very well. She described him to Michael as being very handsome, very tall, and extremely intelligent. I could see Michael's face light up as information was given to him about his son. He looked so proud.

Later on after the conversation he had on the phone, he would tell me how very proud he was of his son, and how badly he wanted to see him again. But Michael was so afraid of what Michael Jr. would think of him, so frightened that he would turn on him, and this would have broken Michael's heart. Of course if that were Michael Jr.'s reaction toward his father, his father would not have blamed him. Michael realized just how badly he had let his son down, and he also knew that there was no way that he could adequately explain to Michael Jr. about his life and everything he was fighting while he was little.

There was no way he knew he could make Michael Jr. understand why he did what he did. But even knowing all of this, Michael did try to get in touch with him, only once though. Bertha had given him Michael Jr.'s cell phone number, but all Michael received was Michael Jr.'s voice mail and an answering machine. He at least got to hear his son's voice for the first time in a long time, and that went straight through his heart and left him speechless. He left no message on the machine. He just hung up the phone and cried. He also knew of the party that Michael Jr.'s stepparents were going to throw for him, a going-away party before he was to be shipped out.

I told Michael, "You have the address?"

Michael said, "Yes."

"You have to go. You really have to go."

Michael just looked at me with tears in his eyes and he said, "I can't. I can't go in there and blow his life apart. I couldn't before, and I can't do it now."

Again I tried my best to persuade him to go. I told him, "So what? If you get a punch in the nose, big deal. At least you'll break the ice, and at least maybe you'll be able to salvage some sort of relationship with your son. You're never going to know unless you try."

Michael just kept shaking his head and telling me he couldn't. He was too ashamed to face his son after all these years.

At this point in Michael Jr.'s life Michael was convinced that he was more likely than not probably not interested in meeting him anyway. I have to tell you the way Michael handled this whole situation came as a shock to me, because I knew Michael was never a man to back down from a challenge, a fight or anything else. After all, he fought his whole life and especially these past few years to regain his sanity and to stay sober. He fought for every day of sobriety, but this seemed to be the one and only thing Michael would not be able to face head on. This was, as far as I'm concerned, the most important thing he needed to face head on. But this was something that just broke his heart, something he knew he would never in his life be able to change. He would never be able to go back in time and make things right with his son, and he was just so afraid of causing him more pain. He was so very proud of his son, but he was never given the opportunity to tell him.

I often wonder to this day if things would have turned out differently for both Michael and Michael Jr. if Michael Jr. had actually answered the phone that day that his father called, that one time that Michael summoned up enough courage to dial those numbers. This was the one and only day he would have been able to actually talk to his son as an adult over the phone. I often wondered if they could have put the past behind them and just started off anew. I wonder if it would have made a difference in both of their lives.

Once again I sit here wondering and longing for the ability to turn back the hands of time. I thought, *If only Michael and I had the opportunity to be able to go back in time, how many things would we have been able to change knowing what we know now. How much quicker would we have acted not only for ourselves, but for Michael Jr. as well?* I should say, especially for Michael Jr., you are only given so many hours, so many days, weeks, months, and years to get it right, and unfortunately you can never go back and redo it. I think that has to be the most frustrating part of life. At least that's what I was finding to be true for myself. Michael had convinced himself of one other thing and that was that Michael Jr. probably had nothing but hate for him. This was the one thing that Michael would never be able to face, one of his children despising him. This was something he could not live with if he were to have to face this fact, so in his heart he once again had to let it go.

Dear God, this year was turning into a butte. The only thing that seemed to be going right for us was Michael's employment. Michael worked as many hours as he could get, sometimes twelve and thirteen hours a day. Many times he wouldn't get home until 8 o'clock at night, but I would be waiting for him with his hot supper. Frequently I would skip supper with the two boys in order to eat with my love when he arrived home. Quite often over these late-night suppers we would find ourselves talking about Michael Jr., wondering how he was doing, and also worrying about his well being. Michael loved Michael Jr. so much, just as much as he loved Teddy and Martin, and it was so sad that he wasn't able to let him know this. Along with all of those other heartaches in his life, the traumas that he had to go through, now this situation with his son would become just another heartache to him, one he would have to learn how to live with.

During these weeks and months that followed my mother would come over the house to visit with her grandsons and me two days a week. We would love having her over. We enjoyed every moment with her, especially the boys. They would often sit in the backyard at the picnic table together playing games, coloring or just talking. She would watch them on their swings and sometimes Teddy would persuade her to go into the front yard so he could show her his latest trick on his bike.

It was one of these afternoons when she was visiting that it began raining so they all came in the house to watch TV. She and I were sitting there in the living room when a commercial for laser eye surgery came on. We both looked at each other, and she told me, "Kyra, quick take down this number," and I did.

After I did, I looked at her, and I asked, "Are you really serious about this?"

"Well, it wouldn't hurt to at least look into it. It would be great if I could get some of my eyesight back at least." She then told me, "With my eyesight a little bit better, I would be able to gain my independence back. I would be able to go for walks when I wanted to and play with Teddy and Martin and read to them." She always read to them before in the past, so her not being able to share this part of herself with them, her love for reading, really hurt her.

We were both big believers in reading to children. My sons had all the Dr. Seuss books right along with a huge book of nursery rhymes and many, many other little stories in between. The one that was Martin's favorite was *Arthur's Good Manners*. He loved that book, and she loved reading that to him. So this was really taking the quality of her life away from her by her not being able to see very well. She also reminded me about how it would probably only get worse.

She said, "What am I supposed to do? Wait until I am totally blind? By then perhaps it would be too late. At least I could think about it and get the information, and then we could talk about it and decide if this is right for me or not."

So I agreed. I called the eye doctors that we saw advertised on television and tried to gather all the information I could over the phone and what it detailed. They explained a little bit about it and told me they would send me the information that we needed that would answer all the questions we had. So we waited for about a week with great anticipation. The more I thought about it the more I realized that this was my mother's best shot at being able to gain her independence again and to be able to see again. I realized I couldn't live in the past. There were new operations coming out every day. Medicine was able to offer people like my mother their independence back, so I felt as though I should do all I could to help her.

After receiving the packet in the mail about the information and the local doctors that were offering this operation, I called her Primary Care Physician and set up an appointment so she could go and have her tests for her sugar, her blood pressure and everything else. She had to be physically able to undergo this operation, and it was only if her sugar was at a good level and her blood pressure as well. She was very healthy. There didn't seem to be anything wrong, and the doctor gave the go-ahead for her eye surgery. I then made an appointment for her to go see the eye surgeon to see if she was eligible for this operation and if it would benefit her at all before she went through it. We had two interviews with this doctor, and everything seemed to be so positive. It seemed to be just what she needed, and the doctor did say that it would help her immensely. She wouldn't have 20/20 vision, but she would at least go back to where she was maybe ten or fifteen years earlier with her sight which wasn't that great, but it wasn't that bad either. So we made an appointment for the operation for the end of June of 1995.

In the meantime Michael was still working very hard with the furniture moving company, and this I have to tell you is a young man's job, because I could clearly see it was beginning to take its toll on him physically. He was now 48 years old, and I could see that every day was a struggle for him. He would come home at the end of the day so sore he could barely walk.

He told me, "I think it's time, Kyra, that I go and apply at the other trucking company, the one that I had been planning to apply for after I received all the

330

experience I could. I don't know how much more my body can take."

I agreed. I said, "Yeah, go for it."

He had one more run down to Maryland before he was going to do this. He hired a couple of helpers that afternoon when he arrived in Maryland to help him move this furniture into storage. By the time he finished it was about 8 o'clock at night. He went to his hotel room and went to bed completely exhausted. The next morning when he woke up he felt a little bit better he said, "But my body's still in a lot of pain." He sat there in the hotel room, he told me, trying to wake up. He got himself dressed and he thought he would go and get a cup of coffee and a good breakfast before heading back with the empty truck. He came out of the hotel room and got into the truck, and while he was backing up he told me his eyes did the weirdest thing. There was a wall behind the truck, and he did not see it at all. He said, "It was something I should have seen, but it was like my vision went blurry." He told me he backed right up into it. Thank God it didn't cause very much damage at all because he was moving slowly, but it was enough to scare him. His eyes had never done that before.

When he arrived back home that evening, is when he told me all of this, and he said, "Tomorrow I'm going to make an appointment at the VA to see an eye doctor, because I don't know what's going on. My eyes are playing tricks on me," and for a truck driver this could be scary as hell and extremely dangerous. So the next morning when we woke up I called the VA, and I made an appointment with an optometrist there for him and also for a physical because it had been a while since he had one of those. Even though he continued to see his psychiatrist twice a week that was a different part of the VA. He had not received a physical since he had been in the detox there in the alcohol program. The psychiatrist handled all of the scripts for him, the scripts for the antidepressants, and that's something the psychiatrist would give you. So as far as seeing one of the doctors went, this was new for Michael.

They were able to see him in only two days. He went first to the optometrist, and the optometrist did find that his eyesight was getting bad. I guess with age this was expected to happen, and he wrote out a prescription for glasses. He also said, "A physical wouldn't hurt you."

Michael told him, "After this I plan to go over to the next building to see a physician for a physical, because I haven't had one in about ten years."

They did all the blood drawing and examined his eyes, a complete physical. They had Michael wait around for a couple of hours. I guess considering what had happened to his eyes, the doctor was rather concerned about what was going to come out in the blood work, so this is why they really didn't want Michael to leave. They wanted him to wait for the test results.

When the test results came back, the doctor called him back into his office, and he told him, "Do you realize you are a diabetic?"

Michael almost fell off his chair. He said, "I had no clue."

The doctor said, "You're not only a diabetic but your sugar level is 450. The normal sugar level is between 100 and 105. That's why your eyes were going all kaphooey on you."

They would not allow Michael to leave the hospital. They put him on an insulin drip.

He told the doctor, "My wife is waiting home for me."

"I'm sorry but you are not allowed to drive right now. You could go into diabetic shock."

So Michael called me from the VA. He told me everything that had happened, and he told me what his sugar was. I realized how horrifying that was because of having a diabetic mother most of my life I knew what the normal sugar level was supposed to be. I told him, "Yeah, well I could understand why they would not let you drive home."

He was rather upset and he thought it was ridiculous that he couldn't return home that evening, but I did try to explain to him, "The doctor's were right, Michael. You could get into a horrible accident, and beside that, you needed that insulin drip or something horrible could happen in your body. You could go into a diabetic comma. Just let them take care of you. They know what they are doing."

We talked for about a half hour over the phone. I calmed him down.

You see we had developed a weird psychological problem about being separated. It seemed as though the only time we really were separated was when we were going through horrifying times like his being in detox or us having really bad arguments and fights while we were both drunk. So this was like a familiar kick in our stomachs, us having to be separated. This is why it hit us the way it did, but we had to overcome it. There were certain important reasons now in our lives when we would have to be separated like. He had to let them take care of him rather than coming home and going into a diabetic comma. Always that underlying knot in our stomachs existed because it was always bad, bad things that separated us before in the past.

We were not used to this anymore. We were used to being together as a family, having supper together as a family every night and just being together all the time now. So when Michael was forced to have to stay away, either through driving truck or now in the hospital, it just hit us rather strangely, differently perhaps than another couple would feel about it. He would have to stay two days there getting his sugar level a little under control. They started him on pills because he simply refused the insulin. He didn't want to stick a needle in his arm every single night. I sort of agreed with this. As long as he could keep it under control with the pills, I really didn't see the need for insulin, myself. This was one of my mother's biggest fears. She refused time and time again to go on insulin. The thought of it frankly scared the hell out of her. This is what I heard all my life, "No, no way would I go on the needle." So when I was hit with this with my own husband, of course I had already been prejudiced all my life. So that is why I so quickly agreed to the pills instead of insulin.

After two days at the VA and at least a dozen phone calls home, I was trying to keep Michael's spirits high and desperately trying hard to get him out of the depression that I could hear by his voice he was falling into. On the third day he was able to come home. I then had to begin setting up menus specifically for a diabetic. I knew what to give him and what not to, and I tried my best to make him follow these guidelines. I tried to get him not to cheat. I knew on his walks with Martin he was getting a candy bar here and a candy bar there. But even that little bit of cheating shouldn't have done what it did to his sugar level. He was exercising all the time and he was walking all the time. He was doing his best to lose weight and to get the sugar under control that way, but it just seemed like no matter what we did, no matter what he ate, he never was able to get the sugar under control. It always stayed at about 250, which of course was a hell of a lot better than 450 but a far cry from what it was supposed to be, 105.

So with his sugar not under control, he was no longer able to drive trucks. No one would allow him to because an uncontrolled sugar level is very dangerous because of the possibility of going into a diabetic coma or shock while behind the wheel. They considered him a hazard to himself and the public, so his CDL License was completely useless. All the months that he had spent at the moving company, breaking his back, moving furniture, and trying to gain all the trucking experience he could, were for nothing.

All of this was occurring just before I was to take my mother in for her eye operation. When it rains, it pours. But on the other hand my mother was never as healthy as she was at this moment. Her sugar level was great, her blood pressure was great, and physically she was perfect and ready to go. It was now July 1, the date of my mother's laser eye operation. Michael stayed home with Martin, and Teddy and I picked her up early that morning, got her to the eye doctor, and I sat there. The whole procedure only took about an hour and a half. I was amazed. After that hour and a half my mother came walking out of the room where they had done the laser treatment and she looked great. She felt great, she said. She had a big patch over her right eye.

We had decided to only do one eye at a time because we thought it would be a lot less stressful for her. She completely agreed because she didn't want to have two eyes patched up at the same time. I remember us walking back to the car at the doctor's office, and she was so happy. She was actually giggling. I don't know if it was from the anesthesia or what it was. She was so looking forward to being able to see again as well as she did ten, fifteen years before, and playing with Teddy and Pat. The only thing that she had to do was simply put two drops in her eye twice a day for about a week and then she would have to return back to the doctor's for an exam.

I asked her if she wanted to come and stay with us for this week, and I would put the drops in, and she said, "No. Drops are easy."

I said to her, "Are you sure?"

"Yeah, Kyra. I can take care of myself."

"Okay, Mom."

I took her home after the operation, and she went to bed and slept for about half of the day. I stayed with her. It was getting late, and I needed to go home. I told her, "Call me in the morning." The next morning the first thing she did was call me as soon as she woke up. On days that we did not see each other we would stay in constant contact with one another, calling each other at least two or three times a day. It was so funny. On some of these calls, all she would do was rant and rave about what was going on with her Soap Operas. Quite often she would confuse me because she would talk about these people as though they were part of our family. God forbid if there was a special on that particular time her Soap Opera was supposed to come on and they canceled it out for that day. Oh, there would be hell to pay for that. After that first day of her recovery I went up there on a daily basis with fresh dinners. I didn't give her the frozen dinners that week because I wanted to check on her and make sure everything was going well because my mother had funny ways of hiding things from me. So the only way I could truly be sure she was truly okay was to go and actually see her.

Everything was going great. Her spirits were so high. It was the happiest that I had seen her in a very long time, and I prayed that this operation was going to work. I prayed she would regain a lot of her eyesight, but we had to wait and that was the hardest part. So far after three days passed, she didn't really see much improvement. She said it was all kind of blurry still, but we waited and we hoped for the best.

She was talking about going for her first walk in many years all by herself and being able to do this with confidence. She was even talking about getting back to drawing which was her first love. She was always such a good artist, and I missed terribly seeing all her beautiful drawings that she used to draw when I was a child and the things that she taught me about drawing. I missed that time that she and I spent together, and I hoped both of us could work with Martin because he seemed to be taking on the artist part of the family. I knew, I could tell, this ran as deeply in his blood as it did through my mother's and mine, and I knew there was much she could teach him.

Finally this day that we had both anticipated so much finally came. She was going to have the patch removed from her eye that day. I would bring her to the doctor's, and he would remove it and examine her eye. He told me everything looked great. There was no sign of infection. There was nothing wrong. Her eye was still a little bit blurry, but he said that would improve over time. She had to wear sunglasses for the following two weeks, and he made an appointment to see her in a couple of days just to recheck because of her age.

After this first appointment where she had the patch removed and she had her sunglasses on, I told her, "Let's go to my house for supper tonight, Ma, and you and the kids can just relax out in the back yard." She agreed. We had a really nice day. I had a cookout with chicken breasts. I had made homemade potato salad, tossed green salad and corn on the cob. She loved every bit and enjoyed every bite.

She told me, "Kyra, you really mastered the art of grilling."

I laughed. I said, "Well, it's not very hard."

The next morning she called me right on schedule. This was a nice habit that she and I had gotten into. When the kids were in school she would wait to call until she knew I had dropped them off and returned back home. Every morning we did this, and we would talk for over an hour over a cup of coffee. She decided to stay home that day. I had offered to pick her up and bring her over to visit for the day, but she said her stomach was kind of upset.

Remembering that she had just eaten over the night before, I said to her, "What are you doing, accusing me of poisoning you?"

She laughed, she said, "No, silly. I'm just not feeling that good. My stomach is a little out of sorts, and besides that tomorrow we have to go out because I have my doctor's visit."

I said, "Oh, yeah." So we just talked for a little bit longer on the phone. Of course later on that day we spoke again and then that night.

The next morning when I called her it was a little bit earlier than usual to make sure she was awake for our doctor's visit. She told me she was awake but she hadn't slept well that night before because of the nausea. She told me that she had thrown up twice that morning. She said, "I guess it's just summer complaint." Sometimes when it was hot out she would get a little bit nauseous here and there but not very often. So we wrote it off to that. I got myself dressed, and I picked her up. At this point she was wondering whether she should cancel the doctor's appointment or not, and I insisted that she went because it was very important. The doctor had to keep a close watch on her eye.

I said, "Ma, you don't want to end up getting some kind of an infection and losing your eye, so this is very important that we go."

I persuaded her, she agreed and we went. The doctor sat there looking into her eye. I sat there watching him, and he told me, "Everything looks great. It's healing, and her eyesight should be improving any day now. It will get better by each passing day."

So now leaving the doctor's with a clean bill of health, I put her in the car, and we drove to her house. I asked her if she would like to come over mine, but again she refused. She said, "I just want to go home and relax." Her stomach was not feeling much better than it had the night before.

I drove into the parking of her apartment and she opened up the door to get out and she ended up vomiting. I said, "Ma, close the door. I'm taking you to out-patient to get you checked out."

She insisted, "No," she was not going. She told me again, "Kyra, it's just summer complaint. I get it every summer. It's nothing big. It will pass."

So being a fool and against my better judgment, I did listen to her. I helped her out of the car, and I walked her to the elevator of her apartment. Upon arriving at her apartment I opened the door, and I brought her over to her favorite chair and began taking her shoes off for her. I went into the bedroom to get a cool summer nightgown that she could change into. While I was doing this she began vomiting again. I then quickly ran to get a basin for her to throw up in, and as she was sitting there vomiting I told her, "Ma, this is bullshit. I'm taking you to the hospital, and I'm taking you now."

I started putting her shoes back on, and she kept telling me, "No, I'll be all right."

I said, "Well, when the doctor tells me that, that's when I'll believe it, but you're going now." I put her shoes back on while she was holding the basin under her chin, and we started walking toward the door. I asked her, "Do you need this basin any longer. Are you able to hold it until we get to the hospital (it was only down the street)?"

She said, "Yea, sure." So I put the basin on the sideboard in her kitchen. We reached her front door and under the archway, as she took one step out of her apartment, she collapsed into my arms. I quickly then pulled her back into her apartment, and sat her in the chair. I looked at her face and the right side of it was completely drooped down as though she had lost all control of the muscles in that side of her face. I had no idea what was going on. I panicked. I went over to the phone she had on the wall, and I looked at this device as though I had never ever seen it before in my life. I couldn't figure out how to work it. I guess you would say I went into complete shock. I tried to snap out of it because I knew I had to get help for her, and I knew "0," just push "0," so I picked up the receiver and I pushed "0." I began babbling into the phone about what just happened. Thank God I could remember the address. I told the operator, "My mother just simply collapsed. I don't know what's the matter with her, but please send help quick."

As soon as I hung up the phone I went over and went on my knees by my mother, holding her head and stroking her hair, telling her it was going to be okay. But I was lying, all the while feeling inside that this was not going to be okay. This was not going to end well.

Thank God the ambulance and the Fire Department got there quickly. As I said, the hospital was only down the street. It took them no longer than four minutes to arrive. I let them in and the Paramedics asked me, "Is this the way she normally is, given her age?" (She was 74.)

I said, "No, not at all. She was always very, very active and very independent. She doesn't sit there in the chair all day with her faced drooped." I told him what had happened just prior to this, about her vomiting when she was getting out of my car. I said, "Oh, my God, if I had just insisted and taken her to the hospital out patient this wouldn't have happened."

He quickly said to me, "No, no. This just would have happened more than likely at the hospital." You see at that moment I was feeling a tremendous amount of guilt, first of all for making her go to the doctor's when she wasn't feeling well, insisting that she go, and then allowing her to talk me into not bringing her to the outpatient when I could clearly see she was very sick. I felt as though I had just made two major screw ups, and somehow what happened to her was all my fault. At least that's the way I felt at that moment. You know hindsight is 20/20 they say. If I could have known what was going to follow after I brought her into her apartment, I certainly wouldn't have brought her there. I would have brought her directly to the hospital, just as I knew I should have. As I said, it was against my better judgment that I listened to my mother telling me that she was going to be okay. I knew deep down inside this wasn't going to be true. But no one can see what's going to happen to them. Ten minutes into the future, an hour, a year, you never know, and my mother certainly wasn't senile. So for me to force her to have to do something was rather ridiculous, because she should have known better herself. She should have known what she felt like, and this had to have been worse than any summer complaint she had had in the past. It just had to have been.

So as they were placing my mother on the stretcher, I just stood in her kitchen in complete utter shock. I simply couldn't wrap my brain around what was going on. With every passing moment she looked more and more out of it. She looked as though she didn't even recognize me any more, and this simply terrified me. I followed them downstairs and the ambulance driver asked me if I wanted to ride in the back with my mother. I said, "No, I have my car, and I'll follow directly behind you," and I did.

Once at the hospital they began running all sorts of tests from CAT scans to X-rays. They even did a spinal tap to make sure it wasn't spinal meningitis. I told them she had never been in as good a shape as she was now. Her sugar level was great, her blood pressure was great, and I told them that she had just had her eye operated on. I said, "So you see, she had to be in good shape to have this done." I was totally dumbfounded. I just simply could not understand what had happened to her. The nurse, one of the nurses that stood by me all the while I stayed with my mom, explained to me that they would run all these tests and they would find out what happened, what was the matter with her, and that I shouldn't worry.

I sat there holding my mother's hand for hours as they poked and prodded at her trying to find out what had happened. One of her eyes remained open, the one on the side of the face that wasn't affected, and the side of the face that wasn't all drooping. I looked into her eyes, and I explained to her what they were doing and what was going on and that they were trying very, very hard to find out what happened so that they could fix it. I could tell by the look in her eye she was scared, but she was unable to speak, not even one word.

About three hours had passed by now, and they decided that they were going to give my mother a spinal tap to check for Spinal Meningitis. I should have refused that test for her and knowing what I know now, I certainly would have. A normal spinal tap would take all of 4-5 minutes at most. They asked me to leave the room while they did this, and they were in there for over a half an hour. After that half an hour passed by I came back into the room whether they wanted me there or not, and I asked them what was taking so long. It seemed that no one knew how to give a proper spinal tap. They were basically using my mother as a fucking pincushion at that moment. I told them to stop, now. I said, "Get a doctor in here that knows how to do this," and they did, and it took him all of two minutes.

By the time I was able to return back to my mother to hold her hand and the sit by her, she had a single tear coming out of the eye that was open. As I sat there watching that one tear streaming down the side of her face, I thought to myself, *Oh, good job, Kyra. You just fucked up again.* She had to have felt that pain. The time that she needed me the most to protect her I failed. I learned quickly, and I never let this happen again. I remained by her side throughout the whole night. Through test after test, they could not find out what was wrong with her. After nine hours I was beside myself with worry. I couldn't believe this was happening. My mind could not begin to comprehend what my eyes were seeing. I was losing my mother, and I knew it, and quite frankly, the stupidity of our hospital's medical staff was staggering.

I had called Michael when they first brought my mother to the hospital to let him know what was going on, and I told him I'm not sure of what happened. The second phone call was about eight hours after this, and I told him everything that they were doing. They were trying to find out what happened to her. They still had not yet.

I could tell in his voice that his heart was breaking for me. He just kept telling me, "Oh, Kyra, I'm so sorry. I'm so sorry, baby."

I told him that I loved him and to kiss the boys goodnight for me because I was going to remain here for quite awhile longer. I didn't bother calling April and Amber yet because again I had no idea what to even tell them. Besides, they were both at work. They worked the second shift. I decided to let it go until morning when I could at least give them some information and they would be freed up to come to the hospital to see Mom.

CHAPTER NINE

This was July 7, and I will never ever forget this date because my life changed forever. It was around one o'clock in the morning when they decided to bring my mother up to the ICU ward. The nurse who had been so very, very kind to me throughout the whole night told me, "Kyra, there is nothing more that you can do for her right now. Why don't you go home and get some rest and come back in the morning?" She assured me that my mother would be in very good hands. The people in the ICU Ward were very, very competent people.

I told her, "How can I possibly go home now, not even knowing what's the matter with her, what happened to her? I'm supposed to just leave?"

She just repeated again that there was nothing more that I could do and just to go home and get some rest. Then she told me I looked terrible. She said, "If you're going to be of any help to your mother, you're going to have to have a clear mind and a rested mind, and the only way you are going do that is to go home and try your hardest to get a good night's sleep, or at least to relax."

So after much protest, I agreed.

I arrived back home around 2-2:30 in the morning. Before I left I gave my mother a kiss, and I told her that I would talk to her in the morning as we always did. I don't know whether she heard me or understood or not. By this time they had started her on sedatives. I came home, and I got undressed. I took a long hot shower hoping that it would relieve some of the pain, some of the stress that my body and mind had just endured, but it did not. I crawled into bed under the covers.

It was about 4 o'clock in the morning by now, and I hugged Michael. Michael woke up, and he asked me how I was doing and how Mom was doing. I said, "Neither one of us are doing very well right now."

He just turned around and he put his arm around me and gave me a huge hug and a kiss, and he told me how much, how really much he loved me, and how very, very sorry he was. I started to cry in his arms, and he began crying as well because, you see, through all these years my mother had become just as much his. He loved her very much, perhaps just as much as I did.

I finally passed out. It must have been about 5 o'clock just from pure exhaustion both physical and mental. I woke up at 8 o'clock to the phone ringing. It was my mother's doctor at the other end. He explained to me that they had finally discovered what happened to my mother. You see they had just sent her to have an MRI in the next town over because Oakland didn't have an MRI machine at the time. The MRI results came back. She had suffered a massive stroke at the base of the brain, one of the most deadly strokes you could have. I told him I don't understand how this happened. This was the healthiest she had been in the past few years, and we had just come out of the doctor's office. He couldn't have seen this coming? The doctor explained to me, no, he couldn't have. This happened in the brain, not the eyes.

I just kept telling him I don't understand how this happened, and he told me the best way he could explain it was, "You know what happened to Christopher Reeves, how it affected the base of his brain? The same thing happened to your mom. They were very similar injuries."

Then I said to him, "She didn't injure herself. She didn't bang the back of her neck or the back of her head."

"You don't have to bang it. It was like a little explosion that happened in her brain. You see, the base of the brain controls everything, the breathing, the speech, and all the vital things that keep a person alive. When you have an injury to that part of the brain, it is pretty much over." Then he went on to tell me about his own mother. He said, "This happened to my mother as well. I don't know your mother very well, but with my mother she was very active. She was very independent, and I could not see keeping her tied to a machine for the rest of her existence, a thing that she would not want to have done to her."

I agreed. I said, "I know. I know my mother would not want this either."

Up to this point, you see, they hadn't put her on life support. They just gave her a breathing tube in her nose to help her with the breathing, but he told me it was only a matter of time before her lungs were going to cease as the rest of her body would.

He asked me then if I wanted a DNR put on her record, and I asked him what in the hell was that. He said, "That's a sign Do Not Resuscitate. If she passes, we let her pass naturally."

Then I asked him again, "Are you sure that there is no return from what just happened to her?"

He told me, "No. The chances are nil that she would talk again, or walk, or even sit up. In fact she is basically dead already." So he asked, "Do you want us to put her on life support to keep her body alive, to keep it functioning for her even though there is next to no chance of her ever recovering from this?"

I asked him, "What if she did recover. What would it be like?"

"She would never be able to get out of bed again. She would be a vegetable because of where the stroke occurred in the brain. The base of the brain is a deadly stroke always." After seeing Christopher Reeves in his wheelchair, (at that point he wasn't even talking—it wouldn't be until later he would be able to) just sitting there in his wheelchair immobile like a vegetable, just barely existing, just barely clinging onto life, I could not see my mother going through this, not the person that she was, without the independence that she desperately needed in her life. This would be a living hell for her, and I knew it. I couldn't do this to her. Our whole family had discussed similar situations before in the past, and we were in the agreement that we were not to be kept alive by machines. We were very independent people, and this would truly be hell.

So you see, I knew already what my mother wanted. Now the only thing that was left was I needed to summon up the courage, enough courage to put her before my own selfish needs to keep her alive even if it meant going to the hospital on a daily basis and looking at her shell. I had to love her enough now to let her go, and this is something that no one should ever have to do to their parent.

So through my tears and my headache, I told the doctor, okay, to put the DNR on her folder. If I were to do anything else, I knew my mother would curse me for it, and I simply couldn't condemn her to a life in hell. What few existing years she had left to be spent like that, I couldn't do that. I had to think of her own best interests, and I must. I knew I must put her first before anything that I wanted. My brain knew that I was making the right decision, but my heart screamed out "NO, NO!" After giving the doctor permission to do this, to place this on my mother's chart, basically giving her a death sentence, I told him that my sisters and I would be at the hospital in a couple of hours. I had to call them and let them know what was going on.

As soon as I hung up the phone, I just broke down. I became almost hysterical. Teddy and Martin heard me and came running into my bedroom.

I tried quickly to compose myself. I told them both what was going on. They just kept asking me, "When is she coming out of the hospital?" They didn't want to accept that she was not. That's when Michael came into the room, and he told them both, "Come on, let's get ready to go. We're gonna go fishing and let Mommy take care of Grandma."

He got them dressed quickly and fed them breakfast and took them out of the house. I first called my sister Amber and told her what was going on, and she no more than I could believe it. Then I called April and she started crying as well. I tried my best to calm her down and comfort her just as I did with Amber, but it was very, very hard because, quite frankly, all I felt like doing was sitting there screaming and pulling my hair out myself.

After a period of crying, both April and I tried our hardest to get a hold of ourselves. I told her I had just spoken to Amber who was going to pick us up in an hour or so. I needed a ride because Michael had taken the car with the boys to go fishing, which, by the way, they both agreed was a good thing in order to spare them as much as we could. After all, this was all new to us. We had not had a death in our family in I can't even tell you how many years now. The last one was my grandmother when I was very, very young.

Of course at this point all three of us were hoping against the odds that my mother would somehow through some miracle pull through this and be our mom again. The thought of anything else happening besides this was simply unthinkable to us at this point. As a matter of fact, I had become so quickly immersed in denial that I insisted Amber stop by my mother's apartment so I could pick up her eye drops so the nurses could put them in her eye on schedule. When she magically woke up, she would be able to see again. As I said so many times in the past, denial is a fantastic place to visit but unfortunately we can't remain there long.

My two sisters and I arrived at the hospital around 10 o'clock that morning. Going in and seeing my mother lying there motionless in bed with the tubes up her nose and in her arms and strapped to a monitor was completely surreal to me. Just two days before she was in my backyard enjoying a lovely cookout with her grandsons. I just felt as though my whole world was collapsing around me. What was happening to all the hopes and the dreams that my mother and I had talked about, the things that we were going to do once she was able to see better again, the drawing, the long walks, gaining her independence. All of these things she had so looked forward to being able to do again, and we had definite plans that she was going to do again. So I thought, Perhaps if the three of us stood there talking to her we would somehow be able to pull her out of this, override everything the doctor told me.

We wanted nothing short of a complete and full recovery and for her to be able to do the things that she wanted so desperately to do for the remainder of her years with my sons and me and her two other daughters. Any other thing but a full recovery in my mind would have been completely devastating and totally unfair at this point. I had to think positive. I had to hope this was going to work, and by talking to her would magically bring her out. She would just simply wake up, and I, in turn, would wake up from this nightmare that was placed before me. The four of us were what you would call cyclically connected. It seemed like when something bad was happening with the other we would pick it up. We wouldn't know of course exactly what was going on. We would just know that there was something off. Each and every time that I would call my sister if I felt as though something was happening to April, something would be happening. Something that she would be terribly upset over whether it was big or little, I would be able to pick it up and she with me. Amber would also along with our mother, especially our mother. She would always know when there was something wrong with us. From time to time this was not all that convenient because I didn't wish them to know every time Michael and I got into a little spat, or something was going wrong at school with Teddy, or I was just having a particularly bad day. These were things that normal people kept private. I was not able to because I would always get their phone call and sometimes from all three of them at once.

So you see, I thought by us pulling our energies together over her that somehow it would help. There was so much love in that room at that very moment and so much psychic energy being directed at my mother. I knew deep down in my heart if there were anything that could have pulled her out of that, it would have been this. But there was one thing that I could not be involved in and that was praying. I had not prayed since my grandmother died. I had not spoken to God. I stood at the window looking out as my sisters April and Amber prayed over my mother instead of talking to God in prayer.

I spoke to God on my own while looking out over the smokestacks and the connecting building to the hospital. I asked God, "Why? Why would He take her now?" and then I asked him, "Are you even there? Are you even hearing me?" Even after so many years had passed since my grandmother's death, so many years for me to think, I never was able to get past the anger that I had toward Him, toward God. As a matter of fact through the years it only grew deeper. So on this day when my sisters were able to gain some solace through prayer, I stood there with a bitter heart toward God, a bitterness that grew through every passing moment that I saw my mother lying there. My sisters and I were very much alike in a lot of things, but this is one where we greatly differed. It seemed as though all three of us carried anger in us, but their anger was toward our earthly father, a father that abused and hurt us all of his life. Mine was to our Heavenly Father, who I felt simply neglected my cries for help through my life.

The three of us were there for about four hours when the doctor came in and spoke to us. He informed us she was in a coma now. He didn't really expect her to hang on much longer, perhaps a few days at the most. I thought to myself, and believe me, I kept this to myself, *You see what good your prayers did, April and Amber? You see how he listened?*

We remained there until about six or seven o'clock at night. I sat there holding her hand for most of this time and stroking her head, her silver hair, her pretty silver hair that was so baby soft. We continued to speak to her because we also realized that people in comas sometimes are able to hear when people talk to them. We asked her to fight, to fight as hard as she could to come back to us. If it was possible for her to do this to please try. Then we began telling her stories of her childhood, funny stories, things that she used to do with us. The way she would play the Platter's music and the Temptations, and we would all dance around in the living room, and the picnics in the park on a Sunday afternoon—our fondest memories. We tried to get her to remember with hopes that perhaps this would pull her back to us.

By the way, on the way to the hospital I had told my sisters about the conversation the doctor and I had over the phone about placing a DNR on her chart because of the condition that she would be in if she were to wake up. They both completely agreed with me, and they were glad that I had the courage to make that decision because they told me they didn't know if they would be able to or not. So the three of us knew where it stood. She was either to make a full and complete recovery, or we would lose our mother forever. It was all or nothing and we knew, believe me we knew.

This is what our mother would have wanted. She was so miserable and depressed and becoming increasingly more depressed as the days went on simply by losing her eyesight. I cannot only imagine how devastating that would have been for her to have woken up some day into the future and found she couldn't move a finger in her body. I knew I couldn't allow this to happen to her, and I knew also that she would curse me if I did. Then I still couldn't let go.

I presented the eye drops to her nurse and explained how she must get them in her eye twice a day so that it wouldn't become infected. The nurse kindly took the medication, smiled at me and said, "I'll make sure that she gets it. Don't worry." I can only imagine what was going through that nurse's mind at the time. I realized that moment I had denial written all over me, but what else was a daughter to do? How else are you supposed to handle this outside of just hoping and praying things work out? Quite honestly, not even in my wildest nightmares could I ever imagine having to say the words, "Let my mother die!" That was exactly what I was saying when I allowed them to put the DNR on her record. Those were the most heart wrenching, heartbreaking words that ever passed my lips. Believe me I had to search deep, deep down into my soul to be able to say them even though I knew this is what my mother would have wanted. That lingering twinge in the back of your brain, that twinge that always eats at you made me wonder, *Did I truly make the right choice?* This would be something I would be forced to live with for the rest of my life.

It was around 7:30 p.m. now. My sisters and I were getting ready to leave planning to return early the next morning. I spoke to the nurse again after giving her the eye drops and told her, "If there is any change, please, please call. I will be sitting by the phone waiting." I also reminded her about my mother being a Catholic, and I knew how important it was for her to have the last rights. If I were not able to make it back here in time, if it were to go bad quickly, I asked her to promise me she would do this, and she did. She promised me this. The three of us gave our mother a last kiss goodbye and told her we would be back early the next morning to see her again. I gave her a hug and told her how much I loved her.

On the drive back home Amber, April, and I began to talk. The three of us felt rather lost at this moment and our conversation seemed to drift back to the old days when we were younger. This seemed to be the only thing right now that would even come close to cheering us up or helping us look to the bright side of things. As Amber dropped me off back at home I gave them both a hug and a kiss, and I reminded them of how much I loved them and they me. Amber decided that she was going to come about 7-7:30 the next morning to pick me up, and we would go back to the hospital to sit by our mother's side. The three of us were so emotionally drained and exhausted by this moment all we could think of doing was crawling into bed and pulling the covers over our head trying desperately to make believe this was not happening in our lives.

As I stood there on the sidewalk watching Amber drive away, I turned and started into my house. I walked to the door, and as soon as I stepped one foot inside my home, this horrendous, completely overwhelming, anxiety-ridden feeling hit me, a complete sense of panic that I had to get back to the hospital immediately. I truly felt as though my mother was summoning me back to be by her side. I thought, *Oh, my God, perhaps she's come out of it. Perhaps everything is going to be fine.* As I was getting this feeling I was also getting a feeling that she not only wanted me there, but she was summoning Teddy back as well. I can't explain this feeling. It was just overpowering, overwhelming. It was as though she had picked up the telephone and called me herself. I knew never to ignore these feelings so I acted quickly.

Michael had just gotten through giving the boys their baths. Teddy was in his pajamas. I told him, "Get dressed quick. We have to get back to the hospital. We have to go see Grandma."

Michael asked me, "Are you okay?"

"Yeah. I just got this overpowering feeling that we must return back, and now."

So he quickly helped me get Teddy ready, and he and I headed out the door. He asked me, "Mommy, we're gonna go see Grandma?"

"Yes. She wants to see you. I know she wants to see you." So, of course, he was very happy to hear this news.

I had no idea what I was doing. I was just following this overwhelming urge that struck me. I knew I had to do what she was asking, and I knew she was asking for Teddy to be there. Whether this was right or wrong, I knew this was something I could not ignore. I must do this.

I drove back then to the hospital with Teddy beside me, quickly finding a parking spot and rushing into the hospital. Almost in front of the ICU Ward was the nurse that had stayed with me for most of the night down in the Emergency Room with my mother talking to me and trying to help me. She asked me how my mother was doing, and I told her she was in ICU. She was in a coma, but I had this overwhelming urge to come back to the hospital. I explained to her that my sisters and I had been there just a few minutes before, but I couldn't ignore this feeling I was getting.

Teddy at that point looked at both the nurse and me, and he said, "Mommy, Grammie is going home today."

The nurse and I looked at each other. I shook my head and said, "Teddy, Grammie's not able to come home right now, maybe in a few weeks. I'm not sure even then."

Then he said, "Mommy, I don't mean that home, and he started pointing up at the ceiling toward the heavens, and he said, "She's going home today."

Well, you can imagine how this statement completely floored me. I was not prepared for my mother to go. I told him, "Stop talking silly. Grandma's not going anywhere."

He said, "Yes, she is. She's going home," and I just nodded my head to the nurse. The nurse stood there with her mouth hanging open because she couldn't believe these words were coming out of a seven-year-old.

Teddy and I then entered the ICU ward, and we went into my mother's room. He stood on one side of the bed, and I stood on the other. He leaned over to my mother and gave her a kiss on the cheek. He said, "Grandma, it's me, it's me Teddy."

His words no sooner left his mouth when everything that she was connected to that was keeping track of her vital signs completely, totally flat lined. It was as though she was waiting for him to speak, for him to be there so that she could go.

As soon as the machines started flat lining, I yelled at him. "What are you doing?"

"Nothing, Mom."

I said, "Did you kick out some…" All I could think of was that he kicked the cords out that were monitoring her vital signs. Then I looked at his feet, and I could clearly see that he wasn't anywhere near the cords. I began crying. As soon as the nurses heard me crying and screaming, they came to retrieve Teddy from the room. I then picked my mother up in my arms and held her until I could feel her take her last breath. I remember looking up into the heavens and asking God, "Is this what you have to fucking offer me?" and I cursed him all the while rocking my mother in my arms.

The kind nurse that sat with me for all those hours the night before came in and placed her hand on my shoulder and said, "You know, she's going to be okay. She's at peace now. Look at her face," and I did. I made myself stare into my dead mother's face. That is when I told her I would love her forever. I would never ever forget all the good times we had together and all the things that she had taught me, not only in life as a child, as a teenager and as an adult, but she taught me how to be a good mother. I would always practice this. I would always remember her teachings, and I would always follow them.

To this day when anyone tells me what a good mother I am, I always say, "That's because I had such a great mother to learn by. Without her love and support and her teachings, I would not be the woman I am now. I would not be the mother and the wife I am now. I owe my life to her." This is what I would always tell people when they complemented me about my mothering. I learned from the best.

After a few minutes passed by, and I sat there looking at her and reminding her of everything she taught me, things that I would always carry in my heart and in my life, I felt something marvelous happen. I couldn't believe it. I actually felt her leaving, that deep physic connection that the four of us always shared. That connection we had particularly between us. I could feel her soul ascending. I could feel what made her leave, and I knew right there and then she was going be just fine. But was I going to be? This was a completely different story.

I knew I had to somehow pull it together especially for my children. I knew this was what she would have wanted and would have insisted upon. I had to be strong for my babies. I had to be a mother that she would be proud of. I owed this not only to her but also to my children and Michael. So while I was sitting there looking at her face, a peaceful, at-rest face, I knew the world would never be able to touch her again. The pain that she had to endure with my father, and the depression that she suffered later on with losing a lot of her eyesight, all the worldly worries were now lifted off her shoulders. She was truly at peace.

After one last kiss goodbye I went out to the waiting room where my son Teddy was sitting, and I held him in my arms expecting him to fall apart, to cry. Much to my surprise he did neither. He told me how much Grandma loved him, and he told me how much he loved Grandma. Then he reminded me about how she was going home. He said, "She's gone up to Heaven now to be with God, Mommy. This is a good thing."

I couldn't believe it. My seven-year-old son was actually consoling me. This was one more thing I was grateful to my mother for; she had taught him so much about God and so much about spirituality. He had completely embraced it as a child. He knew in his heart and his soul she was going to be just fine. It was me that he worried more about than her at that moment, and he told me so. He kept telling me, "Mommy, don't be sad. This is a happy day for Grandma, not a sad one." I was so stunned to find out he had so completely accepted God in his life and in his heart.

One more thing I was grateful for was that he was able to see her for the last time, to be able to say goodbye, and to give her a kiss, something I was not given as a child when my grandmother died. I was so grateful he was able to do this. Somehow perhaps she realized just how painful that was for me, not being able to say goodbye to my grandmother. Somehow she was able to work it that I would bring him back to the hospital at that moment so he was able to do this. Perhaps in the future he wouldn't carry the hatred toward God I have because he was not denied certain things such as the right to say goodbye to his loved ones. Through her teachings he was absolutely certain of where she was going to go, and it was going to be paradise returning back into God's arms, God's loving arms.

But even knowing everything that he knew, he did cry, but not a lot. I told him I suppose we are sitting here in tears, I guess not so much for Grandma but for us because, something so beautiful and so wonderful has been ripped out of our lives forever. We cry for ourselves, not for her. Somehow we have to learn how to go on from here, and in the future hope and pray to keep only the happy memories of her alive, and not remember what she looked like just before she passed. Later on in life we need to talk about the funny things that she used to do with us, and how wonderful a person she really was. These are things that we would have to learn how to do much, much later. For now we have to handle what is before us, and that was me now having to call my sisters who I'm sure haven't even reached home yet.

I first called my sister Amber and only got her answering machine, and this was not a message that I would ever leave on her machine. I simply hung up, and decided to try a couple of hours later after I knew she would surely be home. I then called my sister April and told her what had just happened. I tried to explain to her the overwhelming feeling that struck me as soon as I walked into the house, and that I grabbed Teddy and returned as fast as I could back to the hospital. I told her, "Mom, was summoning me. I know she was, and I had to bring Teddy."

I explained this because the first words out of my sister's mouth were, "Why did you go back to the hospital?" She completely understood when I explained.

She said, "You know, Mom and Teddy had such a close connection. I could see her wanting to hear his voice for the very last time before she left. I knew in my heart she knew she was leaving, and she had to hear his voice one last time before she could go."

April chose not to return back to the hospital to see our mother. We really didn't see the point in this. She had already gone, so I told April if she would not mind, to please call Amber after a couple hours, "after you get through composing yourself." She agreed to do this.

After I hung up the phone with April, I asked Teddy if he would like to return back to Grandma's room to say his last goodbye, and he said, "No, Mom. I don't need to do that. I already have. Remember I stood there, and I told her, 'Teddy is here. It's me, Grandma, Teddy,' and I gave her a kiss on the cheek. That was my goodbye to her, so I don't feel the need to go in once again."

I told him, "Yeah, you're right. I could feel her leave. She's no longer there anyway. She's back up in Heaven, just as you say, with God and the angels now."

Before leaving the hospital I had to sign some papers, and I asked the nurse if she had remembered about giving my mother her last rites, and the nurse said, "Yes," she said, "As a matter of fact the priest came in about fifteen minutes after you left to do so." This greatly put my mind at ease because I knew this was really important to my mother.

All of this is so heartbreaking to look back on now, because you see, when I was getting that feeling, that strong beckoning call from her hospital to grab Teddy and bring him back with me to see her that day, I had hoped and prayed that after hearing his voice she would come out of it. I was hoping against all the odds that in a month or so she would be sitting back in my back yard playing with her two grandsons and enjoying the cookout and the delicious food that she so enjoyed. Teddy seemed to know differently. He seemed to know, yes, he had to go there but for a very, very different reason. He had to go there in order to let her go, to let her go back into God's arms. He had such a better sense of reality and what was going on than I did. To this day I don't understand how he did, but it was obvious that he did.

Again, you can immerse yourself so deeply into denial that when finally, finally reality hits, it can be so extremely devastating—like having the rug pulled out from beneath you. By hearing Teddy's voice, I am now convinced that this was her green light to go, as Teddy would say, "to go home." Yes, it is extremely hard for me to comprehend and to accept, but I knew I had no choice. Of course I must accept what was lying before me, and that was that I had lost my angel, my guidance, my mentor, my best friend, my teacher, my mother—she was all these things rolled up into one for me.

I had no idea how I was going to live the rest of my life without her. I knew all that was left now for me was to try my hardest to make her proud of me every day, and to try to be as much like her as I possibly could. I knew that would be the ultimate tribute to her, her life and her love, was for her to now look down on me and smile. I knew I had a long road ahead of me before I could reach this confidence in my life, this goal. I would have to go through a lot of pain before I would be able to be the person I knew she would be very proud of.

That day was to begin now and here. I had to take Teddy home now and explain to Martin, who was not quite five years old how his grandmother would no longer be coming over, and he would no longer be able to see her. I explained to him the way my mother explained to Teddy about her going home, back to Heaven to be with God. This is very hard for a four-year-old to comprehend, but he tried and he did very, very well I must say. He cried for a few days. He was missing her terribly, just as Teddy did, but again we cry for ourselves for they are fine. They are okay and they are back in God's arms.

I kept my children very close to me through these hard times, and I let them know if they had any questions at all that I would answer them honestly. So between keeping them very close to me both physically and in my heart, and I can't stress this enough, by being completely and totally honest with them, they were somehow able to make sense of it all, and they accepted the fact that Grandma had to go back up to Heaven. They seemed to accept this fact much easier than I did. I had a very, very difficult time, especially the day or so to follow after her death. I lost my beloved mother July 9, 1995. She was 74 years old. This day is burned into my memory and into my heart.

The next morning April and Amber came over to my house. April let me know that she was going to handle all of the arrangements. I'm not proud to say, I was a basket case at this point. It was just so shocking and so sudden. My mother was literally here one day and gone the next, and my mind was not comprehending this at all. I was having a very, very difficult time coming to terms with it, and April and Amber could clearly see this along with Michael.

Michael was so sweet and so loving and kind at this horrible time in my life. I couldn't have asked for a better support system than he gave to my sisters and me as well. April told me that she was going to go to the Morton Funeral Home and set up the arrangements for our mother. I just sat there not saying a word which I suppose was completely unfair to both April and Amber because after all it was their mother as well. For some reason they just seemed to be better able to handle it than I was. Perhaps it was because of their religion, because they did pray. They had that relationship with God that I had thrown away. That's when I sat down, and I told them, "You can do whatever you like. We'll split the expenses, but please don't expect me to attend."

They both looked at me with complete shock in their eyes.

Michael was coming in from the living room and heard what I said. I told them, "I just can't even fathom the idea of walking into a funeral parlor and seeing my beautiful beloved angel of a mother lying there in her casket. This is not an image I wish to have seared into my memory forever." I went on to tell them, "That night, the day that it happened, I spent the whole night there holding her hand watching her go through pain with all the tests that they ran on her, and then the following day holding her in my arms as she took her last breath. I think I said my goodbyes. I think I've done all that I should be expected now to do. Please don't ask me to go and see her in her casket. I don't know if I could live with that image."

Michael and my sisters just sat in the kitchen looking at me stunned. April is the one that said, "Well, Kyra, if you feel that strongly about this, perhaps you shouldn't, and if you feel as though you've said your goodbyes, then maybe you really don't need to see what you're fearing the most, and that is our mother in a casket."

I told her, "I'm very glad and grateful that you understand where I am coming from," and I could tell she did. Everyone is different in this world, and everyone handles things differently, and sometimes the mind can only take so much, and sometimes the heart can only be broken so badly before it is beyond repair.

Then I began having such an overwhelming feeling of unfairness, not only for me, for April and Amber, but especially for Teddy and Martin. You know, as parents we teach our children how to walk, how to talk, and how to go potty, their ABC's, and the colors. You are their first teachers in life, but no one, no one ever prepares you as a parent to teach your children about death especially at the ages of four and seven. Death is not supposed to touch babies, and for me to even have to bring up the subject I found horrifying. This is not something that I was prepared to have to teach my children about at such an early age, let alone it happening to their dearest grandma, a grandma that they loved more than anything in this world and to all of a sudden have to live without her. How do you begin to teach a child about death at that age?

Again I let my heart lead. Through all their lives and all the teachings I would always listen to my heart and what would be the best way to go about these things. My heart always led me, and I'm grateful to say usually it was always the right decision. But this, this was something totally out of the realm of being a parent. There is no way a parent could possibly prepare to teach their children about death at this age. It's just something you have to experience and you have to survive it, live through it and find a way to go on. This is what my children and I are having to learn how to do now and it sucked.

Up to this point I also thought I had finally achieved my dream. It was a simple, simple dream of just leading a normal life, a normal happy family life. It seemed as though Michael and I were doing everything right with our children. We were loving them, taking good care of them and teaching them every day. We provided consistency, love, along with discipline. We gave them a sense of security. They knew that they would always have us. I kept them away from all the bad things, the gambling, the arguing, the alcohol, the drugs. I protected them, as I always will. Michael and I finally achieved normalcy in our lives, and it was the first time that we had this. Everything was going so well, so perfectly before now. I feel as though I just had the rug pulled out from underneath me, and all my dreams just went flying up in the air.

My life now was turning from being normal into anything but, and it was taking every ounce of my sanity to hold on. I knew there was no other option but to hold on. Failure was not an option because I had my two boys counting on me to be able to pull through all of this and to be the mother that they both deserved. I had to get a hold of myself emotionally, and I knew my walking into that funeral parlor and seeing my mother like that was not going to help me at all to do this. It seemed as though no one but April fully understood what I meant.

Amber was upset over this, and Michael was furious. He said, "You're disrespecting you mother by not going and paying your last respects. Kyra, we have to bury our dead with honor and the dignity they so deserve. You can choose to be disrespectful to your mother for whatever reason you may think in your head to be correct, but I will not. I am going to your mother's funeral and wake along with my two sons. If you choose not to join us, then that will be on you."

Another thing he told me was, "Keep in mind that this is a one-time opportunity. If you screw up this, it will be something you will have to live with for the rest of your life, so you better make the right choice."

After April and Amber left I sat there at the table thinking about what Michael said. It was a cross between my heart breaking and being furious at him, and at the same time wanting so desperately to be able to protect my children from pain. He told me that he was going to bring them to pay their last respects to their grandmother that they loved deeply. I realized I could not protect my children from pain or death. It is a fact of life. Life had taken this out of my hands, and Michael certainly has. I realized also everyone has to face death at some point in their lives. I suppose if you have to face it at a young age you at least have some kind of idea of the pain. Perhaps through your life you learn how to live with it a little bit better than a person that has not had to face it for many, many years. Maybe this would be a valuable lesson for our children. Again as a parent, God, you never know. You never know what the right thing at the right moment is, especially when it comes to something like this, something so important.

I kind of felt that Teddy was going to handle it a lot better than I was. He already had, so that only left Martin. What was his reaction going to be once he saw my mother in her casket? What his father started explaining to him was that this person was not really Grandma. This was her shell. Her soul has already gone. As I overheard Michael explaining this to Martin, I realized something, that he was 100% correct because I felt it. I felt her soul leaving that day and that precise moment. So I decided to let him make these choices himself for this moment as far as this was concerned because I think at this time he was making better choices than I was. He was thinking far more clearly and more rationally than I was.

I find children do believe what their parents tell them because Martin accepted this about his grandmother. What made "her" was gone, and all that was left was a shell that we had to bury with respect. He seemed to take to this without question just as fact, and this is the way he began to look at it. Their grandma was good. She was safe back in God's arms, and we all need to bury our dead. Michael once again proved to be the strong one, and I thank God for him, because just as he supported our two sons, he held me up too. He prevented me from sinking so deeply into a depression, a great abyss of despair. At this moment he held my heart in his hands and he treated it ever so gently and ever so lovingly.

But at this time in my life the anger that I felt toward God had never been stronger. I truly hated him now and this would serve to help no one, especially me. It left me in a horrible predicament, because while trying to reinforce my two sons' belief in God in hopes that it would help them through this most horrible time in their lives, every word that I would say to them about God in my heart I felt was a lie. I felt no, God was not good. God was not kind, and God certainly wasn't going to protect any of us. That's the way I felt. I never ever let those words pass my lips to my children.

I reinforced everything that my mother had taught them already and what their father was teaching them now in order for them to be able to get through what they had to get through over these next few days. This was so incredibly hard for me to do because you see, up till now I had never ever lied to my children about the way I felt. Being honest with my children was always very, very important to me. I felt that the only way I would have a good relationship with my children was to be honest with them and them honest with me, because only through honesty can trust be built.

A child needs to be able to trust the parent so that later on in life when they come up against obstacles and they ask your help or your advice on some things, they will listen to you because they will trust you and trust your judgment. Honesty is crucial in building any good relationship, and honesty is something I have always had with my children, so for me now not to be was just another heartache on top of the heartache that I was already feeling and went against actually everything I believed in. But I knew it was for the greater good, and I realized that perhaps sometimes in a child's life, you cannot be totally honest with them about absolutely everything, and this was one of those times. Also I would find that without true honesty in life you would never have an open line of communication between one another. You would always be having a guarded conversation, and this would not be good in a relationship because no relationship could survive without honesty, communication, and trust.

I tried my hardest to build the best relationship I could possibly build with my two sons with honesty and love always coming first. Through my children's childhood I slowly built this trust, this honesty, and this open line of communication in the hopes that in their teenage years, what everyone refers to as the terrible teens, perhaps wouldn't be so terrible after all if they knew they could always come and talk to me. I would never stand in judgment of them but always keep that line of communication open.

I was always looking into the future into the time that they were going to be teens and young adults. I began setting up these building blocks for this honest relationship among the three of us. I realized you see that even though their father and I both talked to them about not drinking, doing drugs and smoking and all the bad habits people can pick up along the way, they may still be tempted by things that can destroy your life. I hoped and prayed that they would always be able to come and talk to me whenever these things tempted them. I knew that line of communication that I spent their entire lives building up between them and me would come in handy at these moments because they would feel free to be able to come and talk to me about it. I hoped I could help them head off any kind of temptations that may flow their way. I knew that these temptations would come to them. These temptations would occur in their lives even though Michael and I spent our entire lives trying to teach them the right way to live and the things to avoid, the things that can destroy your life.

We knew what we had created when Teddy and Martin were born. We realized that more than likely, they were born alcoholics because they came from two alcoholics, so I believed the temptations in the future for them would be much greater than a normal teen. My point to all of this is to help them avoid that first drink, avoid that first joint, and avoid that first cigarette before they even took it so that they wouldn't have to fight an addiction, a monkey I knew would instantaneously appear on their back as soon as they tried these things for the first time. So I hoped love and honesty would win out over blood over their genetic makeup.

This was the first time since they were born that I sat there and outright lied to them. My only concern was about them at this moment in their mental frame of mind. I had to somehow figure out how to carry them through this heartbreaking time. I kept them close to my heart and close to my side. Now with the sudden death of my beloved mother, I somehow had to figure out how to handle this in my heart and my soul.

I think, what truly made this so devastatingly hard on the entire family was the suddenness of her death. She was literally here one day and gone the next, without any warning. There were no signs of her being ill. You simply cannot imagine the shock unless you have been through it yourself. Then the day following her death I sat in my chair in the living room looking at Teddy and Martin and Michael watching TV and thinking to myself, *Is this really happening? Is she really gone?* It was so surreal, a nightmare that I just wanted to wake up from. We had so many plans for when her eyesight got better. She was going to do arts and crafts with the boys and teach Martin how to draw just as she taught me. These were not going to happen. The walks, the long walks that she wanted to take, and the independence she was so looking forward to regaining. It's all gone now along with her. I had to face this fact.

This was something my heart and my mind were nowhere close to accepting. My tears and my heart break I would share in private never letting my children see the pain that I went through because in no way did I want to make their pain worse. I thought if they saw me in such agony and such heartache, it would only hurt them further. I could not allow this, so I kept my pain private, away from everyone that I loved.

I was very, very proud of Teddy and Martin at this moment because they seemed to have been handling it a hell of a lot better than I was. Perhaps it was because of my mother and what she taught them about God and about Heaven. They accepted this as fact. They knew in their hearts that she was okay and she was back in God's arms. This is what carried them through that painful time, and they did it with more grace and dignity than I could ever summon up at that moment. My hat was off to both of them. They showed their true inner strength when I could not. For this I will ever be grateful to my mother because it was her words that saved them from tremendous heartache.

I found April shared her strength as well. She somehow held it all together. She made all the funeral arrangements. My mother's funeral was held at the Morton Funeral Home. Mr. Silva was the Director there and he was a tremendous help to our family. He showed love and compassion to perfect strangers.

We were in a horrible financial situation. We had no money. My mother had no life insurance, so we were working on a very, very tight budget. He showed us the utmost respect even though we were financially strapped. He did the most marvelous things for my mother. He helped my sister April arrange the most beautiful floral arrangement. He arranged for a priest to be at the ceremony and set up the church time. He did this all on out-of-pocket expense because we had to set up payment arrangements. We had nothing at the time, so without his generosity and kindness, my mother would have been buried in a very, very simple manner with no flowers, no church, nothing. For this I will ever be grateful to him.

The next day when my sister first went to the funeral home and first met Mr. Silva, she sat there in tears and told him the whole story about our money situation.

He said, "Don't worry about it, April." Then he asked about her other children, if she had any siblings.

She said, "Yes. I have a sister Amber and a sister Kyra." Then I guess she went on to tell him about what I said about not attending my mother's funeral or wake. He thought this was absolutely horrifying.

Mr. Silva said, "It's not for your mother, it's for her. She needs closure. Grief is a whole process," he explained to April, "and part of that process is saying goodbye. Without this next step that Kyra must take, I worry about her mental stability." He convinced April that it was very, very important for me to attend.

April said, "Well, that's easier said than done. When Kyra stands, she stands solid, and trying to get her to change her mind about anything is next to impossible."

"Well, let me try. Perhaps I can convince her that this would be the best thing for her to come and see her mom for the last time for the sense of closure."

She gave him my phone number and said, "Good luck." She then left the funeral home and came back to my house. She and I spoke, and she told me what Mr. Silva said.

I told her, "This is ridiculous. I've already had closure. Mom died in my arms. How much more closure could I have? What more do people want from me? I just want to be left alone, and I don't want to see my mother like that."

April told me she understood. She said, "It's not me. It's Mr. Silva that really thinks that you need to do this, and he's going to be calling you." She asked me to please be kind to him, because he had been a great help to us.

"Of course I'll be kind to him, but I don't feel as though he understands where I am coming from at all, and he certainly doesn't understand the relationship that Mom and I had."

My mother's wake was going to be in two days. The day before my mother's wake the phone calls began, and they were relentless. Mr. Silva was not going to give up on me. He was going to keep ringing the phone until I answered. He rang that entire day on and off all day long. I knew who it was, and that's why I didn't want to answer. That night I finally picked up the phone, and sure enough it was Mr. Silva.

He said, "Kyra, I've never met you. I don't know you, and I certainly don't know the relationship that you had with your mom, but your sister April told me you were very close. You loved her so much that now you do not want to see her in this state."

I said, "Yeah, you're right."

Mr. Silva said, "It's a process of grieving, and it's an important process. It's the last thing you will have to do in order to begin the healing."

I then told him, "I helped take care of her while she was alive. Every day we spent together, if not physically, over the phone. When she left I was holding her in my arms. I don't see where I could get more closure than that."

He began explaining to me that this was different. It is a different type of closure. It was like a finalization of life, and this is the last process, and he told me, "If your mother and you were that close, I'm sure she would want you to be there." He also explained to me how good an artist he was. He said, "I will make her look like an angel. I promise you that. She's just going to look like she's sleeping."

I then told him I would consider everything he just told me, and I would have to think about it. I wasn't sure.

Then he said, "Kyra, I hope you make the right decision. Remember, this isn't something you can go back in time and do over again. This is a one-shot deal, and it's a very, very important step for you."

I thanked him, and I hung up the phone. I sat there in tears, not quite sure what to do next. If I were not to go, would I be letting my mother down? My children down? My husband and my sisters down, but maybe more important, myself down? Maybe this is something I had to face. I had to see her for one last time, but I simply did not know how I was going to handle it.

Then it hit me like a bag of bricks. I had to, I had to face my fears, and I would have to learn how to face my fears in the future head on, each and every one of them. I would have to learn how to overcome them, and this was my start. This would be my first lesson of being able to gather up all the inner strength that I had to face my fears, to face death. I had to begin somewhere. I had to be stronger now than I ever had been before in my life in order to be able to fight my own demons, to fight my own fears and to stand up and face them all. That strength comes from deep, deep within, an inner strength that is only built over time and through pain, and this was the beginning of my pain and the beginning of me finding my true inner strength. This was something I never knew before I had in me.

I was also facing one other thing in my life and that was realizing that you cannot control everything. You can only control you and how you handle situations. I realized I was always a control freak but when you're faced with death, it is one thing that hits you like a bag of bricks. No, you don't have control over everything, especially death. You cannot control whether people live or die, and me being the control freak that I was, this just made everything that was going on around me even harder to accept.

With this major personality quirk that I had and that I always struggled with my whole life, it seemed as though when anything bad ever happened I would always blame myself for it. I always thought I was in control, and I could have stopped it. I could have prevented it. But in reality there is very little anyone else can do to save someone, especially from death.

I realized at this time in my life, this was something that I was really going to have to start concentrating on changing in my personality. I had to accept the fact that no, I couldn't be in control of everything. This was one of the hardest things I have ever had to do, to let go. Let go of the urge to control everyone and everything around me. To try to keep all my loved ones safe and happy, when in fact, I had to come to the realization that the only ones that I truly was responsible for were my two sons and my husband's happiness. My life was the only thing that I had control over, not everything around me. This would take a long time for me to completely accept. So in the meantime I would struggle with this personality quirk along with the grief of losing my beloved mother and my best friend.

It was now the day before my mother's wake. April stopped over my house and asked me if I would go to our mother's house to pick out some jewelry and clothes so Mr. Silva could dress her. I told April, "Yes, I will," and I thought of something much better. I had this very beautiful pink and white dress that my mother always liked. I wanted her to wear this for her wake, but I did go to her house, and I picked out some jewelry along with the mother's ring that I had bought her a few years earlier. I gave all of this to April to bring to the funeral home.

After she left I sat there, and for the first time since my grandmother died, I spoke to God. I asked him to please show me the right way. I begged him for guidance, but unfortunately I felt nothing. I felt as though I was just talking to a blank wall. There was no connection there whatsoever. It felt nothing like it did when I was a child and I prayed. I felt so completely empty and all alone.

It's the most horrible feeling when someone you love as much as you love your mother passes. It's as though you get kicked in the stomach while falling into a deep dark hole. You feel pain but numb at the same time. It's as though you're entire body just goes into shock. The only thing you can feel is pain, and you just look forward to the day and then pray for the day that this subsides, that this hopefully passes. But only in time will this happen.

While you're in all of this pain, you have to be the responsible adult and you have to do things you don't want to do. You have to make arrangements, and you have to pay your respects to your loved one that now has passed on. Most importantly you have to face the fact that they have passed on. That is one of the hardest things you will ever have to do in your life, but that is life. People are born, and people die every day. I suppose it's what we do in between those times that are truly important. The people's lives that we touch, the people that we love, the legacy that we leave behind can either be very good and very loving or very bad. It's everyone's choice. So that night before my mother's wake I didn't get a wink of sleep.

The next morning Michael and the boys woke up early. I could hear Michael in the bathroom getting ready and getting his suit out of the closet. He started getting the boys dressed in their little suits. I lay there listening, and I said to myself, *I can't do this. I can't just lie here. This is my responsibility as her daughter, as a mother and as a wife to get myself together, to get a hold of myself and my emotions, and get up and do what I am supposed to do, and that is, go and pay my respects, a respect that my mother so much deserved, and say good bye to her for the last time.*

So I got up out of bed, and I tried my hardest to do this. I got my hair done, my makeup on, and I got my dress on.

Michael said, "Honey, you're making the right choice. You know you are."

I said, "Yeah, Honey, I know I am. I couldn't do anything else."

As the four of us arrived at the funeral parlor, my knees were shaking. As I was walking up the stairs, I felt like throwing up. Michael held onto my arm, staying as close as he could throughout the whole thing. He helped me in the door and I introduced my family and me to Mr. Silva. Mr. Silva took my hand and told me, "Kyra, you've made the right decision you know."

I looked at him, and I said, "Yes, Mr. Silva, I know."

Then he asked us if we would like to go in to see her now, and I said yes. So he escorted us into the viewing area where my mother lay in her casket. Mr. Silva did such a beautiful job with the makeup and the hair and her clothes. She looked exactly like an angel. She looked so beautiful. As soon as I saw her I knew I made the right choice, and I knew Mr. Silva was right, I did need this closure.

As Martin and Teddy kneeled by my mother's casket in front of Michael and me, Michael stood there with his arm around me and whispered in my ear, "I love you, Kyra."

I whispered back, "I love you too, Michael."

He began praying with Teddy and Martin. I stood there with my head bowed not joining in with their prayers. At this moment I just felt as though the prayers that they were saying were just words. They meant nothing to me. After Michael and the boys were done with the prayers, the four of us went and sat down by my sister April and Amber. I sat there as though I were hypnotized. I couldn't take my eyes off of my mother. I just sat there looking at her remembering everything that we had done in our lives together. All the fun that we had and most recently all the fun that she had with her grandson and the cookouts and her laughter—most of all her laughter.

As more and more people came I sat there feeling like I was sitting in a black hole disconnected from everyone. I guess the best way I can put it is I was feeling numb. Then my mother's sisters with their children, my cousins that I hadn't seen in years came in. After giving them hugs and greetings, I sat back down, and I looked toward the door. I was so happy to see this one man. His name was Robert Clay. He was an old family friend. I had known him since I was eight years old, and at certain times in my life he was almost like a brother to me. He in a lot of ways was very much like my mother. He would literally give you the shirt off of his back. If there were anything that you ever needed and you called him, if he was able to do it, he would do it in a heartbeat. He was a good, good soul and a good man. He came along with his five children. His oldest was John; the next one was Steven, then Scott, then Holly and Robert, Jr.

We always tried to keep in touch, our family with his, and his children were kind of like my nieces and nephews. They all gave my sisters and me such loving embraces. With tears in their eyes they all told us how horrible they felt about what had just happened, and what a lovely, loving woman my mother was, and I told them, "Yes, I was lucky to have her as a mom," and all the while thinking though they were very, very lucky to have Robert as a father. Oh, my God. He was the most perfect father you could imagine, everything a father should be and more.

At my mother's wake while talking to his children, we promised to keep in touch. We realized that many years had passed by where we were not close, and we should have been because our families had always been so close. So we made this promise, and I fully intended to follow through on it.

With Michael by my side and my two sons and the love and support from our family and friends, we got through this day. I am so, so glad now that I went. If I had not done this, it would have been a major regret I would have had to carry on my shoulders for the rest of my life. I couldn't believe that I was stupid enough to think, to even let the notion enter my mind, that I would not go.

As our time there was coming to an end, as the wake was ending, I went up to view my mother by myself and knelt down beside her casket remembering how beautiful she was in life, only wishing to take away those memories, not the memories of now, not the memories of today, and not the memories of her being gone now to me forever. When I looked at her I tried to imagine her just simply sleeping and not being dead. I leaned over, and I kissed her hand, and then I got up and took my place beside Michael once more.

This is when Robert leaned over and said to me, "Kyra, that sight was so incredible. It looked as though your mother wanted to lean up and touch you." It was a very odd thing that he said that because as I leaned over her I could feel her energy, I could feel her spirit there beside me, and for the first time in my whole life I was actually glad that I had this gift. This was the one and only time that I ever found this gift comforting, because yes, I could feel her, and

I could also feel that she was okay, that she was happy. It was a very, very light feeling. I can sense the different spirits. I can sense the difference between a child, a woman and a man, and I can also sense when these spirits are angry or hurt and upset. I found through experience that a child's spirit is like a whisper. It's very light, almost carefree, but I could feel it. A woman's is a bit heavier, and all depending I suppose on the way she died or on the way she lived. I could pick up anger or I could pick up just peacefulness, just a fleeting whisper. Men are always stronger. Their spirits always come through stronger, more masculine, more domineering. That's how I am able to tell the difference between a man and a woman. More often than not I have found men's spirits to be much angrier than women for some reason, I don't know.

There is a definite difference between the spirit of a child, a woman and a man and a happy, a sad or an angry one. The angry ones are the bad ones I don't like. They leave you with such a heavy feeling in your heart, and sometimes this feeling I wouldn't be able to shake for some time. I was touched by one and this feeling lasted a couple of days. I don't know whether he stayed in the presence beside me for that long, but the emotion that was left behind certainly did, and I didn't like it at all. But I found I have no control. Whenever I am in the presence of the spirit, I will pick it up. No matter how hard I try to ignore it and to ignore them, it doesn't work. They are always somehow able to get through to me no matter how hard I block them. So by this stage in the game I've just about given up trying. Whatever happens, happens, and I have to handle it the best way I can, still though, always trying to ignore it. I thought perhaps if I did ignore them and they didn't see me seeing them or picking them up, they would just go away. I do think this actually does work because when I am in the presence of the spirit it doesn't last usually very long, maybe a half an hour and then I feel nothing. So they come and go, but I'm certainly not going to put out the welcome mat for them.

So when Robert made this remark about my mother looking like she was ready to reach out and touch me, I just laughed and said, "Yeah, really?" and of course said nothing about how I felt and what I was able to feel.

As everyone began leaving, Michael, Teddy, Martin, and I told April and Amber that we would meet them at our house. I made dinner for them that night. We all sat around talking about Mom trying to remember only the good days. Trying to keep only good memories in our heads, but it was too soon for this. Our memories caused us only pain for this moment. Being able to laugh at the things she used to do and remember fondly our relationships would not come until much later. Our broken hearts were still too raw to accept laughter into them right now. Only time would repair our broken hearts and we all knew this.

After supper April and Amber returned back to their homes, and Michael and I gave the children their baths and put them to bed for the night. We returned back down to the living room to watch TV. We sat there on the couch, and he held me in his arms for most of that night comforting me and loving me and reassuring me everything was going to be fine. I honestly don't know how I would have gotten through this most painful time without Michael and my two sons standing beside me and holding me up. They are the only ones that gave my soul the strength to go on and not give up and allow my broken heart to consume me. If not for them I don't know what would have happened to me.

It never ceases to amaze me how children can be so resilient to accept fact likes Teddy and Martin did about my mother's death. They knew where she was and that she was in Paradise and much happier than I certainly was at this moment. They just accepted this as fact, and I thought how much easier this would be on me if I could do the same, if I could somehow summon up that resilience, that courage. Even though they cried, they released their pain, and I think deep down inside they realized they were crying for themselves, of course, because Grandma was in Paradise now and she could no longer be with them. She would no longer be able to watch Teddy do his jumps and his stunts. I'm sure she was standing by him watching him from time to time afterwards. Martin with his drawing, the sensitive artist, she was going to teach him so much. I knew they were crying for this reason and this reason alone, and in time their hearts healed as well.

As a family this was our first test of our strength as a family unit. Were we going to fall apart and separate or were we going to come together and be strong and hold each other close? I am so glad to say that we did. As a family we got through this by being honest and loving toward one another and caring about each other's feelings and keeping each other as close as you possibly could be. This was our first test as a family, and I am grateful to say we passed it with flying colors. We actually came out of this first horrifying heartbreak that we all had to face even stronger than we were before.

The next morning when we all woke up we began getting dressed and preparing for my mother's funeral. My mother was to be cremated. This was her wish and she wanted me to take possession of her ashes, which I did.

So the morning of the funeral we all got dressed and went to the funeral home, and I was glad to see Robert was there again along with his five children for support and love. I always knew he loved my mother very much. My mother loved him. She never had a son, and I think she looked upon Robert as the son she never had. The priest came to the funeral parlor and said a few prayers, and then they put my mother in the hearse and we all went to the church where they had a ceremony for her.

Walking into the church again I felt that kick to my stomach, that familiar pain in my heart. I knew I lost my mother, but also I was having bad flashbacks about losing my grandmother as well. It was heartache on top of heartache, and as I sat there in the pews looking at my mother's casket, all the memories of when my grandmother and I used to go to church came rushing back. As I sat around watching everybody crying, me included, I once again asked God for guidance and for strength. But even in God's house I felt nothing. All I felt when I prayed was blank, just nothing, no communication. I felt as though I was just praying to a blank wall. This was devastating to me. I felt as though I had turned my back on God many, many years earlier and now he had turned his back on me. This left me completely empty inside. I guess most people would call it a spiritual crisis. I don't know. All I know was it was the most horrible feeling of just complete utter emptiness, and when I needed him the most I felt as though he was not there for me.

This of course only added to the anger that I was feeling toward him. I don't know what that blank wall was. Was it a wall that I put up throughout the years, a wall that just got thicker and taller? Was it a wall that was built with my anger toward God? Was this his wall blocking me out of his divine presence, blocking me out and keeping me away from his love now? Was this His wall or my wall? I hadn't a clue, and I had absolutely no idea how I was going to be able to begin to tear this wall down and to have God in my life again in my heart and to stop hating him. I had no idea how to begin to go about doing this or if this was even possible.

Maybe too many years had passed by now for anything to be fixed. Perhaps what I've done in his eyes, my turning my back on him, is just so unforgivable that he never wanted to hear from me again, never wanted to hear my prayers again or hear my voice again. Again I had so many questions and no answers.

While sitting there becoming completely emotionally drained, trying to endure all the pain that was going on around me, I looked over at Michael (he was, of course, sitting right beside me as usual), and I put my head on his shoulder. He put his arm around me, and I knew I was going to be okay. His love overpowered all of this pain I was experiencing and all of this doubt that I had with God. I always felt that Michael had some magical way of protecting my heart, and he did. He truly did. I felt as though with Michael beside me there was nothing I couldn't do. I felt as though I could literally walk through hell if I had to as long as I knew he was waiting on the other side for me. His love overpowered all of this pain and carried me through.

The service came to an end and everyone began coming out of the church with my mother's casket in the front to be loaded back in the hearse to be taken to the crematoria. While I was coming down the stairs of the church, my knees buckled out from underneath of me, my head spun, and I felt as though I was just going to pass out. Of course Michael was there. He was holding my arm, thank God. I didn't fall. He caught me just as he always caught me throughout our whole time together.

He always had a way of lifting me up above it all, above all the pain and all the sorry in my life. He was such an amazing man, a man I truly felt blessed to have in my life. He was always my protector, and most importantly always my hero.

Now I was faced with having to go the rest of my life without my mother in it, and my children were faced with the same. I would try desperately to keep as much normalcy in their lives as possible in the days that followed. Through all our tears and the grief that we had to go through, we would stay strong, though I have to admit it hit Teddy perhaps the hardest, maybe even worse than April, Amber, and me. She was like a second mother to him, and she had been with him practically every day since the day he was born. His reaction was rather odd. I observed him one day throwing out a lot of things that she had given him. One thing in particular was pogs, these little round cardboard disks that were popular in 1995. All the kids wanted to collect them. There were all different pictures on them. She was always adding to his collection.

One day I saw him standing there at his bedroom window just throwing them out, one by one, and I asked him, "Teddy, what are you going? Why are you throwing the pogs away?"

He wouldn't answer me. I never did get a straight answer from him. So it was one of the weird things that he did after this. He did retreat to his room by himself and just sat there and watched TV. This was a slight personality change for him, because as I said earlier, he was always the physical type always wanting to be outside doing things. I kind of backed off for a while thinking maybe he needed some space to think and absorb everything that just happened. I was right. He did. After a few days, about a week, he slowly started coming back. I also let his best friend Joey know that Teddy's grandma had just passed. I asked him, "Do you know what that means?" He wasn't too sure. I told him, "She went back to Heaven to be with God, and Teddy right now is going through a bad time because he misses her."

Joey was only eight and a half years old around this time. He seemed to understand this. After I let Joey know everything that was going on, he and Teddy became even closer. I would often see them playing basketball together and see them sitting together on the sideline talking. Joey was a tremendous help to Teddy through this most painful time in his life, and for that I will be forever grateful.

It was I would say a week after my mother's funeral when I began smelling flowers in my bedroom. At first I thought perhaps I had knocked over a bottle of my perfume, although I didn't have any perfume that smelled quite like this. The smell was just so strong but very, very pleasant, and I wondered where it was coming from. I looked all around and it was on my side of the room and it seemed to radiate along my bureau, so I had Michael help me move it, (it was a huge bureau) and we found nothing. There was absolutely nothing that could be causing that floral scent. At the time, Michael and I just simply shook our heads.

It was also around this time that I had begun to pray every night, but I'm sorry to say always with the same results—that wall and nothing, nothing more. There were days in that first couple of weeks following my mother's death that I just simply didn't want to get out of bed, and there were a few days that Michael told me, "Just relax, Kyra. I'll take care of the kids." He knew I just needed to be by myself for a while to begin to heal my broken heart.

Through these few days that I was able to just spend in my room by myself, I tried to pick up on my mother's spirit. I tried so hard to do this, but I felt nothing, just like when I prayed. This feeling of complete utter blackness of just being dropped into a black hole was getting worse instead of better.

One day when Michael took the boys fishing, I sat in the living room and watched TV. They had a rerun of a movie called *Flat Liners*. This probably was the worse possible movie I could watch at this time in my life. This movie showed a group of college students experimenting with life and death. They figured how to bring people to the brink of death and then bring them back just so they could experience the other side for even a few moments to at least know that there was something else other than here other than this, other than this life.

Now through the years since I first injured my hand and was diagnosed with R.S.D., I had always been offered painkillers and sleeping pills, both of which of course I refused because of my alcoholism. I couldn't run a risk of becoming dependent on pills and becoming a legal junkie, but I knew with one phone call I could get a prescription. My mind took over and began thinking about how I could go about seeing the other side, dying but coming back just in the nick of time, being pulled back like they did in that movie.

Believe me, I realize now just how stupid those thoughts were, and I would never ever suggest anyone do that. I didn't want to kill myself. I just wanted to get a glimpse of Heaven, a glimpse of where my mother was and my grandmother was so that I would be able to go on with my life in fact knowing that they were truly okay. Up to this point, no, I wasn't sure, especially after I began starting to pray again and found nothing there. I started to doubt whether there was even a heaven and perhaps even a God. All these doubts consumed me and consumed my thought. I was so desperate to find out one way or the other.

This was at the beginning of the week, and I knew Michael took the boys fishing every Saturday. He would take them early at 9 o'clock and not return until 6 or 7 that night, so I would have an opportunity to try this experiment on my own, to die and get pulled back into life before it was too late. All I wanted was a second just to see for myself, to have no doubts. Then I could go on with my life happily. So after watching the movie and giving it much thought, I called my doctor, and I asked her for a prescription of sleeping pills. She phoned it into the pharmacy, and I picked them up the following day.

It was now Friday the day before my plan was to come into action. I had it all planned out very carefully. I knew Michael would arrive back home no later than 7 o'clock that night, so I planned to overdose around 6:30 quarter of 7 and leave a note about what I did and why I did it and for him to call for help as soon as he saw this on the table. I know I was playing a very dangerous game, a very stupid and selfish game and things could have gone terribly,

terribly wrong. But at that moment I just didn't care. I couldn't think of anything else. I just had to have a glimpse of where they were and if they were truly okay, and also if there really was a God. So that night Friday night I went to sleep with all these thoughts in my head, and I could barely wait until that next day came, that Saturday, when Michael would take our boys fishing, and I could do what I knew I must do.

So that Friday, with all these thoughts going through my head, I finally went to sleep. I do not know how long I was asleep. I began to dream, and all of a sudden my mother's face appeared to me, and we were literally nose-to-nose. Her face looked like it did when she had her stroke, all drooping down on one side, her hair was all a mess, and she screamed one word to me at the top of her lungs. That word was "NO!"

I woke up screaming, my heart pounding in my ears, and I said, "Oh, my God; oh, my God." I took the bottle of sleeping pills from the night stand, and I ran into the bathroom with them, and I flushed them down the toilet. I realized what I was thinking was so stupid but it would take a shock like this to snap me back into reality, and she was able to finally reach me through my dream. I will never forget what her face looked like and the anger in her voice.

Michael sat up in bed as I was coming out of the bathroom with an empty bottle of pills. He asked me, "What was going on?"

I just told him, "Nothing. I'm fine. I just had a bad dream."

He went back to sleep quickly, and I lay there thinking about how stupid I was and what I almost did.

That next day I woke up, and I said, "Okay, now you really have to snap out of this. There will be no more pity parties, Kyra, and there are no more selfish thoughts. Your children and Michael certainly deserve better." That was the day I snapped out of it, and what I'm going to tell you next is completely unbelievable. I packed their lunch for them to take fishing as I always did, and 3 o'clock passed by, and then 6 o'clock, and 7, and I began to worry because they were never later than 7 o'clock. That's when the mosquitoes would start coming out, and Michael didn't want to get eaten alive by them so he would always make sure he was home by them.

Seven thirty came, 8 o'clock came, and it wasn't until 8:30 quarter of 9 they came driving in the driveway. I ran out to the car, and I said I was worried sick that something had happened, and Michael told me, "No, Honey. We just had a flat tire." He had trouble with the jack and getting the bolts off of the tire. It hit me like a bag of bricks.

If I had gone through with my foolish, foolish plan, they would have come home and found their mother dead because unlike every other weekend when they were home at 7 o'clock on the dot, they would have been almost two hours late. That would have been long past my being able to be revived and brought back to life.

I knew at that moment also that my mother was fine, and her spirit was fine because she could see, unlike me, what was coming down the road. She knew that I would not have been able to be revived. I truly would have died. Knowing her love and her strength, I knew she was not going to allow this to happen. When I finally came to this realization that she was truly okay and she was seeing what was going on, therefore there must be a Heaven and there must be a God.

I continued to pray to that blank wall every single night, but it just simply didn't change. I did know deep down inside that they were okay, and for whatever reason this wall was there. Maybe through enough prayers, through enough days of my hoping and chipping away at it, it would eventually come down. I had to try. So every day I prayed, and I prayed for grace and for strength. Through every passing hour and passing day and week our hearts began to mend. I am very happy to say that Robert did keep his word, and he did keep in touch.

It was about three weeks to a month after my mother's funeral when I had a really nice cookout in her honor, and I invited them all—his five children and him. We had a great time. The boys splashed around in the pool. They took to him so easily. He is just that type of man. He loved everybody, and he loved children especially and everybody loved him. It is really rare that you can say you have never heard one bad word about a certain person, but I can truly say that about Robert. I never heard anyone say anything bad about him. It's because I guess there isn't anything to say. He was just good, and his family and my family seemed to mesh together really well. My kids got to know his, and he got to know mine, and I in turn got to know them. Throughout the rest of that summer we would have a few more cookouts where he would join my family and also my sister April and Amber. They loved him as well and they had known him for a lot longer than I had.

I also found out something else was starting to happen over these part three weeks. I had begun waking up in the middle of the night. I don't know if I was sleep walking or what, but I would find myself on the phone in my room trying to dial my mother's number in a complete panic state, panicked because I had not spoken to her for so long. I worried about how she was getting her food and who was taking her to the doctor and who was looking after her. This went on for months. It was so bizarre because it was much like Michael's night terrors, night terrors where he would wake up not knowing where he was and do things while he was in the middle of one that he had no recollection of doing. This was what was going on with me, but instead of me being violent and hitting him, I would jump out of bed and try to reach the phone to call my mother. This was very, very disturbing to both Michael and me, and if it had gone on for much longer, I would have had to start seeking professional help.

I would also have a lot of during my dreams about my mother. I would dream about just the four of us sitting at the table, my two sisters, my mother and me, and we would be talking. Then all of a sudden my mother would disappear, and I would wonder where she went. In my dream whenever I asked April and Amber, "Where did Ma go?" they would just laugh.

In other dreams it would be just simply April, Amber and me sitting there, and I would begin to ask, "Where's Ma?"

They'd say, "Who knows?"

I'd ask them, "What do you mean, who knows?" Then I'd ask them if they had called her or if they had been in touch with her at any point. I then realized how long it had been in my dreams that I hadn't had any contact with her, and I would start going into a panic mode again. These dreams would become so disturbing I would wake up either crying or yelling.

Even though these dreams let up over the years, they lasted for years. At first they were quite frequent. Perhaps three or four times a week I would have one of these disturbing dreams. Over the months they eased up to once, maybe twice a week. Then I would go months. It took many years for me to stop having these dreams. This lasted probably about five years.

People go through many, many things when they lose someone so close to them, but you can't give in to these nightmares. You can't give in to your fears. You can't give in to despair and heartache. You have to keep getting out of bed, and you have to keep fighting sometimes on a daily basis if need be because our loved ones, the ones that have crossed over would want you to do this, to go on and to be happy, certainly not destroy our life in memory of them.

This took me a long, long time to figure out, and the learning process is quite painful. Every day I dragged myself out of bed even though I truly would rather have lain there all day. I became stronger as the days went on. I learned that the living are the important ones—your children that you must take care of and that rely on you and your husband as well. You and your family can become stronger through horrifying painful times such as these when you keep things in perspective. The living is what's important, and the dead, I know, would agree with this.

Through this very painful learning process, the process of learning how to carry on without your loved one beside you, without being able to pick up the phone and simply call them. I learned many, many other things, and I had to go through many things, stupid little things that you never, ever thought would bother you like simply grocery shopping. One day about a month after my mother passed when all of this was really, really raw to me and the learning process had really just begun, I was in the middle of a grocery store, a grocery store that my mother and I always shopped at. Music was playing, and I couldn't even tell you what the song was. (I also had developed at this time an aversion to music. I couldn't listen to music without crying. It didn't matter what kind it was. I didn't know why.)

So while shopping one day in the middle of the grocery store, the music started. I was walking down my mother's favorite aisle which happened to be the cookie aisle. I began crying uncontrollably. I just lost it right there in the middle of the grocery store. I never was so embarrassed in my life, but I simply had to get the hell out of there. I had half a grocery cart full of groceries, and I just left them. I knew if I didn't get out of there, I was simply going to embarrass myself further. So I walked out leaving my grocery cart there. I realized I couldn't shop there for a while. I had to go to another grocery store, one that she and I didn't shop at too frequently.

I had to make little changes like this in my life in order to survive, in order not to just crumble. I avoided driving down her street, past her old house. I avoided the coffee shop that she and I would always go to for that morning cup of coffee before we would go to the doctors or shopping or just driving around. I figured if just even for now that I did all these things, all these changes, at least until my heart was healed this was okay.

In the future I hoped that I would have the strength some day to go back to that grocery store, to go to that coffee shop and to drive by her house. I knew when I was able to do these things again, I would know that my heart was healed. For now, I must avoid them. I just missed her so much. So with all these little adjustments that I would have to make and the praying that I did every single night even though I continued to get that blank wall, our family pulled together and stayed strong. In time we began to heal.

It was about a month after my mother's funeral when Mr. Silva, the funeral director, called me and told me to come and pick up my mother's ashes, that they were ready, and I did. He kept me in his office for at least an hour and a half talking, making sure that I was okay. I assured him that I would be, and I explained to him how close my family was, my two sisters included, and that, yes, our hearts are broken still. I told him about the adjustments I had to make, certain places I had to avoid, for now anyway, until my heart was healed.

He agreed, "He said, yes, if you feel more comfortable going somewhere else, you should." He reminded me, "You know, Kyra, it just takes time. The heart needs time."

I told him, "I know."

After that nice conversation I brought my mother's ashes home. I never bought an urn to display them. I just kept them close to me in my night stand by my bed in the box that they were originally in. I never intended to keep them for very long. I wanted to set them free into the four winds, to release the rest of her just as her soul was released on the day she passed.

The weeks would pass by, or should I say drag by. The healing process is so long and so hard. Michael was still out of work because of his diabetes. He was collecting unemployment, and with the cost of my mother's funeral spreading it three ways between April, Amber, and me, we had very little money to spare, so we decided to have the phone turned off just for a little while until we could get caught up on the funeral expenses. We did this around the end of August. Weeks and months passed by. It was the beginning of November now and our hearts were still trying to recover from this great loss. But it's true with every passing day, weeks and months it does help, and the pain is less every day.

One particular day in November, it was around the 6th or 7th, just the beginning of the month, Michael and I were sitting out in front of our apartment, right underneath the kitchen window, when all of a sudden the phone rang. Now mind you this phone had been shut off since August, nearly two and a half months, and it was completely dead. There was no dial tone whatsoever. When the phone began to ring Michael looked at me, knowing what he knew about me and about what you would say was my gift.

He looked at me and said, "Well, Kyra, I think that's probably for you."
I just looked down on the ground and I shook my head, and I said, "No."
He said, "Go answer it."

I still couldn't believe I was hearing my phone ring. I walked into the house and picked the phone up and at the other end was just silence. Then a clicking began to happen, and I asked, "Is this you, Mom?" I said, "If it is click twice for yes." It clicked twice. I asked her if she was okay. Then the phone went completely dead again, as it was just before, and it was to never ring again until we had the service turned back on.

This was a one-time thing, and I knew it was her reaching out to me letting me know once more that she was okay. I went back outside and sat down beside Michael again, and I told him what had just happened.

He looked at me and said, "Are you really surprised, Kyra?"

"No, I guess not." This was a really, really nice communication, a gift that she gave me. I believe it was for the first time since my mother's death that I actually laughed. I laughed at this notion because this was our main communication. At the end of her life we were constantly on the phone together. This was just a remarkable thing, and I did have a good laugh. It made me feel really good.

As Michael and I sat there watching Teddy do his jumps on his ramp as he always did and Martin chasing the bugs and jumping into piles of leaves, I knew then my mother was standing right there watching it all and taking it all in. That phone call was a way to let me know that she was not gone, and this made me feel so happy inside. For the first time in months I actually felt my heart lightening and repairing itself. This was truly a special gift that she gave to me. A gift from beyond that only she could give me. It was also at this moment I realized that love never dies. Love lives on long after death. I can't begin to tell you how I so desperately needed this gift from my mother at this moment.

With the holidays quickly approaching I knew how hard this was going to be. This would be the first holiday without her, and I knew that the first holidays were the hardest on a family after such a tremendous loss. I had already gotten through Halloween with my two boys. I dressed them up as I usually did. Teddy was a Vampire and Martin a little cowboy. I tried to keep my spirits high and theirs as well. I took them out trick or treating and we did have fun that night, but I knew the worst was yet to come and that would be the first Thanksgiving and the first Christmas without her at our family's table.

Thanksgiving came and we dealt with it. Of course it wasn't business as usual. Of course there was a huge gap and of course she was greatly missed, but with my sister April and Amber there to enjoy Thanksgiving dinner with us, we made it through. Quickly following Thanksgiving was Martin's birthday on the 26th. We gave him a nice birthday party and took him to the Christmas Parade, but after what my mother showed me, the gift, the last gift she was able to give me being that phone call, I knew deep down in my heart she was right there with us. She was celebrating that Thanksgiving dinner and she was seeing Martin's 5th birthday. I just knew it. I could feel her there. I could feel her love.

As the weeks past now it was the middle of December and most of my Christmas shopping was done. We were able to get enough money together to make sure the children had a happy Christmas. Throughout the years, actually ever since Teddy was born, I began this tradition in our family. We would all go and pick out our family's Christmas tree. It just happened to be on my mother's birthday this year, December 13. So the four of us got all bundled up. We got into the car, and I said before I left, "Mom, be with us please," because this is the time that she enjoyed spending with us. She would come with us to pick out our family's Christmas tree. Sometimes it would take us nearly an hour to find the most perfect one we could possibly find. It couldn't be too big and it couldn't be too small. It had to be just perfect, and this would take time.

Michael and Teddy, Martin and my mother would often become a little impatient with me and tell me, "Come on, Kyra. One tree's as good as the next."

I'd explain to them, "No, it's not." I wanted my family's Christmas tree to be perfect.

So after finally finding the one I liked the most, we would get it tied to the top of the car, and then we would go to the Morton Green where they would decorate so beautifully with millions of lights. On the Green was Santa's House, and every year after picking out our perfect Christmas tree we would go to the Green and the boys would have their pictures taken with Santa. After that we would walk around looking at all the displays and the lights. Everything was so beautiful especially if it had just snowed that day. All the lights would glisten and the snow would look like millions of little diamonds. We would always stop for hot chocolate.

After doing all this we would return back home quite cold and frozen, but this experience was well worth it. This was a family tradition that I so look forward to every year. This year, of course, it was bittersweet. This without a doubt was the hardest thing I had to face after losing my mother, going through this family tradition now without her. I tried my hardest not to think about it too much and to just live in the moment and enjoy what was going on at the time for my boy's sake. I knew deep down inside all along in my heart this was not a tradition she would want me to break simply because she was no longer physically able to be here with us. I knew she was here in spirit so this kept me going. When we arrived back home with our beautiful tree Michael would place it in the Christmas tree stand we had already set up in the corner where we always put it.

It was about a week after this, after we went and got our tree and came home and decorated it, and a week before Christmas when Teddy came running home after playing in a neighbor's back yard and told me that he saw Grandma standing there by a tree, and he ran over to her.

He said, "I almost didn't recognize her because she was young, but I know it was Grandma. She leaned down and asked me how I was doing and how Martin was and Daddy and you, and I told her we were all doing fine."

When he told me about this it floored me and it also scared me, because this was a part of myself that I never wanted my children to have. I thought the worst at that time. He was given the gift, the same gift I had been given, a gift that ran in our family. I didn't want this for him. I didn't want this for Martin. I was hoping my children would be spared. At that moment I wasn't quite sure whether it was this gift starting or perhaps just an isolated incident, and it was just my mother reaching out to him. Maybe this was his Christmas gift. I didn't know, so I didn't get into great detail at the moment with him about things. I did explain to him, though, a little bit about our family's history.

I said, "Sometimes Mommy, Grandma, Aunt April, and Aunt Amber see and feel and hear things that other people cannot." I told him how very glad I was that he was sharing this with me, but I told him not to share it with anyone else. Keep it to himself, and if anything else happened for him to come and let me know right away. If he were to see her again or to feel something else, I asked him to let me know. I told him he was always able to talk to me about it, and I understood.

So he was happy. He was happy to actually be able to see my mother once more, and I was very happy for him. I hoped that this was just an isolated incident and not something more. This was something I had always protected my sons from. I never spoke of anything that I had experienced in my life in front of them. I always made sure that they were not in earshot. This was the one and only secret that I would have kept from them because I didn't want to influence them in any way. I didn't want them to start thinking and trying to do perhaps what I was able to do naturally and that was to pick up on spirits. I didn't want to put this into their brain. I kept them as far away from it as I possibly could until now; anyway I was able to do this. I had to communicate with Teddy, and I had to let him know that he wasn't losing his mind. That's the only reason I spoke about it with him. Even then I kept it very, very short in order not to plant seeds. I was afraid if they started trying to feel things, it would come and it would come very strong. So I didn't want them even beginning, and I did downplay this as much as I possibly could with Teddy.

However, after his experiencing this, a child's natural curiosity started kicking in. It was a couple of days afterwards when he came to me in my bedroom just before I was getting ready to go to sleep. He started asking me questions, questions like "What do I see? What do I feel? What exactly did I mean when I said this to him?"

I knew then that I had to be honest, and I told him, "Mommy has only seen one what you would want to call 'spirit,' in her whole life, but I had my mother touch me and many, many others; I could feel their presence, and sometimes it's not so good. That's why I never spoke about it to you. I hoped that you and your brother would not have this." I told him also, "It's a family trait. It's like having blond hair and blue eyes. We have this."

Then I gave him the same warnings that my mother gave me first and foremost about the Ouija Board. He had never heard of this game. I told him it is a game people use to contact spirits. You don't need it. If someone pulls this game out, you are to get the hell out of their house.

Through the years I would educate him more about these things, and also keeping whatever he was feeling to himself. I should be the only one that he spoke to about these things, if he were to see or feel anything more. I knew when he came to me because of what he had seen his curiosity I knew was peeked. However, I believe after talking to me about this and my explaining the basic things that I experienced in my life and the rules that he would have to follow, he did feel a little bit better about it. At least he didn't feel like he was going crazy or seeing things. I had to assure him that he was not crazy, and he wasn't seeing things. I told him hopefully it would end here. Hopefully he won't feel the spirits, and he won't feel what I felt during my life. It would just be an isolated incident, a one-time shot. I said more than likely that's what it was even though I felt in my heart differently. I had to make sure he knew he wasn't alone, though.

I said at the end of our conversation, "Please, please come and talk to me whenever you experience anything. I am always here for you."

He told me, "Mommy, yes I understand." Then he just got back into his bed and fell back asleep.

That Christmas was hard particularly on Martin and Teddy. Now both of our mothers were no longer able to join us for Christmas dinner. Michael's mother was sick in the nursing home wasn't able to make it to our home for dinner, and of course my mother was gone. We tried our hardest to put up a front of happiness and joy. I have to tell you that was the best acting job we ever did.

It was now the night before Christmas. Teddy and Martin's stockings were stuffed. Their presents were laid out from Santa and Mommy and Daddy underneath the tree. Michael and I then snuggled up on the couch in each other's arms sitting beside the soft glow of the Christmas tree lights. I looked up at him, and I said, "Michael, do you remember one year ago to this day how I felt and how I started crying uncontrollably?"

"My God, yes, Kyra. I do remember now."

I knew at that moment why I was having that feeling. I was going to have to face the most painful time in my life, my mother dying in my arms. I was picking up all that pain that was yet to come, and that was the worst foreboding feeling I ever felt in my life. I always got these feelings but never that deep and never that heartbreaking as what I did just the Christmas before, and I told Michael that has to have been what it was.

I thank God at that moment that I could not look into the future and see everything that I was going to go through that year, but unfortunately I felt it. I felt all of that pain all at once that Christmas Eve just a year ago to the day. I said to him, "That was our last Merry Christmas together." Our family holidays after that last Christmas would never, ever be the same, for my mother would always now be gone. After this there would always be an empty plate at our family's holiday table, and every Christmas after this would always be just a little bit emptier and never, never the same again.

This is true. I never felt the same way toward Christmas again, but for my children's sake, I never let this show. I knew my mother would not want me to. After this talking and snuggling on the couch, it was about 1-1:30 in the morning when we finally made it to bed, and we snuggled, warm under the covers together only to be rudely awaked out of our nice dreams by Teddy and Martin jumping on us both.

It was morning, Christmas morning, and I can't even begin to tell you how much I dreaded going down those stairs knowing that my mother was not going to come over that day and look at all the gifts that were given to the boys and play with them. But I sucked it up, and I walked down those stairs with Michael. The boys ripped through their presents as they always did and then started in with their stockings. As usual they were thrilled with everything they got.

After I watched them rip everything apart and all the wrappings were everywhere, I picked them up and tried to straighten up the living room. I then put my turkey in the oven. I knew April and Amber would be there at three o'clock on the dot, and I was looking forward to seeing them, and I know the boys were as well.

As I sat there and placed my Christmas turkey in the middle of the table, I looked over to the chair that my mother always used to sit in during these holiday dinners. I was hit with such a wave at sadness and emotion I just choked on it, but I swallowed my tears, and I put on a smile. Michael was good at reading my face, though, and he knew exactly what I was thinking and how I was feeling because he gave me that look of "Oh, Baby Doll," that look that told me everything was going to be okay, a look of pure love that was in his eyes. I gathered my strength from his love. It was actually getting to that point in our relationship where he didn't have to talk anymore to encourage me and give me the inspiration and the strength that I so desperately needed many times. All I had to do was look into his eyes, and I saw it.

After dinner, after that most difficult dinner, Michael retired to the living room with Teddy and Martin, playing with their gifts. April and Amber stayed in the kitchen talking with me and helping me clean up. I told them the feeling that I had just that Christmas before, that feeling of foreboding.

I asked them if either one of them had experienced this last Christmas, that feeling of foreboding, and they both told me, "No."

I felt like I received my feeling on top of both of theirs at the same time. It was just a huge incredible painful tidal wave. The three of us spent a couple of more hours cleaning up and talking. I noticed April seemed to be the one that was taking my mother's loss the best. Amber, I could tell was completely

devastated and her drinking was getting worse and worse by the day. She had
dealt with the hatred toward my father for so many years and now she had to
deal with the loss of our beloved mother. She was the only true parent to us.
She kept us safe and loved. Now she was gone. This was very hard for her
to bear, and I worried about her very much. I knew I had Michael and the
children to carry me through this but she had only started dating this man most
recently. His name was Rocco. He was a kind man, but they didn't know each
other very well yet. I hoped that he would be a little supportive of her, and he
seemed to be. But still, it was a new relationship, and she was in a lot of pain
and drank to help numb this pain.

After she and April left that Christmas, Michael and I brought our very, very
exhausted boys up for their bubble bath that night. We tucked them lovingly into
their beds with a kiss. They didn't put up much of a struggle, because they were
so exhausted from playing with their toys all day. Michael and I went back
down stairs and snuggled by the lights of the Christmas tree. We didn't even
turn the TV on. We just thoroughly enjoyed each other's company. We talked
about how much fun the kids had that day with the new toys. Michael seemed
to be trying his hardest to keep my mind off of my mother.

After a couple of hours of just enjoying each other's company and relaxing
in each other's arms, we went to bed and fell fast asleep. Before we knew it
the sun was up and the two boys were jumping on our bed itching to go out and
play in the new fallen snow. It had been snowing through the night, and it was
still snowing in the morning so there was about 3-4 inches of accumulation, just
enough for their brand-new sleds. They would get new sleds every year for
Christmas, and they kept yelling out, "Let's go to the hill. Let's go to the hill,"
and we knew what that meant!

We got up, and I gave them their breakfast, and they scoffed it down as fast
as they could. Remember, they had to be the first ones on that hill! We bundled
them up, but we told them on the way there that we were not ever going to bring
them here again if they gave us a hard time like they gave us the last time we
brought them that New Year's Day of last year.

They both promised us, "No, we won't. When you call us we'll come. We
promise."

I said, "Okay."

So we got to the hill, and of course they weren't the first ones there. I don't
know who these other kids were. They must have lived right around the corner

because they had to have been there at 5 o'clock in the morning in order to beat us there. We arrived around 6:30. Anyway, we got our boys up to the top of the hill and they slid down screaming and yelling all the way. Then of course there was the nasty trek up the hill trying to avoid all the other sleds coming down. This time that our family would spend on this great snow mountain I suppose became a tradition in itself. We would do this time after time and year after year. Our boys so enjoyed it.

Christmas this year it was especially important to me to be able to put a smile on their faces. I knew nothing could make up for the absence of your grandmother, but I knew it was very important to keep up traditions, traditions that would make them happy, traditions that they would be able to look back on as adults, fond childhood memories that would last them their lifetime. This was very important to me and it was very important to my mother so we kept this up. It was amazing, the more I heard my little boys' laughter the happier I became and the more I could feel my heart healing.

Before we knew it, it was New Year's, 1996. A new year was starting. Michael and I celebrated New Year's Eve just as we always did, cuddled up on the couch with a few snacks that both of us enjoyed, watching Dick Clark ring in the New Year. We sat there by the soft glow of the Christmas tree lights, and we would make love. I guess you could say this was Michael's and my tradition. We celebrated one another, and we celebrated our battle over alcoholism. We celebrated our sobriety and our life and our love. This was how we began every New Year, celebrating the simple little things in life that we fought so hard to achieve. Every year we stood as a team, strong and proud.

Before we knew it spring was here. Michael was not able to return to his truck-driving job, the one with the moving company, because of his sugar level. It never got below 180, and he had become quite desperate for work. So he went and spoke to his uncle who owned one of the funeral parlors in Morton. Michael did have landscaping experience he gained while working for Smithville College, so his uncle put him to work keeping up the grounds of the funeral parlor and his private house. Michael was very grateful to get this. We were finally able then to get our phone turned back on and able to get caught up on some of the bills we had to let go, at least make a dent in them. Michael did enjoy working outside. He was very good at what he did. The grounds had never looked better, and his uncle was very happy with all of his work.

CHAPTER TEN

In March 1996 Michael would start working at the funeral parlor. Michael had the problem with his diabetes, and I had the problem with my arms. We were both facing challenges health wise at this point. During the month of April my arms became so sore and so bad so quickly that I had to go see my doctor about it. I explained to her how they had been feeling for the past year and a half and how the numbness was becoming much more frequent and more painful. She told me that I should see a neurologist, and she set me up with an appointment for one. She gave me the tests, EKG's, on my arms and we found out that I had a very severe case of Carpal Tunnel Syndrome. On a scale of 1 to 10, my left arm, the one that also had the RSD was a 9 and my right arm was a 7. I would also find out that any kind of operations that they offered for Carpal Tunnel I would not be eligible for because of the RSD. Literally there was nothing they could do for me. It was just something I was going to have to learn to live with. It was just so aggravating and so painful. I had to watch out how I grabbed anything, and how I picked up anything. Even just drawing or writing a simple letter would cause me pain. So I tried doing just as I did with the RSD and that was blocking a lot of the pain out. I knew this was going to be a long drawn out process, and it was going to take a long time for me to be able to perfect it, but I knew I could if I tried hard enough.

After my diagnosis I started this process immediately. I came home, and that night, in my bedroom, when everything was quiet, I tried focusing on one picture on the wall and putting all my thoughts and energy into that. It was working. It would take my mind off the pain. So between that and the Excedrin, it helped a lot. As I said, I knew I was going to need time to perfect this, and I was fully confident that I could.

It was now the end of April, actually the last day of April, when I was in the middle of cooking supper when there was a knock at the door. I opened the door, and I saw Holly standing there with little Robert, Jr. and two of

Robert's children. Holly asked me if she could please come in, and I said, "Certainly." She sent Robert, Jr., into the living room.

She and I remained in the kitchen talking, and she told me that her father was at Mass General Hospital in Boston. It seemed as though a heart valve he had had put into his heart when he was 18 years old had dissolved over the years, and it left him pumping blood into his chest. They did an emergency operation on him, and they were able to save him but he remained brain dead. She told me she would have let me know earlier what was going on but there just wasn't any time. She said it all happened so quickly. This was yet another heartbreak, because we had just begun close family ties. As I said earlier, he was like a big brother to me at times in my life, and I very much looked forward to him and his children being a part of my life and my family's life in the future.

I was in shock, and I did something that was totally out of character for me now in life. I punched the wall. It was a knee-jerk reaction in a fit of anger, and this action did not help my hand at all. I couldn't believe this was happening. The man was only 45 years old, and I had not even begun to recover from losing my mother. Now I would have to lose a man that I had known since I was 8 years old. It just seemed to be one thing right after the other, one heartbreak after the other.

She then asked me if I could please watch little Robert for her. He was 13 years old. She was 25, but she didn't want him there when they had to remove her father from life support. She didn't think he would be able to handle it. I agreed. I told her he could stay as long as she needed him to. So she and her brothers went back to the hospital that evening. On May 1, 1996, they removed him from life support. He quickly passed away. How my heart broke for her and her four brothers because I knew only too well the pain of losing one of your beloved parents. I knew they were going to have to face everything that I had already been through, and it was not something I would wish on anyone.

That following day Holly returned to pick little Robert up, and she told me all about that night. All of his children were there around him as he left. The poor girl was so broken up and so brokenhearted, and I knew there was nothing, there were no magic words I could say to her to help ease the pain. I told her how much I loved her father and how much I loved her and her brothers.

I also told her, "You can consider us a part of your family. You can come here any time you need to, just to have a cup of coffee, just to talk or visit. I'll always be here for you and your brothers, Holly."

She went on to tell me, which didn't surprise me at all, that her father was going to be an organ donor. This was typical of Robert. He gave and he gave and even after his death he still was giving.

After she left I sat there and I thought I wished I could get in touch with each and every one of these people that were to receive a part of him and let them know just what kind of special person this man truly was, and how very lucky they are to be carrying a part of him in them. He was a truly, truly special soul, and a man I will never, ever forget.

After I gathered my thoughts that evening and got hold of my emotions, I then called April and Amber to let them know the tragic news. They couldn't believe it any more than I could. Forty-five years old is just too young. He had too much life ahead of him. He would never even be able to see his grandchildren being born now or watch his youngest son graduate from high school. It was all just too heartbreaking to comprehend, and our losing our own mother just 10 months before. It was like picking a huge scab off of a very painful sore, a sore that had just begun to heal.

I knew that I, Michael and of course April and Amber would be going to support the family, his children and to pay our respects to this kind, kind soul. But I chose to spare the children yet another funeral. I felt it was just too soon after losing their beloved grandmother to expose them to this. After losing their grandmother just months earlier I did my best to protect them from any unnecessary pain. I lived in fear of all this death warping their brains and the way they looked at life. They were at such an impressionable age. I knew I had to be very, very careful of what I exposed them to. So this is why I chose not to let them attend Robert's funeral.

It would take two weeks for the family to get Robert back because he was an organ donor. In that two-week time Michael lost two of his friends. One was Lester, a friend that Michael had known for over 20 years, and the other one was Alex. Michael protecting me much like I protected our children would not let me go to Alex or Lester's funeral. He told me, "Kyra, you don't need to see this again. Just stay home with the boys. I'll be fine."

My heart broke for Michael. I realized just how close he and Alex had been. They were like brothers even though they fought all the time. I could see it hurt him. Alex went in a rather odd way. Both he and Corey had never stopped drinking, so the alcoholism did begin affecting their health. It certainly affected their relationship because they had broken up years earlier. Michael and I were the only two in our group of friends that were able to sober up and stay sober, and our relationship grew ever stronger. We saw theirs deteriorate, relationship after relationship, divorce after divorce.

Alex was alone, and he had been partying with one of his friends that night and drinking heavily as usual. He made the remark to his friend that he felt like he was going to die. I just have to go lie down for a while. Sure enough, his friend found him dead the next morning. Alex was only in his late 40s. Our other friend Lester was about the same age as well. He went pretty much the same way, in his sleep after getting severely drunk the night before. So, in the next two weeks Michael would have to attend three funerals, Lester, Alex and then Robert's.

This year, 1996, was turning out to be equally as heartbreaking as 1995. Michael and I sometimes would just look at each other and shake our heads wondering when it was going to end. It seemed like neither one of our families had many deaths in them before 1995. It had been years and years, and now all of a sudden we were being hit all at once with all of this horror and heartbreak. Thank God Michael and I were as close as we were because we held each other up and we supported and loved each other through it all.

At the end of that two weeks Robert's family finally received his body back. It went to the same funeral parlor as my mother's did, Morton Funeral Home, where Mr. Silva was. I had a neighbor watch Teddy and Martin while Michael and I went to the wake. As we got out of the car walking up the stairs, it was just all way too familiar and way too painful. It was exactly the same as my mother's. I walked up those exact stairs. It was just like a bad flashback.

Michael and I went into the funeral parlor, and Mr. Silva met us. He shook both our hands and said, "I'm sorry to see you again under such sad circumstances."

I said, "Yes." I explained to him that Robert was a very beloved friend of the family, a friend that I had known since I was 8 years old. Then we proceeded into where they had the viewing, and I couldn't believe it. I simply could not believe it. It truly was like a bad instant replay, a horrifying and heartbreaking instant replay in my mind. The casket was in the same exact spot in the same room as my mother's. The only thing that was different was the person lying in it; instead of my mother, was now Robert. As Michael and I approached the casket, we kneeled down beside it and Michael prayed. I didn't even dare to try. Instead I kneeled there looking at Robert lying there peacefully, and I thought to myself, *I'm not going to pray. I'm going to remember all the laughs and the fun times that we had, and most recently the family cookout we all enjoyed together.* I tried so desperately to remember the good times. Not now, not here, not the present, and certainly not what my eyes were seeing, him lying dead before me.

Instead of praying I read his funeral card. This is a card all the funeral parlors hand out with the deceased person's name, date of birth, and date of death. They also include either a passage from the Bible or just a poem.

Robert's read, "My Dearest Friends. You toiled so hard for those you loved. You said good-bye to none. Your spirit flew before you knew. Your work on earth was done. We miss you now. Our hearts are sore. As time goes by, we miss you more. Your loving smile. Your gentle face. No one can fill your vacant place. Your life was love and labor. Your love for your family true. You did your best for all of us. We will always remember you. The Lord be with you, Robert, now and forever more."

I thought that saying hit the nail right on the head. This is what type of man he was. He was hardworking for those he loved, and he was caring for everyone. They simply could not have picked a more perfect card for him.

After Michael and I were finished paying our respects, we went over to sit with Robert's children, April and Amber. I could tell by looking at April and Amber's face, they were as numb as I was. I could tell they were thinking the same thing I was. This was all just a bad horrifying instant replay of ten months' earlier. I looked over to Robert's children as they sat there sobbing. My heart broke for them. I just wished to God that I had some sort of magic words to help ease their pain, but I knew whatever I said would change nothing. Their father would still be dead, and they would be sitting here brokenhearted. All you can do is offer your love and your support at times like this because there is little else you can do. I found it extremely frustrating.

After the wake Michael and I returned home. April, Amber and Rocco joined us and we had coffee and doughnuts. We sat there discussing the next day, the day of the funeral. All of our hearts went out to each and every one of Robert's children. Although they were older children, we knew that their pain and this terrible burden that they now had to bear would be equally as hard on them as it was on us. Robert's oldest son, John was now 30. He had a younger brother Steven who was 29. Scott was 27. Holly was 25, and the youngest, Robert, Jr., was 13. I promised myself that night that I would keep in close contact with each and every one of them. If I could not visit them in person, I would call them at least once or twice a week over the phone. I knew Robert would appreciate my doing this, and I did. I kept close contact with each and every one of them after this. They truly did become like my nephews and niece. After the four of us visited for a while, April, Amber and Rocco went home. Michael and I were so emotionally exhausted. We just flopped into bed.

Of course, before we knew it the morning was here and it was time for Robert's funeral. I once again had our neighbor watch Teddy and Martin. Michael and I then got ready and arrived at the funeral parlor just as the priest was delivering the eulogy. We then went to the church and then the cemetery to place Robert in his last resting place. Michael and I decided to skip the gathering after the funeral, and we just returned back home. I didn't want to impose on my neighbor any longer than we had, and I knew Teddy and Martin were waiting for us. Michael then changed his clothes and went to work. I spent the remainder of the day sitting outside with Martin and Teddy watching them play.

A couple of days past by, and I gave each and every one of Robert's children a phone call to make sure that they were doing okay. I spent half the day on the phone with them trying somehow to relieve their pain even if it was just a little bit. Again I prayed, I prayed every single night and always that blank wall was there. Even though I was praying for someone else now, for their happiness, for their heartbreak to pass quickly, there was nothing. I felt nothing but I wouldn't give up. I knew perhaps someday that wall would come down.

It was now quickly approaching June, and it was starting to get hot out. The children were both after me to get a new pool and to start setting up the yard for our summer fun and cookouts. I agreed to do this even though all I felt like doing was crawling into a hole. No matter what was going on inside of me, inside of my heart and inside of my head, I always tried my hardest to keep a smile on my face for my children. I never wanted them to see my pain. It was also around this time that our next door neighbor, Joe, who had only lived there for about a year and a half passed away one day. In his case it was more of a relief than anything else. He had suffered from stomach cancer for the past two years, and he was in a great deal of pain. Then about two days after his death across the court, across the project, there was another death. This woman also was suffering from cancer, and her death also was a relief.

My God, it just seemed like one thing right after the other. We hardly had time to catch our breath, and of course we attended Joe's funeral, the one that lived right next door to us. After this I remember we returned back home, saying, "Please God, no more, for a while anyway."

I then began trying my hardest to set up the backyard for my children. I went and purchased a brand-new pool for them and a brand-new grill for our summer cookouts. I tried to concentrate on their happiness and hopefully some of it would rub off on me. It was the second week in June, and I would have my first family cookout. April, Amber and Rocco would attend, and the five of us gathered in the backyard. We all sat there watching Teddy and Martin splashing around in the pool and having fun. April brought her famous baked beans and Amber her delicious potato salad. After a couple of hours of laughing and talking I began setting up the grill. I had bought four beautiful steaks, some chicken breasts and hamburgers, and everyone enjoyed every bite. That first cookout of the season is really special, and it is the most delicious one of them all. We seemed to anticipate it all through the winter this first day, this first cookout. On this day we did enjoy watching the children splashing around. We had fun and we did laugh. Then I noticed something was a little off with Amber, and I didn't know quite what it was. Of course given the circumstances of what we had all been through, I wrote it off to that. Maybe she just wasn't rebounding as quickly as April, Michael, and I were. Unfortunately I would find this wasn't the case at all.

At the end of the day when we were all cleaning up and she was bringing the things from the backyard into the kitchen, the condiments, potato salad, and baked beans, she and I were alone in the kitchen. She began to tell me that she had just been diagnosed with lung cancer. My knees instantaneously went weak, and it was all I could do to fight back my tears. Then she quickly told me that the good news was it was caught very early. With an operation and chemotherapy, her outcome looked really, really good. She was given about a 70% survival rate. She went on to tell me that the doctor had to run a few more tests. At the end of the week she would have the results and when they would be able to operate. They were going to have to set all of this up.

She had no sooner gotten through telling me all of this when Michael walked into the kitchen and saw my face. He asked me, "Kyra, what's the matter?"

I just shook my head, and I looked down and said, "I'll tell you later after everybody goes."

Amber turned and walked back out into the back yard. I quickly followed.

I went over to April and whispered in her ear, "Did Amber tell you what was going on with her?"

April just nodded her head yes. We said nothing more about it for the remainder of that day. We gave each other big hugs at the end of the day. It was now around 7:30-8:00, and everyone was pretty tired, so April and Amber decided to call it a day, and they left. I sat there in the backyard, completely numb.

Michael offered to give the boys their baths for the night, and I accepted. I could hear them upstairs in the bathroom laughing and splashing around in the tub, but all I felt was hollow inside. After Michael was done and he was beginning to tuck them into bed, I went up and kissed them goodnight, and then I went into the bathroom and threw up. I could no longer keep the food down in my stomach. I just wanted to crawl out of my own skin.

Michael could hear me vomiting, and after I came out of the bathroom he asked me again, "Kyra, what's the matter?"

I then told him, and he said, "Oh, my God."

We both sat there, crying, in total disbelief. At this point it just seemed like there was a horrifying, disgusting black cloud over our entire family, and it wasn't going away. I remember telling Michael, "Thank God she has Rocco to help her through this most difficult time."

We were all very close as sisters, but neither April nor I were able to be with her the way Rocco was 24/7. She would need that extra love and all the support that only a man that loved her would be able to provide. Amber called me at the end of the week after she heard from her doctor about all the test results. She said that they wanted to operate right away. So at the end of June she had her operation. They removed part of her lung and two ribs from her back. This was a very difficult and very painful operation for her to endure. She had always been very thin and very frail, and this itself worried me because I realized when people went through chemotherapy they would lose a lot of weight, and she had no extra weight to lose. But she did it, she got through the operation with flying colors, and started the chemotherapy a month or so later. To my relief and surprise she actually gained weight on chemotherapy, which really pissed her off because she had always struggled so hard in her life to maintain her weight to be as small as what she was. She was always on one cockamamie diet after another. I remember her telling me, "Damn, I must be the only woman in the doctor's office that is actually gaining weight instead of losing it."

But I thought to myself, *Good, I'm glad to hear this.*

She went through a couple of months of chemotherapy and things seemed to be looking up. The cancer seemed to be gone and her back was hurting less every day. I guess her back pain is what originally brought her to the doctor. It seemed as though her back just started hurting her one day, and it never stopped. I guess with lung cancer this is the first warning sign I suppose. Of course I kept in very close contact with her. Every other day I would call her on the phone along with April, and she would always tell us how much better she was feeling. She was even looking forward to returning back to work within the next few weeks which was now in the middle of September.

This entire summer I spent worrying about my sister and praying, still with no results. In the middle of October of 1996 she was ready to return back to work but she felt rather self-conscious because she had lost a lot of her hair during the chemotherapy. I invited her and Rocco over to dinner one night, and she said, "Oh, this is great. I can give it the kid test," she said, "If the kids don't say anything about my hair, then I know I'm presentable enough to go back to work."

I laughed. I said, "Oh, Amber." So after telling me this of course I had to sit down with Teddy and Martin and threaten them within an inch of their lives not to say anything about Aunt Amber's hair loss. I told them she was very self-conscious about it so be very kind. They both promised me that they would.

That dinner went over fantastically. We all had a great time. Amber sitting there laughing at the two boys and their jokes and their school projects, Martin with his bug project and Teddy with his little Eskimo project. We had to build an igloo, so she really got into it with the kids that day, and she had a lot of fun with them. This was something that my heart needed to see after so many months worrying about her. Seeing her sitting there laughing with my boys, it was as though the weight of the world had lifted off my shoulders. For the first time in many, many months I could say I was happy.

So she returned back to work and back to thankfully a normal life. She and Rocco were closer now than they had ever been. They truly loved each other and you could clearly see this. Michael and I were so happy for them, but unfortunately, I'm sorry to say, they were both drinking. Amber had been so much help with Michael and me, leading us in the right directions to get help for our drinking. However, even though she tried many, many times in detoxes and programs, it just never took. She was never able to stay sober for very long, and Rocco unfortunately was drinking just as much as she was. I suppose all that mattered was that they were happy together. They truly were, and I was happy for them. I looked at them as two little lost souls who had finally found each other after many, many years of having the wrong people beside them. They finally found the right person.

It was now the beginning of November and we were looking forward to the holidays this year. Our whole family felt as though it escaped a tragedy, a tragedy that could have so easily taken our sister Amber, but spared her instead and in turn spared our family from yet another heartache. So we had even more to be grateful for this Thanksgiving, and we looked forward to sharing it together. It seemed as though just as we were being grateful for the outcome of my sister's health, something else was to hit us.

It was around the 13th of November when Michael's mother began taking a turn for the worst. It seemed as though she suffered a stroke. Michael and his brother Joe were called in right away. She remained in the nursing home and Michael and Joe both started a vigil. They were by her bed constantly giving her drops of water. Michael would refer to her as his little birdie as he placed little drops of water on her lips to keep them moist. This lasted for three days and she passed on November 16, 1996, with Michael and Joe by her side. She was 76 years old at the time of her death.

After her passing, Joe came to our home with Michael. I gave them both a huge hug, and I told them how very sorry I was. Of course they were both crushed. They did realize that their mother was in a lot of pain and had been bedridden for over a year. Again I don't know if this is terrible to say, but when a person is suffering so greatly, isn't it more of a release than a tragedy at this point? The true tragedy was that she suffered at all and for so many years. Both of them did realize this which did ease their pain if even so slightly. That night in bed I held Michael in my arms just as he held me in his through the most painful time in my life, the passing of my mom.

Through these next few days I would not leave his side for anything. I was grateful for one thing and that was that her funeral was not going to be held at the same funeral home that my mother's and Robert's were held at. At least I wouldn't have that instant replay of horror. It was held at their family's funeral home, the one that Michael was working for, and of course Teddy and Martin did attend the wake and the funeral. I sat there with Joe, Michael, Joe's wife Susan, their children, Teddy and Martin watching Michael and Joe cry.

Then Teddy began to as well, and I felt so horrible for my boys. I felt so horrible for Michael and Joe. What a life. What a beginning my children were having, facing such sorrow at such an early age and the tremendous loss. Now both of their grandmothers were gone from them forever.

I really, really worried about how this was affecting them psychologically and emotionally. I kept them as close as I possibly could, and I kept the lines of communication open. As a parent that's about all you can do. You can never prepare yourself for having to teach your children about such horror as death at such an early age. You can only explain to them that it is simply a part of life, and it's the most painful part. Martin was just two weeks shy of his 6th birthday, and Teddy had just celebrated his 9th. My God, we were not prepared as adults to handle such pain. How could we possibly expect children to do so, but yet they had to. They were forced to. Of course, my sisters were there along with Rocco as well to show their love and their support in Michael's time of need.

While at the wake Amber and I had a private moment in the corner of the funeral parlor. We sat together alone talking, and she began to cry.

"This is horrible," she said. "I feel so bad for Teddy and Martin especially to lose two grandmothers within a year."

I told her, "Don't worry about them. They will be fine. I'll make sure that they're fine. I keep them very close in my heart, and I'm constantly talking to them and keeping a clear line of communication open so I know exactly what they are thinking."

She was very happy to hear this. Then she began crying again.

I told her, "Amber, come on; snap out of it."

She said, "I can't." She went on to tell me how she was feeling. She said, "I feel like Michael's mother was taken in my place. I feel like I'm the one that is supposed to have died."

I told her, "Stop it; stop it right now. What you are saying is ridiculous. You're only 49 years old."

She said, "I know, but I just can't shake this feeling that she was taken in my place."

I felt so sad to hear her say that, and the comment itself was just so odd. I didn't know what to say to it or what to make of it, but I guess after the pressure that our whole family had been under for this past year, well over a year now, we were liable to come out with any kind of strange statements at this point. I put my arm around her, and I gave her a big hug. I told her how much I loved her and how proud I was of her. Her whole life she's fought. I told her she was the most beautiful one of us all. She was always so thin, petite and beautiful, and she always worked so hard both in her marriages and in her work. She never gave up and now with the cancer and how she fought that. I just kept telling her how proud I was of her and how much I loved her. I began telling her about Joey helping Teddy through these most difficult times and he was such a good friend to him. I also started explaining to her about this new family that had just moved in. Martin was now developing a friendship with one of the boys in this family and his name was Nick, Jr. He seemed to be getting as close to Nick, Jr. as Joey and Teddy were. I told Amber, hopefully between me keeping the children close along with an open line of communication, and the friendships, the important friendships that they were building with these two boys, this would carry them through the difficult times.

She agreed. "Yes, friends will help. It's very important."

I said, "Yes, I know."

This family was funny. The head of the household, his name was Nick, and he was a single Dad. He had two daughters, one Teddy's age, one a year younger and then one son Martin's age, and that was Nick, Jr. He was a fun-loving guy. Just like our family did with our cookouts, he also had cookouts. Practically every weekend he was out there, and Martin really took to his family and to him. Up until now Martin really hadn't had a close friendship with another guy, so I tried to cultivate and encourage this because I though it would be good for him. The four of them were always having sleep overs. Either Teddy was sleeping over Joey's house, or Joey was sleeping over our house. The same was beginning to happen with Martin and Nick—either Martin slept at Nick's or Nick slept at our house. The fun and the distraction was just what my children needed. I knew when Joey ever stayed over or Nick, Jr. stayed over, and I heard them laughing and playing just as normal children would, I knew that they were going to be okay. Then perhaps hopefully they weren't going to be as scared as I feared they would by all of this trauma in their lives at such a young age. I really liked Little Nick's father, Nick. He was such a free spirit and such a kindhearted soul. He was like a breath of fresh air over all this doom and gloom that seemed to hang over my family at this time.

So as Amber and I sat there at the back of the funeral parlor talking privately, I told her all of this, and this seemed to raise her spirits just a little bit knowing that Teddy and Martin were handling this well, and they did have help from their very special friends.

She then started asking me about my arms.

I said, "Boy, you can't leave well enough alone, can you?"

She said, "Well, you know me."

"Yeah. No, they're not doing very well." I told her what I did to try to control the pain, and she was actually quite impressed that I was able to do this. I said, "I've been practicing this now for eleven years since I hurt my hand in 1985. Just an added thing for me to have to try and block out." I told her, "I know I can do it."

She asked me if I had applied for SSI yet, and I told her I thought I was too young, and she said, "No, you can be any age. If you really can't work and you're in pain then you should apply for the SSI."

I thought about it for a moment, and I said, "I'll look into it and see if I'm eligible."

"You really should, because it would certainly help with the income."

After about half an hour of talking to Amber in private, I returned back to Michael's side. He leaned over and asked me if everything was okay, and I said, "Sure, Honey. Amber and I just needed a few moments to talk in private.

He said, "Okay."

It was becoming late and people were beginning to leave after paying their last respects. We, of course, would be there the next morning for the funeral, so we went home, took our baths and went straight to bed because we knew what was awaiting us the following day. We got up early the next morning and the four of us got ready, the boys in their little suits, me in my dress and Michael of course in his suit. We got into the car and arrived at the funeral parlor.

We were the first ones there. That's when Michael's uncle, the director of the funeral parlor, told us about John's coming in just prior to our arriving at the wake yesterday. They allowed him to attend his mother's wake, but he was heavily guarded. When Michael's uncle told us this, I felt terrible for John. I knew how hard it was for all of us to go through this, but we had each other to lean on. He had no one. He was completely alone, but I realized also John did do what he did. He took another human being's life, and for that he had to pay. This was just one more price and that was having to grieve by himself when family tragedies such as this occurred.

397

After hearing this news we went back to the main parlor and we paid our last respects. The priest came in and read a few passages from the Bible and then we began the procession to St. Paul's Church where we had the ceremony. After the ceremony we went to the cemetery where she was laid to rest right beside her husband, Michael's father, where they would be together side by side for eternity. After the funeral we had a little family gathering at Michael's aunt's house which was his mother's sister. We stayed there for a couple of hours talking with relatives that Michael had not seen in years. They were so happy to meet Teddy and Martin. I remember one of them commenting on how handsome they both were, and I said, "Yes, thank God they take after their father." Michael just shook his head and laughed at that statement.

We arrived back home. It was around 5 or 6 o'clock. The boys asked me if they could go and play over their friend's house, and I agreed. I helped them get out of their suits and into their play clothes. I knew this would be a good distraction for what they had just been through. While they were over their friend's house playing, Michael and I just lay there on the couch together snuggling up and watching TV. Our love and our closeness made all this pain bearable, and it was the only thing that did. Later on that night after the children returned home from their friend's, we gave them their baths, skipping supper because we had enough to eat at the gathering after the funeral. We then tucked them into bed. Martin insisted I read him his favorite story, "Arthur's Good Manners," and of course I was only too happy to. I was very, very glad to see a smile on both Teddy and Martin's face after the day they'd had. After that they fell fast asleep.

Michael and I found ourselves both mentally and physically exhausted. We crawled underneath the covers and held each other close. He began slowly caressing my neck and our lips met in a soft embrace. We began making love, and all the while we made love there was something else there. Something else that had never been there before and that was pain. I could feel the pain in his heart, and as close as I held him and tried hard to break through that wall of pain to reach his heart, I found it almost impossible to do for I knew he needed time, he needed time for his healing to begin. But I did what my heart needed to do, and that was hold him close and make love and just try desperately to forget not only this past day but also this past year and a half. For a moment while we were in each other's arms making love, we could if only for now if only for a few moments anyway, we could find refuge in each other, in each other's arms and in each other's hearts as we always had in the past.

We were finding through the passing of years and time that this love grew into something that was so incredible and so strong. We could feel each others heart beating and we always seemed to know exactly how the other one was feeling. I could never begin to find the words to adequately describe the tremendous love and respect that Michael and I had toward one another. The longer we were together, the more this grew and the stronger we became. All of these emotions would come to a fever pitch every time, each and every time we would make love. We also began to realize through all of this heartache and pain we were experiencing together, there was literally nothing after this we could not face as long as we remained together, and we remained as strong and as in love as we were now. Love was truly our weapon against all of life's heartaches.

It was now exactly two days after Michael's mother's funeral when the grim reaper decided to pay us yet another visit. This time it was a neighbor two doors down. It appeared he had suffered a massive heart attack in his basement. When they carried this man out on the stretcher, I had never seen anything like it before in my life. His face, his skin was a white as the sheet that partially covered his face. I looked at Michael and Michael looked at me. We were at a loss for words. This was becoming so incredible. It was like some sort of a sick dark comedy. Who was going to be next? This neighbor's name was Alex. He left behind a six-year-old daughter and a wife. While at the other end of the court Nick saw all the ambulances, fire trucks, and police cars coming in and thought the worst. He realized that we had just buried Michael's mother a couple of days before, and he thought, *My God, did Michael have a heart attack or did something happen to one of them?* I think our neighbors were beginning to think the same thing as we were, because, keep in mind, we had lost a lot of the neighbors as well. It seemed as though every time an ambulance came in, a dead body went out.

Our neighborhood, our lives had become truly sick, and we all just prayed for this to end. We wondered if this was ever going to. The body count now had reached eight, eight people since July, 1995. In the span of sixteen months eight people had been taken from us. It began with my beloved mother, then our neighbor Joe next door, then Robert, then two of our old dearest friends, Lester, and another neighbor across the court who suffered from cancer,

Michael's mother, and now Alex. Michael and I felt like we were in a boxing match, and we just kept getting hit with left and right hooks. We stood there punch drunk. That's the way we were beginning to feel, punch drunk. All of this was completely surreal. But again we had our two sons to worry about here. While all of this death was happening around us, we tried desperately to keep as much normalcy in their lives as we could keep.

After all of this, the holidays were quickly approaching. I did look forward to them, and I thank God that my sister Amber would be at our family Thanksgiving table as she always was. So I knew I had this to be grateful for, and I truly was. That Thanksgiving we spent together just as we always had as a family: April, Amber, now Rocco, Michael, our two sons and me. After Thanksgiving was of course Martin's birthday, and we had a big cake, and I decorated the house. I tried my hardest to just keep things normal. After his birthday we took him to the Christmas Parade just as we always did. We tried to keep these traditions going. We went for our Christmas tree and picked that out, and they had their usual picture taken with Santa during our walk around the Green. We tried our hardest to shield them from all the pain and all the emotions that their father and I were going through at this moment. I truly believe we were successful at doing this. Thanksgiving came and went. Martin's birthday came and went and then it was Christmas, and again the family was all together at the dinner table, and I thanked God for this.

Because we got so much snow that year the boys wanted to use their sleds right away after dinner. So I remember Amber and Bruce along with Michael walking them over to the little hill by the side of our house where they would sled almost on a daily basis during the winter. As long as there was a half an inch of snow, they would be out there. Amber really seemed to be enjoying herself and she looked well.

From December to March we had three, I'm very grateful to say, uneventful months. They were calm, and Amber was doing well until about a week before my birthday. She called me and let me know that the cancer had spread. The cancer had returned to her lungs and spread down to her liver. She was going to start chemotherapy again because as far as operations went, they didn't see a chance of her surviving them, so they went with the chemotherapy instead. After this phone call I hung up, and I sat at the edge of my bed, and I broke down, and I prayed harder than I have ever prayed in my life. I said, "Dear God, I don't know why all of this is going on, and I'm not even going to try and understand why you're doing what you are doing. Please stop, and don't do this to my sister." I sat there begging God, and I got no response. I got no good feelings. I got nothing but that blank wall again.

Michael heard my crying from downstairs and he came up to ask me what was the matter, and I told him. He said, "Oh, my God." He was floored just as badly as I was, but I told him Amber seemed convinced that this round of chemotherapy would knock the cancer out of her again.

The doctors seemed very, very hopeful, and again they gave her about a 70% chance of survival which was really good. Eighty or ninety would have been better but I was willing to settle for 70. I remember just sitting there at the edge of my bed with Michael holding me in his arms crying my heart out. I knew things weren't going to be good, and I knew my sister wasn't going to survive this. It was only a matter of when, but deep down in my heart I knew. I felt that sick feeling like I had just been kicked in the stomach.

My God, I was barely able to wrap my mind around all the deaths that had already hit our family. I was not in any way prepared to bury my sister next. I had no idea how I was going to face this.

Michael just kept telling me, "I'm here, I'm here with you, Kyra, and I love you."

It was at this point I turned to Michael, and I told him, "I don't know what you have planned for my birthday party this year, but I want it canceled, and I don't ever, ever want to celebrate my birthday again. I can't. It's just too fucking heartbreaking."

At this point in my life I just wanted to even forget the day I was born, and certainly the beautiful woman that brought me into this world now was gone out of my life forever. I had no desire to celebrate this day. A celebration just didn't seem right anymore.

Michael for the moment agreed, but he said, "We will talk about this later. It just doesn't seem right to me."

I looked at him, and I said, "Well, it seems right to me, and it is my birthday, after all, that I choose to erase from time."

It was in April that my sister Amber began her second round of chemotherapy. April and I would visit her often. She went through hell. She was very sick and throwing up all the time. She could barely keep anything down at all. On top of her dresser in her bedroom medication stretched from one end to the other. I had never seen so many bottles of medicine in my life.

We tried our best to keep her spirits high. We knew that having a positive outlook, especially with cancer patients was really very, very important, but nothing seemed to help. My heart went out to Rocco. He took such good care of my sister, and he loved her so very much. He made sure that she had her medications when she was supposed to, and he went with her to every chemotherapy treatment. He had truly become her main support system throughout this most horrifying time in her life, and for that I will be forever grateful.

Amber's chemotherapy ended around the middle to the end of May, and they were going to run some more tests to find out if it had worked. The day that she went to the doctor for the testing, Rocco of course was by her side. She had to wait four days for the results to come in, and I know these were the longest four days of her life. It was now the beginning of June of 1997 and the results were not good. The chemotherapy did not work. She was dying of cancer. It had gone from her lungs and completely attacked her liver.

This news needless to say was completely devastating to our family. We had no idea just how long she had left. All the while I was dealing with this, I tried my hardest to keep a smile on my face for my children. When I set up their pool and the grill for our family cookouts, a family that was dwindling year by year, I sat them down and talked to Teddy and Martin about what Aunt Amber was facing now, what our whole family again had to face and that was yet another loss. I told them I didn't know how much longer she had with us, and they both began to cry.

The three of us sat there crying together for a few moments, and Teddy asked me, "Mommy, why does God keep calling everybody that we love home?"

I had no answer to this question. My faith at best was on very, very shaky grounds. All I could tell him was, "Mommy doesn't know." I also said, "I don't understand any more than you do about why God does what he does. I suppose he has his reasons."

I then reminded them both that Grandma and Nana along with Robert would not like to see us crying and feeling such pain. After all we do know, that they are in Paradise again, and this is what we have to keep in mind. They are home in God's loving arms, and Amber unfortunately will soon be joining them. I also knew that my mother would come for Amber and help her cross over. I told them both that too.

After this I tried my hardest to keep their minds occupied and not think so much about Amber. I didn't want their lives to be consumed with waiting for this fateful day to come. I knew I had to keep them busy, and perhaps I had to keep myself busy. So I would work every day with Martin and his drawings and play board games with him, and I would encourage Teddy to do his stunts on his bike with the ramp and go skate boarding and roller blading just as he did ever summer. I would try so hard through these horrifying years of their young lives to keep as much normalcy in their lives as I could.

Unfortunately, as the years passed by and our losses just became greater this would be very, very difficult to do. I just focused on what made them happy and what they had fun doing and tried my hardest to encourage this and join them. I had to do this with a smile on my face with my heart breaking inside all the while. I would do this week after week after coming home from visiting my sister Amber and seeing her become more and more consumed by cancer. She slowly was turning into someone that was becoming totally unrecognizable to me. The cancer was literally eating her up. She went from about 125-130 pounds down to 80 in a span of a year. She was literally skin and bones. Her face had become sunken, and her hair was almost nonexistent due to the chemotherapy. I slowly watched my beautiful vibrant sister turn into a skeleton, and it seemed to me to be practically overnight.

It was the first two weeks in July that I hadn't gone to see her. Up until this point I was visiting her every other day. I needed a break. I needed to shut my mind off for a few days. I needed to concentrate on my children's mental health and the spend time with them just thinking about them. So I took this time. I took these two weeks. In the process of these two weeks I called her quite often. I always kept in touch, and she would tell me that she was actually feeling better. She and Rocco actually went to the grocery store, and she went shopping. I was saying to myself, *Jeeze, you know, hopefully she'll be around a little while longer. Maybe she's getting stronger.* You know as I said in the book before, denial is a great place to visit but unfortunately you can't live there. She was in denial, and I was in denial. We didn't want this day when she was going to pass to ever, ever come. We didn't even want to think about planning for it at this point so of course when she was giving me this good news, I eagerly accepted this as fact.

It wasn't until April came over for one of our cookouts. It was just April, me, Michael, and the two boys who were there. She and I began discussing

Amber, and I told her, "I think Amber seems to be getting a little bit better."

She looked at me and she said, "Kyra, what are you talking about?"

I said, "Well, I've been talking to her on the phone, and she told me that she went shopping with Rocco."

"Kyra, she never went shopping with Rocco. She sat in the car and waited while Rocco ran into the grocery store and grabbed a few items of food, mainly popsicles because that's all she's eating right about now."

That's when it hit me, that old denial that through my whole life I so eagerly embraced when times got hard or when I didn't want to face what I knew I was going to have to face. Believe me when I say it is so easy to step into denial because it is a nice safe place. You can make up a whole new world. Anything you want to happen in that world of denial can happen, but it's just a trick of the mind. It is not even close to reality, and it is something that everyone must really look out for because it is such a comforting place to be but it's not real.

I was so eager to believe Amber. I was so eager to throw myself into the world of denial yet again in my life that I couldn't see what was right in front of me. I couldn't believe that I actually allowed myself to do this, but I wanted it so badly. I wanted to fantasize that my sister was going to be fine. How stupid I was. So when April told me all of this, it hit me like a bag of bricks. I realized what I had done in accepting what Amber was telling me about how she was doing. Now I had to face reality once more and accept that my sister was dying.

It was about the third week in July April and I went to visit her, and we spent a few hours just talking. She relaxed on the couch with her bandana on. As she sucked on one Popsicle after the other, she told me jokingly as she poked me with her elbow, she said, "You know, Kyra, these can become very addictive," she said. "I can't seem to get enough of them."

She especially liked the cherry ones, and I laughed and said, "Well, I suppose given our family's history, becoming addicted to popsicles would be the least of our worries."

She said, "Yeah, really."

April and I had a nice visit with her. For the next couple of weeks we visited on and off. Thank God for one thing and that was she wasn't in a huge amount of pain, but it was always her back. Her back is what hurt her the most.

A strange thing occurred with me. It was about the third week in July after one of our visits. I don't know if it was psychosomatic or what it was, but my back starting hurting me, and for the following week it progressively got worse, and worse, and worse. It got to the point where I could barely bend over to tie my shoes. Of course, I thought to myself, *Oh, oh. Do I have the same thing Amber does? Perhaps I should go see a doctor because this is how her cancer started out, with back pain.*

All through Amber's cancer treatment her back pain really never went away. I thought I would wait a little before going to see my doctor. It was now the first of August when April, Michael, the two boys, and I went to visit Amber. This was the first time I brought the boys up to see her in a couple of months. I wasn't sure how much time she had left, so I wanted them to have one last visit with her. On this day I could barely walk, because the pain in my back had become so severe.

After sitting at the kitchen table where the six of us were having a nice little visit, the boys were so strange. I guess it was a good thing that they didn't seem to be able to pick up on what she looked like now. They didn't see her the way April, Michael, and I did. It was like there was nothing wrong with her. This was the way they acted. They didn't whisper to me, "Mommy, what's the matter with Amber?" or "Why is Amber so skinny?" or "Why does she have a bandana on her head?" It was as though they didn't see any of that at all. They just saw their Aunt Amber sitting there looking the same way she always did. I don't know. Perhaps they were in their own little world of denial.

After a couple of hours Amber was becoming very tired, and it was time for her medication, so we decided it was time to end our visit. We all gave her a huge hug and a kiss and told her how very much we all loved her. April, Michael and the two boys had already left the apartment and I straggled behind. While I was standing at the door with Amber just before she was ready to close it I gave her one last hug, and she whispered in my ear, "Pray for me, Kyra."

I can't even begin to tell you how those words cut through my heart. You see, I never let anyone know, including Michael, the struggle that my soul was having right now and how I was unable to pray, or should I say not unable to pray, but just feeling as though there was nothing there. Her words while cutting through my heart also angered me, and in my blind anger I said to my dying sister, "Why should I pray? What good would it do? What good has it done me so far?"

She stood there with a horrified look on her face, and she said, "Oh, Kyra," and she gave me a kiss on the cheek. I again told her how much I loved her and how proud I was of her, and then I just turned and walked away.

I remember that drive on the way back home after leaving Amber's. How hollow I felt inside, how terribly empty. I could feel my eyes welling up, and I literally choked back the tears, thinking about God and praying, and about my immortal soul. Have I been damned and if so what in hell did I do to deserve this? What in the hell did Amber do to deserve this and my mother? There are so many questions and absolutely no answers. That night I could barely sleep my back was hurting so badly. I called Amber that morning and we spoke, not very long, maybe fifteen minutes because she wasn't feeling well at all. As usual we ended our conversation with, "I love you, and I'll talk to you tomorrow."

This was now August 2, and I could barely get out of bed my back was in such pain. I remember telling Michael that day I was going to make an appointment to see the doctor because I didn't know what was going on, and it wasn't getting any better. It was just getting worse, and he agreed, of course.

On the morning of August 3, 1997, I woke up realizing I had slept through the night. Obviously the pain in my back wasn't that bad anymore, and to my surprise I got up and stood up with absolutely no pain whatsoever. It was like I didn't even have it to begin with. Then it hit me. It hit my heart so hard. I knew Amber was gone. I can't tell you how I knew. I just knew. That backache was completely gone. Now the feeling in the pit of my stomach was there, that feeling of being dropped into a huge pit, a huge black hole, replaced the pain in my back, and I knew. I sat at the edge of the bed, and I cried. Michael asked me if I was crying because of the pain in my back, and I said, "No, I'm crying because there is no longer a pain in my back, and my sister Amber's dead."

He said, "Kyra, how could you possibly know that? Call her."

I said, "No, I don't want to because I know."

He went out to the doorstep to pick up the morning paper, and I sat at the kitchen table with my cup of coffee trying to gather my thoughts and my emotions, knowing all the while what I was going to have to face that day. He opened the paper to the obituaries and saw her name right there because she had died that night. They were able to get it in the morning *Gazette*. I remember this so well, Michael reading it and looking over the paper at me and telling me how very sorry he was. After those words left his lips, my heart shattered into a million pieces. You see, it's very different feeling it and thinking it, and then absolutely without a doubt being told it. Once the words are spoken, once you know for fact, once it is there in black and white, that's when it finally hits you and it hits you like a bag of bricks. I just got up from the kitchen table. I took my cup of coffee into the bedroom, I closed the bedroom door, and I went back to bed. I lay there, crying my heart out, in a fetal position, for hours.

It was after lunch that April came over, and she told Michael that she was with Amber when she passed that night. She also told Michael that she didn't realize that the Gazette would have time to put Amber's name in the obituaries, and she was going to come now and tell me what happened last night. Michael said, "There is no need to. She already knew." Then I read it from the Gazette to her.

Michael told April, "Kyra knew that Amber was dead before the Gazette even came."

April just nodded her head. She said, "I know," she said, "You know our family and the weird things that have gone on."

He said, "Yes, I'm familiar with all the stories."

I pulled myself together enough to go downstairs to talk to April, and she told me that Amber went peacefully on the couch. She was sitting beside her watching TV, and it was as though she just went to sleep. All the while I just simply couldn't get out of my head my last words to my sister, who I loved dearly, and what I said to her when she asked me to pray for her. These words will now haunt me for the rest of my life until my dying day. I will never forgive myself. This will be a major regret that I will have to live with that concerned my sister Amber. How could I have ever been so cold to her and become so angry at her words when she was simply asking me to pray for her. I went to my room and was crying my heart out in a fetal position for hours right after getting the confirmation from the obituaries in the paper that she truly was dead. That was all I could think about.

Those words haunted me and made my heart hurt even worse. My last words to my sister Amber were cruel instead of loving and supportive, and I will never ever be able to forgive myself for that. April went on to tell me that Mr. Silva at the Morton Funeral Home came to pick our sister up. That was where her funeral was going to be held, the same place as Robert's and my mother's. I said to myself, *Oh, God, another horrifying instant replay.* It truly was right up to those same familiar stairs that my knees always shook at, that same familiar handshake by Mr. Silva, and then walking into the viewing room. Again there was no difference except for the person who was lying there—the same room, the same positioning of the casket, the same everything. Again, I chose not to bring Teddy and Martin to this. I did ask them if they wanted to go. I kind of left it up to them, since they were so close to Amber. They both told me, "No." They wanted to remember her as she was the last time we visited. I was very relieved to hear them say this, because I knew when I walked into that funeral home, and I saw my sister and what she looked like, as an adult I could barely keep control of my emotions. I can't even begin to imagine how they would have, because what we buried did not resemble my sister whatsoever.

All the past deaths and now my sister, it all came rushing back to me all at once—all the pain, all the anguish, and all the heartache. I just felt like my guts were being ripped out. When I leaned over to kiss my sister's hand, a hand that was so cold to my lips, I was just horrified by her appearance. Even though Mr. Silva did the best job he could, there is only so much you can do. Again, as Michael stood there by my side praying for her, I sat there reading her funeral card, just as I did with Robert's. Her funeral card would become something very special to me. In a few more years it would become my most favorite poem. The name of the poem was "Footprints in the Sand," written by Mary Stevenson. I tried desperately to gather as much comfort from this poem as I possibly could at this moment. This poem describes a person seeing himself walking on the beach, a walk that represents his life. The man notices that when things were going well there were two sets of footprints, he presumes his and the Lord's, but when he was having a difficult time there was only one. He confronts the Lord about abandoning him when he needed him most. The Lord answers, "My dearest sweet child, don't you know that that one set of footprints was mine? Through these times of trouble when you needed me the most, I was carrying you."

I thought to myself after reading this, *Why, why isn't the Lord now carrying me?* I suppose at this time I just couldn't see the truth. My heart was still so filled with hate toward God, and it seemed like through every passing death it just grew stronger and stronger. Even though I tried to pray and I tried to talk to him, that blank wall remained. So why was I now being denied? Why couldn't I be like that man on the beach and feel the Lord carrying me and helping me? Perhaps it would have overridden my hate if he had shown just the slightest bit of compassion toward me, but I realized that maybe my hate was just blocking all the good from coming in, all of God's good and God's grace from healing me now. I truly did not know.

After we paid our respects, Michael and I went over to sit by April and Rocco, and I couldn't help but to look around at everyone, the few of us that were left now, and wonder who was going to be next. Who was going to be the next person lying in that casket there in the same room in the same spot? It was just so overwhelming. The pain, the sorrow, and the heartache were all consuming to me at this point. All I could do was close my eyes and just try to remove myself from where I had to be at this moment. I sat there, and I could no longer stand looking at my sister Amber in the condition that she was in. I closed my eyes and tried my hardest to remember the happy days, the days when I used to watch her and her boyfriend dancing to the Temptations and to the Beatles. The days not too long ago when she was so beautiful.

I tried to block all my pain out with memories of happy times, but also, along with these memories of the happy times came memories of my father, who was around at these times that I was trying so desperately to remember. He was a part of it all as well. In my heart and in my soul I held him directly responsible for my sister's death now. He's the one that planted the seed of hate toward him, a hate that she was never, ever able to overcome. A hate that ate at her like a cancer long before she was diagnosed with it. When you carry this hate and this resentment in you for as long as she had in her life, almost her entire life, I truly believe it can become toxic and poisonous to you. This was my father's legacy that he left behind, broken daughters in one way or another. Amber was psychologically affected by him and began this hate toward him that lasted until the day she died.

April told me about the conversation she and Amber had a couple of year's earlier. When Amber ever started talking about my father and the things that he did to her. It was as though it happened yesterday. I truly believe in her mind at that moment, it did happen yesterday, the pain was so strong and that hate was so real. That's why she was never able to completely stop drinking even though she tried time and time again. I credit her for Michael's sobriety and mine. Without her guidance I don't know if we would have been able to find the right people to help us. She was able to save Michael and me, but she was not able to save her own self. This is the saddest part of all. So, yes, I held my father completely, utterly responsible now for her death.

April came away from the relationship, if that's what you want to call it, with my father with a different set of problems. Her personality was slightly different from Amber's. Instead of drowning herself in a bottle, her fixation for food was what drove her because so many times we went hungry. I suppose if you go hungry enough times as a child, when you become an adult you always need to make sure that there is plenty of food in the house. This was April's fixation. Amber had the alcohol. April had the food, and both of them had the lowest self-esteem that I had ever seen in my life. He took everything from them, things that he was not able to take from me. But then again, they were forced to live with him for a lot longer than I did. Neither one of them ever felt good about herself, about her appearance, about where she lived, or how she acted. There was nothing that they felt good about, and that's a horrible, horrible way to live. To actually think that your own father was the one that condemned you to feeling like this for the rest of your life has to be one of the biggest tragedies of them all, the biggest tragedy in our family. It was even worse than all the deaths now. To look back and remember what he did to them, all I can hope and pray for now is that he has found his proper place in Hell.

These were all of the thoughts that ran through my mind as I sat there among the few loved ones that were left in my life: Michael, April and now Robert's children who had joined our family. Again, I couldn't help but to look around and wonder who was going to be next. Who among us were we going to have to say goodbye to? Which one of us was to be the next one lying in that casket? I realized I had to stop thinking this way. I had to stop these negative thoughts from entering my brain. Michael, as supportive as he always was, at that moment put his arm around me. I can't tell you how much better that made me feel, feeling that sense of deep connection and deep love that just radiated off of him toward me. He carried me through all of this pain and all of this heartache.

I was concerned about April more so than anyone because she and Amber were very, very close. They shared everything growing up because they were closest in age, and they had remained close all through these years. They were more than sisters. They were best friends, and I realized how horrible this was on April because she was not only losing a sister, but also a best friend. I told her after the wake to come home with Michael and me and have something to eat, but she refused. She said, "No, Kyra, I'll be fine. I just want to be alone right now." So I respected that. I told her if she needed to talk to me, just pick up the phone, and I'd be there. She gave me a big hug with tears in her eyes, got into her car, and left, just as Michael and I did.

The next morning we all met back at the funeral parlor where the priest came in and gave a little service. My sister Amber was to be cremated. When we went back into the funeral parlor, we went into the viewing room again to pay our last respects. I told her how much I loved her, and how proud I was of everything that she accomplished in her life. I also told her what a hard worker she was, what a good big sister she was to me always, and what a marvelous aunt she had been to my two boys. Something hit me as I was kneeling by her casket with Michael beside me. I thought to myself, *I know Mom came and got you, and I know you're with her.* A sense of peace came over me, the only peace I felt through any of this, through all these heartaches and all this time. I knew she was finally going to be okay. Her misery here on earth was over. Her torture from all the memories our father pushed upon her was all over now. I knew. I could feel it. She was at peace. This realization did give me much comfort. I just kept thinking to myself, *My God, she was only 50 years old.* Maybe her work here was done. I don't know. I don't think anyone truly knows the answers. Maybe this is what we find out when we pass. Maybe then and only then are we presented all the answers to all the questions that we have ever had in life. I hope so anyway.

After the church ceremony they took my sister to the crematory, and I again asked April if she would care to come home with Michael and me to be with the kids for a while and not be alone. But again she said that she would like very much right now to be alone. She needed to collect her thoughts and her emotions. I agreed. I said, "Okay," but I told her I'd call her that night, and I did.

The day after the funeral when I went to bed that night it seemed as though I was bombarded by memories both good and bad, but mostly bad. I remembered how much Amber and April protected me from my father and how much courage that must have taken for them to do so. They took beatings for me, slaps, and punches. They went without food to make sure I did not. Thinking back on these times something else also entered my memory. Something that I had long forgotten and never, ever wanted to remember again, but it came back to me this night. This was only the tip of the iceberg. This was only one incident that stood out in my memory. There were many others.

This one day I remember I was six years old. I was in first grade, and I came down with the mumps. I also had tonsillitis on top of it. I could barely swallow. My mother and April went to the grocery store because we were completely out of food and they had to get my medicine as well. So, my father was left in charge. My mother thought this was okay as long as he was sober, and he was sober at the time but evidently hung over. I lay there in my bed in my room sucking on a cough drop trying to get some kind of a liquid down into me. I had trouble swallowing my own saliva. At this point my father yelled to stop making such noises. I guess I was making too loud a noise while I was sucking on my cough drop because I couldn't breathe through my nose. I couldn't make out what he was saying. I just heard him yell but didn't know what he yelled. The next thing I knew the door to my bedroom flew open and my father charged me like a rampaging bull. He ran over and grabbed me by my throat that was extremely swollen already because of the mumps. He picked me up by my throat and held me up against the wall, my toes just barely touching the floor.

He kept screaming at me, "When I tell you to do something, do it!"

I had no idea what he was talking about.

He said, "I told you to stop sucking on the cough drop."

That was the last thing I remembered. I must have blacked out because of the pain. The next thing I knew I woke up in my bed, and he had left my room. I could hear him out in the kitchen, slamming pots and pans around, and I just lay there crying, asking myself, *Why, why does my daddy enjoy hurting me so much?*

Thank God it was only a few minutes after that I heard my mother and April's voice in the kitchen. My father just stormed out of the house. I didn't tell them what happened. I didn't tell them what he did, and I never would. I knew even at that young age he just enjoyed inflicting pain not only on children, but he would go out to the bars and fight the biggest guy and win. He wasn't a coward. He was just insane. I made it my life's goal for as long as I had to endure living with him too never, ever show anything, not pain, not love. This was only one of the reasons why. I decided if he had no love for me in his heart, I would have none for him. Certainly picking a six-year-old girl up like that by her throat, there was no love there and there was certainly no compassion. My heart just went cold toward him, and it never changed. There was nothing that he did after that that showed me he was even human. So this was why I stayed the way I stayed toward my father.

My sisters on the other hand, I don't know. I guess their love for him was never completely extinguished as was mine, because they always seemed to care about what he thought where I could have given a fuck less. I found when you shut yourself off from a certain person there is no way that they can hurt you, because the only way a person can hurt you is if you love them or you feel something toward them, and I simply did not. But the ones I did love were my mother, April and Amber. They were always so good to me and so protective. They truly deserved all of my respect and all of my love, and I showed it to them. We built a bond that would never be broken even through death. I still feel my mother and Amber's love. Laying there that night remembering all of these memories both good and bad, I also remembered that love does live on and it got me through.

I lay in bed a couple of days just resting. Michael insisted that I do this, just take a little time to myself, a little time off. I would speak with April over the phone but that would be about all the communication I would have with the outside world. Michael spent a lot of time with the boys over the next two days taking them fishing or just out walking. Michael allowed me that time, the precious time that I needed to begin my healing and it helped immensely.

On the third day I got up out of bed and the first thing I did was grab my sketchbook. Even though my hands were sore I still enjoyed drawing. I found this to be very therapeutic and a release of my energy and pain. I guess you could call it my little escape right now. I had been actually working on some sketches over the past six months. Again, it was a good diversion and good therapy. I had started drawing inventions that would just pop into my head, things that I thought would be useful. Over the past six months and into the next couple of months I would work on perfecting these inventions. I was actually seriously considering making this my career, so I worked very hard on it. I did find a company who would help me submit my inventions to certain manufacturers. Yes, they did. The manufacturers thought that it was a good idea, but they just didn't have the resources at that time to put into making prototypes, and I didn't have the resources either. So it kind of went nowhere, but it was a good distraction. It was something to take my mind off of my pain.

It was shortly after Amber's death that I was approved for SSI because of my arms, so the added income did help immensely in our family's finances. It was now September, and I had been trying my hardest to deal with this great loss in my life. I was constantly distracted by the children's activities, distractions that I very much needed at this time. They were starting school and gathering new school clothes. There were meetings with their new teachers, getting them straightened out in their classes, and doing everything parents do with their kids at the beginning of the school year. I also tried to get involved with their school. It was not only good for them but it was good for me as well. Psychologically it kept me busy. I knew this is what I needed to do right now.

Before we knew it, it was Halloween. I did a lot of extra work with the kids this Halloween. I dressed Teddy up in a Werewolf costume. I got a bunch of cheap wigs from the store, and I glued the hair to his arms, his chest, and his head and his face. He looked absolutely fantastic. I would have done the same with Martin, but he insisted on being a cowboy. I would bring Rice Crispy treats to their class party for Halloween. This is something I did every year. We went out Trick or Treating that night. I remember these years so fondly, and I remember having so much fun with my two babies.

You know, I was hit with a lot of heartbreaking things in my life and most recently some very overwhelming ones, but my kids made life worth living. They provided such a beautiful, beautiful distraction from all the pain. They are the ones that helped me through all of this right along with Michael. I know they don't know what they did for me, but I guess they will now, now that it's actually in writing, in print. I will forever be grateful to Michael, Teddy and Martin for pulling me out of Hell, pulling me out of that pit of despair. They truly saved me, my three little angels.

It was now the second week in November when something odd started occurring. I began getting dizzy spells, and my hearing was going kaphoey. My hearing would become really, really sharp at one point, and then at another point almost deafening and my eyes would become sharp as well and then go to almost where I couldn't see. I had no idea what was going on with me. I went to my doctor and explained everything that I was feeling, and she sat there just looking down at her paper and she shook her head.

She said, "Kyra, I don't know how to tell you this, but you have all the classic systems of MS."

I just sat there, numb. I said, "You have to be kidding me."

She said, "No, let's just have some tests run, and we can take it from there." So she set up an MRI for my brain. I would have to wait a couple of days.

When I arrived home I didn't tell Michael. I didn't let on that anything was wrong. I told him, "The doctor just wants me to have an MRI done just to eliminate certain things." I didn't let on how worried I was. I couldn't frickin' believe it.

Thank God the days passed quickly. I had my test, and then I returned back to the doctor and she told me great news, "No, it's not MS. They couldn't find anything wrong at all."

At this point I said, "Well, what in the Hell is going on with me? Why am I dizzy? Why are my eyes and ears doing these things?"

She said, "Have you been under a lot of stress? Sometimes that will happen." I then sat there and began explaining to her what our family's life had been like since 1995 when my mother passed.

She said, "Oh, that's probably it. The stress has just caught up to you." Then she went on to tell me the exact results of this MRI that was done on my brain. She said, "There is one odd comment that they made. The technicians that read the MRI said that you have an old brain."

I laughed. I said, "What do you mean, an old brain?"

She said, "I don't know exactly what that means. That was their finding."

So, I just laughed and shook my head in relief that I didn't have MS, but then I thought, *What exactly does an 'old brain' mean?* I don't know. I never did find out. I just let it go. Weird enough things were happening in my life as it was.

When I got home I told Michael what the results were, and we just held each other in complete relief for the longest time. Then I told him the comment the technician said when he read the MRI about my having an old brain, and he just laughed.

He said, "Of course, the most bizarre thing that could happen would happen to you."

I think all the stress of course from all the deaths had just caught up to me, and I knew we were facing the upcoming holidays; Thanksgiving, Martin's birthday, Christmas and New Year's. I knew I was going to face them with yet another family member gone. I'm grateful to say in a couple of weeks these symptoms did pass and they never returned.

So we had Thanksgiving Dinner. Michael, Martin, Teddy, April, and I enjoyed a beautiful turkey dinner that year, and after a day or so it was Martin's birthday. We had his party and took him to the Christmas Parade just as usual. April and I didn't talk much about all the deaths. Instead we chose to look toward the future, and the future for us seemed to be going well. She had just started a great paying job at Johnson & Johnson. The money was very good there, and with the added money she was able to do more things with my sons. She would take them to the movies, to the mall, or just for ice cream. She spent a lot of time with them. She was such a great aunt, and she gave them lovely childhood memories just as their father and I tried to do even through all the sadness. We knew as long as we stuck together and that great love was there it would carry us through everything, and it did.

With the passing of Amber, April and I did become even closer as sisters than we were before. We did become really good friends as well. She began sharing a lot of her life with me, what she was thinking and what she was feeling. That family gift that we shared was becoming even stronger as the years passed and with the passing of our loved ones. We always felt that deep connection to them. Even after their death we could feel them now and again around us. Each and every time we did it was so comforting. Every time she felt it she'd let me know, and every time I felt it I'd let her know. It got to the point where we would laugh, and it got to the point where we would now be able to talk about these feelings freely without feeling sad. We would talk about the fun times and the laughs that we all had together. That's what is so important, to remember the good times. That's what carries you through the grief in your life.

Christmas came and went. We had our traditional gathering which of course now was only April, but we tried to live in the moment and enjoy every second that we had together. It was now 1998, or I should say it was going to be because this was New Year's, and Michael and I spent it the way we always spent it, together in each other's arms on the couch by the soft glow of the Christmas tree, watching the clock ringing in the New Year. Of course, we would make love, a love that just grew more and more by the passing years. After we made love Michael and I both toasted the New Year with a cup of eggnog.

Our boys were growing up. Teddy was now 10 years old and Martin 7, and we were both really proud of them. They were growing into good, good young men. What I started to notice about their personalities was that through all the pain that they had suffered through the years of their young lives, it gave them a great sense of empathy toward other people's pain. I noticed that whenever I would take them to the mall or the grocery store and we would see a handicapped person in a wheelchair, or on crutches they would look at them with much sympathy. At that young age I thought that was a great thing.

I knew in my heart they were going to be okay. They had made it through these horrible years unscarred by all the pain. It actually seemed to have made them stronger children and much more aware of the pain that other people have to go through. Because of the things that they went through, they were much more aware of life and what life can throw at you than most other children their age. They seemed to be more mature, and I thought perhaps this wasn't such a horrible thing after all. I hoped and prayed as adults maybe they would be able to help other people through horrible times, such as times that they had to endure in their lives. Perhaps they would be counselors or psychiatrists. This I hoped for, but of course I wouldn't push my ideas onto them. They were way too young yet. I thought maybe as they grew older they would make these decisions on their own. All of this was yet to come. As I said, they were only 7 and 10 years old.

Lying there that night that New Year's Eve, New Year's Eve of 1998, Michael did discuss this. We talked a lot about the boys and how well they were doing and how proud we were of them. We looked forward to watching them grow into young adults, and we looked forward to the coming year with great expectation. Michael also wanted to start taking Martin out with Teddy target shooting. He said this is another fun thing that I can enjoy with my sons. I kind of just grunted and said, "Well, we'll see." Keep in mind Martin was not like Teddy. He was the quiet, sensitive artist, where Teddy was the He Man, so I wasn't quite sure if I was ready to let my little baby, my sensitive little artist baby go yet. After this a sense of normalcy did start returning back into my family's life, thank God.

It was now February and things were going smoothly. April was coming over quite often, mainly on the weekend, and she and I would sit at the kitchen talking over cups of coffee. It was then I began telling her about the dreams that I was having, rather disturbing dreams about Mom. I told her they were not that bad now. They were really bad before I told her. I was waking up with night terrors and running to the phone in my sleep needing to call her. It was such a sense of urgency that I would feel totally anxiety ridden. I told her this lasted for about three months after Mom passed.

She said, "I had no idea you were going through that."

I said, "Yeah, but thank God it passed. If it hadn't I would have had to speak with someone about it, but now I'm beginning to have dreams, odd dreams. In my dreams now we're having a family gathering, and everyone's there but Mom, and all of a sudden I go into a panic, and I start asking people, 'Have you spoken to Mom lately?' and I remembered in my dream that it had been months since I had spoken to her. I then go into that panic state again. I can't seem to shake it, and I can't seem to be able to stop these dreams."

She told me, "Oh, I'm sorry, Kyra, that you're going through this."

She had no answers. Of course, there weren't any answers. These dreams now would go on for years on and off. They would become less frequent but nevertheless traumatic, and every time I would have one of these nightmares, I would break out in a cold sweat shaking beside Michael. It would take me almost the remainder of the night to get over it, to get over this trauma.

I guess it was around March, about a month after I told April about all of these dreams I was having, when Martin told me as soon as he got into the car after I picked him up from school that he saw Amber. He was playing Hide and Seek at recess with a few of his friends, and he said, "I went around a tree to hide, and she was standing there. She was just standing there." He said, "Mom, she was beautiful. She had long, black hair and the biggest brown eyes, and she was dressed in white. She leaned down and asked me how I was doing, and how my dad and Teddy were, and especially how you were. She told me, 'You take good care of your mom now.'"

When he told me this the hair on the back of my neck stood up. It was just his description of her that made this ring so true. This is what she looked like when I was younger. This is what I remember growing up seeing her look like, exactly the way he described, and he, of course, did not know her then. I didn't have very many pictures of her. Unfortunately while growing up poor, taking pictures is the last thing on the list. The first thing would be food, so there weren't very many family pictures taken. He had no idea what she looked like when she was younger, so for him to describe her now to a T, I just wanted to cry. How I prayed that she could have visited me in the way she visited him, but I guess that wasn't to be. I then had to have a little talk with him, the same as I had with Teddy after he saw my mother. I just gave them a little information, as little as I possibly could just so they wouldn't think they were losing their mind or seeing things.

I told him no, "What you saw was very real," and I told him if he saw anything else to please always come and talk to me about it because you can. I told him, "You should feel like a very, very special little boy right now because Aunt Amber just gave you a gift. She was actually able to come back and talk with you."

He was thrilled over this. He was just so happy. There was not one ounce of sadness in his voice or in his eyes as he described all of this to me.

Again, it was just simply matter of fact, but also those old worries started hitting me. He now had the same experience that Teddy had and that was seeing a loved one that passed. I was hoping that door wouldn't open any further for them both. But just in case it did, I had to stress the point to them that they were not to talk with anyone else but me about these things, and for them to let me know immediately after seeing someone that passed. They both promised me they would; they would follow my instructions. I remember giving him a huge hug and reminding him just how special he was and what a beautiful gift he was just given by Aunt Amber.

Now it was April, and Teddy did have yet another gift given to him, which was very similar to the one before. It was in the back of Nick's house by a tree in his yard. Both my mother and Amber were there, and they were again young and beautiful. Teddy went up to talk to both of them, and their questions were always the same. "How's your mom doing, your dad, and your brother?" They asked him if he was being a good boy.

After seeing and talking with them he came running back home to tell me immediately, just as he promised he would, and I was floored because I knew now they were together. Mom was protecting her little girl as she always did, and I also knew that I was right that Mom did come for Amber and helped her cross over just as I felt. Teddy was so thrilled to tell me this. Again there's not one ounce of sorrow to be felt by these spirits, only good, and only love. Love is what lives on and love was the emotion that they gave off whenever they talked to Teddy or Martin.

Again, I reminded Teddy of how special this was and what a great gift this was. This was their way of letting you know that they're always watching out for you and that they will always, always love you. The look of joy that was in Teddy's eyes was indescribable. I thought to myself, *If my children are going to be given this gift, what a great way for them to find out.*

What a great introduction this was, and I hoped they would always be able to see them every now and again to feel that love that would radiate off of them. Now that's a gift. That's something that I would love to have been able to do, to be able to experience, and I hoped and prayed that they would experience this many, many more times in their lives. Perhaps it would happen when they needed to feel that love the most. Perhaps then they would come back to visit

Teddy and Martin to offer love and support to them both when they could see them going through difficult times and knew that they needed them now. Perhaps they could come and visit them, my mother and Amber both, through heartbreaking times in my children's lives as they grew older. It would be wonderful if they could always just do this and perhaps even help guide them, guide them to the right choice or just carry them through it with that feeling, that great feeling of love that they both felt toward Teddy and Martin. If they could have this happen to them many more times, I couldn't think of a better gift they could be given.

It was now the end of April, and Michael and I were sitting at the kitchen table one evening after supper having coffee. Michael told me then about these weird feelings he was getting in his mouth, that he felt these little lumps on the roof of his mouth. He then went out to the car and got the flashlight. He said, "I've been putting this off for a couple of weeks now. I felt these now for a while. I just keep forgetting to bring the flashlight in the house so I could look at them."

Michael and I then went up the bathroom and he shined the flashlight in his mouth, I could see on the roof of his mouth three or four little white speckles, and I asked him, "What the hell is that?"

He said, "I don't know, but I have my doctor's appointment tomorrow." He had to go to the VA not only for his psychiatrist sessions, but also for his diabetes. They were treating him and giving him his medication for that as well. He said, "I'll show the nurse tomorrow," and he did that next day when he went.

She immediately had him go and see the dentist at the VA. The dentist quickly transferred him to the ENT (ear, nose, and throat doctor). The doctor took a little biopsy, and Michael had to wait a few days to get the results back, which coincided with his visit to his psychiatrist. So he figured, "Well, this is good. I can kill two birds with one stone."

After his psychiatrist appointment on the fourth day, he went to see the EMT. It wasn't good news. The EMT told him that he had soft-palate cancer, but the good thing was it was right at the beginning stage. He then found out what they were going to have to do. They were going to have to remove that portion of his palate and also remove all of his teeth in order to be able to make a prosthesis to fit in his mouth so that he would be able to eat.

He told me he sat in the car out in the parking lot of the VA for over an hour, trying to comprehend what was just told to him, and he clung to the fact that they assured him it was at the beginning stages, and his survival rate was very, very good. They also told him that most people that did catch this at the beginning did survive.

So that night when he returned home after supper while the children were playing in the living room he gave me all of this information, and I'm telling you right now you could not have hurt me any more if you had literally taken a sledge hammer to my heart. This completely and totally floored me. This was about the worst possible news you could ever imagine we could have received, even though the prognosis was good and it was at its earliest stages. We couldn't even wrap our mind around it. I couldn't wrap my mind around even the slightest possibility of me losing this man, this part of me, a part of my soul, and a part of my heart. I couldn't even let my mind go down that road at this time even if there was one chance, one percent, and one possibility that I would lose him. This was devastating to me even though he kept telling me the prognosis was very good, the doctor's told him, and he kept reassuring me that he was going to be okay.

The thought of everything at that moment just came crushing down on my soul and on my shoulders, a pressure that I had never, ever felt before in my life. Even through all these losses, I never felt this way or this bad. It devastated me to even think of the possibility, the possibility of his having to endure even more physical pain now than he ever did mentally, and the possibility of my children now having to face a life without their father in it and my having to face a life without the only man that I ever truly loved in it. At that moment I felt like my brain was going to snap. All I could feel was my heart breaking and my soul being crushed, and then it quickly dawned on me, the children.

I drew back away from Michael, and I said to him, "What are we supposed to tell Teddy and Martin after all their recent losses and all their little heartbreaks? How were we now going to be able to tell them something like this?"

Michael said, "We aren't. Don't tell them about this cancer, because they are going to think, "Cancer, this is what Aunt Amber had. This isn't like that at all. It's not that type of cancer, but that's what they're going to think if you say the word 'cancer,' so don't. Just tell them that Daddy has something wrong with the top of his mouth, and he has to go and have a little bit of surgery done at the dentist."

This is what we decided to first tell them, that Daddy had to have his teeth out and he had a little something wrong with the top of his mouth, but he was going to be fine. He was going to have to go to the hospital to have a little operation. So this is what we did. We went into the living room and sat Martin and Teddy down and told them this, and when they heard the word, "dentist," I could see a sense of relief come over their faces. They had been to the dentist, so this wasn't anything big. Then we told them that Daddy would have to stay in the hospital three or four days until he was a little bit healed before he could come back home. They asked us when this was going to happen. When was Daddy going to have to go away? Michael told me it would take about a week and a half for them to make the prosthesis and they already had him booked into surgery two weeks from now. The prosthesis would be done by them, so as soon as his teeth were removed, they would be able to put the dentures in.

Our children, unfortunately, were too smart I believe to swallow all of this as just being a very light thing or a simple dentist visit. They had experienced already too much in their lives. I say this because for the rest of the night both of them sat in their father's lap and would not leave his side watching TV with him all night long until they fell asleep right there in his arms. We then carried them upstairs and tucked them into bed. Michael and I went to bed and held each other close. We talked a little bit more about the operation and the process. Then Michael came out with the oddest thing. Of all times to be thinking about this. He said, "Kyra, you know what I realize? This year, November 4, we're going to be celebrating our 20th anniversary.

I thought about it for a moment, and I said, "Oh, my God, you're right. Twenty years!"

We both just shook our heads because it didn't feel at all like 20 years had passed by. It was like we were stuck in some sort of time warp, and again like a few years earlier, he said, "It only feels like we have been together maybe 5, 6 years. Time passes by so quickly."

I just thank God that I was smart enough to be able to enjoy every moment of him, every moment of every year that we were together. Sure we went through our hard times, but that made the good times even more enjoyable and more precious to us. This I kept to myself, because he didn't need a big head, but damn, even after 20 years this man was still able to make me weak in the knees. I also thought if we had 50 years more to spend together, I know I would feel the same exact way still. There was just something so electrifying between us, so real and so honest. This love was so strong, and this was just so incredible because it simply got stronger as the years passed by. The longer we were together, the more we wanted to stay together, the more we wanted to be by each other's side all the time.

It was now a couple of days before the operation was to happen, and Michael was beginning to get a little bit nervous. I could tell by the look on his face. I would give him back rubs quite often to try and relax him. This did help a little bit but it was very hard. He didn't seem to want to talk about it. I think it made him more nervous talking about it. I suppose it didn't help matters much that he had to go all the way to Boston for this operation. It was in the Jamaica Plain VA, and we lived in Morton. It was quite a ways away. I was going to take a bus in with Martin and Teddy to see him, to be there when he was in recovery, but he insisted that I did not do this. After everything the boys had been through he didn't want them being dragged to a hospital. He told me, and he insisted upon this that I just stay home and take care of the boys, but he would call me as soon as he was able to talk. Thank God the VA provided transportation because Michael hated driving in Boston traffic just as much as everybody else does, and with his nerves on edge it would be really, really stressful for him.

It was now the day before his operation the end of May, 1998, when the VA van pulled up in front of our apartment. This was very hard for the boys and me to see. We were having to say goodbye to their father, sending him off to face this operation by himself. My heart was breaking inside. I gave Michael a huge hug and a kiss and Teddy and Martin did the same. It was so hard and so traumatic on them knowing that they would not be able to see their father for four more days when they were used to seeing him every single day. This was not easy, and knowing that I would only have a few damn phone conversations between us in the following four to five days. Michael and I had always done everything as a team, and I so needed to be there by his side when he woke up from that operation. I felt as though my heart was being torn in two choosing to stay here with our two sons or to be with him there. I simply had no choice, and I had to follow Michael's instructions on what he wanted me to do. He would have been very, very upset with me if he woke up and saw Teddy and Martin standing there alongside of me after what he told me. So I had to respect his wishes and stay away, stay at home and wait for his phone calls.

The next day just before his operation he called, as Teddy, Martin, and I sat there by the phone eagerly waiting to hear from him

All the boys kept asking him was, "When you coming home, Daddy? When you coming home?"

He just said, "Oh, you sillies, I'll be home before you know it."

So I decided to mark off the days on the calendar to show them exactly when Daddy would be home again. This made them feel kind of better about the situation, a little more at ease knowing that on a certain day Daddy would be arriving back home. So each day that Daddy was gone we checked off one more day on the calendar until that day finally arrived when he was coming home. The boys were so excited they were hardly able to control themselves. Michael had only been able to call home twice in the five days now that he had been gone because he wasn't able to talk. It was very painful and very difficult for him to speak with the new prosthesis, but what he told me was very good and that was he was doing very well. The operation wasn't that horrible.

The day finally arrived that he was coming home. I remember clearly this day. Teddy and Martin sitting out on the sidewalk waiting for the van to drive up and bring their Daddy home. They sat out there for an hour and a half before the van finally arrived. It seemed they were running a little bit late. As soon as Michael got out of the van, Teddy and Martin jumped on him almost knocking him off his feet. The only other times I have ever seen Martin and Teddy this happy was on Christmas morning when they were running down the stairs ready to attack each and every one of those presents underneath the tree. Actually they looked even happier than Christmas morning. This beats any present they could have ever received in their lives and that was to have their Daddy's lap to sit on while they watched TV every night.

Later on that night they did exactly that. They wouldn't let their father be. They sat on his lap, one on each knee, watching TV, and I heard Teddy ask Michael about what the hospital was like, and he also let Michael know that he was afraid Daddy was going to die.

Michael then explained to him, "Honey, people get sick all the time. It doesn't necessarily mean they're going to die because they get sick. People go to the hospital all the time. That doesn't mean they're going to die there. Millions of people every day go in the hospital and come out just fine. You go to the hospital because there is something wrong, and the doctors most of the time can fix it."

I knew Teddy had this in the back of his mind. I knew he was feeling and thinking this. He just didn't tell me about it. You see, in Teddy's mind, up until now, everyone that had gotten sick or went into the hospital died.

Michael said, "Well, see? I'm living proof," and he told Teddy, "I'm going to be around for a long, long time. Don't you worry about that."

Then Teddy just snuggled up closer to his dad and hugged him, and soon they were both asleep right there in their daddy's arms once more.

This was a picture my heart needed to see. My three men, the men that I loved more than life itself all together again snuggling up in Daddy's favorite overstuffed chair, and I thought to myself, *God has taken a lot from me over the past few years, but he has also given me a lot.* I looked at my beautiful family sitting there, and I did thank God. I thanked him for all our love, and I did truly feel blessed, truly blessed. I also realized at this moment if God were to take one of them from me, this would be completely unbearable. This is the one thing that I would never recover from, and I pleaded to God to never let this moment change. To keep my three men, men that I loved more than life, always by my side, and always keep this love that we share in our family forever. This was the only one thing that I ever wanted in my life was to have a close, loving, caring, normal family, and this is what stood before me. This is what I was looking at while I was sitting across the living room. My beautiful family.

God did help us. Michael was recovering from his surgery nicely although it left him with a slight speech impediment. Believe me, I could deal with that. That was nothing, but he on the other hand was slightly self-conscious of it. I told him it was barely noticeable. He was recovered enough to join us for the Junior Olympics at Teddy and Martin's school. This is a little event that they would have every June at the end of the school year where the whole school would participate. It was grades 1-4, and they would set up little games running, passing balls, Hula-hoop, throwing rings. They had so many games and we had so much fun. They even gave out ribbons for the best participant in each event. Teddy always got the first place ribbon in the event of throwing the baseball the farthest, and Martin always seemed to get the first place ribbon in running. Boy, was that kid a fast runner. This was an all-day event, and it was great for all the families to gather, get together to talk, enjoy our children, watch them have fun, and cheer them all on.

After everybody had their fun and all the ribbons were handed out, Michael and I would always take Teddy and Martin to McDonald's for Happy Meals to celebrate their little victories and then out for ice cream. This year though I have to tell you it was a little bit more special because of what Michael, well actually the whole family, had just gone through. Our sons walked away from their little Junior Olympic Day with four Blue Ribbons for first place but I felt as though our family walked away with a Gold Medal. We survived this last test, this last hurtle, and as a family, once again came out that much stronger for it. Yes, we truly felt like winners on this day.

Something else really funny happened. On the way to McDonald's Martin tapped me on my shoulder as he was sitting in the back seat, and he said, "Mommy, did you see Grandma and Aunt Amber there?"

Michael looked at me, and I looked at Michael, and we both started laughing. Michael just shook his head, and he said, "Oh, God, Kyra, this is your area here."

Martin said, "Grandma and Aunt Amber were sitting on the next bench over from you and Daddy."

Michael said to Martin, "You saw this?"

He said, "Yes, they sat there for about 10 minutes, 15 minutes watching me running back and forth until I won. Then I looked over, and they were gone."

I asked Martin, "Why didn't you tell me this at that time, the time you saw them?"

He said, "I don't know, Mommy. I assumed you saw them, too."

I said, "No, I couldn't." I told him, "I guess they just wanted to sit there and cheer you on, and they wanted to give you another gift besides your First Place ribbon."

Then he looked at me because Michael and I had laughed, and he then asked me if I believed him.

I said, "Oh, yes, Honey, I do believe you, most definitely. I have no doubt."

Michael just continued to shake his head, and it wasn't until later on that evening when he and I were alone he asked me if I had been talking to them about this. I told him I had after they told me that they had seen my mother and my sister already. This was something that I didn't share with Michael because it did make him feel uncomfortable. But I guess I had to share it now. I had to let him know.

He then asked me, "Do you think they are going to be able to pick up spirits like you can? Are they going to have to face these strange things?"

I told him, "I don't know yet. I guess we'll just have to wait and see, and I'll just handle it as it comes and explain a little bit more if they need to know more."

I could see Michael wasn't any happier about this than I was, but again what are you going to do? It's not as though you have a choice. I knew the only thing I could do for my children was to help them navigate through these very strange waters and accept the gift if it is going to be given to them. All I could do was help them through it. I didn't have the ability to stop it, no more than I had the ability to stop my own.

Meanwhile, Michael's recovery, thank God, was going very well. He had to do his daily salt rinses which sometimes would sting. The salt rinse just consisted of bottled water with table salt in it. He would have to remove his teeth to do this rinse. He showed me one day what it looked like. It was a big gaping hole at the roof of his mouth and it led all the way up to his sinuses. So whenever he took a drink of anything without his teeth in blocking that hole, it would come right out his nose. This rinse he would have to do for the two weeks following his operation and our family's menu had to change ever so slightly, although I was still able to keep cooking the baked chicken breasts and the roasts that our family loved. Before giving it to Michael I would have to put it in the food processor. This was something I had bought when Teddy was a child so that I could make homemade baby food for him. I never thought in my wildest dreams that I could actually put an entire roast dinner in a food processor, and that's basically what it looked like, baby food.

Right now this was all Michael could tolerate eating because he couldn't stand to have pressure of any kind put on his gums or the roof of his mouth. Unlike the salt rinses that only went on for a couple of weeks following his operation, I had to do this for months afterwards. This was the only way he was able to eat, and then the VA began sending Ensure, these little cans of liquid food supplements, so that we could be sure he was getting the proper amount of vitamins and minerals that he needed. His diet consisted of, for breakfast either Cream of Wheat or very, very lightly scrambled eggs. Not even oatmeal because oatmeal would tend to get underneath the teeth and underneath the prosthesis that would lead up to his nose. Often it would come out of his nose if anything were to get under it, so feeding him was quite difficult and keeping his body nourished was even more difficult. He ate very small portions because that was all he could tolerate trying to swallow. At lunchtime he would have cream of chicken soup. He did like the taste of cream of mushroom, but I would have to put that through a strainer first before serving it to him because the mushrooms were still too big and way too chewy. I would alternate between the two soups for his lunch and then at supper everything would just be thrown into the food processor. I did the carrots; the potatoes were already mashed, and then the meat.

I found myself basically going back and trying to remember exactly what I fed Teddy and Martin in their younger years before they had their teeth and they were able to chew. I didn't like giving them baby food out of the jar. I wanted to make my own baby food for them, so I just went back to that time, and I tried to give Michael the same texture and the same things that I gave Teddy and Martin when they were very little. This seemed to work fine. He was able to get enough down, but again the vitamins and the nutrients were an issue. That's where the Ensure came in and this helped a lot in keeping him healthy.

So in short, you see for months after the operation he was basically on a liquid diet which he hated so much. He enjoyed the cookouts, the steaks, the broiled chicken breasts, the hamburgers, hot dogs, the ribs, and especially my turkey dinners. All of this for the time being he was no longer able to eat, and this made him absolutely miserable. The one thing he did enjoy doing was eating, especially my cooking. He always loved my cooking. To make things worse he had to sit there across from me, Teddy, and Martin and watch us eat the foods he so dearly loved the way he liked to eat them, with a knife and a fork, not with a straw.

His next doctor's appointment for a checkup for his mouth would be in July, and we were all looking forward to this because hopefully they could possibly fit him with something a little bit better, something that would allow him to eat like a normal person again. That morning he went for his checkup, the van picking him up, and he went in to the EMT. After the EMT looked at him and looking in his mouth, he handed him the worse possible news he could and that was the cancer spread to yet another part of his mouth still remaining at the soft palate but just over to the right a little. So he would now have to go through another operation to have that part removed.

When Michael came home and told me this it was devastating. We were looking forward to his being able to eat like a normal person again, to enjoy his food. He had so little else in his life. He had stopped drinking. He had stopped eating sweets because of the diabetes, and now he couldn't even eat food. Thank God he was still seeing his psychiatrist because he needed him now more than ever, and before he left the VA he told me that the oral surgeon set up the date for his next operation and that was going to be in a week.

So in a week my two sons and I had to prepare ourselves for yet again more worry and more time away from their father. I asked Michael, "What does this mean? Are they going to have to make another prosthesis to attach to your teeth?"

He said, "Yes. I guess so."

So once again we found ourselves having to sit down across from Teddy and Martin and tell them that their father was going to have to go in the hospital yet one more time. They didn't take this well. They were looking forward to a summer just as they always had with their father, a summer filled with fishing and bike riding. He was going to teach Martin how to target shoot. All of this now, this whole fucking summer had to be put on hold, and after everything our kids had already been through, they didn't even have this to look forward to.

I kept in close touch with April from the first time I found out about the cancer in Michael's mouth. She called me practically every night when she couldn't come over because she worked a lot. She always watched out for the boys and me and was there to help in any way possible that she could. She was floored herself, and she thought this was absolutely horrifying.

CHAPTER ELEVEN

It was in the middle of July 1998, a couple of weeks before Michael's next operation. Again he tried his hardest to keep as much normalcy in our children's lives as he could. In those two weeks he took them fishing practically every day, and he was even able to take Martin out target shooting for his first time. I had the pool always set up in the backyard. He was with Teddy and Martin constantly, either in our backyard or out doing things with them trying to keep his mind off of his next battle, his next operation. Again, he was only able to eat the food that I put in the food processor, basically mush. All through this Michael really didn't want to talk about this upcoming operation. Both of our hearts were in so much pain at this point, and we were both so very scared.

Our children were about the only things in our lives right now that were providing any kind of happiness at all. They were the ones that kept us sane. At night Michael and I would just hold each other close. During these intimate times that we would spend together, our love for each other was enough to push reality and the horrors of the world away at least for this little bit of time each day. But unfortunately with every rising sun breaking through our windows, we would have to face a new day and the worries would just come rushing back to us. I'll tell you, these next two weeks passed by quickly at some times and dragged in others. We just wanted it to be finished with. We wanted to make sure he was cancer free.

So when the day came that the van from the VA came to pick him up, I gave him a big hug and so did Teddy and Martin. We knew again we would not see him for another five days. He called me from the hospital when they were prepping him for surgery for the next day, and he let me know that he was feeling well. Then he spoke to the two boys and let them know that he was doing well and that they were to behave themselves for me. After we said our *I love yous* and our *goodbyes* and hung up the phone, Teddy then asked me, "How many days again?" and again I went over to the calendar. This was a comforting thing, because they could actually see and count the days off. Every passing day we would put a big X on it. While Michael was in the hospital I tried to keep the boys as busy as I could in their pool and playing games in the backyard, and encouraging Teddy to ride his bike and Martin to do his drawings.

April at this point was a tremendous help to us. She would pick the boys up and take them out for the entire day either to the mall or to the movies. Quite often around this time she began taking them for the weekends to give them a break, a change of scenery, and to try to take their minds off of what was going on.

On the fifth day after Michael's operation and recovery he returned home. It was on the last day the calendar was marked off just as I promised the boys. Again they sat out there on the sidewalk waiting for that big, blue van to come driving up with their Daddy in it. Again they nearly knocked him down as they jumped on him as soon as he got out of the van, and he came over to me and gave me a huge hug. He had the best news that he could possibly give me and that was that the doctor reported to him that they got ALL of the cancer. Every little spot they saw, they took and at this point he was cancer free. Tests would still have to be run, and he would still have to be examined on a regular basis, but for now this was a huge relief.

I actually know what it feels like to win the lottery, because that's what I felt like on this day. I felt so lucky and so thrilled I could have jumped up and down. In my relief I began to cry, and Michael and I just held each other. At this moment I also felt like someone had just lifted the world off of my shoulders, this tremendous weight that I had been carrying around since the loss of my mother. I felt a huge release of all the pain and all the heartache. Everything just flowed out of me all at once with this fantastic news. I felt like I was reborn again.

Before we knew it things were returning back to normal in our home. Michael was out in the yard with the boys raking the leaves, the children had returned back to school after the summer vacation, and everything was going great. We were a happy little family again even though Michael still had to eat only dinners I would put through the food processor. He still was on a soft diet, but this was nothing. We dealt with this happily. The important thing was he was here, and he was healthy again.

I sat there at the kitchen window one autumn day with the leaves blowing around and the trees still having their beautiful colors, orange, yellow and red, and I watched Michael and Teddy working on our car getting it ready for the winter. It's funny; he was teaching Teddy everything he taught me about cars; spark plugs, how to tune it up, where to put the antifreeze, how to test all the fluids.

It was so funny to watch and so heartwarming to see just how close Michael and Teddy really were. There was a little secret that I was keeping from Michael, and that was I was putting a little bit of money away every month, enough money to save up to get him a brand-new recliner. His old one was literally falling apart. Between the weight of him and our two sons on his lap practically every night, it just about had it. I really wanted to surprise him. With his birthday quickly approaching October 20, I had just enough money saved up. Teddy, Martin, and I went to at least three or four stores before we found the perfect one for their dad. It was beautiful, big, over-stuffed recliner in blue, his favorite color. Sitting in it was like sitting in a cloud. It was absolutely perfect, and I had the delivery date set up a day before his birthday.

It just so happened that it was about three days before Michael's birthday that he had his next checkup. He had quite a few checkups after that last operation because they wanted to keep close watch on the cancer and make sure that it didn't return. As I said, this was about three days before his birthday when he had this checkup and the news was not good. The cancer it seems reappeared. They found more little white spots and again they would have to be removed. After this last operation he would only have about 50% of the roof of his mouth left which would make it even more difficult for him to return back to a normal sold food diet. At this point we had no idea when this was going to happen, when he was going to be able to sit at the dinner table and be able to eat a normal hamburger, piece of roast, or chicken without it being turned into mush first.

They set up this next appointment a couple of days after his birthday. We tried our best to keep it together because all we felt like doing at this point was screaming our brains out and ripping our hair from our heads. It was so surreal. This just simply could not be happening to us, to our family. Again that nightmare that you just can't seem to wake up from. Just when you think it's been beat, just when you think things can finally return back to normal again, you get the rug pulled out from underneath you. This is the most horrifying feeling and the most horrible thing for a family, especially children, to have to go through.

In the meantime it was Michael's birthday. I had the cake, and I decorated the house. Of course the fantastic present arrived the day before. He was absolutely thrilled. At least with this gift I was able to put even the smallest smile on his face. A small one was better than nothing. Once again the day came and the van from the VA picked him up to take him to Boston. He again called me that night and talked to the children and me. Once again we marked the days off on the calendar.

This all seemed to be turning into some sort of sick family routine in itself, one that can only be compared to a nightmare, a nightmare from which you can never wake up and a black hole of which there is no way out. This is what it was beginning to feel like. Once again on the fifth day, Michael finally returned back home, and the boys ran out to greet him as they always did. Once he reached the door I gave him the hugest hug and all the love in my heart just poured out to him.

With this last operation to his mouth it made it even more difficult for him to eat. Even after me putting all the food in the food processor and turning it into mush, he now had great difficulty even being able to eat this. It seemed as though every time he would close his mouth the dentures and the prosthesis that were attached to the dentures would move. When this happened the food would come right out of his nose, because if it moved there would be nothing blocking it from reaching his sinuses. Eating became a challenge in itself. Drinking was no easier. It broke my heart every day to have to sit there and watch him struggle to get anything down at all. Thank God the VA was sending these Ensure drinks because this would become his main source of nutrients. I hate like Hell to think what would have become of his body if he were not able to at least get a little bit of nutrients in him.

I was becoming numb watching this and seeing the man I loved more than life itself going through this on a daily basis. I was too numb to even shed a tear anymore. I was completely drained emotionally. For me to have to sit here day after day and watch Michael and my family go through this was the worst crushing blow God had ever given me in my life. You see, when you are that close as a family and you share that much love, it's not just the person that's going through the pain and the suffering; it's the entire family as well.

I just prayed in time things would get better with his eating and perhaps they could make him a better fitting prosthesis so that he would be able to eat a normal dinner again and once more enjoy the cookouts that he so enjoyed. I just tried to keep in mind, "All he needs is time, time to heal," but watching him every day go through all of this was just so heartbreaking and so frustrating to me. My brain could not even begin to comprehend my heart's pain. It was at this point in my life where I was trying my hardest to prepare myself, to brace myself for the worst, and the worst would be having my sons grow up with no father and me spending the rest of my existence without my love by my side. I realized this was nothing you could ever prepare yourself for, although I did try.

I tried my hardest to prepare myself for the worst and at the same time hold on to every strain of hope I could find to hold on to, because your heart could never truly prepare you for that kind of crushing blow or even thinking about the possibility of that crushing blow. You hope for the best. You try to prepare for the worst, but in reality there is no preparation, there is no way your mind or your heart could ever prepare to be ripped apart like that. So for now, for this day, I had to pray that this was all over with, that all the cancer truly was gone and that our family was back on the road to recovery and normalcy.

Throughout all of this Michael was so very brave and so very strong, just as he always had been. Again he lived by this motto, "It's okay if you're tired to take a break, take a step back, gain your strength again, and come out fighting, but never give up." This is just what he did. He fought so hard through all of this. I guess that's true about what they say, "You can't keep a good man down." He was a living example of this through battle after battle in his life, time after time. He won. He beat the odds, so I thought, *Why not now? If he beat the odds against alcoholism, and if he beat the odds against keeping his brains and his sanity together after Vietnam? We beat all the odds, and we have a beautiful family to show for it. We are fighters, and this is just yet one more battle that we have to fight together.* I knew if anyone could beat cancer it would be him, because quite simply I knew he had that spirit, that soul, and that inner strength to do so. I only wished I could say I shared all of his strength. I was strong but not nearly as strong as he was, because all of this worry, all of this heartbreak I guess was beginning to take its toll on me.

It was around the middle of November now of 1998 when I was packing the kids into the car one morning to bring them to school. It was a snowy, slippery morning. I'd always bring Joey along with Teddy, Martin, and Joey's little brothers A. T. and Angel, Jr. to school, and I'd pick them up every night after school. One morning, Izzy, Joe's mother, came out to the car to help me get the kids packed in and to make sure the snow was removed from around the tires so that I could get out. When she looked at my face, I guess my face spoke volumes. See, up until now I hadn't really spoken to her although I liked her. That wasn't the point. The point was I was just so tied up in my own grief, my own losses and heartache. I guess socializing wasn't high on my list at that moment. I just kept my pain to myself. So when she got a good look into my eyes that morning, she asked me if everything was okay, and I just kind of shrugged my shoulders and said, "Yeah, I guess so." I don't know if Joey had been telling her everything that was going on with Michael. I'm sure Teddy had told Joey, but she didn't seem as though she knew very much about my family situation at the moment, so I told her that my husband was sick right now and everything that's come down on my family has just started catching up with me. I told her, "I'm more emotionally drained than anything." That's when she offered to have me over for a cup of coffee after dropping the children off at school so that we could talk. I accepted that offer.

I first went home to make sure Michael was all set for breakfast, and then I went over to her apartment. It was only a couple of houses down. As I entered her house I noticed it was really pretty. She loved dolphins. She collected all sorts of dolphins, statues, and crystal figurines. Everything was so pretty and shiny. She invited me into the kitchen where we sat and we began to talk.

Before I started speaking I thought to myself, *Could I, or even should I begin to tell her what the past three years have been like for me?* As I mentioned earlier, throughout all of my grief and my pain over the past three years, there was little time for socializing. I just felt like I got kicked down time and time again. The more you get kicked down, the more you begin to realize maybe the next kick won't be so hard if you just stay down and don't try to lift your spirits too high and hope for too much, because you find time and time again you just get disappointed. So sometimes you just stop hoping that it will all stop because it never seems to, and if I were to tell her about my pain over the past three years, would she even be able to comprehend what I was saying. This isn't something that you can just talk about. The only way you can truly know how other people feel after such a loss in their lives is to actually experience it yourself. That's the only way your heart truly knows that pain by going through it. Even if I were to speak of it, if I were to get her to try and comprehend it, is this a good thing to do to another person? No. It certainly isn't. Why would you actually want to make someone feel and comprehend so much pain? So running this over quickly in my mind before I even spoke to her, I realized, no. I wasn't going to do this.

So now I decided to keep it as light as I possibly could and only let her know a little bit of what was going on right now. I told her that my husband was diagnosed with soft-palate cancer, and he was just now recovering from his third operation. I said, "All of it is just kind of, I guess, catching up to me. That's why I look withdrawn and tired."

Then we started talking about the kids, and she began telling me about her husband Angel. The more we talked, the better I was beginning to feel. I don't know. There was just something about her. We hit it off right away. She seemed happy, and her upbeat spirit sort of rubbed off on me, and we sat there talking over coffee for a couple of hours, and I did feel much better when I left.

When I walked through the door, Michael asked me, "How did your little visit go?"

I said, "Oh, great. She's a really, really nice person, and an intelligent woman."

He was very happy to see a smile on my face, something he hadn't seen very often over the past six months at least. He said, "Well, that's good. You should go over a couple of mornings a week and have some coffee and talk with your friend."

I agreed. "Yes, it probably would be a good thing for me to do."

A couple of days after that I went over again, and I met her husband, Angel, for the first time. He was such a sweet guy, and also very polite and very intelligent. They were just a great family, and I was so happy for Teddy especially to be involved with such a nice family at such a young age because he was so close to Joey. Again I hoped that this relationship would go on well into their adulthood.

I'm glad to say that the three of us quickly became very close friends. We would help each other out whenever one of us needed help. They became friends that you could truly rely on in times of need. Izzy came from a very large family although she only had one brother and a sister, Cathy, whom I also got close to, who was also a very intelligent and loving woman. They had a large, large extended family—a lot of aunts and cousins that they were very close to. Each and every family gathering on holidays or birthdays, their house was completely overflowing with people, loving caring people, family-oriented people, people that I wanted my children around. I'm glad to say they all got to know my two boys and me very, very well. They took us in as part of their family, and we felt welcomed with open arms. This was Izzy's side of the family.

On Angel's side of the family were his mother, father and sister. They were also at these family gatherings, and I got to meet them and liked them very much as well. His parents were only in their 50s, and they still did a lot together. They traveled and went on vacations and just enjoyed each other's company. Izzy's mother and father were also still alive and only in their 50s. Her mother's name was June. Although her parents had been divorced for years, her mother and she were very, very close just like my mother and I were. Her mother was a hairdresser and owned her own salon, and she was very good at what she did. She was very beautiful. She had long, flowing black hair and was always dressed so beautifully. June loved her family tremendously. I have to say Joey had a relationship with his grandmother just like my mother had with Teddy. It was the same kind of relationship. Joey was her first-born grandson, and I think there's always a special bond between a grandmother and her first-born grandchild.

This introduction of Joey's family to mine came at such an incredible time in our lives, a time when we truly, truly needed a spiritual uplifting. This was a time when we needed to be able to just laugh and have fun and try our hardest to forget our heartaches. They say that God never closes a door without opening a window. They were our windows. Their laughter and their love helped my children get through so much and for this I will forever be grateful and beholding to them. But even with all the love that they showed us and all the laughs that we had at these parties, at this moment it could not change our reality, the reality of life.

This Christmas, the Christmas of 1998, was so incredibly hard for me. I tried my hardest to go about business as usual and so did Michael. We went out and got the Christmas tree, and we had the children's pictures taken with Santa. We tried to keep to the family tradition that we had started. It just felt so hollow because right now I was only doing it for my children. I grinned and bared it.

I would have rather forgotten that Christmas was even here. Michael and I were just beginning to be able to laugh again, and we had a good time setting up the Christmas tree. However, always in the back of my mind I wondered what else was going to happen now. Is there going to be any more cancer? Are there going to be any more deaths? I just couldn't shake it. I couldn't get it out of my head.

I tried so hard to live in the moment, to be happy seeing my children sitting on Santa's lap, or walking around the Green and looking at all the pretty lights. I just couldn't remove myself from fact, the fact of life and the fact of death. It lingered in me like a dark, black cloud, one that was becoming harder and harder to push away, to get rid of. But I allowed my children to see none of this in me. I kept that smile on my face while my heart was breaking inside. I would not ruin one more thing for them. I would not ruin their Christmas, but I just was simply going through the motions now. I always felt so happy around the Holidays. Michael used to call me, "His Little Christmas Girl." I would be the first one to decorate the outside of our apartment and to decorate the house long before we got the tree even put up. The presents were mainly bought by September. By the time Christmas Day came I was all set. I so enjoyed Christmas and the Holidays with my mother, Michael's mother, Amber, April, Michael and the two boys. I loved having my family every Holiday at my table.

This is something I looked forward to every year, and now I was finding every year was getting harder and harder to face, especially the dinner table with one fewer person at it. Now it was Michael and I, Martin and Teddy, and my sister April. All of us put on that smile and all of us made Teddy and Martin's Christmas the happiest it could possibly be because we also knew inside that Amber, my mother and Michael's mother would not accept us acting any other way.

I guess it was a couple of weeks now after Christmas. We were starting a new year, 1999. One night when I walked in to our bedroom I saw Michael sitting there at the edge of the bed praying.

As soon as I realized what he was doing, I apologized, and said, "I'll leave you alone," and I started closing the door.

He told me, "Kyra, what are you doing?"

And I said, "You're praying."

"Yes."

I then asked him, "Well, don't you want your privacy?"

"No," he said, "Come and sit beside me. I'd like us to pray together. After all, we are both praying for the same thing."

Of course I agreed, but I told him before we started to pray together about what I had been experiencing since my mother's death. I told him I found it very, very hard to pray. The words came, but that's all they were: just words. The feeling, the connection to God, I didn't feel. In fact, I hadn't felt it since the last time I prayed with my grandmother, which was many, many years ago.

I then began to explain to him how it felt for me whenever I prayed now, how I felt nothing, how I just imagined a big, blank wall being there. I felt no spiritual connection to God. I felt as though at this point in my life God had just turned his back on me perhaps because I spent so many years with my back to him. I told him, "Michael, I have no answers. I don't understand, myself."

He felt horrible for me. He gave me a big hug, and when I put my head on his shoulder he said, "Kyra, how come you never spoke of this before? How come you never let me know?"

I told him I felt ashamed. I felt I just must have been such a terrible person that God now no longer wanted to hear my voice. It's truly amazing because we shared absolutely everything else in our lives. Michael and I knew each other inside and out, but this was the one thing that I kept from him because I was ashamed and sad. I just couldn't shake the feeling that there was something wrong with me. Like it was some kind of dirty little secret that I was keeping to myself. I don't know why I felt this way, but this is the truth. That's the way I felt. I honestly believed if I just kept trying, if I just kept praying, some day, somehow I would be able to tear that wall down. I would once again, just as I did as a child, feel as though God was truly listening to me and hearing my prayers.

So I just kept trying night after night since the death of my mother, and night after night it was the same, nothing. So I thought to myself as Michael was holding my hands and asking me to pray with him, *What good is this going to do? What difference is this going to make?* If anything, I was afraid of hurting him further. If God put up this wall in front of me for a reason, if he had become angry with me, would he now take it out on Michael if Michael were to pray with me and help me break that wall down? I was afraid to actually pray with Michael, afraid to hurt him. You see, Michael never ever turned his back on his faith or his belief in God. Throughout all his life and the trauma that he had suffered, he always prayed. He always had that open communication with

God, and he always felt like God was listening to him. He never wavered in his faith like I did, and he never had that hate or anger toward God that I had.

So all these thoughts ran through my mind while Michael sat there insisting, holding my hands, telling me to pray with him. As we were saying "The Lord's Prayer" together, I looked up at Michael's face, a face that held so much love and so much compassion, a face I always looked to for strength.

I thought to myself, *I suppose if anyone would be able to break this wall down to give my faith back to me, in fact to help me reconnect with God, it would be him.* So I was very, very disappointed when at the end of our prayers I felt the same and that was the blank wall. I guess I knew all along this wasn't going to work, but again, I had to try, and I had to keep trying. I knew this.

I had this weird feeling inside that God was somehow making me work my way back to him. My faith would now have to be forged through pain and suffering, and perhaps when the day came when my heart couldn't stand anymore pain, maybe this is when God would start listening to me again. I had a feeling He was just making me work for it now.

I couldn't help what I did next because Michael looked at me with such hope in his eyes such hope that somehow he was able to help me through all of this. When he asked me if this helped at all, I lied, and I told him, "Yeah. It made me feel a little bit better," but in fact it changed nothing. I just didn't want him to know that, and because Michael's faith was as strong as what it was, I truly don't believe he completely understood what I meant when I said, "All I felt was a blank wall whenever I tried to pray." I don't think he was completely able to comprehend everything I felt, even though I tried to explain it to him the best way I could.

I think all he thought was, *If you believed in God, God would always have his ear open to you.* I guess in some cases this isn't true, and I don't think he quite grasped the notion of praying your hardest and feeling nothing, as though there was no one listening.

After this night Michael and I would pray together every night. It was on the third night of our prayers when Michael asked God to please help me find my way back to him, all of a sudden it happened. I could feel that wall breaking down, crumbling before my eyes. In my mind's eye, there was nothing but light where that darkness hung. I found just as I did as a child praying with my grandmother, I could actually feel the light on my face, the light of God. I knew he was listening to me now.

I will forever be grateful to both Michael and God for bringing me out of the darkness. Finally after almost five years I could feel God, and I could feel his love, just as I could always feel Michael's. This lifted my soul up out of the darkest pit. I felt so much joy all at once rushing over me. I almost cried. The feeling was just so uplifting and so remarkable. No words could adequately describe the emotions that came rushing over me. My heart actually felt lifted and light again, not heavy and bogged down as I had felt over the past five years. I felt my soul come back to life, and I felt joy for the first time in a very, very long time deep, deep down inside of me. I felt like a lost child that finally found its way back home, and I felt God's arms embrace me with love.

I will never, ever forget this experience, this first time after working so hard to try to make that connection with God and actually now breaking down that wall and feeling Him again. This first time in so many years was utterly remarkable, and also for the first time in many years now I felt hope. I saw that light at the end of the tunnel, and at the end of the tunnel that light was God. He was there for me with open arms, and I embraced Him and swore on that day I would never, ever turn my back on Him again. I would always try to behave in my life the way I knew he wanted me to and to live every day of my life honoring him. I promised God this after he gave me a second chance. I will live the rest of my life with that love inside of me, that love that only God and God alone can show to you.

As I sat there by Michael's side with him still holding my hands, the light must have just been flowing out of me, because he told me, "Kyra, your face even looks different."

I told him, "Michael, I really can feel it now. You helped me."

He helped me. That wall is gone completely, and I went on to describe to Michael how I could feel a light on my face, a light coming from within. This was a light only God can give to you, and I thanked him and hugged and kissed him. I told him how much I loved him. I thought to myself, *This man, this beautiful man that I've loved so deeply for so many years, has given me so much to be grateful for, and now he's given me one other thing perhaps just as important as our children that he gave to me, and that was my faith back. Michael led me back to God and gave me my faith back.* I truly don't believe anyone else on the face of this earth could have done what he did. How on earth do you even begin to thank someone for doing such an incredible thing?

After this day the bond between Michael and me grew even deeper and deeper after sharing such a spiritual experience. We both knew right then and there that there was nothing we would not be able to face and overcome together. Now not only did we have this bond between us, but we also felt that God was standing behind us leading us and guiding us. We knew we were not alone. I also knew going through this cancer scare that Michael and I went through, this too made us stronger and brought us closer together than ever before. I just felt I could have this lifetime with him and a hundred lifetimes with him and it still wouldn't be enough time. I wanted him by my side forever, for all eternity. This I was sure of now more than ever, and I felt so very, very lucky to have known such a love in my life, because I did realize there are so many people that never ever find such happiness and never find such love.

I was one of the lucky ones, and I realize this. You see, once you find this kind of love, you never ever want to live without it, and that's just the way I felt. A hundred lifetimes would not be enough. Five hundred years of this love would not be enough. You just never ever want it to end once you experience this, and once you have it you never want to let go of it. So you see, Michael now not only held my heart in his hands, but he held my soul as well. It was my soul that he freed from Hell. It was my soul that he led back to God and to the light, and I truly believe that only a love as strong as ours could have done this. I think it was the love that Michael felt for me that actually broke that wall down and led me back to the light.

Every night after this Michael and I would pray together, feeling that spiritual bond between us grow ever stronger. I looked forward to these times together, these quiet times at night in our bedroom where we would just sit side by side holding each other's hands and praying. The feeling was just so incredibly uplifting. It made everything else that was going on in our lives with the cancer and having to deal with our children and explain things to them about the cancer, it made it bearable. Alone at night in our bedroom when we prayed, this was our refuge. This was now our special time together, and I also found by having God back in my life and in my heart and being able to feel Him, this made it easier for me to talk to my children about what was going on, about the cancer and about the people that had passed in our lives. They knew before I did that they were all fine and all back home again in God's arms. Someday when it is our time, we will all be together again.

It is so funny, but after this when I started speaking openly to my children about God and about my feelings, sometimes they would just sit there in amazement. Like, "Ma, you didn't realize this before now?" I never let them know about the struggle that I went through in my prayers and not being able to feel God in my life. They never knew this. Having this back in my life now was confirmation that no, we are not alone. He is here with us and He is always watching over us.

I also accepted one other thing along with God and that's His wisdom. I realized I could not question the decisions he made in taking who He had to take at a particular time. Everything happens for a reason and when it is your time to go, no matter where you are, I believe, whether you are in a 747 or your own bathtub, you're going to go. I believe there is a date and a time we are born, and I believe there is a date and a time we must go. If you are truly meant to go, there will be nothing that will be able to save you, even the love of a daughter or the love of a sister. It just won't matter, because it will be God's will. I learned not to question Him but to accept and ask Him for grace and guidance in getting through the horrible times, the sad times because truly, He is the only one that can help you.

It is now the end of January 1999, and Michael got picked up by the van that would take him to the Boston VA. This was his annual checkup. They kept close watch on his mouth especially after the third operation. I thought to myself, *Oh, God, please, please let this next year be better than the past few. It's a brand-new year. Please let my family just have some peace and love for this year. Please let him come back home with some good news.* So the doctors at the VA examined his mouth, and they found no cancer, thank God, but they ran a few other tests on him just to make sure there wasn't any cancer anywhere else in his body. We would have to wait for the results of that testing for about four days, and they would call us and let us know.

So as he arrived home with good news that there was no cancer left in his mouth, or should I say what was left of his mouth. This was good news. I remember just sitting on the couch in each other's arms watching TV that night after supper, talking about it and making plans for the summer. We were going to go fishing and have picnics. Michael had been teaching Martin target shooting, and he was going to continue doing that with Teddy as well. In fact we found we were planning our entire year because we got such good news for a change.

This looked like perhaps it was going to be the best year in five years. I could actually see the look of relief on my boys' faces for the first time in almost five years. That grief seemed to be disappearing I thought perhaps I could salvage a normal childhood for them. A look of innocence was beginning to shine once again in their eyes. As Michael and I would play out in the snow with them helping them make their snowmen, their laughter lifted both Michael's heart and mine. Could it be possible that we could be a happy family again? I'm sorry to say this was short-lived, and we found this time to be little more than just a dream, a beautiful dream that we would rudely be awakened from.

It was the beginning of February when the test results came back. Michael had no more cancer in his mouth, but it had gone down to his lymph nodes in his neck. The doctor's told him that they had to remove these lymph nodes and also start radiation therapy. They wanted him to come in immediately so that they could begin making the mask, a mask that would have to be worn during the radiation therapy. This mask fit his face perfectly, and through each and every therapy session of radiation, he would lay on a table, the mask over his face, and they would have to screw it into the table keeping his face perfectly still throughout the whole time. So his operation would be scheduled for the beginning of March because it would take time to make this mask and to set up all the necessary appointments for the operating room.

Michael and I were both completely, utterly petrified at the thought of this horror and once more trying to explain to our children so that they were able to understand what was going on. It was so incredibly hard to do. Teddy was only 11 and Martin only 8. Of course we didn't go into any details. We just let them know that their father was going to have to have another operation, and hopefully this would be the last one. After these last three, they learned not to ask too many questions. I don't think they really wanted to know the answers. We kept them close, very, very close to us and always provided a deep sense of security for them. They always knew that Mommy and Daddy loved them, and they always knew that Mommy and Daddy loved each other. Sometimes for children this is all they need to know to feel secure.

About a week before Michael's operation in March the doctor handed him a sheet of paper. On the sheet of paper was his radiation schedule. It was on a daily basis, five days a week. You see, in order for the radiation to work you have to have so many hours of it. Every day we knew he was facing having to get into that van and go to Boston for this treatment and come back home.

So much traveling when he was feeling so sick was incredibly difficult. I didn't know how he was going to do it. Whenever I looked at the sheet of paper, it floored me. It was literally every single day he had to have this treatment for a month and a half.

On that last visit to the doctors about a week before the operation was to occur (it was actually the day that Michael showed me the schedule of radiation therapy he was going to do) and that night after we got through praying as we always did, we went to sleep. I was awakened by Michael sitting at the edge of the bed. He had such a strange look on his face.

I sat up quickly, and I asked him what was the matter.

He said, "Oh, Kyra, you wouldn't believe me if I told you."

I said, "You forgot who you're talking to. I've experienced weird things all through my life, and you know that."

He said, "Okay, I'll tell you." He then went on to tell me he had gotten up to go to the bathroom and before lying back down again he noticed in the corner of his eye coming from the corner of our ceiling, and the best way he could describe it was like a cloud of stardust all sparkly and just bouncing around. He said, "It floated around the ceiling for a while, and then it went past my head and straight into our closet." He looked at me and he said, "Well, you know about these things. What the Hell was that?"

I just looked at him, and I laughed. I said, "Welcome to my world, Michael. No, I have no idea what that was. Just like so many things that happen in my life, I have no answers for them—so many questions and no answers. I told him it could have been any number of things. It could have been Joe next door that passed, because you liked each other so much. Maybe he was coming for a visit. Maybe it was your mom. Maybe it was your eyes playing tricks on you. I don't know any more than you do, Michael."

He then lay back down, and I put my arms around him, and he said to me, "I think you're rubbing off on me, because shit like this just doesn't happen to me. I've never experienced anything weird in my life, Kyra."

Once again I told him, "Welcome to my world."

Mind you, he only knew about a quarter of the events that happened to me as far as the spiritual world went, because he never liked talking about it. It always made him feel uncomfortable. I could see he was clearly uncomfortable now seeing just the little thing that he saw. He never liked talking about such things, never mind something like this actually happening to him. It really threw him. I reassured him about one thing, and that was it's nothing that was going to hurt him. He just nodded his head, and I could tell he wasn't anywhere near ready to go back to sleep again but I was, because I was used to things like this. I feel asleep in his arms.

I don't know how much sleep he got that night, but when we awoke the next morning he didn't look very rested at all. I just told him, "Michael, forget about it; let it go. You know the same advice you've given me over the past 20 years? Well, I'm now handing it back to you. Just let it go."

He did finally.

The day before his next operation came. Just as usual, the boys and I each gave him a huge hug before he got into the van and drove away, telling him how much we loved him. I thank God for one thing, and that was the boys were in school. At least their little minds would be occupied for a certain amount of hours every day because this time their father was going to be away a little bit longer than that 5-day period. It was almost two weeks before he was able to return back home. Again we marked it off on the calendar. Every night Michael would call. At first his voice was very, very raspy, and I could barely make out what he was saying. Actually looking back on it now I'm amazed that he was able to talk at all, but each day I could hear his voice getting better and clearer. Each and every night the boys and I would take turns talking to him and sending our love over the phone.

I tried my hardest to keep the boys as busy as I possibly could while they were not in school. We did arts and crafts together and watched movies. I even dug out their ice skates. Although I didn't have enough courage to put a pair on myself, I put theirs on and just let them play around. It was a particularly cold winter, and the ice was still safe so I thought maybe this would be a nice break in their daily routine. I picked them up early from school. We stopped at Dunkin' Donuts to get hot chocolate before we went to the pond, and we spent the whole day there.

I would desperately try and think up things to do with them, things that would bring them joy and take their mind off of their father. Even if it were only for a few hours it helped immensely, but every night we were by that phone waiting for his phone call. It just seemed that with every phone call all those worries, all that anxiety just came flooding back. This pain that we felt could only be blocked for a matter of hours, and then the real world, reality, would come crushing back in on us. All we knew is that we wanted Daddy home so that the four of us could sit as usual in the living room cuddling one another, especially on a cold winter's night, and watching TV or talking about the day. This is what my family desired and this is what my family needed more than anything in the world was just to have Daddy back home again.

There was one night during these two weeks that Michael was gone that I sat in our room just as we had always sat together and prayed. I never prayed so hard in my entire life. I felt that light on my face, and I felt that connection. I began pleading to God to please, please make this right. Please cure Michael, and I asked him, I begged him, if one of us had to go, if one of us had to die, let it be me, not Michael. I truly felt in my heart that our two sons needed their father more than they needed me. He had so much more to teach them, and I knew he would be able to guide them much better than I would. I began begging God to please just leave Michael alone. Give me the cancer and leave him alone. He's been through enough pain in his life, enough traumas. He has suffered enough. Whatever else you have to give him, give it to me and let him alone. I prayed, and I begged God to do just this. I told him I would gladly take his place. With every fiber of my being, with all my heart and all my soul I truly, truly meant this.

It was now exactly two days before Michael was expected back home again, and as we marked the days off on the calendar the boys became more and more excited to see that last day coming. After school I picked the boys up and after supper we were sitting down in the living. They were doing their homework, and I was watching TV and there came a knock at the door. I wasn't expecting anyone so I had no idea. I was rather surprised. I opened the door to see Michael standing there. He wanted to surprise us. He knew he was going to get out a day early, and I'm telling you we all went into shock. We started yelling and screaming. We grabbed him and just hugged him, never wanting to let him go again.

I said, "You sneak, you. How come you didn't let me know you were coming home a day early?"

That's when he said, "I just wanted it to be a huge surprise for you guys."

I said, "Well, you achieved your goal." I couldn't remember the last time I was so happy. I was absolutely thrilled to have my love back in my arms again, and the boys were thrilled to have their Daddy's lap to sit on that night.

After peeling Teddy and Martin off of their father, which believe me took some doing, I remember Michael telling them, "I'm not going anywhere, boys.

I'm here to stay. I'm not going back to the hospital."

After the boys began calming down, I then started helping Michael take his coat off, and then he began removing his scarf, which to my horror revealed the operation incision. The incision went from one ear to the other. They had completely cut his throat open and the staples that they had put in were still there. He was not going to be able to have them removed for another week. I felt like I was going to pass out when I saw this. I was absolutely horrified to see what they had done to my sweet love, but I knew I had to contain my emotions.

I'm sure Michael saw the horror that went over my face at that moment. I just remember Teddy asking him, Daddy, does it hurt?"

Michael said, "No, actually it doesn't hurt at all."

I looked at him as if to say, "You have to be kidding." Evidently when you have an incision that deep a lot of the nerve endings are also cut. Thank God, because that did take care of a lot of the pain.

It was very strange that the boys seemed to hardly notice their father's neck. I guess they were just so thrilled to have him home again that little else mattered at this moment. I brought Michael's bags upstairs and he followed, getting into his pajamas and getting comfortable again in his own home. He told me this is something that he looked forward to every night he was stuck at that hospital. He looked forward to this first night back at home. So he got into his pajamas and his slippers and housecoat, and we both came back downstairs. He sat on the couch with Teddy on one side of him and Martin on the other, and me sitting in my chair looking at my three beautiful, loving men and thanking God Michael was back home again where he belonged. That night we all stayed up very, very late, and the children didn't go to school the next day. I kept them home so that they could spend the entire day just being with their daddy.

The next morning after we woke up Michael told me that we would have to wash his neck two or three times a day so we could remove all the dead skin so it could start to heal and dry. I brought out one of the old washcloths that I used to use on Teddy and Martin when they were babies. It was the softest one that I could find. First he tried doing it himself. He soaked the washcloth in warm water. I stood by him holding a towel so he wouldn't get soaking wet, but he was having too much difficulty doing this himself. It is very hard to wash your own neck when you can't stretch it out too much to lean over the sink properly, so I told him just hold the towel over your chest, and I'll wash your neck. The first time we did this I was absolutely horrified. I never ever thought in my wildest, most horrific nightmare that Michael and I would now have to do this, that Michael would have to go through such a horrific operation. With every stroke of the wet washcloth to my love's neck my heart broke a little bit more. I ended up by doing something that I fought so hard not to do and that was break down in tears.

My heart just couldn't take any more. I could actually feel it crumbling into pieces inside my chest. I dropped the washcloth back into the sink, and I held Michael in my arms so close and so tight, and we both cried. We just stood there crying until we had no more tears left to shed. Perhaps both of us needed this release. This release of pain, heartache, and sorrow just came flooding out of both of us all at once. After a long period of time we were able to gain our composure once more, and we both just went to bed and held each other close. I held onto Michael so tightly. I never wanted to let go.

We were now as we always were in our former life, still the strong team, but this fight was unlike any other fight that we had fought in the past. This was now a fight for Michael's life, for our life together, and for our life as a family. We had no idea if we were going to win this one. Perhaps this was what petrified us the most. Now every day, a couple of times a day, I would wash Michael's neck, and I would pray silently, all the while I was doing it, *Please, God, let this be the end. Let this be the end of the cancer and the end of our family struggle.*

A week passed by now and his neck was healing really, really well. It was time for them to remove the staples, and they did so uneventfully. Everything seemed to be going as scheduled. His neck was looking great, the doctor said. In a week they would begin the radiation therapy to make sure that they get all the cancer. When it was time for his radiation therapy to begin, the VA van would pick him up every morning. He would go in for his therapy and be dropped off later on that afternoon. He would always have to carry a basin with him because he always became physically ill on the way back home. This radiation therapy took so much out of him. He was vomiting all the time. This went on for a month and a half. He looked worse after all this therapy than he ever did while he had cancer in him.

Every day when he returned home after his therapy he would immediately go to a bathroom and begin vomiting which in itself was not a good thing considering what shape his mouth was in and now his neck. There was a lot of pressure added to his head with vomiting. I would just hold the cold compress on his forehead as he was throwing up and rub his back while he desperately fought to get the nausea under control. I felt so frickin' helpless just standing there with a stupid washcloth on his forehead. There was nothing else that I could do. There was no way I could stop his pain, and that to me was the most heartbreaking thing of all. No matter what I did, it just didn't seem to be enough. Not for me anyway. His take on it was completely different. To him I was an angel, but to myself I was a useless piece of shit.

This went on for a month and a half on a daily basis. Every day after his daily therapy, after he returned home and after his vomiting sessions in the bathroom, he would gather himself, get into his pajamas and come down and sit in what was now his favorite chair, the one his boys and I bought him for his birthday the year before. He would just try and relax. All through these days, these days of our struggle, our struggle to rid Michael of this horrible disease, we fought this as a family. It affected each and every one of us. Every morning that we would get out of bed, we knew we had to fight one more day. Day after day after day, and you know when a person in your family is suffering from cancer there are no good days at all, just some days slightly less painful than the day before. That's all you can hope for. That's the best you can hope for because your whole world now truly becomes a fight, a fight for survival, a fight to overcome this cancer, a fight to simply survive this cancer.

As hard as it was for Michael and me, we knew it was even harder for our children because we knew what they were thinking. They knew that there was a possibility that their daddy was going to die. So Michael and I had to put on a front for them every single day. We had to make it appear much better than it actually was. We had to shield our children from reality. It was our job as parents to protect them until that day came when we could protect them no longer. If that were going to happen, if they were going to lose their father to this disease, then let them have to face it when the time comes and not contemplate it on a daily basis. This is what we tried to protect them from. I tried to keep them as busy as possible and as uplifted as possible, and this was so incredibly hard because all the while my heart was just breaking.

Finally when the radiation therapy was over, you could see it on Michael. You could see it on his face. It had taken such a toll on his body on his mind and on his spirit. He had lost so much weight. He looked like he had aged twenty years. He had become so frail it scared me. I could see he was slowly slipping away from me, and there was nothing I could do. In order to be able to fight this horrible disease, you have to believe you can win. You have to keep a positive mind set, and this is something that both Michael and I both desperately tried to remember and keep in mind at all times. We tried to only allow positive thoughts to enter our minds and keep away horrible negativities, thoughts of the possibility of Michael losing this battle, of our family losing this battle. We would not let these thoughts enter our mind. We beat everything else in our lives against all the odds, and now we will beat this. Michael and I gave each other every single day these words of encouragement. We simply refused to think otherwise.

It was now the beginning of June 1999, and Michael was recovering nicely from his operation and his radiation therapy. He had started gaining some weight back, and he was looking a little bit better. That healthy glow was slowly starting to come back in his face, and so far test after test proved there was no cancer left in Michael. So now we have to start his recovery. He started walking around and exercising again, and spending time once more with his sons fishing and target shooting. He even started working on the car again.

One afternoon he brought our car up to his mother's house. Of course there was no one living there, and they had yet to sell it. So he used the yard to work on the car because he had to get underneath it. He told me one day what happened to him when he returned back home from working on the car.

He said, "I was underneath the car, and my legs were sticking out, and I had my knee bent. The most amazing thing happened, Kyra. This little tiny finch landed right on my knee and it stayed there for the longest time." He said he had never seen anything like that before in his life. Birds usually are very afraid of people.

I said, "Yeah, I know." I was blown away by this too. I had never heard of this.

It wasn't until later on that evening when I thought to myself, *I wonder if this was a good sign, a sign maybe his mother was watching out for him, because that's what he used to call her as he sat by her bedside dropping drops of water in her mouth and wetting her lips just before she passed. He called her his "little birdie."* I thought maybe she was sending him a little sign that she was watching out for him.

I told him that, and he smiled and said, "You know something, Kyra, I thought the same thing. I could almost feel her there with me. This is what made me think of this."

After this rather strange thing occurred with Michael, I could really sense and see a positive attitude come over him even stronger than before, the positive attitude that he always tried to keep. I think this little sign that he was given was just that added push that he needed, that added help. This was a loving gesture from beyond. A loving gesture only his own Mom could give him at this most horrible time in his life. I think she was letting him know she was there beside him and that she loved him. I know he felt this.

So between this happy little incident and every night when Michael and I would pray together, our positive attitude grew as the days went on, and emotionally our family began to heal from the trauma we had just experienced. Every night in our prayers the first thing, the most important thing to Michael and me, was to get help from God for our children, so we would give them the proper guidance and do right by them and to make them strong people. Then we would pray that Michael's cancer would not return. We also asked God for grace and strength to help us through every single day.

These things we prayed for every night, and through these prayers Michael and I grew ever closer and ever stronger. There was also one other thing that began happening to me once I was able to start praying again once I regained that connection to God. The weird personality quirk that I always had, that feeling of always needing to be in control of everybody or I wasn't comfortable was slowly disappearing. I now knew the only one that was truly in control was God, not me, not anyone else. That was one of the hardest things I ever had to do was hand that control over to God, but once I did (and believe me it took a long time) I felt much more free. I felt like that weight of the world was removed from my shoulders, and now I didn't have to be perfect. I didn't have to be in control all the time, and the world would not collapse if I were not. I guess you would call it blind faith. Handing over your life, your feelings, and your emotions to something that you can't physically see or hear, but nevertheless you know it's there. I knew I had to take that leap of faith in order to be able to get over my control issues and lift that weight of the world off my shoulders. I knew I was going to have to take that step and I trusted in God, and I knew he was there. In time I did it.

I found this time to be a very crucial time in my life. This was a time of much change in both the way I looked at the world, the way I felt toward God, and the way I felt toward myself. I realized I was still dealing with so much old pain, or should I say not dealing with it because I tried to avoid it and tried not to think too much about my mother, Amber and Robert. Every time thoughts of them came into my head I would try to push it out instead of dealing with it and learning how to put it in its proper place.

Pain is a very, very real thing, and grief is as well. You must go through grief when you lose people. It's a healing process, and hopefully some day you can look back on all of the fond memories you shared together with the people that you will always hold close in your heart and laugh, laugh at the good times and not remember them in that casket. Don't remember the heartache, only the love, because the love is what lives on and love is what is important. If you can remember only the love, then and only then will you be healed. The other is to move on in your life, to have a happy life. I realized all of this, and I knew I had to find a place to put all this pain so that I would be able to remember only the happiness, the laughter and the love.

An idea just popped into my head one night as I lay there in Michael's arms thinking about this past year. I thought, *Wouldn't it be perfect if you could have just a large wall full of cubby holes, little compartments like the children have in kindergarten to fit their little hats and lunch boxes in? Wouldn't it be great if you could just place in each and every one of those cubbyholes all of your pain and all of your heartache that you suffered through your life so that you could keep them in their proper place in the past and only remember the good? One cubbyhole would be for my mother's death, the other for Robert's, the other for Amber's, and now the pain that my family has endured with us fighting cancer. Each and every cubbyhole would hold a moment, a moment that changes your life forever. Then lock that door right after you put it in only allowing the love, the happiness and the joy that are in your memories to remain out so that you can carry them in your heart forever, laugh about them and remember them fondly. Wouldn't this be a perfect, perfect thing to be able to do?* I actually started practicing this.

In my mind's eye I imagined that huge wall of cubby holes, and I worked at putting away each and every heartache that I ever had in my life and locking that door right after placing it in, and it actually worked. This is something that my mind devised so that the rest of my life I could live in happiness forgetting all the sorrow just as I know everybody that passed would want me to do, put all the heartaches in those cubby holes. They would want me to do this. They would want me to be happy and they would want me to move on with my life, not remain stuck in grief and heartache. This is what I would want them to do if I were one of those who had passed.

Now I believe the worst thing that you could possibly do is to be stuck like that in grief and heartache and carry that with you until the day you die. How is that honoring the ones that have gone? The legacy you have made for them is now filled with grief and pain. You must find a way to move on, and find a way to honor their memory and laugh about the good times, the fun times. This is what makes them happy, to look down and see us living and not wasting our life in grief. All of these people that I have lost already I will always love, and I will always hold their love in my heart. I feel their love around me even today. I will never ever forget them. Even though I have devised this wall of cubbyholes in which to place my pain, I have not placed them in it, just the pain. They live on in my memories and in my heart for always. Remember me saying, "Death is just a part of life. People are born every day, and people die every day. It's what you do in between that really matters. That truly counts at the end."

Each and every one of my loved ones left behind a beautiful legacy. A legacy filled with love and caring, and I honor that legacy every single day. Every day when I'm faced with different situations, I quite often think to myself, *How would my mother handle this? What would my mother's reaction be, or how would Amber or Robert handle it?* People that are this good I was very lucky to have in my life and learn something from them, and I was. That's what I carry with me today—all their love and all of their strengths because love is truly strength.

Evil is weak. Evil will always try to take the easy way out, and evil doesn't care. Basically evil is very stupid. That is one thing we have going for us. We have the decent people. We can always count on evil screwing itself. That's why good people, the ones that were ripped away from me, need to be honored every day and their good deeds need to be remembered and repeated by other people that they touched through their lives. I believe God needs us all now more than ever to think positively and to do good deeds. When we do good deeds in our loved ones names, loved ones that we lost, I think that's even more special because they truly do live on that way. Goodness and love truly never die.

This summer Michael spent as much time with the boys as he possibly could, and things were really, really looking up. He had many checkups, and he came out of them clean as a whistle. There was no cancer left in him. Come the fall, about a week before Michael's 52nd birthday, he was awarded a disability from the veterans for his post-traumatic stress. This first check was quite substantial because they had to pay him from when he was first diagnosed with it. It was a retroactive check, but being sneaky, as he was at times, he kept this from me and the boys until the right moment. That moment was when he came driving into the driveway with a brand new, red, 4-door Ford Escort right off the showroom floor.

I remember this like it was yesterday. Teddy was sitting there doing his homework when he saw the headlights driving in, and he thought it was his dad. He got up to look out the window and he said, "Who's that?"

I said, "Is it Dad?"

"No. That's not our car." We had had an old broken-down blue LaBaron that Michael got from his mother, and this, of course, was a cute, brand-new red, Ford Escort.

I said, "I don't know who that is."

Then Michael got out of the car, and Teddy said, "It's Dad; it's Dad!"

We all went outside, and I looked at Michael. The next question out of my mouth, of course kidding, was, "Where'd you steal it from?"

Michael then told me about the check that he received from the Veteran's Administration, the retroactive check, and he said I went, I bought it, and I paid cash for it. He handed me the keys, and he said, "Here you go, Kyra; it's yours, fresh off the showroom floor."

I was speechless. My mouth just hung open. I was pleasantly surprised, of course. I was shocked, but also then I thought to myself, *He never, ever agreed with anyone about buying a brand-new car off the showroom floor because it just depreciated so quickly. It was like a waste of money to him.*

Then I thought to myself, *Is he buying it for himself or is he buying it for me because he knows he wasn't going to be here to be fixing our old blue car much longer? Does he want to make sure that the boys and I are all set with transportation?*

I never thought I could feel so sad while being presented with a brand-new car. I quickly asked him, "Is there something you're not telling me about your health?"

He adamantly denied being sick again. He said, "No, no, Kyra, I'm fine," he said. "We needed a new car. I had the money, and I went and bought one."

Again this was not like him. This is not something he would buy for himself, so I was a bit confused through the whole thing.

He said, "Come on, let's take it for a test drive." The boys jumped in the back seat, and Michael drove. We drove all around for about an hour and a half, and he said, "Do you like it? If you don't like it, I'll bring it back and get something else."

I said, "No, I like it a lot. This is what you picked out for me, and I want it."

He then told me he had his choices of blue or white, but he chose the red color. He said, "I thought it would go best with your blond hair. I thought you'd look very pretty driving it."

That very next day after we dropped the boys off at school, Michael and I went for a long, long drive. We ended up basically at the beginning where all of this started at our favorite spot down the lake. We sat there looking at the beautiful fall colors of the trees, the brilliant reds, oranges and yellows and smelled that crisp fall air. We sat there and talked for hours just as we always did in the past, although in recent years I guess we just became so busy between the children and the tragedies in the family, we hardly took any time out for ourselves just to simply sit and be together and enjoy each others company always looking out over that lake.

After so many years we find ourselves back at the beginning. We must have been on our second date when we first came to this spot and discovered it and made it our own. We'd forgotten just how special this spot was to us, but all the memories came flooding back, both the good and the bad. Our 21st anniversary was just around the corner, November 4, and both of us just shook our heads and said, "Twenty-one years. My God, where did all the time go?" Our minds were boggled at the thought, and I told him how much I loved him and also that I would not have traded one minute with him for anything in this world. Throughout all the good times and the bad times, we just grew ever stronger. We grew into ourselves. We would not be the people that we are today, I guess, unless we went through everything that we went through. Throughout all the trials and tribulations our love just grew stronger with every passing year.

It was now two days before our 21st anniversary when Michael and I, Teddy, and Martin were walking through the mall. Michael wanted to buy the boys new winter coats and boots. I noticed an art store. They had all different kinds of beautiful pictures hung, and one particular picture that I was drawn to was of a lighthouse with a deep, deep blue background, a midnight sky, and there was a storm going on. The waves were crashing against the shore. In the lighthouse itself there were three little lights, two at the base and one at the top to guide the ships in. The name of the picture was "Nature's Majesty" and under that was written "A Beacon of Hope." I thought to myself, *How very appropriate that was for my life at this time.* How I had searched for that beacon of hope and finally after so many years found it with Michael's help. Anyway, I stood there staring at it. I could barely take my eyes off of it.

Michael came up beside me and said, "Oh, that's very pretty isn't it?"

I said, "Yeah, I love it."

He said, "Oh, come on. We have to go look at the coats for Teddy now." I followed behind him.

Two days later on our 21st anniversary Michael came walking through the door holding this picture, and he said, "Happy Anniversary, Baby Doll." He told me, "You know what? This is so appropriate for you because you have been my Beacon of Hope."

I was so touched by what he just did and what he just said that I cried, and I told him how much I loved him and hugged him. I felt really bad about the whole thing, because all I had was a watch for him. Even though he loved it, it hardly compared to the loving gesture he just paid to me. It's so funny. I always looked at Michael as my Beacon of Hope, the source of all my strength. I found it incredible he actually felt the same way toward me as I felt toward him. I guess you could say we just held each other up.

Later on that night my sister April came to pick up Teddy and Martin so that Michael and I could have the evening alone together, and even though he still was not able to eat solid foods very well (it was still difficult, and he still had to have his food put through the food processor), he was able to eat a piece of anniversary cake. He at least enjoyed that part of the meal. I set up some candles in the living room, and he and I snuggled on the couch.

I turned to him and asked him, "Michael, do you remember that perfect, perfect weekend that we had down the cape, that weekend that we danced half the night away?" I then asked him if he remembered playing one particular song, my favorite song, "Only You" for me, and then we went back to our hotel room and made love all night long.

He looked at me with a huge smile on his face, and he said, "Of course, Baby Doll. I'll never forget that night."

"You know something? Neither will I." I told him, "I wish people were allowed to freeze just one moment, just one perfect moment, and be allowed to go back to that moment just every now and again when times are so bad or when your heart is breaking so maybe it could help you heal a little."

He said, "Yeah, that would be great, but unfortunately that's not possible, Kyra."

I said, "I know. I just think it would be a great thing to be able to do."

We then begin kissing, and he started caressing my neck, and then we began making love. It never ceased to amaze me how the fires of our passion never grew dim. Each and every time we would make love I would find myself completely consumed by the love that Michael had toward me and I toward him. After 21 years we both found that this was a passion so strong that time nor grief or any heartache that came our way could ever extinguish. We always felt like we had been together all our lives and perhaps maybe even before, but at the same time realizing 21 years had passed and it only felt like 5. How is it possible to feel as though you have been with the same person all of your life and before, and yet at the same time only feel like you've been together for a few years?

Time is very strange and time passes so quickly in a blink of an eye. After this last cancer scare Michael was clean and clear of it all. Now we could actually make plans for the future, and make plans for the next year and perhaps the year after that even. All I knew was that after coming so close to possibly losing my only love, I didn't want to waste one more minute. I wanted to make every day count. I felt as though we had been given a second chance now, and I promised not to take one more second for granted. From here on out Michael and I did just that. We lived for every moment. He was getting up early along with me and getting the boys ready for school, and as soon as we dropped them off we would be off riding around, getting coffee and talking.

It was now a couple of weeks before Thanksgiving and Martin's birthday when Michael had his next doctor's appointment. They were constantly checking him to make sure the cancer hadn't spread. When the day came for his doctor's appointment, the van pulled up as usual. I gave Michael a big hug. The boys were at school already. He was off to his doctor's appointment in Boston. It wasn't until 4 or 5 o'clock when he arrived back home. I had picked up the kids from school and started supper. I could tell by the look on his face as soon as he walked in the door that this was not going to be good news, and sure enough it wasn't. He told me, "I'll talk to you later about it," but I knew what it was. The cancer had returned somewhere.

After we finished supper and I cleaned up, the boys went into the living room to do their homework. Michael and I stayed in the kitchen talking and this is when he told me that the cancer returned in the same area that he had it before, in the lymph nodes, so they had to schedule another operation.

I asked him, "How can you go through another operation? You haven't even fully recovered from this last one yet. You're so weak physically, how can you do this?"

He said, "I don't have a lot of choice now, do I?"

I couldn't believe it. I got up from the kitchen table, and I gave him a hug reminding him of how much I loved him, and I went upstairs to the bathroom. I turned the shower on, I flushed the toilet, turned the faucet on in the sink, and I sat there crying my eyes out, hoping the water would drown out my tears.

Once again I just felt my heart crumbling inside of me. I just simply didn't know how much more Michael could take, or I could take, or Teddy and Martin now could take. How much more fucking bad news is our family expected to take. I stayed in the bathroom by myself for about a half an hour until I was able to compose myself enough to go back downstairs and face Michael and my children again.

I remember walking past Teddy and Martin, who were sitting on the floor doing their homework on the coffee table. They looked up at me and they asked me, "Mommy, what's the matter?"

"Nothing, I'm okay. I just think I'm getting the bug or the flu. My stomach's kind of topsy turvy right now, but Mommy's okay."

They went back to their homework, and I went back out into the kitchen where Michael sat there looking at his medical reports. They also had him down for another round of radiation therapy. I knew this would kill him. There was no way he was physically able to go through that all over again. To make matters worse all of this was to take place around the second week in December. That would mean this would be the first Christmas that my son's would have without their dad being there. It was hard enough with his being gone all the other times. At least it wasn't on any holiday or birthday. It just added to the pain. The idea of looking over at his chair and not seeing him sitting there enjoying the holidays with us, in my mind was now inconceivable. I didn't know how the children were going to be able to bear it.

Michael could have stopped now; he could have stopped at any time. He could have just simply told the doctors, "No more surgery, no more radiation therapy, no more," and let himself go, but that was not what Michael was made of. Michael was a fighter, and that's how he was going to go down, fighting every inch of the way.

He once jokingly said to me years earlier, "They're gonna have to drop kick my ass into that grave, because I ain't gonna go without a fight." This turned out to be exactly what was going on. He fought through every round of radiation therapy, through every surgery. He fought and he fought hard, and now he had even more to fight for, and that was his two sons he refused to leave fatherless, and me all alone.

He looked over the table at me and he said, "Kyra, remember me telling you it's okay to sit back and take a break when things get just too hard to handle? Take a break but never give up, never stop fighting, and once you get your strength back, that's when you come out fighting and you win?" he said. "I have to win. I have no choice. I'm now fighting for our two sons, and I can't fail them. I won't fail them!" He told me then, "I'm going to make damn sure that I'm here to teach Teddy and Martin how to shave, how to drive, and I'm gonna be sitting there right on the couch right beside you waiting for them to come back after their first date. I won't give up, and I won't quit. I can't."

After I saw the determination in Michael's eyes I knew that if anyone was going to beat cancer, it was going to be him. He just simply refused to accept anything short of victory over it. Now the only question in my head was if his body was going to give out well before his spirit would. Was he going to be able to physically survive this? I had no idea. At this point all I had was hope and my prayers.

After we got through talking about this next surgery and this next round of radiation therapy that he was going to go through, he started talking about Martin's birthday which came right after Thanksgiving. He said, "I want to make this a special birthday for Martin, one that he will always remember. Where do you think he'd like to go? What special place can we bring him?"

The first thought that popped into my mind was Chuck-E Cheese's. He always loved Chuck-E Cheese's. So he told me, "Call and make the plans. Set up reservations for his birthday party. I want it to be held there. Invite all his friends from school."

So I did just that the next day. I called and made reservations to have his birthday party held there, and I sent invitations out to all his friends to join us just as Michael requested. Holly, Robert's daughter, offered her camcorder to me so that I could tape this special memory so that Martin would have something to watch later on as he got older in case his memory grew dim, this special birthday party for my angel and Michael's little peanut. Then I invited Izzy, Joey, her two other sons, A.T. and Angel, Jr., and Angel, and took them along as well, along with her sister Cathy and her son Michael.

That camcorder came in handy. It allowed me to tape the whole birthday party, and on this night I just brainwashed myself into trying to forget everything, everything that was going to be up and coming in the following two weeks. I tried to forget Michael's next surgery for just this one night so that my sons would enjoy themselves and that we could have found memories to look back on. It was a challenge, but I was able to do it at least for one night. I got some great footage of Michael with his little boy Martin, the birthday boy, and Teddy, Joey, Angel, Jr., A.T., Michael and a couple of friends from Martin's school, along with Izzy and Angel. I have to say it was one of the best birthday parties I had ever been to, and for kids Chuck-E Cheeze's is paradise. They all enjoyed themselves that night.

It wasn't until a few days after this that Michael and I sat down with Martin and Teddy and let them know that he was going to have to go back into the hospital for one more surgery.

Martin began crying and saying, "No, Daddy, no."

Teddy leaned over to Martin and he said, "Stop; stop crying. Daddy's going to be fine; you know that."

At this point I didn't say anything. I had to get up and walk away because when I saw Martin crying that's all I wanted to do myself, but I knew I couldn't in front of them or in front of Michael.

So Michael just sat there between Martin and Teddy holding them and watching TV for the rest of the night. Martin finally calmed down, and then Teddy asked Michael, "How are we supposed to get our Christmas tree?"

I told Teddy, "Well, I guess it's just going to be me, you, and your brother this year, but we'll be able to get it. Daddy showed me how to tie it onto the car and get it home. Don't worry about that."

He asked, "Is Daddy going to be home before Christmas?"

We weren't sure, so that's what we told them. We were honest. We didn't know how much time he was going to have to spend in the hospital after this operation.

I said, "It's a good possibility that, no, he's not going to be home for Christmas."

That's when Michael quickly jumped in and said, "Well, we could talk on the phone for hours that day. It would be like I'm here."

Teddy just looked down after Michael said that and said, "That's not going to be the same thing, Daddy."

I said to Teddy, "Well, right now we really don't have any choice in the matter. It has to be done. Your dad really needs this next operation."

I hated seeing that look on my children's faces, that total disappointment and complete heartache and not being able to do anything to stop it, to take their pain away. I was barely able to deal with my own. I remember making a comment to Michael in the kitchen after we talked to Teddy and Martin. I told him, "I don't even want to put up a Christmas tree this year. I just have no spirit, no Christmas spirit left in me anymore."

He told, "Don't you dare. Don't you dare say that," he said. "You've always been the Christmas Girl to me and to our two sons, and you're not going to let them down now." He made me promise him right there and then, "No matter what happens, as long as our kids are still kids, as long as they're still young, they will always have a beautifully decorated Christmas tree and house," he said, "You promise me this right now, Kyra," and I did.

I said, "I don't know how I'm going to do it, but I'll do it."

It turned out that year Michael was going to be able to go and pick up our family's Christmas tree with us. We just got it a few days earlier than we normally would have. The boys were thrilled about this, and again we stopped after picking up the tree at Santa's Little House where the boys had their pictures taken with Santa and we did have our family walk around the Green looking at all the pretty lights. At least this was one family tradition that we were thankfully able to stick to this year. The next day I had the traditional Christmas dinner that I always cooked every year. Although it was three weeks before Christmas I wanted us to just make believe that it was Christmas Day. The tree was up already, the lights were on and everything was decorated. So I thought to myself, *Why not have a Christmas dinner?* because of course, I knew Michael wasn't going to be here Christmas Day. I was able to put everything in the food processor except my homemade giblet stuffing that Michael loved so much. That for some reason just didn't work out too well in the food processor, but he was able to enjoy the turkey, mashed potatoes, squash, and of course we had our traditional eggnog with our dinner. Everything was as it would be for Christmas day. It just occurred three weeks earlier that's all.

The next week passed by so quickly, too quickly. Before we knew it, it was time and that van from the VA was pulling up to pick up Michael one more time. I kept the boys home from school on this day so that they would be able to say goodbye to their Dad and watch him get on the van. We all gave him hugs and kisses, and he promised to call that night. It was that night before he had to go to the hospital that Michael and I spent the entire night cuddling on the couch by the soft glow of the Christmas lights with all the other lights out. We kept the TV off and concentrated on each other. We didn't speak much; we were just taking each other in and holding each other tight for comfort. Neither one of us at this point knew what was going to happen next. There was no way to look into the future. All we knew was whatever fights lay before us, we would take on just as we always had in the past, together as a team and as a family. On this night we just prayed and hoped for the best because at this point that was all we could do.

CHAPTER TWELVE

That night when Michael called from the VA we spoke on the phone for well over two hours. This was the night before his operation. I remember the last words he said to me just before he hung up the phone, "Kyra, pray for me, please. Please, pray harder than you have ever prayed in your life." Those words that he said just sounded so familiar in my head. Those were almost word for word what my loving sister said to me just before she died and that brought back that memory. I thought to myself, *Dear God, this can't be happening again, not now, not to Michael.*

I told Michael, "Yes, of course I will, and everything is going to be fine." I tried to reassure him as much as I could, and I told him how much I loved him and how he was the world to me. I told him to remember those words before he went into the operating room and to come back to us, come back to his family and come back to the woman who loves you more than life itself. I told him to stay strong because he was in the battle of his life. He was in fact in the battle for his life now and he must remain strong.

That night in our bedroom I did pray. I prayed harder than I ever had before in my life. I also tried to talk to Amber that night in my prayers. I asked her for her forgiveness for the cruel way that I spoke to her, and in fact the last words that I said to her I would live to regret for the rest of my days. I told her how very, very sorry I was, and if I could take those words back I would in a heartbeat. I told her also that she had no idea of the spiritual crisis I was in, how I was just not able to pray, and how badly I felt about it. Her words cut right through me when she asked me to pray for her. I just let her know how much I loved her and missed her along with Mommy, Robert and Michael's mother. I asked them all if there was any way possible they could help us now and help Michael, would they please do so, because we could really use all the love and support we can get right now. Yes, on this night I prayed harder than I have ever prayed before in my life.

That next day after Michael's operation I called his doctors at the VA, and I spoke to one of them. I asked him how everything went, and he said everything went great. He says it seems we have all the cancer now. Unfortunately I didn't put much stock in that statement because that had been told to us time, and time, and time again. But for now those words still came as a relief to me, and maybe, just maybe everything was going to be okay.

It was now the day before Christmas and Michael had spent about a week and a half recovering from his last operation. He was doing very well. We of course spoke every night on the phone for hours although I could tell it was very difficult for him to speak. I guess with kids all you have to do is let them do the talking. Teddy and Martin every night would tell their father about their day at school. How they were so excited now to be going on Christmas break, and of course Christmas break meant being able to use their new sleds, have those snowball fights and build their snowmen. So they were really excited this time of the year.

On the 24th of December I asked Izzy if she would mind bringing the boys and me to see their father in the hospital in Boston. You see she was very familiar with the Boston traffic because that's where she came from. So this was a breeze to her, and of course she said, "Yes." So I did something that Michael never really wanted me to do. I brought our sons to the hospital and to see him lying there in bed. For some reason he just did not want me to do this. He didn't want our children seeing this. So going against his wishes, we took that drive to Boston. We brought all of his presents with us so that he could open them. I had bought this beautiful long men's housecoat. It was so soft, like a baby's blanket, in blue, his favorite color, pajamas, brand new slippers, and I bought him two hand-held games. One game was *Wheel of Fortune* and the other one was *Jeopardy*. I was hoping they would provide a little distraction for him during his long stays in the hospital.

So Izzy, Teddy, Martin, and I arrived there about two in the afternoon. After I found out where his room was, we went up to his room and stood there as he lay sleeping in his bed. He opened his eyes, and he had the most amazed look on his face. He rubbed his eyes and said to me, "Am I dreaming?" He actually thought he was dreaming. He thought he was hallucinating. As the three of us stood there before him holding all of his Christmas presents, he then sat up in bed and laughed. We all just hugged him and kissed him.

I told him, "I know this goes against what you told me to do, but I just couldn't resist. It's the day before Christmas, and the boys desperately wanted to see their father, and I desperately wanted to put my arms around you and hug you. We need this, Michael, and I think you do, too."

He nodded his head and said, "Yeah, I did."

He was glad that I went against his wishes, but I was shocked to see his condition. He wasn't doing as well as what he was telling me over the phone. I could see he was deteriorating. He had lost all the weight that he was able to gain back again, and he looked so pale and frail. He was only 52, and he looked like he was 80. The most amazing part was I don't think the boys even realized how much their father's appearance had changed. Children are so strange sometimes because they were just sitting by him like nothing else was going on, like this was an everyday thing, just as they sat on the couch watching TV every night. They made no comment, and they said nothing to me afterwards. Really, it was as though they didn't even notice or maybe in a child's mind they block out what they don't wish to see. I don't know. I think they were just so happy to be able to finally touch their father and be with their father again that's all that mattered to them.

I knew this was the best Christmas present that I could ever, ever give my children, and that was being in their daddy's arms for Christmas. Izzy helped me achieve this. She had become like a little sister to me now. I loved her like a sister, and Angel, her husband, like a brother. They were so kind and so caring. She did this I know mainly for my boys because she knew also that they needed to see their dad for Christmas. They needed to be in his arms just as much as I knew this to be true.

After about three hours of us visiting, Michael told me that he wanted to speak to me in private. He had something he wanted to tell me, and could Izzy take the two boys out for a little walk in the corridor while we did this. So I whispered to Izzy to take the boys out for a few minutes so Michael and I could talk, and she did.

Michael then began explaining to me what they wanted to do to him next. Besides the next round of radiation therapy, they wanted to insert a feeding tube in him because he was losing so much weight. Due to the condition of his mouth, he wasn't able to eat very much at all. Michael was very, very concerned about this. He didn't like the thought of having a feeding tube inserted into him, and neither did I, but I asked him what's the alternative.

Perhaps if you don't have one put in, you'll just waste away, and the weaker you get, the less you'll be able to fight the cancer.

So he came to a decision that day, and he told me, "Okay, I'll have them put the feeding tube in me. I'll agree to it."

At this point he just looked so horrible I really didn't see any other alternative. I thought perhaps if he was able to gain some weight back and to get stronger, then we would be able to handle all the other things and he'd be able to recover. He needed to get stronger, and this was our only option. So a couple of days later they put the feeding tube in Michael's stomach, but they found he was so weak and his body had been torn down so badly, he was not able to take a feeding on a regular feeding schedule. I guess some people who have feeding tubes can be fed three meals a day through the tube, but Michael's body couldn't stand this, so they had to put him on the feeding tube 24/7 at a low rate. That meant only a little bit of food at a time was being pumped into his stomach throughout the entire day, which was what his body was able to tolerate.

Just before Izzy, Teddy, Martin, and I left Michael, Teddy and Martin jumped on him and gave him hugs and kisses and their love. Michael smiled so brightly. Then it was my turn, and I gave him the biggest hug I had ever given him in my life. I didn't want to let go of him, and I told him, "You are my heart, and you do whatever you have to do to come back to me."

He looked at me and smiled and he told me how much he loved me and he promised he would. He said, "You know, I'm still the fighter, Kyra."

I said, "I know you are."

Leaving him there like that was one of the hardest things I've ever had to do in my life. I had to fight with everything in me the urge not to just jump into bed beside him and never leave his side, but I knew this was not realistic. I knew that I had our two sons that I must think of first, and I must take care of and keep their spirits high and protect them. This is what Michael wanted me to do. So it took every ounce of self-control that I had to turn and walk out of that room and leave him there. I just kept looking at Teddy and Martin and knew I had no choice.

When we arrived home later on that evening, I felt so cold and so hollow. A huge void was here, and we all felt it. I knew that Christmas Eve was going to be incredibly, incredibly heartbreaking for me. This was our time together. This was the time we set up all the gifts underneath the tree and filled the stockings and then cuddled in each other's arms for the rest of the night beside the soft glow of the Christmas tree lights. Tonight I would now lay here alone and pray that next Christmas my love would be back in my arms just as he always was.

So I did just what Michael and I always did and that was place all the presents underneath the Christmas tree for Martin and Teddy and fill their stockings. Instead of lingering in the living room sitting on that empty couch alone (I couldn't bear to), I just simply went to bed and tried my hardest to forget. I just kept thinking of Michael, and I prayed for our whole family that night.

Of course the morning came with the light breaking through our bedroom blinds. So harsh and so cold was that light I knew I would now have to face Christmas Day alone watching our children open their presents and having so much fun. I didn't even bother looking outside to see if it had snowed. That was one of the first things Michael and I did every Christmas morning. As soon as those rays of light came through the blinds, the boys were up and ready to go, attacking the tree and all their presents. So I sat there as they ripped open package after package. They then attacked their stockings. With wrapping paper almost waist deep in my living room, I began picking up all the mess and watching my boys playing with their new toys.

After they were through examining all their new toys and playing with some I turned to Teddy, because he was now 12 years old, and I asked him, "Would you like to help Mommy in the kitchen today?" I thought perhaps I could keep his mind busy and off of his father's not being here today. So I had Martin help me with the cranberry sauce.

Teddy just stood there in shock. I guess he really didn't realize exactly where the stuffing went in the turkey. As he stood there watching me push it in he said, "Oh, Ma, how gross is that?"

I said, "I do this every single year." Evidently he had never seen me stuff the turkey before, so he was quite grossed out over the whole thing. I said, "Well, maybe then you could start peeling the potatoes."

He said, "Yea, that I can do."

April was coming over around 2:00, and they were looking forward to showing her all their gifts and getting the gifts that she brought them. Sadly as far as family went, this was now the only thing my children had to look forward to. There was no more Aunt Amber, there were no more grandmas, and now even their father wasn't able to sit down and have Christmas dinner with us.

April was very, very important to Teddy and Martin. She was always doing something with them, either going to the movies or just out for a ride to get ice cream. She even took them on a hayride that her work sponsored one year. She was very, very much a loving hands-on Aunt, and thankfully she absolutely loved the holidays—Halloween, Thanksgiving, Christmas, and Easter. Easter, I guess, was her favorite holiday. She loved it more than any other, and she would always bring all these beautiful pastries from the bakery especially at Easter time. She would bring cupcakes that were made into baskets and Easter bunny cookies. She would also give them gifts, always of course the coloring books and crayons for every different holiday along with bubbles to blow. The gifts depended on what the kids were into that particular year, because their tastes changed in different toys of course. Teddy was into the Game Boy, so she got him his favorite game boy game and Martin a bug kit where he could make his own bugs.

I remember that particular year very well. She was always, always thinking of them, and they were very close to her. So she was the only thing that took the sting out of their dad not being able to be there for this Christmas. Even though I did a lot of baking for the holidays, she would always show up with two or three boxes of goodies from the bakery, a huge cake, all kinds of cookies and candies. I'll tell you, the sweets just poured out of my house on every holiday. Most of all she just really loved spending time with Teddy and Martin. They were very, very lucky to have such a loving aunt, and I was very lucky to have such a loving sister.

One o'clock came and April arrived with her usual goodies and her presents. The children were thrilled to see her. We sat down and had a lovely dinner again trying our hardest not to look over to the empty chairs. After dinner she sat in the living room and they opened up the gifts that she bought them, and then she opened up the gifts that we got her. Everyone was having fun. I was trying very hard to keep up our spirits and just trying to enjoy the moment, as I would find myself doing quite often in my life in the past. I was just trying to live in the moment, enjoying what was going on around me and not letting the pain in.

So after this day of fun, around 5 o'clock Michael called. We must have spoken on the phone for at least two or three hours, and the boys told him everything that Santa had brought them. Yes, everything that "Santa" had brought them. I hadn't told Martin yet that there was no Santa Claus, Easter Bunny or tooth fairy. He still believed all of that. Teddy, on the other hand, played along and let me believe that he still believed, and of course never saying anything to his brother about it. So they talked on the phone, and the boys described every little thing that they got, and then it was my turn.

Michael and I began talking about our own little Christmas tradition that we had Christmas Eve of cuddling on the couch after all the work was done, and he told me how much he missed that last night. I told him I couldn't even bear to sit there on that couch by myself. I went straight to bed.

He said the strangest thing after I said that. He said, "I'm sorry, Kyra."

I laughed, and I said, "What in the hell do you have to be sorry for? This is something that was put on our family. We had no control over this. All we can do is fight it now. Don't feel sorry for me; I'll be okay. Our love will carry me through."

The love that I could feel from him all the way from Boston would carry me through, and it did. It kept me strong both for myself and for our sons.

That following week passed by with our heartbreaking phone calls every night, and before I knew it was New Year's Eve. Of course how Michael and I were to spend this New Year's Eve was drastically different from any New Year's Eve we had celebrated before. Our tradition of cuddling on the couch and making love by the soft glow of the Christmas tree lights of course could not be this year. I lay on the couch by myself trying to feel his presence and watching the clock. Just before the stroke of midnight I called his room at the hospital, and we counted the New Year in together. It seemed funny that the rest of the world was so worried about all the computers crashing, about this big catastrophe going on when all I could worry about was my little corner of the world, my little family and my true love lying so far away from me. He was all I was worried about. I could have cared less if the rest of the world just came crashing down, because as far as I was concerned my world already was. I lay there, and we counted in the New Year together over the phone, and it was all I could do to choke back my tears.

He said, "Happy New Year, Baby Doll."

I said, "Happy New Year, Teddy Bear."

It was now the beginning of the New Year, the beginning of a new century, New Years Eve 2000, but I had not lost all hope. I clung to the littlest hope like a baby clings to its mother. Perhaps this year things would turn around, Michael would make a full recovery, and our family would be back to normal again. I hoped and I prayed as hard as I ever did, but I could tell by Michael's voice that he was growing weaker, and I needed to see him. So a couple of days after New Years I asked Izzy to bring us once again to visit Michael, and she of course agreed. He was now in a private room hitched up to this feeding machine that kept a constant slow flow of food going into his stomach from this long tube. Whenever I saw him all I could think of was that my world was just crumbling down around me and there wasn't a fucking thing I could do about it. The boys ran over and jumped on his bed, Teddy on one side and Martin on the other hugging him and kissing him, and I just stood there in horror. This strong, handsome loving man that I had known since I was sixteen and a half was now reduced to such a frail whisper of a man. My heart was just shattering. I then went over and gave him a huge hug and kiss and told him how much I loved him, and he told me how much he loved me.

I knew I had to do something, but I just didn't know what. It always seemed to me that our family got us through so many hard times because we were able to stay together, we were able to have daily contact and keep each other strong. Now every day he was just so far away. I thought perhaps if he were closer to home the boys and I could see him on a daily basis, this would help with his recovery because I did know that a positive attitude played a huge role in this. Now with him on a feeding machine, I didn't know quite how to go about handling all of this. I just knew I had to do something.

The day after we returned from this visit, he called me on the phone and told me, "Kyra, I didn't want to tell you in front of the kids, but I swear if I don't get out of this place, I'm going to die."

Those words were all I needed to hear. I called the head of the hospital, and I explained what was going on. I explained how far away his family was, how very close we were, and he needed to see us. I knew this would help in his recovery.

The head of the hospital agreed, "Yes, this probably would be a good idea, and actually outside of his being on the feeding tube, there was really no other reason to keep him in the hospital." So the head of the VA set up all the arrangements to have him sent to a nearby nursing home where he could recover and get physical therapy as well. I thought this was a good idea and a positive move. So within a couple of days Michael, thank God, was back in town where the boys and I could see him on a regular basis now and give him the love and support that only a family can give.

It was now the middle of January 2000, when they transported Michael by ambulance to the nursing home only about five minutes away. I was there by his side an hour after he arrived there. Right after dropping off the children at school I went to see him. This nursing home was very, very nice. It was very clean and everyone there was very loving and supportive. I have nothing but good things to say about them, but Michael still looked horrible. The feeding tube was not agreeing with him. They changed the formula they were giving him, and they kept changing the rate on the machine that regulated how much would go into his body. It seems like they just couldn't get it right, because if too much was allowed to enter his stomach at once, it would make him vomit, and too little would not provide the nutrients that he needed.

So we spent weeks trying to get this just right—the timing on the machine and the formula that was being fed into him. In the meantime he would be sick and vomiting. It was like his body was just rejecting this food supplement. In the meantime our family's daily schedule just became so crazy. I would get up in the morning and get the boys up and ready for school, drop them off and then I would head straight to the nursing home to sit by Michael's side.

As soon as I arrived at the nursing home every morning, I would wash his face and shave him and collect the dirty clothes from the day before so I could bring them home to wash. One day I asked the nurse about the physical therapy part. I said, "When is he going to start this?" They were in between physical therapists. Right now they had none, so I began my own physical therapy with him. After washing and shaving him every morning, I would get him into his clean pajamas, and we would walk all around in the nursing home inside, going very slowly but keeping a steady pace. I wanted him to do this twice a day, once in the morning and once in the evening after what would normally be supper time, but for Michael it was the third bag of feeding formula. I asked one of the nurses at the nursing home if at this time of the day, after supper, they could do this, take him for a walk because I was at home at that point giving my children their supper and getting them ready to come and visit their father.

She said, "Kyra, we've already tried this. He just gives us this look, just to leave him the hell alone."

I know that look she was talking about, and it can be very intimidating, but please, the man is so sick, I don't think he was able to fight anybody. But even though they felt intimidated, they really didn't push the subject, so that left me trying to get back to the nursing home as quickly as possible to give him that walk after picking the boys up from school and giving them their supper.

Come to find out Michael was the perfect patient. He never complained, he never argued about anything that I had to do with him or give him, but it seems like I was the only person that he was this cooperative with. Everyone else he would give a hard time to. He didn't want anybody but me touching him.

So after the nurse told me this, I went back into Michael's room, and I told him, "Why are you giving them those looks? Why are you giving them such a hard time?"

He just smiled at me from ear to ear and turned his head away not answering my question.

I said, "You little shit. I know what it is. It's the team. I'm the only part of that team, aren't I?" and he still said nothing. So the schedule was, after I dropped the children off I went to the nursing home, washed and shaved his face, changed his clothes, walked him around, and then we would go back to his room. He would get back into the bed, and we would sit there holding each other's hands watching TV for the rest of the day until it was time for me to pick up the boys from school. I then would pick up the boys, bring them home, give them their supper, and then bring them back to the nursing home, where the four of us would go for that walk around the nursing home inside so that Michael could get the exercise that he needed. Then the boys, Michael, and I would return back to the room, and Teddy and Martin would begin their homework.

This is where they would do their homework every night until their father was to come back home. They would sit there by the large windowsill in their father's room doing this, trying to study and trying to keep their grades up. This was becoming more and more difficult as time went on because of course their concentration level was not as it was before. We were all doing our best and just trying to get through this horrifying time in our lives. As I sat by Michael's side holding his hand and quite often caressing it, we would watch our two boys as they did their homework, answering whatever questions they had.

One day Michael asked me to bring him some soft-serve vanilla ice cream. I said, "Oh, really, you're up to doing that?"

He said, "Yeah, I've been craving that."

"Okay." So the next day the boys and I stopped at Friendly's and got some soft-serve ice cream for Michael and some sundaes for us. Michael thoroughly enjoyed his ice cream. I realized, though, by doing this I was probably breaking every rule in the book as far as having a person on a feeding tube went. But, you know, he had been through so damn much, and he was so miserable I thought if I could just put a little bit of a smile on his face, all the other consequences would be worth it.

He did take it well, and he didn't get sick, but I told him, "Honey, we can't do this too often, you know."

He said, "I know."

Week after week passed by now. It was toward the end of February 2000, and Michael didn't look any better than he did the first day he arrived at the nursing home. Actually he was starting to look worse. His spirit was being crushed there, and I could tell he was going downhill fast. I also saw something in his eyes that I had never seen before in all the years that we were together, and that was a look of giving up. He looked like he just gave up on everything, and I knew I couldn't let this happen. I couldn't allow him to just give up now, not after all of this. I knew I had to do something.

I asked him, "Do you want to come home."

He said, "How can I with the feeding tube?"

I said, "I'll learn how to run this feeding tube. I'll learn how to run the machine. I'll take care of you. I come here every day and take care of you anyway. It will just be a lot more convenient because you will be home."

"Are you sure that you want to do this, Kyra?"

"Of course I do. Of course I'm sure. Remember, we always did everything as a team. What's different now? There is no difference. We need each other, and you need to get the hell out of here. You need your spirits lifted up again, and your family will do this for you."

So I went and spoke to the head of the nursing home, and I told her that I wanted my husband home as soon as possible. She asked me why.

I told her straight out, "This place is not good for him. He's too young, and he has too much to live for. He looks like all the fight has gone out of him. He just looks like his spirit is crushed, and I have to do something. I want him home, and I want him home now."

She said, "Well, you have to learn how to run the feeding machine."

I said, "Gladly. Just show me. I'll be able to do it."

So in two days I picked Michael up and brought him home. We left the nursing home, and they set up an appointment for a visiting nurse to come and show me how to run the feeding machine, how to take care of his feeding tube, and how to give him all the medications that he needed.

On the morning that I picked him up from the nursing home, before going home I took him for a long ride in our new car that he had just bought. He cracked the window just a bit to let some of the fresh air in, and I could see on his face the change already in just a few minutes out of the nursing home. His spirits were beginning to lift once more, and we ended up down at our spot down by the lake where we sat for a couple of hours holding each other and talking. I knew I had made the right choice by getting him out of there. I only wished I had done it a week earlier. As we sat there cuddling looking over the frozen lake and the beautiful winter scenery that only New England could provide, we were together again as a team and as a team we would fight once more.

The visiting nurse arrived at our apartment about an hour after we got home. She was very, very nice and very patient with me, going very slowly and showing me everything that I needed to know. When I realized just how easy this was, I kicked myself for not bringing him home immediately after his leaving the VA instead of spending over a month in the nursing home. I could have been doing this. Running a feeding machine is very simple. You put the formula, whatever formula the doctor prescribes for the patient, in to this bag (you pour it in). It looks like an IV bag, and there's a thin hose that runs from the bag through this machine. On this machine that had digital numbers, you set the numbers to the speed that the formula is dripped into the patient, the proper flow of the food. Then from the machine you take the long tube and you put it into the tube that is stationary in the patient and has been surgically placed into him and you connect it. It's as simple as that.

The only difficult part I found was keeping the tube clear, the tube that came from his stomach that I would hitch the other long tube to. The tube that remained in his stomach was very difficult to manage. It was very difficult to keep it clear so that the flow of food could go in easily, because this was also the place of delivery for his medicine. His medicines were all liquefied and the ones that were still in pill shape I had to crush into a fine powder and mix with water. Then it had to be sucked out of the cup with a large syringe and inserted into the small hose going into his stomach. No matter how fine you were able to grind them, the powders would sometimes clog this tube. So what I figured out was to hold onto the end of the tube that was closest to his stomach and with my other hand pull on this tube and this would release a paste-like substance and it would clear it.

I did this until one of the nurses showed me a little secret and that was to take a tiny, tiny bit of ginger ale every day and with the large plastic syringe that I would deliver his medicines in put a little of that through the tube and that would clear it out every day. It did work like a charm. Even with me following all the instructions to the letter and giving him the medicine that I was supposed to give him, he still occasionally would get sick and start vomiting. Now his vomit was becoming black and it stunk to high heaven. It looked almost like tar, and each and every time he would have one of these episodes, I would take him down to Out Patient so the doctor could take a look at him. At this point we had a fantastic Oncologist Dr. Shrew who came highly recommended. He was the top in his field in Morton, and he was affiliated with Dana Farber Institute, so I had full confidence in his abilities. Once he began seeing Michael he wanted to start him on chemotherapy to knock out the rest of the cancer if there was any left in him. So that is what we did.

It was around the middle of March now and he began the chemotherapy treatments, but every appointment that Michael had with the doctor and every treatment that he had would have to be at a very limited time because during this time that he was out of the house he was not on the feeding tube. He was supposed to be on the feeding tube 24/7, so it was always like a rush in and rush out type of thing. Of course, the chemotherapy, even though the doctor gave him medications to counteract the nausea, it still didn't work. He was still throwing up from it. The doctor one day prescribed this bottle of medicine in liquid form to help with the nausea. Whenever I picked it up from the pharmacy, I was completely blown away. This bottle, although it was large, cost over $900. Thank God we had medical insurance. I tried it on him, and it didn't work. He was still vomiting.

There were no normal days now, either Michael suffered from diarrhea or constipation, one or the other or just throwing up from all the nausea. We went through all of April like this, and all through this horrifying time Michael never complained to me once. I was told his visiting nurse said, "He is such a marvelous patient," and she offered another service and that would have someone come in and help me wash him and shower him.

Michael and I both looked at each other and our reactions were exactly the same, "Thank you, but no thank you." He told me, "Kyra, I don't want anybody but you touching me."

I wholeheartedly agreed with this. I didn't want anyone touching him either, so we thanked her very much.

She said, "Well, at least let me get you a shower chair in case he gets dizzy in the shower," because they worried about that. I agreed to that and went and picked it up. Every other morning Michael would sit on the shower chair, and I would wash his hair and rub his back and wash it and shower him down.

These times of the day were our very intimate moments and our loving and caring moments, moments I will always remember. Even now, today, we were that team and we stood strong side by side just as we always did. Through this time I often remembered our past and our fight with alcoholism, and I thought, *You know, this isn't much different. We were fighting for our lives back then, and we're fighting for our lives now.* If we were able to conquer that and win, I felt in my heart that we would be able to conquer this and come out even stronger than we had ever been in our lives before. It was our deep, deep love for each other that got us over each and every hurdle in our lives, each and every heartbreaking moment and each and every disaster. We pulled together and we became one. Our hearts became one, and our love was invincible. Through our love an incredible strength grew, and we needed all that strength right now at this moment to fight this cancer. I knew we had it in us, and I knew neither one of us would give up. I knew this was not a time for tears. This was the time for strength. I would shed no more tears, and I would not be weak.

I felt as though I was a new person now. I had God back in my life. I was able to pray. I was able to draw strength from Him. Michael was the one who gave that back to me, and now, no, I won't shed any more tears. I'll just be strong. I'll be strong for Michael. I'll be that strong woman that he so deserves to have standing beside him. This I promised myself, and I promised Michael that no matter what else was to come our way, we would handle it together just as we always did in life. This was now not a time for tears but a time to fight, and we fought with everything we had.

So Michael continued with his chemotherapy treatments. These treatments would be given to him right at Dr. Shrew's office right in our Town. I would be able to sit with him all the while he was receiving them and hold his hand, and again, thinking only positive thoughts. Meanwhile I did my best to protect our children from seeing too much of the things that they didn't need to see. While still always remaining honest with our children, we told them just what they needed to know and that was Daddy was getting medication that hopefully would kill the cancer that was in him.

We told them we were hoping everything was going to be fine, but unfortunately this medication that their Daddy had to take in the meantime was making him very sick and that was why he was throwing up. I don't think they quite understood why something that was supposed to be making you better seemed to be making you sicker. I tried to explain to them the best way that I could, that sometimes you have to kill bad things in you, and when you do, when you kill the cancer cells, the process of this is so strong that it can actually make you sick to your stomach. But it wouldn't last forever, I told them. As soon as the chemotherapy was over, their Daddy would not be throwing up so much, and then hopefully we would be back on the road to recovery, Michael's as well as our family.

This is what I told our children. After each chemotherapy treatment that Michael had if he wasn't feeling too sick right away, I would always try to get him to come with me to that spot, our special spot, our special place by the lake before we went back home, before I had to attach him back to the feeding machine. I am grateful to say that some days he was able to do this, and we enjoyed every second of sitting there, holding each other and remembering.

It was now toward the end of April of 2000 when the chemotherapy ended. Michael was to wait a week and then they wanted to run an MRI on his head to make sure all the cancer was gone. So on May 5 I brought Michael to have this test done at our hospital in Town. Coincidentally this was the same day that Holly, Robert's daughter, had given birth.

I thought, *Oh, my God, this was such a lovely thing,* and I asked Michael, "Would it be okay if I went to visit Holly, her husband and their new baby upstairs in the Maternity Ward while you're having your test done?"

He said, "Certainly, Honey, go and have some fun."

I was absolutely thrilled and stopped at the Gift Shop to get this big bunny that you hung from the ceiling, a ballerina bunny. They had a beautiful baby girl. I brought her some flowers, and I went upstairs, and I stood at the window looking at all the babies, and I saw hers. I thought to myself, *If Robert could only be here to see her,* and I really felt deep down in my heart like a stand-in for Robert, where he couldn't be there physically to see her, to see his beautiful granddaughter, but I could, and I could lend my support to his daughter, just as I know he would have. I knew he was not physically there, but I could feel him there in spirit. I knew he was seeing what I was seeing. She was such a beautiful baby girl. This day was so bittersweet. A beautiful life coming into the world and the grandfather that would have taught her so much and loved her so much was not here.

I then went into the room and gave Holly and her husband Mark a big hug. I told her how very proud her father would be right now.

I said, "You take very good care of that little girl because Daddy's watching." She just swallowed back the tears, and she said, "I know."

I explained to her that I had to keep our visit short, although I hated to do so because Michael was downstairs getting a test, and I only had a short amount of time before I had to go and pick him up.

She then asked me how we were doing, and I told her, "Well, we're hoping for the best. He just went through his last rounds of chemotherapy. This was what the test was for; to make sure that all the cancer was gone. That there weren't any more tumors."

I remember her giving me a hug and telling me, "I'll pray for you, and I hope to God everything goes very well for you and your family."

I thanked her, and I took one more look at that precious angel that just came into this world. Then I went back downstairs to where Michael was after completing his tests.

He looked at me and asked, "What does the baby look like?"

"Just like Robert," and he laughed. I said, "She's a beautiful, beautiful girl."

Michael and I then returned home. We would have to wait a few days for the test results which the doctor would have for us at our next doctor's appointment.

The second week in May something horrible started happening with Michael. It was the day before his next doctor's appointment when we were going to get the test results back. He started vomiting violently. The smell was just so horrific and the color jet black like tar and thick. It was the worst vomiting spell he had had so far. I tried to give him his anti-nausea medicine, and I did something really, really stupid. His tube had become clogged, and when I went to try and squeeze out what was clogging it, my finger slipped from his stomach. I had one hand on his stomach holding the tube close to his stomach while I pulled on the other end to release whatever was clogging it when my finger slipped and the whole tube came out in my hand. I looked at Michael and my mouth just dropped.

I said, "Oh, God, no!"

Michael looked at me and he said, "What did you do?"

I said, "Oh, Honey, I just ripped the frickin' tube out. We have to go to the hospital so they can put it back in."

So I got him up and dressed and out to the car, just barely making it. He was barely standing. I got to the Emergency Room, and they said, "Actually that's no big deal. They can reinsert the tube just fine. Don't worry about it. It isn't a catastrophe."

I thought it was. I said, "Well, what about this black vomit? I was trying to give him his anti-nausea when this happened. I was giving it to him because he kept vomiting this black tar."

A few doctors came in and looked at him. He had stopped vomiting by that time. They said, "Well, he looks okay now, but we have to get the tube reinserted." They took him up to the operating room, and it only took about 20 minutes. Everything was fine, but they wanted to keep him overnight just to make sure.

I told them, "Tomorrow we have an appointment with Dr. Shrew," and I let them know about the test results we were supposed to get in.

They said, "Don't worry about it. Dr. Shrew can see him while he's in the hospital." So Michael spent that night in the hospital.

The next morning after dropping the kids off at school, I went right up there. I spent the morning with Michael, and then toward the afternoon Dr. Shrew came in. He asked us how we were doing, and I said, "Well, not too well." I told him what I did with the feeding tube and he kind of chuckled.

I said, "Yeah, laugh. I was horrified."

He told me then that he wanted to run a few more tests on Michael because the first one was kind of iffy, and of course, we agreed. So Michael stayed for about a week in the hospital while further tests were being done on him. That week was like turning back the hands of time, to the time he was in the nursing home. I went right back onto that schedule, dropping the kids off at school and going and spending my days with Michael and then picking the kids up after school, giving them their supper (although now we began eating in the cafeteria a lot), and then we would go up to see their father and spend the evening up there with them doing their homework. We would get home about 9 o'clock.

That week the doctor got to meet Teddy and Martin, and all three of them hit it off very well. The doctor really seemed to like them.

One morning a couple of days before Michael was scheduled to come home, I arrived just as Dr. Shrew was getting onto the elevator. I was getting off, and I called him aside to talk with him. I asked him to please tell me the truth. Please tell me honestly what was going on. He hemmed and hawed around, and I gave him a brief description of what our lives had been like over the past five years and how many loved ones I lost. I told him I can handle the truth, but I what I can't handle is having sunshine blown up my skirt and then the rug ripped out from underneath me. I asked him, "Please, be honest with me. What's going on?"

That's when he told me that Michael had developed yet another tumor, a cancerous tumor between his neck and his brain, and it was inoperable. The cancer had gone to his brain. There was nothing at all medicine could do for him now. "He is going to die."

I was floored. I know I should have seen this coming. I should have tried at least to brace myself for the worst, but I couldn't allow myself to think that way. I couldn't allow myself to be negative. I had to hope always for the best, always that we were going to beat this until I was faced with a cold slap in the face of reality, and this was my cold slap in the face.

I asked the doctor how much longer did he have. The doctor looked at me, and he just shook his head. He said, "Kyra, I couldn't even tell you. Michael is such a fighter, and he is so strong, I really, honest to God, don't have any idea or I would say," he said. "It could be three months; it could be six months. I guess only God knows."

I was so numb. I remember feeling like I was walking on a cloud. I guess I was just in shock. Dr. Shrew got on the elevator, and I walked into Michael's room. I went over to him, and I gave him a big hug and a big kiss, still fighting back my tears and still just feeling completely numb. I looked at him and he looked at me and it was like we both knew at the same time. He told me Dr. Shrew just came to see him, and then he went on to tell me everything Dr. Shrew told him and of course later told me at the elevator.

He said, "Dr. Shrew was leaning over me with his tie dangling in my face, so I grabbed him by the tie, and I asked him, You tell me how much time I have left?"

He told me the doctor refused; he just kept saying, "I don't know, Michael," and that's when the doctor called him a fighter.

I told Michael then that it was almost identical to the conversation that I just got through having with him. It was like the doctor didn't want to tell us. He didn't want to take away that last shred of hope that we had, and I could see it in his eyes.

That day Michael and I just sat there, side by side, him lying in his bed and me sitting in the chair holding his hands. We barely spoke a word. I guess there was nothing left to say. We were two crushed people. You know it's weird, but when people are in shock they can behave so strangely. Never ever did the words, "Michael, you are going to die," cross my lips. I just could not bring myself to say these words, and if fact, I never did say them, and neither did Michael. It was as though in our hearts and our souls we felt if these words didn't come out, if these terrible words didn't pass our lips, it wouldn't be true. I suppose you could say this was just another form of denial. I stood up and gave Michael a huge hug and kiss and again told him how much I loved him and how much he was my heart before leaving to pick up my children from school.

I picked the boys up that day, and I brought them right back to the hospital. We had dinner in the cafeteria. I was not able to eat one bite. After the boys got through with their supper, they brought their backpacks up to the hospital room where their father was, and after giving them a hug and kiss, they began their homework.

In the meanwhile Dr. Shrew returned back to Michael's room, and he said to both of us that he would like Michael to go back to the nursing home. They would be able to take care of him there, and he can also receive rehabilitation. I can't even begin to tell you the outrage that I felt at that statement. REHABILITATION!

I went over beside Dr. Shrew, and I whispered in his ears, "Rehabilitation for what? To leave a better-looking corpse? No. He's not going anywhere but home."

The boys at this time had no idea what was going on and that their father was going to die. It would be later on that evening after we returned back home that I would have to tell them this. As soon as we got into the house I sat them both at the kitchen table, and I told them that the medicine that they were giving their daddy did not work, and the cancer is still there. Their father was not going to be able to make it. He was going to go home with Gramma, Nanna, Amber, and Robert.

All I can remember is Teddy jumping up from the table and screaming to me, "You mean Daddy's going to die? Daddy's dying?" He went over to our front kitchen window and put his fist right through it in a fit of anger and despair.

Martin just stood there with tears streaming down his face screaming at me, "You lied to me, Mommy! You lied to me! You told me Daddy was going to be okay. You lied to me!"

He just kept saying that over and over and over again, and I told him, "No, Martin. I didn't. I was holding out hope, just like Daddy and the doctors were. We had to hope that this was going to be fine. Your daddy was going to be fine."

I jumped up out of my seat, and I grabbed Martin and Teddy and held them in my arms. We fell to the kitchen floor, the three of us, crying uncontrollably with our hearts breaking in millions of pieces simultaneously.

You see I knew on the way driving back home what I was going to have to do to them. Once we arrived home, I was going to have to deal with this devastating news. All the while I was driving home, I thought to myself, *How am I going to do this? How am I going to rip their little worlds apart? How am I going to tell them, "Daddy's not going to be here to teach you how to shave, or how to drive, or even be at a grammar school or high school graduation or to see your children being born. There will be no more fishing trips, no more target shooting, no bike riding, and no more cookouts with Daddy flipping the burgers on the grill."* There would now be no life with their father. Their father would be ripped from their lives now forever very shortly. How does a mother do this to her two sons that she has spent a lifetime protecting? How do you rip their hearts apart just as yours has been ripped apart?" Nothing in life could possibly prepare you to do such damage to your children, nor should a parent have to. All of this was simply so unfair.

That night the three of us slept in my bed together, holding each other close and crying half the night. I knew it was important to keep my children close to me both spiritually but physically as well. Through this closeness I knew we would get through this. We finally fell asleep from pure exhaustion from crying. The next day I called the school, and I told them that they would not be in. I called Michael at the hospital, and I told him that I told our boys what was going on, and I said, "We're just taking today off. We're spending it in bed together. We're going to watch TV, and we're going to talk and cry and just relax and try to heal each other's souls and hearts." That's exactly what we did.

Through this day I talked to Teddy and Martin about what Dr. Shrew said and how he wanted their father to go back to the nursing home and receive physical therapy. They were as confused about that statement as I was when Dr. Shrew made it to me.

They said, "Physical therapy for what, Momma? Daddy's going to die."

I said, "Yeah, I know."

You see, I already knew what the right thing in my heart was to do, of course, and that was to bring Michael right back home. But it wasn't just me that this was now affecting, of course; it was affecting our children, and I had to take their feelings and their thoughts into consideration as well. Were they going to be able to handle this? I didn't want them to suffer psychologically throughout their whole lives over this small moment. I had to make sure that we were all in the same mind frame and all wanted the same thing.

They said to me, both of them said, "We want Daddy home. Daddy's not going back to that nursing home, Momma."

I said, "Oh, thank you." I was so relieved to hear them say those words, and again we all hugged and we cried.

So that was the family decision. Their Daddy was going to be brought home as soon as possible.

So the next morning the three of us went to the hospital and we told Dr. Shrew, "Dad's coming home, so whatever you have to do, do it. Whatever you have to set up for visiting nurses then do it. This is the way it is going to be. He's not going to a nursing home."

I had in my mind that when Michael died, he was going to die in the same bed that we had made love in, that we had made our two beautiful sons in, that we had spent so many happy years in. This was where he was going to take his last breath, and I would not have it any other way. It was my sons' strength, their strong souls and their strong hearts that helped throughout all of this. They stayed strong, and I had never been so proud of them.

Dr. Shrew told me he would need a couple of days to set up the hospice nurse to start coming on a regular basis and setting me up with the medications Michael would need.

I said, "Fine, you've got two days, and then he's coming home."

In that two days at the end Dr. Shrew said, "The nurse will be there this afternoon to meet you and explain certain things to you."

I said, "Good."

So I brought Michael back home. We went upstairs. I helped him get undressed, and I gave him a nice warm shower, nice clean pajamas, and a nice, clean bed. By the time the boys were ready to get out of school, Michael was home in his bed waiting for his children.

It was about an hour after supper that the hospice nurse first came. She introduced herself, and she explained the services that hospice provided to the family as well as the patient. She told me about counseling sessions and spiritual guidance as well.

I told her, "Yes. We're very interested in those things."

I also told her about the priest that Michael, and I met this last time at the hospital. His name was Father Post. He was the priest at St. Paul's Church, a church that Michael's family were members of and had gone to all the time when he was younger. He would soon start visiting us on a regular basis as well. My boys loved him, and he loved my boys.

Our family, thank God, had a lot of good loving people around us to help us through this most difficult time including Izzy and her family, and of course Joey who helped Teddy, Nick who helped Martin, and always my sister April. She now went into overdrive. She was taking the boys constantly trying to keep their minds occupied and off of what was going on in their home, trying to keep their spirits high. This I was ever so grateful for because 90% of what went on my children thankfully did not see. Some days were particularly bad. It seemed like they were either at school, out with April, or over at Izzy's house with Joey.

At this point in my life I felt cursed but I also felt blessed at the same time, because when I truly needed help and love it came to me. Father Post and I became good friends as well. He was more than just a priest; he was such a good soul and a good human being. I could talk with him which I never, ever thought in my life I would ever be able to do with a priest. After all, so many years earlier I had turned my back on the church, and I certainly never would consider a priest as a friend, but my eyes had been opened so much over the past few years. I guess this was just a natural process. God lived in my heart again and in my soul, and I was able to communicate with him. Perhaps this is what made being able to communicate with one of his most precious helpers so easy. Father Post and I had a true friendship and a true connection, and like God he carried me through all of this pain.

From the middle of May to the end of May huge, huge changes occurred in my life. For one I had to become almost a doctor overnight. I had to be able to measure out certain potions of medicine for Michael. Our dresser looked only too familiar. It looked like my sister Amber's dresser with medicine from one end to the other given at all different times of the day. I devised a chart which hung right over the bureau in order to keep track of it all. It was a checklist that I went through every single day. After every medicine I would give Michael, I would put it toward the back to make sure I never repeated. I had the times and the medicines that I was to administer to him right there, and of course I had to keep check of his sugar level which ironically at this point was absolutely perfect. It was 105. The normal sugar level was between 95 and 105, and before now we had never been able to get it under control. It always hung around 185. His heart rate was fine. His blood pressure was fine. Yet he was dying.

The nurses from hospice truly were angels on earth. They were so, so kind and so gentle and loving and understanding. They were simply incredible each and every one of them. They let me know they were there for me 24/7. If I ever needed anything no matter what time of the day, I could just pick up the phone, and call them. There was always somebody on call, and I knew I could count on them. Again they asked me if we would like any assistance with Michael's personal care, and Michael again shook his head. "No thank you. No, everything is fine. We will just continue doing what we have been doing for the past couple of months, and I have a shower seat. I'm able to handle it."

She told me, "Well, when the day comes, if it comes that you cannot, please just let us know because we have nurses that will come in and give him a bath in bed."

Again, Michael shook his head, no, and the nurse and I both laughed.

I said, "No. It's okay. Everything's under control so far." I promised if I needed help I would ask.

They made sure the medicines were there right on time, and the drugstore, CVS, always did everything super fast for me. As soon as I called the prescription in for Michael, they knew I was working through Hospice and they would have it immediately done. Hospice was top priority. They were great, and I can't say enough about the CVS Drugstore.

I remember these days like it happened yesterday. As soon as I would drop the kids off at school, I would come back home and crawl back into bed with Michael, and I would stroke his head and his hair. We would lie there talking for hours about anything and everything. It was on one of these days that I asked him if there was any way he could come back to me to please find a way, and let me know he was all right. He just smiled and nodded his head, yes.

In these last days he told me what was important to him. He wanted to be buried with his mother and father in their family plot, and I promised him I would make sure that this happened. He said that he would also like it to read in his obituaries that he was an infantry soldier in Vietnam because he was very proud of this. I thought to myself, *How funny that was that he was proud of something that tortured him for so many years,* but he was. He survived it and he was proud of serving his country and of course I was proud of him. He was always a hero to me.

So I promised him, "Yes, that will be in your obituaries as well." These I guess were really the only two requests that he had outside of his children, and before he even said a word I told him, "You know our two sons will always come first above everybody and everything else. I will always take care of your sons, Michael."

He just smiled and said, "I know."

He also told me while he was at the VA he talked to them about getting his medals, medals that were coming to him from his term of service. They were supposed to be mailing them to him. They came around the 4th or the 5th of June, and he was thrilled. I brought them up to his bed, and I showed him.

They came in a box, and I opened up the box and he said, "Oh, I never thought I would get them." So this put another smile on his face. He was proud to be able to show his sons what he had earned in the service.

Every day after school the boys would come home and spend an hour or two lying in the bed beside their dad watching TV and telling him about their day. Right to the end we stayed a family. But it's funny; other than these little conversations about what Michael's last requests were neither one of us spoke about his death still. We were not able to say the words. We were just ever so happy to live in that little place called denial even if it was short lived.

Quite often through these nights Michael and I would both be abruptly awakened by the beeping of his feeding machine, the feeding tube. If he turned over the wrong way and pinched the tube together, the flow of food would stop, and the little alarm would go off. At this point I just poked his back, and I told him, "Michael, roll over, will you?" He'd roll over, but unfortunately the alarm would not shut off. I would have to get up and re-start the feeding machine all over again. Sometimes this happened once or twice a night.

On the days that I would drop the boys off at school, I would then come back home and crawl back into a nice warm bed with my darling, my love. Some of these days we would just lay there listening to soft rock music and just enjoy being together. As I would lay there watching him nap during the afternoon, stroking his hair, a song came over the radio and it struck my heart so deeply like a knife piercing it. The song was, "I Don't Wanna Miss a Thing" by Arrowsmith. I thought how appropriate that song was right now. Listening to this song I began to cry, and I just held Michael closer than I ever had before in my life, not ever wanting to let him go, and praying that we would have at least six months left.

It was now around the 8th of June, and once again I was lying beside Michael listening to music after dropping the children off at school. I sat up in bed, and I looked him square in the eye, and I asked him words I don't think he ever, ever thought would come out of my mouth. These words I don't think he ever thought in his wildest imaginations he would ever hear. I asked him to marry me.

He sat up in bed and he looked at me and said, "Kyra, how many times did I ask you to marry me, and now you're asking me to marry you? Of course I'll marry you. I would have done it eighteen years ago, but why, why now? You know, I'm not going to be here much longer."

I said, "I know," and I went on to tell him exactly what he meant to me, how he was my heart and my soul and was my only love. I simply did not want anyone else. I told him, "When it's my time to go, I want my headstone to read, *Mrs. Kyra Jones.* I want your name, Michael. Please give me your name."

We kissed and hugged and held each other for the longest time, and he became a little agitated and angry. He said, "You realize if you said 'yes' to me all those years ago we could have had a nice church wedding, a normal wedding, a normal reception, and maybe even gone on a honeymoon."

I told him, "I know. This is on me. I know it's my fault, but what's important now is that when it's my turn to go I will be buried with your name, my husband's name." Again I told him, "I don't want anyone else. There will be no other love for me." I also told him that I considered myself a very lucky woman to have known such love in my life, and I seriously didn't think the chances of me ever finding something like this ever again were not good. I was lucky enough to have it once. I think twice would probably be out of the question. No one on the face of this earth is that lucky. So I wanted to be "Mrs.

Michael J. Jones, III." That was my last request to him. I wanted to carry his name with me now for the rest of my life.

The next day when the Hospice nurse came, I let her know that Michael and I wanted to get married. She was absolutely thrilled. She thought that with all this sorrow if something wonderful could come out of it this would be beautiful, and she said it would be uplifting for the boys as well.

I said, "Yes, I know."

She said, "I'll help you. We can set this up for you," and they did.

They had the people from City Hall come to our house to do all the paper work, and Hospice took Michael's blood work. I only had to go to the Walk-in Clinic to have my blood work done for our marriage license. Father Post agreed to perform the ceremony. We had a Catholic wedding ceremony right in our bedroom. He was as thrilled as everyone else was. They had one question though, and that was, "Why on earth didn't you get married years ago?" They all agreed that it was obvious how much Michael and I loved each other and having two children on top of all that love. I told them about the family history. "I was just too scared. I was always scared of losing Michael." Ironically enough, I found I was losing him anyway, so therefore, I had nothing to lose. I told them I wanted his name. I wanted to carry his name with me for the rest of my life. Until I draw my last breath, and until we're together again.

Only when I knew everything was all set up, everything was planned, all the work was done, and Michael and I truly could get married did I tell the boys. They were absolutely thrilled. They couldn't believe Mommy and Daddy were actually going to get married. I asked Teddy if he would be the one to give me away. He said, "Of course, Mommy." Martin was going to be our ring bearer, holding Mommy and Daddy's rings.

I called Michael's brother Joe to let him know about the wedding ceremony, and I told him I wanted it to be very intimate and very quiet because of Michael's condition. I said, "I think he wants you to be his Best Man, Joe."

He was honored. He said, "Oh, my God, of course I will."

So on June 12, 2000, Joe and Susan arrived. My sister April, of course, was there. She's the one that bought the wedding cake, and Joe and Susan bought a lot of the food. Izzy and Angel were there as was Joey, Angel, Jr. and A.T., and Holly, Robert's daughter with her brand-new baby stopped by.

My sister-in-law Susan asked me if I would like her to tape the wedding ceremony, and I cringed at this thought.

I said, "No, I don't. As a matter of fact I don't want any pictures taken at all of this day. This is an extremely bittersweet day. The love of my life I'm finally marrying, yes, but I would still have to say goodbye, and I don't think I want any pictures and certainly no films to remember this."

I didn't think it would be good for the boys to be able to look back on and see how their father looked and what occurred on this day, as they grew older. I wanted them to remember him when he was out fishing with them, target shooting and bike riding. I wanted them to remember him looking like that and not leave these pictures as Michael's legacy. The cancer had ravaged his body so badly. As I said he was only 52 years old and he looked like he was 80. No, I didn't want any pictures to remind us of what he looked like at the end. I wanted us to have our memories of the better times and the happy years, and I knew Michael would feel the same way.

So I told her, "Thank you, but no thank you." I told her not to bring any cameras because I didn't want any pictures. So there were no pictures allowed at this wedding. This was a very small intimate ceremony.

Just before Father Post was to perform this wedding ceremony for Michael and me, he told me he had to get permission from the cardinal to do this because I had not received my Confirmation. Michael had received his, though, and he gave the okay. He said, "I explained to the cardinal what kind of family you are and how much love is between all of you and how long you had been together. It is certainly a loving ceremony." The cardinal agreed, so Father Post was able to perform it. Michael and I were in our bedroom with Joe, Susan, my sister April, Izzy, and our two sons were in the room. Michael sat there in bed, and I stood beside him. Father Post read us our wedding vows, and we repeated them. As we placed the rings we had for one another on each other's fingers and sealed our bond of love with a kiss, now after twenty-one-and-a-half years of being with my only love, I was now Mrs. Michael J. Jones, III. This was a most sacred day, and I was both so happy and yet so devastated at the same time.

That night after everything was all done with and everybody had gone, Nick and Kim, his new girlfriend, came over to visit and congratulate us. They had just gotten out of work. We did have bottles of champagne, and I did sit there drinking a couple of glasses of it. Even though I probably shouldn't have, I did anyway. We had it for the champagne toast that we had in our room following our wedding. We had little glasses that said, "Bride and Groom," on them. I handed Michael his glass of champagne and we clicked it together for a toast. I drank mine and he handed his back to me full.

I looked at him, and I said, "Michael, aren't you even going to take a sip?"

He said. "Kyra, I've been sober for over eighteen years now. I'm not going to meet God with liquor on my lips even on this most special day. No, I don't want a drink, Honey."

So Joe took the glass and drank it for him.

After all of this when I was sitting in the kitchen with Nick and his girlfriend, Kim, and sipping on my glass of champagne, I asked them, "How long have you been together now?"

They told me, "A couple of years."

I told them, "Don't wait. If you are right for each other and you love each other, don't wait until something like this happens. Have that perfect wedding and a nice honeymoon. Have something to look forward to like a life together instead of like me now, having to plan a funeral. That's what I was having to face now."

They both looked at me rather strangely, but I think they could understand where I was coming from at that moment. April had taken the two boys for the night, so Michael and I could be alone.

After Nick and Kim left, I cleaned up a little bit, and then I went back to bed to be with my husband. I got into bed and snuggled up close beside my love. We lay there listening to music for hours, and just before he was ready to fall asleep, he gave me a kiss, the sweetest, most loving kiss he had ever given me, and he said to me, "Good night, my wife."

I looked at him and smiled and said, "Good night, my husband," and we both sort of chuckled.

Every night from here on out that's how we would end the day with that sweet kiss good night, and him telling me, "Good night, my wife," and me replying, "Good night, my husband."

Then he rolled over and went fast asleep. I lay there, unable to even close my eyes trying to take in all the emotions and understand what I was feeling at this moment. I thought to myself, *How can I honor him? What can I do for him after everything he's given me in my life? What special thing can I now do for him?* and it hit me—his eulogy. I wanted to write down and deliver for him the most perfect and loving eulogy that had ever been written. When the time came I wanted to stand before all our family and friends and just scream out how much we loved each other, how much we loved our family, and how he was simply my hero. I wanted everyone to know exactly what kind of father he was and how much love he had for his sons and everything that he taught them and also everything that he taught me over twenty-one-and-a-half years. I wanted everyone to know everything good about this man, this man that held my heart, this man that I would forever love.

So I began first of all telling them how much of a hero he was in my eyes and in his sons'. Then I began describing exactly what he would do with his sons and how they went fishing, bike riding, and target shooting. I went on to our Christmases together and our traditions that we had built in our family and how much love our family shared together. I just simply wanted everyone to know everything about him, and about how wonderful a person and how strong a man he truly was. I needed everyone to know this, to know him as I did.

At the end it was a three-page eulogy. I know I still could not have possibly covered everything, but I tried my damnedest to do so. So this is how I spent what you would consider a "honeymoon," the night of my wedding, lying beside the man that held my heart, writing my goodbyes to him, and trying desperately to honor him the way I knew he should be honored.

To this day it never ceases to amaze me when I look back on all of this, all the things that Michael went through, all the things that I had to do to him in order to take care of him. Even the showers—they were very, very difficult, but through all of this he never, ever once complained about anything. I just found this so amazing. He was so appreciative and so grateful for everything that I did for him, and it amazed me because to me it was nothing. It was something that I wanted to do. That's what you are expected to do when the man that you love becomes ill. You should take care of him, and you should stand beside him through everything. So this was something I felt in my heart was a normal process.

This was nothing out of the ordinary for me, but everybody kept complimenting me and commenting on how well I kept Michael. How he was always so clean and always looked like his spirits were high. Little did they know it was him, not me. He fed my spirit and lifted my spirit. In return I was able to help him and lift his spirit. Again, that "team" just came into play. No one else knew it but this was business as usual for Michael and me. We had always worked together. Instead of us working on the car giving it a tune up, it was now changing his feeding tube bag. It's the same difference. If you're a team, you're a team through everything in life. If you're ever lucky enough to find this, hold onto it with everything you have because I certainly did.

In these following days Michael and I would find we added two more to our team and that was Teddy and Martin. They were so much help in taking care of their father. They would help me carry the large water bottles from downstairs up to our room and the cases of the liquid food that Michael needed for his feeding tube as well as spending every spare moment keeping his spirits high. They helped me so much, and they stood by their father's side. We were a team of four now, not just two.

Teddy and Martin now were out of school for the year and their summer vacation had begun. I remember one day walking in on the three of them, Teddy and Martin sitting beside their father on the bed. He had all of his medals laid out in front of them explaining to Teddy and Martin which medals meant what. He had a medal for sharp shooting, a medal from the Vietnamese Government for their gratitude, his platoon's medal, the Cavalry Medal. He was telling them a few stories about his days in the Army although he kept it very light, of course.

I remember him telling the boys, "You know, something that I learned through life was to use this, and he pointed to his head, before you use this, and he pointed to his fist. Before you use your fist, use your head, and it will keep you out of a lot of trouble in life." He told them, "This is something I had to find out the hard way."

On Father's Day of this year I brought them to pick out their own Father's Day cards for him. They spent a lot of time finding just the right one. They were very loving, but funny. I of course picked out my own for him. I didn't know what exactly to get him for a Father's Day gift this year. Just then I saw these little statues. One of the statues said "Father of the Year."

I said, "That's perfect!" So I got him that, which was like a little award, and a huge bouquet of flowers to put by his bedside. He always loved flowers, especially blue ones, daffodils and blue tiger lilies. The boys and I spent that whole day in bed with him, watching TV and talking.

It was now around June the 21. Teddy was over Joey's house playing, and Martin was over Nick's. In this private moment that Michael and I had alone together, I asked if we should now talk to boys about their Uncle John and their brother that they had never met. I told him I wanted them to know this because I didn't want them to be sideswiped by this information. At this bad time in their lives I didn't want this to come as a shock out of the blue to them.

Michael was hesitant. He really didn't want to talk about it, but he finally agreed. He said, "If you feel as though you need to, Kyra, go ahead."

I really did. I thought it was the right thing to do at this moment. It was the right time. I just wanted them to be prepared. You see, we had already spoken to both our sons about our past, the drinking that we did and the mistakes that we had made in our lives in the hope that they would not repeat them. So we were always very honest about everything with our children, except these two points, their uncle and their brother. We were waiting for them to get a little bit older before we were going to speak with them about this. We just didn't feel as though it was something that they needed to know at a very young age, but now I had no choice. I didn't want this coming out at Michael's funeral. I wanted them to know.

So that night when they got home after supper I sat them both down in the living room, and I told them about their Uncle John and what happened and why it happened which was because he was on drugs and alcohol and he really had no idea what he was doing. I told them how long he had been in prison and that he was still in prison. That was the easy part. The more difficult and heartbreaking part was explaining about their brother, and basically how we let him down. I reminded them both of what Michael and I had told them about our drinking years, the crazy years. I said we were not capable of taking care of a child. We couldn't take care of ourselves, let alone someone else at that point in our lives. I told them that their brother had been adopted, and I had not seen him since he was five years old.

They both just sat there rather shocked and the first question out of their mouths was, "Did I know where their brother was?"

I said, "No, Honey, I have no idea. I do know that he was a marine in 1995, but short of that I know nothing about him."

I went on to try and explain to them that by the time Mommy and Daddy were ready to have children, and I was pregnant with Teddy, we got the adoption notice in the mail. I told him, "Daddy never signed it," so that later on in life if Michael Jr. were to see these papers, he would know his father did not just write him off. They were glad to hear about that part of it, but they were confused. I suppose this just added more stress to what they were already under, but I just thought it was something they really needed to know.

Through this time we were receiving counseling from Hospice. They would come to the house and talk with Teddy and Martin and me on a regular basis.

Father Post would also visit now on a regular basis as well. He was coming three and four times a week. He would give Michael communion and pray with us.

I believe it was now about the 24th of June when Michael really started taking a turn for the worst. The cancer was catching up to him, and he was growing weaker and weaker by the day. He was still refusing to use a bedpan and insisted in getting up and going to the bathroom. The only thing he would use was the urinal by his bedside. On this day when Father Post came on the 24th he gave Michael his Last Rights as I sat beside Michael holding his hand. The three of us did have a very spiritual uplifting visit, something that Michael and I desperately needed. I made sure that Teddy and Martin were included in this visit. Father Post later would talk with both of them. It seemed as though they were doing much better at this point than I was, or just maybe perhaps they were in their own little world of denial. I don't know.

After Father Post left on that day the funniest thing happened. Michael jumped out of bed, and as weak as he was, this was quite a feat. He said, "Kyra, I have to go to the bathroom." I quickly undid the tubing and helped him into the bathroom and gave him his privacy, standing out in the hall looking out of our window.

As he came out of the bathroom I noticed the wedding ring was gone from his hand. I helped him back to bed, and I said, "Michael, where is your wedding band? Where is your wedding ring, Honey?"

He pointed over to the closet, which wasn't making any sense. I said, "Oh, no." So I called the boys up to help me look for the ring. We looked all over, all around his bureau all around the closet, and then we looked in the bathroom. It was nowhere to be round. I finally figured out. It must have slipped off his finger, because he was losing weight on a daily basis. The ring was very loose on him, and it must have been flushed.

So I said to myself, *There is no way in hell my husband is going to his grave without a wedding band on. It took twenty-one and half years for that wedding band to be placed on our fingers, and I'm certainly not going to let him go without it now.* I actually went out and purchased another wedding band.

I called Father Post the next day and explained to him what happened. I said, "Is there any way possible that you can perform a little ceremony so that I can place this ring his finger?"

He said, "Certainly, Kyra."

The next day he came, and we repeated our wedding vows, just the three of us, Father Post, Michael, and I. I took my wedding band off so that he could place it back on my hand, and I placed his new wedding band back on his. I said, "Now, please keep it there."

Michael laughed. He said, "I'll try," and that night, just as we had always done since the 12th of June on our honeymoon, our wedding night, we kissed, and I said, "Good night, my husband."

He said, "Goodnight, my wife," and we went to sleep.

The next morning, the 26th of June when I awoke and leaned over to give Michael a kiss as I did every morning I noticed there was something drastically wrong with him. He seemed to be out of it, like he was there, but not there, and I became very, very alarmed. After changing the feeding bag, I got on the phone, and I called the hospice nurse. I told her to come over immediately. There was something wrong with Michael. She came.

By that time he had begun shaking, his muscles contracting in his face and in his body, and I asked her, "What is going on?"

She told me, "Kyra, he's having seizures, and it looks like they are very painful seizures."

The cancer now had completely spread to his brain, and this was what was causing the seizures. She got on the phone immediately and called CVS for a prescription. She told me that this medicine would help ease the seizures and would make him sleep. At least while he was asleep he wasn't suffering with seizures. She went quickly to get it, and as soon as she gave it to him, the seizures stopped and he went to sleep. I could see the peaceful look again come over his face. I could tell he wasn't in any pain. The medicine worked, thank God.

From that day on I did not leave his bedside for one minute except to go to the bathroom. I also made sure the boys were out of the house most of these days, over to Joey's or over to Nick's, anywhere but here. I didn't want them seeing this. The medicine worked great, but the only thing was it only worked for two to three hours at a time. As soon as he began waking up, he would immediately go into another seizure.

My heart was breaking beyond belief to have to stand there and watch my only love go through such pain where he had fought so hard over these past two years and to end it like this. We had fought so hard all our lives to have a normal life and a normal family, and we had it. If only for a short time we had it, and to end up this way like this to me was inconceivable. Again, it was that horrible heartbreaking nightmare that you just couldn't wake up from. I felt like I was back in that dark pit again. Every single time Michael started waking up, the seizures would begin, and I would have to immediately give him some more medicine. This would stop the seizures and knock him out again. Every two and a half hours this occurred.

It was now the 27th of June and the nurse came again to examine him and see how well the medicine was working and took his vitals. She and I were standing together at the foot of the bed after she gave him another round of medication and she actually began to cry. She said, "This is just so heartbreaking, Kyra. You guys are so young, and you have such a beautiful family. This is just all so heartbreaking. I wish I had an opportunity to get to know Michael when he was well because he must have been a really great guy."

I said, "He was. He truly was, and he was always my hero." I told her that I had had so many people ripped from me so cruelly, but yet I knew that they were all okay. I knew Michael was going to be okay as well. I have a lot of confidence in this.

She then asked me how I was able to sleep, and I told her, "Well, I wasn't really. I set my alarm clock for every two hours so that I would be ready when he awoke and started with his seizures. I would then be ready to give him his medicine."

She said, "Where are you sleeping?" I pointed over to the little corner of my bed that was left because I had him more to the middle of the bed because I was afraid he would roll off onto the floor if he started shaking.

She just shook her head and said, "Oh, my God."

I said, "I can do this. I'll be okay. I'll do this for him. He deserves nothing less."

So for three days it was a procession of every two and a half hours medicating Michael as soon as he would start waking up and start shaking.

It was now the 28th of June when I was about ready to collapse from pure heartache and also physical and mental exhaustion. It was on this day as the nurse was visiting when she and I began talking and she told me, "Kyra, you really have to start considering now taking him off of the feeding tube. You realize one thing, if you can realize nothing else right now, and that is that Michael is gone. All that you are keeping alive is his shell, and all that you're doing is feeding the cancerous tumor that is eating away at his brain. You're no longer feeding Michael. You're feeding that, and you really have to consider taking him off of this."

I knew, once I did he would be gone to me forever, but I had to use my head, and I had to think rationally. I had to realize and accept the fact that he was already gone. Keeping him alive now would only cause him more pain and more suffering. He wasn't alive. He was asleep the whole time, and I pray to God he felt no pain. I know I had to be strong now for him just as he was strong for me all my life. I could not be selfish in order to keep his shell here lying beside me. I had to let go and now had to somehow find the strength to let him go, to free him. He had suffered so much throughout his whole life, mentally and now physically and his soul needed to be freed. I knew I had to do it, and I knew I was the only one that could.

I had to love him enough now to let him go, and this called for more strength than I ever, ever imagined I had. He was my entire world, my heart, and my soul. My heart beat only for him, and I knew if he were to go now that he would take half of my heart with him, the half that belonged to him. How was I going to be able to bear this? At this point I thought I'd gladly throw myself in front of a Mack truck than take his life, than let him go, but I knew I had to stay strong. I had to do what was right, and I had to take care of our sons just as I promised Michael I would.

So after the nurse left that morning, I prayed harder than I ever had in my life, harder than even before when I was asking God to take the cancer away. This was an entirely different feeling, an entirely different prayer. I was asking for the strength to do the right thing, to please give me the strength to let Michael go. I was so exhausted. I was literally walking on my knees. I had nothing left inside of me. I just felt so hollow and so empty. All that was left in me now was a shattered heart and a fractured soul, and I knew God was the only one that was going to be able to repair this. I stood in front of the bureau with all that medicine in front of me, reaching from one end of the bureau to the other, and the bottles of water, the water that I had to give him every day. I stood there, and I just broke down, completely, utterly, and totally broke down in tears.

This was the most broken I had ever been in my entire life. I never knew a person could feel such pain and survive. As I stood there completely drained and exhausted, I prayed, and I asked God for the strength, for the energy to keep going. I asked it for Michael, not for me. Michael deserved my being able to take care of him in his last hours on this earth the best way I could, and I felt as though I was letting him down because I was so exhausted. I prayed to God to just give me the strength just until the end came, just so I could take care of him properly until that moment came. "Please," I begged Him, "please give me the strength because I simply have nothing left inside."

It was then, just then that I felt something behind me, and I thought to myself, *Oh, God, please, not another spirit.* I just couldn't handle feeling something like that right now and trying to ignore it as I always did in life, but this was something entirely different. This was something I had never, ever felt before. I had never experienced this. As I said it came up from behind me, and it was like an angel wrapping his wings completely around me. I felt totally engulfed in love. A love such as this I had never, ever felt in my life before, not even with Michael. It was like taking Michael's love and mine and multiplying it by a million. It was the most pure, purest of love that I have ever felt and the most uplifting love I had ever felt. I felt like I was being reborn, renewed and replenished in that instant. In that moment I could feel my strength coming back to me. I could feel my heart repairing itself, and most important, I felt my soul not only being repaired but also lifted higher than I could ever imagine.

This all happened to me in an instant. After this energy, this entity left me, it left me completely repaired, completely whole again. I hadn't had such energy since I was sixteen years old. I had not felt so good and so loved in my whole life. I had been completely and totally engulfed with love. I don't know what you want to call it. I don't know if it was a spirit or if God took pity on me and actually sent me perhaps my guardian angel. I don't know. All I know is what I felt.

That completely overwhelming, completely engulfing love I will never, ever forget. Once you experience something like this, there is no denying, there is no denying God. You simply cannot feel the same way after an experience like this toward anything in life now. You look at everything differently. It makes you want to be a better person. It makes you want to please God. It makes you want to show love and compassion to people, because I think I was able to truly feel what Heaven was like in that split second. If that truly is what Heaven is, all it is, is love, the purest of pure love. A love no one here on earth will ever experience, unfortunately.

If that's truly what Heaven is, I knew Michael right along with all my other loved ones were truly in Paradise and truly in God's arms. If they felt that love as soon as they crossed, I knew they were okay. Without a shadow of a doubt now, I knew it because I was shown it. Somehow God took pity on me and helped me help Michael, and He showed me all the proof that I will ever need again in my life in that split second. Everything that I wondered about, everything that I'd hoped Heaven would be was shown to me by that feeling and that uplifting spirit that was sent to me.

Right after this happened I lay beside Michael in bed, and he opened his eyes, and he started looking at the ceiling, and a huge, huge smile came over his face, a smile like I had never seen before.

I said to Michael, "Oh, my God, Baby. I wished I could see what you're seeing right now." I truly believe at that moment he was seeing perhaps his guardian angels, his mother and father, Amber, Robert and my Mom all waiting for him. I believe this is what he was seeing.

I then explained to him what I was about to do and that I was going to take him off of the feeding tube. The look on his face was just so strange. He wasn't conscious, but he wasn't asleep either. It was like he was asleep but his eyes were open. I don't know exactly what was going on. All I know is that look that he had on his face when he was looking up at the ceiling. I'll never forget the smile he had.

I then got up and went to the side of his bed, and I disconnected the feeding tube, and I shut the machine off. I then went back, and I lay beside him, and I told him what had just happened to me, and the good feeling that I got from it. I don't know if he heard me or not, but I wanted him to know. Then I held him in my arms and told him just how much I loved him, and I told him I couldn't wait until we were together again. I asked him again if he could, if there was any way possible for him to come back to me, would he please show me signs afterward, signs that would let me know he made it to the other side okay. I knew in my heart, however, after what I had just been shown, he was going to be okay.

A couple of hours after this we remained lying there in each others arms, and Father Post knocked at the door. I went down to let him in, and I led him upstairs to our room.

I told him what I had done with the feeding tube. He said, "That was a good thing, Kyra. I'm glad to hear you had the strength to do that."

I told Father Post, "I didn't have the strength. Michael gave me the strength. The strength that I have now comes from years of him teaching me how to be strong."

Then when we were down in the living room, we talked a little bit more, Father Post and I.

I sat across from him looking directly into his eyes, and I told him, "I really, really hope you don't think I'm insane, but I have to tell someone about what just happened to me," and I went on to explain to him just how tired I had been and just how exhausted my soul felt and how broken my heart was. I told him how I stood there crying at the bureau and how I felt. The best way I could explain it was, just completely engulfed in love like an angel's wings wrapped around me, safe and protected. I told him I prayed for the strength to be able to do what I knew I had to do, and I prayed for the strength to be able to take care of Michael to the end just as he deserved. He deserved to be taken care of with love until he passed with as much dignity as possible, and I prayed to God to give me the strength to be able to help Michael.

Father Post's eyes started welling up with tears, and he shook his head and he looked down and he said, "You know something, Kyra? I've only heard of these things happening. I have never been blessed myself. No, you're not going crazy, Honey. It did happen. You have been truly blessed, and you have been shown things most other people never get to see or feel. Yes, God is the one who gave you the strength to do what you had to do. You have been touched by the Holy Spirit."

I thought to myself, *This man is a priest, and he has never been blessed like this?* I felt truly, truly special at that moment, and I thank God that I talked to Father Post about it so I didn't think I was losing my mind. He confirmed exactly what I thought it was, and that was God giving me the help when I needed it desperately. God sent a helper, an angel to fill me back up with the love and the compassion that I needed so desperately at that moment. God answered my prayers and there was no going back for me now, and there is certainly no denying what was shown to me.

After now being replenished in both my mind, my body and my soul, I should say especially my soul, I knew I was going to be okay. I would be strong enough now to do the things and to carry on the way Michael would want me to, in fact expected me to, and take care of our children. This was the most important thing to Michael, our two sons, and I knew now I would have the strength to do everything I needed to do, because now I knew without a shadow of a doubt I had God standing beside me every step of the way.

It was on this night, June 28, that I pledged my heart and my love to God. I told Him, "I will follow you now for the rest of my days, and I will never ever forget what you showed me, all the compassion and the love that you showed me. I am yours to use in whatever way you see fit. I will stand up for you always now, and I will never waiver in my loyalty to you." I pledged my heart and my soul to God on this day.

It was also this night that I sat down with Teddy and Martin in their room, and I explained in detail what was shown to me, what happened to Mommy during the day. I let them know the time was growing near that Daddy was going to be leaving soon, and they both looked at me and said, "Yes, Mommy, we know." The three of us sat there and said The Lord's Prayer together, holding hands, gathering strength from one another and from God. Our deep sense of spirituality right now is the only thing that kept us sane. If it had not been for that, I don't know how we would have gotten through all of this. I then gave them kisses and tucked them into bed. Then I returned to my love.

I lay beside Michael, holding him in my arms all night long, and I began talking about that one special weekend that we had down the Cape years earlier, and the fond memories that we had from that weekend. I don't know if he heard me, but I had to pick our most perfect moment to reminisce about. This moment I wished both of us could just travel back to even if it were only for an hour to spend together in each other's arms. I just reminded him of this day and the love that grew ever stronger as the years went by. I told him, "You are my love. You are my heart. You are my only love forever."

Before falling asleep, I set that alarm clock for two hours. Every two hours I was still giving him that medication because he was still having severe seizures. I fell into a deep asleep, until I was abruptly awakened by that screeching alarm. Then I got up at 2 o'clock in the morning and gave him his medicine before his seizures would start again, but it felt much, much different from how it had in the previous two days. I felt good. I felt uplifted, and I felt rested. I knew that light at the end of the tunnel now for us was God. I got through these painful hours knowing He was standing beside us ready and waiting for Michael when the moment was right.

The next morning about 8 o'clock Father Post came to the house once more to see how Michael and I were doing. He again gave Michael his last rights, and after we talked for a little while he left, and I got the children up and gave them their breakfast. They asked me if it was okay if they went over Joey's and Nick's, and I said, "Certainly. I'll call you if I need you." Again, I was trying to shield them from as much pain as I possibly could.

It was around 10 o'clock that morning when Michael started having really loose bowel movements. I had a undergarment on him at this point because over the four days he was not able to get out of bed. He was not really conscious. So I changed him and cleaned him up, and then as soon as I had a new undergarment on him, he had another loose bowel movement. I knew this was now beyond me. I needed some help, so I called Hospice and let them know what was going on. I told them, "I have changed him now four times and it just keeps coming. The bowel movements won't stop." You see I didn't know at this time that this was a natural process that the body goes through before death. It's called "emptying out," and this is what Michael was doing. They told me they would send a nurse and a volunteer to help me wash Michael properly.

They arrived about 11 o'clock, and they were upstairs with Michael for about an hour. They got him all cleaned up, and I went back upstairs after they were done. I hated to have to call them, because Michael and I had always handled this on our own. This is just a very personal thing to us and again as I said, the team, we always worked as a team. But again, it was beyond me at this point.

When I went back upstairs the two of them were standing at the foot of the bed and Michael was lying there with his eyes open but still unconscious because I had just given him the medication. When his breathing began to become shallow the nurse turned to me and told me to look closely. I could see his breathing was becoming lighter and lighter yet his eyes remained wide open. I asked them both to leave so that Michael and I could be together alone. I knew these were his last moments. I quickly thought of the boys, though, and I knew that they would want to be there, so I called over at Joey's and Nick's and told them to send the boys home.

They come upstairs, and Teddy sat on the one side and Martin on the other side of their father and me at the foot of the bed. All three of us held hands, and we held Michael's hands, and we said The Lord's Prayer. We prayed that he be taken quickly. We all told him how much we loved him The boys were allowed to say their good byes although they did not shed their tears in front of their father. They waited until they got into their room. I could hear them crying. I then went closer to Michael sitting right by his side holding his hand

and praying, all the while his breath becoming shallower and shallower. I began feeling him slip away and his soul leaving, and I stared deep, deep into his eyes as I saw the light of life grow dim, a light that had showed me so much in my life, so much love, so much guidance, so much compassion and so much strength. That light that he had in his eyes, that love that he always showed while he was looking at me came from that light.

That was my guiding light for twenty one and a half years. That light, that light of love in his eyes guided me through so much, so much pain and so much heartache while he remained so strong and taught me how to be strong as well. These lessons I will carry with me for the rest of my life now. This man was everything to me. He was my lover; he was my love, my heart, my father and my brother. He taught me things my father should have taught me. We were buddies just as a brother and sister would be. He was absolutely my entire world, my best friend and my confidant. This light in his eyes stood for everything to me as I sat there watching my love slowly slip away from me.

It was on June 29 at 1:25 p.m. I was watching this light forever now be extinguished. I sat there by his side holding him and staring deeply, deeply into them, into his eyes, into that light until the moment it was completely gone, until the moment he took his last breath in my arms. My only love forever now was gone from me now, forever, and I knew now I had to find some way to carry on, to gather all the strength that was in me that was given to me from both Michael and God. I needed to call on this now, and I needed this to guide me now more than ever. I had a lot of work left ahead of me, and I knew this. First and foremost I had to make sure our sons were okay.

After Michael took that last breath I went into the boys' room, and I held them in my arms. It was just then that my sister April came knocking at the door. I hadn't expected her to come. Thank God she did. She came upstairs, and I told her that Michael was gone. By now the two nurses had returned back to my bedroom and were preparing Michael to be picked up by his uncle, the one that ran the funeral home. That was another request that Michael had that he go to his family's funeral home and be taken care of by his Cousin Troy.

After they were done preparing Michael, April asked me, as she was wiping away her tears, if it was all right with me if she went into my room and sat by Michael and said a prayer for him. I said, "Of course, of course it is. Michael would like this."

504

After she had her private moment with Michael, she came back out of the bedroom and suggested to me that she take Teddy and Martin out while Michael's uncle came to pick him up. I said, "Yes, thank you, April." I thought that was a good idea as well. They didn't need to see this. So April took Teddy and Martin downstairs. Joey was knocking at the door at this time wondering what was going on. I guess they knew the time was drawing close as well. Joey was family. I had kept close contact with Izzy so she did know this was coming. So April, Teddy, Martin, Joey, and his two little brothers went for a ride. She stopped to get ice cream and sat on the bench underneath some trees.

While the nurses were still there I called the funeral home, and I let Michael's Cousin Troy know that he had just passed. "Oh, Kyra, I'm so sorry."

"I know."

He said, "I'll be there immediately to get Michael."

So when Izzy looked out her window and saw the hearse she knew exactly what happened. Nick's girlfriend, Kim, also knew and both of them came down to be with me. Troy went up with the stretcher to my bedroom with a helper and now I could hear him saying, "I'm so sorry Buddy, I'm so sorry," while he was standing at Michael's side.

I went down to the kitchen because this was one sight I didn't wish to see, and I know I didn't have to. Kim and Izzy stood by my side as I sat down in the kitchen. I could hear them coming down the stairs with the stretcher. Going around the corner it was quite tight and they banged into the wall.

A rush, a tidal wave of pain, of heartbreak after hearing this sound all at once came over me, and I broke down. I just started crying. To see him carried out was more than my heart could bear. I couldn't hold it in. They placed Michael in the hearse. Troy came back into the house and told me I needed to go down to his office as soon as I could that day. I needed to gather myself up because I had to figure out what was to be put into the obituary for Michael. Of course I knew, the Infantry Soldier was going to be the first thing, and the Vietnam vet, the Proud Honorable Vietnam vet was also going to be placed in his obituaries.

It took me a little over an hour to compose myself, gather my thoughts together enough to speak with Troy and go down to that funeral home. Izzy came with me for support. I then told Troy everything that I wanted written in the obituaries, and of course that he was a veteran of Vietnam, Infantry Soldier, an avid fisherman, hunter, and he enjoyed spending time with his two sons.

Then it dawned on me, he doesn't have two sons. He has three sons. I told Troy, "I don't know if you know this or not but Michael had an older son, Michael Jr., and he was adopted a few years ago." All I could remember was Bertha's name and that was Summer, so I gave Troy the name I knew Michael went under before he was adopted, and that was William Joseph Summer, and that he was a marine. In 1995 he had joined the Marine Corps. So Troy put that in as well right alongside Teddy and Martin's names, and mine as his proud wife. We then began discussing the casket and the funeral arrangements, and I told him where he was to be buried. Michael wanted to be buried in his family plot right alongside his Mom and Dad so that was to be.

I also started thinking to myself about the funeral, and I said, "I want a military funeral for Michael."

Troy looked rather surprised at this statement. He said, "I thought Michael hated the government."

"Yeah, he did. So do I, but that's beside the point. The point now is that I want him to receive the honor and the respect that he should have received all these years that he was alive. He will now receive them in death." I told Troy, "He may have hated the government, but the military is something else. It's different. The military is filled with men just like he was, men that should be honored every day. He respected every branch of the service, and he respected every man that served in it. Now I'm going to make damn sure he is going to get the respect and honor that's due him."

Even if he wasn't alive to know it, I knew he was watching, and I wanted to do this for him and for our sons. I wanted our sons to see their father being buried with honor, the honor that so eluded him in life. I thought just maybe through all of this disaster and this heartbreak, I could pull something positive out of it all, some kind of a positive memory for my sons to show them that our country truly did appreciate everything that their father did for it. I would stand for nothing less now than a military funeral, and in a way this was my little extra to Michael, my last gift that I knew I could give him to make sure this was done. He never asked for this, but I think he would be happy to have this honor bestowed upon him. This would be the last gift that I would be able to give him, and I feel the most important one. It made me feel so good inside to know that he is now going to get the respect he should have always received.

So after all of this was setup, Troy began making some phone calls to make sure that we were able to give him a military funeral and that the guardsmen would be able to be there. He quickly found out that because there were so many deaths of veterans it seemed like at this time, the Guardsmen on the Cape were so busy attending to those funerals, they would not be able to spare the time to come up to take care of Michael's. So these Guardsmen that we did eventually get had to come all the way from North Carolina. It took Troy a couple of hours over the phone trying to get in contact with this person and that person to assure a Military Funeral for Michael. Thank God he eventually was able to do so.

So after making all of these arrangements and getting everything straightened out, the times, the day, and his wake which was to be on July 2 and his funeral July 3. I had also brought along with me to the funeral parlor one of Michael's best suits, a navy blue suit that he always looked so handsome in and his favorite pair of boots. You see Michael was also an avid western boot collector. He had about thirty pairs of boots and he would shine them up and keep them looking so nice. When he first started getting sick with cancer a couple of years ago he started this, and he would just keep adding and adding to the collection. I didn't realize that he actually had thirty pairs. That's how he spent his spare time just shining up boots and taking care of them.

One day he was taking so much time doing this, I jokingly said to him, "I'm gonna bury you barefooted if you don't drop those boots and leave them alone right now." I wanted him to do something. I don't know, I couldn't remember, but it went like that.

I said, "I will bury you barefooted."

He said to me, "You better not. I'll come back and haunt you!"

He always felt as though he had a previous life in the old West. He would say, "I must have been a cowboy in my past life because I love horses, dressing that style, and I love boots." He loved everything about the old West. So for me to make that threat about burying him barefooted, he took it rather seriously. He did, "He said, I swear I'll come back and haunt you if you bury me without my boots on."

So of course I made sure that I had his best most beautiful pair of boots. These boots were a cherry mahogany color. They were absolutely gorgeous, and when I handed them to Troy along with Michael's suit, I said, "Please, you have to get these boots on him."

Troy said, "Kyra, I don't know if I can."

I told Troy, "Give me five minutes alone with him. I'll get them on him. I have to make sure he is buried with his boots on."

Troy laughed and said, "You've gotta be kidding me."

I said, "Sadly enough, I'm not."

He said, "Don't worry about it. I'll figure out a way to get them on."

So he was buried with his favorite pair of boots and his favorite suit.

Troy also began discussing Michael's brother, John, and what was to be done with him. He said, "I know John is going to want to come and pay his last respects."

I said, "Of course. He should be able to."

So Troy called the prison to make sure John would be allowed to come and see Michael for the last time and to pay his respects. Thank God they approved. I knew this was going to be hard on John and so terribly heartbreaking to him because I knew how much he loved Michael. He loved his big brother so much, and he already had to go through his mother's death by himself, to grieve by himself with no love or support from the family. Now he was going to have to face this the same way, by himself and my heart went out to him. I had no idea what kind of faith John still clung to if any at all. I knew what was carrying us through this horrific time, but I had no idea what would carry him through it.

When I returned back home that afternoon, Izzy stayed with me. I then called Michael's brother Joe and let him know what had happened. He of course was crushed as well. After all it was just a little over two weeks ago when he was here, and Michael and I were getting married. You see, we were all hoping and praying for the best, hoping that Michael would remain with us for at least six months, and not go so quickly. I told Joe what I had arranged, a military funeral for Michael. I told him that he was to be buried with honor and dignity and all the respect he deserved. Joe was very happy to hear about this and thought it was a great idea. After calling Joe, Izzy, and I went back out to order the flowers for the funeral. I wanted a beautiful blue cascade for the casket, and then I got a beautiful red, white and blue corsage mix in the shape of a huge heart from his sons. After this Izzy and I went home. I was so exhausted I couldn't think any longer. At this point in time I just wanted to shut my mind down and shut my heart and emotions down. I felt so drained.

It was also about this time that April was returning back home with Teddy, Martin, Joey, Angel, and A.T. Later on that evening the whole neighborhood came over my house. Sam came from next door. He was a sweetheart, and he would talk to Teddy and Martin quite often about what was going on. He let them know that he was their friend, and if they ever needed anything to always come to him. He was over with his three children. Izzy was over with hers and of course remained by my side being always supportive like my sister April.

That night I got a phone call while everyone was still there from Izzy's mother, June, with whom I had also become close and talked to quite often. She knew what was going on as well, and she told me over the phone how sorry she was for the boys and me and how her heart broke for us. Then what she came out with next simply amazed me. The size of her heart was so large and the depth of her compassion so deep.

She told me, "Kyra, I know you don't have your mommy anymore, but you can consider me your black mommy. I'll stand in place for your mom, and my heart is with you right now."

These were June's exact words to me, and they made me feel so good. It also made me laugh just by the way she came out with that statement. It was just so funny.

So my boys and I, you see, were surrounded that night by so much love and so many caring people that it did ease our pain greatly. Later on that evening Izzy's sister, Cathy, even stopped over with her son, Michael. I never felt more supported in my whole life as I did that very minute. It's true what they say, friends can carry you through the most horrific times in your life, if they are true friends as these people were to me. Between the love that Michael had for me and I had for Michael, having God back in my life to carry me through this most horrific time, and having friends such as these, I knew my children and I were going to make it through this. We would survive. Believe me when I say these friends would not leave my side. It wasn't until 10 o'clock that night that they all started leaving after I let them know how tired I was, and that the boys and I right now needed to get a good night's sleep.

That night Teddy and Martin slept with me in my bed, and as I lay there with them in my arms keeping them close I thought to myself, *How strange life truly is. This is the very bed that both of them were created in. This bed was here throughout all the good times and the bad, and how this bed witnessed all the tears that I shed for my loved ones that had passed. Now we were lying here, the three of us together, a family, because this was my family now, my two sons.* As we lay there I thought, *Throughout all of those times and right up until now, this is the bed that Michael was lying in when he drew his last breath. In this bed I felt so close to Michael. So many nights we just held each other so close. I still feel that today.* Right now, lying here with Martin and Teddy by my side, I could feel Michael. I could feel his spirit and his love lying right alongside of us and carrying us through this night, this first horrifying night without him.

I was once again awakened, as I was so many mornings before with that sun peeking through our blinds. I woke up Teddy and Martin, and I told them, "We have to start looking for suits." I realized that they had outgrown their dress suits that they had worn to the funerals that they had attended in the past. So after a little bit of breakfast, because none of us had very much of an appetite, we began looking through the closets trying to find something that would fit. We found nothing, so what I decided to do was to bring them to the Mall and rent really nice suits for both of them. I couldn't afford to buy them at this point. I didn't know how much money all of this was going to cost, and I was working on a limited budget, so I thought renting a really fine suit would be much better than buying a cheap suit.

While they were being fitted for their suits at the store, I sat there, and I just became overwhelmed all at once. I guess an anxiety attack set in. I just started thinking of all the things that Michael and I had done in our lives, and all the fighting that we had done to gain a normal life and a normal existence. What was all that fighting for? What was it all about for it to end like this? The more I thought this way, the more helpless I felt and the more overwhelmed I became. I now was trying to plan my husband's funeral and to make everything as perfect as it possibly could be because at this moment it was the only thing I truly had control over.

Hospice came back the following day and sat there talking to Teddy, Martin, and me, making sure that we were handling things the way we should. Just like my main concern was for the boys, theirs was as well. I had to protect their mental health. I found as a parent there was no way that you could shield your child from absolutely everything obviously, but I did my best to shield them from what I could, and I prayed it was enough. I prayed that my protection over them would be enough, the open communication that we always shared between us would be enough, the honesty that I always showed them would be enough, and most of all our belief system, our belief in God. I hoped these would all be enough to prevent them from having any permanent scars. I so desperately did not want my children's lives to be ruined over this, and I knew Michael felt the same way I did. He tried to protect them as much as he could as well. I guess only in time will we find out if everything that we tried to do was enough.

So now after being fitted for their suits, we had about an hour to spare until we could pick them up, so we just walked around the Mall. We passed that art gallery where Michael had bought me that beautiful picture of the lighthouse just a few month's earlier, and of course the memories flooded back. I tried to block them as much as I could and keep a smile on my face for my children. We went and ate at the food court, spending the remainder of our time there until we knew the suits were ready to be picked up.

By the time we got back home April was there waiting for us. She had brought Chinese food, but we had already eaten so we just picked at it. She just wanted to make sure we were all okay. She worried so much about the boys and me. She didn't want me driving around at this point. We had found something odd had happened to us whenever we were hit with a loss, and that was our driving skills dropped dramatically. We would go through red lights and Stop Signs and not even see them, so she really worried about my driving, especially now after this horrendous heartache. She offered to pick the boys and me up the next day to go to the wake. I told her, "No. It's okay. I can drive down the street. I'm okay." And I was. I kept my faculties about me. Although it was hard from time to time to do so, I did.

July the 2nd now was here. The boys and I woke up that morning and that feeling like I got kicked in the stomach was right there just as it always was before every wake. I prayed. I prayed for God's grace and his help and guidance, and it made me feel just a little bit better. I got the boy's up, and they didn't even want to talk about breakfast. They had no appetite of course. I told them we would have to get dressed around one because the wake was from 2 to 4 and then 6 to 8. I would only allow them to go the one time and that was 2 to 4. I didn't think they needed to sit there for an additional two hours later on that evening listening to the crying and meeting all our old friends, or should I say the ones that were still alive, the ones that were still here, which were only two. So I thought it best that Teddy and Martin just attend the one time and then of course go to the funeral the next day. My friends and April all agreed. They thought the two viewings would be a little bit too much on them. So 1 o'clock rolled around, and I started getting the boys in their new little suits. Martin was

9 years old now and Teddy was 12. I got into my black dress and we got into the car and left for this most heartbreaking experience.

We got to the funeral home and went in. Troy, Michael's cousin, met us at the door, and he told me first about John. It seems that John had been there earlier that day in chains and shackles just like he was for his mother's wake. I had left a ring for Troy to give to John. It was one of Michael's rings, and I hoped it would provide just a little bit of comfort where he was not able to grieve with the family. Troy told me that the Guards would not allow him to give John the ring. He had to stay far away from John. Troy told me he stood far away just as instructed, and he watched John enter the viewing area where Michael was.

He said, "Kyra, I felt so bad for him. He dropped to his knees when he saw Michael and cried." The cancer had changed Michael so much and aged him so drastically. Instead of looking his age, 52, he looked like he was 80, and John was absolutely horrified by this.

My heart for that moment broke for John. I felt so bad for him. I felt so bad to hear about all of this and especially Troy not being able to give him that ring. I know holding onto something of his brother's would have helped him through the grieving process, but he was not allowed to. There was nothing left to say. There wasn't anything we could do to help John.

Troy then asked the boys and me if we were ready to go in to view Michael. I looked at him, and I said, "Yes." We started walking toward the casket, and there Michael was lying in his beautiful blue suit, the one he adored so much. Beside him was his military picture, the one I gave Troy to display. One thing threw me and that was that the cascading blue flowers that I had picked out for his casket weren't there. They were draped over the lid of the casket instead and in its place was the American Flag. The whole scene was simply breathtaking. He was honored. He finally, finally got the honor and the respect he always deserved. I was so proud to see that flag over my husband's casket.

The boys and I went up and kneeled down by the casket and said The Lord's Prayer. I asked Michael at that moment to help his two boys get through this, and help them as much as he possibly could. I knew through experience, they could. Michael would have been so very, very proud of Teddy and Martin. They stood tall, proud, and full of honor. They were loving young men. They didn't break down and cry. In public they didn't shed a tear. They kept a strong upper lip and were brave just like they knew their father would want them to be. On this day both of them stood tall and strong together, and I was so very, very proud of them. They both acted just the way Michael taught them to, full of honor and pride. That's exactly what they did on this day. They were there to honor their father, and that's exactly what they did. They honored him by behaving just the way they did.

After we paid our respects and said our prayers beside their father's casket, we then went to sit down. April was right by my side. Joe, Susan, and their children then came in and paid their respects. They took their place by me in the family line. As Joe sat there crying, I slipped onto his finger another one of Michael's rings. Michael had accumulated four or five really nice rings, and I gave one to each of the men in our family. One was for John, one was Joe, one was for Teddy, and one was for Martin.

As I was slipping on the ring, he looked at me and he said, "What's this?"

I said, "That was one of your brother's favorite rings, and I know he would want you to have it."

He gave me a hug and a kiss and thanked me.

I knew these rings would mean a lot to the men, to his brothers and his sons. To carry this little piece of their brother and father with them would possibly help through the grieving process. As we sat there and the relatives came up to greet us and give us hugs of comfort, a few of them did ask about John. I realized that, yes, I was right to let the boys know about him, because now was when they would have been blindsided and would have asked me, "Who was John and why didn't you and Dad tell us about him before?"

So I knew I made the right choice then, and I answered the questions from Michael's relatives as clearly as I could. I just told them, "Yes, he was allowed to come, but no one else could be here." They found it just as sad as I did that poor John now had to grieve in solitude.

I guess it was around 3:30 when Troy came to me and let me know that a man had called earlier that day. He had forgotten all about it. He said this man claimed to be Michael's older son, and I almost fell out of my seat. I said, "What?" I couldn't believe my ears. He was actually contacting us after all these years. He said that he wanted to get in touch with you, and that he needed to talk to you then. Troy told me he told Michael he could not give him my phone number. That was private information. I again was just blown away.

I couldn't believe it. I said, "Troy, you did what?"

He then thought quickly and said, "I think I got his phone number."

I said, "Oh, my God, I hope you did."

He went up in his office and looked all around. He finally found it. I then called it immediately, and I spoke to a woman whose name was Alice. This was Michael Jr.'s stepmother. I explained to her what the situation was with Michael when he was little. I told her how I always wanted to raise him as my own and that I always loved him.

She began then describing him to me, and she said, "You know, he has a lot of tattoos and he was in the Marines. He's a big guy."

I said, "Yeah, fine." I didn't know what point she was trying to make with all of this. Perhaps she thought these tattoos would scare me off or something. I don't know, but of course she knew nothing of my life's history. Tattoos were the least of my worries.

I told her I didn't care about the tattoo. He could be covered from head to toe with tattoos as long as I could see his eyes.

She laughed. She told me that he wasn't there right now, and she didn't know where he was, but as soon as he came in she would give him my phone number, which I gave to her.

I said, "Please, please. Have him call me." I realized that he must have gotten a cold reception from Troy, who just probably wanted to protect Teddy, Pat, and me. Nevertheless it was a cold reception for a child to get when calling about his father's funeral.

I can't even begin to tell you how upset I was over all of that. I just so wanted to see Michael Jr. again and hold him in my arms again, but most certainly not under these circumstances.

It was now 4 o'clock and it was time for everyone to leave and return back at 6. The two boys, April, and I went out to dinner. I chose the place that Michael took me on our second date, Ann's Place right by the water, the lake that we always sat by to talk or to just relax or fish. So we went there and the most incredible thing happened. Because it was almost the 4th of July, all the tables had red, white, and blue carnations on them. Each table only had one flower. It was either a red, blue, or a white one. We sat down at a table, and I looked over at the table where Michael and I sat on our second date. That was the only table in that entire restaurant that had a blue flower on it. Chills went up my spine. I told April and the boys all about it, and they laughed. Amazing, out of that entire restaurant, that one table that Michael and I sat at on our second date was the only one that had the blue flower, Michael's favorite color! I knew he was around. I could feel him carrying us through this, and this was just one more little confirmation.

It was around 5:30 after we ate our dinner, or should I say choked it down because I did not feel hungry at all at that point, but I knew I had to keep up my strength, I told April she should take the boys home and I would go back to the funeral parlor. She agreed to do so. I told her to please make sure as soon as the boys hit the door they got out of their suits. She said, "Don't worry. I'll make sure they do." So they went home and got undressed. Teddy went over to Joey's house, and Martin went over to Nick's. Through these two viewing times, Izzy and Angel were taking turns watching their kids. At one point they did bring their kids, Angel, Jr. and A.T., and of course Joey was there standing right beside Teddy through all of this.

Throughout those two hours from 2 to 4, there was one point where Joey and Teddy went and sat off in a corner by themselves. I could see the wheels turning. They were cooking something up. Whenever they got together like that, it led to no good, so I said, "Oh, my goodness, what's going on?"

They both came up to me and said, "Could we talk to you alone?"

"Of course."

Teddy then told me, not asked but told me, that he was going to be a pall bearer for his father, and Joey wanted to stand by Teddy's side and do the same.

I was completely floored. I told Teddy, "I have no idea how you are going to do this. You know what this entails. You've been to enough funerals now and you know what a pall bearer has to do."

"Yes. They have to carry the casket, and I want to carry my father's casket."

Believe me, I tried talking him out of this because I thought this was just too much for him. He was only twelve and a half, and he had already stood tall through so much. He was so insistent. There was no talking him or Joey out of it.

I went over to Izzy, and I told her what they had just said I asked her, "Is that okay with you and Angel if Joey is a pall bearer?"

She said, "If Joey really wants to do it, of course it is. He wants to stand by his brother's side." That's what Teddy and Joey had become, brothers. After she said this, I got such a lump in my throat it was all I could do not to break down in tears.

I was so proud of Teddy and Joey at this moment but scared as well. I hoped they would be able to do it without breaking down. After all I had known many a man who in no way would be able to do such a thing after the death of their father or mother, and for a twelve and a half year old and a fourteen year old to do this now, it was completely incredible to me. This was something I know I wouldn't have had in me to do.

So I told Troy, "You can add Teddy and Joey to Michael's pall bearer list along with Angel," Izzy's husband who wanted to do this as well. There was so much love and there were so many friends I was grateful for. So the pall bearers were the three of them along with Michael's brother Joe, Michael's Uncle Charlie, the one that I had known for so many years and was friends with his daughters, and then John, Robert's oldest son. These were six men that Michael had the utmost respect for. I couldn't think of a more perfect set of pall bearers.

Over dinner after the 2 to 4 viewing hour I told April all of this, and she was as blown away as I was. I told Teddy just before he got into the car with April to go back home to just enjoy himself and be a kid. I told him, "Go out and ride your bike with Joey. Just go and try to have some fun and take your mind off of tomorrow."

He looked at me and gave me a big hug, and he said, "I'll try my best, Mom."

So April headed home with the boys, and I headed back to the funeral parlor. When I arrived, Joe and Susan were already there. I went up to the casket, and I looked at Michael, and I told him what Teddy and Joey were going to do tomorrow, and I said, "You can be so proud of your boy. He is growing into such a good man."

As the evening went on, Izzy stayed close by my side just as Angel and Cathy did. I saw Michael's uncles and aunts, ones that I hadn't seen for years, and my old friend Corey, Alex's ex-wife now, was there with her new husband. They looked very, very happy together, and I was happy for her. She told me that they had stopped drinking several years earlier, and they were doing very, very well.

As I sat there in the receiving line talking to Izzy and Joe, I happened to glance up at the door where this tall, handsome young man was standing with his girl beside him. He walked up to the podium where you signed the guest book. He picked up the pen and looked directly into the viewing area at Michael. Then after looking at Michael his eyes turned to me. As soon as our eyes met, I knew who he was. I remember those eyes from years and years ago, and I said to myself, *Oh, my God, that's Michael Jr.*

I must have been sitting there with my mouth hanging open in amazement. He was so tall and of course so much older. He was 24 years old now and a marine, to boot. As soon as he took his eyes off of me, he ran for the door, and I got up and ran right after him, thinking all the while to myself, *Oh, no you don't. Not after all these years. I am not going to lose you again.*

I went out the front door to see him standing leaning over the banister crying his heart out. I went up to him and wrapped my arms around him and held him close. I kept telling him, "Michael, it's going to be okay; it's okay; it's okay, Michael."

The girl that was with him told me his name wasn't Michael; it was Steven.

I said, "Steven?" Then I just started rubbing his back, and I called him by his correct name—he had chosen to change from Michael to Steven. I told him, "Steven, it's okay. It's all right, Baby."

He stood up wiping the tears from his eyes and he told me, "I've been looking for my father for two years now, and I find him like this?"

I asked him how he found out. He said, "My grandmother read it in the Gazette and knew who my adoptive parents were and called them to let them know. That's how I knew where to go and what was going on."

Then I told him we just lived down the street.

He said, "Oh, my God. I go by that house all the time. I go down the street all the time." He simply couldn't believe it, and quite frankly the whole thing was surreal.

After seeing me run out the door, Izzy came out because she was wondering what was going on, and I told her then who Steven was. I said, "This is Michael's first son, Steven." I introduced him to Izzy.

Then Izzy asked me, "Do you want me to go get Teddy and Martin?"

"Yes, yes!"

I thought that would be a great idea, so she hopped in her car and went and picked up Teddy, Martin and Joey. Joey, of course would not leave Teddy's side, and brought them back to the funeral parlor where Steven and I and his girlfriend stood standing outside while he cried in my arms.

I told him, "You have two brothers, Teddy and Martin. Izzy is going to bring them here any minute now."

He just looked in shock at the whole thing. He couldn't believe what was going on. Again that sense of surrealness.

As we stood there on the porch of the funeral parlor, Izzy came driving up and Teddy and Martin got out of the car and started walking up the steps. Steven couldn't take his eyes off of them.

I said to Teddy and Martin, "I know how ridiculous this sounds, but I have to introduce you to someone very special." I said, "Teddy, this is your brother, Steven. Steven, this is your brother, Teddy." Then I turned to Martin, and I said, "This is your brother, Steven. Steven, this is your brother, Martin." They shook hands, and they stood there just speechless. I told Teddy and Martin to give their brother a hug.

Poor Cathy and Izzy were crying in the background. They couldn't believe what was unfolding in front of their eyes. That's when Izzy turned to me and said, "Kyra, you really need to write a book, because Hollywood could not make this up."

I looked at her and laughed and said, "Yeah, right."

So with Teddy and Martin by Steven's side I told Steven that we were going to have a military funeral for his father the next day. "I would really, really like it if you would be able to attend and to ride with his family, to be with the family on this important day."

He said that he was not sure if he could get the time off from work, but he would do his best. He would try very, very hard.

I asked him if he would like to return back into the funeral parlor to pay his last respects, and he said, "I can't do it. I can't."

I took his hand, and I told him, "We'll do it together. Come on. This is important for you to do." Remembering back to the time I lost my mother. Closure is very, very important. I took his hand and we walked back into the funeral parlor together side by side and he kneeled by his father's casket. I said The Lord's Prayer out loud with my hands on his shoulders. Then in my mind I asked Michael to please, please help Steven get through this. "I know you're helping Teddy and Martin. Now you need to help him as well."

I can't even begin to tell you how good it felt to be able to hold Steven in my arms again after so many years, but too bad it had to be under such heartbreaking circumstances. I wished to God years before in 1995 when Michael had the opportunity to break the ice and to bring him back into our lives, he had taken it, but you can't go back in time. You can't turn back the hands of time. It just felt so good to have him here now. I always felt like he was the part of my life that was missing.

On this day I felt so much pain but also joy in having him back in my life. I always wanted to be his mother. I always wanted to raise him as my own, but I was realistic. I knew at the age of 24 he didn't need another mother. The one that he had for so many years had obviously done such a great job because he was a good man. But nevertheless I did want to try and be that mother to him that I always wanted to be, and I would try. I was given a second chance here, and I wasn't going to blow it again.

One funny thing did happen. After we got through paying the respects and I got through praying in silence for Michael's help, I took Joey by his other hand and he flinched back. I said, "What's the matter?" and he showed me his hand and his knuckles were all cut up.

I looked at him and said, "What is that?"

He said, "Oh, I got into a fight a few days ago," and I laughed. I know it was inappropriate but I laughed right in the middle of the funeral parlor because I had seen his father's hands look like that so many times. You talk about "like father, like son." This is a living example of it.

By this time it was time for all of us to go. It was getting late, and his brothers asked him if he was going to be able to come tomorrow. They really wanted him to, and he agreed. He said, "I will."

So that's how we left it. After not seeing him for so many years, having to watch him drive off in his little white jeep was more heartbreaking to me than you could imagine standing there, wondering all the while if I truly ever was going to see him again, if he was going to have enough courage to return back the next day for his father's funeral. All I could do was stand there and pray that he would.

CHAPTER THIRTEEN

That night when we arrived back home, Teddy and Martin could not stop talking about their Big Brother, a big brother they had just now met. The feeling was just so, so strange. It was like one side of us was happy and thrilled to have Steven in our lives now, and the other side devastated because we lost so, so much with the passing of their father and my only love. I felt like I was torn right down the middle with both of these emotions, and then adding in you could say the anxiety of it all, just wishing that Michael could have been here to meet his son and speak with him. I wished Steven had had the opportunity to know Michael. Just pure regret was all I felt toward Michael and Steven's relationship. I was so filled with emotions right now, all of these and then some. I felt like I was going to lose my mind. I was feeling so badly for Teddy and Martin, but I was feeling even worse for Steven because he never got to say good-bye to his dad, and this is how he found him after a two-year long search.

This night the boys slept in their own bed for the first time since their father's passing, and I lay in my bed feeling completely and utterly alone, never again being able to roll over and put my arms around Michael and never again to feel his arms around me. He was my protector and he kept me safe, and that I would have no longer. I did not get much sleep this night, and I awoke feeling so sick, my head pounding, my stomach twisted in knots, and my heart broken. My body was in so much pain I felt like I had fallen down the stairs. I remember sitting at the edge of my bed as soon as I woke up that morning and praying so hard for strength and for guidance. I asked God to please show me the right way, show me the right things to do. But as I did throughout my whole life, I let my heart lead the way. I let my heart tell me what the right things would be to do, and I asked my heart to give me the strength that I needed to get through this day. I knew I was going to somehow have to find the strength to stay strong, to stay strong for Teddy and Martin and now for Steven. I knew if I let God help me he would, and he did.

I was finding now looking back on all my heartbreaks over the past five years that for each death and for each heartache I grew ever stronger in spirit. I was learning how to turn my pain into my strength, and this God did for me. When I got up it was about 6 o'clock. I went down and made myself a cup of coffee trying desperately to pull myself together and gather my strength. Then I went upstairs and woke up Teddy and Martin. We then began to get dressed. Before I knew it April was there and Izzy, Angel, their children, and Cathy. Even though I had a house full of people that loved me, I still felt so empty and alone inside at this moment, and my stomach was still tied in a knot.

It was about a half an hour before the family limousine was to pick us up when I saw Steven drive up in his little white Jeep. I was surprised but not surprised at the same time. I didn't think he would miss this day this opportunity to be with his new-found family. He walked into my house and April was the first one to greet him at the door.

She said to him, "I guess you can consider me your aunt now. My name is April and you can call me Aunt April."

He knew he was welcomed with open arms. He then came into the kitchen where I was sitting, and I stood up and gave him a big hug and a kiss on the cheek. The feeling was just so surreal and so bizarre as he stood there in the kitchen standing beside me. I began getting this overwhelming feeling as though he had been there all along, as though he had always been with us somehow. Perhaps it was because he should have been. I don't know. All I know is that it felt like "old hat." It didn't feel like he was in my kitchen for the first time standing here.

We talked for a few moments, and I tried to explain to him a little bit about our lives and about his new family. I began telling him about the times that his father and I would pick him up and bring him to the lake and out for pizza, to the playground, or fishing, hoping to jog his memory because his memory was very vague. Of course, he was very young, and he really couldn't remember a whole lot, but I could, and I tried to remind him of all these times. I tried to remind him of how close we were, but he had a hard time remembering.

So all the memories of him that lay in my head, he could not share with me because he was simply too young to remember. I knew him, but he didn't know me, and I realized at that moment, *Teddy and Martin, and I are strangers to him. We were family but we were still nevertheless strangers,* and this I hoped to change. I wanted to make him a part of his brothers' lives. I felt as though actually he needed them more than they needed him at this moment. You see they had each other and they had me. He had no one, and I wanted to change that. I wanted so desperately for him to get to know Teddy and Martin and to get to know just how truly great they both were. From this day on I will try my hardest to do this.

I welcomed him into the family with open arms, and I treated him no differently than I did Teddy and Martin because now he was also my son, not by birth, but he was a part of the only man I ever truly loved in this world just like Teddy and Martin. I wanted to love him just as I did Teddy and Martin, and to keep that promise I made to Michael before he passed to take good care of his sons. His sons now also included Steven. I told him on this morning as we stood in the kitchen that I loved him, and I wanted him to be a part of this family, part of his family again. He was free to come and go as he pleased. Whenever he felt like coming over, please come for a visit just to sit and talk. It didn't matter, but he was always welcome here.

I told him, "This is your home now, just as it is Teddy and Martin's."

He began to cry.

I told him, "Don't, it's okay. We'll make it through this day as a family."

Just as I was saying those words, Troy drove up in the family limousine to take us to the funeral home. We all got into the limo and arrived at the funeral home. I took Teddy and Martin right along with Steven up to the side of their father's casket to pay their last respects. I stood there alongside Steven as Martin and Teddy kneeled, and I said The Lord's Prayer, and again after I said the prayer there was a moment of silence. In that moment of silence I begged Michael to please, please send a little more of his strength my way, and to please help his three sons get through this horrifying day.

We then began placing in Michael's casket the things that we wanted him to be buried with. I put in his last three Father's Day Cards that the boys had just bought him. Teddy placed his brand-new Nike ring in the casket, giving it a kiss before laying it beside his father. Martin put a little yellow duckling, a little plastic figure that he always used to have on his father's feeding tube machine to make his father smile. He placed that in beside his father.

For me I left him with nothing but that very, very important wedding band. To me this one gold band spoke volumes of our dedication, our relationship and our love. That was all I needed to bury my husband with. I knew after he was buried he would go through eternity with that symbol of love that we had toward each other, that little gold band around his finger. I would always carry mine on my finger symbolizing our love. I would cherish it every time I would touch my wedding band in life and the times that I would lay there in our empty bed feeling my wedding band on my finger and holding it close to my heart telling Michael how much I loved him. Every night before I would go to sleep there, I would always know in his casket with him was that matching wedding band, that symbol of our love. He would for always have that on his finger just as I would mine. This in my heart would be our connection, a connection that would never be broken, because I knew every time I touched that ring I would be touching a part of him. I would always be able to keep a part of him close to me and to my heart never, ever to be removed from my finger.

When the four of us were done paying our last respects, I leaned over and I kissed Michael's hand and kissed the wedding band that I placed on it and told him, "I'll be seeing you when my time comes. Please be the one to come for me."

I then started walking back to my seat and sat down while Teddy, Martin and Steven remained by their father's casket for a few more moments. To see the three of them standing there, Michael's three handsome sons standing beside their father's flag-draped casket, was so surreal and heartbreaking. I will never until my dying day get this picture out of my mind. Just then Steven also placed something in the casket with his father. Then Steven and Martin came and sat by my side, Martin sitting on one side and Steven on the other. Steven placed his head in his hands and began crying. Martin looked on fighting back his own tears.

I handed Steven a tissue, and then I asked him, "Honey, what did you place inside your father's casket with him?"

"My medals from the Marine Corps."

I thought to myself, *Oh, my God.* I had no idea how many medals there were. All I could see was this huge cluster of little tiles, blue and green and white. It was quite large, and I thought to myself, *I have to find out exactly what he did to deserve all those honors.* I knew in time I would, but for now I was so honored for him to show such love for his father that he would want to give him his medals, medals I know he worked very, very hard for. I know Michael felt the same way I did right now. I know he was watching, and I know he was with us. He must of just been bursting at the seams with honor and pride to see his older son bestowing such an honor on him at this moment, to give him what he worked so hard to achieve, all the medals he worked so hard to get where Michael can now carry them through eternity with him.

So while Steven sat beside me and Martin on the other side, Teddy took his place with the pall bearers, Joey, Angel, Joe, John and Uncle Charlie. It was now time to start calling the funeral procession and the cars that would follow the hearse. We were to get into the family limo and go to the church.

I pulled Troy aside for one minute, and I told him, "Look, I know Teddy is doing an incredible thing, but please keep in mind he is only twelve and a half, and his best friend Joey is only fourteen. I don't want them exposed to anything that they don't need to be exposed to." I asked him to please make sure they were not in the room when they closed the casket. This, in itself, is a traumatic experience for a loved one, a finalization, and I didn't want Teddy seeing this.

So Troy told me, "Yes, of course. I'll make sure they're not in the room," and he did.

So as everyone left the funeral parlor, getting into their own cars, Izzy, Angel, April, Steven, Martin, and I sat in the family limo. We sat there in front of the funeral parlor watching the casket being brought out. Teddy and Joey together with Angel on one side, Joe, John and Uncle Charlie on the other side. We sat there in the limousine watching them bring out the casket. Steven sitting on one side of me was just in tears throughout the whole thing as Martin sat on the other side of me.

I told him and Martin, "You don't have to watch this. Just look down." But I did have to watch. I had to watch while my son Teddy honored his father. I had to pay Teddy that respect, and so I watched every painful step he took. I had never been so proud of him as I was that very second. I knew he was growing into a wonderful, wonderful man, a man with honor and pride, just as his father taught him to be. He showed more strength on this day than I could even begin to imagine me being able to do. As they placed the casket into the hearse, he rode in the limo that they provided for the pall bearers and again at the church. I had to watch the same thing. Step after step I watched him take, and with each step my heart broke just a little bit more for him.

We all took our seats in the church and as Father Post was delivering the Mass he came over to Martin, Steven, and me sitting there, and he made the sign of the cross over us. I gave a sign for him to come closer to me, and he did.

I whispered in his ear, "Father Post, I don't know what you're going to think of me but there is no way I can possibly do Michael's eulogy," a eulogy just a few days before I knew I was going to be so proud to give, but there was no way now that I could possibly do this. I was going to describe in great detail all of the good things that Michael did with me and with his two sons, Teddy and Martin, and all the fun that we had fishing, having cookouts, and the target shooting, all of that. "I simply cannot do this now." I told him I would explain my reasons later, but for him to please take it from here, and do Michael's eulogy for me.

I knew with Steven sitting beside me, when the time came for me to deliver this eulogy, to stand up in front of everyone and speak these words, I felt now would be paramount to me reaching my fist into his chest and ripping his heart out. How could I now talk about all those good times that Teddy and Martin had with their father, everything Steven was denied? How could I do this to this man now? I couldn't.

It just broke my heart because I wanted everyone to know what a good man Michael truly was, but I thought to myself, *I'll do this in private later.* I will revisit Michael's grave, of course, and I will read to him what I had written. I will deliver his eulogy in private some day after this, but not now, not here and not in front of Steven. I just simply could not be that cruel. Thank goodness Father Post had come to know the family very well, so he was able to give a beautiful eulogy in my place. He spoke of how close Teddy and Martin were to their father, and how we were always together. Most importantly he spoke of how well Michael was taken care of always and how much he was loved by his family. So it was a beautiful eulogy anyway, but it wasn't my own. It wasn't the one that I so desperately wanted to give.

When the service was completed they began bringing the casket back out, and I said one last prayer before leaving the church. I felt so good in God's house. I asked him again for the strength. As we were walking out of the church ready to get back into the limos to go now to the cemetery, on those same exact stairs five years earlier after the service for my mother, the same stairs that I almost fell down because my knees became so weak, the same exact thing happened to me again. My knees almost buckled from underneath me, and my head began spinning. Now, instead of Michael catching me, Steven was the one that caught me and prevented me from falling.

The whole thing to me was completely amazing and completely surreal. Just five years earlier in that same exact spot his father carried me through the most horrific time in my life until now. We stopped for a moment on the stairs after this happened so that I could regain my composure and my stability. Then we proceeded to walk down the remaining few stairs and get into the family limousine to make that final heartbreaking ride to the cemetery.

Once at the cemetery everyone began getting out of their cars and the family out of the limo. Teddy made those last few heartbreaking steps to take his father's casket out of the hearse and place it in its final resting area in our family plot. As we stood there the flag that laid on Michael's casket waving in the warm, warm summer's breeze, Father Post read from the Bible as I looked directly across from me where Teddy was standing alongside the other pall bearers, staying so strong and not shedding a tear but standing there full of honor just as Martin was and Steven alongside me. After Father Post was done the Guardsmen shot off their rifles in the background. Then they retrieved the flag from the casket. They picked up the casings from the bullets and placed them in the middle of the flag. Then they began folding the flag as taps played in the background. The head of the Guardsmen came over and presented it to me, and I thanked him.

Standing there like that beside Michael's casket and his family's headstone was almost more than my heart could bear but I knew I must. I must be strong. I must bear whatever pain my heart felt now for our three sons. This ceremony came to an end and everyone began getting back into their cars. I sat in the middle between Martin and Steven, Martin to my right and Steven to my left. I then took the flag that I was hugging and clinging to desperately and handed it to Steven, a flag that represented everything to me, all the honor that my husband stood for in life. I handed it off to his oldest son now. He looked at me with amazement in his eyes.

I told him, "Here, this is yours. It doesn't belong to anyone else. You are Michael's oldest son, and you should have it." I then hugged him, and I told him I loved him.

He said, "Thank you so much, Kyra."

Then I placed my arm around Martin and held him close as well. The longest and most heartbreaking ride of my entire life was that ride from the cemetery back home. It was just so final then. Michael was now in his family plot instead of at home sitting on the couch with his two sons watching TV or fishing, target

526

shooting, or working on the car. He was now taken from us forever, and we would have to learn how to live the rest of our lives without him. But for right now, for today, I just couldn't even begin to think about it, and I could not even begin to comprehend the pain that I was feeling in my heart. I was just still very numb at this point.

After we arrived home we were to pick up our own cars and go back to the church. Father Post had allowed us to set up a little meeting area in the basement of the church, a little gathering. Susan had made all the food for this gathering, and I appreciated it very much although I was not hungry whatsoever. My appetite I feared was dead forever. It was a good opportunity for me to introduce Steven to everyone. Robert's children were all there, Izzy and Angel, their children, cousins he had never met, Joe and Susan's two girls and boy. It was some sort of sick family reunion I guess you would say, but it was a good opportunity for him to meet all the relatives that he never even knew he had.

After this gathering Steven came back to my house with Teddy and Martin. April, as long as she knew I was okay, went home to rest and try to take in these past few days. Steven, Teddy, Martin, and I had a really nice visit. It was so funny but once they started talking about their hobbies, their likes were so similar it was like they all grew up in the same household. Their personality quirks were so similar it was bizarre. It was as though Steven had been with us always.

He then began telling us about his time in the Marines and how he was in the platoon that was dropped into Bosnia to help rescue Captain O'Grady. He was in the Special Ops in the Marines, so I guess he did a lot of dangerous things like that. I know Michael would have been just as proud of him as I was at that moment when he was telling us all of this. I could tell Teddy and Martin were so impressed with him, and they kept commenting on all of his tattoos. He did have quite a few.

I then told him I would really, really like him to come at least once a week to have dinner with his family. "You know, you're welcome here any time you want to stop by, but I would at least like to have one evening. You can pick the day and time. Whatever day is good for you." I realized a 24-year-old's life is probably very, very busy, but I was hoping he would have enough time to spare to have at least one dinner a week with us.

We spent hours talking this day, and I reminded him about how this was his house, just as it was Teddy and Martin's now. I told him it was completely up to him. "I don't have the right to ask for anything from you, and I won't. It's all up to you whether you want a family or not. It has to be your choice, Steven. It has to be your decision and your decision alone."

He looked at me and he said, "Yes, yes I do. I want this. I want a family, and I want to get to know my brothers."

I was so happy to hear him say those words because I could tell Teddy and Martin wanted to get to know him as well. There seemed to be almost an instantaneous bond between the three of them. Their personalities just meshed so well together it was as though they all grew up together. But again, I knew it was all up to Steven now. We were here for him. Whether he was to accept us or not was another story. So far, he did, but whatever decision he was to make, I would have to respect and stand by and allow him to make. Right now it was all up to him.

It was quite late that evening when he left. He gave us all hugs good-bye, and I told him I wanted to see him back in a couple of days for dinner. I told him, "I'll make my homemade lasagna." This was something that Michael, Teddy and Martin always loved.

He said, "Do you know what? It's funny that you say that because that is my favorite dinner."

So after Steven left promising to return in a couple of days for dinner, the three of us went upstairs and got ready for bed. Teddy and Martin fell asleep right away. The poor things were so exhausted, emotionally exhausted. After getting into my nightgown I sat there on the edge of the bed. I said my prayers, then I happened to notice that smell, that floral smell that appeared right after my mother's death was now gone. It had stayed there all this time right up to today, but now it was gone. I just shook my head. I couldn't understand, *Why now?* Then I thought, *Maybe my mother was somehow attached to that smell, and she was helping me through the years that were going to be so hard for me, the years of much loss to come after her death. Maybe she was helping me and carrying me through, and now I no longer needed her?* I couldn't understand. All I knew was that smell was now gone.

The same night after Michael's funeral when I noticed the smell gone, I noticed something else beginning to happen. Something that wasn't so pleasant. After I said my prayers and I put my lights out, I held onto Michael's rosaries, the ones that were wrapped around his hands during his wake and funeral. I asked Troy to give them to me. I wanted a part of him to pray with just as we held hands and prayed every night together. I felt like if I had his rosaries it would be almost like him sitting beside me saying the prayers that we always said.

So I lay there holding the rosaries, and I began picking up these spirits, a presence in my room, a presence I hadn't felt before. It didn't feel good like that spirit that came to help me when I so desperately needed it, and there was more than one. Actually my room was full of them and they didn't feel familiar at all. It didn't feel like Michael's, my mother's, Amber's or Robert's spirits. They were unfamiliar to me, and it was extremely disturbing to feel so many all at once when in the past I had only felt one at a time and never as strong as this. My room was actually packed. Just as in the past, I tried my hardest to ignore them, to just go to sleep, but trying to go to sleep when you have perhaps ten people standing there staring at you is difficult. This is the way it felt. It was only after a couple of hours, after exhaustion had taken me over completely, was I able to fall asleep.

In the morning when I awoke I felt nothing again, and I thank God because I thought this to be just an isolated incident. I prayed it wouldn't happen again. I never felt bombarded like that before in my life. There were so many all at once. So many that I couldn't distinguish whether they were male, female or child. Again, this never happened to me before. I actually thought as far as things like this went in our family it was calming down because after Teddy and Martin saw Amber and my mother that seemed to be it. They never saw them again, and I never saw the little girl again or felt her. I hadn't felt actually any spirits in maybe a year and a half, so when this hit, it kind of sideswiped me because I was hoping perhaps all of this was over with now. However, I guess if you are given a gift, if that's what you want to call it, it's never truly over with. You are always susceptible to certain things. What I experienced that night in my bedroom was completely mind-blowing. Just so many of them all at once was just so overwhelming to me.

The next morning when I awoke I got the boys up for breakfast. It was so very, very strange not having Michael here. This was something our minds and our hearts would have to get used to, but the pain was just so new and so fresh. These first few months I knew were going to be incredibly difficult. I tried my hardest to get back into a normal routine with the boys, but I realized there would never be a normal routine again because of the absence of their father. It would be just them and me, and this is something that is incredibly hard to wrap your brain around but you must, you must find some way to get back into as much of a normal routine as you can because you have to accept this now as a part of life. I realized that after all my previous losses, but I also realized that it was going to take a long time to do this because unlike all of the other losses, I was not going to be able to have Michael here to help me get through. I had to stand alone, I had to be strong, and I had to keep the promise that I made to Michael and that was to take very good care of our children, now not two but three. Today was the first day, the beginning of this new life for my sons and me.

It was July 4, 2000, and it seemed like everyone around us was just so happy and celebrating the 4th of July with the fireworks I could hear going off in the distance. Everyone having cookouts. We would sit there simply numb in the backyard listening to all of their laughter. On this day I told the boys, "Come on, let's have a cookout. Mommy will throw some burgers on the grill, and we'll eat outside."

They really weren't even in the mood. They were just sitting around thinking about what just happened and I guess trying to get their hearts to comprehend all the pain they just went through and were still feeling now. So that's what we did. We just sat around the house, and I went out and threw some burgers on the grill and brought them back into the living room. We sat there watching TV, just relaxing and trying to recover from the past few days.

April came over later on that evening and we all sat in the living room talking and she was asking me about Steven. The boys of course chimed in and were telling her about all of his stories that he had told them the day before about his days in the Marine Corps. They also told her about all the tattoos he had, and she said, "Yes, I noticed." They were so thrilled to have him in their lives. Again it goes back to that old saying, "God never closes a door without opening a window." Right now I guess Steven was their window and mine as well. He gave us something to focus on other than our extreme heartache that we felt at this moment. He was a very, very pleasant distraction, and one that we hoped would be in our lives forever now.

That night after I got the boys to bed, I again went into my room and began praying just as Michael and I always did, again with Michael's rosaries, rosaries I would always keep on my night stand now so they would always be close to me and my heart. It began to happen again just as it did the night before. My room was once again jam packed with spirits, spirits that I couldn't hear or see, but I could definitely, most definitely feel. This feeling was just so disturbing. I couldn't block them out. They were just too strong and there were too many of them. When morning would come they would disappear. They would leave, but as soon as night fell, as soon as I was trying to sleep they would then come back ever stronger.

This would happen to me night after night after night now. Some nights they were so strong, they gave off such a strong presence that it was almost impossible for me to sleep. It was getting that bad, but I knew I could not allow this to start affecting me. I had my life to take care of here. I had my boys to take care of, but I didn't know how to stop it. I didn't know how to push so many of them away. So every day I would wake up exhausted, not getting much sleep the night before because of this and trying to deal with my children and my life as usual. I had to do this. My children were counting on me to stay strong for them, and right now this was the last thing I needed going on in my life.

Steven would come for that weekly dinner, and we so looked forward to this time to spend as a family. He would also pop in during the week on his lunch breaks every now and again. The boys and Steven became very close. I did everything I could to cultivate this new relationship that they were now building to encourage it every step of the way. I even began inviting Steven to Izzy's family gatherings as well. Her family welcomed him too with open arms just as they did with Teddy, Martin and me, and I would always introduce him proudly as my son. But in the meantime unfortunately I was having to deal with these nightly visits, ones that were becoming more and more disturbing to me.

One day I actually sat down and told April about everything that was going on, about how I was feeling at night and what was going on at night in my room. She told me, "Kyra, sometimes when you open that door, you know what door I mean, that door we always desperately try to keep closed, that door to the other side, that day that you asked for help for Michael and you felt what you felt, that marvelous love," she said, "perhaps that made your little light glow just a little bit bigger and brighter. This is what they are now all attracted to." She told me, "You don't have to put up with it. If you truly want them to leave, they have to leave," she said. "Just say your nightly prayers and then ask God to help you. Tell God that you can't handle this right now in your life and help Him lead them away from you. Try it."

I said, "It sounds too simple."

She said, "Well, it kind of is just that simple. They are spirits, and for whatever reason they're drawn to you right now. I know God is the only one that can lead them away and make them leave you alone."

So that night in my bedroom I tried that. I said my regular prayers, and then I asked God, Please for whatever reason all of these souls are in my room every night, please help them find their way back to you, because I can't deal with this right now. I have too much else to deal with, and I need to be able to at least sleep at night."

I went to sleep still feeling their presence. But at least that night I was able to sleep. The next morning they were gone, as usual. That following night after I said my prayers all I could feel was God's presence. All I could feel was good. There were no more spirits in my room. God had helped me once more, and I'm glad to say I never felt anything like that ever again. I still pick up on spirits here and there, but just as I always had in my life. That was normal to me, but nothing like this, nothing of this quantity again.

Something else unusual did happen to me. Actually this was quite life-changing for me and just as spiritually uplifting to me as when I received so much help from God on that day before Michael passed. It happened this way. I was sleeping, and I leaned up, sensing something in my room. I leaned on my elbow and in front of me was this huge angel. Believe me I know how this sounds. If it did not happen to me I would not believe it myself, but it's for real and it truly did happen to me. I saw him or her; I couldn't tell you whether it was a male or a female. It had shoulder-length hair. It didn't have a huge wingspan. It didn't have its wings out but I could see the humps on both sides of his shoulders.

It was obvious what it was, and what amazed me the most beyond the obvious amazement was the color of him. It was a gray color from head to toe. It had no color but gray. There were no white lights, clouds, or harps playing in the background, it was just this entity standing beside my bed looking down at me. He kneeled beside my bed and with the back of his left hand, he caressed my left cheek, and he said to me, "Kyra, everything is going to be fine." He said this without his lips moving at all. It was as though he spoke to me but didn't. His lips never moved, and I'll never forget the look in his eyes, the kind loving look. After he caressed the side of my face with his hand, I lay back down, and I went back to sleep.

In that moment that I was looking at him I felt as though I had felt him before, I think he was perhaps my guardian angel, the angel that was sent to me to help me when I needed it the most, to help me help Michael. I truly believe that's what that was, and unfortunately this would be the first and the last time that I would ever receive a visit like this. This good feeling, this knowing that there is something beyond this here on earth, beyond life, is what carries me through every day now knowing what I know. I received that confirmation from God that I needed to carry on the rest of my life. Without a doubt in my mind I know this is not it. This is not the end. There is so much more that none of us here on earth, us humans, even know about yet. I think it is so terribly sad and unfortunate that we have to wait until our death to find all of this out. That's why I felt so blessed to be shown just a peek into heaven, to be given just a little bit of knowledge, enough to know this isn't it.

Now after being shown what I've been shown over these past few months, there really is no going back and there's no denying. I cannot deny God's existence after everything that I've been shown and after everything I have felt. I simply know what I know now, and this does give you a different view of the world, to know how other people feel. I can pick up people's pain. I have great empathy for them because I felt so much in my life, so much pain, but now with God's help I've also felt so much love.

I do realize that is what Heaven is all about, love, the purest of pure love. There is no killing love. Love never dies. It just simply moves from our earthly bodies that have grown old or decayed through disease. It simply moves from the body back up to Heaven, back home where we began. This is my belief and through much, much pain in my life this is probably about the only thing I know to be true. Love never dies, and love is what keeps the people you loved so much on earth close to you, close to your heart and drawn to you because that love is still there. It has just simply taken another form. Because I believe in this, I also believe this is what our souls are based on. That is what is in the inner core of our souls, that beautiful bright light of love that we carry all through life and into death. That bright light is never extinguished. Our souls go on. Our love goes on hopefully learning more and more through every experience we have. Honestly, feeling this way now, and feeling as though we all came from the same place, we are truly all brothers and sisters. We are all God's children and equal in his eyes.

Feeling all of this now has given me such a different outlook on life. I live my life now never, ever wanting to hurt anyone and always trying my hardest to uplift people's spirits because I know that is what's truly important. I know what God wants us to do is to treat each other well in this world and love each other just like He loves us. Every day I try to live my life like this because I know it's just simply the right thing to do. There's too much pain and too much grief in this world, and if I can do anything at all to help even one person feel better, I take that opportunity when it arises, whether it be getting a neighbor a loaf of bread when I go to the store or lending a few dollars to someone a day before pay day. Whatever I can do for my family and friends and even strangers, I will do.

I know this is a tremendous way to show my gratitude to God, a God that saved my life, a God that showed me all the support I needed to be able to help Michael at the end of his life and to make me feel whole again as a person, to heal my heart and heal my soul. I know without his healing, without the love and kindness He showed me on that day, I would not have been able to do it, and I would not be the person that I am today. He's the one who showed me how to turn my pain into my strength. To live my life this way would be the greatest thank you I could possibly give God. Sometimes I think to myself, *My God, I can't believe how much my life has changed since I was a child.* When I was young my grandmother taught me so much about God, and I wanted to follow Him before all the anger set in.

All of this anger I felt after my grandmother's death was just negativity, but it was so real. This anger to me was so real and this is how that wall started getting built, brick after brick. With every angry moment, every bad emotion I felt, more bricks were laid. I blocked God's love out, His goodness and His compassion for so many years. For so many years I felt nothing toward God but anger, and this was so hurtful to me and so destructive. It's sad, because through my life, when I could have used his love, perhaps if I tried to pray and get guidance, maybe I would have felt a lot better. After so many years of anger toward him, I was like an empty shell. So when all of these deaths started happening in my family, and when all of this heartbreak came to me all at once, I had nothing to lean on. I had nothing to fall back on. Then when I began starting to try to pray again, I found there was nothing there for me to pray to because that wall was so big and so thick, that wall of anger I had built. It was I. It was never God. That was my wall, not His, and I was the only one that could break it down. With Michael's help, thank God, I was able to.

Anger and hate are such powerful emotions, just as powerful as love, but unlike love, all anger and hate will do is destroy you. If you carry it around long enough inside of you, it will become toxic and kill you. That's why now, today, I try so desperately to keep negativity away from me, negative thoughts. I refuse to hate. I won't even let it enter my brain, and my anger I always try to keep a check on and keep under control because all of these emotions are so devastating to the body and to your soul. I work hard every day keeping only positive thoughts and positive people around me. People that are spiritually uplifting. Happiness and laughter, these are the surroundings I try to stay in and the surroundings I try to provide for my two sons to keep their spirits high and their souls strong.

In the following weeks after Michael's death, of course, our family went through tremendous changes, but the one bright spot was Steven. He would come for his weekly dinners and stop by quite often during the day. The day came when he wanted me to meet his step mom and dad, and of course I jumped at this idea. I thought it would really be a great thing to do, to meet the woman who raised such an intelligent and honorable young man as Steven. Izzy, her boys, her nephew Michael, along with Teddy, Martin, and I went for a very lovely visit. She had a rather large aboveground pool, which of course the boys absolutely loved. They couldn't wait to jump in it.

Meeting her for the first time was really nice. Actually she reminded me a lot of my mother. She was very small in stature but had a huge heart, just like my mother did, and she told me all about Steven's younger years. He loved playing football and was quite good at it in high school. I had an opportunity to show her the photo album that I had started for Steven. It was all about his family. I included in the photo album pictures of Steven's great-grandparents. His great-grandfather was still alive. He was 100 years old. There were pictures of his grandparents and of course Michael and me with his two brothers, Teddy and Martin, but I only filled this album three-quarters of the way. The other quarter I told Steven was for the pictures we would be taking of the family in the future. Pictures of all of us together. Steven was so overwhelmed by this he was speechless.

He was so grateful to be able to look back and see pictures of his grandparents and great-grandparents so he could make some sort of family connection. I think this was very important for him to be able to do. He would have something that perhaps in the future if he did have children he would be able to show them pictures of all their relatives. I enjoyed very much this first visit meeting with Steven's parents, and I think they liked us as well. After spending a very, very delightful day there we came home, and Steven came over that night for supper.

That night while I was getting ready for bed something funny happened. There was an overwhelming smell of coconuts in my room. It was the funniest thing. It seemed to replace the smell of flowers that I had for almost five years in my room. In its place now were coconuts? I thought to myself, *Well, if my mother sent me the flowers, perhaps Michael was now sending me this coconut smell.* I laughed. I said, "Michael, you can't do anything better than that, than coconuts?"

It actually wasn't until years later when I sat down and began writing this book it finally hit me what the coconuts represented. This smell lasted for about a week in my room. As I said it wasn't until I sat down to write this book that it finally hit me what it was. It was during the early years that Michael and I spent together when we were drinking. We had that one absolutely perfect weekend, that one weekend I have in my memory to always look back on now. I try to remember that one weekend before things become so difficult, that loving perfect weekend. I always drank piña coladas, and it was the smell of a piña colada. It wasn't just a coconut. It was a piña colada drink.

While I was writing this book this hit me like a bag of bricks. I just sat there and began laughing. I told Michael, "Sorry. I hadn't made the connection up to this point. Well, better late than never, Honey." The smell of coconuts that I thought was coconuts at the time, did only last a week. I think perhaps my laughing at Michael and his sending me this strange smell probably didn't help matters. I think after a week he gave up on me, but looking back on this, I do think this was his first little sign that he was happy to see what I was doing with Steven and to let me know he was okay.

Before we knew it, it was September and Teddy was now going to celebrate his thirteenth birthday. I tried to keep it as uplifting and as happy as I possibly could. I had a cookout, and I had a big, beautiful cake with one of his baby pictures in the center, a baby picture that I took of him completely naked, lying on my fur coat, when he was about eight months old. I thought it was absolutely adorable, myself, but of course it embarrassed the hell out of Teddy. At least it kept his mind off of his father. Everybody came. Of course Aunt April, Steven, Izzy, Angel, Joey, and a few friends that Teddy had from school. We all had a good day. Again I was trying to distract Teddy from the absence of his father.

Thankfully they were back at school now and this took up a lot of their time, although what was happening was not good. Their grades were beginning to slip drastically. Their concentration level was not as it was before, so I tried my best to address this problem. I called Hospice back in to have one more counseling session with them. It seemed as though Martin was affected really badly, especially in math. It was during math class he would tell me when everything was silent and they were taking the test, he began to hear his father's feeding machine. This machine made a low droning sound, and this was playing back in his head and it was breaking his concentration. This all came out during the last counseling session with Hospice. Martin told me it then went away very quickly. He said, "It seemed like all I needed to do was talk about it, and it fixed itself."

I said, "Yeah, that's good," and again I reminded him, "You come and talk to Mommy whenever you need to." I always tried to keep that line of communication open between Teddy, Martin and now Steven to always talk about their feelings and to get their emotions out because that is the only way they could deal with them and heal. But yet their grades just didn't seem to be doing any better even after this last counseling session, so I had the counselor at Martin's school start talking to him. They met about 2-3 days a week at school.

This counselor was really good. In talking with him I found out that he experienced a very similar thing with his father. His father passed away at home with cancer as well, and he was around Martin's age when it happened, so he knew exactly where Martin was coming from and what Martin felt. I thought, *This is marvelous. He can have a man to talk to and relate to who actually went through it as well.* Yet still the grades just never seemed to rebound. He always got A's and B's. He always was very particular about getting his homework done. As a matter of fact he wouldn't want to go to school the next day if he wasn't able to get it all done. He would always have an argument with me, and every day he would come right home from school and start his homework. He was a very, very good student and so was Teddy, but I slowly saw their grades go from A's and B's down to C's and D's and then D's to F's.

I tried my best to get them the counseling that they needed. Teddy was just so steadfast in his religious beliefs, he knew that everyone was fine, and he didn't see the point in really talking much about it. So counseling with Teddy was very, very hard. He just simply didn't want to talk about it. The good counselor that Martin had was a great help to him psychologically. His grades just didn't show it, and they just never improved.

So now I was trying to deal with my children almost flunking out of most of their classes when before they had A's and B's. I really didn't know quite what to do about it. I guess this is how all of this tragedy over the past five years and the last one ending with their father dying affected them. While at school their concentration level seemed to drop down to zero. I would go into parent teacher meetings all the time, and I would explain to the teachers what just happened in their lives and possibly this was the reason why their grades were dropping so badly.

Neither the teacher nor I had a solution for this problem at this moment. We just tried to drag along the best way that we could. I thought to myself, *For now I would just kind of give them a break this year, and perhaps next year they would rebound as long as their conduct level stayed the same, and that was always excellent.* They were always very, very, respectful. They knew this was one area I would not waver in. I would not stand for them to be anything but gentlemanly to their teachers, principal, police, and authority figures. This was how they were brought up and this is how I expected them to behave no matter what else was going on in their lives. They did. They were always great kids. The teachers had nothing but good things to say about them outside of their grades being miserable.

Halloween was here before we knew it, and I dressed Martin up. I think he went as a ghost that year. Teddy chose to stay home and hand out the candy. Izzy and I, along with her kids and Martin, went around trick or treating up and down the streets that we always went to year after year. Then next was Thanksgiving and Martin's birthday.

Martin was going to be ten years old this year, and I wanted to throw him the biggest most uplifting party that I could possibly give him because I knew how deeply he missed his dad. These first birthdays, these first Christmases, the first holidays without their father were going to be tremendously heartbreaking. I tried to not even think about it. I just went on autopilot and did everything I could to keep uplifted, and it did work. It took the sting out of it anyway. Everybody was at Martin's birthday party and we all had a good time. There was a lot of love in that room. I know Martin could feel it, and I also had a feeling Michael was standing right there, too, supporting his baby.

A week after Martin's birthday party was Steven's. Steven was born on December 5, 1975. Since this was the first birthday party that we would spend together as a family, I wanted it to be spectacular. I decorated the house beautifully, and I let the boys pick out their brother's birthday cake. The picture that was to be put on it was Taz running with the football. I thought it was cute. I got shrimp cocktail, and I made a turkey for everyone to make sandwiches out of. His brothers got him presents; sweaters, a beard trimming kit, and I gave him a $100 bill in a card. I told him go out after his birthday party here and celebrate with his friends and just enjoy yourself. He gave me a huge hug, and I told him how much I loved him.

Before we knew it Christmas was here again, and this I knew was going to be the worst of all the holidays that we had to celebrate. The Christmas cuddling Michael and I always did, I couldn't even let myself remember right now. The feeling was just too raw. The heartbreak was too new. After filling their stockings and putting out the presents, I just immediately went to bed and fell asleep.

A week prior to this, a week before Christmas was the first time that I had visited Michael's grave, and I placed a beautiful wreath around it. I took ornaments, Michael's favorite ornaments, from the tree and decorated the wreath with them. That day is when I read Michael's eulogy to him. I hadn't been able to bring myself to go to his grave site before this day. As I stood there reading his eulogy and all the wonderful things that he did with us and especially his two sons, I felt a chill come over me like he had walked right through me. I stood there looking out over the cemetery and all the headstones with the wreaths and the red bows hanging from them. I felt love, but I also felt so cold inside at the same time. I knew each wreath represented a broken heart just as mine did.

On this day, this first day of my visit to Michael's grave site I could not bring Teddy and Martin with me. I knew the pain was still too new and too raw. I finished placing the wreath on his grave and reading the eulogy and then I said a few prayers, and I spoke to him. I asked him if he liked everything I had been doing with his three sons, and I hoped that I was making him proud of me. I told him how very, very much I loved him and how he was my heart always. I then looked down at my feet and at my feet were two military plaques, one for his father who died in 1968 on July 3, and the other one right beside it was Michael's. "Vietnam War veteran," it said. It gave his date of birth and his date of death. There was something I noticed when I looked at his father's date of death, and I just shook my head again as a shiver came over me. Michael was buried on July 3, the same day his father died 32 years earlier, and I thought to myself, *Out of all the days in the year, to coincide those two particular days with the father and son, a date of death and a date of burial on the same exact day is surreal.*

Things like this just leave me speechless. Coincidental? Who knows? I stopped trying to figure it out. After noticing this I just simply turned and walked away back to my car and drove off again shaking my head. When I arrived home I didn't let the children know where I had been. I just wanted to keep this as a private moment between Michael and me.

The following week when Christmas came I remembered back to that moment when I placed the wreath on his grave. That is how I spent my Christmas night with memories, only memories now. The next morning when we woke up the kids went downstairs and they were opening their presents with no enthusiasm whatsoever. It was as if it was something they were expected to be doing, so they did it. That cheer, that happiness, that laughter was not here, and I don't think it will quite ever be the same again. That most important person in our lives, the person who we loved more than life itself is now at the place where I placed that wreath down and not here with his family, as he should have been. So after they were done opening their gifts, they were playing with the new games, the new game system that I had bought, and they just turned on the TV and sat there on the couch watching.

I prepared Christmas dinner as I always did, but this time the feelings of numbness and sadness hung in the air on my family's Christmas Day. Steven spent the day with his stepparents. April came over for Christmas dinner, and we sat there at the table, the four of us eating and not even really feeling hungry but just simply going through the motions. After dinner they went into the living room, April and the two boys, and watched some TV as I cleaned up. Then Steven arrived. It was around 6 o'clock. He brought a present for me, and he told the boys he was going to take them out shopping for their presents because he really didn't know what to get them. They were thrilled to hear this.

A couple of days after Christmas he would take them out. What he got me blew me away. I opened up the package and there was a lighthouse. I had told him about the picture that hung on my living room wall, the lighthouse picture that Michael had bought me for our 21st anniversary and how very special that was to me. So he wanted to get me a lighthouse. He thought it would be special for me and it was. It was very special. It was truly a gift from his heart, a gift that he gave much thought to, and a gift that I truly appreciated. After opening his gift, I made him a turkey sandwich. Then it was time for him to open his. The boys got him some cologne and a couple more shirts. I gave him some outerwear to use—gloves, hat, scarves and a beautiful sweater. He was so thrilled to be spending his first Christmas with his family, and we were very, very happy and grateful that he was there to share this beautiful holiday with us.

It was two days now after Christmas 2000 when I went to bed, and I had the most amazing dream that I had ever had in my life. It was so real. In my dream Michael came to me and he took my hand and he said, "Kyra, come with me. There is something I want to show you."

We walked up a little hill, and this hill was covered with the most beautiful emerald green grass I had ever seen in my life. It was close to a cliff. We were standing at the edge of the cliff and you could see the whole ocean. It was magnificent.

At the top of this hill there was a beautiful white house. On the front lawn of this house was a bell. It looked like an old well, but instead of a bucket being there, there was this gold bell that you could ring. We passed this and started walking up the stairs of the house. Everything was white, pristine white, beautiful. We walked into the house, Michael leading me by the hand. The floors were all hardwood and shiny like glass. The curtains, the furniture, everything else was completely white. He then began taking me for a tour through the house leading me upstairs showing me each and every bedroom. There were five bedrooms altogether. In each and every bedroom were the same colors; white curtains, white bedspreads, white everything except the hardwood floors that shined. We went into our bedroom and beside the bed next to the wall was a whole line of Michael's boots, all thirty pairs of them. They were all shining just like he would keep them.

I laughed and said, "You collect boots here as well?"

He said, "Sure, why not?" and he held my hand and said, "Kyra, this is our house. This is where we are going to live together. When it's your time to come to me, this is where we are going to live."

I was completely amazed. I said, "Michael, why can't I stay now?"

He said, "It's not your time, Kyra. It's not your time."

The second he said it wasn't my time was when I woke up in my bed, and I woke up with a huge smile.

This didn't make me feel sad at all. Actually it just added more confirmation to what I always suspected to begin with. We had always been together, and we would always be together. I do believe in reincarnation. I do believe in past lives, and I do believe that we were always together in past lives. Maybe in the other lives we experienced pain as well, just like in this one, and maybe in this one we've experienced so much maybe we don't have to return if we don't want to. Perhaps this truly was where we would spend all eternity now, where Michael showed me, our house.

I felt as though Michael had just given me a Christmas present by this dream. I felt so good and so uplifted. I said out loud, "Michael, thank you," and I returned back to sleep. I don't know to this day if this was just a dream, a beautiful, marvelous, wonderful dream, or if this was real. I guess I'll find out some day.

Before I knew it New Year's Eve was here, the beginning of 2001, and Izzy invited Steven, Teddy, Martin, and me to her New Year's Eve party. Of course we accepted the invitation. I thought to myself, *I have to do something to get out of this house, because there is no way I am going to be able to sit in that living room at the stroke of midnight on that couch by myself without my true love being there beside me as he always was.* I had to do something to distract myself, and this was the perfect way to do it, a house filled with loving people and me away from that couch and all those memories. So Steven, Teddy, Martin, and I went over. We had a great time. We rang in the New Year together.

Before we knew it the end of January was here. This year was a little bit warmer than most. The grass was starting to grow early. It was February 14 now, the first Valentine's Day without Michael. How my heart was aching for him, to feel his touch, to feel his caress just one more time. I would have given anything for this.

On Valentine's Day I went to his grave side to lay one single red rose and to talk with him and pray. As I got out of the car I noticed the grass was beginning to take seed and grow a little bit around where he was buried, everywhere but up where his head would be. In this spot only there was a huge heart shaped dirt spot where nothing seemed to be growing. But the shape of this huge dirt spot was undeniable a heart, a large heart just like the heart-shaped chocolates Michael would buy me every Valentine's Day. That is exactly what this looked like except much bigger. It was something that there was no way I could miss. I took pictures of it because I simply could not believe it, although given my family's history I don't know why I had such a hard time believing it. It seems like whenever something weird like this happens, I still question it, and I still wonder if this was true.

A huge heart was where his head would lie. I stood there in amazement, and I began to cry and I told Michael, "Thank you; I get it. Thank you, baby, my only love." I told him he would always have my heart.

It was a couple of days after this that I was talking to April, and I told her about the heart lying there in the form of dirt, and that's when she told me, "Kyra, you have to go take a picture of that. I think that's incredible."

That's when I did. I went and purchased a disposable camera and went to the site, and I took quite a few pictures.

April told me herself. She said, "You know, that's your Valentine's present from Michael."

I said, "Yeah, I know." You see, love lives on.

It was springtime now, around the middle of March when I knew I had to get his name put on the headstone. Up till this point I just couldn't face doing this. It was like that final, final thing. I went to the company that did the engraving for the headstones in the area, and I told him where the site was and the name.

He asked me, "What else would you like to have put on your husband's headstone?" I thought about it for a second, and he said, "Well, usually people have, *Loving Father and Husband or Son.*"

I looked at him rather strangely because that was the last thing I was even thinking of having done. I wanted something that meant a little bit more. Something that stood for our lives and our love together, and then it came to me. I knew exactly what I wanted. I then told the man, "I want on my husband's headstone engraved for all eternity, *My Only Love Forever,* because that is truly what is in my heart, and that's truly how we felt toward one another. We were each other's forever."

The man looked at me rather strangely. I can't believe this is the first time that anyone hit him with such a request. Perhaps he was just used to writing the same old thing. I don't know. Nevertheless he did give me a rather strange look.

Then I asked him, "When would this be able to be done?"

He said, "Because it is in the English writing, Old English, it will take a while, because I'll have to get the machines down from Maine to do it."

"That's okay." I told him to call me when it was completed. It took a month and a half for them to be able to do this.

It was now the first week in April and everything seemed to be going very well with Steven coming for suppers every week and also stopping during the days most of the time throughout the week. He and his brothers were really getting to know one another, and I thought, building a bond, although I could tell something was changing with Steven. He seemed to always have one foot out the door this last month whenever he visited. It was like he was there but not there, and I couldn't quite place my finger on it. I thought perhaps he was having girl problems or job problems. This just started to occur the last two weeks in March. Before that it seemed as though he and his brothers were growing closer and closer, but something happened.

I had always given Steven the opportunity to talk to me, to ask me any questions that he had. I tried to keep an open line of communication with him just as I did with Teddy and Martin, and he did ask me a few questions. I told him all about his father, all about our past, and the struggles that we went through, and how when he was little his father and I were barely able to take care of ourselves let alone a child. How the atmosphere in our home because of the drinking was not one for a child to be in.

But all of these explanations that I would give Steven just rang hollow, because the fact of the matter was I could not go back in time and change things. That was probably the only thing that I could do to help him feel better, to give him his childhood back, but there was no way I could possibly do that. The one thing that he truly needed now was to be able to speak to his father and not me, but his father was no longer here. He needed to build a bond, a relationship with his father, not me and his brothers. This of course was not possible.

So it seemed like the closer we all got, the further away he became, and I was trying to deal with this as well as I could at the moment. I wasn't using my head correctly. I had just gone through the shock of my life losing my only love. I was barely holding on, myself, and I was desperately trying to protect Martin and Teddy and keeping them close. At that moment it just seemed like I couldn't do anything right. All I could do was keep trying, trying to reach

Steven and trying to make this bond that was developing between him and his brothers even stronger—just take it a day at a time.

Unfortunately it was around this time that I found myself in a financial hardship. All through the winter I had spent a lot of money on oil, but it just didn't seem to last long. I found myself in need of oil and not having the money to purchase it. I remembered something that Michael told me that if I ever had any problems paying my electric or oil bill to go and see the veterans' representative at the City Hall, the one he used to speak with all the time. So I remembered this and said, "Well, I'll give it a shot," figuring I would walk away with nothing anyway, but it was worth a try. So I went down to the veterans' representative and explained my situation to him. I told him, "I was able to heat all through the winter but I am out now and don't have the money to buy any more." He was more than happy to help me. They did give me money for oil.

It was at this time when the agent began discussing Michael's death and the type of cancer that Michael died from.

I told him, "No. There was no history of that in his family at all. This was quite a shock to us and our whole family that he would come down with this now."

This was when the agent asked me if I had ever heard of Agent Orange Poisoning. He began to describe what it was, a defoliant that they sprayed in Vietnam to kill the foliage.

I told him, "Yes, Michael told me about that." I also told him that I had heard a little bit about the soldiers that had returned from Vietnam dying within a couple of years of their return, and others having children that were badly deformed. I told him that was 32 years ago. Michael had been out of Vietnam for 32 years. How could that possibly affect him now? I didn't understand.

That's when he told me that it can store itself in fat cells, and he said, "A lot of these guys that are having problems with diabetes now, such as Michael did, when they go to lose the weight sometimes this is what happens. It kicks right back up again. It comes out of its dormant stage, and that's when it can cause the cancer."

Whenever he told me this, I can't even begin to tell you how this made me feel. I almost fell off my chair. I sat there with my mouth hanging open in between wanting to cry, scream, and throw up. Could this even be possible? Michael had fought for 32 years to regain his sanity, to regain his life and something that happened to him over there was now killing him so many years later? I couldn't wrap my frickin' brain around it.

The agent told me he was going to look into it, look into the areas where Michael was and see what was going on at the time.

I just remember saying to myself now, *This can't be.* I thanked him for doing this, and of course never in my wildest nightmares did I think anything was going to come of it. I thought the poor man was just wasting his time.

I remember shaking his hand and leaving his office then, going out to my car and sitting there, my stomach coming up in my throat. I just kept saying to myself, *No, no. It isn't possible.* At this moment I would not allow my mind to go down that path. I couldn't start thinking of such things. All through Michael's life for the last 32 years, it was as though Michael left Vietnam, but Vietnam never left Michael, and it finally killed him now? I couldn't think it. I wouldn't allow myself to think it because I had no idea how I would handle it if it were true, but yet I couldn't shake it. Once these words were spoken to me, I couldn't shake it. In the back of my mind I began to wonder, and it began eating at me.

It was now two to three days after this conversation with the VA Rep that I began getting pains in my left arm up to my shoulder and into my heart. I thought, *God, I'm having a heart attack. It's all just caught up to me now.* I called my sister April to come and keep an eye on Teddy and Martin while I went to the hospital. I told her the feelings that I was having.

She said, "Yes. You better get there immediately." So Martin came with April and me to the hospital, and all I could think of was, *Am I going to have a heart attack and die?* I did not want to have it happen in front of Martin. I told April to just leave, take Martin home, and I would call her when I was done. I told her why, and she hesitantly agreed.

They ran all the tests, x-rays, EKG, everything, and they found out in the x-ray that I was having a blockage which is very similar to a clot. That's when I found out that this is one of the side affects of the RSD. It can cause blockages, and if one of these blockages goes to your heart, your lungs or your brain, you're dead. Up to this moment I had never been told this. I lay there for a couple of hours in a lot of pain because the blockages are very painful until they dissipate in my blood stream.

Since then I have had a few, but I know what they are now, and I just deal with it. I try to relax, and again I try to focus my brain on blocking the pain out, and it does work. I began to wonder when the blockage would come that would take my life. Then I made myself stop thinking that way. You see, we're all going to die. I just have a pretty good idea more than likely how I am going to go that's all. That's the only difference between me and everybody else. Then again, I could go out tomorrow and get hit by a MAC truck. I mean, who knows, but these painful blockages were just another thing that I had to deal with now. Again, when you're time's up, it's up whether I'm taking a shower or flying in a 747. If I am meant to go at that moment, nothing will stop it. That's the way I feel.

Also, what is truly important is what you do with your life in between that time, in between the time of birth and time of death. What difference you make in other people's lives and how you conduct yourself in your own is what people need to think about. That's what I need to think about, and I did just that. I wouldn't let death consume my thoughts or worry when the next blockage was going to hit. I just wouldn't do that. I refuse to take precious time, whatever time remains here on earth, and fill it with worry about what day would be my day. I had too many good things to focus on now to allow this to happen. I had Teddy, Martin, and now Steven to concern myself about. I would not steal one moment away from them with thoughts of such things.

But with my finding this out about myself and this latest revelation about Michael and what he possibly died from, believe me, it was taking every ounce of energy that I had to keep pushing all those negative thoughts out of my mind and to just try to stay happy and uplifted. I needed to be able to feel the love from my children and for my children. In my mind negativity and vengeance are just evil. Evil is set up to bring the soul down, to rob you of that love that God wants to share with you. I did my best to keep that out of my life and out of my children's lives. I just would not allow myself to dwell on negative thoughts, and when bad things hit, I would accept them, deal with them and let them go, not hold onto them.

Now it was going on to the second week in April, and as I mentioned earlier Steven's behavior was becoming rather odd. He was becoming distant. Around the 12th of April when he wanted to take his brothers to see a movie with him and his girlfriend, of course I agreed. I thought this would be a good thing, and it was. They all had a lot of fun and they went out to dinner afterwards. But when they returned, Steven's behavior was even more bizarre than it had ever been before. I just couldn't quite understand the feelings I was getting from him.

After they returned home from the movie I had made brownies for them to munch on. As he was sitting there eating the brownies, he had such a distant look in his eyes again like he was there but not there. When it came time for he and his girlfriend to leave, he gave me such a huge hug, a hug that I remembered only too well. That was a hug like he gave me the last time I saw him when he was about five or six. Just as this hug, that hug I will never forget either. Deep down inside I surely knew that this was it. I wasn't going to see him again, and unfortunately my feelings were correct.

I called him a couple of times after this leaving messages on his answering machine, and he never returned my calls. Martin called a couple of times as well, and still, no response. This hit the boys really hard. Teddy and Martin were both broken hearted over this. For nine months their brother was back in their lives, a brother that they were just starting to get to know and build a bond with. They had lost their father, and now they had lost their brother.

I did my best to try and explain to them that maybe it was just to overwhelming for Steven and perhaps too hurtful to hear about all the things that his father did with his brothers that he never did with him. I tried to get them to look through Steven's eyes and how he might be feeling. I suppose they did kind of understand as much as 10- and 13-year-old boys could understand. Sadly we just looked at it in time like another death in the family of somebody else that we loved and lost.

Thinking back on it now about a month before Steven did leave for good, he and I during one of his lunch breaks sat at the kitchen table, and we were talking. He was telling me about the anger he was feeling toward his father. I told him he had to let it go. He had to find some way to let it go or it would kill him. I explained to him about how Amber died and what her life was like and all the hate and anger she held onto toward our father, and how I believe it became toxic to her. I did tell him, "It will kill you. If you don't let it go, it will kill you, and you are going to have to find some way to do this."

I guess he did by simply trying to erase all memory of his father, along with us. If this was the only way that he could do it, to move on to survive his life, to get rid of the hate, then I would just have to learn to accept it, and so would his brothers. As long as Steven was happy I knew it was the right thing for him. If this was the only way he could do it, then so be it. After these couple of phone calls not being returned, I got the idea, I got what he was doing, and I respected his decision. Although I hated it, I had to respect it, and I never tried to get in contact with him after that.

It was now the middle of May and Michael's headstone was engraved. The man from the engraving company called me and asked me if I would like to go down and inspect his work. I said, "Certainly." That following day I went to the cemetery, and when I first saw those words my heart broke. Saying those words was very different than actually seeing them in writing, but I knew I was right to have that written there for all eternity because that's what we stood for forever, our love lives on.

Each day I look at Teddy and Martin I see Michael. I hear his laugh in their laugh. I see that twinkle of light in their eyes that he had and the characteristics, their personalities are so much like their dad's. They are a living tribute to our love, and they are a part of Michael that I will always be able to hold onto. Each and every time I give them a hug or a kiss goodnight, I will always have a part of Michael with me. In my two son's eyes, he lives on. I will always keep the promise I made to Michael, I will hold our sons close forever and protect them and raise them just as he would have wanted me to. I would always, always put them first no matter what. So as I stood there by Michael's grave looking at the engraving, the lettering, *My Only Love Forever*, I kneeled down beside it. I kissed my index finger, and I ran that kiss across each letter, and I told him how much I loved him just as we always used to tell each other.

It was now June the 29, our first anniversary exactly one year to the day that my heart was ripped from me and both my sons' world changed forever. On this day at exactly 1:25, we went to the cemetery with a bouquet of flowers to pay our respects and to show our deepest love. From this first anniversary on every June 29, at 1:25 that is where you will find us, at that exact moment that Michael left this earth and went back home. We honor this day by going to the grave site with flowers and holding hands with the rosary that was in Michael's hands at the time of his funeral. We pray and we reflect back over the year that has past, a year without their father, a year without my only love. We remind Michael just how much we miss him, how much our hearts ache for him, and how much we truly, truly love him. This right along with the other traditions I have to say, happier traditions, has become a tradition. We will come here every year from here on out to honor the hero in our lives, because that's what he truly was, a hero, a fighter, a survivor, and the strongest man that I had ever met in my life. Yes, he truly is my hero and forever will be.

I'm happy to say this gift that I was given in life, to be able to sense spirits, this was probably the first time in my entire life that I was actually happy and actually did consider it now a gift because I can pick up on Michael. I can feel when he is close to me. It's not all the time. If it were, I would be worried because I would be afraid he didn't cross over. It's just every now and again, maybe once a week, twice a month, here and there. I can feel him. I can feel his strength, and I can feel him helping me. Love never dies, and quite often he is able to come to me in my dreams, always wonderful dreams, and we're always having fun. We are either at a party or just walking along the beach, but it's always a pleasant dream, and I feel so refreshed after awakening from one of these. I feel as though I was able to spend a little bit of time with him, at least in my dreams anyway.

It was now July and after Steven removed himself from our lives and after the first anniversary of their father's death, we were needless to say gloomy inside. As I thought to myself and began looking around, I said to the boys, "Why don't we redo the apartment?" Financially we couldn't afford to move, and I didn't really want to anyway. We had a strong community and good friends nearby, so why would I want to move? But I knew I had to make some sort of a change. After all, the apartment remained the same actually since my mother passed away in 1995.

Through all the deaths and all the sorrow, it was the same thing that we looked at, the same walls, the same furniture. We needed a change, a positive change, and that's when I thought of redoing our apartment. I talked to the boys about it. We didn't have a lot of money to work with but it didn't cost that much. It was paint and some carpeting. The furniture was not in great shape. After all, there were many years we were not able to purchase anything new. We were always struggling to make ends meet.

I began looking at new furniture trying to find a way to fit it into my budget. We were in the furniture store one day, and I mentioned to the salesman who was helping us look at the furniture that my boys and I needed a change and that we had redone the apartment. I told him everything that had happened and that this was more a spiritual uplifting than anything, and it's important.

So we tried to work things out in our budget. That's when I mentioned the car, and he said, "You can use the car for the collateral." I thought to myself for a moment, *Would Michael approve of my doing this seeing he is the one who bought it for me and the boys?* The loan wasn't that big, and I thought Michael would approve. I was improving the apartment and the children needed new beds, new mattresses. Everything was just pretty much worn out.

So we did it. We bought a brand new living room set, a kitchen set, and the two boys got bedroom sets.

It took us almost three weeks to redo the apartment, painting all of it, adding new swinging doors, new rugs, and linoleum. The three of us worked so hard together. It took our minds off of our heartache at least for a little while anyway. The end results were fantastic. It was a completely different apartment. It was just the uplifting that we needed at this moment in our lives. We were thrilled.

It was also about this time that Izzy's sister Cathy found an abandoned litter of kittens behind her house, and she nursed them to health. Izzy asked me if Teddy and Martin would like a kitten. Well, whenever the boys saw the four kittens (there were three black ones and one little gray one), they each wanted one for themselves, Teddy taking the little black one and Martin the gray one.

I said to myself, *Oh, no. I have just redone my apartment, and here are kittens that are going to be clawing everything up.* Then I stopped and thought again, *You know, this will give them something to focus on, a positive really beautiful thing, a beautiful little baby kitten that needed a home and love.* They had more love than anyone I know to share with an animal.

They did just that. They kept them by their sides and showed them all the love one animal could ever be shown. They took good care of them, and of course they stayed in the house. The kittens were not to go out. We took them to the vet and, had all the shots and had them fixed.

For being brothers, the kittens were so completely different. We named the black one Angel, because he was the one that almost died at birth, so I thought that was an appropriate name. The little angels came down to save him. The gray one I named Spanky. It just hit me when I looked at him to name him that. I asked Martin, "Would you care to?" and I told Martin what that name was from. Michael had a little mule when he was growing up. It was cute and he loved that mule. His name was Spanky, and he was all gray, so I thought that connection was really nice. Every time I called Spanky I would think of that. Martin said, "Yeah, Ma, that sounds great."

So they both had their loving distractions and things were really looking up. We had our brand-new apartment, two beautiful sweet little kittens to love and the boys actually seemed happy for the first time in quite a while. I was finding myself actually not dreading getting out of bed every morning. To have something happy to look forward to for a change was quite delightful.

It was now the beginning of September. Teddy and Martin had just returned back to school, and we were settling into the routine for the year. I guess it was about September 6, just a regular, routine day. I dropped the kids off at school, came home, did my housework, prepared my supper, visited with Izzy for a while, and then it was time to pick the children back up from school. While the boys sat in the living room doing their homework, I cooked supper, and after supper we just sat in the living room watching a little bit of TV and relaxing, talking about the day.

That evening I got ready for bed as usual, saying my prayers. I could hear the boys laughing in their bedroom watching TV and playing with the kittens. I remember yelling at them, "C'mon guys, it's time to go to sleep. You have to get up early in the morning to go to school!" So I heard the TV go off, and I saw their lights go out, and I lay down and fell fast asleep.

I began dreaming of this old, old church that we had in the Green near City Hall, and I found myself behind City Hall in the dream at one point. Coincidentally, the place that we had just purchased all the furniture from was in my dream as well, and it was located right next to City Hall. Behind the buildings was a huge parking lot, and I looked out onto the parking lot and down the street, and all I could see were Gurneys with white sheets on them as far as the eye could see.

There had to have been thousands, thousands of dead bodies, and in my dream I could remember trying to figure out what was going on, and I was becoming more and more alarmed when all of a sudden a man appeared from the furniture store. He looked rather ghoulish. He was dressed in a black suit very much like the one the undertakers' use, and his hair was all wild, long and white. His face was drawn in, sort of skeletal looking. He stood there at the podium with this large book in front of him, checking off people as he rolled them in to the furniture store. I could see the smoke stacks coming up. They had to make a makeshift crematorium, and he was rolling one body in after the other.

As I was looking out onto the remaining bodies (there were still thousands of them left), I was getting this panicked feeling. I know this sounds absolutely ridiculous, but I've always had a fear of zombies. Some people are afraid of vampires, some people werewolves, some people spiders, some people snakes. I know it's not realistic. I know it could never happen, but it still just hits that core of fear in me, and that's the feeling I was getting in my dream. I was panicking more and more because I expected them to start sitting up, all of these thousands of bodies. I have learned through my life how to wake myself out of nightmares, so I did this, and I leaned up in bed. All I could see was red, a veil of red wherever I looked in my room like a film of red which had covered my eyes, and then I was not able to stay awake.

I fell quickly back to sleep and went right back to the exact same spot I was in my nightmare, the spot that I had so desperately tried to awaken myself from. I was right back there again, and again that fear set in, and the man said to me, "I have much work to do. I can't stand here talking to you," and he proceeded to go from one body to the next, rolling them into the furniture store to cremate them. I stood there alone in the middle of this vast parking lot with bodies on Gurneys as far as the eye could see covered with white sheets. I tried desperately again to bring myself out of this horrifying nightmare, and I found myself leaning up once more in bed to that veil of red. This time I made myself sit up even further. I had to desperately, desperately try to get myself out of this nightmare. Thank God, I finally did. My eyes began to clear, and I no longer saw the red veil.

This nightmare was so disturbing to me. There was no way I was going back to sleep again that night. I sat at the edge of my bed, and I prayed, then I went downstairs and I had some tea. Before long it was time to wake the children up for school. I could not shake that feeling of complete and utter dread. I knew from past experiences after these dreams when I have them this bad, when they're that horrible, usually something does occur, and I had no idea what it could possibly be. Something of this magnitude where thousands of bodies would be gone, thousands of souls would be lost, I couldn't even comprehend it in my mind. I began thinking of earthquakes, fires, I didn't know. All I knew was something bad was going to happen and a lot of people were going to die.

I was so sickened by this dream and by this feeling that when April came over for a visit that day I told her all about it. She said, "Oh, my God," and then she began to think and wonder what could possibly happen. These dreams are just so frustrating. Again, you don't get details, you don't get where it is or what it is, the disasters to come remain unknown to you. You just get a sense of the horror, perhaps the horror that they felt just before they died and the panic as well. I got all of that all at once in my dream, and I couldn't shake it for days. I couldn't shake it.

It was now September the 10, and that night was the first good nights sleep that I had gotten since I had that nightmare. We woke up early that morning. I got the boys gathered up for school and fed them their breakfast. It was now September the 11, 2001. I was actually feeling good on that day. The skies were crystal clear blue, so beautiful, and the air was crisp. I just thought to myself, *I'm just going to take today off. I'm going to run a nice hot tub after I drop the boys off at school and give myself a manicure and a pedicure and just spend today relaxing, listening to music.* That's exactly what I did. I dropped the boys off at school, and I came back home. I drew a nice hot bubble bath, and I lay there relaxing. As I was lying there I watched the two kittens playing with their new toys on the bathroom floor. I laughed because they were so cute. I got out of my tub and went into my bedroom where I began giving myself a manicure.

While listening to the music playing on my radio I just felt so relaxed, when all of a sudden, at 9 o'clock, my radio went dead for a few seconds, and then came back on. As it did the news reporter announced that a plane had just driven into one of the Twin Towers in New York. I just sat there glued to my radio, my nails imbedded into the side of my mattress listening to the reports. I guess it was around 5 minutes later when he came back on and said, "You are not going to believe me when I tell you this, but the second tower has just been hit as well." All the while we thought the first tower was hit by mistake by a stray plane losing its path or the pilot having a heart attack. Never in our wildest nightmares could we have ever imagined what was unfolding in front of us. So when they said on the air that the second tower had been hit by a second plane, I knew exactly what that dream meant. I dreaded the thought of hearing how many people were going to be killed or how many people were dying at that very moment, and my heart broke just as every other American's did. I knew at this time it wasn't just my heart breaking; it was all of the nation's. I felt as though I had just been kicked in the stomach.

Listening to all of this was quite surreal, and all I could do was remember back to that night now that I had and the panicked feeling that I felt, complete utter terror. I wondered to myself, *Is that what these people are feeling at this very moment? Did I pick up on all of that before it even happened?* I sat there listening for most of the day.

It was about an hour before I was supposed to pick up my sons from school when April called me in a complete state of panic and asked me if I knew what was going on. I said, "Yes, I've been listening to it all day on my radio." Come to find out her radio station just went off the air at that moment. Instead of broadcasting what was going on, it completely died out, and it wasn't until an hour or so later that she turned her TV on and saw all the horror that was unfolding.

She said, "Oh, my God, Kyra. Oh, my God." It was strange. I didn't think to call anyone, not April, not Izzy, no one. I just simply couldn't bring myself to talk or to take my attention away from the radio that I was listening to so intently. It was like I had lost all sense of time. I guess I was just in shock.

After talking to April, panic mode started setting in. You see, living with a Vietnam vet for 22 years kind of rubs off on you, and you start picking up on their personality quirks. The traumas that they suffered in combat rub off on you. I picked up on these from Michael. Sometimes paranoia, trauma, and the sense of terror would just overwhelm me. So as soon as I snapped out of this state that I was in while listening to the radio, all of this hit me, and all I could think of was going and getting my children from school and bringing them home to protect them because no one knew what was going to happen next. Were we going to get bombed or what? We just didn't know.

So I had to go early to my children's school. I tried to get into the building, but they were in complete lock down. They blocked out the news. They didn't let the children know anything at all. It was at this time when I first heard the name, Osama Bin Laden. The principal at my children's school was telling me that he more than likely was behind these attacks, and I asked him the name again. I told him I had never even heard of him. They released my sons to me, and on the way home I tried my best not to panic them, but to alert them to what was going on, and that we were right now under attack and what happened to the Twin Towers in New York. The principal also told me that they had to black out and lock down the school not only to protect all the children, but also to particularly protect the ones that he now knew were orphaned because both the parents were in those towers working. So I did my best to try to explain to Martin and Teddy what was going on because it really didn't make any sense at all. How do you try to make sense out of something that makes no sense? Why would these people want to take innocent lives? Why were the innocent being killed? No, it makes no sense and it never will.

When we got home I put the TV on, and on the news station that we were watching and on every station now were scenes of these people, terrified people running down the street with this huge cloud of smoke chasing quickly behind them. They were running for their lives as the towers were beginning to collapse.

Teddy turned to me, and I will never forget these words, he asked me, "Mommy, this is in America? This is happening right now in New York?"

I looked at him, and I said, "Yes, Teddy, it is."

He just shook his head, and he looked down in disbelief, just as so many of us did.

Just then it dawned on me, and I never, ever in my wildest nightmares thought I would be saying this, that I was actually grateful Michael wasn't here to see this, because I know this would have set him back in his therapy years. I was having a hard enough time dealing with this myself. As it was, I could not imagine what this would have done to Michael. How it would have traumatized him all over again. As I said, when you live with a person long enough, you start picking up on their personality, on their quirks, and when you live with a Vietnam vet for as many years as I did, all of the feelings that they had toward the government, toward Vietnam rub off on you, all of the stress and trauma. I found myself being startled when people would walk up behind me, jumping just like Michael did, and not trusting, not trusting the government, not trusting people. Trust was another huge issue that Vietnam vets had to deal with and still do. Also the deep-seeded need to protect your loved ones, your family at all cost. All of these personality traits rubbed off onto me. I actually do feel like a Vietnam vet myself, and after 9/11 I began sleeping with a knife under my mattress and a baseball bat handy at my side in the corner of my room so that I could protect my two sons and our home. A deep-seeded panic set in me after 9/11. So you see, if Michael were still alive I know it would have been almost impossible for him to control himself and his fears. If it was affecting me so badly, I can't even begin to imagine how it would have affected him.

As my two boys and I sat there in the living room watching TV and all of this horror unfolding in front of us, we began hearing about the other planes, the one that hit the Pentagon, and of course Flight 93. All these brave souls, each and every one of them a hero in my heart, who chose to crash that plane in the field instead of letting it reach its destination. I would like to think and believe that I would be as brave as any one of those people were at that moment. I pray that is something I will never have to face, a decision I'll never have to make.

After this day the communities came together and we were all very angry. It was as though our mind set was "I dare them. I dare them to come over here and try to take our freedoms away from us, a freedom that not only my husband fought for, but so, so many others."

No, we weren't going to allow them to do this, and as a nation we stood strong, and I was so proud to be an American. Other communities just as our own came together. Just little points of light, little points of hope, and in each of these points of hope and these points of light we sent a message to Osama Bin Ladin and all the other evil people that wished America harm, and that message was "Fuck you. You're not going to do this to us! We will stay strong and we will stand together," and that's just what Americans did. We stood together against evil, an evil that wished to cripple our society, to make us scared, to make us not want to go to school, or work, or to take planes, or subways. No way, that's not what Americans are all about, and I think they found this out.

Our little community like so many others held candlelight vigils where we gathered and said prayers for all those lives that were lost, all those lives that were so cruelly taken. On these days following 9/11, we showed the world what America was made of. In these days I was never prouder to be an American. And, no, I would not keep my children home from school, or stop going to the grocery store, or laundry mat, or wherever I damn well pleased. I carried on with my life as usual just as so many other Americans did. We stood strong and tall and we made our stand against evil.

CHAPTER FOURTEEN

It was a couple of days after 9/11 when I went to Michael's grave site, and I prayed. I said to him, "Do you see what's been done to us?" It's remarkable that I'm still gathering strength from him. He still lends his support to me because after each and every time I visit him, I do feel stronger, and I feel better like my heart is lighter. At this time in particular after all this horror just happened, I needed him more than ever, and I could feel him carrying me through this most difficult time and lending his support and strength to me just as he always did in life.

After the weeks of turmoil that followed 9/11 and watching them digging through the rubble every day on TV, it was all just so overwhelming and heartbreaking. The holidays now were quickly approaching. Halloween was just around the corner. It was now the first week in October and everyone was talking about not letting their children go out Trick or Treating I guess because of 9/11.

But I told my boys, "Yes. You'll go out trick or treating just as you always did. I guess it was particularly the Malls that people were afraid of. There was a rumor going around that one of them might be hit so I thought to myself, *Well, as long as we stay out of the malls we'll be okay.* Just go on the route that Izzy and I always took when we took our children trick or treating. This was just the side streets around our house. Again I had the attitude that I wasn't going to let the terror take me over. We just can't let them win, and canceling Halloween certainly would be one of the steps, one step toward letting them win. So, no, I wasn't going to. I planned to spend Halloween as usual.

It was about a week before Halloween when I received a letter in the mail from the Veterans Administration. It was a rather large letter, a lot of papers explaining their decision. I opened up the letter sitting at my kitchen table and began reading. The more I read, the sicker I became. They had deemed Michael's death a "service-connected death," but of course nowhere in any of the papers that they sent me would you ever find, "Agent Orange-related cancer." They went on to explain about diabetes and not healing and quite frankly just a lot of bullshit. I don't know about you, but I had never heard of anyone getting cancer from diabetes, and this is basically what they were claiming.

They went on to tell me that they would be sending me a grant every month because it was a Service Connected Death. How on earth could it be a service-connected death when he had been out of the service for 32 years? I could not wrap my mind around it, and I still can't. I read on through all the bullshit in the letter regarding the diabetes and the healing. They never really spoke of the cancer, the thing that really killed him.

I think I suffered a mild nervous breakdown. My body went numb and the side of my head particularly went numb. I felt like I wasn't in my body anymore. I was here but not here at the same time. I had never felt that way before in my life. After finishing reading a few pages that they sent me explaining everything and feeling this way, I went upstairs and threw up.

We had just finished supper when I read this, and there was no way I could keep the food down. I became violently ill over what I had read. I could not even begin to comprehend anything that they were saying with their screwed up explanations. Nothing made sense at this point.

After throwing up my entire dinner I came back downstairs where Teddy and Martin were sitting watching TV, and I walked by them. I told them, "Mommy has to go somewhere. I'll be back in a little while." I had to get the hell out of there. I could not let my children see me in such a state. I got into the car, and I just started driving, crying uncontrollably and feeling like I was going to throw up again.

I went to the cemetery, and I sat there in my car parked in front of Michael's headstone. I played the radio as loud as it could possibly go. I rolled up all the windows, and I began screaming my brains out. I could actually hear myself screaming. I could hear my own voice. Again, it was like I was there, but not there. I screamed and I cried, yelling every profanity that I had ever heard in my life, all the while beating on the steering wheel like a mad woman.

At this moment I was unleashing all my anger, all of my hate that I had built up in my 39 years of life. It all came rushing out of me all at once like a volcano erupting. I exploded right there in the car. All I could think of was how was I going to live with this. How was I going to live with the knowledge that Michael died a service-connected death? That Michael was poisoned by Agent Orange. It was as though they had put a bullet in his head 32 years earlier and it just now exploded. What was the past 22 years for? I thought of all the fighting, all the heartache we went through together sobering up, this struggle to become normal, and all of his years of therapy and medication just to have a normal family, to lead a normal life and for it to end up like this. It was too heartbreaking to even think about anymore, but yet I couldn't get it out of my head.

I then began thinking about all the times that the hospital had told us that Michael had a good chance of beating this. Had we been lied to time and time and time again? Did they already know what the end results were going to be? I really thought for sure they had to know. After all, Michael couldn't have been the first one, the only one with this that was dying from this. They had to have known. I know they knew, and this just fueled my mistrust for the government even more. After Vietnam Michael never trusted the government, and he taught me to do so as well. Now this just confirmed everything that we had felt. All the government does is lie to suit its own purpose. Obviously in Michael's case this was something that they couldn't deny. Their decision was extremely fast because in talking to other people, I was told they had never heard of it being decided so quickly. I guess it was that obvious, and yet they wouldn't admit it to me, and I knew they never would.

Now I have to live with this, live with the knowledge that the government killed my husband and try to deal with that hate and anger, a hate and anger that I never wished to have to live with. This was something I always tried to push away from me and keep away. I would now have to deal with this. This was the last straw to me, after all the other heartaches in my life. It was all just too much losing the man I loved and now having to deal with the way he died along with knowing it was unnecessary. After all, how much can a woman's heart take? How much pain? How much loss? I now had to deal with this anger on top of it all.

After my explosion in the car, I got out and went over to Michael's grave. I kneeled down beside him. I prayed so hard for guidance, so hard to remove this anger and hate from my heart. I just remember repeating over and over again, "They killed you, Michael. They killed you." It was at that moment that I felt a deep sense of revenge. I knew I was going to have to find some sort of justice and extract my own revenge. I just didn't know how I was going to go about doing this, but I knew it had to be done. I knew me, and I knew this was something that there was no way in hell I was going to simply be able to let go of. Until I did something, I knew that hate and that craving for revenge would not leave my heart. My heart would be broken now for the last time, and I swore that night at Michael's grave that I would have revenge for him. I would find some sort of justice for him and his two sons, and I wouldn't rest until I did.

After I gathered myself together both physically and emotionally, I then said to Michael, "I now have to go home and keep the promise that I made to you and that was to take care of our sons, but with that promise I now had another one to keep, and that is to find you justice, justice for my hero."

Revenge was quite a new emotion for me to be feeling. I had never felt this before in my life. I know that's hard to believe but I hadn't. I had never been out to get anyone, so this was entirely new to me, and I didn't like the feeling at all because it made me feel very angry as well. I just felt like I wanted to punch something, but I controlled myself. I controlled that anger. I tried to keep check on both that deep sense of revenge and hate that was boiling up inside of me at this moment.

That night when I returned back home after my mild eruption and breakdown at the cemetery, I calmly explained to the boys about their father and how they deemed it a service-connected death. They didn't understand any more than I did of course, but they weren't stupid. They put two and two together and realized that the government killed their father. Again, you don't get cancer from diabetes. I've never in my life heard of that connection, and neither had my two sons. Now the boys felt just as I did. They wanted justice for their father. On this night we could feel Michael here with us. Again at the most difficult times I can feel him, and I know for a fact that love lives on long after the human heart has stopped beating. Just by these feelings of his being present I know this because I can feel his love still with me.

Now needless to say these upcoming holidays were extremely hard on the boys and me. I found myself sitting in April's kitchen one day just before Christmas telling her in the middle of an anxiety attack I was having about how I believed they knew all along what the outcome was going to be with Michael's cancer and how we were lied to repeatedly. If we had just known what the outcome was going to be, all of those operations would not have been necessary. He wouldn't have had any, but they just hacked at him and kept hacking. Those two years we could have spent going on vacations that we never took and thoroughly enjoying our family instead of in a constant recovery mode and putting the children through what they went through seeing their father hacked up. All of that was unnecessary if they knew what the outcome was going to be.

How could I live with this? How could I allow myself to live with this? Each and every time I thought about it, my anger just grew deeper and deeper and my sense of revenge grew stronger. As I was sitting there telling her all of this, I just broke down in tears. My heart, my brain, and my mind just couldn't stand to think about it anymore.

All of these thoughts constantly occupied my mind now, and every day that passed by, all this hate and vengeance ate at my soul just as cancer would to a human body. Now even though I knew I had God back in my life and God's love touched my life as it did, it was still not enough to help me. Not enough to push all this sense of revenge and hate away.

It started eating at me now, not only at my soul but also it was beginning to affect me physically as well. I found myself vomiting at least three or four times a week. I was not really able to keep food down. I prayed every night for grace and for strength to help me push all this negativity away from me and allow my soul to heal, but nothing, nothing seemed to be working. There would come times in my life with my two children when the pain was too overwhelming, important moments that I wanted Michael so badly to be here for and to be sharing with his sons.

Teddy is fanatic about the Red Sox. He puts the fan in fanatic. I swear that boy has not missed one Red Sox game in the past eight years, and he was there sitting right beside me on the couch as we watched the Red Sox win the World Series in 2004. We finally broke the curse, and the Red Sox Nation had never been happier. Teddy just leaped up off the couch and jumped up and down, "Yea! Yea!" At that moment I knew if his dad were here he would have been there at the game, the two of them together sitting in the bleachers watching this little piece of history unfold. This broke my heart.

Things like this, moments like this, like him teaching them how to shave and how to drive a car were just out and out stolen from us. They were irreplaceable memories, irreplaceable moments in time that will now never take place, not with their father. To this day Teddy has never been to a live baseball game with the Red Sox. He can only watch it on TV because we can't afford the tickets, but this doesn't seem to bother him. He enjoys it just as much, but I know deep down in his heart the wish of all wishes would be for him and his father to be sitting there in the bleachers together watching the Red Sox win a game. It's just simply unfair that this will never be. It's moments just like this that add to that sense of hate and revenge that I'm feeling.

Teddy is Teddy. He is still the man's man enjoying the sports and bike riding and all the rough housing. Martin is more like me. He is quiet and sensitive and still enjoys art. His sketches are becoming quite remarkable. He was able to do one thing I wasn't, and that was draw from his own imagination. I always had to copy off of another picture and add my own twist to it, but it always had to be in front of me for me to be able to draw. I was never able to draw from my imagination the way Martin seems to be able to do. My hat's off to him for that because that's quite remarkable. His taste has gone from insects now to scorpions, iguanas, and lizards. He has tanks set up and he does a very, very good job of taking care of all of them. He is quite a responsible person. Both of my sons are responsible and honorable men just as their father wanted them to be and just as their father taught them to be.

I am proud of both of my sons. As hard as it may be to believe, they both have great senses of humor considering everything that they have been through in life. They were at least able to retain this, and as I said, Martin seems to be turning out a little more like me than he was his father, especially where that gift is concerned. He has it stronger than Teddy does although Teddy does have it slightly, but not like Pat. Pat's is even stronger than mine. I don't know if it's because of his age maybe because he's in puberty (he's 17) or he is just simply stronger, because he can pick up on a lot more than I can.

This is very strange as well. He also had a very, very important dream when he was the same age as I was and that was ten. He had a dream about this little boy drowning in sand, in a huge sand pit, and all he could see was the boy's arm sticking up out of it. He woke up in the middle of the night, and he told me. The very next day it was on the news. This little boy, I guess you could say, had basically drowned in sand. He had lost his footing on top of a sand hill and sunk into the center of it, and Martin saw it. It was then that I explained to Martin about the dream that I had when I was ten about the hunter and how I saw that on Television the next day. I sat him down, and I explained everything to him then.

You see, outside of them seeing my mother and my sister Amber, they hadn't really experienced anything else, and they hadn't seen them since that time. So he was startled at first, but I explained it to him.

I said, "It sort of runs in the family, like blue eyes and the blond hair do. Well, this runs in our family, and it's something you are going to have to learn how to deal with."

I warned him about the Ouija boards and about trying to contact these people. I also warned him about not talking to other people about this. I know times have changed a lot, but I wasn't sure just how much. I have never told anyone this outside of Michael and of course my family for fear that they would think I was crazy just as my mother warned me. So I gave him the same warnings that she gave me, and I told him that you could block them out. When you feel the presence, you can just simply choose to ignore it and ask God for his help. Simply just tell Him this isn't something you can handle right now and to please take it away.

The three of us do speak about this often and sometimes we just compare notes about how we're feeling, again keeping that open line of communication that is very, very important with your children no matter what it is about, and honesty as well. If they don't feel that you are being honest with them, how can they trust you, for trust and honesty go hand in hand. After all, you can't trust a person that's lying to you. How would you ever know when they are telling you the truth, so I've done just that. I have told my sons the truth always, and I always will. I want them to know that they can count on me and they can trust me with anything in their lives no matter how old they get.

It was now February 2002 when April came for a visit as she did often. She began talking to me and telling me how she was feeling, how she felt like she had never really accomplished anything in her life, anything important anyway, and how she wanted to make a career change. She couldn't stand working where she was working any longer. In her words it was a soul-sucking job and there were constant back-stabbings going on. It was just becoming unbearable for her soul to go there day after day.

She said, "I want to make a difference in the world," and she told me, "I know through all the people that have passed and the feelings that I felt that this isn't the end. That there is something beyond this."

I told her, "April, I know, I know there is."

She said, "When I meet God, when it's my time, I don't want to go to Him without accomplishing anything. I don't want my life to have been meaningless. I want to touch people. I want to help people." That's when she decided to become a home health care aide working with the mentally challenged, working with people with Down syndrome or slight retardation or other mental problems.

She started working in a group home taking care of four women, and she had never been happier and felt more fulfilled. But you know at that moment when we were having that conversation about her job change, I wished I had told her how I truly felt. I guess I'll have to do it now in this book. I wish I had told her then, actually spoken the words, and let her know what a fantastic big sister she had always been to me, just as Amber was, and how very, very much I respected and looked up to them and loved them. What a great aunt she had been to my two sons, and what a difference she did make in my life and in theirs. How wrong she was to think that she had not touched other people's lives and done good for other people, because she certainly had for me, my two sons and Michael.

I never knew until that moment when she said this that she felt that way. Most important, I wished I had told her I don't know what I would have done if it had not been for her and Amber protecting me from our father. How do you even begin to thank someone for that type of protection, to thank her for every punch, every slap, and every kick that he truly wanted to give to me that she took instead, and so did Amber. How do you begin to thank someone for doing something like that for you for protecting the baby of the family? She sat there thinking her life meant nothing, and that she gave nothing. How wrong could one person be? I should have, and I wish to God I did tell her all of these things face to face while I had the chance.

It was during this visit when it began snowing rather heavily, and I asked her if she wanted to stay for the night instead of driving home on the slippery roads. She said, "Yes, I'd rather," because she didn't like driving in the snow very much which was a hindrance in itself considering we lived in New England. I gave her my bed, and I took the couch. Something funny happened to her during the night that happened to me actually quite often. She felt the corner of the bottom of the bed slope down as though someone was sitting on it.

The next morning at breakfast she and I began talking, and she told me this. She asked me if this ever happened.

I said, "Yes, quite often it does. I think it's probably Michael."

She just laughed and said, "Yeah, it probably is. Always keeping an eye on you."

So as April began her career change my life in a way remained stagnant, stuck in sort of a limbo. Of course I was always doing things with my sons trying desperately to live in the moment and enjoy myself. I found this very difficult to do because just as before as I struggled while I was having my spiritual crisis and not being able to pray, I could pray now. I could feel that connection only now ever stronger, but it didn't seem to be helping me push out this deep, deep sense of hatred and revenge that was building stronger as the days went on. It was beginning to take its toll on me. It was now starting to affect me physically.

It was around 2003 when I began experiencing my feet going numb, and I had no idea what was going on. My doctor set me up for a full MRI. They found three of the discs in my back were herniated, and deterioration was developing between the others, along with arthritis throughout my whole body. When they did my blood work they found I was extremely anemic, and my thyroid had gone totally nuts. It was so bad that I felt like I was literally walking on my knees all the time. I was so very tired.

This explained a lot, but I knew deep down inside carrying all these negative feelings as I was doing was not helping at all. I had to find some way to deal with them and purge myself of them. Praying just was not helping. The doctor started me on the proper medications for my anemia and my thyroid, and this helped immensely, but the pain in my back and my arthritis remained. Just one more pain I had to deal with. I struggled physically for the following year trying to get my thyroid under control so I would not be so exhausted all the time. Just as I was beginning to feel a little bit more human, a little bit better, another tragedy hit.

In 2004 my dearest friends, Cathy and Izzy, lost their mother, June, one of the sweetest, most beautiful and intelligent woman I had the privilege of meeting. The poor things were as devastated of course as I was when I lost my mother. This seemed to affect me deeply as well. It was like all of the pain from all of my losses just came rushing back, that old familiar pain, that feeling of being dropped down into a dark hole and kicked in your stomach.

Then only a few months after their mother's death, their father passed away. I almost felt like my bad luck was rubbing off on them. So with this ever so familiar pain, a feeling like you've been dropped into a black hole returned once again, and the physical pain I was feeling with my back, it was all very overwhelming. I had to separate from Izzy for a while to get my bearings back, to crawl out of that deep black hole and try to regain my sanity, all the while still retaining all that negativity and anger. I felt as though it had become toxic inside of me now. I felt as though I had to do something drastic and quick before they all found themselves sitting at my funeral because at this point I was feeling so sick both physically and emotionally.

I truly felt as though I was dying. At this time I just felt as though life had used my heart as a punching bag, and it was growing old, tired and thin. I was so afraid that one last punch, that one last blow would break it wide open.

It was now the 5th anniversary of Michael's death. The boys and I went to the gravesite as usual on this anniversary at 1:25. I asked Michael for some guidance after our prayer and asked God for strength to show me the right way. I needed both of them to give me their help now more than ever.

It was now maybe a couple of weeks after this 5th anniversary when I was sitting in my room one evening thinking. It dawned on me to write a book but I thought how ridiculous this was. I thought back to the day that Izzy said that to me, but I had never written anything more in my life than a simple letter. How was I now going to sit down and write an entire book, but I had to try.

The next morning April stopped in for coffee as she usually did after work. (She worked the 3rd shift and would show up around 7-7:30 a.m. We would talk for a couple of hours.) This is when I first told her that I was going to start a book.

She looked at me like I had three heads. She said, "Kyra, how are you going to do this? Why would you want to do this? You're going to write a book about your life and revisit all that pain? How could you do this?" She just couldn't understand.

I told her, "There are many, many reasons why I feel as though I have to do this. I really have no choice but to try. I can't imagine God giving me the life that he gave me and showing me what he showed me, helping me so much and carrying me through all this pain for me to now just keep it all to myself. The world needs to know. It needs to understand. We do have help. God is there to help us."

I pointed out the evening news to her. I said, "Evil is very much trying to take a foothold in society. Can't you see it? All you need to do is turn on the evening news and see the horrible things that are happening with really no logical explanation as to why people are doing what they are doing."

I thought to myself, *If there is no logical explanation as to why people do these horrible things, there's only one explanation then, and that's evil.* I think each and every one of us has that capacity of good and evil inside of us. It's our own individual choice which way we want to go. If we want to be weak and allow the evil to take us over, it will. It's stronger than ever now. On the other hand we can be good and build our spirits, our souls up, and help other people. I truly believe I should be talking about my experience, and I really also believe that God would want me to and as I said, not just keep it to myself.

I also told her, "People that have had experiences such as I have should also talk about it. God needs help here on earth. We need his help, but he also needs ours. He needs us to spread the good things that he does. By me telling my story even if it helps just a little bit and counteracts some of the evil that is going on in the world today, then I need to do this. Another reason is I need to release this toxic sense of revenge and hate that I have been carrying around for three-and-a-half years now, because I feel like it is killing me.

"I have to find some way to get justice for Michael, and this is the only way I can realistically think of doing so. I want to tell this story and tell everyone what a good man he was and what happened to him, what happened to our whole family. How far do you think I would get in a court of law run by our government against our government if I were to take our government to court? How far do you think I would get? I'm a poor disabled widow with very few resources. I could stand up against the government with their unlimited resources and their twisting of the truth? No, I knew how that would play out. I would lose and no one would hear this story."

I also told April I knew that it would take years in the court system for any kind of justice be given to Michael if any at all. I knew Michael would not want me to spend the last remaining years of my life going in and out of court rooms rehashing and replaying all of this over and over again and destroying my soul along with my heart. I knew Michael wouldn't want me to go down that road.

"So this you see, April, is probably the only way I'm going to be able to get the justice Michael so greatly deserves. In addition, by writing this book I'm praying to release all of this revenge, this anger and this hate, these toxic emotions that are slowly killing me. I have to hope that this will help me and will release all of this poison from me. It is sort of a self-analysis without the benefit of a psychiatrist at hand. All I know is that I have to try. I have to do something. So instead of choosing a court of law I chose a court of public opinion."

I told April I would stay truthful and honest throughout the entire book. There will be no exaggerations and there will be no lies. There will be nothing but the truth, and for better or for worse it would be what it will be. I truly hope after all is said and done that my book in some small way may be able to help somebody.

I also told April, "I would love to memorialize Michael, Mom, Amber, and Robert, because they were very, very strong people, and they were very, very good people, people that this world and my children and I sorely miss. I want to do this for so, so many reasons, so many important reasons, and I want to get started immediately."

After I told April all of this, all of the reasons, she agreed. She said, "Yes, you probably should do this then. It would be a good thing."

I then told Teddy and Martin what I was about to start, and I told them that Mommy might have good days and bad days, but just kind of ignore it because it has nothing to do with you. I'm not mad at you.

They understood. At first they didn't quite get why I wanted to do it, but I explained to them just like I explained to April, and they were behind me after that 100%. But now being a single mother and having all of the responsibility placed on my shoulders to not only take care of my home, but my two children, it would prove extremely difficult for me to find the time that I knew I would have to spend concentrating and trying to remember so that I would get everything right, so that I would write down only the truth.

I will try to remember each and every little detail that I possibly could, but I knew what that meant and that meant revisiting that huge wall of cubbyholes, that huge wall that I had created years before in my mind somewhere to place all that pain, to keep it away so I could go on with my life and be able to take care of my children.

I now find myself having to revisit, to open up each and every one of these painful cubbyholes, but in doing so I found I had a lot of fond memories as well tucked away in them along with the bad. I was able to keep those fond memories with me in my heart and in my mind and only put the bad back, only the sadness and the heartbreaks.

This worked. I was able to do it. Now I live with only love, joy and fond memories of my mother, my sister, Robert and Michael. I kept out the good and returned the bad, keeping it tucked away, away from my life so that I can be happy.

I would try very hard to get all of my work done one or two days a week, the housework, the shopping the laundry and whatever the boys needed to do to try to get it done before I began writing every week. I didn't want to be interrupted when I was in the middle of my thoughts.

This was very, very difficult. Having two teenage boys that want to go here and there and over their friend's house and go to after school activities. It was quite a challenge. Some of the very sad parts in this book I would be crying over, and I would have to stop and gather myself together to bring Teddy over his friend's house. It was really hard, but I did it.

This took me over a year to complete. With the pain in my heart and the pain in my arms, I had to handwrite this book. Because of my arms, the carpal tunnel, and the RSD, it's really painful for me to type. It's a lot less painful to write which of course left another dilemma. After the whole book was written out, what now was I going to do with it? How was I going to get it into print?

Teddy and I did the first hundred pages together. I read them, and he typed it out on the computer. I felt as though I couldn't go any further than that with him. It was just too much, and I didn't want to put him through any more in his life than he already had been through. I was able to revisit all this pain, but I didn't want to inflict this onto Teddy, so now I found myself in the beginning of 2006 trying desperately to figure out how I was going to get this printed up.

April was a typist and she was very good at it, but she told me there was no way she could do this. There was no way that she could revisit all this pain. She simply couldn't take it, so she was not able to help me on this.

It was also around this time that a friend suggested that I get in contact with a publishing company before I go any further or put any more work into it. I told him that I had already put a year and a half into it, and I really didn't think there was any turning back now. I went on the computer, and I found a publisher that was willing to look at my book, but still that left me having to get it printed out.

In the meantime a lot of other things were going on. That Easter April showed up with two huge Easter baskets, one for Teddy and one for Martin. Now mind you, Teddy at this time was 18 years old and Martin was 15. They just about grabbed April and dragged her in the house so that none of their friends could witness her bringing them Easter baskets.

After this they both sat her down and explained to her the ribbing they would get if any of their friends ever saw this, and to please, please never do this again. They appreciated her thought and her love, of course, and she was always doing things like this, but they made her promise that she would never do it again. Easter was her favorite holiday, and I knew she just couldn't resist. She couldn't accept the fact that Teddy was now 18 years old already and Martin 15. On Halloween she was still bringing the Halloween cupcakes and loads of candy for them, and at Christmas time, oh my God, all the sweets and the boxes of chocolates. She just loved them so much. Really they couldn't have asked for a better aunt than she was.

So after Easter I got back to work trying to transcribe my book, or should I say trying to figure out a way to do this. One day in a store Teddy saw this transcribing device, one that you can attach to the computer and speak into. There is no typing involved. So we purchased this. We brought it home, and we found it didn't work very well. We had to get a chip to go into the computer for it to work, so we went back. A couple of weeks later we went back for it because I had to come up with the money. Time was ticking away. We finally got the computer chip and the thing all set up for the voice printing and it still didn't work very well.

After this I started getting sick again with my back. I was in extreme pain, and my thyroid also started kicking up. We just couldn't seem to get it under control, and this too was making me feel sick. So I found myself having to take a couple of months off to recoup and regain my strength and recover from the pain.

It was now August of 2006 when we tried the voice thing again, and it worked a little bit better. It's something you have to adjust to, but I was just never able to. I did a few pages, but it was very slow going, very agonizing work. That's the way you had to do it. You had to do it very slowly for it to come out correctly. So in between being a single Mom and having to take care of the household and now contending with this, I felt like pulling my hair out half the time. It was quite maddening. It seemed like after I did all of the work and went through all that pain of writing this book and freeing myself from these toxic feelings, the feelings of revenge and hate were all gone now. It worked. The book worked. But I now had to face another dilemma and that was actually getting it printed out, and nothing seemed to work.

It was now Christmas of 2006 when truthfully I almost felt like giving up. It just seemed like I was hitting one brick wall after the other when all of a sudden it dawned on me. Tape it. Read it out loud onto a tape, and then have someone type it up. So after Christmas that's exactly what I did. I went and got a small tape recorder from Wall Mart for about $20 and some tapes, and I began taping.

I found on those little tiny tape recorders the voice was very scratchy and wasn't good at all. So this wasn't something I felt as though I could just hand off to someone else to type up when they could only understand half of what I was saying. I couldn't do this, but I knew at least now I was on the right track so I went to Radio Shack and purchased a more expensive tape recorder and regular tapes.

This worked fantastically. I found a way now to get my book done, thank God, but again it was a slow process because I had other things to do in my life. I wasn't able to completely give taping my book 100% of my time, but I worked on it for hours and hours at a time in between the grocery shopping, house cleaning and giving rides to my sons and still feeling all the pain my body was in. I knew giving up was not an option for me, not now, so with every spare moment, with every free day I dedicated my time to finishing this.

It was now the end of March 2007, and I found I had only completed taping one-quarter of the book, when one morning April stopped again for coffee just as she always did after work. She really wanted to go Easter shopping. She always started very early to get the best buys and the best merchandise.

I reminded her about the Easter baskets, and she said, "No, I promise I won't." She was just going to get one big basket with all kinds of different candies in it for everyone to pick out. So she and I went out shopping that day and we had fun. We stopped for lunch at a little seafood restaurant in our town. She was telling me she hadn't been feeling very well. She really hadn't been eating very much but she was gaining weight.

You see, three years earlier she had been diagnosed as being type II diabetes, just like my mother. She wasn't very good at staying on her diet and cheated a lot. She was always getting sweets and goodies, and her kitchen was stocked constantly. Again, it goes back to that fixation with food I believe. She always had to have a fully stocked kitchen and bakery goods. It was insane.

I do believe it goes back to when we were children. When you are denied something as a child, I think as an adult you try to make up for it. I believe that was what she truly was doing. She had ballooned up to the weight of 305 pounds, and she didn't have a large frame. She was just slightly taller than my mother was, and my mother was only around 5 feet 4 inches.

It was at this point I started getting after her about this. I told her, "You really have to start taking this seriously. You're on insulin, and stopping at the bakery twice a week is not a very good idea, April."

I quickly realized once I began talking to her about it, it was almost like talking to an alcoholic about drinking. She did get on the defensive, and I realized I had to step back. She was an adult. She was 56 years old, and she certainly was smart enough to make her own choices here. I could clearly see these choices were affecting her physically. She was not feeling well at all, ever. She was always exhausted.

She did work very hard in the group home taking care of these four ladies she was in charge of during the night shift. She was always cleaning and picking up in the house and always bringing things in. She worried about the women and about them being properly taken care of. On the holidays she did lots of extra work there. She would bring in pumpkins for Halloween and scarecrows, and Thanksgiving she would have the turkey decorations up. At Christmas time she did so much. She always made sure that they had beautiful Christmas stockings, and she'd go shopping even though she didn't have very much money because unfortunately this job didn't pay very much. She always made sure they were taken care of as well as my two boys were.

She really enjoyed her job but whenever she told me that she had been buying food, the food I saw when I was with her shopping, not eating it and throwing it away, I was starting to become alarmed. As she was gaining weight, she told me she wasn't eating, but she was gaining more and more weight.

I didn't believe her at first, but when she looked me in the eyes and told me, "Kyra, honestly, I'm not eating nearly as much as what you think I am." I was alarmed because I had no idea what was going on.

It was now April 1, April Fool's day. About 9 o'clock that morning I received a phone call from the hospital telling me that my sister had been brought in at 5 o'clock that morning from where she was working. I couldn't believe it. It was like a bad April Fool's joke. I know April always had a wicked sense of humor, but this was just a little too much. At first it was like denial. I didn't believe it, but they told me, "No. It's for real. Please get here as soon as you possibly can. So of course I did.

By the time I got there they had put her in the ICU, and she was on life support. I was very, very upset to say the least. I was her health care proxy, and she was mine, and because of all the deaths in the family, we had discussed this in great detail of course about what we wanted and what we did not want. This was actually something she did not want. She never wanted to be put on life support.

I began trying to get information from the doctor who was tending to her, and he explained to me that she began hemorrhaging an extreme amount of blood out of her mouth at about 5 in the morning. They were now trying to figure out where the blood had come from. They were running all sorts of tests on her.

I thought to myself, *Well, if this is just an isolated situation where she was bleeding, maybe from her stomach, maybe from an ulcer, I would want her on life support so that we could repair the damage, and she would be okay.*

So they ran tests after tests after tests. They tested her for hepatitis. They tested her for absolutely everything. Then they asked me about the drinking, if there was drinking in our family.

I told him honestly, "Yes, there is," I said, "I'm an alcoholic, although I haven't had a drink in twenty years. April is one as well, although she hadn't had a drink in at least 22 years." I stressed this point to him that this was not the issue now. She hasn't had a drink in 22 years.

I said, "My whole family consisted of recovering alcoholics. Unfortunately for her, our sister Amber was the only one that wasn't able to completely stop drinking, and she passed away a few years ago." But again I kept telling him and reminding him that it had been 22 years since April drank, so it wasn't an issue and to look elsewhere for what was going on with her. I explained to him that she was a diabetic and on insulin. I tried to remember everything else that I could to help him. I didn't get out of the hospital until about one o'clock that morning.

When I got home I called the woman that was covering April's shift at her work to try to get some information about what happened to her. They explained the scene as looking like a murder scene. April had hemorrhaged so badly the bathroom was completely covered. Thank God she was able to make a phone call before this happened in order to be able to get a relief person in there to cover her. She was taken by ambulance from her job. I was just dumbfounded. I couldn't understand what was going on. April had been seeing a doctor on a regular basis because of her diabetes. She always had to get prescriptions for her insulin, and they were always testing her blood. I just couldn't comprehend the whole situation.

April spent four days in the ICU, and I was there almost constantly. I held her hand, and I talked to her. Again that feeling of that room being full was once again what I was picking up. I was sure it was our mother, Amber, Robert and Michael all there to help her, and hopefully to help me make the right choices for her. I could definitely feel each and every one of them. That was the only way I got through this. I held April's hand, and I talked to her. She was completely unresponsive and relying on the life support.

Finally after the third day they found out where the bleeding was coming from. It was coming from her esophagus. For some reason a hole had developed there. Also, with all the other testing that they did, they found that she had severe cirrhosis of the liver, a condition they claimed she had for many years.

How could this be? How on earth did the doctor miss this, a doctor that she saw on a regular basis? Cirrhosis of the liver is not easily missed. There are very distinct symptoms, especially if she had it for years.

Again I just couldn't wrap my mind around it. Sitting there looking at her, totally blown up like some sort of human balloon. I couldn't get my brain to comprehend what my eyes were seeing. I couldn't help thinking back to what Michael told me he witnessed when he first walked into the ICU unit and saw his father lying there the day he returned back from Vietnam. He told me that his father looked like some sort of human balloon. He looked like he was pregnant his stomach was swollen so badly. This is what Michael must have been seeing. The doctors kept insisting that they would be able to pull her through. They kept giving her transfusions of blood to rebuild her body.

It was on the fourth day when they knew they could do no more for her, they asked me if it would be okay if they admitted her into Mass General in Boston. They have much more resources than our town's hospital had, and they thought if anyone could pull her through, it would be them.

So, of course, I agreed, but in the back of my mind I was wondering all the while if this was the right choice, if this was what April truly wanted because of our discussions years before. She told me she didn't want to be put on life support, and here I was keeping her on life support now for four days and allowing them to run all these tests. I guess at this point I was being selfish. I just simply didn't want to lose my last sister, a sister I loved so much. So I hesitantly did agree to this.

They brought her to Mass General by ambulance the next day. While talking to this doctor about Mass General I told him, "I need a few minutes alone with my sister. I need to talk with her." He left the room. I told April as I held her hand and kissed it that I was very sorry, and that I hoped I was making the right choice. I also told her that it was okay for her to go if it was her time to go. The boys and I would be okay, and for her not to worry about us.

I went on to talk to her a little bit about our childhood, the recent years and also the book. I said, "What do you want—to add another chapter to my book, now?"

She was 100% behind me with this book. She would ask me quite often, "How's it going? How are you doing with it?" She was so curious to see the end results, and I think she was proud of me for doing it.

I essentially said my goodbyes to her there at that time in that room, because I had no idea if she was going to be able to be saved or not, if this was her time to go or not. I wanted her to be able to go with a clear conscience and no worries. I told her it was okay to go. After that I signed the papers for her to be transferred to Mass General, and of course their diagnosis was the same as this hospital's, and that was severe cirrhosis of the liver.

The bleeding started up again when she arrived at Mass General, and they got it again under control. They spent days running more tests on her as she remained on life support and in a comma.

It was now April 10. For ten days she had been in limbo while being poked and prodded. The doctors called me from Mass General wanting to run a stent from her brain, into her neck and down into the liver. The things that they were describing were horrible, and I knew, I knew April would come back and haunt me if I allowed them to do this. I really had done way, way too much already, much more than she wanted me to do.

So I told them, "No. You're not to do anything like that." I told them to let her go. "Take her off the life support. If she stays alive, then she stays alive. If she goes, then she goes."

I also let them know a little bit about our family's history of the recent years and the deaths. I told them, "My sister, April, and I are very, very spiritually sound, and we do believe when it's your time it's your time."

I told the doctor, "I don't know what kind of religion you follow, but that's what we feel." I also told him, "I've already done much more than she ever wanted me to do, and I feel guilty about this. For me to allow you to do any further work would be horrifying."

He agreed once I explained everything to him, and they took her off life support.

I made sure, and I told them, "The only important thing to me now is that she doesn't feel a thing. That there is no pain."

He assured me, "No, there is none. She is heavily sedated."

I said, "Okay. Now take her off the life support."

I sat at the edge of my bed praying. This was about one o'clock in the morning. Three o'clock. Then three-thirty. He called me back and told me she was gone. She passed. I thanked him for respecting my wishes and hers. I told him I realized that there really wasn't anything that he could do. From what I understand her liver was just about completely gone anyway.

I also said, "I am a true believer that when it's your time, it's your time, and I know I did the right thing."

After I hung up the phone I sat there, and I prayed, and I cried, but that only lasted for a few minutes. I didn't cry very much because I knew she was okay. I knew she was back in Paradise, and I knew she was with Mom, Amber, Michael, and Robert, because I could feel them by her. They were waiting for my stupid ass to do the right thing and let her go. This, I took much comfort in knowing.

Something funny did happen. About four hours after April passed away my phones went completely insane. At some point I was able to call out, other points I wasn't. Some points other people were able to call me, and other points they weren't. In between there was static, and the phone would ring and no one would be there. It was completely insane, and I knew April was letting me know, "Thank you, and I'm okay." I knew this is what it was because I had no problem with my phone before now, never.

Now all of a sudden it goes completely haywire on me. I even had the phone company come out and check all the lines a day or so later to make sure something hadn't happened. They said they were all fine, but still the problem continued. This all started the next morning about 8 o'clock I had tried to call Mr. Silva at the Morton Funeral Home, who had now become our family friend because we had seen him so much. I let him know what had happened and asked if he could pick April up. We were going to have the funeral at his Parlor. He told me how sorry he was to hear this, and how shocked he was. She was only 56 years old. My two boys were devastated.

It seems like no matter how many deaths you do have in the family, whether it is the first or the last, the pain is equal and certainly a great, great loss, but we cry for ourselves, not for them. They're okay and we know this. We cry because there will never again be Aunt April standing at our door holding Easter Baskets, coming over for Christmas Dinner, or just spending time talking and laughing with me. There will be no more, and that's why we cry. We cry for ourselves, but I simply knew I had to let her go. I couldn't be selfish like that just to have her here, to hold her here when she shouldn't be here any longer. It would be selfish to keep her on machines just so that I could go and see her and spend time by her side holding her hand. I probably could have kept her alive for months on life support, who knows, but that would have been horrifyingly selfish on my part. I loved her way too much for that. She certainly did not deserve to be kept alive like this.

It was Friday, April 13, 2007, when I delivered my last sister's eulogy, when I buried my last sister. It was a small ceremony. There was a wake and then the viewing room, where she lay just as my mother, Amber, and Robert had. Again there was that sick instant replay. The flowers were gorgeous, and I had all the pictures put up, pictures of her with my two sons, pictures of her and me when we were younger. Everyone from her work came. It was a very nice ceremony, and at the end the preacher read from the Bible, and then it was my turn.

This would be the first eulogy that I would give. I always had a fear of speaking in front of people, but there was no fear in me now. There were no negative feelings. I felt as though I had to lift everyone up just as God lifted me up. I stood there, and I spoke from my heart.

I told everyone, "This is not it. April is in a good place right along with Michael, Amber, Robert, and my mother. They are all together now, and they are in Paradise again. This is not the end. This is just simply leaving and going back home where we all came from originally."

I also let them know a little bit about the strange experiences that April and I had after each and every death, that were proof that this is not it. "Our souls go on because the souls of our loved ones have come back to visit us in one way or another. That's how I know. This isn't it. What heaven is, is love, and that's what God wants us to do.

"We are all brothers and sisters here on this earth, and God is our Father. Each time we hurt one of our brothers of sisters, we hurt Him. It's like being a mother with children that are fighting. It makes you feel bad inside to see your children fighting, to see them not getting along, or not treating each other with love and respect just as you would like them to. I imagine this is the way God must feel when he looks down on us and sees us at war or hating each other simply because of the color of our skin, or the way we dress, or where we live. Spreading that negativity is the worst thing you could possibly do, and in God's eyes, probably the most hurtful."

This is basically what I said for April's eulogy. I let them know that she was the best big sister I could ever hope for, and what a fantastic Aunt she was. She touched so many people's lives in such a positive way with her love and caring. At the end of this eulogy, I said The Lord's Prayer.

I turned to April in the casket, and I said to her, "Dear sister, I know we will be together again some day when it's my turn, and I love you."

After I spoke, everyone came up in the line to pay their last respects and to shake my hand. A distant relative (one who knew my mother very well) said to me, "Well, kid, you hit the nail right on the head with that eulogy." He felt the same way that I did. I imagine a lot of people do.

I told him, "I know you knew my mother very well."

"Oh, yes, I did."

They were very close, and I asked him, "Do you think my mother would be proud of me now, proud of that eulogy?"

"Most certainly, because I know that's exactly the way she felt as well."

I can't begin to tell you how fantastic that made me feel. My sister was to be cremated, and I would take her ashes and place them right alongside my mother's by my bed in my night stand.

I made one decision, though, when I was placing them in there. I wanted to release them, and I decided that this Christmas of 2007, December 13, my mother's birthday, that I would do so. I hope and I pray that there's going to be a snowstorm on this day because this was their most favorite time of the year. To release them to the four winds in the middle of a beautiful snowstorm would be the perfect way for their earthly remains to go back to Heaven. So this is what I plan to do with Teddy and Martin, wait for this day.

On April 1, April Fool's Day, April first got sick, and I was delivering her eulogy on Friday the 13th. I sat there and I put the connection together, and I couldn't help but laugh. I said, "Boy, you do have a good sense of humor, April."

There was one pleasant surprise, I have to say, and that was that Izzy, Angel, and Cathy showed up for April's wake. I had not seen them in over a year because of everything I was going through physically, writing this book and trying to just purge myself of all the toxic emotions. That took every ounce of energy I had. I was now seeing them and talking to them. It was as though no time had passed at all. They were such good and loving people who truly cared about me and Teddy and Martin.

Izzy told me she had been trying to call me, and that's when I explained to her about what the telephones were doing and that I had someone come out and look at it, but there was nothing they could do. We both rolled our eyes at the same time. I think we were thinking the same thing. It wasn't an earthly or a phone problem. We did have a little chuckle over it. We began talking again a couple of days after the wake, and I explained to her what was going on with me and what I was trying to do, basically trying to regain my sanity. I just needed a break from everyone, even the good people in my life.

The following week I began packing up April's apartment, and I wanted to do this by myself. I don't know why. I guess I just didn't want anybody else touching her things. Once everything was packed up, it took me over a week to do, Izzy and Angel rented a U-Haul for me, and all the guys got together and helped me move April's things out. I put them into my basement. Then it took me over a month to get all of her finances straightened out.

It was now the end of June, and it was the seventh anniversary of Michael's death. The boys and I, of course, were at the gravesite saying our prayers. When we got done and got back home, I said, "I really, really have to finish this book. I have to finish it, and I let Izzy and Cathy know that I was once again going to be absent from their lives for a short time." I had to now throw myself into this book and finish it.

They also thought it was incredible that I was writing a book, although I did remind Izzy, "Well, you suggested it at Michael's funeral."

She said, "Yeah, but I didn't think you'd take me seriously."

I now consider Izzy and Cathy my two sisters. They have seen me through so much, so much pain that would have sent other friends running in the opposite direction. Their hearts have always remained open and caring to me, and for that I will be forever grateful. So in this time that I threw myself back into the book, although I did not see them very often, I kept in contact with them over the phone. It was around the middle of August that Izzy moved, and I gathered up Teddy and Martin, and we all pitched in and helped.

As Izzy was bringing me through her new apartment, first she showed me the basement. This is where I would rather not have my ability to pick up on things at these times. As soon as we went down in the basement I sensed a spirit, a very, very strong one, although not bad. It was a man, and I could almost pick up on what he would look like. It was probably one of the original owners, an older man in overalls and a plaid shirt. I was actually starting to get better at picking things up like this now and not resisting them as much as I did in the past. I tried very hard to realize there is really nothing wrong with it, I suppose. If you're able to do this, perhaps you should just go with the flow. I don't know. I stopped resisting anyway and it did become a little bit stronger. I could pick up on a lot more detail now than I ever could before. Then we went upstairs, me not saying anything, of course, about any of this to her. She has no idea that I am able to do this. Then she showed me her apartment, and it was fine. There was nothing there. It was a rather nice apartment. It was a couple of hours after this we began moving in.

With all the guys helping, before we knew it most of her things were moved in. Everybody was famished, so I went home and made some subs and brought them back. It was then that they began talking about their mother, June, and I told them, "You know, she's with you. I know she's always watching out for you guys." I looked at Cathy and Izzy, and they gave me a strange look that indicated that they felt it too. They told me a lot of strange things that happened to them immediately following June's passing, like the lights going on and off in the house, and all kinds of electrical problems happening. So they kind of knew where I was coming from. But there was one thing that I can't tell my best friend and that was how I knew her mother was watching out for her. How I knew was because her mother was standing right next to her when I said that. How do you tell someone this? Again I was always afraid of people thinking I was insane. That's why I never, how do you say, "came clean" before now, but in writing this book I have found it to be extremely liberating.

I am able to speak now of things I have never been able to speak of before. I feel a sense of freedom and relief for the first time in my life, like a sack of potatoes has been lifted off of my shoulders. Don't get me wrong. I still do not wish to go any further with this gift that I have. I'm happy just to keep it the way it is. I don't want to be able to start hearing these spirits or talking with these spirits. If things just stay the same, then I'll be fine. I no longer look at it as a curse. I do look at it as a gift, a gift that God gave me, and I'm grateful for it.

After taking these few days off to help my friend move, I threw myself back into finishing the taping of my book. After completing it, I never felt so good in my whole life as I do now. As I said before, this book has been extremely liberating for me. I have never felt stronger and more confident in my whole life. Spiritually sound, spiritually strong, I now look at my life before this book as being the first part of my life. I still now have a whole second part of my life to look forward to. I just realized this as I was finishing the book. I realized that 45 years I found my niche in life, and that is writing. I found the perfect escape, the perfect high, so to speak, that I could ever have, better than any drugs or alcohol. I found I had the ability to be able to just pour all of my pain, all of my heartache, all of the things that happened to me in my life out onto paper and free myself from all that pain and sorrow. Writing this book was an incredibly marvelous, life-altering experience.

My writing this book has made me so strong I truly believe there is nothing I couldn't face and beat now. Something else that happened to me throughout writing this story. I learned how to turn my pain into my strength by allowing myself, when I returned to that huge wall of cubby holes, to keep out and keep in me safe all the love and the good memories and the happiness and put only the pain away so that I can continue with my life, continue with the second part of my life carrying only the people's strength and love with me and not the pain. That's what added to my strength.

Now I sit here today almost finished taping this book. It is now October 5, 2007, and I am ready, more than ready to begin that second part of my life. I actually feel as though I've outgrown my life now. I feel like a butterfly emerging out of its cocoon and ready to go. I want to continue writing. I have many more books that I want to do. I also want to get into painting and develop that art form, an art form that lay dormant in me for a long time now. I want to get into photography. I also am going to start volunteering at the V.A. where Michael went.

Then of course there are my children, my beautiful sons that I am so, so very proud of. They have become honorable, loving, caring men that I am proud to send out into the world. I know they are going to do good and hopefully make a difference, a positive difference in other people's lives. I know their father would be really proud of them just as I am.

So I find myself really looking forward to beginning that second part of my life now, and I wanted to have this book end on a high note by telling you that my boys are doing fantastically, and I am as well. We have been through a lot in our lives, but that has just made us stronger people and more compassionate people.

Quite honestly now, looking back on it all, I would not have traded one second of my life, the good times as well as the bad, for all the money in the world because it has made us what we are today, and the three of us are very, very strong individuals and very happy. For the first time in a long time I am able to truly say that and mean it.

Sitting here today I also think back to that very special time when God helped me. I still find the help He gave me incredibly amazing. He gave me the help when I needed Him the most. As I wrote, it was like I was being shown just a little piece of Heaven by that touch, that purest of pure love.

Mind you, now this is just my opinion, but I think in a lot of ways I actually found out on that day what the meaning of life was and that is love. We are here to love one another. I swear to you, that's all that I felt, the purest of pure love. Maybe that's what our souls are made of. Deep down in the very core of our souls we carry that little piece of Heaven with us, that love from Heaven. If this is true, then most of us spend our entire lives ignoring it, never truly letting it out or feeling it because if we did, we would treat each other much better than we do. But I truly think that's what the meaning of life is. We are here for love, and yes I do, I think it's just that simple.

Please believe me when I say I am not a religious fanatic. As a matter of fact I don't even go to church. I find I have a very personal relationship with God, and I don't feel as though you need to go to a huge building every Sunday in order to talk with Him. He is our Father and we are his children. We can talk with Him any time we want, in our living room, in our bedroom, or wherever. I just think it's a very personal relationship.

But don't get me wrong; I'm not knocking church, either. I believe people should do what makes them feel good. If you feel better by going to church, then by all means do so. What's most important of all is that you keep that connection with God and that you do talk with God because He is always there for us. Whether that means going to church or simply saying your prayers before you go to sleep. The important thing is that you keep that connection, and when you do need help, He will be there to help you.

As humans we might not understand everything that He does. As a matter of fact we may curse Him for doing the things he does, but it's not up to us to question it. We don't know what's going to happen in the future, but He does, and I've learned the hard way not to question Him. Now I just keep Him in my heart, and I talk to Him quite often, but I never question.

The way I look at it is everything happens for a reason, and we just don't know what that reason is until we pass and go back home. Then I suppose we'll get the answers to all the questions that we have had in our hearts and in our minds all our lives. Until then I just have to believe that He knows best.

I should also say I don't believe in beating people over the head with the Bible, and I am most certainly not preaching to people. I don't believe in that. I believe we all have to find our own way in our own time. This was now just my time to find my way back home, to find my way back to God, I think. My whole life led up to that very moment that I was shown what I was shown.

And now with me writing this book I can only hope and pray that I have found the justice for Michael that he so deserved. He overcame so much, and he worked so hard to gain a normal life. Actually we both did. We successfully broke the cycle of alcoholism and abuse in our family, against all the odds. We did this. We won. After all the fighting, after all the battles against our demons, we won. We had that loving, normal family that both of us wanted so desperately, only to have it horribly ripped away from us.

I live now with all those beautiful memories that Michael and I created together, memories of our love and memories with our children. These are all I have to hold onto now, and I do hold onto them for dear life, remembering every day. Most importantly I remember Michael's words of encouragement. He taught me to never give up no matter what. If it becomes too much, sit back and take a break but then come out fighting, and come out to win. These words keep me strong to this day, and they will keep me strong until the day I die. Just as Michael used to say, "They're gonna have to drop kick my ass in that hole." I say the same thing, and I feel the same way. I'm not going to go down without a fight.

Every morning I get up, and I put on my makeup, and I fix my hair. No matter how much pain I feel, I somehow have the ability to visualize and keep the pain at bay. This allows me to fight every single day, fight to be strong, fight for my children. No, I will never give up, because I also know that I have all the love and the support from the people that have passed, because I can feel it. I can feel them, and this only makes me stronger.

Michael has taught me so much. He taught me how to live and how to love, and that's exactly what I intend to do with the rest of my life, live each moment to its fullest and not take anything for granted, especially the love of my children. I now know I have the love of God with me and the love of my family, the ones that are still here and the ones that have passed. With this love I know I can accomplish anything I set my mind to. They are my support system.

I now would very much like to end this book with a few personal thoughts and comments. First of all I would like to make it very, very clear that I am a true patriot. I'm a proud American, and I am extremely proud of our country. I truly believe that we are the most honorable country in the world. My family has fought in every World War, my grandfather World War I, my father World War II and my husband Vietnam. I am proud to say this, and I am proud of them for doing this. I am equally proud of all the men and women who are now serving and fighting for us, for our freedoms for America. I know that they are giving a part of themselves, a part they will never get back, because once you have seen the horrors of war, you're never quite the same again. To make such a sacrifice to me is the definition of honor. I immensely respect and love each and every one of these honorable soldiers and greatly appreciate everything that they are sacrificing.

However, you know they aren't the only heroes in our society. We have many, many others. Those brave firefighters who went rushing into those buildings on 9/11 right along with the police. Their bravery was simply amazing to me. They actually went rushing into buildings that other people were running out of, without a second thought. My God, that's a hero. I respect our firefighters and our police so much for doing this and for making the sacrifices they made. They truly are the heroes in our society, right along with our soldiers that are fighting for our freedoms.

To the soldiers I would like to pass on just a little bit of life's experience in dealing with my husband, who also gave a part of himself, who also left an important part of himself over in Vietnam. If you have trouble dealing with all the memories and all the horrors that you witnessed, in trying to get back into your life and into society to please, I beg of you, get help with it immediately.

Don't waste ten years of your life like my husband did. Don't try to self-medicate to forget. Do not crawl into a bottle of liquor or a bottle of pills to help you cope. There is help for you. Demand it. They owe you that and so much more.

My husband was haunted by memories until the day he died, memories of all the fellow soldiers that died there in front of him. I guess you would call it survivor's guilt. I don't know.

Every time Michael would bring the subject up of all those soldiers that died around him and him not getting a scratch, I would always tell him, "Michael, do you think for one second any of those guys would want you to now come back and waste your life when their lives were so cruelly taken from them? Put yourself in their shoes for a second. If you were the one that was dying, and died there, would you want your fellow soldier, this soldier that fought beside you, to regret the rest of his life simply because he made it back alive, or would you want him to live it to the fullest, to enjoy every second that he was given? Would you want that soldier to come back and just live with regret or honor you and live each day to its fullest and make a life, a life that he will now never have? What would you want?"

I tried very hard to have Michael put himself in that person's shoes, the poor man that died in Vietnam beside him, and ask what would that man want him to do with his life now? I was never able to quite get it through to Michael, and he was never able to forget, even with the medication and the therapy sessions that lasted years. He was never able to forget.

It was people like Michael and all the other soldiers right down to the soldiers of today that have made this country the great country it is, and I think somewhere along the line the government has forgotten all about this. The people are the ones that make America great, fellow Americans like us, the fighters, the warriors, the heroes, not the few elite. Every day the gap between the haves and the have nots grows ever wider. We have a few in America that are rich. Most of us are just getting by struggling every single day. I hate to see this on my fellow Americans' faces in the supermarket, other stores, and the park, that look of just being beaten down, of being exhausted, of making little pay and paying ridiculous amounts for rent, ridiculous amounts for electric, and having nothing at the end of the week. Forget going out to dinner. You're lucky if you can afford to eat now, and it's only getting worse by the day.

I know three people as I sit here today that are going to have their house foreclosed on. Where are they going to go? To the street? They work three jobs. I know one woman that goes to work at 5 o'clock in the morning and doesn't come back home until 12 o'clock at night. Her mortgage is $3700 a month, and she by no means lives in a mansion. It is just a normal little regular house. How long can she keep this up? She is almost my age. She is going to end up by collapsing. My sister, April, the one that was the home health-care aide, made $8.50 an hour, and her rent for the month was $700. She had nothing left at the end of a week except an exhausted, broken-down body and a broken spirit. Is this what America has turned into?

People are killing themselves working not only one job, but two jobs and a lot of times three jobs. You don't even have time to stop and think. These people are exhausted. I don't know what the hell happened in America, but it used to be, not too many years ago, that a man would be able to support his family, have a home, have a car, and perhaps even put his children through college. What the hell happened? Things changed drastically, and not for the better. For instance I got a delivery of oil about three months ago during the summer, because I was completely out. I use it for hot water. So unless I wanted to take an ice-cold shower I had no choice. I paid $600 for a half a tank of oil. I have no idea what I am going to do during the winter when it actually gets cold.

America, for the poor, has become a very scary place, and there are many, many more poor people who are just struggling to get by than there are rich. How many homeless at last count? I think there were 40,000, 40,000 Americans sleeping in cardboard boxes under bridges. This is great! Our government is doing such a great job. I figure as long as they have their $1,000-a-plate dinners, their $2,000 suits, their huge mansions, and their limos why should they be concerned? Why should they care? And believe me, they don't.

Our forefathers would roll over in their graves if they could see what was going on in America today. This great country of ours was built by people like us, by the true Americans. Our first politicians were not rich. They were hard-working people that cared about their fellow Americans.

We no longer have that today in our society. Our government is the elite, and as far as I'm concerned our government is corrupt and evil. How could our government consciously spray poison onto their own men in battle, as they did in Vietnam with Agent Orange? They had other choices. They had other options. How much thought did they put into that before they dumped it on our men? I'll tell you, none. I honestly don't know how much worse things could possibly get: people losing their homes, losing their apartments, becoming homeless, people that are working two and three jobs, this is what is happening to them. This is not what America is supposed to be, people, and we have to start thinking. I think it's time for Americans to take America back.

We need somebody in the White House who actually knows what a struggle is and is not born with a silver spoon in their mouth. Trying to explain the daily struggle to one of our Congressmen or our president himself is equal to talking to an alien. They have no idea, and I suppose the only ones we can blame are ourselves. We are the ones that keep electing these people into office, these people that have unlimited income and run and place TV and newspaper ads, instead of trying to pick one of our own from our communities.

I think we need to start doing something like that. We should elect the man that has to go to a grocery store every week with $40 in his wallet and feed two children. A man that can do this is the man that I want sitting in the White House, because this is a man who knows pain, who knows the frustration of trying to run a household and raise a family with nothing. That's the man I want in the White House, because he is the one who truly understands.

We need to start electing our own fellow Americans, people who have their fellow Americans at heart and know what's best for us, not people who, behind closed doors, after the session is over, vote themselves a huge pay increase. Congress has done this so many times, and then the very next day they knock out the increase in the minimum wage (quite frankly minimum wage is a joke anyway). They have the audacity to do this. These are not people who have our best interests in mind, only their own. They will hold onto that limo, that mansion, those suits, and those dinners for life. Where do the rest of us sit? We sit in an ice-cold apartment working three jobs, barely being able to feed our family.

No, that's not what America is supposed to be. I think our government has run wild, and I'm calling for a change. Americans have to start taking America back. We have to put our own in the positions that can truly benefit us, because these people that we have now don't give a shit about us, and we have to know that.

I have a perfect proposal. Anyone wishing to run for any office, for senator, governor, congressman, even for president should be made to live in a project, work two jobs or three jobs, whatever number of jobs they want to work, and try to make ends meet, get down with the people that have to live their lives on a daily basis just like this. I don't consider it cruel or unusual treatment. After all, this is the way most of us have to live every single day, so why shouldn't they? If after a year's period of time, if they can pass this test, then I say, yes, they have every right to run for president, Congress, Senate or whatever. But until they pass the test, no. Now let's see how many of them would step up to the plate and actually do this. I challenge each and every one of them, including the president. I truly don't think they have the intestinal fortitude to go through what we go through on a daily basis.

I would also like to go one step further and make another proposal. A law should be passed that all the men and women who have ever served in our military and have given that precious part of themselves, when they get back home, they should be tax exempt for the rest of their lives. They should never have to pay taxes and should be given a home at cost, interest free. That's the least America can do for its heroes. Until changes like these are made with our government, I don't see a happy ending for us at all, because it is just going to get worse, not better.

Personally I plan to become more politically active in the future, and I call on my fellow Americans to do the same. We have to start making some changes before it's too late. We need to start taking a hard look at the person who is running for Senate or for Congress, researching thoroughly their background and what they stand for. I say, if we don't like anyone, don't vote. Don't vote simply because he is the lesser evil. I believe that is the way most of us have had to make our choices. Who's going to hurt America less?

Perhaps with fewer people showing up at the polls on Election Day, we will send our message loud and clear then, and only then will we start looking to our own communities for the good people and for the caring people. We need people who will make a difference for the better for Americans instead of just the elite people who have never struggled a day in their lives and certainly have never had to concern themselves about where their next meal is going to come from.

But again, these are only my thoughts, my opinions. I'm sure that not everyone will agree with me, and that's their right, but my husband gave his life, right along with so many other Americans to protect these liberties and freedoms that we take for granted today. So I do feel as though I have the right and maybe even the obligation to voice my opinions in this book.

Sometimes you have to walk through hell to find God.

BIOGRAPHY

My name is Kyra Jones. I am a 46-year-old housewife. All I ever wanted was to simply have a normal life with a husband and children. Due to a string of events, I realize now a normal life for me is an impossibility. I have learned with God's help to accept the life He has given me, and just ask Him for help to get through it.

I am a proud widow of a Vietnam veteran, a hero, and the proud mother of two intelligent, loving, caring, and handsome sons. My story is of heartache, loss, pain, and finding my faith. My whole life has been a test of love and faith. I dedicated my life to Michael, and now I dedicate this book to him.